The Ultimate Pet Duck Guidebook

All the things you need to know before and after bringing home your feathered friend

2ND Edition

Written & Illustrated by

Kimberly Link

Majestic Waterfowl Sanctuary

www.majesticwaterfowl.org

A Happy Duck Publication™

Copyright © 2009, 2014

All rights reserved. No part of this book may be used or reproduced in any manner whatsoever without written permission except in the case of brief quotations embodied in critical reviews.

Other Happy Duck Titles...

www.majesticwaterfowl.org

A portion of the proceeds from the sale of Happy Duck books are donated to Majestic Waterfowl Sanctuary!

For:

Young Matthew & Young Jeffrey

Ducky Acknowledgments...

Special Thanks to Majestic's amazing vet team for their ongoing generosity:

Dr. Otka & The Noank Mystic Veterinary Hospital

Additional Thanks to Majestic's other friendly vets:

Dr. McGee & The Collierville Animal Clinic & Surgery Center

Dr. Poster & The Poster Animal Hospital

Expressed Thanks to:

Mary Gentry

Smidge's Army

Jenn & Mike at Feathered Angels Waterfowl Sanctuary

And all of our Majestic Friends, Supporters, Rescuers, Volunteers & Adopters!

Table of Contents

INTRO-DUCK-TION 19
PREPARATIONS 21
   VET CARE 21
      Finding a Waterfowl Vet 21
         Ask your vet questions 21
         Find a back-up vet 22
         Confirm only qualified waterfowl vets will be handling your duck 22
         Ducks hide when they're sick! 23
   STOCKING YOUR MEDICINE CABINET 23
      Purchase a Pet Carrier 25
   FEED 25
      Choose a Feed Brand 25
         Duckling crumbles 26
         Avoid medicated feed 26
         U.S. brand options 26
         U.K. brand options 27
      Feed Brand Research 28
         Sequential production 28
         Quality control 28
      Milling/Manufacturing Plants 29
      Feed Bag Ingredient Labels 29
         Feed label facts 29
         Generic labeling 30
      Vitamin Fortified Feed vs. Mixing Your Own Grains 30
         Seeds & cracked corn 30
      Feed Bag Expiration Dates 31
         Feed recalls 31
      Fresh Feed 31
      Feed Storage 32
         Peppermin oil & dearth 32
         Feed and rodents 32
         Rodent prevention & control 33
         Rodent facts 34
      Grit 34
      Feeding Egg-Laying Ducks 34
         Added calcium source for egg-laying ducks 34
         Laying formulas 35
         50% laying formula for egg-laying ducks 35
         Adjust the ration of laying formula as needed 35
      Avoid High Oxalic Acid Foods 36
      Feeding Ducks on Public Ponds 36
         Don't feed ducks bread 37
         Other dangerous foods 38
      Determine a Feeding Schedule 38
      Feed Dispenser 39
         Duckling feeder 39
         Adult duck feed bowl 39
         Adult duck automatic pet feeder 40
   DRINKING WATER 40
      Make Water Available 24/7 40
         Make multiple water sources available 40
      Duckling Water Dispenser 41
         Weighted water bowl 41
         Water fount 41

- *Adult Duck Water Dispenser* ... 42
  - **What doesn't work** ... 42
  - **Rubber water bucket** ... 42
  - **Heated water bucket** ... 43
- DUCKLING ACCOMMODATIONS ... 46
  - *Housing for Ducklings* ... 46
    - **Draft free room** ... 46
    - **Brooder** ... 46
    - **Bedding** ... 48
    - **Heat source** ... 49
    - **Feather duster** ... 49
    - **Food** ... 50
    - **Water** ... 50
    - **Nutrient packs** ... 50
  - *Supervision* ... 51
  - *Swims for Ducklings* ... 52
  - *Ducklings grow fast!* ... 53
  - *Naps for Ducklings* ... 53
  - *Ducklings and Pecking Orders* ... 54
  - *Warning Signs of Duckling Illness* ... 55
  - *Inside to Outside* ... 55
    - **Preparing ducklings for their move** ... 56
    - **Moving ducklings permanently outdoors** ... 57
- BUILDING YOUR DUCK PEN ... 57
  - *Finding the Perfect Location* ... 57
  - *Keeping Predators Out* ... 59
  - *Sturdy Building Materials* ... 59
  - *Unknown Predators* ... 60
  - *Predatory Determination* ... 60
  - *Predators* ... 60
  - *Free-Ranging* ... 67
  - *Determine the Size of Your Enclosure* ... 68
    - **250 square feet for two ducks** ... 68
  - *How to Build a Predator-Proof Enclosure* ... 69
  - How To Build a Predator-Proof Enclosure ... 69
    - **Structural supports** ... 70
    - **Roofing** ... 70
    - **Doors** ... 72
    - **Perimeter fencing** ... 72
    - **Underground perimeter** ... 74
    - **Digging predator barrier** ... 75
    - **Electric fencing** ... 76
    - **Motion sensor lighting** ... 76
- BUILDING YOUR DUCK A HOUSE ... 77
  - *How to Build Your Duck House* ... 77
  - *Barn Flooring* ... 80
  - *Barn Windows* ... 81
  - *Internal Pen and Barn Fencing* ... 81
    - **Chain link** ... 81
    - **Poultry wire** ... 82
    - **Portable playpens** ... 82
    - **PVC welded wire mesh** ... 83
- BEDDING FOR YOUR DUCKS ... 84
  - *Hay and straw* ... 84
  - *Pine shavings* ... 84
  - *Avoid litter* ... 85
- PROTECTION FROM THE ELEMENTS ... 85
  - *Summer & Shade* ... 85

Shade cloth	85
Shade trees	85
Air conditioning	86
Misting systems	86
Winter & Heat	87
Staying indoors	87
Heated Barns	87
Insulation	88
Seal windows	88
PROTECTING WEBBED FEET	88
Remove tripping obstacles	89
Planting grass	89
Safe Catching and Handling	90
SELECT YOUR WATER FEATURE	91
Drowning	91
Swimming Accomodations	91
Kiddy pools	92
Concrete ponds	92
Preformed pond liners	93
Ponds	95
Pumps	98
Water Sources Must Be Kept Clean	99
Prevent Slipping & Tripping Hazards	99
PROVISIONS FOR SEPARATIONS	99
A Pair of Drakes	100
Warning Signs That Help is Needed	100
How to break up a fight	101
Who's Fighting and Why	101
Personalities	101
Spring fever	101
Weather	102
Temperature	102
Medical science	102
Visitations and Distractionary Tactics	102
Separating Ducks	102
Portable playpens	102
Temporary fencing	103
Permanent fencing	103
Multiple Females & Males	104
Life on the Other Side of The Fence	105
Double the supplies	105
Duck Identification	106
How to put a leg band on an adult duck	106

CONSIDERATIONS ... 109

LIFE EXPECTANCY	109
Where Will You Be Ten Years From Now?	110
Leaving to college	110
Apartment living	110
Will provisions	110
YOUR HOME SITUATION	111
Family Agreement	111
Other pets	111
Indoor Ducks	111
The Mess	112
FLOCK SIZE	112
Two ducks are ideal	112
Mirrors	112
Ducks and geese together	113

GENDER SELECTION ... 113
   All Male Flock ... 114
   All Female Flock ... 115
   One Male and One Female Flock ... 115
   One Male and Multiple Females Flock ... 116
   Multiple Males and Multiple Females Flock (Adhering to Ratios) ... 116
   Gender Identification: Ducklings ... 117
   Gender Identification: Ducks ... 117
      Determining gender by the tail feather ... 117
      Determining gender by the quack ... 118
      Muscovy gender vocalizations ... 119
SIZE OPTIONS ... 120
BREED OPTIONS ... 120
   Exotic & Wild Duck Breeds ... 120
   Keeping Different Duck Breeds Together ... 121
   Breed Standards ... 121
      Comparative weights: males vs. females ... 121
   Breed & Feather Colors ... 122
      Crested ducks ... 125
   Bantam Breeds ... 126
      Call ... 126
      East Indie ... 127
      Miniature Silver Appleyard ... 128
      Australian Spotted ... 129
      Mallard (Captive-bred) ... 130
   Lightweight Breeds ... 131
      Indian Runner ... 131
      Khaki Campbell ... 132
      Magpie ... 133
   Middleweight Breeds ... 134
      Ancona ... 134
      Blue Swedish ... 135
      Blue Swede mixes ... 136
      Buff Orpington ... 137
      Cayuga ... 138
      Welsh Harlequin ... 139
      Abacot/Hooded Ranger ... 140
   Heavyweight Breeds ... 141
      Aylesbury ... 141
      Pekin ... 142
      Muscovy ... 143
      Muscovy mixes ... 144
      Rouen ... 145
      Saxony ... 146
      Silver Appleyard ... 147
DUCKS OR DUCKLINGS ... 148
   The Benefits of Ducklings ... 148
      The bond of imprinting is strong ... 148
      What exactly is imprinting? ... 148
      Filial imprinting ... 148
      Sexual imprinting ... 149
   The Benefits of Ducks ... 150
      Guaranteed gender ... 150
      Guaranteed size ... 150
      Ducks and ducklings don't mix ... 150
      Ducks require less chaperoning than ducklings ... 150
      Helping a displaced animal ... 151
   Acquiring Ducklings ... 151
      Grain store ducklings ... 151

- **Hatchery ducklings** 151
- **Pet store ducklings** 151
- **Animal shelter ducklings** 152
- **Breeder ducklings** 152
- *Acquiring Ducks* 152
  - **Adopting a rescued duck** 152
  - **Determining the age of a duck** 153
  - **The nature of an adopted duck** 154
  - **Charging & retreating** 154
  - **Ducks as companion animals** 154
- *Quarantine* 155
  - **Bio-security** 156
- *Transporting Ducks* 156
- *No-Spill Water Bowl* 157
- *Shipping Adult Ducks* 157
  - **Never ship ducks in extreme weather** 158
  - **Prepare your post office staff** 159

EXPENSE 159
SEASONAL TIMING 160
WEATHER 160
- *Summertime Care* 160
  - **Keeping cool** 161
- *Wintertime Care* 161
  - **Keep an open water source** 161
  - **Bathing and preening** 161
  - **Warm feet in cold water** 161
  - **Snow on your aviary net** 162
  - **Snow on your electric fence** 162
  - **Sanding icy pens** 162
  - **Unsafe, ice-covered ponds** 163

FAMILY PLANNING 163
- The Birds and The Bees 163
- Ask The Stork 164
  - **What's that spiral thing hanging out of my drake?** 164
  - **Why are my same-gendered ducks mounting each other?** 164
  - **Why does my drake keep biting at my hands and wrists?** 165
  - **Why are my ducks jiggling their heads at me?** 165
  - **Do ducks mate for life?** 166
- *Planned Parenthood* 166
  - **Collect all eggs daily** 166
  - **Egg addling** 167
- *Hatching* 167
  - **Avoid incubating eggs** 167
  - **Let your duck do the work** 168

TIME INVESTMENT 168
- *Personal Schedule* 168
  - **Morning routines for ducks** 168
  - **Evening routines for ducks** 169
  - **Weekend routines for ducks** 169
  - **Vet trips** 169
  - **Continual care for ducklings** 169

FINDING A DUCK SITTER 170
LETTING GO 171
- *Euthanasia* 171
  - **Timing** 171
  - **Together or alone?** 171
  - **Medical procedure** 172
  - **Cremation** 173
- *One Without The Other* 173

  Duck mourning 173
  Human mourning 173
  A Momma Duck's grief 174

ENRICHMENT 176

My Ducky Diary 176
Water 176
Kiddy Pools 176
  Kiddy pool safety tips 176
Garden Hose 177
  Garden hose safety tips 177
Ponds 177
  Pond safety tips 177
Your Swimming Pool 178
  Swimming pool safety tips 178
Your Bathtub 178
  Bathtub safety tips 179
Walks & Foraging 179
Keep Your Eyes Open to Danger 179
Taking New Ducks on Walks 179
  Feeling entirely at home 179
  Flock cohesiveness 180
  Friends & small steps 180
  Portable playpens & a helper 180
  Waddle wands and hand signals 180
Healthy Treats 180
Earthworms 180
Cricket Box 181
Watermelon 181
Leaf Lettuce 182
Toes! 182
Transplanting Foliage 182
The Language of Ducks 183
Vocalizations 183
  Happy quack 183
  Content muttering 183
  Warning quacks 183
  Competitive boasts 183
  Trumpet displays 184
  Hissing 184
Body Language 184
  Tail wagging & catching rain 184
  Splayed tail 184
  Head bobbing 184
  Head vibration 184
Fun Sounds 185
  Duck callers 185
  Cell phone apps 185
  Recorded bird song books 185
Welcoming New Flock Members 185
Tag 186
Love at First Sight 186
Aggression 186
Introducing Ducklings to Adult Ducks 187
Naming Your Ducks 187
Dressing Up Your Duck 188
Costumes 188
  Play it safe 188

SPRING FEVER 188
EGGS 189
   Enrichment for Ducks 189
      Egg counting 189
      Egg rolling 189
   Enrichment For People 190
      Cooking eggs 190
      Egg hunts & coloring 190
      Egg art 190
ARTS & CRAFTS 190
   Footprint Art 190
   Sculpture 191
   Feather Art 191
   Photography 191
   Scrapbooking 192
SLEEPING 192
   Naps 193
VOICES & SINGING 194
   Songs & Rhymes 194
BECOMING A DUCK WHISPERER 194
   Response to Touch 194
      Positives 194
      Negatives 195
   Response to Children 195
   Response to Gender 195
VISITORS 195
   Frogs 195
   Wild Mallards 196
TOYS! 196
   Fun Can Sometimes Be A Little Scary 196
      Safety first 196
   Mirrors 197
   Cups 197
   Parrot and Baby Toys 198
   Lettuce Maze 198
   Plush Animals 199
   Remote Controlled Toys 199
HAPPY DUCKS = A HAPPIER YOU! 199

MEDICAL CARE 201
   Knowledge is Power 201
   Signs That Vet Care is Needed 201
   Medication Safety 202
      NSAID medication 202
      Aspiration & injection 202
      Medicating egg-laying ducks 202
      Safe antibiotics 202
   Dosage Verification Table 202
   Gelatin Capsules 206
   How to Give Your Duck a Pill 206
   Ducks as Pilling Patients 208
   Vet Visits & Rechecks 209
   Surgery 209
      Blood work 209
      Intubation 209
      Withhold food & water 210
      Anesthesia 210

- **Proper hygiene** 210
- **Friendship therapy** 210

STRESS 211
INTEGUMENTARY SYSTEM (BILLS) 212
- *Freckled Bill* 213
- *Peeling Bill & Rubber Bill* 213
- *Scratched Bill* 215
- *Broken Bill* 215
  - **Non-exposed tongue** 215
  - **Exposed tongue** 216
  - **Muscovy ducks with trimmed bills** 216
  - **Garden tools and bill injuries** 217
- *Punctured Bill* 218
- *Swollen Bill* 218
- *Prosthetic Bills* 219
- *Genetic Deformities* 219

INTEGUMENTARY SYSTEM (SKIN) 220
- *Bee Sting* 220
- *Frostbite* 220
- *Skin Coloration Changes* 221
- *Lacerations* 222
- *Puncture Wounds* 223
- *Abscess* 223
- *Cysts* 224
- *Follicular Cysts* 224
- *Bruises* 225
- *Melanoma* 226

INTEGUMENTARY SYSTEM (FEATHERS) 227
- *Molting* 227
  - **Why do ducks molt?** 227
  - **When do ducks molt?** 227
  - **Molting of sexually monomorphic ducks** 228
  - **Molting of sexually dimorphic ducks** 228
  - **Molting of Muscovy ducks** 229
  - **Molting tidbits** 229
  - **A duck who hasn't molted** 229
  - **Things to consider during the molt** 230
- *Feathers and Sunshine* 230
- *Random Feathers* 230
- *Yellow Feathers* 231
- *Impacted Oil Gland* 231
- *Overactive Oil Gland* 233
- *Underactive Oil Gland* 233
- *Infected Oil Gland* 234
- *Ruptured Oil Gland* 236
- *Wet Feather* 236
- *Minor Wet Feather Resolution* 237
- *Severe Wet Feather Corrective Procedure* 238
- *Plucking a Broken Blood Feather* 240
- *External Parasites* 241
- *Lice* 242
  - **Common types of waterfowl lice** 242
- *Mites* 243
- *Maggots* 245
- *Houseflies* 245
- *Flesh flies* 245

MUSCULOSKELETAL SYSTEM (HIPS, LEGS, FEET & TOES) 246

Basic Leg Anatomy 246
Therapy for Hips, Legs, Feet & Toes 246
   Hydrotherapy 246
   Duck cradles & wheelchairs 247
   Recovery items 248
   Stretch therapy 248
   Physical therapy, acupuncture & massage 249
   Weight management 249
Cold Feet 249
Sprains 249
Limb Amputation & Prosthetics 251
Dislocated Limb Joints 254
Foot & Leg Deformities 255
Niacin Deficiency in Ducklings 258
Splay Leg 258
Slipped Tendon 260
Broken Bones 260
   Symptoms of a healed broken bone 261
   Symptoms of a newly broken bone requiring attention 261
   Calcium supplementation 262
   Egg-laying ducks 262
Osteosarcoma 262
Arthritis 263
Toe & Footpad Injury 263
Torn or Punctured Webbing 264
Curled Toes 265
Broken Toenails 266
Infection 267
   Symptoms of an infection 267
Staph Infection 268
   Reading lab results 269
Bumblefoot 272
Synovitis 274
Osteomyelitis 274

MUSCULOSKELETAL SYSTEM (WINGS & TAILS) 278
Basic Wing Anatomy 278
Wing Clipping 278
Sprains 279
Angel Wing 284
Drooped Wing 285
Dislocated Wing 285
Broken Wing 285
Pinioned Wing 286
Wing Amputation 286
Wry Tail 287

MUSCULOSKELETAL SYSTEM (HEAD, NECK & ABDOMEN) 288
Keel Split 288
Broken Bones 288

REPRODUCTIVE SYSTEM (FEMALE) 290
Female Reproductive System 290
Treatment of Reproductive Disorders in Female Ducks 290
   HCG injections 290
   Leuprolide injections 291
   Utilizing both injections 291
   Hormone implants 291
   Expense 291
   Salpingohysterectomy 291

Egg Binding	292
Preventative Egg Binding Treatment Options	296
Dietary adjustments	296
Lighting adjustments	296
Environmental adjustments	296
Hands-off approach	296
Calcium gluconate to remedy soft-shelled eggs	296
Calcium carbonate to remedy soft-shelled eggs	296
Manganese to remedy soft-shelled eggs	297
Hormone injections	297
Obturator Paralysis	297
Oviduct Prolapse	298
Salpingitis	299
Metritis	299
Peritonitis	300
Cysts (Ovarian, Oviduct & Ovotestis)	301
Benign Reproductive Tumors	301
Ovarian Cancer	302
Oviduct Cancer	302
Inflamed Vent	303
Gender Change	303
Biological changes	303
Henopause	304
Tumors	305
Male role reversal	305
REPRODUCTIVE SYSTEM (MALE)	306
Male Reproductive System	306
Prolapsed Penis	306
Penectomy	308
Testicular Cancer	309
Testicular Cysts & Benign Tumors	309
Testosterone Overload	312
NERVOUS SYSTEM (EYES & EARS)	313
Ears	313
Hearing Impairment	313
Eyes	315
Eyelids	317
Sticky Eye	317
Eye Infection	317
Eye Trauma	318
Irritated Tear Duct	319
Sinusitis	319
Eye Dryness	320
Cataracts	320
Blindness	325
Transitioning	325
Pen safety	325
Simplicity	325
Routine & consistency	325
Rubber mats	325
Water safety	326
How to Build a Slope-Banked Pond	326
Companionship	327
Exercise and stimulation	327
Harness and leash	327
Signal sounds	328
NERVOUS SYSTEM (BRAIN & SPINAL CORD)	329
Seizures	329

Congenital Neurological Disorders 330
Brain & Spinal Cord Tumors 330
Environmental Neurological Disorders 330
Neurological Disease 330
Metabolic Bone Disease (Vitamin Deficiency) 331
Incubation Errors 331
Brain & Spinal Cord Trauma 331
Ingestion of Toxins 334
Hardware Disease 336
Lead Poisoning 337
Zinc Poisoning 340

RESPIRATORY SYSTEM 343
Chronic Respiratory Disease 343
Aspergillus 343
Pneumonia 345
Aspiration Pneumonia 348
Air Sac Injury & Infection 348
Air Sac Mites 349
Avian Chlamydia 349
Whistling 350

DIGESTIVE SYSTEM 351
Malnutrition 351
Internal Parasites 352
    Avoid home treatment plans 352
    Treating the entire flock 352
    Follow-up testing 353
    Preventing invasion 353
    Earthworms acting as hosts 353
Removing Parasites from Barns and Pens 353
    Additional cleaning tips 354
Capillary Worms (Roundworm/Nematode) 354
Cecal Worms (Roundworm/Nematode) 355
Strongyloides (Roundworm/Nematode) 356
Ascaris (Roundworm/Nematode) 356
Subulura (Roundworm/Nematode) 356
Tetrameres (Roundworm/Nematode) 357
Gizzard Worms (Roundworm/Nematode) 357
Gape Worms (Roundworm/Nematode) 357
Eyeworms (Roundworm/Nematode) 358
Fluke Worm (Flatworm/Trematode) 358
Tapeworms (Flatworm/Cestodes) 359
Trichomonas 359
Coccidia 360
Oversized Pebble Consumption 360
Lost Voice 361
Eggshell Craving 364
Feather Craving 365
Feather Biting 365
Appetite Changes 365
Medication & Appetite Loss 366
    Make food available 24/7 366
    Adjust the dosage 366
    Dosing at bedtime 366
    Measuring food consumption 367
Post-Surgical Appetite Loss (Intubation Irritation) 367
Bacterial Infection & Appetite Loss 367

- *Syringe Feeding* 368
  - **Recipe** 368
  - **Amounts** 368
  - **Instructions** 369
- *Tube feeding* 372
- *Dietary Aids* 372
  - **Energy water** 372
  - **Healx® booster** 372
  - **Vibrant Health® Rainbow Vibrance** 372
- *Probiotics* 373
- *Excess or Rapid Weight Gain* 374
- *Dehydration* 374
- *Diarrhea* 375
- *Crop* 375
- *Specialized Crop Diet* 378
  - **Automated feeders** 378
- *Sour Crop* 379
- *Crop Impaction* 380
- *Pendulous Crop* 381
- *Crop Injury* 382
- *Fatty Liver Hemorrhagic Disease (Hepatic Disease)* 382
- *Aspergillus Parasiticus (Aflatoxicosis)* 383
- *Botulism* 383

URINARY SYSTEM (RENAL SYSTEM) 384
- *Renal (Kidney) Disease* 384

CIRCULATORY SYSTEM (CARDIOVACULAR SYSTEM) 386
- *Heat Stroke* 386
- *Hypothermia* 387
- *Heart Attack (Myocardial Infarction)* 388
- *Cardiomyopathy (Heart Muscle Disease)* 388
- *Heart Murmur* 389
- *Congestive Heart Failure* 390
- *Endocarditis* 390
- *Anemia* 390
- *Sepsis (Septic Shock)* 391
- *Thymic Lymphoma* 391
- *Lymphocytic Leukemia* 392

ENDOCRINE SYSTEM 393
- *Endocrine Disorders* 393
- *Hypothyroidism (Underactive Thyroid)* 394
- *Hyperthyroidism (Overactive Thyroid)* 394
- *Endocrine Cancers* 394
- *Diabetes* 395
- *Pancreatitis* 395

LYMPHATIC-IMMUNE SYSTEM 397
- *Fever* 397
- *Immune Deficiency* 398
- *Thymic Carcinoma (Lymphosarcoma)* 398
- *Viral Disease* 399
- *Duck Virus Enteritis (Duck Plague)* 399
- *Duck Virus Hepatitis (DVH)* 400
- *Avian Diphtheria (Fowl Pox)* 400
- *Avian Encephalomyelitis* 400
- *Avian Proventricular Dilatation Disease (PDD)* 401
- *West Nile Virus (WNV)* 401
- *Newcastle Disease (NDV)* 401

- *Avian Influenza (Bird Flu)* 402
- *Bacterial Disease* 402
- *New Duck Syndrome/Disease (Infections Serositis)* 402
- *Avian Cholera* 403
- *Salmonellosis (Food Poisoning)* 403
- *Reticuloendotheliosis* 404
- SURVIVING PREDATORY ATTACK 405
- MY DUCKY MEDI-TRACKER 406

WATERFOWL RESCUE 408
- ABANDONED DUCKS 408
  - *Confirm the Duck is Abandoned* 408
- RESCUING DUCKS ON WATER 409
  - *Large Bodies of Water* 409
  - *Jet Ski* 409
    - **Two-seat jet ski** 409
    - **Single-seat jet ski** 409
  - *Kayaks, Canoes & Rowboats* 409
  - *Luring Ducks to Shore* 409
  - *Rescue Pen Assembly* 410
  - *Rescue Time* 411
  - *Rope Over The Water Rescue Method* 413
  - *Rescuing Tips* 413
    - **Fake left, grab right** 413
    - **I thought you had him!** 413
    - **We've got a flier!** 413
    - **Never grab a duck by the legs** 414
    - **Don't flinch** 414
  - *Ideal Catching Times* 414
- WILD WATERFOWL 414
  - *Wild Duck Emergency* 415
    - **Safe place** 415
    - **Water** 416
    - **Food** 416
    - **Drive & donate** 416

INDEX 417

Ducky Anecdotes

Glory's Staph Infection	252
Jessie's Broken Toe	256
Joven's Bumblefoot	270
Roberta's Bone Cancer	276
Lil Ms. Bee's Broken Wing	282
Alice's Ovarian Cancer	294
Young Jeffrey's Private Parts	310
Crocodile Stanley's Missing Eye	314
Deirdre Dear Heart's Cataracts	322
Tricia's Toxins	332
Daphnee's Hardware Disease	338
Lil Bo Peep's Pneumonia	346
Mercy's Refusal to Eat	362
Mercy's Diet	370
Neo's Crop	376

Intro-duck-tion

When I wrote the first edition of this book, I'd been a Momma Duck for seven years and the President and Founder of Majestic Waterfowl Sanctuary for five of those. Today, I have a total of twelve years of duck mothering under my belt and another two hundred pages of ducky knowledge to share with you that you won't find anywhere else (aside from our sanctuary's website).

In those twelve years of caring for over 165 rescued ducks (most of who were removed from ponds and lakes where they'd been abandoned by their prior owners), I've come to learn a lot about their care. Whether you're interested in the kind of standardized care that will keep your ducks safe, happy and healthy, or the type of individualized care for ducks with special needs, you'll find everything you need in these pages.

I remember when I first brought home my own little ducklings, Young Jeffrey and Young Matthew. Back then I only had two books to help me through my adventure and neither of them were any good. I was a loving and doting Momma Duck who needed an actual pet guide, not pages-upon-pages of breed standards, tips on fattening them up, or lousy advice about culling sick birds rather than providing them with quality vet care. Everywhere I turned all of these so-called "guides" were exactly the same, all offering me a whole lot of nothing when it came to quality pet advice. I knew I had to change all that.

And so I've written this *Ultimate Pet Duck Guidebook* for other Momma (and Poppa!) Ducks like me. In the pages to come I'm going to be very specific when it comes to some of the items that I like to use, and I'll often include brand names, detailed descriptions and supplier websites to help you source them for your own ducks. While websites can change and products might improve and/or become unavailable, this information should still set you up with enough information to find what you need.

Beyond that, this guide will help walk you through the preparations you'll need to make before welcoming your ducks home, bringing to mind those special things you may not even know to consider. And to top it off, I've included a fun and duck-proven enrichment chapter. But even more so, my book contains *the most* comprehensive compilation of medical information you'll ever find pertaining to domestic waterfowl injuries and ailments, including the knowledge of how you and your vet can properly treat them. You'll find lots of duck books out there offering advice in every other area, but *none* will help you in that desperate moment if something goes wrong. This medical chapter has proven itself to be the key selling point of the entire book, saving hundreds of known ducky lives and preserving the hearts of their loving families all around the world.

No matter what anyone else tries to tell you, ducks are a high-maintenance pet; they require a lot of care and attention and they *do* get sick (they're just better at hiding it than most animals). To help you find quick answers to your questions, I've set up the most detailed table of contents I could possibly provide along with an exhaustive index because I know when you and your duck need help you usually need it *fast!*

Please keep in mind that you won't be reading about hatching techniques in this guidebook. As a caretaker of so many homeless ducks the last thing I want to do is hatch out ducklings. This means I have absolutely no hands-on knowledge to share with you in this regard. My only advice is to tell you to let your ducks do it themselves because they know *exactly* how it's done and are far less likely to make incubating mistakes that frequently end extremely badly for the ducklings.

REMEMBER: Although I've written this guidebook to help you and your duck, I'm *not* a veterinarian. No book can replace the assistance of a board certified, qualified and experienced vet. This book will provide you with the information you need to ask your vet educated questions, but it's in no way intended as a substitute for proper vet care.

Preparations

Preparations

So you're looking at that cute duckling and thinking, *"How much trouble could that little thing be?"* Before you hold that tiny darling against your cheek and smell the sweet scent of their fluff and the pleasant odor of their crumbled food, consider carefully. This little fellow won't be much trouble now, but in a few weeks, you're going to have your hands full. There are many preparations that need to be considered and addressed *before* you bring a new duckling home and become a Momma Duck (sorry, fellows, but even daddy ducks are referred to as Momma Ducks in this book because that's how your duckling sees you!).

As with any pet, ducklings need a lot of care and attention—and *a lot* of protection from predators. You'll need to find yourself a good vet, purchase waterfowl supplies and build an enclosure for your duck to live in—not to mention all the cleaning you'll need to do. So, put that duckling back down, read this book, and if being a Momma Duck still sounds perfect for you, then go back and buy a couple—one for each cheek (or better yet, adopt!).

Preparation #1
Vet Care

First and foremost, on the top of your list, is always vet care. Finding a doctor for a duck can be extremely difficult—not at all what you're used to when finding vet care for your other animals. For this reason, I highly recommend that you call your local vet hospitals *before* bringing a duck home to make sure you have access to health care and information for your duck prior to their arrival. Don't make the mistake of assuming that just because an avian vet is qualified to see birds that they're also qualified to treat your ducks. Birds such as parrots, parakeets and canaries require very different care and medications than ducks. What is safe for some birds isn't necessarily safe for your ducks, and in some cases, can be quite harmful.

Finding a Waterfowl Vet

I've begun a nationwide registry of waterfowl vets on our sanctuary's website in an attempt to help folks find a duck-tor for their feathered friends. Families who have waterfowl vets provide us with their vet information through our site, so I can contact the vet office, confirm the information and then add them to our website's national *"Vet Finder."*

Another good way to find a waterfowl vet is to do an internet search for avian vets in your state. Begin calling each of these vets to determine which ones specifically handle ducks.

- **Ask your vet questions**

Never assume anything when it comes to your duck's vet care. There are questions that you'll need to ask them to be sure they're a good match for your feathered friend. If they're not available for direct consultation you can always ask a knowledgeable staff member your questions.

Before establishing a relationship with a particular vet practice make sure to find out what kind of service you'll be getting after-hours, on weekends and holidays. If they're the only waterfowl vet in the vicinity, will they answer their pages during off-hours and under what conditions? If another vet office covers their emergencies when they're closed do they have a waterfowl vet on staff? Weigh all of your options and design a vet plan that you and your duck can rely on.

Keep in mind that staff changes occur in vet offices, so it's a good idea to periodically check in and confirm that the same qualified vet is still on their team and available for appointments should the need arise.

Here are some good questions to consider when screening a potential vet:

1. How many duck patients does this vet have?

2. How many ducks does this vet see as patients in any given month/year?

3. What formal education has this vet received that has directly prepared them for the special handling of waterfowl, including any training seminars attended (in the U.S., the *Association of Avian Veterinarians* meets annually and often includes a seminar on waterfowl).

4. Is this vet experienced with reproductive issues that may occur in egg-laying ducks and do they know how to properly treat those issues should they arise?

5. Has this vet operated on ducks in the past? If so, what types of surgeries have they performed and what were those outcomes?

6. What reference books does this vet recommend you read in order to better care for your ducks? *(If they can't think of any... be wary!)*

If at any time in the future this vet should become stumped by your duck's medical condition, what resources will they tap into for assistance? *(Ideally, you're looking for a vet who's willing to consult with other vets. They're the best. Avoid vets who will "read up" or "surf the internet" as their sole means of research.)*

HINT: One tell-tale indication that a vet doesn't have a lot of experience with waterfowl is often demonstrated in their inability to easily open up their bills. A vet who tries to pry a duck's bill open at the *tip* is demonstrating their experience with parrots and their inexperience with waterfowl. You want to see a vet who knows to pry their bill open at the *base*. A vet who can't manage to open a duck's bill within a few seconds most likely doesn't have many waterfowl patients (see *"How to Give Your Duck a Pill"*).

- **Find a back-up vet**

I don't know what it is about my ducks, or any of my animals for that matter, but it seems if they're going to get sick, injured, or just start acting funny, they always seems to do it after-hours, on weekends, over a long holiday, or during that particular week that my vet just happens to be away on vacation. This is why it's vital to have a back-up plan if your vet is unreachable.

I highly recommend finding a second, emergency veterinarian willing and qualified to take ducks into their care as patients 24 hours a day, 7 days a week. You should do this *before* you bring your duck home. You don't want to spend precious time in an emergency situation calling dozens of vet offices, trying to find someone willing to assist your duck. Worse yet, this would be a terrible time to discover that there aren't any emergency waterfowl vets around you. I keep track of the waterfowl vets in my area, and in addition to my main veterinarian I have a back-up vet *and* an emergency 24/7 vet office with multiple qualified vets on staff.

While having a 24/7 waterfowl vet is ideal, there still may be times when they aren't available—especially depending on where you live. There may be periods of time when your vet offices change their hours, when your vet switches practices completely, or when both your vet and your back-up vet are out of the office at the same time (which is not uncommon when avian vet conferences are running). As long as you know this ahead of time, you can plan for it and be prepared.

- **Confirm only qualified waterfowl vets will be handling your duck**

Anytime your duck is being treated while you're not right in the room with them, make sure that the vet handling them is the actual qualified waterfowl veterinarian you've selected. This is especially true in emergency situations or when operations are being performed. You don't want your duck being passed into unqualified hands after you leave the room (and trust me, this does happen). There's only one way to be sure that your duck is being handled properly and by the appropriate people and that is to step up and *ask*.

- **Ducks hide when they're sick!**

My cat vet once told me to never trust anyone, not even a vet, when it comes to the diagnosis of one of my animals. She said no matter how hard your vet tries to convince you that they can't find anything wrong with your pet, if you still don't feel comfortable—*trust your instincts* and call on another vet. You know your duck better than anyone else because you're with them every day and know their normal behavior. If you see them acting a bit peculiar trust your eyes and your heart. This is another reason to have a second vet contact available ahead of time—to get a second opinion when you need it.

When cared for properly and kept in clean quarters, ducks tend to be very healthy and very resistant to disease. However, when they do become sick or injured, ducks are well known for hiding their ailments as a defense mechanism against predators, so they won't be the first one targeted. It's easy (and sometimes impossible) to miss early warning signs and suddenly end up with a seriously ill duck and wonder how this all came on so quickly—ultimately, it didn't. You've been tricked like many Momma Ducks before you. And once things have progressed this far, the need for vet intervention will be immediate. This is why the early recognition of subtle warning signs can be life saving. Closely monitoring behavioral changes in your ducks and contacting a vet early-on with your concerns can often prevent a hidden health condition from worsening.

This advice should also be shared with your family. If you sense that something is wrong with your duck and a family member tells you not to worry, take it with a grain of salt. Always trust your instincts when one of your ducks is not behaving normally, no matter what anyone else tells you. Place a call to your vet and have your duck seen by a professional.

Preparation #2
Stocking Your Medicine Cabinet

Now it's time to stock your medicine cabinet and get your supplies ready. These are some of the items you may want to have on hand if you're going to bring home a duck. You'll most likely never need most of them, but if you do, it's a good idea to be prepared.

Important Items to Have On Hand:

- **Carry Box:** Fish & tackle boxes and small tool organizers have various compartment dimensions that are perfect for storing your duck's medical supplies. They come in a wide variety of convenient shapes, colors and sizes and are often very affordable.

- **Disposable gloves:** You may need these for applying topical ointments / medications.

- **Needle nose pliers:** You may need these to pluck out a blood feather if it breaks.

- **Small, lightweight towel:** You may need this to drape over your duck's head in an emergency. Covering their eyes with a towel can sometimes calm a duck in crisis. Try to find one that isn't too heavy and just the right size for your duck, keeping in mind that dark colors block light better than white ones.

- **Clothespin:** You may need this to hold a towel *loosely* in place over your duck's head during an emergency. Be careful to only clip the towel to itself without catching any part of your duck or their feathers in between.

- **Blood coagulant (styptic powder/swabs):** It's wise to have this on hand for any pet emergency in your household. For ducks, you may need this in the case of a feather break emergency, or to control any excessive bleeding of the bill, feet or legs.

- **Cotton swabs:** These can be handy for cleaning out small wounds or for applying ointments or styptic powders.

- **Gauze pads:** You may need these to control bleeding if an accident occurs.

- **Vet wrap flexible cohesive bandage:** A roll of vet wrap can come in handy when you need to wrap a sprained wing or leg (2" x 2.2 yards).

- **Reel of adhesive tape:** You may need this to hold gauze bandaging or vet wrap in place.

- **Delousing powder:** You may need this in case you need to delouse your ducks.

- **K-Y® Jelly / Lubricant:** You may need this to moisten a prolapsed oviduct.

- **Saline solution (optic formula):** You may need this for flushing out eye injuries, which aren't uncommon during the mating season. A sensitive eye formula is ideal.

- **Non-sting, first-aid wound wash:** You may need this to clean out a cut or treat broken skin to help stave off infection. Try to find this in a spray bottle to help make application easier. Use wound wash sparingly around feathers since some formulas may interfere with waterproof effectiveness.

- **Oral Syringe:** You may need this to dose medication or for feeding a sick or injured duck.

- **Sav-A-Chick®:** These small nutrient packets come in multiple formulas that contain electrolytes and probiotics as well as essential vitamins and minerals. They're perfect for an emergency situation with an under-the-weather duckling, or even an adult duck.

- **Avi-Culture® probiotic powder:** It's good to have a probiotic designed specifically for birds on hand. It can be stored indefinitely in your freezer. You may need this when your duck is on medication. It protects their intestinal flora, and it's also a great preventative during stressful times including when they molt.

- **General antibiotic:** Ask your vet to provide you with a few antibiotic pills to keep on hand for your duck. I recommend having 4 doses available (enough for one dose every twelve hours for a total of two days). Remember previously when I mentioned those times when you might not have a 24/7 back-up vet available? Having this medication on hand has proven to be a life-saver for many families in this situation. Keep in mind, vets are less likely to give you emergency medication if they don't believe you'll bring your duck in for an exam at the first available moment. These medications are not intended to *replace* vet care, but to hold your duck over until you can get there. Long-term clients, trusted for their commitment to their pets, are far more likely to receive this kind of consideration. If your vet is willing to provide you with this medication, be sure your duck's dosage information and clear instructions are printed on the label for you, so you'll know exactly what to do in an emergency.

  As with any medication, remember to periodically check your duck's medicine cabinet and review all expiration dates, properly discarding/refilling any old prescriptions as needed.

- **Anti-inflammatory/pain medication:** Leg sprains aren't uncommon in ducks and having this type of medication on hand can really help reduce pain and swelling until you can make it to a vet.

- **Pill cutter:** You may need this to cut pills into optimal dosages.

- **Sting Free Bacitraycin Plus®:** You may need this topical ointment if someone gets a small scratch or cut. Whereas wound washes will rinse away, ointments tend to stick around longer. This tends to work best on the legs and feet, but it can also be applied (under vet direction) to irritated vent areas. Be careful not to get it on your duck's feathers.

- **Antibiotic eye ointment:** Ask your vet to provide you with a tube of antibiotic eye ointment. You may need this if someone gets a poke in the eye, which is not uncommon during the mating season. This is another medication that can be administered in an emergency situation until you get your duck to the vet for a much-needed eye exam.

I have a well-stocked first-aid kit for sanctuary emergencies

Purchase a Pet Carrier

In addition to having a fully stocked medicine cabinet you should always have a pet carrier on hand for emergencies. I have a lot of ducks at my sanctuary, so I keep multiple carriers on hand. There've been times where I needed to bring a few ducks in at a time, which can be simple or complicated depending on which ducks need to go to the vet. Some ducks like to travel together while others don't, so it's best to have more than one carrier on hand in case of an emergency involving two or more ducks.

Preparation #3
Feed

Your next step in preparing for your new ducks is to decide what brand of feed you'll serve and what type of feed dispensers you'll utilize. I've tried many things, and through trial and error, my Young Jeffrey and Young Matthew (along with a myriad of other ducks) have taught us what works the best.

Choose a Feed Brand

I remember when I was first researching my feed options. I read long-winded advice about percentages of this and percentages of that. I spent hours reading bag labels, flipping through guidebooks and punching numbers into calculators. I felt like a chemist. I'm going to spare you all of that and make the process much simpler for you.

If you buy duck feed that is *specifically designed* for ducklings, and later for ducks, the companies have already worked out the math for you. The only thing you have to keep in mind is the age of your ducks, the gender of your ducks and the quality of feed you want to give them. You can choose whatever duck food you want and even change your mind down the road.

The first time you go to the grain store it may take a few minutes to review brand options with a counter person who knows their product lines. If they don't know the answers to your questions, then they aren't the informed person you're looking for. If this is the case, ask them to call someone to the counter who can be of better assistance.

- **Duckling crumbles**

If you plan on adding ducklings to your family, then you want to get yourself some brand name, quality duckling crumbles. Most brands will recommend feeding for the first four to eight weeks, but I recommend feeding it for the first seven to eight weeks. When you feel your duckling can easily swallow adult-sized pellets, mix their crumbles in with the pellets for the first couple of days and once you're sure they're eating the adult food, phase it out completely. My ducks all made the transition in a matter of days, usually no later than three and sometimes as quickly as one. Transitioning your ducks to a new type of feed tends to be relatively simple. I've never seen a healthy duck have an adverse reaction (i.e. diarrhea, vomiting) resulting from the introduction of nutritional feed, progressing through staged feed formulas, or while upgrading their diet to a higher quality feed formula.

- **Avoid medicated feed**

Ducks require non-medicated food, which is different from other poultry foods. Never feed your ducks medicated food. Ducks have a very good immune system. If you feed them medicated food you can affect this, and it can be deadly.

- **U.S. brand options**

1. Mazuri®

I highly recommend the Mazuri® line for your pet duck. It costs more, but this food is designed for long life expectancy and the maintaining of good health for your pets (and it floats on water which is its own fun when you have a duck!). I've seen it work miracles at the sanctuary, so if you can get your hands on it, it's worth its weight in gold. Mazuri® has a very helpful dealer locator on their website or you can have it shipped directly to your home. If they don't carry it, some grain stores will special order it for you.

 Mazuri® Waterfowl Starter (0-7 weeks)
 Mazuri® Waterfowl Maintenance (8 weeks and up)
 Mazuri® Waterfowl Breeder (mature egg-laying ducks)
 For more information: www.mazuri.com

2. Nutrena®

Nutrena® is another recommended feed option for your pets and is my second favorite brand.

 Nutrena® NatureWise® Chick Starter Grower (0-7 weeks)
 Nutrena® NatureWise® All Flock (7 weeks and up)
 Nutrena® NatureWise® Layer Feed (mature egg-laying ducks)
 For more information: www.nutrenaworld.com

3. Blue Seal®

Blue Seal® is another option also formulated with your pets in mind. They have two formulas available for pet ducks.

 Blue Seal® OrganicLife® Starter Crumbles (0-3 weeks)
 Blue Seal® OrganicLife® Grower Crumbles (3 weeks and up)
 Blue Seal® OrganicLife® Layer Pellets (mature egg-laying ducks)

 Blue Seal® Home Fresh™ Grower-Cal Mash (0-3 weeks)
 Blue Seal® Home Fresh™ Grower-Cal Pellets (3 weeks and up)
 Blue Seal® Home Fresh™ Layer Pellets (mature egg-laying ducks)
 For more information: www.blueseal.com

4. Purina®

Although they don't have a specific duckling formula (which I highly prefer) Purina® also has a couple of products that you can feed your ducks.

Purina® Start & Grow® SunFresh™ Recipe, NON-medicated formula (0 – 7 weeks)
Purina® Flock Raiser® SunFresh™ Recipe (8 weeks and up)
Purina® Layena® SunFresh™ Recipe (mature egg-laying ducks)
For more information: www.purinamills.com

- **U.K. brand options**

Pet ducks are quite popular in the United Kingdom., so here are some quality waterfowl feed brands for all of our U.K. friends:

1. Mazuri ® Europe

   Mazuri® Waterfowl Starter (0-7 weeks)
   Mazuri® Waterfowl Maintenance (8 weeks and up)
   Mazuri® Waterfowl Breeder (mature egg-laying ducks)
   For more information: www.mazuri.com

2. Small Holder Range®

   Small Holder Range® Goose & Duck Starter Crumbs (0-7 weeks)
   Small Holder Range® Goose & Duck Grower and Finisher Pellets (8 weeks and up)
   Small Holder Range® Ornamental Poultry Pellets (8 weeks and up)
   Small Holder Range® Goose & Duck Breeder Pellets (mature egg-laying ducks)
   Small Holder Range® Breeder & Show (mature egg-laying ducks)
   For more information: www.smallholderfeed.co.uk/

3. Fenland/Fancy Feed Company

   Fancy Feed Chick Crumb (0-7 weeks)
   Fancy Feed Fenland Waterfowl Pellets (8 weeks and up)
   Fancy Feed Breeder & Show Pellets (mature egg-laying ducks)
   For more information: www.fancyfeedcompany.co.uk/index.htm

4. The Organic Feed Company

   Organic Feed Baby Chick Crumbs (0-7 weeks)
   Organic Feed Grower Finisher Pellets (8 weeks and up)
   Organic Feed Layers Pellets (mature egg-laying ducks)
   For more information: www.organicfeed.co.uk/

5. Garvo

   Garvo Waterfowl Starter Mini Pellets #805 (0-7 weeks)
   Garvo Duck Starter/Grower Pellets #832 (8 weeks and up)
   Garvo Duck & Goose Pellets #831 (8 weeks and up)
   Garvo Waterfowl Condition/Show Pellets #816 (8 weeks and up)
   Garvo Waterfowl Breeder Pellets #803 (mature egg-laying ducks)
   Garvo Waterfowl Floating Pellets #4222 (8 weeks and up)
   For more information: www.garvo.co.uk/

Feed Brand Research

You can't always know how good your own brand stacks up until you compare it with others. For this reason, I encourage all Momma Ducks to do their own feed brand research. The first step is to do some reading, both in books and on the internet. Next, contact your feed company and other feed companies and ask questions. Check their reputation by researching their parent and related companies.

1. Find out about their in-house Quality Control procedures.
2. Ask them questions about their suppliers.
3. Find out where their grain is milled.
4. Find out what else is produced at this mill.
5. Find out what drugs may be used at this mill.
6. Ask them about the "sequential production" of their grain.

- **Sequential production**

A company's attention to sequential production is a very important consideration when choosing your feed brand. You want to be absolutely sure that the manufacturing plant that produces your duck feed pays close attention to the type of feed they're mixing just before running a batch of your duck's food. Batch-to-batch contamination can be dangerous if they're producing a very different type of diet (especially a medicated one) for another species of animal just prior to processing your duck's next meal.

In other words, if they're bagging monkey food right before they bag your duck food and a few kibbles accidentally spill over into your bag, you want to know that those monkey kibbles won't hurt your duck if accidentally ingested.

Quality sequential production means that companies purposefully order the production of their various feed lines in such a way that any minor run-over from batch-to-batch will be absolutely safe for your duck. Some mills will also flush between runs as an added form of security and in some cases, medications that may be harmful to a particular species won't be bagged at the same manufacturing plant as the feed for susceptible species. Knowing a little about the safety precautions that went into producing your duck's feed can truly help you make a wise brand selection.

- **Quality control**

The following are a few basic Quality Control questions you can ask:

1. What kind of in-house QC testing do they routinely perform?
2. Do they test every ingredient?
3. Do they test every batch they mix?
4. Are their ingredients sourced in the U.S.?
5. Which of their ingredients are sourced from other countries?
6. Which ingredients are certified as tested by their suppliers?
7. Do they check up on their supplier's QC practices? How often?
8. Do they quality test any of their suppliers' certified tested ingredients?
9. Which ingredients aren't tested and why?
10. What kind of consumer guarantees do they offer?

Keep in mind, the more tests they do, the more expensive your feed will be. Companies can't test for everything or their feed would be unaffordable for most of us. But are they covering the basics? The things you're concerned about? You're going to have to ask.

Other things I like to keep in mind when asking questions of feed companies are: How helpful were they? How educated were they about their own product? How was their customer service while you were on the phone? How long did you have to wait for your answer(s)? Do you think it'll be better or worse in a time of crisis—if you ever have an issue with their feed?

Make sure your ducks are on the best diet possible

Milling/Manufacturing Plants

It's in your best interests to know where your feed is produced and what other products are being produced in those plants in case of any spill-over contamination. I find that company representatives appear to know more about their milling practices when they actually own their own manufacturing plants. In 2012-2013 I confirmed the following information from the four leading feed brands:

1. *Mazuri® & Purina®:* Mazuri and Purina Mills both own and utilize their own manufacturing plants. All products within the Mazuri line are manufactured in company facilities. Most of the Mazuri production is done at the Richmond, IN Specialty Mill. This mill has been run completely drug-free (no antibiotics, other meds or hormones) since 1971.

   In addition to manufacturing their own brand line, Purina Mills also mill feed for other companies as well as doing custom formulations for other large customers.

2. *Nutrena®:* In the U.S., Cargill (parent company) primarily manufactures feed at their own mills, although in some areas they have agreements with regional mills to manufacture their feed for them. If at any time they have a mill outside their company manufacturing their feed for them, that mill needs to have the same QA/QC (Quality Assurance/Quality Control) programs in place as Cargill.

3. *Blue Seal®:* Blue Seal is owned by parent company Kent Nutrition Group and Kent owns the mills that produce the Blue Seal® Home Fresh™ feed line. On the other hand, the Blue Seal® OrganicLife® feed line is milled by Kreamer Feed Company located in PA. They're PCO (Pennsylvania Certified Organic) and certified USDA Organic.

Feed Bag Ingredient Labels

You may want to investigate feed ingredient labels as a part of your brand research. If so, you'll soon discover which brands stand out from the crowd and which are simply not designed for the optimal health and longevity of our pet ducks.

- **Feed label facts**

1. Current labeling laws don't require livestock and poultry feed ingredients to be listed in any particular order on the tag.

2. According to these same labeling laws, feed companies do *not* have to specifically list *all* of the ingredients on their feed labels either. For example, if they purchase an ingredient from a supplier, they don't have to list anything that supplier may have added to that ingredient before the feed company purchased it.

3. Ingredients are listed according to the condition they were in when they were first purchased by the feed company, *not* by how they may have changed *after* being purchased. This means that any changes in the state of the ingredient after coming into inventory (whether intended or not) don't have to be listed. For example, if a company adds viable probiotics to their feed, it doesn't necessarily mean they're still viable at the end of manufacturing.

4. If the label doesn't say the ingredient is *"whole,"* it may have had the healthy germ removed. Often times wheat, corn and soybeans have the germ removed prior to processing. This is sometimes done as a preservative measure, but other times it's the result of a feed company using inexpensive leftovers. Check the label to see if the germ is added back in later; if so, it was likely done as a preservative measure. If the germ is not added back in, you may be buying grain remnants that have had all of their hearty centers removed.

- **Generic labeling**

Some feed brands use generic labeling (sometimes referred to as *"Group Labeling"*) on their products. Instead of listing exact grains used in their feed you may see ingredients like: *"Grain"* and *"Grain by-products"* on their label.

This means the grains they're using (and the parts of the grains they're using) tend to vary, making their formulas different from bag-to-bag or lot-to-lot depending on their suppliers, availability and ingredient prices. Rather than having a myriad of ingredient labels, they use one vague and generic label.

<u>Vitamin Fortified Feed vs. Mixing Your Own Grains</u>

My vet has advised me to keep all of my ducks on vitamin fortified feed because it helps them maintain good health, which is the best defense against illness, and I find this advice makes good sense.

Even so, some Momma Ducks prefer their own special mixes. Home mix ingredients should come from a reliable and qualified source--that is, from an individual certified in Animal/Bird Nutrition who's aware of the specialized needs of waterfowl. Any such person should be able to easily produce proof of their certification. Any special diets of this nature should be followed exclusively and exactly to avoid throwing off their nutritional balance.

Before putting your duck on a specially designed home mixed diet, you should review the diet with your vet, providing them with the precise details of what your duck will be eating to verify its completeness and safety. Keep in mind, unlike brand name feed lines, which account for a wide variety of variables, a home-mix diet may need to be adjusted seasonally, reflecting a number of factors including access to sunlight and available foraging.

Before I knew any better and switched over to the Mazuri® line, I followed what one guidebook said and mixed my own grains together to try to make a healthy and complete diet for my ducks. It's okay to do this, but in the end I discovered that a good name-brand formula can save you a lot of time and energy and they can often do things a lot better than I can on my own. It's easy to do more harm than good.

Another issue with home mixes is they can lure in an onslaught of unwanted dinner guests, some of whom just don't have very good table manners. Rodents tend to be more drawn to whole grains than they are to milled and processed grains, so pay special attention to your storage techniques to avoid an infestation.

- **Seeds & cracked corn**

Some seeds (especially those still in their hulls) can be difficult for ducks to digest, so do your research before adding them to your duck's home mixed diet.

While cracked corn is often mistaken as the end-all, be-all food for ducks, it's more like "duck candy." You can give them a little, but too much can result in unnecessary weight gain. Some people will add extra cracked corn to their duck's diets in winter to help their ducks bulk up in preparation for cold weather.

Feed Bag Expiration Dates

Some sources will advise against buying large bags of feed, so that you always have fresh food, but in my area it's only sold in fifty pound bags and there's simply no choice in the matter. If you only have a couple ducks and you can't buy partial bags from your grain store, make sure you use up the last of the bag before its vitamins and nutrients lose their potency.

The expiration date of most feed is usually 60-90 days after the date the bag was filled as indicated by the date stamped on the bag; however, within 60 days of the stamped date is highly preferable. Mazuri feed is the exception to the rule. Their formula locks vitamins in for 6-9 months, so using bags within 6 months of the date stamped is ideal. You'll soon learn how quickly your ducks consume their food and how to judge the expiration date on the bag, so that the food is consumed well before you reach that date.

Some feed companies stamp the actual date the feed was bagged somewhere on the label (or on the bag itself) while other companies stamp what I like to refer to as, "a secret code." Reading these codes can be baffling. If your grain store can't translate this code into a valid date for you, contact the company and they'll help you with the deciphering.

- **Feed recalls**

If you're pouring your fifty pound bags of feed into barrels or bins for easy access and safe storage don't discard the bag until you've written the complete lot/batch number on your calendar (I have a special ducky calendar used for just this reason!).

Feed recalls can occur many months after your duck has consumed their supper. Will you remember what they've eaten? Good record keeping can bring instant peace of mind, or it can provide detailed information for you and your veterinarian.

In addition to visiting a company's webpage for recall information, you can also visit the FDA's website (www.fda.gov) to review a company's feed recall history.

Fresh Feed

It's not a good idea to leave feed exposed to the elements. Moisture on duck feed rapidly ruins its quality. You don't want to feed your duck wet, mildewed food or they could get very sick.

Poor diet or poor quality food can lead to a number of problems. Help keep your duck healthy by throwing out any food of questionable quality. Don't risk feeding your pet anything but the best. Read up on duck nutrition and symptoms of nutritional problems/vitamin deficiencies, so you'll recognize any warning signs early on and have plenty of time to correct them.

While I don't necessarily recommend it, I'm aware that not all Momma Ducks have aviary protection over the top of their duck's day pen. If this situation applies to you, avoid leaving unprotected feed dishes out where they can lure night creatures towards "the water hole," so to speak. Little nocturnal creatures looking for tidbits attract bigger creatures looking for tidbits. Don't teach your local wildlife where to find a snack. You don't want to host a predator-prey function in your duck's yard (even when they're not in it), so be sure to pick up their food at night and bring it into a fully predator-proof location.

Young Jeffrey and I bond over a snack on the pond

Feed Storage

I was once advised not to store my feed in metal trash cans because metal can sweat during temperature changes, which can lead to mildew growth. I tried using plastic trash cans, but the mice were relentless. Too many free meals were given away; they destroyed the plastic trash barrels and they created a terrible mess in my barn. To date, I've never found a better alternative than the metal cans, and I've never run into any trouble with them sweating—and we have frosty winters as well as hot and humid summers.

- **Peppermint oil & dearth**

A few routine drops of peppermint oil onto the wooden pallets that support my feed bags helps keep mice out of my grain storage shed—more so, peppermint seeded and planted all around my grain shed works even better. Mice don't like the smell of peppermint (or perhaps it overpowers the scent of the feed), so it helps keep them from helping themselves to free meals. It really is a great preventative for bag damage and feed loss.

To protect my feed bags from insects and beetles, I spread food-grade Diatomaceous earth (Dearth) between the concrete foundation and floor boards of my grain shed. You can routinely sprinkle it on the ground outside your storage shed for even greater results.

- **Feed and rodents**

Food draws in all kinds of freeloaders; you need to keep your eyes open. If you attract a rat, you'll need to react quickly. There are many opinions regarding the best way to manage rat control, but keep in mind, rats are fast learners. If you don't eliminate the entire colony quickly, the survivors will learn to avoid your traps.

Although I'm fond of all animals and think there is a place for each of them in this world, even if it's on the far-end of my eight acres, I can't have rats in my duck pens. Not only will they wipe out food at a record rate, but they also have a tendency to gnaw through everything in their way causing damage to your pens, barns and duck houses. They're also infamous for making access routes into your pens for other predators to follow. On top of this, they tend to use feed dishes as litter boxes and can introduce parasites and diseases. All of this means that rats are simply not welcome in my pens.

A non-recommended common strategy to solve a rat problem is to cut off their food supply. The theory is that as the food supply dwindles, the stronger rats in the colony will kill and eat the younger and weaker ones until there is only one survivor remaining. I don't recommend it, first because it's extremely difficult to do. A hungry and determined rat will work that much harder at breaking and entering into any food establishment in the vicinity, which results in property damage. Second, I don't recommend it because a starving rat is more likely to turn on your feathered friends. I don't dare risk having a hungry rat looking at my ducks as a food source in the absence of anything else.

Our first defense against rodents are two rescued female cats (spayed of course) who've grown up in my pens and have a healthy respect for my ducks. My cats live in the enclosures with my rescues and move from pen to pen utilizing cat doors and ramps. At night and in cold weather they can be found lounging in cat beds up in the hay loft. It's a safe and enriching environment for them to play in and they live to catch rodents.

If you know where the rat holes are, carbon dioxide smoke bombs are another reliable outdoor solution to your problem. You can pick them up at most grain stores (proving that you're not alone in having this issue). You close up all but one of the holes with soil, setting a healthy-sized rock on top of each one. Next, place a pile of filler soil beside the final hole and have a good-sized rock ready as well. Light the fuse of one smoke bomb and push it down into the open hole. Cover the hole quickly with the soil and then place the rock on top. Stand watch and have extra soil and rocks ready in case any smoke comes out of any hidden holes. Cover those quickly to avoid any escapees. After a minute or two the trapped rodents inside will fall unconscious and suffocate. Return to the hole twenty minutes later with gloves and dig out the used rodent bomb and dispose according to the directions.

I recommend that you bomb a couple more times over the next few days to be sure you've gotten everyone—especially if new holes appear. This type of bomb is safe to use in the vicinity of your ducks as long as you've covered all the holes properly and your ducks aren't near the holes while you're doing it.

Remember, these gas bombs are for outside use only. The gas is colored and scented for your protection, so if you miss a hole, you'll see and smell a stream of yellowish-green gas coming out. Cover it quickly to contain the gas and any "non-friendlies." Continue with this tactic until no more holes are found and the telltale signs of the rodents are completely gone.

Tomcat® Snap Traps can be used *outside* and around your duck pen where your ducks *cannot* come in contact with them. I set these outside and around my perimeter fencing in areas where rodents like to travel. I aim the open mouth of the trap towards the fencing to prevent any other wildlife (or my neighbor's cats) from accidentally triggering the traps and getting snagged. Additionally, I attach a wire tether line to each trap and use a carabineer to latch it to the fencing. This prevents predators for coming for a quick meal and dragging off my traps (a favorite trick of fox and raccoons). Unlike traditional rodent traps, these snap traps are easier and safer to handle and set.

Keep in mind, rats are very clever and they'll quickly outsmart your traps, so it's best to wipe out as many as you can at a time and then switch tactics. They'll learn to backfill their holes with soil to thwart smoke bomb attacks and they'll avoid snap traps or learn to fill them with dirt to foil your attempts. More so, they'll teach these behaviors to their young. For best results strike quickly and thoroughly to prevent rodent invasion.

- **Rodent prevention & control**

There are some strategies you can utilize to help prevent rodents from wandering into your duck pen in the first place.

1. The best fencing we've found to keep out rats is ½" x ½", 16 gauge, polyvinyl coated hardware cloth/welded wire mesh with a galvanized steel wire core (supplier: Academy Fence Company www.academyfence.com). Completely surrounding your pens with this type of wire will keep rodents out, provided your perimeter also goes at least two feet underground. The benefit of this type of fencing is it'll last you and your flock a lifetime; it won't rust or deteriorate.

2. Installing predator skirts around your duck pen will also help keep rodents out (see: *"How to Build a Predator-Proof Enclosure"*).

3. Mounting metal flashing or a lightweight, flexible PVC galvanized wire (19 gauge) around the base of your barn, shed and duck house will prevent rodents from gnawing through and making their own private doorways.

4. Rats commonly live within sixty feet of their food source. Prevent rodents from making cozy lairs in the vicinity of your duck's pen by eliminating lawn clutter, wood piles, stacks of hay or other random debris. Keep vegetation trimmed and grass cut to avoid covered passageways to your pen. Without good hiding places and overhead cover, they're less likely to invade.

5. Lay down a two-foot deep barrier of crushed rocks around your pens and barn to help discourage rodents from digging under and entering.

- **Rodent facts**

1. Mice can squeeze through an opening the size of a dime.

2. Rats can squeeze through an opening the size of a nickel.

3. A mouse reaches sexual maturity in 1 month and twenty days later, can have a litter of six babies, averaging about eight litters a year.

4. A rat reaches sexual maturity in 3 months and twenty-four days later, can have a litter of twelve babies, averaging up to seven litters a year.

Grit

It's important that your ducks have access to grit in order to digest their food properly. If you don't have sand in your enclosure, make a small source of grit available to them. When they eat tiny pebbles, it goes into their gizzard and helps it to grind up and digest their food. Grit can be purchased at your grain store.

If you have a duck that is trying to eat small rocks, it's most likely because they don't have access to a good source of grit. They're attempting to find the smallest thing they can, which just so happens to be too big. Introduce grit immediately if you see this behavior.

Feeding Egg-Laying Ducks

If you're caring for egg-laying ducks, then you'll need to supply a specialized diet just for them. You should begin feeding them a brand name laying formula after the first egg appears and continue until they stop (if they stop; I have year-long layers in my flock).

- **Added calcium source for egg-laying ducks**

You should always have a separate feeder with some oyster shells or food grade calcium chips in it for your egg-laying ducks—even when they're on a seasonal break (they'll often start ingesting calcium again before they restart laying). This is also available at your grain store. Rodents aren't interested in oyster shells, so they can be easily stored in a plastic, covered bin.

Soft eggshells, odd-shaped eggs or shells that have a bumpy texture are a sure sign that an extra source of calcium is needed on the side.

Laying ducks should have access to their calcium supplement free choice, twenty-four hours a day, seven days a week, all year long. Don't mix this extra source of calcium into their food. Your females have the instincts to know when they need it and when they don't. It's not good for them to consume it if they don't need it, but you do want it made available to them for when they do. Male ducks or *drakes* will commonly ignore this source of calcium, although they may occasionally poke around in the bowl to investigate it.

While not all ducks will go for this, another highly recommended and free calcium source is to gather up your duck's fresh eggs, hard boil them and chop them up, shells and all. Feed the eggs back to your girls. Some pickier ducks will only eat hard-boiled eggshells if they're separated from their eggs and then crushed and served.

- **Laying formulas**

Laying ducks need a special diet to support their egg-laying. That being said, I want to say something very important about laying formulas. Although they're a vital part of your laying duck's menu, they aren't the end-all, be-all of her diet.

Laying eggs every day takes its toll on your pets, which some people believe may shorten their lifespan. Having gone through labor myself once, I can certainly believe that going through the stress of it every day would eventually take its toll on me after a while. For this reason and others, I think most Momma Ducks would agree that they aren't interested in forcing egg production, but rather supporting their duck's nutritional needs while they're laying their eggs. In other words, I don't want to push my female ducks to lay more eggs than nature would otherwise intend, I simply want to nurture their body's needs.

This is where researching your available product lines comes into play. You want to select a brand that provides for your female duck rather than demanding extra things of her. Don't be afraid to call your feed company's customer service representative before choosing the right brand of food for your pet duck.

Once you've selected a laying formula, you'll find that the real trick is keeping your drakes and non-laying ducks away from it whenever possible. It won't hurt them to get into it now and then, or to eat it in small quantities or percentages (less than 50% of their overall diet), but you don't want them eating it full force on a regular, long-term basis when they could be on a diet that is better suited for their individual needs.

I have different types of flocks in different pens, so it's pretty simple to keep laying formulas out of my bachelor pads, but in those pens where drakes are penned with laying ducks, rationed laying formula is often the answer to the riddle and, as you're about to read, it's also a vital part of your laying duck's dietary needs.

- **50% laying formula for egg-laying ducks**

Ducks are different from chickens and many female ducks have a hard time laying a healthy egg. If you spend any time talking with other Momma Ducks you'll often hear about some very serious egg-laying issues. Having been faced with many of them myself, I've found that rationing laying formulas can help prevent many of these problems.

Whenever my females are laying eggs, I provide them with a mix of 50% Mazuri® Waterfowl Maintenance and 50% Mazuri® Waterfowl Breeder; that is, 50% laying formula.* By maintaining a low ration of laying formula I don't force egg production, but rather give my girls just enough of what they need to cover their dietary needs.

*In the first edition of this book I recommended a 25% Breeder to 75% Maintenance ratio, but I've come to find that collectively, my female ducks tend to do better on a 50/50 ratio.

- **Adjust the ration of laying formula as needed**

Feel free to play around with the ratio of laying formula and regular food until you find the proportions that best suit the needs of your laying ducks. These ratios can be adjusted daily as you examine your duck's eggs. If eggs are looking perfect, keep the same ration. If eggs are soft or odd textured, add more laying formula to the mix. In spring/summer it's not uncommon to have to boost the laying formula ratio up to 75% or even higher if needed. I do have females who don't do well with anything less than 100% laying formula most of the time (as indicated by consistently soft-shelled eggs).

When your duck's eggs appear normal again, stop increasing the ratio of laying formula and then slowly, over the course of a few weeks, work on reducing it again, never going so quickly or so low as to cause undesirable egg quality.

Using the Mazuri® line as an example, let's say that while on a mix of 50% Mazuri® Breeder and 50% Mazuri® Maintenance your duck lays an egg that has bumpy calcium deposits on its surface. Instantly increase her ratio of laying formula to 75% Mazuri® Breeder and 25% Mazuri® Maintenance. As long as her eggs look normal after that, there is no need to increase the ratio any further. But now let's say that her eggs look normal for the next few days, but on the fourth day, her egg comes out soft. Immediately bump her ratio up to 100% Breeder.

At the end of the laying season (when she's laying less frequently, usually in fall/winter) you can often decrease her laying formula back down to 75% Mazuri® Breeder and 25% Mazuri® Maintenance again to see what happens. If her eggs change for the worse, instantly bump her back up to her 100% Mazuri® Breeder and understand that this will most likely be her ideal ratio until she stops laying for the season (at which point laying formula is not needed). However, if you back her ratio down to the 75/25 mix and find there are no adverse effects, you can try dropping her down again to the 50/50 mix. Once you find your duck's minimal ratio, it tends to stay relatively the same. It may vary slightly seasonally and will tend to decrease as she gets older and lays less frequently, which tends to occur in most breeds around their 5th or 6th year.

Mastering the ratio of laying formula is not that difficult if you understand what you're looking for and how you need to react to it. You just need to bump the laying formula instantly up and then slowly down until you find your duck's equilibrium. Finding this balance is vital to maintaining your duck's good health. Malformed eggs can lead to serious reproductive tract issues that can be fatal. Always remember to foster nature's laying cycle rather than force it.

Avoid High Oxalic Acid Foods

Calcium intake is vital to your duck's good health. This is especially true if your duck lays eggs because additional calcium is needed to form the eggshells as they pass through the oviduct. Birds laying soft-shelled eggs may not be getting enough of this mineral.

Foods with oxalic acid in them naturally bind with calcium, forming calcium oxalate. Your duck can't absorb the calcium in this form, rendering it useless. The higher the level of oxalic acid in a particular food, the more calcium it renders useless, leaving less for your feathered friend to utilize.

There are different opinions about how much oxalic acid has to be ingested before causing any egg-laying interference. While some advise that oxalic acid levels are too low to cause any issues, or that you'd see soft-shell evidence if there was a problem, this isn't always the case. Just because your duck is laying eggs with nice firm shells, doesn't mean that they aren't calcium deprived (only a blood panel can confirm their actual calcium levels). Your duck's body may be compensating for their low calcium levels by robbing what's needed from their bones--entirely invisible to you. For this reason, I always advise erring on the side of caution when it comes to offering foods that contain oxalic acid. You can do this either by reducing the frequency and amounts you serve, or by avoiding these foods altogether.

There are plenty of healthy vegetable snacks for your duck to enjoy without having to put their calcium levels in jeopardy. A few raw vegetables that have more than .3 grams of oxalic acid for each 100 grams that they weigh (which is commonly considered high and which you may want to be careful around) are: rhubarb, parsley, chives, cassava, purslane, spinach, beet leaves, carrots, radishes, collard greens, Swiss chard, snap beans, Brussels sprouts, leeks, watercress, broccoli, kale and some types of leaf lettuce (romaine lettuce, corn salad lettuce, iceberg lettuce, bibb lettuce, Boston lettuce and butter lettuce are all lower in oxalic acid and a healthier alternative for egg-laying ducks).

Feeding Ducks on Public Ponds

This brings me to a good point to talk about feeding ducks on ponds. As I visit my local ponds in search of abandoned domestic animals that need to be removed from a wild setting, I often see people feeding the wild and domestic ducks. It's always best to let wild waterfowl forage for their own food. Feeding a mother duck and her wild ducklings can interfere with how she teaches her hatchlings to search for food, leaving them short of the skills they need in order to survive.

Feeding ducks can also cause overpopulation issues on ponds as well as migratory delays. Unnaturally large congregations of ducks can lead to water pollution and an increase of predators in the area. Feeding can also incline wild birds to lose their fear of people. You may be a nice person only wanting to warm their belly, but keep in mind that other people don't necessarily share your kind intentions and could use this advantage to bring harm to the birds.

I do understand the attractio of feeding the domestic waterfowl on found on ponds, especially when children are involved. Domestics don't necessarily have the instincts to forage properly on their own (and ideally should be removed from the wild and re-homed). If you wish to feed a domestic duck on a pond at least do right by feeding them the right thing. There are certain foods that simply shouldn't be fed to these birds, or to any animals for that matter.

- **Don't feed ducks bread**

Bread is *never* a wise choice for waterfowl. Ducks can choke on bread, so it's a dangerous snack; the same is true of popcorn. In addition, if a duck belly gets filled up with bread, they won't forage for bugs, snails, frogs and other small creatures that are a much needed protein source. A belly full of bread leads to malnutrition in ducks, which can cause all kinds of bone, muscle and feather deficiencies.

Sinking bread can also increase the odds of a botulism breakout as it rots, especially on smaller ponds or in coves where water currents are minimal.

Abandoned domestic ducks being fed on a pond

I'm always amazed when I see folks standing at the shores of ponds throwing chips and snack foods into the water for ducks to eat (even more dismayed when they throw in the bag as well). None of these foods belong anywhere in their diets and should never be introduced. They aren't healthy for humans and are just as unhealthy for waterfowl. Junk food is junk food, whether you're a human or a duck.

Unhealthy snack options for waterfowl

If you're planning a picnic and can't resist the urge to feed the waterfowl and don't have actual duck food on hand, there is a safe and healthy alternative. Plan ahead and bring some round, floating, un-medicated cat kibble with you (no hairball or urinary tract formulas). This is a protein filled snack that is a fantastic alternative to unhealthy human snack foods. Avoid overfeeding waterfowl; only throw in what the animals will consume right then and there. It's important that excess food isn't left behind to sink and decay because (as with bread) this can prompt bacterial diseases.

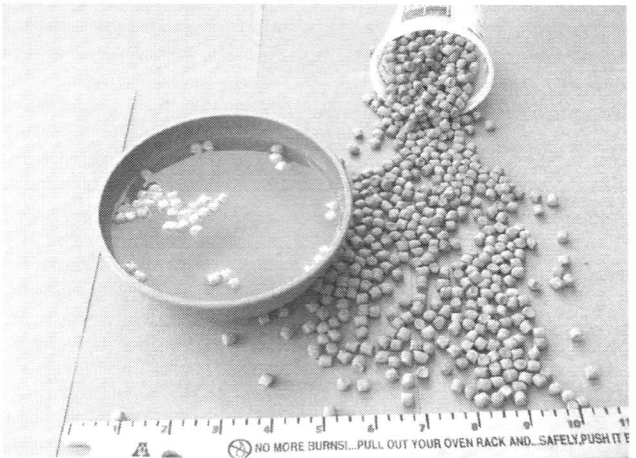

Round, floating cat kibble makes a healthier snack for ducks at the park

- **Other dangerous foods**

Other dangerous foods for ducks include: salted or sugar-coated foods and snacks, grapes, raisins and chocolate, all of which can prove to be fatal.

Determine a Feeding Schedule

I keep my feeders full and available for my ducks throughout the day and night. I did the same when they were ducklings. Some people will advise that this discourages foraging or leads to unhealthy or overweight ducks, but this rarely proves true with most ducks. More so, they often won't eat their duck food if something tastier is available, even if it means they have to hunt for it. Another reason I like to make food available to them all day is many of the ducks that come to my sanctuary have faced starvation and malnutrition. I don't want them ever experiencing a painful hunger pang again, so the food is always fresh and available for them whenever they want it.

Every evening I go around and top off all of the feed dishes and do a quick mix with my fingers to ensure old food isn't forever aging at the bottom of the dish.

If you'd like to establish feeding times, you can offer each duck one measured cup of food, two to three times a day. Timed feedings aren't recommended for ducks who can't actively forage during the day. Long intervals between feeding times can result in ducks gorging down their meals, which can lead to digestive issues.

Feed Dispenser

Now that you know *what* and *when* you're going to feed your ducks, you need to decide on a means to serve up their daily meals.

- **Duckling feeder**

Duckling feeders come in a few shapes and sizes. They're typically a small white jug that screws (albeit frustratingly at times) into a red feed tray, which holds the crumbles. They're a bit too big for two ducklings, so unless you have more than six ducklings, you'll probably end up wasting the excess food they don't eat each time you clean it out. When it comes to feeding two ducklings I prefer to use a small weighted bowl. You can get them at most pet shops, usually in the hamster section.

If you're using a feeding jug, it's important that you don't fill the feeder jug all the way up to the top with feed crumbles, or the bottom can get contaminated with water, saliva and poop and then soak upward like a sponge. To avoid wasting feed with smaller ducklings, just fill the tray with crumbles. As your ducklings grow, you'll get accustomed to how much they eat between cleanings and know how much feed to put in their jug.

Some people will make feeders by cutting a hole into the lower side of a one quart plastic milk jug, but I worry about a duckling getting trapped inside. If you opt to go this route, be sure to find a way to mount the bottle securely in place, so it doesn't tumble over in your brooder and check on your ducklings often. Personally I don't like having a lot of extra strings tying things in place in my brooder either because they can present strangulation hazards, but as long as you're mindful of this, and avoid leaving any dangling stings hanging down, your ducklings should be okay.

- **Adult duck feed bowl**

Ducks are known to spill a lot of their dinner, so my favorite feeders come in the form of bowls. I've tried a few types of feeders and found that they all caused more spillage than the bowls. Two quart rubber bowls are the absolute best for adult ducks because they're easy to clean and unbreakable. *Avoid* metal bowls, which are often galvanized (zinc coated) and can lead to metal poisoning.

Young Matthew enjoys a bowl of Mazuri® Waterfowl Maintenance

- **Adult duck automatic pet feeder**

There are various automated feeders on the market. Some are battery operated and have individual doors that open up on timers, while others are electric "gumball machines" that can be programmed to release a pre-programmed amount of food at timed intervals. These feeders should *not* be used as a substitute for a reliable duck sitter, but they can be used to dispense food while you're at work, or when you have a duck with special dietary considerations (see: *"Specialized Crop Diet/Automated Feeders"*).

An automated pet feeder can be there when you're not

Preparation #4
Drinking Water

Ducks need a source of drinking water made available to them, so finding your duck a water dispenser is the next step in preparing for their arrival.

Make Water Available 24/7

It's not uncommon for a duck to give you a good scare and gulp down too much food at one time and end up with a marble-sized (or larger) lump in their throat. You'll see them stretch and work their necks as they try to move it down and then they tend to go over to their water bucket and take a good drink to help push it the rest of the way. Not only is it humane to have water available 24/7 for your ducks, but it's also necessary to prevent choking incidents—especially when food is also available.

While I used to panic whenever I saw those lumps of food massed in the throats of my ducks, I've since learned that ducks can take care of themselves in this regard. Even so, I'm a softy and will usually coax Young Jeffrey to take a drink before I gently begin massaging his neck, helping to break up the mass of lodged feed pellets until they drift safely down his throat.

If you don't have heated water buckets in winter and your ducks' water could freeze up for any period of time (overnight, for example), then pick up their food dish, so they won't be able to eat during that time.

- **Make multiple water sources available**

As with food, I always have more than one water source available for my ducks. The reason for this is simple, sometimes your pets will have issues amongst themselves, and you don't want one of your ducks hoarding the only food and water source and depriving your other duck of needed sustenance.

Duckling Water Dispenser

How you opt to serve up drinking water to your duck is often dependant on their age and size, although special needs ducks may require individual consideration.

- **Weighted water bowl**

I only brought home two ducklings, so I found a tiny and shallow, weighted hamster bowl was the perfect thing. I realize it's untraditional, but it's my personal preference. I switched out their small bowl for bigger ones as my two boys grew. Mind you, these bowls quickly became fun swimming pools, so if you go this route, make sure your ducklings can get safely in and out of their properly sized bowls.

Young Jeffrey & Young Matthew with their weighted hamster bowl

- **Water fount**

If you're not going to be home continually monitoring your ducklings, I highly recommend going the safer, more traditional route and get them a small, plastic water dispenser from your local supply store in lieu of a bowl. These water founts have very shallow water troughs designed to prevent your ducklings from submerging themselves and possibly drowning.

Always keep your water dispenser clean and the water in them fresh. Stagnant or dirty water can lead to diseases. Botulism is just one deadly example of a disease that can reveal itself and kill your duck within days if you don't keep their water fresh.

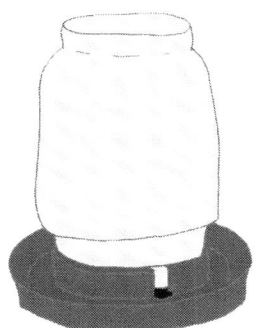

The trouble with these small dispensers (as you'll most likely soon discover) is the cheap, plastic threading that wears out pretty quickly. After a half dozen uses or so, you may find yourself grumbling some unsavory words around your ducklings as you try to screw the red water tray back into the white water jug—and all without getting yourself wet. The threading never seems to work perfectly for long, but you still have to get the unit twisted back together absolutely right, or it'll empty out and leak water all over your duckling house.

Don't try to out-wit the small plastic duckling fount by purchasing a larger metal fount with better threading instead. These larger metal founts have deeper water troughs that are unsafe for your little ducklings.

Whether you opt for a duckling fount or a weighted water bowl, you want your ducklings to be able to submerge their bills to clear their nares (nostrils) without being able to swim. The water should be no deeper than the length of their bill from tip to base. All duckling swim times must be chaperoned by Momma Ducks!

Adult Duck Water Dispenser

The number of ducks you have and some common sense will help you determine what size and how many water dispensers your ducks will require. Before I review what works, I'm going to try to save you some money by telling you what doesn't.

- **What doesn't work**

Many grain store floor personnel are accustomed to dealing with poultry, and an inexperienced staff person (especially one who's never had ducks) will often point you towards a double-walled water fount. While these metal founts work great for chickens, they aren't appropriate for ducks.

Ducks need to submerge the two little nares located on top of their bills fully into water in order to blow air through them and keep them clear of feathers and debris. It's part of their preening routine. They simply can't plunge their long bills under water when utilizing a shallow-troughed water fount.

Even when your grain store sales person shows you how you can keep it warm in winter by setting it on top of a fount heater, you want to stay away. Appealing as this system may be, it's not the ideal solution for your ducks.

- **Rubber Water Bucket**

In the warmer months of spring, summer and fall, when your ducks' water won't freeze, I highly recommend using eight quart, rubber buckets for dispensing water. They're extremely durable, easy to clean and are just the right height and depth for most domestic ducks (with the exception of tiny Call ducks).

If you accidentally misjudge the weather and leave these water buckets out in the cold, they won't crack or break, not even if frozen solid. You can literally smack them with a hammer, stomp up and down on them or kick them around the yard (and believe me, I've done it!) to get the ice out of them without ever damaging them. They're priced right, found at most grain stores, have a very long life expectancy and best of all—ducks love them!

Young Jeffrey & Young Matthew love their rubber water bucket

The number of ducks you have is not the only determining factor in deciding how many water buckets you'll need. You'll also need to take their individual personalities into account. Drakes will sometimes take possession of a particular water bucket and refuse to share it with anyone else. If this is the case, you'll need to add enough buckets to ensure that everyone can get a drink of water whenever they want to. When putting out multiple water buckets among possessive ducks, be sure to space them well apart from each other.

While I highly recommend setting out multiple buckets among possessive ducks, I don't recommend overdoing it. Water buckets should be changed at least twice a day (more often in summer), and you don't want to make this task bigger than it needs to be.

I should also warn you that your ducks are going to love these buckets so much they're going to make a big splashing mess all around them, so choose the locations you put them in very wisely or you'll be on cleaning duty.

A homemade wooden jig set around a water bucket can keep the area clean

- **Heated Water Bucket**

My absolute favorite water dispensing option during cold winter months is a nine quart (2.25 gallon) heated water bucket. It's the optimal sized bucket for most domestic ducks. I've had great success with the Allied Precision® brand (supplier: Tractor Supply Company www.tractorsupply.com). They're built well and have proven the most reliable, rarely shorting out or failing the way other brands tend to *provided* you use them according to their instructions.

The great thing about this kind of bucket is they're weatherproof and can be used inside a barn or in an outdoor enclosure. They turn on and off automatically to prevent the water inside from freezing. The heating element is fully enclosed, safely inside a plastic casing underneath and the electrical cord is protected by a wire spring to help prevent any critters from gnawing at it. I bought a toilet bowl brush that I keep out in my barn to make daily bucket cleaning quick and easy.

A nine quart heated water bucket is perfect for medium and heavyweight ducks

My ducks love to sit around these buckets in cold weather to keep warm and it's completely safe for them to do so. They're durable and look and feel safe, which I know you other Momma Ducks will appreciate. Just be sure to read the instructions carefully to avoid any fire hazards. You can't use them with extension cords, for example; they must be plugged directly into an outlet, and for everyone's safety they should *always* be plugged into a GFCI outlet.

Another great thing about these water buckets is they're just the right size for *"splash-preening."* Splash-preening is when a duck delves their head and neck down into their water bucket and then juts it back out, splashing water over their backs to assist them in their preening. This really helps them in winter, when they may not have daily access to swimming water, but need to keep tidy.

When used outside, I find it best to set the buckets on top of a 16" x 16" square patio brick. This prevents the buckets from sitting directly in mud or puddles. In the wintertime and in freezing temperatures, keeping your outside buckets at just the right height for your ducks can be a little tricky. As your ducks splash-preen they tend to make an impressive mess that freezes into an ever-growing mound of surrounding ice. The ice level will continue to rise and rise every day until they're standing much higher off the ground than the base of their bucket. At this point your ducks will be looking down into a nicely formed hole to get to their water.

A heated water bucket can slowly become encroached in ice

You can either continually chip away at the rising icy shoreline they've created or you can simply keep the patio brick clear of any encroaching ice. I keep my bricks clear by shoveling immediately after snowstorms (or during them if the snow is getting too deep) and also by shifting the bucket's location around on the brick every day. While it may be tempting to keep setting your bucket down in exactly the same place—within the ring of ice that's already formed on the brick, you'd be wiser to set the edge of your bucket over some of that ice. Shifting your bucket to a new location on the brick every day will help melt that circle away.

Keeping the patio brick clear of snow and ice enables you to compensate for the icy build up your ducks are making around its edges. All you have to do is lift up your bucket and stack another patio brick on top of the original one and then set your bucket back down again. Now your bucket is sitting higher up and it won't matter that your ducks are standing on a few elevated inches of ice anymore (although you'll want to spread some sand over this surrounding ice to prevent any slipping accidents). Some of my pens only need one brick, while others require two or three over the course of a winter. How many bricks you'll need will depend on how many ducks you have, whether your ducks are messy or neat and how good the drainage is around your bucket.

A few patio bricks underneath your heated water bucket keeps it elevated above the ice

The heat of the bucket will usually prevent it from directly freezing into any of the encroaching ice (unless it shorts out and you don't discover it in time). If your bucket does happen to get stuck, unplug the bucket first and then use a blow dryer to melt away the ice around its base until the bucket releases. Buckets usually release pretty quickly. Once the bucket is out, bring it to a heated room to defrost. Avoid breaking thick ice in your bucket or you can easily crack the plastic and destroy the pail. More often, only the bucket's cord will actually freeze into some of the splashy mess your duck has created. If this happens, follow the same steps, unplug the bucket and use a blow dryer to melt it out. Attempting to chip the cord out can lead to cord damage. *Never* yank on the cord in an attempt to free it from the ice or you could damage the wire connections between the heating element and the cord.

When spring comes and the ice begins to melt, you can begin removing the patio bricks one at a time as needed to lower your bucket's height again. Watch carefully during these thawing spells because a few inches of water can easily form beneath your bucket if the drainage isn't right. The last thing you want is your electric bucket sitting in a big puddle of water. If you see this happening, you may want to set down a new patio brick a foot or so away from your original one and move your bucket to this new location. Do this as needed to keep your bucket high and dry.

I rely completely on my nine quart, heated water buckets in the winter and on my eight quart rubber buckets in the warmer months. After trying everything else out there with my ducks, I've found that nothing else works quite like them.

For those of you with tiny Call ducks, they make similarly designed heated water bowls that work almost as nicely as the buckets.

A nine quart, heated water bucket

A small, heated water bowl

I've noticed that the bowls tend to be more sensitive than the buckets and are more likely to short out and trip the GFCI switch of their outlet. A nicely constructed, thick plastic bowl will withstand freezing though, and can be switched out with a spare bowl while it's brought into the house to defrost.

The other issue with these small bowls is they're a little too easy for ducks to get in and out of—even tiny Call ducks. Many a petite duck has come to discover the benefit of sinking down into a warm hot tub on a cold winter's night and spilling water everywhere. Even so, there is a trick to compensate for their little party. A friend of mine figured out that he could set their heated water bowl directly into a round, metal cake pan (3.5" deep x 14" diameter). Then, he only filled their bowl about halfway with water to allow his little duck to sit in it without causing a major spill over. The cake pan will catch the small amount of spillage, preventing the surrounding hay from getting water-soaked. If by chance his little ducky does too much splashing, the GFCI switch does what it's supposed to and switches off.

Whenever I have smaller or special needs duck who requires an easier reach, I'll use one of these heated water bowls in winter, which I'll swap out for a two-quart rubber bowl (which I recommended previously in the "feed" section) when it's warmer.

Now that I've covered the smaller alternatives, let's review a bigger one. If you have a lot of ducks sharing one bucket (or ducks with a goosey friend), you can also find these heated water buckets in a five gallon size, but since it's so large it tends to only work with the giant, heavyweight breeds who can easily reach over the rim. Additionally, if you have what I refer to as a *bucket duck* (a duck who loves to hop into buckets of water of any size) and you go with this larger size bucket, they could potentially get themselves stuck inside their warm tub for the day. This happens when they hop in and then reduce the water level with all their splashing around and then get stuck down inside the high walls of the bucket. If you have yourself a bucket duck, this larger size is not recommended.

Preparation #5
Duckling Accommodations

Ducklings have very specific environmental needs and you'll need to address each of these *before* bringing home your new family members.

Housing for Ducklings

When providing safe and comfortable housing for your ducklings, you'll need to consider both the details of their brooder *and* its ideal location.

- **Draft free room**

You'll need to find a warm and *draft free* room that is very safe for your little ducklings; preferably one with a door, so you can close it and keep unwanted guests out. Of course I'm assuming you'll be raising your ducklings in your house (what Momma Duck wouldn't!).

Remember to be mindful of your indoor predators. They consist of your other pets (cats, dogs, ferrets, etc) and your children. Although ducklings are a common and unfortunate Easter gift for children, they're very fragile and can easily be killed by unknowing little hands. Their legs, wings and necks are very fragile. Children should never be allowed to handle ducklings without close parental supervision.

- **Brooder**

Once you have your room selected, it'll be time to set up your duckling brooder. The number of ducklings you're bringing home will obviously dictate the size brooder they'll require. If you're new at this, I highly recommend you begin with two ducklings. Two ducklings tend to get along extremely well, even into adulthood, although boys (or drakes) will squabble now and again once mature (more on this and male-to-female ratios later). I kept things simple and started with two and found that a vacant guinea pig house in my home was a wonderful (and safe) place for my boys to grow up.

Young Jeffrey & Young Matthew's homemade duckling brooder (formerly a guinea pig house)

While you do want your duckling brooder to keep out any drafts, you don't want it to be airtight; they need to breathe after all. My two boys joined us in early April and that year it was still pretty chilly outside, so there were no open windows and not a lot of air currents breezing through our house. For this reason, it wasn't really necessary to have a brooder that kept out the lateral drafts because there really weren't any.

I'm not a fan of keeping ducklings in a glass terrarium because of the lack of ventilation. As your ducklings really start to grow the fumes from the poop can't easily escape and it can become increasingly noxious in there—especially under a heat light. I don't know about you, but I didn't want my new ducklings breathing in potent ammonia vapors between cleanings—especially overnight when those cleanings just aren't happening.

Most Momma Ducks will transform plastic storage bins into brooders for their ducklings; again, I'm not a fan of containers that restrict side ventilation, but… not everyone has an empty guinea pig house at their disposal. My advice in this case is to make sure your bin size increases as your ducklings grow to allow proper top ventilation and prevent fumes from building up inside. Provide each duckling with ½ square foot for their first week and then increase this by about a ¼ square foot each week thereafter. You can do this by increasing your bin size every couple of weeks, or by starting with a larger bin that will meet the needs of your growing ducklings. The measurements of my duckling brooder are: 24" wide x 36" long x 18" high.

Next, carefully cut a large rectangular opening out of the storage bin's cover. Once this is done, drill holes every 3-4 inches all the way around the lid's remaining cover. Finally, zip-tie a rectangular piece of wire mesh over the opening you cut away, weaving the zip-ties through the holes you drilled. Now you have a snap-on cover that allows for ventilation while also offering your ducklings some protection from the outside world.

Whatever you use, it's vital that you keep your duckling brooder clean. If you can smell it, you're not cleaning it enough. You'll need to change out the shavings a few times a day, especially as they get older, poop more and splash more water around. Ducklings can make a pretty good mess around their feed dishes and water founts, leaving you plucking pine shavings out of their food and water. Failure to clean properly can lead to ammonia burns on your ducklings (indicated by red, irritated skin and loss of their duckling fluff) and no good Momma Duck wants that.

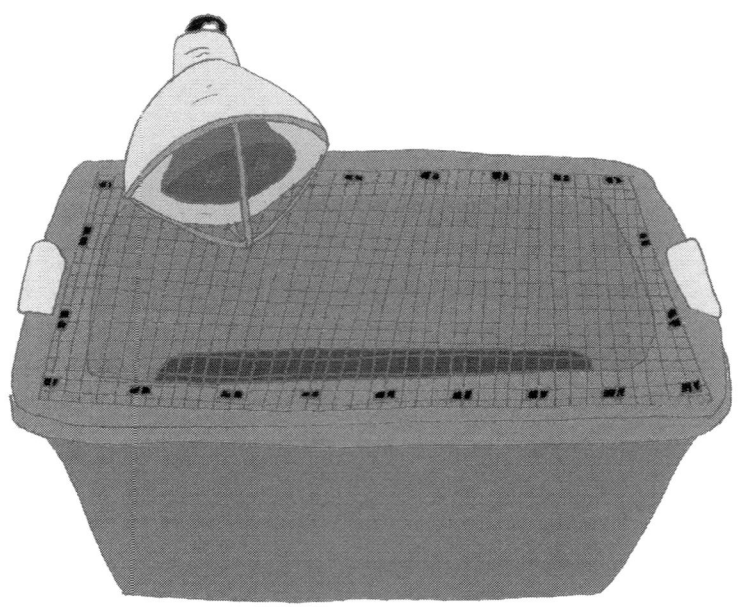

Homemade brooder utilizing a plastic bin, wire mesh and zip-ties

- **Bedding**

Soft pine shavings make the best bedding for ducklings. You can buy them inexpensively by the bale at many pet or grain supply stores. It will soak up messes and is easy for little webbed feet to traverse. Ducklings can easily trip over hay, making it a real obstacle. Avoid using any dyed shavings and stay clear of cedar shavings, which can cause serious skin irritations. Newspaper is also a bad idea since it can strip a duckling of its waterproofing oils.

Young Jeffrey & Young Matthew's brooder bedded with pine shavings

I'm not a fan of wire mesh flooring under your ducklings. Ducks have very sensitive feet and I prefer not to mess around with that. Soft is best when it comes to ducks. Wire mesh flooring is more often required when brooding large groups of ducklings (who make a lot of poop) as opposed to a small family of 2-6 little ones.

- **Heat source**

Until ducklings grow their feathers, they have trouble regulating their body temperature, so watch them closely and don't be afraid to increase or decrease temperatures as needed to keep them comfortable.

Find a place in your brooder for a thermometer, so you can monitor the temperature inside.

Mount your heat source on the outside of your brooder at the top of one of its corners. Fastening your heat source up and in a corner allows your ducklings to move away from it if they get too warm. If you made your brooder out of a storage bin, you can aim your heat lamp down through the wire mesh you zip-tied over the hole you cut out of its cover.

Your heat source can be an actual heat lamp (most have 125 or 250 watt bulbs) or a regular light bulb (60 or 40 watt) protected by a wire guard. If you opt to use a heat lamp be sure to follow the safety instructions carefully to prevent fire hazards.

When I was raising my little guys up in their brooder I heard all kinds of advice about temperature. For ducklings one week old, suggestions often range from 85-95F degrees, but I find 90F degrees to be a good place to start. After that, you can drop their brooder temperature down about 5 degrees a week until their inside temperature is the same as the surrounding room temperature.

The good news is, this really isn't rocket science and truthfully, I didn't even have a thermometer in my ducklings' brooder. A simple 40 watt bulb kept my boys cozy, happy and active through their entire brooding time. If you're good with animals and are an attentive Momma Duck, you'll have no trouble telling whether it's too hot or too cold for your ducklings. Even so, if you're new at brooding, I highly recommend playing it safe and getting the thermometer.

An un-mounted light bulb guard with a 40 watt bulb inside

If your ducklings are moving away from their heat source and skirting to the other edge of their brooder, they're too hot. If you're using a regular light bulb, you can swap it out for a lower wattage bulb (switching from a 60 watt bulb, to a 40 watt), or if you're using a heat lamp, just move it further away from the brooder. If your ducklings prefer huddling tightly together under the heat source rather than coming out between naps to eat, drink and forage then they're too cold. Temperature adjustments should be small tweaks as opposed to drastic measures (unless something's *really* wrong). You're trying to find a comfort zone here, so try to keep adjustments minimal and no greater than 5 degrees at a time.

- **Feather duster**

Hang a feather duster in the corner of your brooder near your heat source (keeping enough distance to prevent a fire hazard). It should be raised 2-3 inches up from the brooder floor. Your ducklings will love this! The feather duster feels like their mommy's feathery tummy, so they'll snuggle under it to sleep. As your ducklings grow, they'll sit around the feather duster instead of underneath it.

Avoid fancy feather dusters with long, narrow or twining feathers. They can tangle around your duckling's throat and result in strangling. You want a plain old feather duster.

- **Food**

Ducklings should *always* have food available to them. They grow fast and have high nutritional requirements that must be met in order for them to be healthy and strong.

One fun thing to do with your ducklings is to dip your finger into their water and then into their duckling crumbles. Your ducklings will love eating off of your fingers and it makes for a beautiful moment for all of you; in fact, if you need to show your ducklings how to eat, this is a great way to get them started. Afterwards, just swirl your finger around in the bowl and they should figure it out from there.

Duckling crumbles tend to get moist and messy pretty quickly as they run back and forth from their water fount to their food dispenser. You'll need to actively empty out wet food and replace it with dry food frequently throughout the day, or the warm, moist environment you've created in their brooder can quickly grow dangerous molds and bacteria that can rapidly turn fatal for your ducklings. To slow down the pace of the impending mess, put some space between their water and food source. As they grow and learn, you'll want to gradually move these two resources a little further apart from each other—but not *too* far, ducklings (and ducks) are prone to choking on their food.

- **Water**

Ducklings also need to have water available to them at all times. Remember to change their water frequently. Duckling crumbles, pine shavings and even poop often end up in their water. To avoid bacterial growth, you want your ducklings to have fresh water. I recommend changing it at least four times a day—more if needed.

Some sources suggest you place a few small round rocks or large marbles into the trays of your ducklings' water fount to keep them from swimming in the troughs. While a nice circle of marbles around the tray of a water fount may keep ducklings from taking unnecessary swims, they can also be quite dangerous. Ducklings are drawn to water and the last thing you want to do is create a little obstacle course in their water trough. Avoid creating places for tiny webbed feet to get pinched and trapped or your ducklings could get stuck and left with injuries that last them a lifetime. If you're worried about the depth of their water trough, pour a thin layer of clean and sifted sand (*not* sandbox sand) down into the trough.

Some Momma Ducks opt to make their own brooder trays to help catch spillage from their ducklings' water fount. Gridded cooling racks are often set onto small cake pans or cookie sheets and then water founts are placed on top of them. While I don't advise it, if you do attempt setting up this kind of device in your brooder be *extremely* careful that duckling body parts (especially tiny feet) can't slip and fall through anywhere or get caught or pinched in any way. These homemade contraptions can quickly become death traps if you don't know exactly what you're doing—and just to be clear, even an expert can mess this up. My advice is to just clean up the mess when the water spills and avoid putting foreign items into your ducklings' brooder.

- **Nutrient packs**

While ducklings kept on proper brand name healthy duckling diets who have properly maintained brooders tend to thrive, there are occasions where someone might get sick. If you have a sick duckling, take them to a vet immediately and be sure to keep them warm for the ride. If you only have two ducklings, you may want to bring them both to the vet together to avoid any separation anxiety and to help them keep warm. As with adult ducks, ducklings with close friends tend to have higher recovery rates than solo ducklings.

Sav-A-Chick® nutrient packets

When bringing home ducklings it's a good idea to pick up a few nutrient packets. Myself, I'm a fan of the *Sav-A-Chick®* brand. You can get Probiotic packets and Electrolyte packets (which have added vitamins). You simply pour the powder from one of the packets into a gallon of water and then use that water to fill your ducklings' fount or bowl. It's completely safe for healthy ducklings, so you don't have to worry about sharing. These packets aren't just great for ducklings, they're also perfect adult ducks who might be a little under the weather or needing a little vitamin boost. I like to pick them up in the spring and keep them around in case of emergencies.

Supervision

I was on maternity leave when my ducklings arrived, which meant I could be with them all day every day while they were growing up. While being with your ducklings to continually supervise them is ideal, not all Momma Ducks have this luxury.

I highly recommend welcoming your ducklings home when you can actually take a week off from work, but at the very least you want to have a three-day weekend ahead of you. During this time you can get acquainted with your ducklings, get them comfortably situated, master their brooder conditions, learn their food and water requirements and have a complete appreciation for their hourly and daily needs. You can't properly prepare them for a day at home without you while you go to work if you don't fully understand what their daily needs are going to be.

Most Momma Ducks will find brief excursions out of the house far less stressful than parting for the day to go to work, but the good news is, as long as you've set everything up properly, your ducklings should be fine until you return.

☑	*Before-You-Go Duckling Checklist:*
☑	1. Water fount and feed dish have both been cleaned
☑	2. Water fount is refilled with fresh water
☑	3. Water fount is screwed together properly and sealed tightly (no leaks!)
☑	4. Water fount trough is filled with small round rocks or large marbles to prevent unsupervised swims
☑	5. Feeder is refilled with fresh duckling crumbles (enough to last the entire time you're away)
☑	6. Water fount and feeder are ideally spaced to prevent excessive mess in the duckling crumbles
☑	7. Pine shavings are fresh and clean
☑	8. Heat lamp is safely and securely mounted
☑	9. Brooder temperature is correct
☑	10. Ducklings' behavior is normal (not panting or shivering / eating & drinking normally)
☑	11. Brooder is closed properly
☑	12. Ventilation is appropriate while also avoiding drafts
☑	13. Door to the room where their brooder is located is closed securely

*Your duckling list may vary depending on your own personal situation!

<u>Swims for Ducklings</u>

When Young Jeffrey and Young Matthew grew a bit, I took them for swims in the bathroom sink a few times a day, although a paint-roller tray is another great idea with its nice ridged slope on one end and its shallow pool on the other. When my boys outgrew the sink, they went for swims in the tub. Ducklings are very messy, so I warn you, these fabulous swims ended with the ducklings sleeping in their brooder while I returned to the bathroom to sanitize the tub.

Swims in the tub are messy, but FUN!

Some sources will say that ducklings can't swim until they're a week old because they have no mother duck to oil them down, but my boys went swimming when they were only two days old and they repelled water without any difficulty (of course I kept their swim sessions brief). As long as your ducklings don't get drenched and they do a good job of preening afterwards, they can go for quick swims. Just be sure their water is lukewarm and they can put their feet down and touch the bottom whenever they want. Keep these excursions brief at first, so they can get back under their heat light again. If your ducklings do get soaked, remove them from the water immediately and put them back into their brooder. If necessary, you can set your hair blow dryer on *low* to send some warm air into their brooder to help them dry off quicker. Test the blow dryer's heat setting and proper distance carefully on your wrist before holding it over your ducklings to avoid any burns. Remember, they're very sensitive.

As my ducklings grew, and they literally do grow overnight (take pictures while you can!), I lifted them out of their brooder and loaded them into a big handled bucket a few times a day. The bucket was my method of getting the boys safely passed my cats. Unfortunately, it didn't take long for those crafty felines to realize I was carrying some interesting take-out cuisine which inspired them to follow me all the way to the door, waiting for a blunder that might end in a tasty treat. Sorry, kitties, not with this Momma Duck. After safely getting by the cats, I headed outside and lifted each of the boys out of their bucket and set them down on the ground a few feet away from our little pond.

I highly recommend getting your ducklings used to the outdoors as soon as they can safely handle the temperatures (weather providing, of course); it's where they'll be living quicker than you can imagine (unless you plan on having indoor ducks, but more on that later). I had a low-to-the-ground beach chair to sit on, which worked out great because whenever they were nervous, their instincts told them to run and hide underneath their Momma Duck—me! Once they felt brave again, they would start venturing out from under the chair and play around my bare feet.

In the beginning, the wind was the most frightening thing in the world to them. Every time a warm, little breeze blew through, my boys ran and hid underneath me again, peeping like a hawk was coming at them. Speaking of which, their instincts are right on the mark when it comes to predatory birds flying overhead; they were underneath me before I ever saw a shadow fall over the land. Ducklings (and ducks) have remarkably good vision.

Don't be worried if your ducklings don't want to swim in anything bigger than a kiddy pool at first. I walked my little sweethearts out to our small pond three times a day, put on wading boots, mucked through a pond bedded with a few feet of sinking mud and quacked like some kind of crazed, half-human duck. *"Come into the water, little ducklings. Look, Momma Duck is doing it. You can do it too!"*

I really began to worry that my growing ducklings would never play in anything bigger than the tiny trickle of the stream that flowed down from the pond. There was just no coaxing them into that water. The truth is I had absolutely nothing to worry about. As it turns out my ducklings knew a super secret mathematical formula that told them exactly when to move onto bigger waters. I believe it relates to their size in proportion to the volume of the water, but I'm still trying to work out the details. Nevertheless, as they continued to grow, they slowly craved the bigger and deeper water. So do yourself a favor, Momma Ducks, and relax in your beach chairs on shore. They'll go into the bigger water when they're good and ready.

Ducklings Grow Fast!

Ducklings grow into ducks in just eight weeks. If you think they'll stay little forever, you're sorely mistaken. My husband and I were amazed when we realized that they were practically growing in front of our very eyes. Every morning when we went in to see them, they were bigger than they were the night before—and that is no exaggeration.

Naps for Ducklings

Like any other baby animal I've ever opened my home to, ducklings tire quickly and nap frequently. Ensure that they can sleep undisturbed when it comes time for them to slumber. A well rested duckling is a happy and healthy duckling.

Ducklings need to rest frequently in order to stay healthy

Ducklings and Pecking Orders

Ducklings placed together will normally get along without much trouble. This is especially true if you start with only two ducklings that are brought home at the same time. You'll likely witness a couple of pokes here and there as they begin working on setting their social hierarchy, which is referred to in the duck world as establishing the *pecking order.*

The day my boys arrived, the bigger Young Matthew immediately set to asserting his dominance over the smaller Young Jeffrey. An occasional poke that says, *"I'm in charge here,"* is perfectly normal. Pecking order pokes are a either a single poke or a quick double poke. These pokes are mild in nature and only occasionally witnessed when a subordinate duckling gets a little too close to the duckling in charge.

If you begin with ducklings who are the same age and bring them home together at the same time, they'll likely get along perfectly. Older ducklings, ducklings of various ages or ducklings who haven't grown up together and who are suddenly placed together often get along, but there is a risk that they won't—and that risk tends to increase as the number of ducklings you put together increases.

This means if you have one two-week-old duckling and put him with a four-week-old duckling, they'll probably get along. Their innate flock instinct will usually compel them to become close friends. However, if you put two four-week-old ducklings with one two-week-old duckling the results could be disastrous for the smaller one. When ducklings don't come from the same brood and are different ages and sizes, you'd be wise to watch things extremely closely and be prepared to set up a second brooder if you need to.

There are times when these pecking order pokes get out of hand and one duckling gets picked on too much. This normally happens when one duckling is larger or older than another one, or when you have multiple ducklings picking on one individual. If you're seeing questionable behavior like excessive poking or chasing, then separations are in immediate order before someone gets hurt. Duckling injuries can result in lifetime disabilities, so it's vital that you act fast.

Ideally you want to divide your brooder safely in half, so that the ducklings continue to all see each other without being able to harm each other. This encourages them to get used to each other and get along. If you have six ducklings and two are having trouble fitting in, then put four on one side and two on the other. You want to avoid putting any one single duckling alone whenever possible. Removing a duckling from his friends can be extremely stressful for them. If one duckling is being picked on a little too much, see if you can find one friend to share his side of the divider. If they still don't get along, change the see-through brooder divider to something opaque. Two ducklings will often get along if there's no one else around.

Once the picked on duckling has had a few days reprieve you'll want to begin reintroducing them again. Remove the divider during closely chaperoned sessions to give them some time to work out their differences. Fun distractions like swimming and eating crumbles off of a Momma Duck's finger can often bring siblings together. When you're absolutely sure the trouble is in their past, you can permanently remove the divider between them.

Warning Signs of Duckling Illness

If all of your ducklings are the same size and age and from the same brood and one duckling is being consistently being picked on by everyone, it could be a warning that the one taking the brunt of the pokes is not feeling well. This is a good time to add Sav-a-Chick® nutrient packs to their water (following the pack's instructions). Watch this little one closely for any signs of discomfort. Next, look at one of your other ducklings and then another.

1. Is the first one's body heaving more than the others (labored breathing)?
2. Is he opening his bill and panting?
3. Is he resting more than the other ducklings?
4. Are his periods of activity noticeably briefer than the others?

Hold one or two of the other ducklings in your hands and get a feel for their body heat, paying special attention to the temperature of their legs and bill. Then, pick up the duckling they've been singling out and hold him in your hands. Can you feel a difference? Are his legs or bill noticeably warmer—or even hot? This could be indicative of a fever.

If you see or feel any of these signs or if your Momma Duck instincts are just telling you that something just isn't right, you'll want to take him to a vet right away. If you only have two ducklings and one falls ill, they've been together anyway, so you might as well bring them both to the vet together too. This will help keep them from feeling lonely and getting over-stressed during the trip. If you have three ducklings and one is sick, leave the two healthy ducks in the brooder and bring your sick one to the vet alone. If you have someone going with you, they can hold the duckling and keep him company while you drive. If you're on your own, then find a safe way to transport your duckling, tucking in little towels safely around (avoid suffocating risks) to help him keep warm. Give him a small mirror, so his reflection can keep him company. Whenever you have a single duckling (or duck) who needs company a mirror can be your best friend—and theirs. A lonely duck will nearly always find solace in a friend in the mirror.

Inside to Outside

Ducks really do belong outside, and for me it was very apparent when the time was upon us to move them. They were two months old and could no longer fit comfortably in their duckling brooder—head room was growing scarce and the wafts of air coming from their brooder were becoming quite offensive.

Before you bring your ducklings to spend their first night outside you MUST make sure their outside enclosure and nighttime shelter are completely predator-proof. Domestic ducks have no means for fighting, running or flying away from predators. If something can get into their house or pen, your pets will be trapped and aren't likely to survive an encounter. Predators are the most common demise of an unprotected pet duck and while the risk of them attacking is 24/7, it increases from sunset to sunrise. While a sadly common approach, a bit of poultry wire in a circle will do absolutely nothing to defend against predators; it'll only trap your ducks with no means of escape—you're basically doing your predators a favor. Your beloved pets need you to do a lot better than this or they won't be with you for long.

I have a nice, secure barn with a few chain-link kennels inside that worked perfectly for Young Matthew and Young Jeffrey. I hung their light in a high-up corner, not for heat, but to help make their new place feel a little more familiar. Then, I set a folding chair in the corner and tied their feather duster to it, so it dangled underneath. The folding chair gave them something to cuddle under, which made them feel safe during the transition from indoors to outdoors—a sort of surrogate mother duck. After all, they were used to having a roof immediately over their heads when they were in their brooder—suddenly the barn ceiling seemed awfully far off.

As the boys grew a little bigger and became more comfortable in their new place, I opened the kennel door and let them venture out into a bigger share of the barn. The feather duster and chair were both quickly abandoned and they never looked back.

- **Preparing ducklings for their move**

Moving ducklings from the indoors to the outdoors will often prove more stressful for Momma Ducks than it will for them. To get both of you used to the idea, take your growing ducklings on frequent and chaperoned trips to their future pen, each visit lengthening in duration. You'll want to do this well before it's time to actually make the permanent move outside. These excursions will do two things for you and your ducklings:

1. Your ducklings will have a chance to familiarize themselves with what will soon become their new home, making the move less stressful for them.

2. You'll have a chance to discover any inherent oversights in their pen. Sometimes things that appear perfectly safe at first, jump out to you as quite dangerous once you've see them in context with your ducklings.

Before taking your ducklings outside you must first consider temperature variances. Ideally, their brooder temperature and the outside temperatures should be no greater than 10 degrees apart. If it's 80F degrees in their brooder, then you don't want to take them outside into 50F degree weather. Ducklings under four weeks of age are far more susceptible to temperature changes than ducklings a little older. Following earlier brooder formulas, ducklings who are four weeks old should be in a brooder that's kept at about 75-80F degrees. If you have them at 75F inside, then you want to be sure the outdoor temperature is *at least* 65F degrees. You also want to prevent bringing ducklings outside if there are extreme variances in humidity levels because these too can be very stressful for growing ducklings.

Good common sense should also tell you that you'll want to avoid bringing your ducklings outside in "fowl" weather (ha!). Ducklings caught in the rain can easily get chilled. I much preferred bringing my ducklings outside on warm and sunny days. If you see your duckling shivering or sitting down to warm their legs, it's already past a good time to bring them back inside to their brooder. Warming up a cold duckling is not nearly as healthy as keeping a duckling warm in the first place.

I brought my boys for their first chaperoned journey outdoors on warm, sunny days when they were just over two weeks old. We would go once a day for about 15-20 minutes. When they were three weeks old, we went out twice a day for the same length of time. At week four, our jaunts lasted 30-45 minutes and took place twice a day and by their fifth week we'd make two or three hour-long trips outside.

Once ducklings are six weeks old and familiar with their new pen, and provided it's completely safe for ducklings and the weather is right, you can begin to leave them alone for brief periods of time. I usually let them think they're all alone, but then keep my eye on them from the window. The object of this exercise is to teach them (and you) a little independence.

While some youngsters will peep and protest against you leaving them alone in their new pen, it's something that all Momma Ducks need to teach their ducklings. I usually leave mine for five minutes and then come back for five. After doing this a few times, I begin leaving them for ten minutes and then coming back for five. There will come a point when you realize that your visits are causing more disruption in their routine than assurances. At this point you can extend the time again to every twenty or thirty minutes.

Experiencing the great outdoors... in baby-steps

- **Moving ducklings permanently outdoors**

When ducklings reach week eight and their new feathers have fully grown in, it's time for them to make the permanent transition outdoors. While it all sounded great in practice, don't be surprised if all those training sessions preparing you for this day did your ducklings a whole lot more good than they did you. It's completely normal for Momma Ducks to worry a little when their nest is suddenly empty.

When the time came for my boys to spend their first night outside, I was a wreck. It took hours for me to leave them alone in the barn. I visited them about five times throughout the course of the evening, and the first night a thunderstorm boomed across the land, I was suited-up and running out to the barn to sit with them and make sure they were alright, which, of course, they were.

While I do recommend checking on your ducklings a few times, especially for the first two or three days, I can honestly say, every time I went out to the barn I found my boys cuddled up and sleeping, or happily engaged in some bug-hunting business. Rest assured, you may worry at first, but once you see for yourself that they're adjusting perfectly to their new surroundings, you'll sleep again at night too.

These days I utilize a little technology to help me keep an eye on older ducklings who are in transition to the barn. Observing your ducklings by camera (or video baby monitors) is a great way to keep an eye on them without disrupting their routine.

Preparation #6
Building Your Duck Pen

There are many details that should be planned out carefully before breaking ground on your new duck pen.

Finding the Perfect Location

Here are some important items that you'll want to think about before beginning:

1. How big do I want my duck pen to be?

The size of your desired duck pen will help dictate its ideal shape and placement. While I love the idea of a humongous duck pen, you'd be wise to finish reading the rest of this book first because there can be a lot of seasonal work associated with a large pen that you haven't considered yet. On the other hand, too small of a pen has its own inherent issues (which I'll soon cover).

2. Where will their duck pond (or kiddy pool) be located inside the pen?

Ideally, you want your duck pond to be downhill from everything else to ensure proper drainage and to avoid splashing and ducky messes in less than ideal places. The size of your pool or pond should also be considered when working out pen dimensions.

3. Where will I be plugging in their heated water bucket in winter?

Remember when I explained about the rising level of ice around their water bucket? I prefer to keep this away from duck houses or pen doors or it can be a real nuisance. When the ice melts you want it to be able to drain away, so an elevated area is a good idea.

4. Have I considered my electrical needs?

Whether you're building your duck pen around existing electrical outlets or running electricity as part of your building plans, consider what you'll be using these outlets for and where they need to be located. Electrical outlets aren't only used to run heated water buckets, but also for fans, heat lamps, pumps, blow dryers, video monitors, etc. If you're installing your own electrical lines, I highly suggest you don't skimp on the number of outlets you're putting in. As you'll learn later, if ducks need to be separated at any time, having extra outlets available can make your reorganization plan much simpler.

5. How will I bring water into my pen?

Pumps and hoses are used to fill kiddy pools and water buckets as well as helping you out with your basic cleaning responsibilities. When planning out your enclosure be sure you consider where your clean water will be coming from. Remember to build your pen in close proximity to your waterlines especially in winter when hoses tend to freeze and you have to carry out water buckets instead. I lucked out; my barn was built with a hydrant pump inside. It's piped below the freeze line and provides water all year long, saving my back a lot of work. While a hydrant pump is ideal, installing them can be expensive.

6. What's my plan for dividing up this pen if any of my ducks need to be separated?

When building a duck pen it's always a good idea to pre-devise a means for future separations. There are times even with the happiest of ducks might need a break from each other. When this happens you'll be looking for a fast, efficient and safe way to divvy up your pen. Select an area and pen shape that allow for this to be done easily, affording each divided area everything you and your ducks will need.

7. Where will I be storing my duck feed?

If you only have two ducks, feed storage is pretty simple. You'll only need one or two bags on hand at any given time. Even so, you won't want to have to go far to replenish their food dishes every day. If you have more ducks and have a grain shed, you won't want your enclosure too far away from it when it comes time to haul bags of feed over. Closer is better.

8. Where will I store sand for winter?

In the wintertime pens will often need to be sanded for duck safety. Find a place to put your sand barrel that enables you to refill it easily while also allowing for quick access to spread around your pen. If you want to have a sand pile, it should be strategically placed in your yard in order to avoid excessive wash away. Make sure your desired pen location won't be too far from the pile or you'll have your work cut out for you.

9. Have I considered the weather in this area? Sun? Shade? Wind?

On cooler days, your ducks will want to sit in the sun, on warmer days they'll want to snooze in the shade. Be sure to choose a location that allows for both. Be careful to place their duck house in a location that utilizes the sun's warmth or the trees' shade as the case may be in your particular climate and location. Forests can be natural wind blocks if you're in a coastal area. If you have a small duck house, feel free to move it around in their pen seasonally to help moderate inside temperatures.

10. What's the water drainage like in this area?

I highly prefer building a duck enclosure on mildly-sloped grounds. Pens on flat grounds have poor drainage and tend to accumulate mud, which can be an invitation to parasites down the road. Ducks will ruin any vegetation growing anywhere near a puddle, making it very difficult to grow grass in their pen.

11. Where's the most efficient placement of doors and windows?

Figure out ahead of time where windows should be place to catch the best breezes or to pull in the most sunlight to light any barns or sheds. Think about the best placement of barn and shed doors as well as duck house doors in relation to their larger enclosure.

12. Can you see your ducks from your house?

Some Momma Ducks forget to take this into consideration because they're unaware of all the times they'll hear a strange noise and want to check on things from the window. Ducks do make an alarm call when something's up and a quick glance out the window can often tell you a great deal about whether their emergency is one you should be concerned about. Besides, it's fun to look out the window every now and again and watch your ducks. Don't deprive yourself of this.

13. What kind of predators might be drawn to this area?

This is one of those questions that must be answered with great attention to detail if you want your ducks to survive. In the U.S., raccoons are just about everywhere. If you think you don't have them, you're kidding yourself. This being the case, don't build your duck pen beneath a tree branch that a raccoon can gain access to. Fox are also quite common, although not often seen. They prefer sneaking up and hiding behind obstacles while making their approach, so try to select an open area that will make them feel exposed and vulnerable. Weasels like water, so don't build your pen near the river at the backend of your land or you may be asking for trouble. When selecting your duck pen location, think about which places have less predator traffic.

Finding the perfect location for your pen and carefully planning out all of the details before you start building will make your daily routines a whole lot easier down the road. Depending on your personal location and situation you may have other details that need to be taken into consideration as well before you start. If your plans include building your ducks a barn or shed, the above questions should be reviewed in regard to that project as well.

If you live in the country like me, count on dogs, cats, weasels, foxes, raccoons, fisher cats, coyotes, bobcats, hawks, eagles and don't forget those savvy owls. These predators are designed by nature to dig under, climb up, bite through, fly over and squeeze through anything they can in order to get to their dinner, and you do *not* want this to be your beloved ducks.

Keeping Predators Out

Addressing the predators in your area is one of your utmost responsibilities as a Momma Duck. If you don't build your pen in the right location, design it correctly or construct it from appropriate materials it won't protect your ducks and keep them safe, so let's spend a little time on it.

To keep wild animals out of my pens I use a number of tried and proven predator-stopping tactics.

1. PVC, heavy gauge wire fencing with a tight wire weave (½" x ½" or smaller) is ideal.
2. High perimeter fencing (at least six feet).
3. Fencing or concrete that goes at least two feet underground around the entire perimeter.
4. Digging predator barriers (predator skirts) that circle the entire perimeter.
5. A well-supported, heavy duty aviary net or a heavy gauge wire roof.
6. Electric fencing around the top perimeter.
7. I also incorporate motion-sensor lighting and a surveillance system.

Unless you have the kind of set up described above, where there's absolutely no way in, always lock your ducks up in a predator-proof barn or shed for the night. You don't want your ducks in plain view, taunting a hungry predator during the stealth of darkness while you're sleeping. Locking them up is also a good idea because it prevents your ducks from being stressed out by predators who might be circling their pen, even if they can't get in.

Sturdy Building Materials

Never underestimate the determination of a hungry animal. You want to make sure the wire you use can't be bitten through or torn apart, that holes can't be squirmed through and that it's strong enough to take a predatory punch. Be certain that your support beams are strong and sturdy and that your wire fencing has a tight fit over them.

Scarce winter months can really motivate a predator that would otherwise not look twice at the effort, so really think your plans through before making a final decision. Choose your stronghold materials wisely by becoming aware of your wildlife and then selecting components that are one step above what you need to keep these crafty animals out of your duck pen.

Remember, the best defense is a great fence. Your ducks have no natural protection against a predator. Your stronghold is their only shield, so make it a really good one.

Unknown Predators

Be careful not to make the mistake of assuming that you're aware of every predatory threat in your area—no matter how long you've lived there. I've lived in Connecticut my entire life and all of a sudden coyotes and fisher cats were reintroduced to the area without any notice. Raccoons have also been repopulated and bobcats have suddenly appeared. I'm not sure who's making all these wildlife decisions, or why they're not required to inform the people who live here, but a safe backyard can quickly turn into a dangerous one without any warning.

Some predators keep a very low profile. Just because you live in a heavily populated area doesn't mean you don't have raccoons and just because you've never seen a fox in your yard doesn't mean they're not around. Foxes are very stealthy and often have their dens far closer than you'd like to believe.

The way it was isn't the way it will be. Predators don't stay in the same place; they follow the prey. While that may sound obvious, many people tend to assume otherwise. Just because your backyard is safe today, doesn't mean it will be tomorrow. They're not going to send you a letter of notification before they come, telling you they're moving into the area.

Predatory Determination

Try to imagine the worst circumstances a predator might face. A starving animal scouting new territory for prey, an injured one who needs to locate prey easily, or one with little mouths to feed is going to be incredibly dedicated to the task of finding food. One summer I continued to find evidence that a predator was diligently attempting to get into one of my duck pens by gnawing on the fencing and digging underground. I reacted by adding extra layers of fencing and putting up additional electric fencing, lower to the ground. One day I happened to go outside at just the right time and discovered it was a fox with an injured front paw. She was my culprit. It explained why she was working so hard to get at my ducks; she couldn't chase down anything else. Situations change and predators can instantly become more motivated. If you want to keep your ducks safe, you have to prepare for this ahead of time or you could lose them.

Predators are extremely patient and have been known to be just out of sight, watching while you're taking your ducks for a walk through the yard. I know people who've run into the house for a second to grab their phone only to see a fox come bursting out of a hiding spot to grab one of their ducks before they even made it to the door. I know families who've watched coyotes lunge through their backyards to grab their ducks while they were only twenty feet away, I even know someone who watched a bald eagle come and hoist her duck up into the air. Predators are exceedingly patient and they're watching and waiting for just the right moment when you're a bit too far away or a bit too distracted. Hunting prey is what predators do and they're exceptionally good at it, which means you have to be even more diligent if you want to protect your ducks.

Your enclosure needs to be strong enough to withstand hours of vigorous attempts at break-ins because at some point a predator is going to try it, and it'll most likely be while you're at work or in bed at night sleeping. Various kinds of jumping, climbing, flying, squeezing and digging predators of many shapes and sizes will be looking at your pen and deciding if it's worth their time.

Evaluate Your Predators

This section will give you a good idea who might be skulking around in your backyard, how they might try to break into your duck pen and how you can best keep them at bay. While this list is by no means comprehensive, it should give you a good place to start in your preparations.

- **Fox**

Foxes are expert and stealthy hunters tending to go unnoticed most of the time. They often live very close to humans without ever being discovered, so don't assume you don't have any just because you haven't seen them around. Foxes tend to grab their prey and run off with it without leaving a trace. If you have a sudden and unexplained duck disappearance with no remains left behind, a fox is a likely suspect and they'll be back for more.

Because foxes are shy and prefer to remain undetected, motion sensing lights around your duck house may help deter them at night. A good guard dog is an excellent deterrent, but because foxes are extremely watchful and patient hunters, dogs can't always be relied upon in every scenario. The scent markings of a dog will usually keep a fox on their toes, but not necessarily away. A hungry fox will watch and wait diligently for an opportunity to seize an unprotected duck. You may not see them, but they definitely see you.

- **Bobcat**

Bobcats can jump as high as twelve feet. They're solitary animals who are very adaptable and can live in very close proximity with humans without being detected. If you do come in contact with a bobcat, they can be provoked to attack, so use extreme caution. Motion sensing lights around your duck pen can be helpful, but a large guard dog can be of greater assistance if this predator is a known trouble-maker in your area.

- **Raccoon**

Raccoons prefer to do most of their dirty work in darkness; however, they can sometimes be seen during the day. One of the top things raccoons like to do is look for food, so never underestimate the determination of this crafty predator. They're lured in by both your ducks and their food. They're really good problem solvers and excellent lock picks, but padlocks are beyond their capabilities. Use this knowledge to your advantage.

A raccoon will employ every tactic at its disposal to get at your ducks. They're capable of tearing and biting through aviary netting and poultry fencing to get at your ducks. Worst of all, raccoons have been known to eat a duck right through the fencing if they can get their paws on any part of your sleeping feathered friend and pull them into their clutches.

Avoid luring raccoons into your yard by keeping attractive food items out of their reach. Predator urine (available at your local grain store) applied frequently around your enclosure may help keep raccoons away, but don't rely on this measure alone. You may have some added success by keeping motion lights around your barn at night, but once they grow accustomed to this, it'll lose its effectiveness. A dog is not necessarily a good idea to keep raccoons away from your pens since a confrontation will most likely end with your dog in a vet's office. As with any wild animal, be extremely cautious of rabies when dealing with raccoons. They're known carriers of this and other diseases in many regions.

- **Weasel**

Weasels are ferocious and blood-thirsty nocturnal predators. They can squeeze through holes as small as an inch and are notorious for killing entire flocks if uninterrupted. They tend to do most of their work at night, but can occasionally be seen during the day.

Significant rodent populations and good water sources are both alluring to weasels. Keep rodents under control to avoid fostering a suitable environment. Large birds of prey (hawks, eagles, owls) can help keep weasel populations in check, but don't count on it entirely. Cats are an excellent deterrent; they'll hunt rodents and weasels (just remember to protect your ducks from your cat). Spreading bobcat urine routinely around the outside perimeter of your pens is another preventative option.

- **Fisher Cat**

Fisher cats are ferocious nocturnal predators. They're very fast, extremely agile and will kill anything they can overtake. As members of the weasel family, they can elongate their bodies and squeeze into small holes and gaps. These solitary predators are designed by nature to climb over, dig under and gnaw through obstacles, so be very wary of them. Fisher cats are blood thirsty predators and will wipe out an entire flock in the midst of a ravenous rampage.

Fishers usually prefer to live near water sources with access to rodent populations or other prey. If you have a dog, have them routinely mark their scent around your duck pen or spread bobcat urine as a deterrent.

- **Bear**

Bears have been known to wander through many areas where they've never been seen before. There's no real protection against a bear other than an extremely strong, fully enclosed pen and a sturdy barn to lock your ducks up in at night—out of sight, out of mind. If bears are a threat in your area, be careful to store food properly, so you won't lure them into your backyard. This means picking up eggs every day and bringing them into your house. Be mindful of where you store your feed; it should be locked up in a building where a bear can't gain access. You may even want to store it in a separate building from your ducks.

- **Snapping Turtle**

Snapping turtles will eat ducklings and have been known to inflict serious damage on the legs and feet of adult ducks swimming overhead. Never let your ducks swim on your pond if there's a chance there could be a snapping turtle dwelling there—and this includes just about any pond that isn't surrounded by fencing with a tight enough wire weave to keep a baby snapper from wandering in.

Snapping turtles have been known to travel long distances, so don't assume you don't have one just because you never have before. A newcomer can secretly join your pond's ecosystem at any time without your knowledge.

- **Alligator**

Alligators will eat ducks and ducklings and can also inflict serious injury during any close encounters. As with snapping turtles, don't let your ducks swim on your pond if there is any chance an alligator could be in it. If you have alligators in your area, be sure to erect strong fencing around your duck pond with a tight enough weave to keep baby gators out.

- **Fish**

While most people don't think about it, large fish like the Northern Pike have been known to lurk in vegetation close to shore and gulp down unsuspecting ducklings. Keep your ducklings off water inhabited by predatory fish.

- **Opossum**

Opossums are nocturnal and generally more interested in eggs than anything else, but they'll strike at a duckling or duck if the conditions are right; that is, if they're hungry enough. Ducks with disabilities make easier targets and are at higher risk of being attacked.

Opossums are often deterred by motion sensor lights and the presence or scent of a good guard dog. If you don't have a dog you can spread coyote or bobcat urine around your duck pen. Remember to pick up eggs daily, so they won't be needlessly attracted to your duck pen.

- **Skunk**

Skunks will eat eggs or ducklings if the opportunity arises. Methods to deter opossums also work for skunks although I wouldn't recommend a guard dog in this situation.

- **Rat**

Rats can fit through an opening the size of a quarter, leap up to three feet in the air and climb walls. They eat eggs, can kill small ducklings, harass larger ducks and spread disease. It can be very difficult to build a rat-proof enclosure. They'll burrow under and around enclosures and barns and chew their way through and into buildings to get at stored feed. They'll literally tear down the barn around your ducks in order to get inside (which can create passages for other predators). Every effort should be made to eliminate them the instant they're discovered on the premises.

Discourage rats by storing your duck's feed in metal containers. Metal flashing can be mounted over base boards to keep rats from chewing through them, but ultimately, the aid of a few good cats is your best deterrent.

- **Snake**

Depending on the species, snakes can either bite or constrict ducklings or ducks and have also been known to eat eggs. Digging predator barriers will keep rodents from digging tunnels into your pen, which will also keep snakes from moving into tunnels and finding a way inside. Cats, dogs and the presence of large predatory birds can also be good snake deterrents.

If snakes are of particular concern in your area, mount ½" x ½" grid, PVC welded wire mesh over the bottom three feet of your existing perimeter fence (easily done with some heavy-duty zip-ties). This will deter larger snakes from just slinking into your pen whenever they want. You can also install solar powered electric fencing around the base of your pen. Attach insulator clips to your perimeter fencing a foot or two off of the ground and then string the wire through them. This will prevent snakes from climbing even higher up the fencing. Be sure to mount *"Electric Fence"* warning safety signs.

Chickens will often eat small snakes that can fit through wire mesh fencing, making them a great addition to your flock. Road Runners are also known to eat snakes. If you have wild populations in your area, encourage them to forage around your pens by keeping pet dogs and cats at bay during their active hours.

Additional tips:

1. Snakes like to hide in tall grass and weeds. Trim plants in and around your pens.
2. Mice and rodents are a pleasant invitation for snakes. Reduce populations.
3. Woodpiles and other moist and dark places are favorite snake hideaways. Remove them.

If you eliminate their food source and their places to hide, snakes have less reason to hang around your duck pen. There are laws protecting some species of snakes, so be sure to check your local legislation before acting.

- **Dog**

Dogs are everywhere. If you don't have one, your neighbor probably does. I once heard from someone who'd left their ducks in their front yard while they went into town on a brief errand. The fencing was by no means predator-proof, just enough to keep the ducks circled inside. A passing dog saw the ducks and jumped over their shoddy fencing and attacked the ducks inside. The ducks couldn't get away from the dog because they were trapped within the make-shift circular fence. If anything, it made the dog's work even easier because the ducks had absolutely no place to go. This is a terrible reminder that if you're going to put up a fence, you best put up one that's actually going to keep predators *out;* otherwise you'll just be doing the dogs in your neighborhood a favor. Build a pen, not a *trap* for your ducks, and never leave your ducks unattended when they're vulnerable (which of course means recognizing when they're vulnerable).

Dogs range in temperament from gentle to ferocious depending on nature and nurture, but even the kindest dog can turn on your ducks in a moment of excitement—even if there's never been a problem before. For this reason, you should *never* leave your dog unsupervised in the presence of your duck. I've heard more stories than you'd care to know about wonderful family dogs suddenly deciding a chase would be in good fun. All it takes is one unexpected flap of an excited duck for a dog to take off unexpectedly. Don't assume that *your* dog would never because they're too old or too well-trained because there's no such thing. It only takes a moment for disaster to strike.

I'm not in favor of introducing dogs and ducks, but if you're going to do it make sure you're working with a gentle and well-trained *adult* dog (who are far more predictable than puppies). Honestly, I find these interactions are more for the sake of the dog's enjoyment than the ducks, so before you begin, ask yourself why you're doing it. Being directly confronted by a predator is extremely stressful for ducks, so if there isn't a sound reason for it, then it should be avoided at all costs. However, if you feel that this closely monitored interaction will help foster harmony and safety in your particular situation, then proceed with extreme caution. Always remain hands-on and in-between your dog and duck during any introductions to prevent any mishaps.

It's often wise to begin by allowing your dog to smell your feathered friend through the safety of a fence. A good way to start is by putting your duck in control of the situation. Do this by crating your dog and allowing your duck to wander around them, permitting them to wander as close or as far away as they prefer. During these exercises, encourage your dog to sit still in their kennel, keep quiet (no barking or whining) and to stay calm. You can reverse the roles later, with the duck inside a safe pen while the dog is allowed to watch from the outside. Again, don't allow the dog to get excited or to circle the duck like a predator. This is a calm and controlled activity where the dog is encouraged to sit quietly. It should never stress out your duck or it needs to come to an immediate end.

- **Cat**

Cats are often even more common than dogs. The temperament of a cat will depend on their breed, gender and socialization. Cats are very high jumpers, excellent hunters and catch their prey much more frequently than they miss.

One pounce from a kitten or cat can quickly be fatal for a duckling, bantam or lightweight duck. Meanwhile a bound from an adult cat can injure just about any duck if it's carried out right. This being said, most cats won't be interested in your medium or heavyweight duck (unless you have somewhat of a monster on your hands).

Kittens can usually be introduced to a fully enclosed duck pen with great success—provided the ducks aren't too small and maintain the upper hand. As long as your ducks start out in-charge they'll usually maintain a certain level of control, thus fostering a beneficial relationship where the cats act as a deterrent for mice, wild birds and weasels. This relationship between guardian cats and ducks should be closely monitored, implementing immediate separations if you see any signs of trouble—trust your instincts on this one and act fast.

- **Hawk, Falcon & Eagle**

Hawks, falcons and eagles are all diurnal raptors who hunt during the day. If your ducks don't have top-cover, they'll be at the mercy of these sky predators. Most attacks occur on free-range ducks, especially when they're in open areas with no bushes, trees or houses to provide shelter.

Diurnal raptors will pluck out a duck's feathers before consuming them, which means their beak marks can often be seen on the shafts of the plucked feathers. If you don't find these telltale marks then the bird isn't your predator, but merely a scavenger. Additionally, if the feathers have small amounts of tissue clinging to the bottoms, they were plucked when cold, which also means the raptor was scavenging. A smooth and clean feather base indicates a warm plucking, which means the raptor *is* your direct problem.

The best defense against flying predators is a well-built enclosure with a strong aviary netting or wire top. Larger birds have been known to attack ducks by pushing down on aviary netting until it's pressed on top of them, so make sure your net is mounted properly to prevent this.

Guinea fowl and geese will often sound an alarm when any large bird flies overhead, which can help warn you and your flock of any incoming trouble. Families of crows can be relentless and will often chase raptors off, so feeding them and encouraging them to settle on your property can be another way of keeping your skies clear of trouble.

- **Owl**

Owls are primarily nocturnal raptors although it's not unheard of for them to hunt during the day either, especially when they're hungry or have little mouths to feed. As with the diurnal raptors, a good aviary net or top wire is in definitely in order if you want your ducks to live a long time (which I'm assuming you do). Owls have occasionally been known to herd ducks into fencing and then eat them right through the wire. Protect your ducks from this kind of attack by providing them a safe nighttime lock-up in either a barn, shed or duck house. Strobe lights are sometimes used as a night deterrent against owls with varying degrees of success.

Remember: All hawks, falcons, eagles and owls are federally protected under the Migratory Bird Treaty Act, which prohibits their possession or destruction. No permits are required to merely scare them off with your presence (unless they're nesting) except in the case of an endangered or threatened species. Check your own state's laws and regulations prior to taking any actions against these impressive birds.

Young Matthew and Young Jeffrey tip their eyes to the sky as raptors fly overhead

Below you'll see a table of various predators to keep in mind when building your duck pen and the range of their skills.

Predator	Digging	Climbing	Squeezing	Reaching	Gnawing	Jumping	Flying	Swimming	Breaking
Coyote	⊕				⊕	⊕			
Wolf	⊕				⊕	⊕			
Fox	⊕		⊕		⊕	⊕			
Bobcat	⊕	⊕				⊕			
Raccoon	⊕	⊕		⊕	⊕				
Fisher Cat	⊕	⊕	⊕		⊕				
Weasel	⊕	⊕	⊕		⊕				
Bear	⊕	⊕			⊕				⊕
Snap. Turtle								⊕	
Alligator								⊕	
Northern Pike								⊕	
Opossum	⊕	⊕	⊕	⊕	⊕				
Skunk	⊕		⊕		⊕				
Rat	⊕	⊕	⊕		⊕	⊕			
Snake		⊕	⊕						
Dog	⊕	⊕			⊕	⊕			
Cat	⊕	⊕	⊕	⊕		⊕			
Hawk							⊕		
Falcon							⊕		
Eagle							⊕		
Owl							⊕		

Free-Ranging

I can't tell you how many people have contacted me at the sanctuary over the years about their free-range ducks. There are a lot of families out there who lock their ducks up in houses at night and then open the door come morning time. They simply let their ducks out and allow them to roam around their unfenced property un-chaperoned (an occasional glance from the window does *not* constitute chaperoning). Some of them mistakenly believe a stone wall or some old disintegrating horse fence is affording their ducks all the protection they need while others believe their dog will successfully keep all of the predators away. Many of them don't even lock up their ducks. They leave them out on ponds all night in some misguided belief that the ducks will thrive there. I'm always dumbfounded when these people come to me surprised that they lost their ducks after tending (or more aptly, *not* tending) to them in this manner.

The truth is no dog will successfully keep every kind of predator away one hundred percent of the time, and I could easily give you a dozen examples where eagles, foxes and coyotes successfully snatched up someone's duck within a few yards of their dog and got away with it. To make matters even worse, once they successfully get one duck, they usually come back looking for more because that's how the predatory mind works.

I've had people argue adamantly with me that fencing ducks in pens is cruel. Although I agree that it's cruel to keep ducks in small and cramped pens throughout their entire lives, I also think it's cruel to allow an unprotected duck to be predated because they have no fencing protection. My ducks live lavishly in spacious pens that are set up like habitats. They have shelter, food, clean water (for swimming and drinking), clean bedding, grass and companionship—human and duck. They're safe from predators and want for nothing. Is that cruel? *Absolutely not.*

Unless your intent is to support your local food chain by providing predators with an easy meal, you need to protect your ducks by giving them a safe and secure pen, or you won't have them around for very long.

<u>Determine the Size of Your Enclosure</u>

Now that we have all that free-range nonsense out of the way, let's talk about space. I once came across information that recommended I build a ten-by-ten pen for Young Matthew and Young Jeffrey—only five square feet per duck! Thank goodness I knew enough to ignore that lousy advice. When looking for any kind of guidance regarding your ducks, remember to consider the source. People who keep ducks for reasons other than for human companionship aren't necessarily the resource you want to be tapping for information. Your goals are very different. While they may see ducks as a commodity, a Momma Duck certainly doesn't.

There are people who sell their ducks for profit and those of us who couldn't be offered enough money. There are people who are trying to maximize their space to its full potential and there are those of us who want our ducks to waddle through spacious and grassy grounds, living fully enriched lives. There are people who pen their entire flock together, unconcerned with any casualties, and there are those of us who couldn't bear it if one of our own was injured. Before following any recommendations from anyone, make sure they have the same goals in mind as you.

- **250 square feet for two ducks**

I've found that a 250 square foot pen is about the smallest you want to go for a pair of ducks. 125 square feet per duck is a far cry from the 25 square-feet-per-duck pen I was advised to build for my boys. A larger pen affords you and your ducks a wide range of benefits:

1. Having ample room in your pen provides plenty of room for a kiddy pool and its associated mess. Keeping water spillage away from your duck house and food is always a good idea to avoid wood rotting and food spoiling.

2. If you have a small duck house, having extra space in your pen allows you to move it around seasonally. It can be placed in shady spots in summer and sunny spots in winter.

3. Larger pens require less ground maintenance. Fewer ducks in a larger space means there's a thinner spread of duck poop and less hosing down and clean-up to be done. The grounds will naturally absorb and handle all decomposition. Also, when it comes to grass, larger pens are far more likely to grow and sustain it, which can make things a lot easier for you.

4. Ducks don't have as many issues amongst themselves when they have larger pens to get away from each other. Smaller pens can lead to excessive fighting—especially if you have more than one drake.

5. Larger pens provide more options for separations whenever the need arises.

6. Larger pens provide more room for enrichment activities. It's hard to assemble a sprinkler system, set up a bunch of colored tubs or play hide-and-seek with treats if you don't have the room.

7. Space is just that… space! Enriched ducks have room to move about, explore, forage and enjoy their days. It also provides a comfortable place for you to set up your chair to relax and visit your feathered friends.

Some signs that your duck pen is not big enough for your ducks include: a lack of sustainable vegetation (no grass), hard-packed soil, piled up feces that can't naturally work its way into the soil, a stinky pen and too many flies.

The benefits of a large pen are pretty wonderful. A bigger pen is more fun to visit and you'll see a lot more activity out of your ducks as they explore each and every corner. For this reason, many Momma Ducks build even larger pens that are twice as large and measure 500 - 600 square feet. Now those are some happy ducks!

While the downside of having a big pen like this may include clearing snow away in winter, fortunately for many of us, that problem only presents itself a few months out of the a year.

"The Gardens" measure: 24' Wide x 36' Long x 6' High
There are one or two ducks in each of its three 12' x 24' sections

How to Build a Predator-Proof-Enclosure

We built a spacious outdoor enclosure for Young Matthew and Young Jeffrey to reside in during the day. You can find all kinds of plans telling you how to build your pen, but remember to keep your own personal needs and the needs of your flock in mind before beginning.

I've found that the most efficient way to build an enclosure is to construct it around your duck house, or if you have a barn or shed, off the side of that building that has an access door. This way, you just have to walk them inside before sunset and then open the door again after sunrise the next morning. This kind of set-up prevents you from having to take your ducks outside of their realm of safety on a regular basis. Having their duck house within their pen also offers double protection against predators.

While there are plenty of duck pen designs out there, not all of them will stand up to the test of time and weather, keep your ducks safe and keep your predators out. To date, I've never lost a duck to a predator and I never intend to. After building a number of different types of enclosures, I can tell you which ones work best and why. The following directions are generic in nature. All construction needs to be carefully planned to ensure adequate weight support and structural integrity.

Remember: Before you bring your ducks into any newly built enclosures or shelters it's *imperative* that you do a thorough visual check and remove all hardware and bits of metal from the site, so that it's not ingested. Hardware Disease is one of the number one causes of death in pet ducks, so take your search extremely seriously and check areas more than once (see: "*Hardware Disease*"). Remove all dangerous debris before letting your ducks explore their new pen. Magnets and metal detectors can greatly assistance you during this pertinent task.

- **Structural supports**

The first step when building your new duck pen is to frame it out. Pressure treated lumber should be utilized for structural support to help prevent future rotting. While there is some controversy regarding the safety of these chemically treated beams, as long as they aren't constantly sitting in pools of water, you shouldn't have any problems. I use them throughout all of my pens and have done so for many years without any related health issues at all among my flock.

The framing out of a structurally sound and predator-proof pen

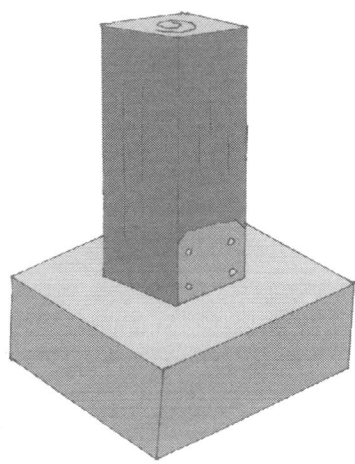

4" x 4" fastened to a concrete footing

Perimeter and interior fence posts should be set in a grid formation *no further* than ten feet apart from one another for structural soundness. I set all of my 4" x 4" support posts on pads of concrete that are 3-6" thick, depending on the pen's size and structural requirements. This helps prevent the bottoms of the posts from decomposing. You want to avoid actually cementing posts directly into concrete because it can promote bottom-of-beam rotting. 16 gauge galvanized post base brackets are sunk into the square concrete pads while they're still wet. Once dry, the posts are securely screwed or nailed into the brackets, allowing them to rest firmly and securely on concrete supports.

- **Roofing**

A wire ceiling or aviary net needs to be raised over any pen where your flock will remain unmonitored to prevent predatory attack.

Once you have your posts in place, cross beams and additional supports can be mounted securely overhead to properly bear the weight of your roofing wire or aviary netting—as well as any snow that may mount on top of it. Be careful not to underestimate the burden of all that snow when you're working through your building calculations. A seemingly harmless cubic foot of light and fluffy snow can weigh as much as *seven* pounds; meanwhile, a more common and wetter snow can easily way *fifteen pounds* or more. Your 250 square foot roof may need to hold anywhere from 1750–3750 pounds of snow following a winter snowstorm. The weight of all this snow can quickly pull an inadequate ceiling down to the ground. Even the strongest duck enclosures may require roof-clearing during blizzards or between multiple snowstorms to prevent any structural damage.

The weight of blizzard snow was too much for my quarantine pen's kennel poles to bear. Fortunately, I was aware of its structural limitations and didn't have any ducks inside.

Aviary nets require less load support than wire roofs, but need to be cleared of snow and debris much more frequently to prevent tearing and collapsing. Additionally, aviary nets aren't effective enough on their own to protect flock members. Raccoons can easily climb up and gnaw right through them *unless* you're also utilizing electric fencing, and even the best, heavy duty nets begin to wear out and need replacing around 8-9 years.

After trying both aviary nets and structurally supported wire ceilings, I highly suggest the latter. There's nothing like heavy 16 gauge, polyvinyl coated, tight weave, wire roofing held in place by beams that you can actually get on top of and walk on. It's easier for clearing snow and debris, and if you have small trees in your pen, it'll be an incredible aid when it comes time to prune their upper branches.

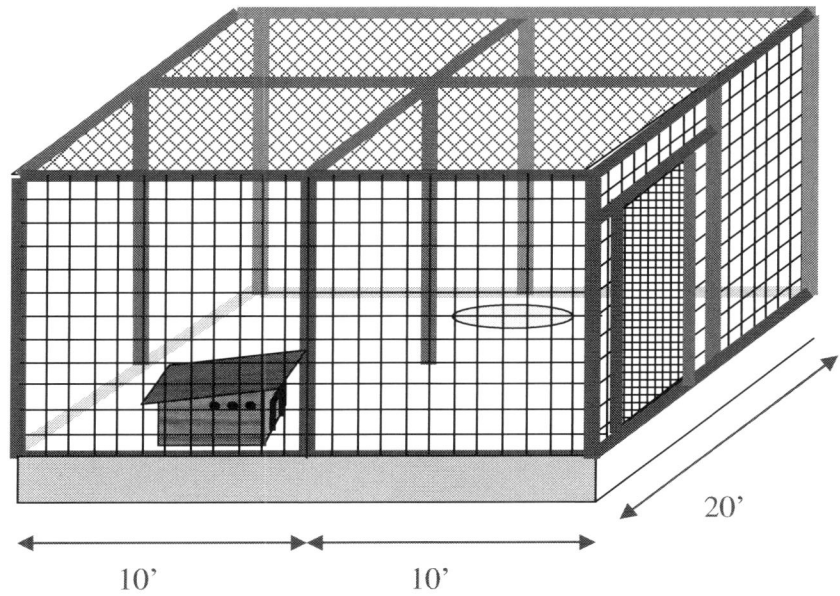

Support posts should be set in a grid pattern every ten feet

I hate dragging ladders around (especially in snow), so I prefer to build wooden ladders and then permanently mount them directly onto one of the pen's exterior walls. If you're going to do this, you have to have an *extremely* secure pen or utilize electric fencing to keep raccoons off of your ladder.

- **Doors**

It's important to get a good seal between your pen's door and its frame, and for me, this is one of the most difficult parts of pen-building. You have to leave enough of a space all the way around to allow for any swelling of the wood, while also avoiding unsafe *gaps* that can make way for predators to gain access into your pen.

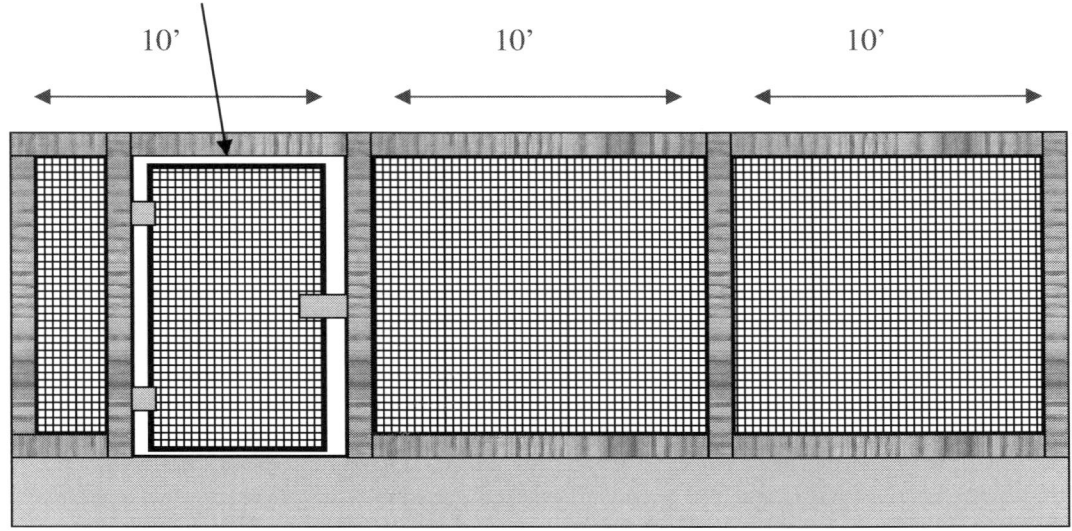

Make sure your door fits nicely into its frame. Avoid wide gaps.

Remember, weasels and rats can squeeze into an opening as tight as ¾ of an inch wide. And while reviewing entryway security, I want to advise you to *always* padlock your doors. Raccoons are notorious when it comes to opening up latches and getting into pens, not to mention disgruntled neighbors.

- **Perimeter fencing**

Your perimeter fencing must be strong. While most people hear the name *"poultry wire"* and assume it must be the ideal selection; the truth is, dogs, weasels, rats and raccoons can bite right through it, so it's best not to use this material as the only barrier between predators and your flock. Remember your perimeter fence is your number one defense against every kind of uninvited guest (including people).

Tall fences make way for comfortable visits to your duck enclosure. You don't want to be all hunched over while you're working in your pen or trying to enjoy the company of your ducks. Place the pen's ceiling at an appropriate height that keeps your back in mind. For human comfort and pen accessibility, I highly suggest a minimum six foot high perimeter fence. This will also discourage most jumping predators from gaining access.

The kind of fencing you utilize will largely depend on your budget. Keep in mind your ducks can live up to fifteen years, so you'll want your pen to last just as long. This makes fencing that can rust (poultry wire, welded wire mesh, etc.) a failing option. Ideally you'll want to use some kind of PVC (polyvinyl chloride) coated fencing if you want your pen to last a long time with minimal upkeep. The heavier the gauge (thickness) of the wire itself, the more durable the fence will be.

Fence weave is another vital consideration. The tighter the weave of wire, the safer your flock will be. Weasels can squeeze through a hole as small as one inch in diameter and rats can squeeze through one that's only three-quarters of an inch. If you want to keep them both out (and I highly recommend you do), a half-inch by half-inch wire weave is the ultimate way to go. I've tried many things here and my personal favorite is ½" x ½", 16 gauge, polyvinyl coated hardware cloth/welded wire mesh with a galvanized steel wire core. While this is the ideal, it's also very expensive. The question is, are you and your ducks worth it? Do you want to leave for work for the day and know that your pets are safe even though you're not home? Do you want to fall into a deep slumber every night knowing that troublesome raccoon has absolutely no chance of getting into your pen? You decide.

*Louisville is one of our sanctuary's most impressive predator-proof pens to date.
This enclosure resides further into our forest than our other pens,
and was subsequently built of exceptionally strong materials.*

If the 16 gauge PVC welded wire mesh is simply out of your price range, you can get lighter 19 gauge PVC wire mesh instead (the higher the gauge, the thinner the wire). If this pricing is still too high, you can get even get 23 gauge PVC wire mesh (which often comes in a ¼" x ¼" weave). The trick is, if you're going to go with a higher gauge wire mesh that offers less protection, you want to layer it with an inexpensive lower gauge wire—and this is surprisingly easy to do.

You can go to just about any fencing supplier or home improvement store and find green PVC 14 gauge welded wire in rolls that are 4-6 feet high and anywhere from 50-100 feet in length (if they don't have it in stock they can probably order it for you). Four foot high fencing of this kind is commonly woven with rectangles that measure 1½" x 2½" while the six foot high fencing usually has rectangles that measure 2" x 4".

Now that you have your lightweight 23 gauge PVC wire mesh and your heavyweight 14 gauge green welded wire, you can install them both, layering one over the other—with your strongest wire placed on the *outside* of your pen, facing your predators and preventing them from biting through the inner and weaker wire that's tucked underneath. This layering of the two fences will keep both the small and large predators out of your pen. Believe it or not, heavy-duty cable ties can be your best friend when it comes to this task. They work amazingly well at pulling the two layers together and holding things in place while you're hammering, and they last a long time.

If this is still too expensive for your taste, you can layer a less expensive welded wire mesh that's *not* polyvinyl coated (commonly referred to as "rabbit wire") beneath the 14 gauge green welded wire. While you may have to replace this wire at some point down the road (how frequently depends on your local conditions), it's a very affordable way to go.

- **Underground perimeter**

The next troublemakers you have to defend against are digging predators and there are a lot of them. The first measure you'll need to take against them is to build in an underground barrier. This can be done in one of two ways:

1. Install an underground, concrete, perimeter foundation.
2. Plant your perimeter fence below ground level.

Personally, after trying both, I much prefer the concrete foundation. It's a little more work at first, but it won't rust, rodents won't get through it, and (if done right) it'll last the lifetime of your pen. I get a can of marking paint and draw the layout of my pen on the ground. Then, I dig a trench that measures one foot in width and two feet down. If you don't have power equipment and think this task is impossible by hand, I beg to differ. We have almost impossibly rocky grounds here in Connecticut and I've dug the perimeter foundations of more than one pen by hand (one while pregnant). If the ground is solid enough, you can simply mix and pour your concrete right into the trench without any framing (or you can have a cement truck fill them for you if it's within your budget).

Another option to achieve this effect is to simply place cement blocks (holes facing down) into these trenches rather than filling them with concrete. If you have muddy soil this is a great way to go. Just set the blocks in place as you dig. If you want to add further strength to this brick foundation you can pound short rebar posts through the holes and even fill around them with some premixed quick cement.

While digging these perimeter trenches, remember to incorporate the plans for your perimeter support posts. You don't want to begin any cement work until you figure how everything is going to fit together.

Once my concrete foundation has had 2-3 days to dry, I use a pneumatic nail gun to securely fasten a pressure treated, pine board into place on top. It shoots a long nail right through the board and into the concrete. Once that board is set, I have a way to attach my wire fencing to my structure.

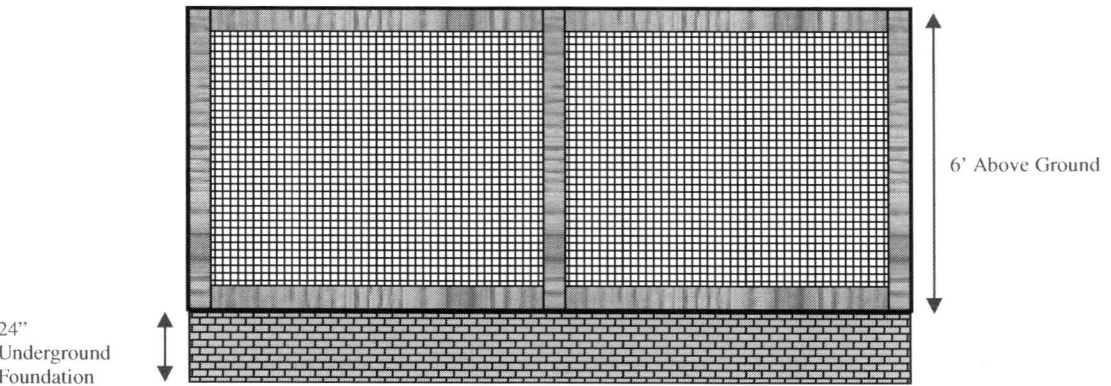

Fencing mounted on top of an in-ground, concrete perimeter foundation

If the concrete option isn't feasible for you, or too labor intensive, you can proceed with the second option. You'll still have to dig a two-foot perimeter trench, but it doesn't need to be nearly as wide—just a couple of inches, enough to lower fencing down into it. If you go this route, you'll likely need to layer your wire in order to make it tall enough.

You can use hog ring pliers/stapler tool (supplier: www.gemplers.com) to quickly ring-fasten a three foot below-the-ground fence to a six foot above-the-ground fence (with a one foot fencing overlap between them). Your underground wire doesn't need to match your above ground wire; in fact, if you went with a more affordable above-ground fencing option, you'll want your underground fencing to be a little stronger. For the underground wire you want to utilize a strong, heavy gauge, PVC wire (so it won't rust)—the tighter the weave the more efficient it'll be at keeping rodents out later.

- **Digging predator barrier**

If you want to be doubly sure that digging predators never get into your duck pen, you can also add a digging predator barrier to your plans. Digging predator barriers are inserted under the ground around the entire perimeter of your pen—like a skirt, and it's normally one of the final things you add to your pen after the rest of the pen-build is complete.

Standing outside of your perimeter fencing, dig a shallow trench. It should go 3 - 6 inches down into the ground and come two feet out and away from the perimeter fencing of your pen.

For this project you'll need long strip of PVC welded wire mesh (so it doesn't rust) that's long enough to cover the entire length of your perimeter (allowing a little extra to overlap at the corners) and 2½ - 3 feet wide.

Begin at the outer edge of your trench, away from your pen. Lay the PVC welded wire mesh down into the trench and unroll it towards your pen. At the two foot mark, gently bend the excess 6-12 inches (depending on the width of the roll you purchased) upward, so that it climbs up the exterior of the perimeter fencing of your pen. Once you have it aligned just the way you want it, secure that top end of this welded wire mesh to the your perimeter fencing (zip-ties work great for this). Once it's tacked in place, work on making a solid crease in the wire where it bends at a 90 degree angle. Repeat this process working your way around the outside of your pen. Some cutting and folding will need to be done at corners to ensure you have good protection in these areas.

When you're finished laying out all of your predator skirts, refill the trenches, placing dirt over the top of the welded wire mesh, burying it completely (and then seed it with grass if you prefer).

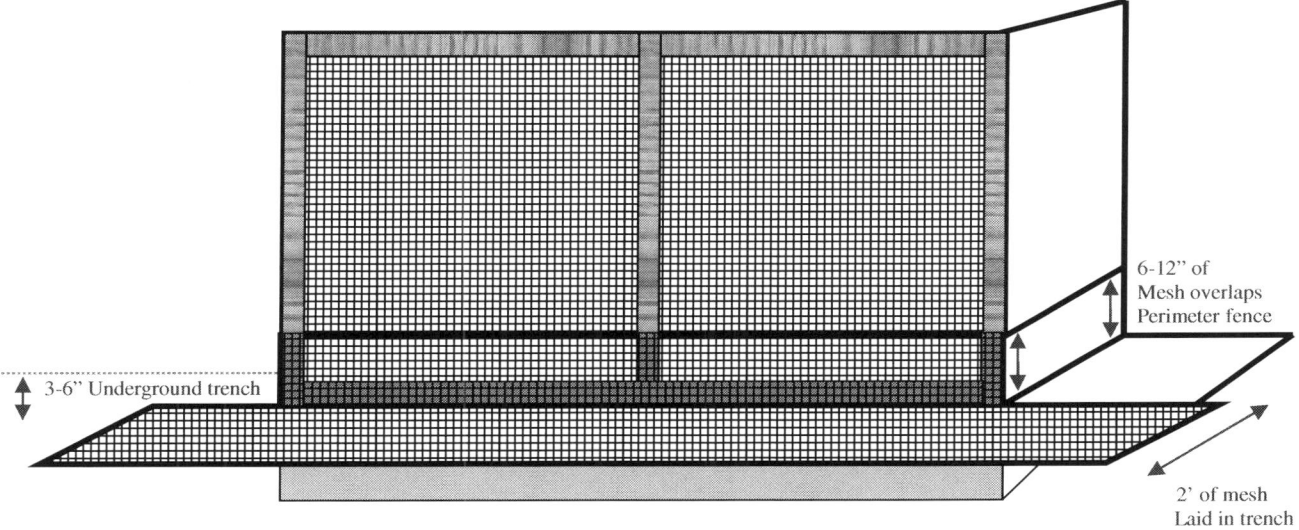

Underground predator barriers

How does your predator barrier work? A predator approaches your duck pen and tries to dig its way under at the base of your perimeter fencing. They hit your underground predator barrier and try moving sideways along the base of your pen's perimeter fencing to try to get in. Unable to gain entry they give up. Predators aren't crafty enough to back up two feet to try to dig-in under the barriers.

- **Electric fencing**

Energy efficient, solar powered, electric fencing can be safely installed around the top perimeter of your pen. This added feature will prevent predators from climbing up on top of the enclosure's aviary net or top fencing. You can purchase a back-up rechargeable battery and plug-in charger for those less-sunny winter months when the battery occasionally has more difficulty charging (you may even want a battery tester). Solar chargers can be purchased to power two, three, five, ten or even a whopping *thirty mile* electric fence (supplier: www.zarebasystems.com).

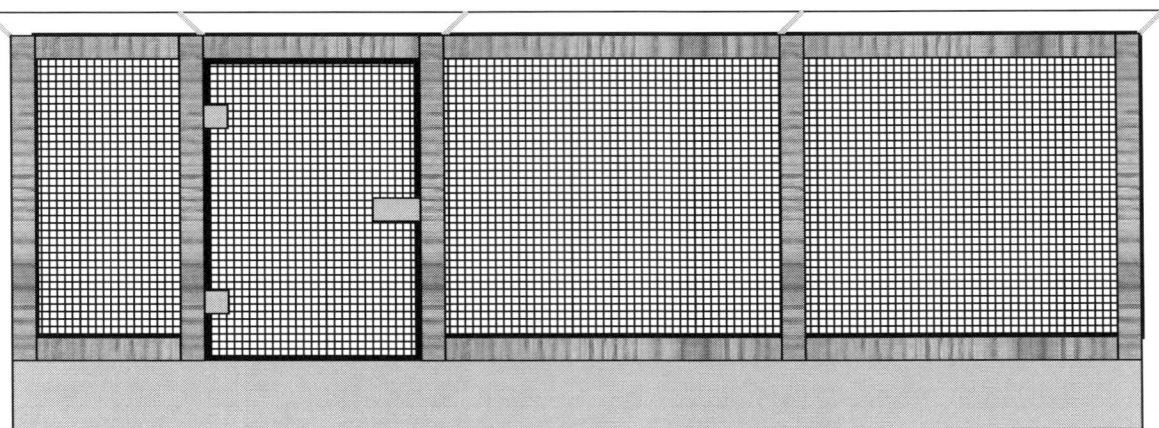

Electric Fencing around top perimeter

In addition to the unit, you'll also want to purchase an electric fence voltage tester for spot checking functionality as well as a small, battery operated Fence Alert® warning light, which hangs from your electric wire and begins flashing a red signal anytime the fence shorts out or runs out of power.

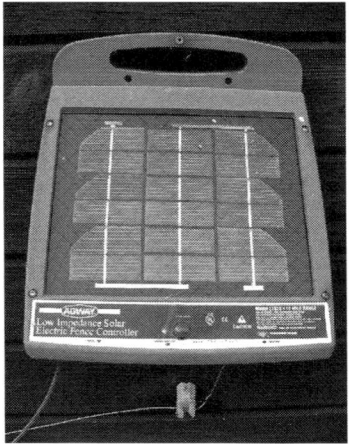

My solar powered fence charger

- **Motion sensor lighting**

If you want even further protection from predators, you can mount motion sensor flood lights around your duck enclosure to alarm predators and alert you whenever a visitor is in the vicinity. Honestly, they do more in the way of showing me who's out there than actually chasing them off, but that works for me. I wake up the second they flash on and then dash to the window to see if I need to go barreling down the front hill after some unwanted guest. Fox appear to be the most deterred by these lights and will often move on pretty quickly when they switch on. Even so, these lights can't be relied upon in and of themselves to protect your ducks.

You'll find a number of products out there that claim to help stave off predators and I've tried a slew of them. While it usually can't hurt to give them a go, if they're not identified here, they can't be relied upon. Think of them instead as an added edge that may or may not have the desired effect when needed.

Preparation #7
Building Your Duck a House

Unless your enclosure is built like Fort Knox and tried and proven effective against predators, always lock up your ducks at night, during prime predatory hunting hours. A great trick to test the effectiveness of your duck pen before your feathered friends begin using it is to set down a pan of raw meat inside for a few nights. This works best in summer and on nights with a full moon when predators like fox, coyotes and raccoons tend to be out and about. If any of that meat disappears, you know you have a problem.

How to Build Your Duck House

If you don't have a barn or shed, you can place a floored duck house inside your predator-proof enclosure and bed it with hay or straw to make it nice and cozy for them to sleep in. The door should lock securely for maximum effectiveness because raccoons have very dexterous fingers and can get past the standard latch. If your ducks *do* have a barn or shed, but don't have access to it during the day, you'll also need to put a duck house in their enclosure.

Duck houses keep food dry, offer a break from the rain, provide a comfortable place for females to retire while laying their eggs and they provide a nice shady place for your ducks to take an afternoon snooze.

Forget that old proverb, *"water off a duck's back."* Not all ducks care to be outside on stormy days (especially Muscovy ducks). My two boys stand like little soldiers at attention, a position they take to assist the water in rolling off of their bodies. You don't want your ducks situated like this all day trying to beat the weather, so give them a nice, cozy place to cuddle-up in during bad weather.

Over the years I've tried a number of different design approaches, in an attempt to continually perfect my duck houses.

- **Duck house #1**

My original duck house had a sloped and shingled roof and a securely latching door. You always want to have adequate ventilation in your duck house, even in winter, or the ammonia fumes can be quite overwhelming. Mine had three holes drilled into each side that were less than ¼" in diameter as added protection from rodents. These original houses were 3' wide x 4' long x 3' high (at its lowest point) and made of plywood. You don't want to go any smaller than this for two ducks. It's the absolute *minimum*.

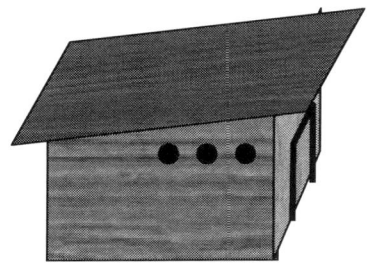
Duck house design #1

Before the door was attached

To prevent the bottom of the house from rotting out, I set it on top of a nice grid of flat patio bricks. Bricks are a much better option than a pad of concrete because you can easily change the location of your duck house if you have a change of heart down the road. If you do want to pour a concrete foundation beneath your duck house, don't do it until you're absolutely sure you (and your ducks) like the spot you have it in. Beginning with patio bricks until you've mastered its location and then pouring concrete later is a great way to avoid the sledgehammer.

While this first approach to a duck house worked well, it was very difficult to manage in the winter. Every time it snowed or any day there was ice melt and refreezing, the bottom edge of the door managed to get caught in it. This constant chipping out of the door eventually took its toll on both the door and the structural integrity of the house.

- **Duck house #2**

My second approach to a duck house was to purchase an outdoor dog house and modify it to fit the needs of my ducks. They measured: 2.25' wide x 3.5' long x 2.25' high and were just the right size for two ducks. Its hinged roof was perfect for collecting eggs every day, but it had a few inherent problems: it had no door and it was raised off the ground.

Because of the clumsy nature of ducks, I'm not a big fan of ramps. My original plan was to cut the four legs off and just sit the house directly on the ground, but rather than cut up my newly purchased house, I opted to give the ramp a go. Today I hate ramps even more so than I did before. My ducks had a hard time with them in winter when the slope tended to get slippery.

I'm a big fan of the other modification that I made, my new door. Rather than having a swinging door that kept getting lodged in the snow, my new door lifted completely out of four brackets and stored on another set of brackets mounted inside the house. Instead of drilling holes for ventilation into the house, I installed a small, three-inch vent into the door and then glued into place. This type of door design is not safe for your ducks *unless* you have your duck house set within a completely predator-proof enclosure.

Modified dog-to-duck house (Right: rebuilt roof)

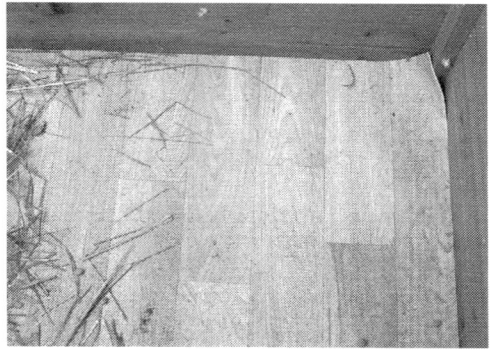

Linoleum flooring inside a duck house helps make cleaning a breeze

This particular style of house came with a three-piece removable floor, which made cleaning a breeze. Additionally, I cut linoleum flooring to size and laid it down inside the house to prevent any premature rotting and to make cleaning even easier. I highly recommend this trick in any duck house. It enables you to roll up and lift out all the poop and hay for easy carrying to the compost pile. It's inexpensive and easy to wash and disinfect.

The major problem with this particular house was the roof, which was poorly manufactured utilizing sub-standard materials. Within six to twelve months of owning a dozen of them, they all began to rot away around the roof hinges due to an inherent design flaw; that is, the back of the roofs didn't extend far enough out over the back of the houses. When water rolled over the sloped roof, it flowed right down into the hinges between the roof and the house, rusting out the wood and screws. Adding to this issue, the roofs turned out to be basically hollow (aside from some flimsy material inside that reminded me of thin balsa wood). Once they began rotting out at the hinges, the damage advanced quickly into the roofing material as well. Not only did the hinges rip right out from the wood, but the green roofing paper began to quickly unfurl—exposing more of the roof to rain and weather.

I actually had to remove each of the roofs and have them rebuilt using higher-quality materials. Additionally, I had someone correct the design flaw by extending the lower edge of the roof, so when water dripped over it no longer went directly into the hinges anymore.

In the end I realized that these "outdoor" dog houses weren't built for the great outdoors at all. It would've been much easier and more time-effective if I'd just built the houses myself.

- **Duck house #3**

My waterfowl sanctuary was running full-fledge when I purchased and transformed all of my dog-to-duck houses. While installing wooden ramps onto them I made arrangements for two other duck houses to be built to accommodate my special needs ducks who couldn't traverse those wooden inclines.

Since my special needs ducks always sleep in the barn at night and wouldn't be locked up outside, this shingled house didn't need a door at all. It was also vital that there was no lip for a limping duck to trip over while getting inside. Ducks with permanent leg injuries need more space to turn themselves around, so I designed this house with a nice wide doorway and with a spacious square floor plan (as opposed to the rectangle of the other duck houses). It measured 3' wide x 3' long x 3' high (at its lowest point).

Benny's Beach Cottage and The Sunshine House are designed to accommodate special needs ducks

This particular duck house design works extremely well and my special needs ducks are still using these today!

- **Duck house #4**

At the same time all this other building was taking place, I was also working on having goose houses built for the other portion of my sanctuary. I utilized the best pieces of all my other duck houses to design these cute mini-barns. This kind of house is a great option for ducks—affording plenty of interior space for two and plenty of head room.

The barn measures a square 4' x 4' and stands 2' at the first rise, 3' at the second bend and 4' at the peak. It has roll roofing overhead to keep it nice and waterproof. This type of design is ideal for two ducks.

The removable door fits into four exterior brackets and has a built-in adjustable vent to control air-flow into the house. It slips in and out easily in winter weather. Because my enclosure is completely predator-proof, I don't have to worry about predators getting the barn's door open, but this is a concern if your set-up is not as air-tight.

Our goose barns ended up making great duck barns!

Barn Flooring

I like to utilize puzzle matting in the sanctuary's quarantine pens. This kind of flooring can also work well inside barns or sheds. You can lay them down on their own or beneath a layer of hay. These soft, lightweight, interlocking pieces are easy to clean and quick to put together or take apart. You just measure the area you want to cover and then purchase the appropriate number of 2' x 2' edge pieces, center pieces and corner pieces (supplier: Mat Depot www.matdepot.com Item #FM28). Quality mats cost about ten dollars each, are stain, mold and germ resistant and will last your ducks a long time.

Your ducks shouldn't be restricted to standing on this type of bare flooring 24/7. Long term exposure can result in foot calluses in more sensitive ducks.

Puzzle mats laid down over concrete

Barn Windows

My duck barn has two windows, and during the summer I like to keep them both open. To do this safely, I nailed a section of welded wire mesh over the entire window frame on the *inside* of the barn (so it's barely noticeable from outside). This simple step prevents raccoons and other predators (who tend to be active nocturnal hungers) from climbing inside your barn and putting the lives of your ducks in danger.

Internal Pen and Barn Fencing

Depending on the size of your duck barn or shed and the number of ducks you have (and how well they get along), you may decide to improve their accommodations by creating some interior kennels. Some ducks really thrive when given some space of their own at night—especially if they can still see all of their ducky friends.

Internal fencing is also frequently utilized in outdoor enclosures as a means of establishing physical partitions between ducks during the day. This type of application can bring sudden peace to a duck pen provided it's done correctly.

- **Chain link**

Chain link fencing is inherently dangerous for ducks because they can poke their heads right through the holes. This can be especially dangerous if you have drakes on either side of the fence because they can fight and get caught in the wire's weave.

I came home one day and discovered Young Jeffrey and one of my newly rescued drakes had been squabbling through opposite sides of their shared kennel fencing in the barn. The rescued boy ended up getting his head and neck pulled right through the chain link fencing. While trying to pull his head backward through the hole again, Young Jeffrey managed to poke the other drake's head in just the right way to get his bill jammed in the incorrect and neighboring hole. The poor guy became trapped at Young Jeffrey's mercy with his head and neck woven through the fencing (see figure on page 82).

Thankfully I freed him soon after it happened. He was a little rattled, but otherwise unharmed; even so, I shudder to think what might've happened if I hadn't discovered him in time.

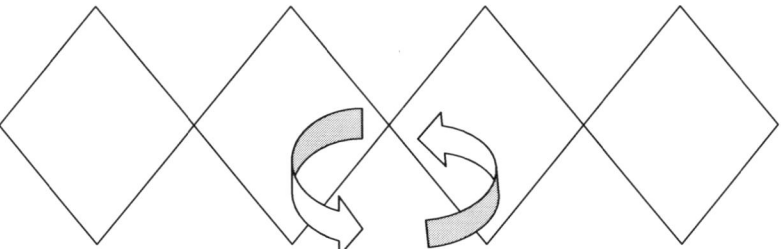

My rescued drake had his head pulled through one hole in the chain link fence and then pushed back through a neighboring hole.

That very night I went to the store and bought a roll of 2½' wide x 25' long welded wire mesh (PVC coated is more flexible and works best around doors) and then cut and zip-tied it directly to the existing fence, so that it was taught and secure over the chain link panels and any other openings a ducky head might possibly fit through.

Chain link fencing in my quarantine pen made safe with a little welded wire mesh and some zip-ties

This type of pull-through accident is not limited to chain link fencing; it can happen with many smaller types of wire weaves as well.

- **Poultry wire**

Poultry wire is another quick-fix pen-dividing solution that doesn't always go well. Whenever using wire with a small weave, consider what body parts might get trapped in its holes. Poultry wire is an infamous trap for duck bills. If you can't glide your duck's bill gently out again without causing further damage, get a pair of wire cutters and quickly cut them loose instead.

- **Portable playpens**

I love my accordion duck playpens. You can find them at most pet stores in the dog section, but in my defense, there *was* a photo of a pet duck on the boxes of the ones I purchased, so I'm fully justified in calling them *duck* playpens.

These eight sided, accordion-like pens fold up quickly and easily and store very well in small spaces. I connect a few together and set them up in the yard when I want to take Young Jeffrey and Young Matthew for some safe and chaperoned foraging expeditions. I unfurl them in my sunroom when I need a quick indoor medical facility and I even use them to create a quick barrier between ducks who don't necessarily get along all the time.

If you want to utilize these pens, you need to be aware of their inherent danger or they can lead to serious and even fatal injuries. You have to know how to set them up properly or you could be doing far more harm than good.

As with chain link fencing ducks can quickly and easily poke their heads through the openings in the wire and they can quickly get stuck there. Ducks will usually do this when they want to argue with someone on the other side, which means if you're using this as a divider between ducks, you'll need to it a particular way to ensure their safety.

The best way to set up these portable pens between your ducks is to double them up. In other words, run two fences parallel to each other with a space of *at least* eighteen inches between them. This wide gap deters the kind of heated debate that incites a duck to even want to stick their head through a hole. As an added measure, even if they both do stick their heads through at the exact same time, they still won't be able to reach each other and connect. Even so, I highly recommend you don't use this type of fencing between sparring ducks. They're much better utilized between a couple of friendly ducks who just happen to need a day or two apart from each other for good health.

Playpen fences can be made safer by doubling them up and placing an 18" gap between them

If your duck somehow manages to get their head stuck in the wire fencing and you can't get them gently back through again (which can be impeded by even a slight amount of head-swelling), you'll need a strong hand and some heavy duty wire cutters to get them out. If you're going to use these portable playpens be aware of the risks with ducks and make sure you have a high quality pair of wire cutters on hand in case of an emergency.

Another way to make these portable fences safe is to zip-tie a flexible plastic mesh right onto them. They'll lose their ability to fold up nicely, but it can make for a quick and safe dividing fence during a time of temporary need. Just be sure the plastic weave is small enough to prevent bills from poking through and getting trapped.

- **PVC welded wire mesh**

Ultimately, a pen or barn with separate built-in and constructed compartments and permanent gates that can be opened or closed as needed is the most efficient and convenient method of separating ducks—not to mention their relative safety when compared with other options.

When building internal fences between your ducks you want to take advantage of safe materials. PVC coated welded wire mesh (a.k.a. hardware cloth) with either a ½ inch or ¼ inch weave are ideal for outdoor applications (Suppliers: Academy Fence Company www.academyfence.com and Louis E. Page www.louispage.com). Remember, the higher the gauge, the thinner the wire, so a 21 or 23 gauge mesh is often more than sufficient in an interior pen situation where your intent is not to keep predators out—just other ducks.

When it comes to using wire mesh in duck barns or sheds that aren't exposed to water and the elements, a non-coated welded mesh is also perfectly acceptable—although not nearly as long-lasting in terms of wear.

Remember to be careful of any gaps around or under your gates. You don't want to leave enough space to allow someone's head to poke through where it doesn't belong. Most ducks (except Call and Muscovy ducks) are inhibited by internal fences and gates that are 3½' high.

Preparation #8
Bedding for Your Ducks

Ducks should always have bedding in their houses, barns and sheds. Not only does it make cozy nesting material, but it also protects their delicate webbed feet, which need protection from hard surfaces in order to stay healthy.

- **Hay and straw**

Find a place to buy fresh hay or straw. Since your ducks don't need feed-quality hay, you can often get a good deal on mulch bales. They consist of the same exact hay, just cut in smaller bits, and they can cost half as much as a regular bale.

My first provider sold me a half-dozen bales and I soon realized that they were jam-packed with thorn bushes. These sharp bristles can do some real damage to your hands and to your duck's webbed feet. Fortunately, most suppliers will guarantee their bales and allow you to exchange them (mine tells me to just toss them and gives me a credit towards my next purchase). While you'll occasionally get a bale that isn't up to par, this shouldn't be a routine issue; if it's, it's time to find a new supplier with a higher quality product.

Another thing to watch for is poison ivy. If you're allergic like me, you'll want to ask your hay provider if their fields are free of it, or things will soon turn terribly wrong.

If you live in hot and humid regions I highly suggest you go with straw instead of hay since it's hollow inside and won't grow mold the way hay can. The type of mold that you're most concerned about is called aspergillus and when inhaled, it can lead to aspergillosis (commonly referred to as *farmer's lung*). This can be a risk to both you and your ducks.

Whether you choose hay or straw, you always want to keep a nice cushion of bedding beneath your ducks' feet to keep them healthy and soft. Ducks have very sensitive feet and can quickly become calloused and sore if conditions aren't just right.

Keeping bedding clean is easier in the warmer months when ducks are outside of their house more often than they are inside. During these periods you can often get away with sprinkling some fresh hay over the messy spots once a day. These soggy areas tend to occur around their water dispensers and in the nests they've made for themselves during the night. During the colder months, when ducks are inside more often, you'll need to refresh their hay at least twice a day—once in the morning and again in the evening. This will help keep your ducks nice and clean as well as keeping their house smelling fresh. Fly infestations can happen pretty quickly if you don't keep their quarters tidy.

Routine duck house or barn cleanings (as the case may be) are a vital part of your regular maintenance routine. It should be abundantly clear when it's time to clean out their building—don't wait too long. Less ducks and more floor space results in less frequent cleanings. While your ducks may be spending more time inside in the winter, you're actually going to be doing *less* barn cleanings during these colder months. The reason for this purposeful change in pace is to encourage hay fermentation. As you set down fresh hay a couple of times a day, you not only create a nice thick layer bedding between your ducks and the cold floor, but the old, poopy hay that's way down underneath begins to ferment and make a little heat for them. Of course when spring comes and it's time to pitch all that hay, your back's going to have to pay for that long winter break.

- **Pine shavings**

While I know a few Momma Ducks who use pine shavings for bedding in their barns, I've never quite understood it myself. I've had to use a bed of shavings more than once as part of a post-surgical care regime to ensure very sanitary conditions for a recovering rescued duck. I can honestly tell you, it gets *everywhere*. It absolutely drives me crazy. Every time a pair of wings flaps, the stuff spreads all over the place. And since it continually ends up mixed up in their food dish or floating in their water buckets, I worry about them ingesting it and it potentially catching in their throats.

- **Avoid litter**

Never use any kind of litter as bedding. You don't want manufactured litter in your duck's mouth, throat or stomach. This is an invitation to disaster.

Preparation #9
Protection from the Elements

You'll need to put a little thought into keeping your ducks cool in summer and warm in winter in order to keep them comfortable and safe.

Summer & Shade

If you have hot summers and your duck pen is in direct sunlight, you'll want to provide some kind of shade for them, so they have a nice reprieve. A duck house on its own is not always enough to keep your flock cool.

- **Shade cloth**

Shade cloth allows enough sunlight to seep through its material to keep the grass and plants underneath alive while keeping your ducks nice and cool. The drawbacks of shade cloth may include unsightliness, seasonal installation and, if not mounted correctly, issues during wind storms.

- **Shade trees**

A non-toxic shade bush inside of their pen is another great way to keep your ducks cool in the heat. I also have a few trees outside of my pens that cast shadows over the enclosures. Just remember that any trees need to be far enough away as to not become ladders for climbing predators like raccoons or to impose danger if any of their branches come down in a storm.

An Autumn Berry tree makes a great shady place for ducks

Shade trees provide a natural setting and require very little maintenance. I utilize Autumn Berry trees in my pens. They were introduced to our area a long time ago and are now considered a local nuisance tree—seeding and spreading quickly. The great thing about weed trees is they're hard to kill and work really well around ducks.

Autumn Berry trees have aromatic flowers in the spring and produce *tons* of non-toxic berries for the ducks to eat in the fall. They're super easy to transplant and grow very fast. A small tree only three feet high can grow to a plentiful six feet in height within just a few months if you plant them in full sunlight. You can literally sink them into the ground in spring and have shade by summer.

These trees can survive even the most brutal pruning, which is frequently needed to restrict their size, and you can train them to grow just about any way you want them to inside your ducks' pen.

- **Air conditioning**

For Momma Ducks residing in hotter and more humid regions, cool water and access to ample shade is good during the day, but often barns need to be air conditioned in order to keep ducks comfortable at night. If you see your ducks panting in their barn it's usually a clear sign that it's too hot for them. If you have installed air conditioning in your barn, you should set the temperature to no less than 75F degrees to prevent chilling your duck, especially when they're molting and can't regulate their body temperatures as effectively.

Most vets will advise to stay within ten degrees of outdoor temperatures with your air conditioning *unless* you're working against extremely hot temperatures and attempting to prevent heatstroke. If this is the case, then bring your ducks inside and slowly lower their barn temperature no more than ten degrees every two hours until you reach 75F-80F degrees.

Be careful to avoid extreme humidity variances as well, which can also compromise the effectiveness of their respiratory system.

- **Misting systems**

Another great way to keep your ducks cool in the heat of summer is to purchase a patio misting system. Multiple systems can often be connected together to reach the desired length and you can purchase inexpensive filters that are simple to attach and help keep the nozzles from clogging with minerals (if that's an issue in your area). While they come with permanent mounting kits that are simple to install, I opt to mount mine to the fence rails in my duck pens using zip-ties, so I can arrange them differently every year if I want to.

Misting systems connect easily to a garden hose that can be attached to a sprinkling system timer. My system is programmed to come on for the duration of two minutes every five minutes between 11:30 – 4:00 in the summertime. The ducks love it and it reduces temperatures in the pen dramatically—almost like you're walking into air conditioning. Timed sprinkler systems are a similar option, but since they tend to make puddles that result in ducky grass mutilation, I prefer my mister.

A secured umbrella makes a nice shady spot

Winter & Heat

In my experience ducks seem better equipped at handling cold temperatures than they are at handling hot ones. Even so, those warm and fluffy feathers only go so far. If you have cold winters you'll want to provide your ducks with some type of insulation to keep them comfortable and warm.

Cold weather tips:

1. Have plenty of hay on hand to get you through winter.
2. Test your heated water buckets at the start of the cold season to ensure they're functioning properly.
3. Have a spare heated water bucket on hand in case yours shorts out or fails.
4. The more ducks you have cuddled together, the warmer their duck house will be.
5. Monitor daily and weekly weather/temperature reports closely.

- **Staying indoors**

Some days simply call for keeping ducks indoors. This will be especially easy if they have a barn or shed because it'll provide them with plenty of room to move around in for the day. If you happen to live in a very cold region of the country this type of set-up is vital, so that your ducks have spacious winter accommodations.

If you have shorter and milder winters and only a small duck house at your disposal then your ducks are going to want some time to get up and move around. In this case, you'll have to let them outside. I know quite a few Momma Ducks in this situation who bring their feathered friends into their homes or basements on these freezing cold days to ensure their safety and well-being. Whatever you decide to do, you'll want to use your best judgment.

The rule of thumb is to house your ducks whenever the temperature drops to 15F degrees or less (taking wind chill into account). This means if it's 19F degrees out, but *feels like* 15 with the wind chill, it's time to load them up. Smaller ducks don't have as much resistance to the cold as heavier ducks, making the bantam breeds even more susceptible to the cold (see: *"Bantam Breeds"*). They should be brought in when temperatures drop below 20-25F degrees. It's vital that you monitor your local weather reports in the winter, so you can plan appropriately. Be aware of weather warnings in your area. Don't leave your ducks outside and exposed to the cold during snow storms, ice storms or other inclement weather.

Muscovy ducks in particular are *extremely* susceptible to frostbite on their bulbous faces--especially males who have more highly developed caruncles. The skin of these facial masks feels very similar to your lips. They should be sheltered any time temperatures even begin to approach freezing levels to avoid the risk of frostbite. Their bean (the red caruncle centered directly over a male's bill) is exceptionally vulnerable to the cold and it will begin to turn from red to yellow and then to bluish when it's in jeopardy. Muscovies can be allowed outside during the day for *brief* excursions during freezing temps when the sun is at its peak and it's not too windy. They shouldn't be allowed to stay outside unless temps are over 40F degrees. Try to imagine going outside without gloves on. If your hands would be cold, so will your Muscovy's face.

- **Heated Barns**

I'm frequently asked if barns (or duck houses) need to be heated in winter. For most regions of the U.S., the answer to this question is *no*. If you provide your ducks with protection from the wind and afford them a thick layer of bedding beneath their feet, they should be just fine in colder temperatures. However, if you're in a part of the country where winter is longer than the typical 2-3 months and temperatures frequently drop below 15F degrees and stay there, you'll probably want to consider it. If you do opt to incorporate a heating system in your barn, be sure it's professionally installed *and* maintained to avoid the risk of fire.

Some sources will tell you that a heated barn will disrupt a duck's molting cycle, but since ducks survive without any difficulty or confusion in the warmer states; I tend to doubt it. What you want to avoid is heating a barn and then suddenly shutting their heat off. In the midst of winter weather, this sudden change in temperature could result in some serious health issues. Whatever you decide, you must be consistent.

While your ducks may appreciate a little heat *never* use plug-in or propane heating devices when you're not constantly present to monitor them. And always have a fire extinguisher handy in case of an emergency.

- **Insulation**

Duck feet and bills must be kept warm. Domestic ducks aren't hearty enough to endure cold winters without protection. They can and do get frostbite on these extremities if you don't make certain preparations and the results can be devastating.

Ducks should always have free access to bedded housing that will protect them from cold winds and freezing grounds. My barn always has 6-12 inches of hay on the floor from November through March (at its thickest in January and February).

In colder regions, barn walls can be insulated by stacking up bales of hay against them, from floor to ceiling, all the way around. In some areas hay is only sold seasonally; if this is the case where you're, be sure to buy plenty before it becomes unavailable. Purchase enough to use as wall insulation *and* enough to freshen up their bedding every day. You don't want to bed the floor at the expense of depleting all of your barn's wall insulation.

For those of you without barns or sheds, you can stack bales of hay all around your duck house. Once these are in place, stack more bales on top of them, using the lower bales to support the upper bales. In this manner you can insulate the roof of your duck house, while keeping the weight of the bales off of it.

Similarly, hay bales can be set up as windbreaks in your duck pen. You can quickly assemble a little area for your ducks to huddle in. Interlock your bales vigilantly for added integrity and be careful not to stack them too high, so you can avoid the risk of bales tumbling down on top of your feathered friends. Once you have your arena set, you can bed it with a nice, thick layer of hay.

- **Seal windows**

My barn has two windows. Before the seasonal cold weather approaches every year, I staple some thick, clear plastic over panes to help keep out the cold. If your barn isn't insulated, you can do this over walls as well. Just be very careful with those staples because if any of them fall down into the hay, your duck could eat them and end up in a lot of trouble.

<u>Preparation #10</u>
<u>Protecting Webbed Feet</u>

I don't know what it is about ducks, but given two paths, a clear one and one mined with rocks and sticks, they always seem to choose the minefield. Ducks tend to be a bit ill-coordinated—ever focused on where they're going, and not too attentive to how they're getting there. They just aren't built for walking the way they are for swimming. They tend to trip and stumble over even the smallest of obstacles making them very prone to leg and foot injuries, some of which can be serious and have lifetime repercussions.

Webbed feet are fragile and must be protected

- **Remove tripping obstacles**

To keep your ducks feet and legs in ideal condition, remove all sticks and rocks and fill in the holes they continually make in their enclosure to avoid any mishaps. Also be wary of plants with thorns, which can do real damage to your duck's webbing.

- **Planting grass**

If your pen is too small for the number of ducks inside, it'll likely require constant attention to keep grass under their feet, and it's vital that you do in order to prevent serious foot afflictions. You may need to reseed from spring until fall in these situations and protect newly growing grass until it's well established. Ducks can wipe out vegetation at an alarming rate—especially females. This kind of upkeep can be very tedious and very frustrating, which is why larger pens, if possible, are often a good idea.

My best advice for growing new grass is to try to keep your female ducks away from seeds and newly growing grass. They're very destructive foragers and will often wipe out new growth within hours—*or less*. Drakes, on the other hand, will usually allow new grass to grow and grow.

I find that grass lasts all spring, summer and fall in most of my pens, but doesn't tend to survive winter wear, so every spring I turn over all of the grounds and reseed all of my pens. Be careful what kind of seed you use and try to avoid those coated in harmful toxins or pesticides, especially if these areas won't be sectioned off because your ducks *will* eat it.

I prefer to combine a few types of seed together in order to get things jump-started. Most of my pens are seeded with an affordable heavy-tread, sun and shade grass seed. I add a few handfuls of super-quick growing grass to this blend and then head out to my pens to spread it around and rake it under. The fast-growing grass helps prepare the way for the slower sprouting seedlings by preventing too much ground compaction, which ducks are very adept at doing with those beautiful, little, romper-stomper webbed feet of theirs. When I get to the shady areas beneath the trees, I mix a shade seed with the super-quick seed.

Trying to grow grass in certain areas of your duck enclosure can be a losing battle, especially around any water sources. Ducks love to forage and drill holes into the ground around their ponds and buckets using their bills. It's always a challenge to keep solid ground around these areas, let alone trying to get grass to grow there. This tends to make for an unsightly border around your pools, ponds and water buckets.

The only way I've ever found to prevent this type of ducky erosion is to place a lip around your pond or pool, going about a foot out and away from the water and to set your water buckets on some kind of base. Any kind of non-slippery mat that they can't pull apart will do the trick, or you lay down a patio brick, which is my solution.

I have multiple duck pens, which affords me some different strategies for seeding and growing grass. First, I seed any empty pens I might have and then when that grass is fully established, I rotate my female ducks into these nice green pens. Once they've moved over I can plant grass in their old pens, which are now empty. Having spare pens also allows me to limit the number of females in any single pen until the grass is growing strong in them.

Another trick to growing grass is to build a simple wooden frame (you can size it to suit your own needs) and then blanket it with PVC welded wire mesh. Next you plant your grass seed and lay the jig down over the top of it. The grass grows up through the jig allowing the ducks to nibble off the tops, but prevents them from disturbing the root systems. Once the grass is well-established, the jig can be moved to a new area of their duck pen.

A grass jig does the trick in my duck pens

<u>Safe Catching and Handling</u>

In order to avoid injuring your duck, it's important to know how to handle them properly. Both ducklings and adult ducks have very fragile hips and legs. *Never* catch them by their limbs or you'll be risking breaks, sprains and dislocations that can lead to permanent lameness.

- **Ducklings**

Ducklings don't appreciate fast movements, so ease in slowly. Carefully cup both of your hands around your duckling and then ease one of your palms beneath their feet for support. You can seal newly hatched ducklings gently within your cupped hands until you have them where you want them; then slowly let them out.

When holding older and larger ducklings, cup one hand around their body while supporting their feet in the other and then brace them against your chest. Allow their head to poke through the circular gap created between your thumb and forefinger; ensuring that their body can't fit through this same hole or they might hop out.

Ducklings are very adept when it comes to jumping out of your hands, and a fall to the floor can be devastating, so be absolutely sure you have a good hold on them before removing them from their brooder. Children should always be sitting down on the floor when handling ducklings; and ideally, adults should be the only ones actually removing ducklings from the brooder and handing them to children.

- **Ducks**

If your duck is friendly and accustomed to being handled, you can just pick them up by placing your hands over their body—one hand over each wing, thumbs over their spine and fingers curling underneath. Once you have them tucked under your arm or braced against your chest, you can slide your free hand under their feet for additional support.

If you have a shy or aggressive duck this can be a little more difficult; even so, you should be able to catch and hold any of your ducks at any given moment in case of an emergency. If your duck isn't used to being handled, you'll need to corral them into a corner of their barn or pen. When doing this, be very careful not to chase them through any obstacles (their kiddy pool, for example). Slowly get them where you want them, then fake left—pretending to reach out and grab them. Then, when they dodge instinctively to the right, be prepared to accept them into your clutches—gently, but firmly of course. Honestly, they fall for this trick every time. Now that you're down at their level, scoop them up from behind by sliding one of your hands under their body and between their legs. Pull their body against yours, bracing them against your chest. Keep that one wing between you pressed firmly against your torso and hold the other wing in place with your free hand. When holding frightened or aggressive ducks it's best if you don't support their feet, so you don't give them the leverage they need to flap their wings. Holding them this way also reduces the risk of getting scratched by their toenails. Now you can stand up if you need to.

Accidental toenails scratches or an occasional wing not held properly in place can quickly cause a bit of sting, but for the most part, catching and holding a duck is relatively painless. Occasionally, a captured duck will try the old *"pinch & twist"* move to escape your clutches. They'll clamp their bill over a hunk of skin (usually on your hand or arm) and then give it a good turn. While they don't have any teeth, this tactic can leave you with a small bruise. If you want to steer away from any of these minor injuries, long thick sleeves will usually protect you.

Preparation #11
Select Your Water Feature

Let's face it, ducks are designed to swim and they *love* water. Placing a water feature in their duck pen will help them stay clean, remain healthy and live happy and enriched lives. Fortunately, they're not all that picky when it comes to the nature of their duck pond.

Drowning

Most Momma Ducks don't even consider the fact that ducks can drown; it just seems so contradictory, but… it does happen.

1. *Feather Quality:* Ducks with poor feather quality, who aren't kept in clean pens or who can't preen properly can become water-laden and drown. The simple added weight of water in their feathers is enough to prevent them from hopping out of their ponds or pools. Ducks with poor feather quality should be monitored closely or kept off of the water when you're not around.

2. *Stepping Stones:* When ducks shed their wing feathers during the molt, their wings can no longer catch enough air to help raise them out of the water no matter how much they flap. Ducklings, older ducks or injured ducks who may have their own special challenges, often face similar entrapment. The situation can become even more punctuated if their pond's water level has gone down (having drained, siphoned out or evaporated away). Always have a stepping stone (or multiple stones in larger ponds/pools) to help them get out of the water—year round.

3. *Mating:* Although relatively rare, even a single drake who's been with the same female for years can make a mistake and accidentally drown his mate. This usually happens in deeper water where females can't place their feet down or when males are significantly larger than females. To reduce the risk of drowning, lower water levels during the mating season when your male is most rambunctious, so that your female can't be completely submerged under water. Remember to make sure any stepping stones are the correct height to enable your ducks easy exit.

4. *Separations:* Multiple drakes mating the same female can easily drown her. Institute separations whenever necessary to prevent accidents.

Swimming Accommodations

There are some things you'll want to keep in mind when it comes to this source of pleasure. Before proceeding with your plans you'll want to consider:

1. The size and shape of your water feature
2. The size and shape of your pen
3. The drainage capability of your pen
4. Your budget
5. Installation effort
6. Daily maintenance
7. Duck safety

- **Kiddy pools**

Kiddy pools are a great swimming option for ducks, but it's always best to dig out a hole and sink the pool into the ground rather than just placing it on top of the ground. Sinking the pool into the ground is much safer than asking your waterfowl to jump up over the lip when hopping in or out. This simple step can prevent hip, leg, foot and toe injuries that can remain with them for the rest of their lives

Kiddy pools come in a few different sizes, but since they have to be emptied and refilled daily, I highly advise you avoid the temptation of anything too big or your back may be in for a shock (unless you have a pump). Multiple medium pools are often easier to empty than one giant pool and your ducks are less likely to get stuck in them (in which case a patio brick or flat rock can work as a stepping stone to help them out). Ideally, and if you built your enclosure on a slight decline, kiddy pools should be placed at the lower end of your pen. The idea here is, when you empty them out, the water drains out of your pen through the perimeter fence rather than making a huge mess in your pen.

You can empty your pool using a bucket. When it comes to scooping out water out of a pond, a bucket with a flat edge works much better than a bucket with a round one. A big bucket and a healthy back will usually empty a medium sized kiddy pool within a minute or two. If you have a larger pool, you may want to invest in a small pump. Once your pool is empty, you can spray it out with a hose and refill it again. In summer your ducks' water can get pretty hot and smelly and may need to be cleaned out twice a day.

As you'll soon notice, the second your ducks get into their pool, they're going to poop in it. After that, they'll begin pulling everything they can reach into the water. When it comes to kiddy pools it doesn't matter if the water isn't clean as long as it's fresh.

Young Matthew & Young Jeffrey enjoy their kiddy pool, which has been sunk into the ground

If bailing out your pond everyday is not quite what you had in mind there are other pond options you can try. Most Momma Ducks start out with kiddy pools and then trade them out for something requiring less effort later. I had kiddy pools in my duck enclosure for the first few years and really didn't mind the emptying and filling. I always saw it as a fun time with my ducks. When it comes time to clean a kiddy pool, ducks are all over you. They love the puddles, they love the worms underneath the pool, they love the house—all good stuff. And there are few things funnier than your ducks standing in a filling pool, waiting for the water to rise up beneath them. It wasn't until I added more ducks and more pens that it became too much to handle.

- **Concrete ponds**

Since I have a natural stream running through my property, I had a few options at hand that most duck families don't. This inspired me to build a water course for the stream to follow. Digging out and creating concrete ponds was actually much easier than you might expect, and it was a lot of fun. I made a foot-long lip around all the ponds to prevent my ducks from reaching over and pulling all the dirt and grass into the water.

The concrete of my cascading ponds was about an inch thick

The constant flow of water from the stream kept the ponds clean and fresh all day long and I no longer had to worry about the daily emptying and refilling of kiddy pools. This concrete approach to ponds had two inherent flaws:

1. After the first winter, when everything thawed, the ponds cracked and had to be patched. This had to be done every spring. Even so, the patch work was relatively simple and much easier than daily bailing.

2. More worrisome, my ducks began hopping over the wide streambeds I'd created, leaping recklessly from bank-to-bank, rather than waddling across. I was very concerned with this dangerous habit and had to put my sledgehammer to work and smash apart the trenches (while the ducks were safely in the barn, of course). In their place, I laid down 4" drain pipes to connect the three ponds and buried them beneath soil and grass. Today my ducks walk safely over the tops of the pipes. No more hopping!

- **Preformed pond liners**

As I added more and more pens (and more and more ducks), re-facing all of the concrete ponds every year began to take its toll on me. Not only that, my ducks had to wait as I worked my way from pen to pen, draining and cementing. Ever see a duck watching their cement dry so they can go swimming? *Pretty sad...*

It was at that time that I tried something new and purchased preformed pond liners. These have proven to be my absolute favorite. I'll admit, it's a lot of work digging out the holes and getting those liners to fit in just right, but once they're set, they're set for good. Some people will also use the flat pond liner sheets to create their ponds, and that's fine too, but since I need to scoop the dirt and sand out of mine every spring, I didn't want to risk piercing them with my shovel.

My favorite preformed pond liners have built in plant shelves. This makes for an easier means for your ducks to get in and out. If your duck still has trouble getting in and out you can place a patio brick or a flat-surfaced rock onto one of the shelves to raise it up higher. Try to put their step in a corner area for added stability and in a favorite ducky access point to ensure they use it.

A lot of work goes into setting a 250 gallon preformed pond into the ground

To keep my ducks from pulling all kinds of debris into their ponds, I simply lay standard red bricks around the edges. I tuck the ends of the bricks under the pond's lip and press them against its main form. Then I fill in around the bricks with dirt or sand. You may need to touch this up as your duck pokes around in these crevices looking for worms, but for the most part, it's pretty easy maintenance.

Standard bricks around the ponds help keep debris out

I utilize a pump system where I draw up water from my main pond and circulate it through hose lines to all of my smaller ponds designed with preformed liners. I set each of my ponds in at a slight angle, so the excess water flows over one of the lips and drains either back into another pond or completely out of the pens following an underground drainage system. These drain pipes are sealed tightly, so that predators can't gain access from outside. Most of my pens have smaller, 50 gallon bean-shaped ponds, but a few of my pens have larger 250 gallon ponds in them (supplier: MacCourt Products www.maccourt.com). I drain and clean these ponds once a year in springtime.

Stream water feeds a 50 gallon preformed pond that is set into the ground at a slight incline. The overflow then drains out and subsequently fills the next pond in line.

If you don't have a natural stream to keep your water fresh and clean, you can purchase a pump and filtering system. If you decide to go this route, I'd suggest purchasing at least a 100 gallon pond for 2-3 ducks and a 250 gallon pond if you have four or more ducks. Remember to buy a filter that can handle *twice* that amount of water. You want a powerful filtration system because unlike koi fish, ducks poop a lot and your system needs to be able to handle this high amount of waste. Closed preformed pond systems like these should be cleaned according to their instructions. If your system includes a *bio-filter* that part of the system should *not* be cleaned, or it'll lose its effectiveness.

- **Natural and human-made ponds**

Building my main pond took a lot of effort and a lot of help, but by doing it ourselves we saved thousands of dollars. My slope-banked pond has concrete walls that are a foot thick and on a whole measures: 15' wide x 32' long x 3½' deep at its lowest point. When I tried to find a contractor to do it for me I was given multiple quotes, each of them over ten thousand dollars. Doing the project myself cost about a thousand dollars, which included the cost of having someone come out to dig the hole (using their equipment), the plywood forms and the cement trucks. When the job was done, I was able to reuse all of the plywood forms to build my original duck houses—nearly a *dozen* of them!

My husband and I designed the pond itself so that water would siphon into it through a pipe laid down in the stream. A drain pipe was set higher up in the other corner of the pond to prevent it from overfilling and overflowing and causing any damage or unwanted soil erosion. The thick concrete walls are reinforced with rebar and metal fence posts embedded inside. This keeps them from crumbling and toppling over.

It took one day to dig the pond, one day (and about a dozen helpers) to make the forms, two days to pour the concrete, one day to pull down the forms and then another year to build the huge pen that would encompass it all.

The excavator operator digs out our sanctuary pond, making a safe incline for my ducks to access it safely

Next, the concrete forms were set into place and a cement truck filled them

Then the truck poured the concrete bedding, which a few of us raked out (continually pumping out water as we worked)

The following weekend we removed all of the forms

We didn't make the pond fully watertight, allowing water to seep through the ground as well as siphoning in from the stream

As nature began filling the pond, me and my boys couldn't wait to try it out!

Pumps

I've utilized a several kinds of pumps over the years:

1. I use a Savio Water Master 6500 GPH, solids-handling, 750-110 watt, submersible pump to move water from my main pond to all of my other ponds (supplier: Webb's Water Gardens www.webbsonline.com). This solids-handling pump is great at propelling stream water, which tends to carry plenty of soil and plant parts along with it (not to mention the duck poop my boys add to it). In my experience, and under the conditions I work them in here, they tend to last me about 4 years and cost about $500 with shipping.

2. When summer comes and our stream dries up my main pond can get pretty low. To prevent it from becoming stagnant and dangerous for my ducks to drink, I pump water over from a natural reservoir about forty feet away. For this job I use a portable stainless steel Wayne 115 volt lawn pump (supplier: AmazonSmile www.smile.amazon.com). I attach my own garden hose to the outlet port on the pump and then switch it on to draw water over to my duck pond. I also use this pump to siphon the water out of my larger 100-250 gallon preformed ponds during spring pond-cleaning. This kind of non-submersible pump system costs about $200 (including the intake hose and nozzle, which are sold separately). Be wary of other brands with plastic handles, which don't support the pump's weight and tend to break quickly.

3. For about $75 you can find yourself a submersible, swimming pool cover pump. These are great for pumping out your duck's kiddy pool if your back just isn't up for the bucketing task. Little Giant makes a highly-rated, lightweight model (PE-1 #518200) that weighs about 4 lbs. You just attach a hose, put it in your pool and plug it in (supplier: Little Giant Pump Company www.little-giantpump.com).

Water Sources Must Be Kept Clean

Like drinking water, swimming water must be kept fresh because your ducks are going to be drinking it. Stagnant, smelly water can lead to health issues that include serious bacterial infections. If their water smells like duck poop, it's already past the time to change it. *Remember:* Fresh water isn't necessarily clear water. Ducks tend to muck up their water very quickly with mud, so it'll often appear dirty. This is fine; water doesn't have to be clear, it just needs to be fresh.

Kiddy pools need to be changed daily (twice daily in summer). Closed system filtration systems may require some filter cleaning (read the instructions and follow them carefully). Stream-fed ponds of any kind need to be cleaned in the spring and sometimes a few more times throughout the year, depending on how well they refresh and how much dirt and silt is carried into them.

Prevent Slipping & Tripping Hazards

It's very important that your ducks can get good traction around their ponds and pools. Slippery surfaces can lead to serious sprains and even breaks.

It's equally vital that surfaces around ponds aren't abrupt or rocky. I've seen many homemade, landscaped ponds that utilize jagged piles of rocks to hold the pond liner in place. While these assorted stones may look really pretty, they're actually quite dangerous for slippery wet feet to traverse.

Level surfaces that afford some kind of grip and without any hazardous crevices are always the best option. This safe periphery should circle all the way around your duck pond, rather than just occurring on one side or in one area. Not only do ducks have minds of their own, but when startled they could easily enter or exit the pond from an unintended access point.

Preparation #12
Provisions for Separations

There may come a time when you need to separate your ducks. This usually happens in the spring and summer when spring fever falls over them, but it can occur at other times as well. Separations may be required when:

1. Multiple drakes are vying for mating rights and pecking order privileges.
2. A drake is being overly passionate with a particular female duck.
3. A bigger duck is picking on a smaller duck.
4. A veteran duck is picking on a new duck.
5. A duck of one color is picking on a duck of another.

You might as well face it; unless you have two female ducks who've grown up together you're likely going to have to separate your ducks at some point—even if it's just for a day or two.

My boys are best friends (most of the time…)

If you have more than one boy in your flock, sometimes they're just going to squabble—no matter how much they love each other. While normal pecking order pokes shouldn't be of much concern, anything more than an occasional prod or tug should be examined more closely. There's a big difference between, *"Hey, don't forget I'm in charge here,"* and bullying.

Even if you have only one duck and one drake, when springtime comes your poor girl may need a day off from all that crazy love he has to offer. In any case, it's always a good idea to have your back-up measures planned out and ready to go should you need to separate anyone from one another for their own protection.

A Pair of Drakes

There are many factors that influence whether or not your male duck will get along with another boy. The more of these in their favor, the better the odds are that they'll get both along.

1. A pair of boys who grow up together *sometimes* get along better than males introduced later in life (especially if they're both the same breed), but this isn't always the case.

2. Boys introduced between September and January (when hormones are at their lowest) have a better chance of establishing a friendship than those introduced in spring and summer, especially as they spend more and more time together.

3. Older boys tend to get along better with one another than younger boys who have more energy to invest into competing. Younger drakes also have greater surges of spring hormones, which can also lead to more squabbles.

4. Calm or lonely drakes tend to get along better with a new friend than secure, energetic drakes who tend to put all their extra pizzazz into wrestling matches.

5. Two males get along better than three or more.

6. Having no females around to compete over usually results in much reduced fighting. Keep in mind, if either of your boys is human-imprinted, they may compete for *your* attention! Alternately, adding 2-4 females for every male (enough for everyone) can also reduce competitive fighting—provided you have the pen space.

7. Certain breeds are sometimes feistier than others. I find that Cayuga drakes are often more steadfast than Pekins. Muscovy ducks don't take no for an answer *(and I love that about them!)* and Mallards can be relentless despite their smaller size.

8. Drakes who are the *same size* usually fight *more* than a pair comprised of one larger and one smaller drake. This is because the same-sized drakes tend to have greater difficulty establishing and maintaining the pecking order—it's always a competition vying for the top, and each boy has equal opportunity. In situations with one slightly larger and one slightly smaller drake, the bigger boy often has an easier time holding onto his throne.

9. Drakes tend to fight less when kept in larger pens with things to hide behind (duck houses, bushes, etc.)

10. As drakes age, fighting sometimes wanes off between them. This is sometimes witnessed around their fifth spring.

Warning Signs That Help is Needed

Some signs that ducks need to be separated include: incessant chasing, eye injuries, someone losing weight or becoming dehydrated and excessive feather loss. An over stimulated drake will often poke at eyes, pluck out feathers and even keep another boy away from food and water sources.

A hormone-charged drake (or drakes) can also get too amorous with females. If you see a growing bald spot on the back of your female duck's neck, or plucked out feathers on her wings or back, your poor girl needs a break. Drakes have been known to stake out duck houses, food dishes, water bowls and/or swimming water in order to get what they want. This will often leave female ducks hungry, thirsty, exposed to the elements or just plain staring at the pond in envy.

Allowing drakes to over-mate females can lead to some serious medical issues, so be sure to give your girls a break from the boys whenever they need it.

- **How to break up a fight**

If one of your ducks grabs a hold of another by the back of their neck, a quick way to get them to let go without them yanking out a bunch of the other duck's feathers is to simply cover their eyes. If needed you can slip the tip of your finger into the crook of their bill to gently pry it apart, but usually your hand cupped over their head and face will coax a gentle release. *Hey, who turned out the lights?*

<u>Who's Fighting and Why</u>

If your ducks aren't quite getting along, there are a few things to evaluate. First, you need to determine who's involved in the bickering. Drakes are usually the culprits in this behavior. Next, you need to figure out why they're behaving this way to see if it's preventable.

- **Personalities**

Ducks have different personalities. Some are on the quiet side and will never give you any trouble, while others will test your patience day-after-day. Ducks have their own unique personalities, mood swings, and feelings. Some conditions lead to resentment among members, others lead to contentment. Dynamics vary from flock-to-flock as much as they do from duck-to-duck.

Young Matthew doesn't always appreciate his brother's friendship

- **Spring fever**

While occasionally another duck is somehow instigating the trouble (often from a neighboring pen); usually, it's the insurgence of spring hormones that's the culprit. If this is the case, there's nothing you can do about it, but wait it out. Here in Connecticut, drake hormones begin to rise in late February, lasting straight through to August before finally declining again in September. This lengthy season is the toughest time when it comes to the misbehavior of drakes.

Before introducing females to my boys, the only time Young Jeffrey and Young Matthew squabbled was when I was around. It turned out they were competing for me. Petting and handling them only made matters worse because that *really* got their hormones going. *Whoops!* Once I presented the boys with females, they redirected their emotions appropriately and I was off the hook.

Once the ladies arrived, the paradigm shifted. After that, trouble tended to occur when one of the girls bobbed her head flirtatiously at Young Jeffrey. Being the alpha drake at the top of the pecking order, Young Matthew took notice of everything his subordinate did. He didn't appreciate it when his best friend and brother made advances on his ladies. Drakes don't like sharing their girlfriends even when there are plenty to go around.

- **Weather**

Rainy and wet spring days often boost the energy levels of males, charging them into overdrive. Additionally, when ducks are faced with a cold spell immediately followed by a marked day of warm weather, it can really spark mating behavior and male competition/aggression.

- **Temperature**

During the summer months, when it's just too sweltering hot to keep up all that fighting, things tend to simmer down. Even so, keep your eyes trained on them because their naughty behavior tends to resurface when they're swimming in cool water and when the sun goes down and they get some relief. Their spitfire behavior often changes in accordance with the temperature.

- **Medical science**

While I've been asked many times and by many Momma Ducks; to date, there is no surgery, dietary changes or medicine that will safely and effectively change a drake's behavior. Avoid experimenting with hormonal drug therapies. They're un-effective and long-term studies haven't been done on waterfowl to ensure their safety. You just have to deal with the fact that this is who your duck is and there's not much of anything you can do about it except separate them.

Visitations and Distractionary Tactics

While separations are in order when trouble breaks out, you may be able to allow them back together when you're around and chaperoning.

I could get Young Matthew and Young Jeffrey to stop squabbling by introducing favorite treats or taking them on a supervised excursion through the yard without the ladies to distract them (to be fair to the girls, I took them on separate walks later). Since my boys are human-imprinted, I could sit down in the grass with them and let them play in my hair and usually keep them entertained enough that they didn't want to quarrel anymore.

Just remember, as soon as you leave, your ducks are going to revert to fighting again, so be sure to separate them at the end of your visit.

Separating Ducks

Separating your ducks can be very emotionally taxing for everyone. All good Momma Ducks like to see their flock members getting along and it can be extremely stressful when they're not. Even though it's difficult, it's far better to separate your darlings than to face the alternative of someone getting hurt.

There are three ways to separate your ducks while keeping them happy and in sight of each other.

- **Portable playpens**

As mentioned previously, you can purchase portable playpens at your local pet store. They come in various heights (30, 36 or 48 inches) and usually cost between $50-60. These fences can be set up quickly and they fold up nicely for storage later. Remember, ducks can stick their heads through them, so double them up and leave a two-foot space between them unless you're present and available to chaperone.

Young Jeffrey & Young Matthew are easily separated with a portable playpen

- **Temporary fencing**

Another way to divide your ducks is to take a roll of 3' high roll of lightweight (21 or 23 gauge), polyvinyl coated welded wire mesh fence, with ½ inch squares (so bills don't get stuck), and use it to create a temporary barrier within your existing pen. While three-foot fencing works well for most heavyweight ducks, you may need to go a little higher if you have smaller ducks who can get enough lift off the ground to glide over lower fencing.

String your fencing across the length of your duck enclosure, splitting up the area in a way that works for both you and your ducks. You can fasten this barrier wire in place by latching both ends of it to your pen's perimeter fencing using a few carabineers or zip-ties.

You can put up this temporary fencing in spring and summer and roll it up for storage in the fall and winter. I used this method for a couple of years, and it worked very well for me and my ducks. The only downfall was having to step *over* the fencing to get to each division, which can actually be dangerous if you're not careful.

With this kind of set-up you want to be careful that your ducks can't get any part of their body under the fencing. If it's tight enough they shouldn't be able to, but if you're worried, you can crease and fold the wire about four inches up from the bottom and then stake it down to the ground with tent-stakes or the like. You may want to bury this in a thin layer of sand or soil if you see your ducks tripping or stubbing toes on it.

- **Permanent fencing**

After a few years of dealing with all those portable fences and temporary tripping obstacles, I finally opted to build permanent gated compartments within my enclosure, dividing it up into easily accessible smaller sections. During the fall and winter, I often keep the gates open, so the ducks can enjoy the full space of their enclosure, while in the spring and summer each alpha drake takes his girlfriend to his own privately assigned space and neighborly visits all take place through the safety of a fence.

Multiple Female & Males:

Maintaining multiple female and male ducks while also preventing any in-fighting and over-mating can be tricky business, especially in the spring. When separations are inevitable, there are different ways to divvy up your flock to help keep the peace. Different strategies may have varying levels of effectiveness depending on when they're used, so remember not to limit yourself to just one remedy.

1. Separate your drakes from one another and divvy up your females between them (try to keep pairs or groups who favor one another's company together).

1 Drake & 4 Ducks	1 Drake & 3 Ducks	1 Drake & 3 Ducks

2. Separate your males from your females; that is, boys in one pen and girls in another. This is a good choice when you can see that your females could use a break as well. Drakes sometimes fight less when they can't actually mate with females; other times, it doesn't work at all.

3 Drakes	10 Ducks

3. Separate your boys from one another, and separate your females into another pen (the girls can all stay together). This becomes necessary when the drakes simply can't get along together and all of the girls could use a break too.

1 Drake	1 Drake	1 Drake	10 Ducks

4. Try other combinations, depending on the personalities of your flock members. Some drakes may get along all year, while others don't. Every flock is different.

1 Drake	2 Drakes	10 Ducks

   OR:

1 Drake & 3 Ducks	2 Drakes & 7 Ducks

Winter harmony among a newly introduced group of rescued drakes

Life on the Other Side of the Fence

Some ducks dread being separated so much, you might be temporarily fooled into putting them back together again. They'll stand next to each other on opposite sides of a shared fence like mirror reflections. It can be hard to watch at first, but they're far better off with a tiny divider between than they would be if they got injured. This initial reaction to their separation is often short-lived—for everyone involved, and your lives will likely be far less stressful than they were before. Although your ducks may want to be next to each other most of the time, they'll usually begin to meander around their pen as well, especially if you're separating drakes and they each have their own girlfriends with them.

Duck alliances can shift frequently; best friends can throw their affections to the wind and turn on each other at the drop of a feather (no pun intended). The good news is, once you know your ducks, you'll become a finely tuned gauge of duck emotion, and you'll know just who to put on which sides of your dividing fences.

You'll learn different ways to separate your ducks as attractions and tolerances mature and the seasons change. Today the girls on one side and the boys on the other, tomorrow this boy with this girl and that boy with that girl, on the weekend each duck in their own kennel as I laugh to my husband, *"I've had enough of all this squabbling!"* I never thought I'd hear myself say to a duck, *"Now you stay there quietly and think about what you've done to your brother."*

Just remember to watch for the telltale signs that someone is getting picked on and do something about it as soon as you can.

- **Double the supplies**

Keep in mind that ducky separations can instantly increase your expenditures. You immediately need additional feeders, water dispensers, swimming pools and little duck houses. You can go from having one of everything to needing two of everything very quickly; or for those of you with bigger flocks, two of everything to four of everything even faster!

If you don't have a barn or shed and your ducks aren't getting along, you may want to turn in your duck house for a duck hotel instead. You can build a bigger duck house with two latching doors and then divide the two apartments by permanently mounting polyvinyl coated wire mesh between them. This allows your ducks to safely visit each other all through the night because no duck likes being alone.

Duck Identification

It can be difficult separating your ducks if you're having trouble telling them apart. When I first started rescuing, it wasn't easy telling who was who, especially when it came to all those white ducks. It can take a while to learn the subtle differences between like-colored flock members. For this reason, I use colored zip-ties (cable ties) as leg bands. When I run out of colors, I start using two-color combinations to identify everyone.

It's especially vital to have leg bands on ducks when veterinary care is required. I once had seven nearly-identical Indian Runner ducks arrive at my sanctuary. They had been removed from a hoarding situation where they had been deprived of food and water before authorities discovered them. Each of these girls had very individual medical needs. By banding them, I could carefully administer medications and monitor progress without any confusion or dosing mishaps.

Seven very similar Indian Runner ducks are given colored leg bands following their rescue

If it takes you a few moments to figure out who's who in your flock, I highly advise you give them colored bands, so there's never any doubt. This is especially true if a family member or pet sitter ever needs to come in to take care of your ducks. I don't want any of my emergency back-up people to have a moment's doubt about who's who in my duck pen.

- **How to put a leg band on an adult duck**

Putting on and removing zip-ties should always be done when you have a helper. You'll be using wire cutters around your duck's legs and you don't want any mishaps, so one person holds the duck in their arms, while the other works on placing or removing the leg band.

Colored zip-ties make excellent leg bands when put on correctly

Loosely coil a colored zip-tie around your adult duck's leg. Slide it above the foot and over that little back toe, but below the "knee" joint (which is actually your duck's ankle). *Never* put zip-ties on growing ducklings. Once you have the anklet where you want it, *slowly* pull the zip-tie through itself until you find the right fit.

Make sure the zip-tie is not so tight as to pinch the skin. It should look comfortable and completely unrestricting with a little bit of extra room. If you think it's too tight, it probably is. Cut it off and try again. You also don't want the ring to be so loose that it can freely slide up and down or slip backward over their little rear toe.

Once you have the zip-tie in place and properly pulled through itself, use wire cutters to snip off all of the excess plastic. This is important because ducks use their feet to scratch their itches and to preen around their eyes. You don't want any little spikes of plastic poking them in the face.

Inspect zip-ties daily to ensure they're comfortable and in place. In colder regions ducks frequently put on weight in the late fall to prepare for winter. Watch their leg bands especially closely during this time and quickly remove and replace any leg bands that need attending.

Considerations

Considerations

Now that you know how to build a predator-proof pen and are aware of the various types of preparations that need to be made, it's time to move on to some of the things you need to take into consideration before bringing home your new ducks.

Consideration #1
Life Expectancy

Most people don't even think to consider a duck's life expectancy before bringing them home. They mistakenly believe they'll have this responsibility for 2-3 years and then the adventure will be over.

The truth is most ducks have average life spans of 6-7 years, with some feathered friends making it 8-9 years. A duck reaching their 10th or 11th birthday isn't as common, but it isn't unheard of either. If properly cared for and blessed with good genes, some ducks can even go so far as to reach a happy 12-15 years, *or even more!* Muscovy ducks and domestic Mallards (bred and raised in captivity under permits) can sometimes reach a hearty 15-20 years.

Ways you can improve the life expectancy of your ducks:

1. Diet plays a major role when it comes to health and longevity. Malnourished ducks have shorter life spans than ducks who are given high-quality feed brands. A smart diet selection is one of the main ways you can keep your duck around for a long time.

2. Serene and stress-free conditions can help your ducks living longer lives. Because ducks thrive on routine, keeping them on a daily schedule is a great way to keep their feathers from getting ruffled.

3. Safe ducks live a lot longer than ducks who aren't properly protected from predators. Their pen is everything when it comes to longevity. Do it right the first time.

4. Vet care is an essential part of healthy living. While many ducks don't require medical care until they're later in years, you never know when something questionable might come up. Remember to respond quickly to even the mildest of symptoms because ducks tend to veil their weaknesses extremely well. A fast reaction time on your part can be life-saving.

Some genetic factors that can influence the life expectancy of your ducks are:

1. Medium and lightweight breeds tend to live longer than heavyweight breeds.

2. Drakes tend to live longer than female ducks. Many ducks have been bred to lay eggs far more frequently than nature originally intended and this can be extremely taxing on their bodies. Reproductive issues aren't uncommon in domestic ducks and can seriously impact mortality rates.

3. Ducks with very horizontal backs tend to have more leg and hip issues than ducks with more vertically-sloped backs. When they occur, these joint issues tend to limit mobility at a younger age, resulting in shorter life spans. If your duck has a horizontal spine, try to keep them in a healthy weight range to avoid excess stressors on their joints.

Dilly has a healthy slope to his back   *Enyo has a more troublesome horizontal spine*

<u>Where Will You Be Ten Years From Now?</u>

Now that you know how long your duck can live, you need to ask yourself if it still makes sense to add them to your family. Think this decision through carefully because *a lot* can change in the next ten to fifteen years.

- **Leaving to college**

Families with teenagers who want ducks should place special emphasis on this consideration. Make sure you think about who will be taking care of the ducks when your teens head off to college, or in other directions. While young adults are leaving the nest (ha!) and moving to dorms or apartments, ducks have to stay right where they are. This usually leaves parents with the responsibility of caring for the ducks, which is perfectly acceptable if they're ready to devote the same level of commitment, but not acceptable if they have other plans. Ducks can quickly go from a beloved pet to a neglected one in this kind of situation.

- **Apartment living**

If you're living in rented space you should seriously reconsider bringing ducks home with you because something as simple as a change in apartments often ends with homeless ducks. It's not easy to find a landlord that will allow ducks as tenants, and you may quickly find yourself in a terrible situation where you're welcome, but your companions are not. This problem often turns from a dilemma to a nightmare as families realize that finding safe new homes for ducks is far from easy. It really is much wiser to adopt ducks when you're in a permanent living situation.

- **Will provisions**

This is a special shout-out to the retired folks out there. While it's a great time to relax and enjoy having a few ducks around, remember to take your health into consideration and imagine yourself over the course of the next ten plus years still tending to your ducks.

If down the road you might not be able to care for your ducks with the same fervor that you do today, you'll need to devise a plan to make up for this variance. When constructing your duck pen think about how it will suit you in ten years and build it accordingly. You want to prevent pen maintenance from becoming more and more difficult as time prevails. Having a handyperson available can also be a solution.

None of us knows when our time will come, but if you're up there in years you should at least consider whether your ducks are likely to outlive you and what will happen to them if they do. Animals of all kinds get left behind every day by families who haven't laid out any provisions for them in their Will including a place to go to and funding to keep them in the manner they're accustomed to. Beloved pets can quickly end up in precarious situations when families don't plan ahead.

Consideration #2
Your Home Situation

Everyone has a different home situation. Before bringing home pet ducks you'll want to consider your family's normal routine and how well ducks fit into it.

Family Agreement

Although you may really want a duck, not everyone in your family may feel the same way. Make sure you're all on the same page and understand the needs of a new family member before welcoming them home. Surprise pets are never a good idea. Discussions and preparations are always the ideal way to go before adding a pet to your family.

- **Other pets**

Your other pets are part of your home situation and they have an opinion too. If adding ducks take time away from your jealous family dog, perhaps it isn't the best way to go. On the other hand, if your dog or cat will think the addition of ducks would be absolutely wonderful, you may want to rethink their motives. Remember, ducks aren't playthings for other pets.

Dogs and cats can lead to real trouble for a pet duck, and if you think your dog is too old or lazy to be interested, I can give you a whole list of names of people who learned the hard way that their dog was actually quite spry. These mishaps can quickly escalate to a devastating and costly trip to an emergency vet, or worse yet, in the death of your beloved feathered friend.

Indoor Ducks

While most people opt to keep their ducks in a pen outside, it isn't the only way to go. You can keep your ducks inside your home with you. *It's true!*

While I'm a fan of my ducks living outdoors and playing in grass and puddles, some people have ducks who spend their entire lives indoors. As long as a duck has been raised indoors they tend to be perfectly happy there. It's not necessarily a great idea to turn an outdoor duck into an indoor duck because they do understand what they're missing.

If you have indoor ducks, be mindful of keeping them on a nourishing diet intended for waterfowl and avoid feeding them unhealthy table scraps. If you think a dog can be convincing, wait until you have a cute duck quacking at the table for goodies.

While ducks don't respond to potty training, you can go online and purchase a machine-washable diaper harness for them (supplier: The Goose's Mother & Father: www.themothergoose.com and Feathered Fashions: www.fashionmyfeathers.com. For other suppliers see: *"Therapy for Hips, Legs, Feet & Toes/Recovery Items"*). All you need to do is provide a few simple measurements and someone will custom make your harness and ship it right to you and your duck. The harness itself snaps into place around your duck and holds a pad or baby diaper in it, so you don't have to worry about your duck pooping all over the floor. When going this route, it's best to start when ducks are young because trying to train adult ducks to wear a diaper harness isn't always as easy. They often have their own ideas about fashion and a diaper isn't one of them. Your supplier will have additional training information to help assist you in this process.

Ducklings grow fast, so you'll need to swap out harnesses as they continually grow. Since harnesses take some time to make, you'll want to talk to your ducky seamstress about estimating sizes and making your harnesses *before* you begin this diaper-training venture.

Don't try to save yourself a buck by attempting to make one of these harnesses yourself—especially if you're new at this. I've seen make-shift harnesses that didn't fit their ducks properly. They can rub incorrectly against the skin and cause irritations that often result in ruined feathers and bald spots. Diaper harnesses need to fit properly. If you see any feather breakage or damage or anything questionable at all, you should permanently discontinue use and allow feathers to re-grow.

The Mess

Ducks are very messy, especially females. They poop a lot, they make huge, splashing messes around their water buckets and kiddy pools, *they poop a lot,* they can wipe out vegetation at an alarming rate, *they poop a lot,* they burrow their bills into the soil and make an impressive muddle—especially where mud puddles are concerned and… *they poop a lot.* No kidding, if you take pride in the appearance of your front yard and you plan to let your ducks out into it, you'll soon be in a tizzy. More ducks have been tossed out and abandoned as a result of the unexpected chaos left behind in their wake. If you have a sense of humor, you'll find this fun quality most endearing about them, but if you're the more serious type think hard before welcoming ducks into your home, unless you plan to build them a spacious pen that they won't need to wander out of in order to have fun.

Consideration #3
Flock Size

Ducks are flock animals. This means they're most content when they're in the company of other ducks. I have known many Momma Ducks with only one duck who thought their duck couldn't possibly be any happier, but when they adopted a second duck they were amazed by the difference in the spirits of their feathered friend.

- **Two ducks are ideal**

To avoid depriving your duck the companionship of their own kind, you should always start your flock with a minimum of two ducks. I wouldn't recommend starting with any more than two if you've never had ducks before and don't know what you're in for. You can always add more ducks to your flock later if you want to—carefully selecting your new flock members to ensure their long-term compatibility.

- **Mirrors**

If you have a solitary duck that has never seen another duck before and you'd like to get an idea whether or not they'd enjoy a friend, add a reasonable sized, non-breakable mirror to their nighttime quarters. Leave it in there for a while and see what their long-term reaction is. Keep in mind, initial hissing reactions aren't the same as long-term reactions, so give your duck time to get used to it. If they grow to enjoy watching the other duck, it's a good indicator that they would benefit from some ducky companionship. Mirrors really are a great way to prepare a solitary duck for the coming of a new friend.

More often, people have two ducks and one passes away, leaving the second duck extremely lonely. If you temporarily have only one duck, placing a mirror in their pen is a great way to give them company until you can find them a new companion. Lonely ducks will often spend a great deal of time sitting and sleeping in front of their reflection, finding solace in the company of their friend until someone new arrives.

A friendly face can really help

- **Ducks and geese together**

While considering flock size makes most people think of only ducks, a few Momma Ducks may also be considering adding geese. Not all ducks and geese are compatible, so you'll want to consider this move carefully before proceeding.

The trick with ducks and geese is to chaperone newly introduced birds carefully until they're fully cohesive. I've had geese that preferred the company of ducks over their own kind and I've had geese that didn't care for all that quacking one bit. Geese tend to be pretty set in their ways, whatever they are, so their personalities really do need to be taken into consideration before mixing your flock.

Watch ducks and geese closely in the spring

When mixing ducks and geese together in one flock you're really watching your ganders more than anything—especially during the mating season which tends to fall somewhere between Valentine's Day and Flag Day when their behavior tends to be a bit unpredictable. You want to make absolutely sure that your gander isn't throwing interested glances at your female ducks. A gander could easily drown a duck by accident when mating her on water, or he could break bones if attempting to mount her on land. Another thing to you need to watch is how your gander reacts to a drake who's mating a duck. Some ganders are extremely protective of their ducks and will drown a drake who attempts such an act with his flock member.

Keep in mind, how animals behave in front of you is not always the same as how they act when you're not around. I find it best to separate my ducks and geese from each other during the mating season to avoid any accidental mishaps.

The benefit of having geese with your ducks is that they're very protective of them once they become cohesive. The myth is that they'll protect them from predators, but this is simply not the case. Predators will take a goose just as quickly as they'll take a duck. A goose will give you a warning call when they perceive any danger, and I love that about them. Even though I have predator-proof enclosures, I like it when they let me know that there's a fox lingering around. Truth be told, my geese are even better than my dog when it comes to quickly alerting me of any high jinks in my backyard.

Consideration #4
Gender Selection

When putting together a flock of ducks, it's vital to consider the compatibility of its members. This is one of the most frequently overlooked considerations and sadly, it has some of the direst consequences for the ducks. Many Momma Ducks learn this lesson too late and find themselves having to either build new pens or find new homes for some of their drakes.

Gender selection is an important consideration

There are five recommended types of duck flocks regarding gender; by this I mean, the ideal number of males and females you want to keep in any one pen area at any one time.

1. All males
2. All females
3. One male and one female
4. One male and multiple females
5. Multiple males and multiple females (adhering to male-to-female ratios)

All Male Flock

Having a flock of all male ducks has its own unique set of benefits and drawbacks, each of which you'll want to consider before piecing together your flock.

- **Benefits**

1. Drakes often get along pretty well if there are no females in sight or earshot to fight over. I know of a number of families who keep all drake flocks and I've utilized this strategy at my own sanctuary. As long as males grow up together or are introduced outside of the mating season, they tend to work out.

2. A benefit of this type of flock is Momma Ducks have no concerns over special dietary considerations revolving around egg-laying ducks. The feeding ritual is straightforward and the same for everyone.

3. One of the most common and serious veterinary issues are reproductive issues among egg-laying females. These worries disappear from the picture entirely when you have a flock consisting of only drakes.

4. Since most farm and waterfowl shelters are brimming with unwanted, homeless drakes, a flock of adopted drakes provides help where it's needed most.

5. If you enjoy tranquility or live close to others, the voices of drakes are soft and pleasant and will keep you happy and in your neighbor's good graces.

- **Drawbacks**

1. If you like eggs for breakfast, I'm afraid you won't be getting any from your male ducks.

2. Drakes will still have disagreements and pecking order disputes can sometimes arise (especially in the spring) even when there aren't any female ducks about. Some drakes may occasionally need to be separated from one another if things get too out of hand. Pay special attention that no members of your flock are being denied access to food or water.

3. Drakes enjoy the companionship of females and are unable to enjoy this natural part of their lives when they only have other males as companions.

All Female Flock

A flock of all female ducks can have its own inherent benefits and drawbacks.

- **Benefits**

1. All eggs will be unfertilized. This means you'll have a healthy breakfast food on hand and you're certain to avoid hatching out any unwanted ducklings.

2. A flock of all females is usually a very peaceful flock. Disputes tend to be very limited and brief in most cases. A newcomer may shake up the pecking order momentarily, but it's usually resolved relatively quickly.

3. Concerns regarding your females being over-mated by males simply don't exist.

- **Drawbacks**

1. Unless you're adopting adults, it can be difficult to obtain a flock of all females.

2. Egg-laying ducks require more attention to their special dietary needs and are more susceptible to reproductive issues that may require vet attention.

3. Because many people buy into the concept of the all-female flock being ideal (especially in terms of eggs), many homeless drakes are left without options. Denying a single drake into your all-female flock prevents one needy boy from finding his forever family.

4. Multiple females tend to be *loud*.

5. Female ducks enjoy the companionship of drakes and are unable to enjoy this natural part of their lives when they only have other females for companions.

One Male and One Female Flock

A simple male/female pair of ducks has its own set of benefits and drawbacks.

- **Benefits**

1. Both members experience the joy of having a mate of the opposite gender and are completely enriched in this regard.

2. A flock of only two ducks require less pen space and maintenance than larger flocks.

3. If they grow up together or are matched compatibly (taking size, color and age into consideration) male and female couple will rarely fight with one another.

- **Drawbacks**

1. Over-mating can occur if you have an overzealous drake, but separations are often brief when needed.

2. Eggs must be collected to prevent unwanted hatchings.

3. Males and females have different dietary needs, which will require your attention.

4. Although you only have one female, she'll likely still be loud.

One Drake and Multiple Females Flock

Maintaining a flock that consists of one male and a group of females comes with its own list of benefits and drawbacks.

- **Benefits**

1. This is the ideal flock. All members experience the company of the opposite gender.

2. The over-mating of any one female tends to be avoided when a male has so many to choose from. Separations are rarely if ever needed (provided that they're size, color and age compatible).

- **Drawbacks**

1. Eggs must be collected daily to prevent any unwanted hatchings.

2. Males and females have different dietary needs, which will require your attention.

3. Multiple females tend to be *loud*.

Multiple Males and Multiple Females Flock (Adhering to Ratios)

If you're going to have multiple drakes in your flock, it's vital that you keep a standard male-to-female ratio in place to help prevent fighting and over-mating issues. If left unresolved, these types of problems can lead to ducks being kept from food and water sources, from gaining access to proper shelter and they can lead to serious accidents and injuries or even to death.

- **Male-to-female ratio standards:**

1. If you have *two* drakes you should have 2-3 females for every male.

2. If you have *three* drakes, you should have 3-4 females for every male.

3. If you have *four or more* drakes, you should have 4 females for every male.

Having a good ratio of males to females will keep your flock in good order and your own personal stress levels in-check. As with any other, there are benefits and drawbacks to keeping this type of flock.

- **Benefits**

1. Adhering to proper male-to-female ratios helps prevent problems of drakes over-mating with just one duck and lessens the fights between drakes because there are enough females for everyone.

2. You have the opportunity to alleviate shelter overfill by adopting more than one homeless drake along with a bunch of females.

- **Drawbacks**

1. Larger flocks require larger pens, which cost more money to build and take more time to maintain.

2. Eggs must be collected daily to prevent unwanted hatchings.

3. Males and females have different dietary needs, which will require your attention.

4. Unless pens are very spacious and include visual obstacles that act as hiding places (duck houses, bushes, etc.), separations may still be needed here and there. You'll need to watch for excessive fighting between any particular boys while also paying attention to any females who may be getting too much attention. Keep a close eye that no members of your flock are being denied access to food or water.

5. Multiple females tend to be *loud.*

6. Multiple drakes fighting over one female can sometimes lead to the accidental drowning of that female.

Gender Identification: Ducklings

Now that you've put some thought into the size and shape of your flock in regard to gender, you'll need to be able to tell the boys from the girls in order to achieve the end result you're looking for. While the gender identification of ducks is relatively straight forward, determining the gender of a duckling can be quite difficult.

If you plan to purchase your ducklings at a local grain store, you'll probably see them sold *straight-run.* Straight-run ducklings aren't vent-sexed by the grain store (although they probably are by the supplying hatchery), so when you select your ducklings, you get what you get. Many folks report getting ¾ drakes to ¼ females when they purchase straight-run ducklings. Whether this is nature's way or the hatcheries' way, well… who can say for sure. In any case, it can be a bit of a crap-shoot getting the ducklings you're looking for. This sad little guessing game frequently ends in disaster when male ducks mature and fight with each other (especially as they approach their first spring) and their frustrated families react by irresponsibly abandoning some of them out on public ponds. This is simply *not* the appropriate answer.

Although many sources will offer instructions on how to sex a duckling yourself, it can actually be quite harmful to the duckling if it's done too early or by someone inexperienced. This should be left to professionals to avoid permanent damage to the duckling.

If you truly have your heart set on ducklings (and I understand if you do), the only way for most Momma Ducks to get the proper mix of boys and girls is to go directly to a hatchery or breeder. Keep in mind though, unless you're local to them, they'll likely have a six-duckling purchasing minimum (so that the ducklings keep each other warm during shipping and survive the trip).

If you're anything like me, and far away from any duckling resources that are willing to identify their genders, you're probably just going to have to wing it (it just never gets dull) and pick out *two* straight run ducklings. When the ducklings mature, their gender will become obvious. At that point, you can increase the size of your flock by adding sexually mature and identifiable ducks or drakes to your flock

Gender Identification: Ducks

Determining the gender of an adult duck is far more straightforward than figuring out the gender of an itty-bitty duckling.

- **Determining gender by the tail feather**

When they're around two months old, many drakes will begin to sprout a curly tail feather that sits on top of the rest. It's pretty distinctive once full grown. If you see these curled tail feathers you're *most likely* looking at a drake.

Drakes molt their tail feathers once a year. If you're looking at the tail feathers of a duck during this time, you may be temporarily fooled into believing you're seeing a female—until a new tail feather grows back in anyway (and sometimes they don't grow back, which is nothing to worry about).

There are rare occasions when a female will sprout a deceptive curly tail feather making this method even more unreliable, but generally speaking, a very curled tail is a male.

Young Jeffrey sports his curly tail feather

- **Determining gender by the quack**

Determining a duck's gender by the sound of their quack is the most effective way of telling males from females. As early as five weeks of age, the voices of most female domestic ducklings begin to take on an inherently different characteristic. The trouble is, unless you know what you're listening for, it can be tricky to hear. It's easier to make this distinction if you have a boy and girl duckling together and can successfully compare the two.

Basically, females begin to develop their deeper (and louder) voices first and you can usually start hearing them right after bath time, during their preening ritual. An attentive Momma Duck can usually make out the indicative little guttural noises of a girl when they're tidying their tummies. Girl ducklings make noises outside of the standard duckling peeps while males don't. In fact, boys will retain their unwavering little peeps right into their eighth week of life—well after they have their adult feathers, and to the point where it starts to get a little silly. This means if your duck is still peeping well after six, seven and eight weeks of age, you're most definitely looking at a baby boy!

Once ducks reach adulthood there is a vast difference between the quacks of males and females. This makes gender identification by means of their voices much more reliable than looking at tail feathers, which are a fluctuating characteristic. I've been on many calls where I've asked the person on the other end of the line to place their duck on the phone, so I could hear their voice.

"It's a boy!" I announce to a curious caller.
"How can you tell?"
"He told me."
"He told you?"
"Yes, I speak duck."

Adult female ducks have a *loud* and repetitive quack, which sounds like: *"QUACK-QUACK-QUACK!"* or a sound more accurately described as a loud: *"UHT-UHT-UHT!"* They need this obtrusive call to round up and warn their ducklings. Adult drakes, on the other hand, have a quieter, much more soothing and drawn-out quack that's more like a soft: *"quuaaaaccckkkk..."* or more accurately: *"Mmmwhappp..."* The difference is so discernible that I can teach any of my sanctuary's visitors how to sex a duck within seconds. Remember, this only works once a duck's peeps have fully evolved into quacks. This measure of determining gender is so reliable that I've added audio clips of both ducks and drakes to our sanctuary's website to enable Momma Ducks to properly identify their own flock members.

- **Muscovy gender vocalizations**

While male and female adult duck quacks sound different, this exact technique doesn't work for every breed. For example, Muscovy ducks are much quieter than other breeds (and are great in this regard if you have neighbors). They actually don't quack at all, but you can still tell them apart by their vocalizations.

Adult female Muscovy ducks make a quiet trilling sound (and sometimes even squeak!) while males make a breathy, "hut-hut-hut," sound combined with some *snorky* nostril sounds. Trust me; you'll know exactly what I mean by this when you hear it.

Here are other ways to gender identify Muscovy ducks:

1. Females have less elaborate, less bulbous facial masks than males.
2. Males often have these red caruncles going down the backs of their necks.
3. Adult males are noticeably larger than adult females.
4. While both genders will wag their tails (yes they do!), males tend to do it far more often than females.
5. While both genders will fluff up their feathery crowns, male Mohawks are decidedly larger than females.
6. Male ducklings will often have noticeably larger feet than females, becoming more and more apparent as they grow.

Dutch is a rescued male Muscovy drake

Princess is a rescued female Muscovy duck

Consideration #5
Size Options

The size your duckling will one day grow up to be is also a very important consideration. It's important to make sure your drakes aren't too much larger than your ducks or the girls won't stand a chance in trying to fend them off. If your females are too small for your males you may have to separate them during the mating season to protect them from their over-eager boyfriends. On the other hand, as long as you're selecting ducks outside of the Bantam breeds, it's okay if your females are bigger than your males.

Ducks come in four basic sizes based upon their average weight:

1. Bantam (1-2.5 lbs.)

2. Lightweight (3-5 lbs.)

3. Medium weight (5.5-8 lbs.)

4. Heavyweight (8.5-12 lbs.)

Keep in mind, ducks are individuals and not everyone fits perfectly into their weight class. I've had plenty of "heavyweight" Pekin ducks who barely tipped the five pound scale and a few lightweight ducks that pushed their way into the medium weight championships.

You can find lots of size-compatible friends for your ducks

Consideration #6
Breed Options

Your next step is to do a little who's who breed research. Have a look around and consider your options carefully and then choose a breed (or breeds) that appeal to you and fit well into your lifestyle based upon their size, shape, energy level, quack volume and flight capabilities (or lack thereof).

Exotic & Wild Duck Breeds

This guidebook is *not* intended for the care of wild breeds and the information provided herein doesn't always apply in the case of exotics.

Keeping Different Duck Breeds Together

While you don't have to select ducks of the same breed for your flock, I've noticed that most ducks have an uncanny preference for other ducks who look just like them.

If you raise a brown duck and a white duck together and then a year later decide to add another brown duck to your flock, you may find that after an initial period of getting used to each other, the brown ducks pair up (sometimes to the point of excluding the white duck, depending on their personalities). Similarly, if you have a brown duck and a white duck and add a black duck, they may not know what to make of the stranger at first.

Although ducks tend to get along with other ducks, they certainly do prefer what they're used to.

Breed Standards

In order to keep this next section relatively simple I'm going to avoid overly complicated breed standards and just go over some of the most common types of ducks you'll find available out there—and what they tend to look like (as opposed to what they *should* look like according to other sources). This section is best utilized as a quick reference for Momma Ducks to help you find a good match for your family, or to help you identify ducks already in your care.

- **Comparative weights: males vs. females**

Every book on breed standards that I've ever seen will tell you that males are typically larger than females. In Call ducks this difference can be as small as a quarter pound, while in Muscovy ducks it can be as much as nine pounds or more!

While males may be heavier than females when breed standards are properly adhered to and achieved, it's not necessarily the case when it comes to your general, over-the-counter, grain store quality ducks. I'm telling you this so you won't panic when your ducks are a pound heavier than your drakes, which is not all that infrequent in the casual world of ducks, where what's out there and what's in books tend to collide.

For this reason, aside from making general comparisons, I'm not going to go into the ideal weight perimeters of any particular breed while reviewing their physical traits (unless you're in a vet's office, who weighs their ducks anyway?).

Hey, who's holding up the line?

Breed & Feather Colors

Duclair: A white duck who has symmetrical colored markings on their back and wings (a.k.a. their saddle) and tail feathers *only*.

Magpie: A white duck who has symmetrical colored markings on their saddle, tail and head feathers *only*.

Bibbed: A duck with a white area on their chest.

Grey: A duck bred to have Mallard colorations.

Trout: A duck bred to have washed-out Mallard colorations with white or light dappling.

Pied: A white duck with symmetrical colored markings.

Irregular Pied: A white duck with non-symmetrical colored markings.

Canizie: A Muscovy duck with contrasting white feathers on their neck and head. This trait can emerge as your duck grows and matures, or over the course of a few years.

Laced: A duck whose feathers are trimmed in another color.

Double Laced: A duck whose feathers are laced with a concentric arc inside.

Striped: A duck whose feathers have vertical stripes.

Rippled: A duck whose feathers have horizontal stripes of two different colors.

Barred: A duck whose feathers have horizontal stripes of two different colors, one of which is white.

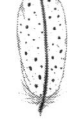
Peppered: A duck who has small gray or black dots on some of their feathers.

Penciled: A duck who has concentric arc-shaped stripes on their feathers without border lacing.

Spangled: A duck who has black tips on the ends of some of their feathers.

Mottled: A duck who has white tips on the ends of some of their feathers.

Splashed: A duck who has irregular color variations on some of their feathers.

- **Crested ducks**

I absolutely *adore* crested ducks! Ducks of any size, breed or gender can be *crested*. A crest is merely a feathery pom-pom on top of a duck's head and like ducks, they come in many colors (some ducks have more than one and are double crested!).

Asaru is a Crested Swede mix *Bindy is a Crested Pekin*

Crested ducks are plumed in a wide variety of colors. Some color varieties are sexually dimorphic; in which cases, males will eclipse molt (see: *"Molting/Molting of Sexually Dimorphic Ducks"*) and appear similar to females in coloration during that time.

Bills can range in color from charcoal, brown, olive or orange. Legs and feet can be any mixture of charcoal, brown, olive or orange.

Bantam Breeds

The most common examples of Bantam breeds include: Call, Black East Indie, Mallard, Miniature Appleyard and Australian Spotted. Because Mallards weigh between 2-3 lbs, there is a slight difference of opinion as to whether they should be considered bantam ducks or lightweight ducks. Since all Bantam breeds can fly, I like to include them in this weight class.

These pint-sized ducks are little balls of pizzazz who tend to zip around pretty quickly. They're a high-energy duck and seem to get into a little more trouble than their larger counterparts. They also tend to be more vocal than other breeds and females can be alarmingly loud and disruptive, as well as quite pleasantly chatty.

- **Call**

Jellybean (White Call) & Tic Tac (Grey Call), Photo courtesy of Heather Grandstaff

Call ducks only weigh about 1–1 ½ pounds and are plumed in an exceptionally wide variety of colors including: Apricot, Bibbed, Black, Blue, Buff, Chocolate, Fawn, Grey, Lavender, Magpie, Pied, Saxony, Silver and White. Males of some color varieties (i.e. Apricot, Grey, Fawn and Silver) eclipse molt.

Bills can range in color from charcoal, brown, olive or orange. Legs and feet can be any mixture of charcoal, brown, olive or orange.

White   *Magpie*   *Black*

- **East Indie**

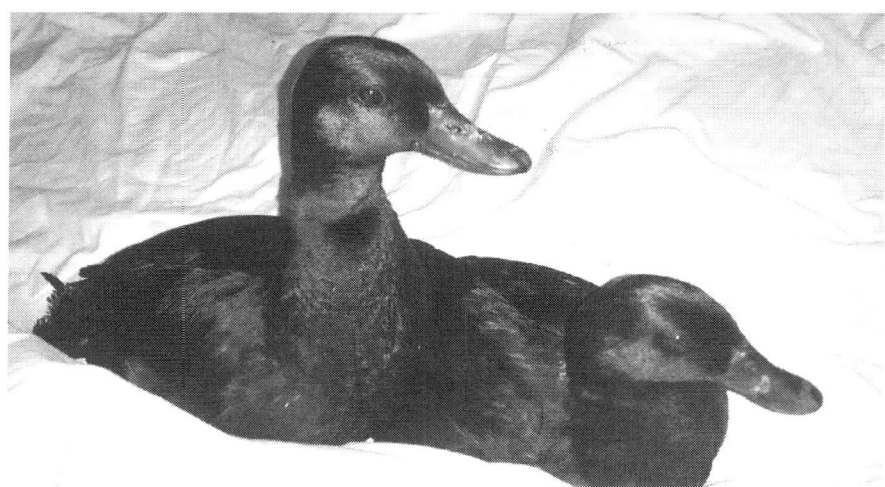

Emmy & Oliver, Photo courtesy of Charrisse Robertson

East Indie ducks look like small Cayuga ducks from the middleweight class. Males and females appear generally the same; both have black feathers with an iridescent green sheen to them.

Bills are usually charcoal, but they can sometimes be olive or have olive in them. Legs and feet are commonly charcoal although they can have orange or olive mixed into their palette as well.

- **Miniature Silver Appleyard**

M/F Pippen & Apple, Photo courtesy of Abby Perata *Yard (M) in eclipse with females Silver & Apple, Photo courtesy of Sandy Lee*

Miniature Appleyard ducks look like small versions of their heavyweight counterparts except that they sometimes have a little more white in them. Males and females are sexually dimorphic. Some families report that their males eclipse molt, while others do not. Whether your drake will eclipse molt depends on their particular gene pool (with more pure-bred individuals usually taking part).

Bills range from orange to brown in females and are olive in males. Legs and feet are commonly orange although they can sometimes have a mixture of brown in them.

- **Australian Spotted**

Photo courtesy of Julie Shere

Male and female Australian Spotted ducks are sexually dimorphic. Males can have either green, blue or silver feathers on their heads and go through an eclipse molt.

Males have olive bills (often with charcoal markings) while females have bills that range from orange to brown with freckles being very common. Legs and feet of both genders are orange although they can have a mixture of brown in them.

- **Mallard (Captive-bred)**

Removing Mallard ducks, ducklings or eggs from the wild is illegal in accordance with the Migratory Bird Treaty Act. However, with the proper permits, they can be bred in captivity and purchased legally. I myself am not a fan of people acquiring captive bred Mallard ducks *unless* they plan to build them proper flight aviaries and provide them with a lifetime of love and care. The trouble is, people tend to buy Mallards from their local grain stores, have their fun with them as ducklings and then release them to fend for themselves when they get older. I honestly don't agree with releasing captive-bred and raised birds into the wild for a whole myriad of reasons including the fact that they fail to learn migratory paths, which can then lead to local population explosions and subsequent human complaints. Buying and releasing Mallards perpetuates an unnatural situation that usually ends badly for the animals.

Peter & Peabody (L) and again with their friend Paul during the eclipse molt (R), Photos courtesy of Lew & Sally

Male and female Mallard ducks are sexually dimorphic. Males have white undercarriages, auburn breasts, white rings around their throats and green iridescent heads while females are speckled with light and dark browns. Males eclipse molt.

Males have olive bills while females have orange bills. The feet of males and females are orange although they may have brown or charcoal highlights.

Lightweight Breeds

The most common examples of lightweight breeds include: Indian Runner, Khaki Campbell and Magpie. While the ducks in this lightweight class have a pretty high energy level, they're not nearly as zippy as their tiny Bantam counterparts. Because of their smaller size, the ducks in this group, like the Bantams, can be very prone to hawk attacks, making extra overhead protection a more than necessary precaution.

- **Indian Runner**

Joker & Riddles are fawn & white Runners

Cleo is a Chocolate Runner

Echo is a Blue Runner

Indian Runners stand upright like bowling pins and are plumed in a wide variety of colors. The most recognized varieties of Runner ducks are: Black, Blue, Buff, Chocolate, Fawn, Fawn & White, Grey, Trout, Silver and White. Males of some color varieties (i.e. Grey, Trout, Fawn and Silver) eclipse molt.

Bills can range in color from charcoal, brown, olive or orange. Legs and feet can be any mixture of charcoal, brown, olive or orange.

Chocolate   *Blue*   *Fawn Runner*

- **Khaki Campbell**

Marvin & Lil Ms. Bee (L) and Marvin during his eclipse molt (R)

Khaki Campbell ducks have brown feathers. Males and females are sexually dimorphic. Males have darker heads and wing feathers than females. Males eclipse molt.

The bills of both males and females can range from charcoal, olive, brown or orange. Legs and feet can be orange or brown or a happy mixture of both.

- **Magpie**

Switch has a black cap on his head

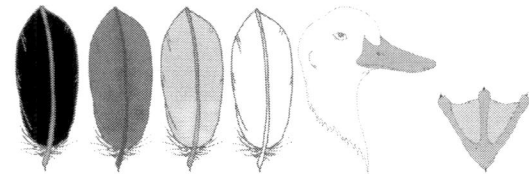

Magpie ducks have mostly white feathers with dark symmetrical markings that stretch from shoulders to tail and also include a matching cap on top of their heads. Males and females appear generally the same.

Bills are generally orange although you may see some brown or charcoal markings on them. Legs and feet are orange, occasionally with brown or charcoal highlights as well.

Middleweight Breeds

Common examples of medium weight breeds include: Ancona, Blue Swedish, Buff Orpington, Cayuga and Welsh Harlequin ducks.

- **Ancona**

Notice how the solid, brown marks under Vida's eyes dissipate as she ages (L-R)

Ancona ducks are mostly white with brown or black markings including a pretty brown mark directly under their eyes. Males and females appear generally the same.

Their bills are mostly charcoal, although a bit of orange may show through here and there. Legs and feet are dark brown, often with orange highlights.

- **Blue Swedish**

Blue Swedes can be gray or black with white throats

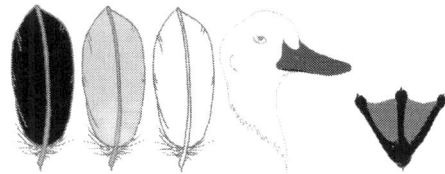

Blue Swedish or *"Swede"* ducks can be gray or black with a splotch of white over their throats. Their color depends on the combined genes of their parents and a single set of mating adults can produce both colors of ducklings along with a percentage of whom are silvery white, in which case you'll see a bit of gray on their heads and wing tips. Males and females appear generally the same.

Bills are usually charcoal although you may see olive highlights. Legs and feet are usually charcoal, although you may see some orange peeking through.

- **Blue Swede Mixes**

Blue Swede and Pekin ducks are both very popular breeds and are frequently crossbred and sold in grain stores. A duckling resulting from this fusion is often marked in an array of colors and commonly referred to as a *Blue Swede Mix*. Because most guidebooks don't feature them, they're one of the most frequently misidentified breeds out there.

Shorty is a cross between a Blue Swedish and a Pekin duck

His head and body darkens (losing the green) during his eclipse molt

Blue Swede Mixes can have any combination of brown, white, gray or black feathers (often with a green sheen as the Mallard genes in their ancestry are unlocked). Males and females appear generally the same. Males *sometimes* eclipse molt, depending on their genetic awakening.

Bills can be charcoal, olive or orange (if orange they may have brown or charcoal markings). Legs and feet can be charcoal or orange—some are even spotted!

- **Buff Orpington**

Left: Bean (left, rear) has a light gray head, unlike his two ladies *Right: During the eclipse molt his gray fades away (right)*

Buff Orpington ducks have beautiful beige feathers. Males have light-gray heads and eclipse molt.

They can have brown or orange bills. Legs and feet are orange.

- **Cayuga**

Kayla has a charcoal bill

Young Jeffrey has an olive bill

Beautiful Bonnie-Bonster was once completely black!

Cayuga ducks have black feathers with a green iridescent sheen that transforms in summer to include brilliant blues, maroons and purples. As Cayuga ducks age, some of them will turn more-and-more white every year during their annual molt. Males and females appear generally the same.

While breeders often strive for charcoal-colored bills there are quite a few Cayuga ducks out there with olive bills. Breeders also strive for dark legs and feet, but many have orange or olive showing through.

- **Welsh Harlequin**

Spencer is a male Welsh Harlequin   *Laci is a female, Photo courtesy of Feathered Angels Waterfowl Sanctuary*

Salt & Pepper are males in eclipse molt, Photo courtesy of Angie Neuman-Hahn

Welsh Harlequin ducks are sexually dimorphic. Males appear very similar to Mallards except they're larger in size and have more white dappled in their feathers. Females are mostly white with dark markings on their wing and tail feathers. Males eclipse molt.

Bills are usually charcoal in females and olive in males. Legs and feet are orange in males and charcoal in females.

- **Abacot or "Hooded" Ranger**

Abacot Ranger ducks appear very similar to Welsh Harlequin ducks except that they're a little larger and females have a fawn or buff "hood" that tends to fade with age. Honestly, unless you aquire yours from someone who knows for sure what they have, you might not be able to tell the difference between an Abacot Ranger and a Welsh Harlequin duck.

There seems to be some discrepancy about the proper weight classification of Abacot Rangers. While some people recognize their ideal size as 2-3 pounds and prefer to list them among the light-weight breeds, most Abacot Rangers these days are actually a little larger than this (weighing 5-6 pounds) and fall easily within the medium-weight category.

Liddy & Dick: (L) Ducklings (R) Adults, Photos courtesy of Kate Harland

Abacot Ranger ducks are sexually dimorphic. Males appear very similar to Mallards except they're larger in size and have more white dappled in their feathers. Females are mostly white with dark markings on their wing and tail feathers. Some families report that their males eclipse molt, while others do not. Whether your drake will eclipse molt depends on their particular gene pool (with more pure-bred individuals usually taking part).

Bills are usually charcoal in females and olive in males. Legs and feet are often orange in males and orange or brown in females.

Heavyweight Breeds

Common examples of heavyweight breeds include: Aylesbury, Muscovy, Pekin, Rouen, Saxony and Silver Appleyard ducks. Heavyweight ducks tend to waddle around a little more casually than smaller ducks—especially deep-keeled Aylesbury and Rouen ducks. Heavyweight ducks also tend to be clumsier than other ducks and more prone to foot, leg and hip injuries.

- **Aylesbury**

Aylesbury ducks have white feathers, light peach-colored bills and are boxy-shaped with spines that are horizontal to the ground and pronounced breast keels. In some cases, breeders punctuate this exhibition quality to the point that the ducks have a difficult time getting around.

In the U.S. Aylesbury ducks tend to look a lot like Pekin ducks (due to crossbreeding), but if you put them side-by-side with one another you'll notice that Aylesbury ducks have lighter colored bills, whiter feathers and a square body type. If you'd like an Aylesbury duck as a pet, try to find this more utilitarian version of the breed with less-pronounced keels, so they can get around easier and are less prone to leg injuries.

Utilitarian (L) and exhibition (R) Aylesbury ducks, Photos courtesy of Chris Taylor/Pen Rhiw Garn Poultry Supplies

Aylesbury ducks have white feathers and white skin (as opposed to yellow). Males and females appear generally the same.

Bill is ideally peach, but more commonly light orange in over-the-counter acquired ducks. Legs and feet are orange.

- **Pekin**

Pekin ducks are the most common breed available and since they've been domesticated for over 2000 years, they're (in my opinion) the friendliest of all of the breeds. If you've never raised ducks before or if it's been a long time, I highly recommend starting out with a couple Pekins. When human imprinted, they tend to cling to their Momma Ducks more than many of the other breeds.

When bringing home a Pekin duck for a pet you may want to avoid selecting *Jumbo Pekin* ducks since they've been bred to be too large for their own wellbeing (9-11 pounds as opposed to 6-8 lbs. of normal Pekins). Their hearts simply can't withstand the pressure and often give in after 2-3 years.

Pekin ducks are often mistaken for Aylesbury ducks, but if you put them side-by-side with one another, you'll notice that the bills and feet of Pekin ducks are deeper in pigmentation (ranging from yellow-orange to orange) and their feathers have a mild, cream-colored hue to them (which really stands out in winter against a snowy backdrop). In addition, their bodies are less boxy and more upright. Since the two breeds are frequently confused with one another, they commonly end up interbred, which is why you may spot a few Aylesbury qualities in your Pekin.

Young Matthew

Oh Henry!, Jocamo & Ranger

Pekin ducks have white to creamy-white feathers. Males and females appear generally the same.

Bills, legs and feet are all orange.

- **Muscovy**

Muscovy ducks are the only domestic ducks who can't trace their roots back to wild Mallards. They're loaded with personality and tons of fun. The females tend to be bossy while the males crave human interaction. Females are especially docile and love to be held and petted when they're broody (overwhelmed with motherhood inclinations). Muscovy ducks often prefer land over water (especially larger males who don't float as easily and readily begin to sink like funny submarines) and can often be seen taking sand baths, which can lead to a pretty dirty duck.

Muscovy ducks can *fly* and because so many have escaped and interfered with wild bird populations in warmer states, laws about owning and allowing them to multiply continue to change. Be a responsible Momma Duck and provide full aviary protection and/or clip wings to prevent any escapes.

Bella (female/left) and Billy (male/right)
Bella still has her youthful peppery spot on top of her head

Females: Bella (White) and Tricia (B&W Pied)

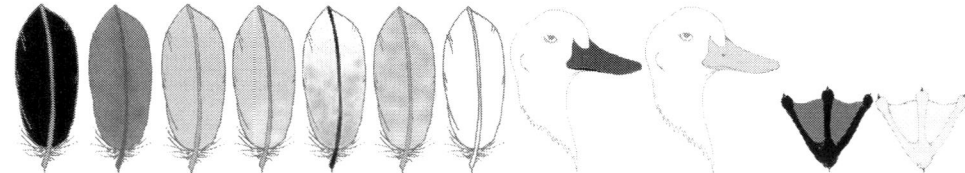

Muscovy ducks are plumed in a variety of fun colors including: Black, Blue, Chocolate, Lavender, Pied, Silver, White and many of these strains are Barred or Rippled. Light-colored Muscovy ducklings have a peppery black patch on top of their heads that stay with them for most of their first year before fading away. If you see this dot, you're looking at a youngster.

Bills are usually peach with charcoal or red highlights although they can be fully charcoal. Feet and legs are usually yellow and occasionally charcoal, sometimes with spots or highlights.

White   *Blue*   *Silver & White*

- **Muscovy mixes:**

1. When a male Muscovy mates with a female Pekin their offspring is referred to as a *Mulard*.
2. When a female Muscovy duck mates with a male Pekin their offspring is referred to as a *Hinny*.
3. When a Muscovy duck mates in general with any non-Muscovy duck their offspring is referred to as a *Mule*.
4. Mulards, Hinnies and Mules are infertile. While females may lay eggs, they won't hatch (even so, go ahead and pick them up).

Talulah is a Muscovy Mule

Muscovy mixes can be plumed in just about every color in the ducky rainbow. The same is true of their bills, legs and feet.

- **Rouen**

While breeders aim for an exhibition quality, deep-breasted keel that makes getting around much more difficult for a Rouen duck, you probably won't find them this way in your grain stores or hatcheries. More likely, you'll find the utilitarian version of a Rouen without the pronounced keel.

Big Boy is a male Rouen

O'Malley during his eclipse molt

LeeLoo is a female Rouen

Rouen ducks remind me of giant Mallards. Males eclipse molt.

Bills can be orange or olive. Legs and feet are usually orange although some will have brown highlights.

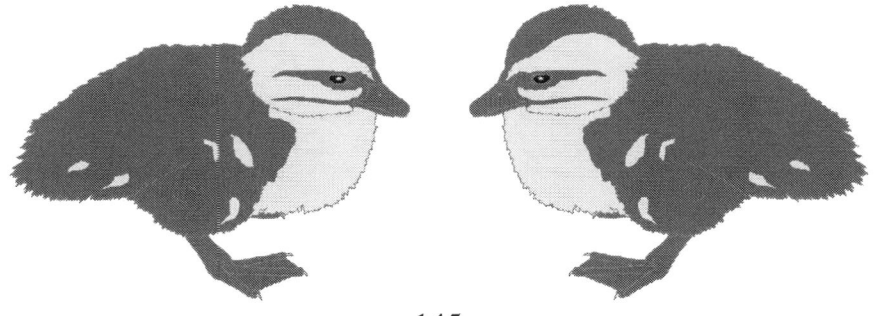

- **Saxony**

Hansel, Klaus & Custard
Photo courtesy of Lisa Steele/Fresh Eggs Daily

Tupelo Honey is a female with less obvious breed traits
Photo courtesy of Mary Winder

Max is second in line with his four ladies...

And Max again during his eclipse molt, Photos courtesy of Katharina Davitt

Females Saxony ducks are tan and white in color with a white streak over their eyes and a bit of gray in their wingtips. Males have white undercarriages, brown chests, gray-tipped wings, white rings around their necks and bluish-gray heads. Males eclipse molt.

Bills are usually orange, but some males may have a slight tint of olive. Legs and feet are orange.

- **Silver Appleyard**

Teddy Crispin (L) and again during his eclipse molt (Ctr.), Photos courtesy of DucksAndClucks.com   *Jezebel (R) is a female*

Silver Appleyard ducks are sexually dimorphic. Males appear very similar to Welsh Harlequins except that they're larger in size. The white ring around their neck can be clear or rather indistinct. Their white undercarriage comes up and stops just below this ring on some males while on others it reaches all the way up their throats. Males also have white stripes on their face that travel over and under their eyes as well as across their cheekbones. Females look like giant Mallards, except that they have a lot more white in their feathers, a brown stripe down the back of their neck and a brown stripe over their eyes. Males eclipse molt.

Males can have olive or orange bills while females only have orange. Legs and feet are orange, sometimes with brown highlights.

Consideration #7
Ducks or Ducklings

Many people have a *love-at-first-site* experience when they see ducklings in a store. There just aren't many things in life more appealing than these peeping little balls of fluff. While they poop a lot and go through a plenty of towels when sitting on your lap, or in the crook of your neck, they're purely warm and wonderful.

The Benefits of Ducklings

Put simply, the mother-to-duckling bond you'll form with your little peep-a-doodle will be like nothing else you've ever experienced before. They'll always look at you with loving eyes and trust you implicitly in a way that no one else in this world ever does and that is an amazing feeling. But… all this joy comes with enormous responsibility. Your duckling will be relying on you for *everything*—not just today, but in the long run too.

If you're able to meet all of their growing needs and provide them with a lifetime of quality love and care, ducklings are absolutely and positively marvelous.

- **The bond of imprinting is strong**

If you spend a lot of time with your ducklings during their first six to eight weeks of life, they'll bond very closely with you. This human-imprinting can last a lifetime as long as you continue to spend time with them.

Keep in mind, once human-imprinted ducklings mature, they may not appreciate your adoration quite as much anymore, especially once *the birds and the bees* kick in. As they grow, many ducks prefer to keep both their feet on the ground in lieu of sitting on their Momma Duck's lap. Some of them decide they want to limit some of that petting as well.

And speaking of petting, most ducks favor being touched on the sides of their long necks or on the fronts of their bellies and prefer you *don't* pet them anywhere along their spine (including their neck), wings or back. There are two reasons for this:

1. When predators attack ducks, they commonly aim for their backs. When you come at your duck in this manner, you can accidentally incite their natural fear reflex.

2. Males especially prefer not to be treated as girls. When you pet them on their backs and wings, they often think you're attempting to mount them. Females on the other hand, may enjoy this kind of petting, especially when they're broody.

- **What exactly is imprinting?**

If you're new to ducklings you may be wondering what *human imprinting* even means. Basically, it refers to the instinctive bond that ducklings form with their Momma Ducks. There are two types of imprinting that occur among ducklings: *filial imprinting* and *sexual imprinting*.

- **Filial imprinting**

Filial imprinting occurs when ducklings hatch out and quickly learn to recognize their parent—or the first moving object that they consider to be their parent. This commonly takes place within a day and a half of hatching and for obvious reasons. Put simply, Mother Nature can be unforgiving, which means those ducklings who form fast and tight bonds with their perceived Momma Ducks are more likely to survive.

Lil Bo Peep was imprinted on a plush toy when she arrived

While imprinting tends to occur quickly, it's not so steadfast as to have exact time lines or conditions. Older ducklings can still imprint on humans especially if there are no other ducks around and you're their only alternative. While I don't recommend you purposefully keep a duckling separated from their own kind, sometimes temporary situations arise while you're waiting to find them a friend.

The longer your mother-duckling time together lasts, the more solid the imprinting will be. Momma Ducks who enjoy a close bond with their ducklings for a full eight weeks will likely enjoy a close connection with them throughout their lives provided you work at keeping the relationship going. On the other hand, Momma Ducks who only have one or two weeks to establish a bond may find it a bit fragile and will probably have to put more effort into keeping it going.

You don't have to bring home ducklings to experience a human-imprinted duckling. Sadly, because so many people are abandoning their ducks, shelters often have them. Given a little time and some careful effort, a former human-imprinted duck will bond with their new Momma Duck.

- **Sexual imprinting**

Sexual imprinting occurs when a duckling internalizes those traits that they'll one day find attractive in a mate. As adults, ducks are attracted to mates who share the appearance of their parent.

If your duckling experienced filial imprinting on you because you were their caretaker upon hatching, they'll also learn that your human physical traits are quite attractive. When they mature, they'll begin to see you in a whole new light and will often try out their courtship displays on *you* as opposed to other ducks!

Sexual imprinting is not necessarily permanent. Although hatchlings may sexually imprint on you in the beginning, this tends to change once they mature and encounter other adult ducks. Commonly, by their first spring, most ducks will figure out what's-what and will appropriately redirect their impulses, although they'll still hold a special place in their heart for you.

If your female duck has sexually imprinted on you, your presence alone can be enough to entice her courtship behavior as well as stimulating nesting and egg-laying activity—never mind all that snuggling and petting. It's for this reason that vets will sometimes advise less handling of your duck when attempting to slow down her egg production (more on this later).

The Benefits of Ducks

As my two boys reached sexual maturity I slowly transformed from "Momma Duck" into "Hot Momma Duck." It was very apparent when it became time to introduce a couple girls. There were a few reasons I chose adult females over ducklings.

Young Jeffrey

Young Matthew

- **Guaranteed gender**

While determining the accurate gender of a young duckling is often questionable, telling adult male and female ducks apart is relatively simple and wholly reliable. You're absolutely guaranteed to get the exact number of ducks and drakes you're looking for, and this allows you to choose the precise type of flock you'd like to have—rather than leaving that decision up to chance.

- **Guaranteed size**

If you have a duck who needs a friend, adopting an adult duck is a great way to ensure that their new pen mate is size-compatible. Remember the needs of your females in relation to your males. A drake that is too large for your duck can be trouble. While some breeds may boast certain weights and sizes, these estimates aren't always accurate, especially when you're purchasing your ducklings from a general grain store or from a farm down the road.

Even when breed ranges are accurate, buying a female duckling who's expected to grow and reach 6-8 pounds when you already have a male who weighs 7 ½ pounds can be pretty risky business. What happens if she only makes it to 6 pounds? She'll be a pound-and-a-half less than your larger drake and that's not so good for her.

- **Ducks and ducklings don't mix**

Bringing home adult ducks gives you greater control over your matchmaking, and it also prevents any delayed introductions.

When Young Jeffrey and Young Matthew were ready for girlfriends, they were *really* ready. I didn't want my adult boys to have to wait two months for them to meet their new ladies while waiting for them to grow up.

Ducklings need to be kept separate from adult ducks who aren't their hatching mothers, especially drakes. Ducklings can be easily killed in a pecking order confrontation, premature mating, or in a drowning incident.

- **Ducks require less chaperoning than ducklings**

Anytime you're bringing home baby animals they're going to require more time and diligence than adult animals. When I had ducklings I was frequently monitoring them and their brooder. I was continually refreshing their food and water, cleaning out dispensers, changing their bedding, taking them for swims and sanitizing the bathtub afterwards. I spent a lot of time and energy fulfilling their every need, including preparing them for their move outdoors to their barn and pen.

Adult ducks need your attention too, but they don't require the kind of constant care that ducklings require. If you have a tight schedule and a lot going on in your life, ducks are simply a lot easier than ducklings. Even so, be careful not to mistake caring for ducks as *easy*. Because as you're beginning to see, there's a lot involved.

- **Helping a displaced animal**

When you adopt a displaced animal, not only are you helping to provide a home for someone who needs one, but you're also making space at a shelter, so they can assist more animals in need.

Finding new homes for shelter ducks tends to take a long time because most people want to free-range them. Good homes with quality safe pens and loving families are few and far between, so when they do come along, they're heaven sent.

Acquiring Ducklings

- **Grain store ducklings**

Pekin, Blue Swedish, Indian Runner and Khaki Campbell ducks are usually easy to locate at grain stores in the spring. Some states have two or six duckling purchasing minimums to try and help prevent impulsive single-duckling Easter shopping, which is largely considered irresponsible.

Springtime really is the best time to acquire ducklings. By the time your ducklings are ready to make their permanent move out to their pen, it's usually warm enough for them to do so. If you don't time things out correctly, your young ducks can be facing transitional temperatures that are either too hot or too cold than what they're accustomed to, leading to stress and illness among growing waterfowl.

- **Hatchery ducklings**

Another option is to purchase your ducklings from a hatchery and have them shipped to you. Think carefully before selecting this option. The last thing you want is to receive a heartbreaking shipment of ducklings where not everyone has made it safely to you and, sadly, it does happen. If you still opt to go this route, do some research on the hatchery and make sure they have a good reputation before proceeding.

As mentioned previously, hatcheries often have a six duckling shipping minimum to ensure the ducklings can huddle together in the box and keep warm enough for the trip. It's practically guaranteed that there will be more than one boy in there. If this is too many ducklings for you, or you can't handle multiple drakes, it really isn't the best way to go.

Before having ducklings shipped to you, make sure you have a few clear days of nice weather, avoiding unsafe high or low temperatures that might bring harm to your ducklings in route. Planes and overnight warehouses aren't often good places for ducklings to stay in inclement weather. National emergencies occurring between your ducklings shipping origin and destination should also be considered before placing your order.

- **Pet store ducklings**

Pekin ducklings are available in pet shops in some areas around Easter time—and often *illegally*. Pet shop staff and owners rarely know anything about their proper care and couldn't tell you a thing about them. Worse yet, accidents often take place that result in permanent injuries and losses (and you'll sometimes see them there). For these places, ducklings are a quick buck and most of them have absolutely no plan for any lef over ducklings who don't sell.

Avoid buying ducklings from pet shops and perpetuating their irresponsible behavior. If they don't make money off them, they won't sell them again next year. If you find a pet shop selling ducklings illegally (many towns, cities and states have laws against it), take responsibility and report them to the authorities (your local humane society is a great place to start).

- **Animal shelter ducklings**

Unfortunately, many schools partake in irresponsible hatching programs in the spring and early summer. These frequently end with dozens of homeless ducklings who are then brought to animal shelters.

Some duckling owners will discover that their impulse purchase wasn't a good fit for their family and bring them to shelters while others will dump them out on ponds. Only a few of those abandoned on ponds will be lucky enough to make it to shelters where they await their new homes.

Imagine the difference you can make in the lives of one or more of these little darlings.

Teary-eyed Piper was abandoned at only five weeks old

- **Breeder ducklings**

If you're trying to find a less-common breed, you may want to try to find a breeder. Like hatcheries, breeders will often ship ducklings directly to your doorstep, but the risks and drawbacks are the same.

Depending where you live, you may be able to find a breeder who is within driving range. If so, you can go out and personally select your ducklings and then safely bring them home. This is a great way to avoid six duckling shipping minimums and many breeders will even vent sex your ducklings for you.

Acquiring Ducks

If you'd like to bring home adult ducks, you can explore your local animal shelters or check your own local ponds for drop offs and rescue them yourself. Helping an animal without a home is one of the most rewarding things you can do.

Although I highly recommend it, you don't have to adopt a rescued duck if you want an adult duck. You can explore the internet, check your local farms, or put an ad in your local paper. You may even be able to take a day trip and go visit a breeder—just make sure you make an appointment first. Breeders will often sell ducks that they don't want to breed or show.

- **Adopting a rescued duck**

Adopting a homeless duck from a shelter may take a little more effort on your part. You may have to make more than one trip to a shelter, fill out forms, allow visits to your home, provide photos of their pen and housing, and so on.

Sometimes shelters are brimming with homeless ducks; other times, they have found happy homes for all of their ducks (and that's a good thing!). If you plan on adopting a duck, apply a few months in advance, receive your pre-approval for adoption and then be patient while you wait for the perfect duck to arrive.

- **Determining the age of a duck**

If you're adopting a duck you may not know how old they are, but there are a few clues you can look for to get a general idea.

1. If the duck was abandoned on a public pond of some kind and then subsequently rescued, they most likely hatched out that same year. If someone is going to throw away their duck, they usually do it pretty quickly—when the duckling stage is over. Most ducks don't survive their first year in the wild, especially in colder regions where ponds freeze over. Many will succumb to serious injuries and predation within the first year as well, but occasionally someone will tell you that a particular duck has been there for a few years.

2. A duck under a year old will have small points at the tips of their tail feathers that are more defined than older ducks. These points help push out a duckling's fluff when they first grow their feathers.

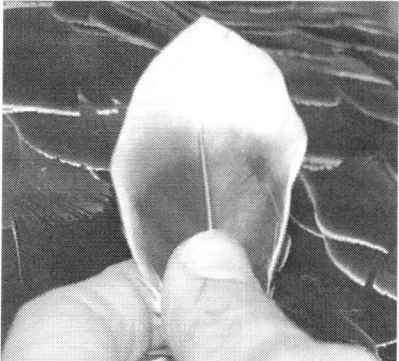

A pointed tail feather

3. The eyes of older ducks are more sunk into their sockets than eyes of younger ducks. You'll see a deeper crease and a more inset eyes on older ducks.

4. Older ducks often have a thicker fold of skin beneath their bills.

 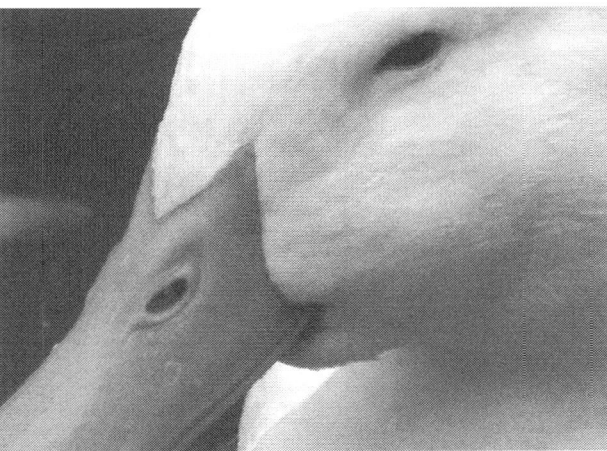

Young Matthew at three years old *Young Matthew at ten years old*

153

- **The nature of an adopted duck**

Although ducks have similar tendencies, they each have very distinct personalities. Some are very affectionate greeters while others are shy and prefer to keep their distance. Some are mild mannered while others are fussy trouble-makers and avid protestors. Some are curious investigators while others are infamous lazy bones who simply can't be bothered.

It's important to understand that the type of bond you'll have with your newly adopted duck will depend on their individual history, breed, age and how much time you're willing to spend with them. Not all ducks are human-imprinted, but that doesn't mean you won't earn their trust and establish a mutual understanding and loving relationship with them.

Adopted ducks go through an initial adjustment phase, the same as any other animal. Don't get disappointed if your new duck won't come near you or runs in the opposite direction whenever you enter their pen. Time and patience will eventually bring most ducks around.

It usually takes a new duck about *three days* to adjust to their new surroundings. This is especially true if you stick to a clearly defined routine. If your new duck is shy, try to limit going into their pen for these few days. Visits should be restricted to feed, water and cleaning duties only. After this initial grace period, you can gradually begin to spend more and more time in their pen. Give them plenty of space while they get used to you and over the course of the next month or so, work on making friends with special treats. You'll be amazed at how quickly a shy duck can come around if you do it on their terms.

I think all adopting families would agree that the true reward of adopting a rescued duck wasn't only giving that duck a happy and healthy life, but also feeling the gratefulness the animal exhibited towards them. There are very few things more rewarding than having a mistreated and fearful animal grow to love and trust you. Under the right conditions this bond can sometimes be even stronger than raising a duck up from a duckling.

- **Charging & retreating**

If you've adopted a shy duck who avoids you when you enter their pen, but then bravely charges after you as you leave—with their neck stretched out and bill focused on your ankles, count this as a blessing. Don't worry, they'll rarely come close enough to make contact; in fact, they usually only come near enough to convince themselves (and any other ducks watching) that they're chasing you out. Honestly, the second you turn on them, they'll instantly retreat (often while bragging). Let them think they have this power over you as you go. It's a great way to boost their confidence, giving them a feeling of control that can eventually assist you in establishing a friendship.

- **Ducks as companion animals**

I'm often asked if ducks are companion animals and the answer is: absolutely and without a doubt! Ducks benefit emotionally, physically, socially and behaviorally from human companionship and humans are winners in this relationship as well. They're affectionate animals with individual personalities and quite clearly able to express their love.

Over the years I've had quite a few ducks in addition to Young Matthew and Young Jeffrey who were extremely fond of giving me hugs. I'd only have to sit down in the hay and they'd jump up and tuck their heads over my shoulder and into the crook of my neck. While I realize most of them are expressing a little more than platonic affection during these moments; they're precious anyway. A hug from a duck simply can't be beat.

An experienced veterinarian once told a friend of mine that of all the human/animal connections he had witnessed throughout his long career, the relationship between humans and ducks (and humans and chickens, incidentally) had always impressed him as one of the most profound bonds of all. Having had plenty of companion animals throughout my lifetime, I'd have to agree, and I think it's because of the level of imprinting that makes this bond so amazingly different. It's something dogs, cats, rabbits, horses and guinea pigs simply don't do. And while parrots can, they tend to maintain a certain level of independence from humans; something ducks simply don't do. A pet duck is willing to surrender themselves *completely* to you.

Isabel with Gulliver

Quarantine

Before adding new ducks to your existing flock you would be wise to consider a quarantine plan first. This is a good way to prevent any new ducks from sharing any little critters or diseases with your own ducks. Beware of making clean health assumptions and skipping this step.

There are six steps you can take to help keep your duck yard clear of invaders. The more steps you take, the safer you're from trouble:

1. *Sanitize:* Clean and sanitize the pet carrier that brought your new duck home to you. Do this far away from your duck pen. If you walked on someone else's property to acquire your duck, clean and sanitize your boots *before* you walk into your own pen to avoid any cross contamination from someone else's duck yard to yours. If you can, set up a kiddy pool inside a portable playpen (away from your duck pen) and let your new duck take a bath. Give them time to preen and remove any transient fecal matter from their feet and feathers. Sanitize the pool when they're finished.

2. *Fecal Exam:* Bring a separate poop sample from each new duck to your vet and ask them to check for parasites *including* coccidia (the lab won't necessarily check for it unless you ask). Results often come back within 24 hours.

3. *Precautionary de-worming:* If you're especially concerned about the conditions your new duck was living in before getting to you, general wormers are available. Ask your vet for details. Do *not* follow internet instructions, which frequently have incorrect and dangerous dosages listed along with misleading advice.

4. *Precautionary delousing:* Apply delousing powder on any new ducks (more on this coming in: *Medical Care*) to prevent lice or mite infestations.

5. *Precursory medical exam:* Consult with your vet before bringing home your new flock member and pre-arrange for your new duck to go in for a baseline medical exam.

6. *14 day minimum quarantine:* While not everyone has the space for this step, if you can pull it off, it would be wise to do so. Because ducks hide their illnesses well, it can take time to notice if something is a little off. While relatively uncommon, this is your only defense against bringing a disease into your existing flock.

If nothing else, I highly recommend you do the fecal exam. Once parasites get into the grounds of your pen they're extremely difficult to remove. If you don't have the space to quarantine your new duck, a large pet carrier kept in a safe and cozy place with food and water inside will more than suffice for the night.

- **Bio-security**

It's vital for the safety of your flock that any of your farmer friends don't come wandering into your duck enclosures with the same shoes and clothing they wore into their pens. This is how contagions are introduced from one property to another. Keep visitors outside of your duck pens unless they come to you with clean clothes and clean shoes.

To keep trouble out of my pens I have all visitors step through a *Footbath Mat* (supplier: Gempler's www.gemplers.com). A 24" x 32" mat can hold up to a gallon of sanitizing solution. I fill the mat with a solution of Virkon S ® mixed with water according to instructions.

Virkon S ® solution is great for cleaning and sanitizing your duck pens, pet carriers, kiddy pools, buckets and bowls as a part of a quarantine regime or just for basic clean up care in and around your pen.

Transporting Ducks

Transporting ducks is simple and safe if you have the right size and number of pet carriers and some cozy bedding inside. I prefer plastic pet carriers, but you can use pet cages as long as they have a solid floor. You don't want wire caging directly under your ducks' delicate webbed feet.

Duck carrier (left) & Isabel sits on my goose carrier (right)

If you're going on a long trip, use carriers that allow your ducks to stand up, stretch and resettle. At the same time, avoid carriers that are too roomy. Your duck shouldn't have enough space to flap their wings. Too much mobility can lead to injury in a moving vehicle.

If you have multiple ducks, consider whether or not they'll get along for the full duration of the trip. You may want to utilize more than one carrier and face the doors towards each other, so that your ducks can still see and comfort each other during the trip. If your ducks are good friends, get a carrier that allows them to travel together.

Hay or straw bedding tends to work best inside pet carriers because shavings tend to get into water bowls and all over the car. Avoid using newspaper, which can remove vital oils from your duck's feathers. Towels can get messy and toe nails can get caught in loose threads, making them a less appealing choice.

Ducks can get car sick, and they do sometimes vomit. Be sure to keep fresh air moving through your vehicle (or air conditioning in hot weather) to help prevent this. A drink of water will help them to feel better and prevent any choking.

No-Spill Water Bowl

If you're going on a trip with your ducks you can purchase a no-spill water dish for the ride. They're specially made for car journeys and you can usually find them in the dog aisle of your local pet store. If you want to save yourself a little money, you can quickly and easily make your own no-spill water bowl.

1. Purchase a disposable container that is the perfect size for your duck.

2. Carefully cut a large hole in the lid, leaving only 1 inch of plastic around the border.

3. Snap the lid onto your bowl and fill it halfway with water. It's dishwasher safe or disposable if it gets really messy.

Homemade no-spill water bowl for traveling

Shipping Adult Ducks

While I do *not* recommend shipping adult ducks, I don't want any Momma Ducks out there making mistakes that could cost lives. If a breeder will be shipping your adult duck to you, the only carrier willing to transport them is Express Mail.

Not all locations qualify for overnight shipping. You can enter origin and destination zip codes on Express Mail's website to ensure a *one day* delivery time. *Never* ship ducks who won't arrive within 24 hours!

If overnight shipping is available from the duck's origin to your destination the following steps can help ensure that your new best friend will arrive safely.

1. *Purchase a shipping carton:* If the shipper doesn't have access to a post office approved poultry box, you can purchase one and have it mailed directly to them (supplier: Horizon Micro Environments www.hm-e.net). While a breeder might suggest utilizing a small, single-stall waterfowl box, these boxes are *very* tight and I wouldn't recommend letting anyone squeeze your future pet duck inhumanely into one unless they're sending you a tiny Bantam breed duck. For all other breeds, I highly recommend purchasing the *Economy N.E.S.T. (Natural Environmentally-Secure Transporters)*, which measures 16" x 16" x 16" and is ideal for shipping one adult duck. They also sell a larger *Swan Nest* (32" x 16" x 20") that can be divided into halves for two ducks.

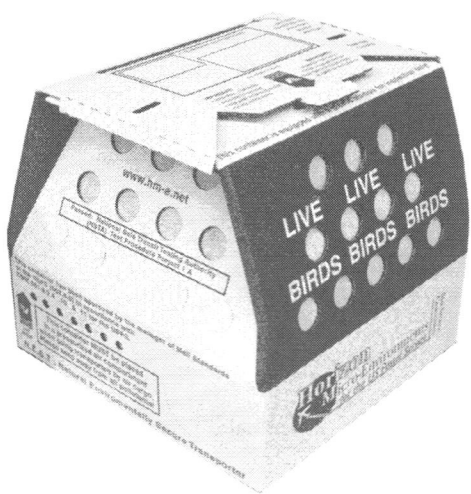

Economy Nest shipping carton
Photo Courtesy of Horizon Micro Environments

2. *Shipping carton preparations:* When the folded box arrives at the shipper's residence (which I'm assuming is a breeder) they can assemble it, set your duck safely inside and then ship them out to you. They should know, but it can't hurt to remind them, to allow your duck a good drink within a half hour of putting them into the box. On the other hand, withholding food 2-3 hours before shipping can help prevent poop pile up. The carton should be bedded with pine shavings to help absorb some of the poop during the trip.

   Some breeders will poke holes into a covered cup and zip tie it into one of the inside corners of the carton. They'll fill the cup with sliced cucumbers to help keep the air inside moist.

3. *List a toll free emergency number:* Be sure to list the toll free cell phone numbers of the shipper (the breeder) *and* the recipient (you) on the carton and actually write "TOLL FREE CELL PHONE" next to each of the numbers. Postal employees won't call you at their expense, so you need to make it free.

4. *List addresses clearly:* Always list shipping and return addresses *clearly* on the carton. Avoid using labels that can peel off. Instead, write on the carton itself in black permanent marker. Seal the address beneath a piece of clear packing tape to prevent any possibility of smudging. You never know if the box might pass through rain on the way on or off a plane

5. *Guaranteed shipping:* Be sure to have the shipper write "RETURN SHIPPING GUARANTEED" clearly on the carton. If the mail system breaks down anywhere along the way and a duck becomes trapped in route, you want the postal system to know they can send the duck back and have their costs covered. Assure the breeder that you'll cover those costs and they'll be happy to write this for you.

6. *Ship during full weeks on Mondays:* You'll have to coordinate this shipment well—a life is depending on you. It's best for the breeder to ship your duck on a Monday or Tuesday during a non-holiday week; this way, if the duck is delayed in shipment for any reason, they aren't at risk of being locked up in a post office or warehouse over a weekend.

- **Never ship ducks in extreme weather**

Never ever ship ducks in the heat of June, July or August—or any time when weather conditions are extremely hot or cold during the transit route since this could lead to a horrible death for your new duck. Also take into consideration any national issues that might hold up shipping or delivery (hurricane threats anywhere along the flight route, for example).

- **Prepare your post office staff**

Talk to your post office staff *before* arranging the shipment with the breeder. They'll tell you what times they receive shipments, so you can arrange to be at home. Talk to them again after you make arrangements with the breeder, so they'll know ahead of time when to expect your duck and to call you immediately upon their arrival. Actually hand them a note they can post for whoever is working that day:

> *A live duck will arrive at this postal location on:*
>
> *Tuesday, April 10th 2014*
>
> *Please call **Kim Link** as soon as they arrive!*
>
> *Local Phone: 888-555-1212*
>
> *Toll Free Cell Phone: 888-555-3434*
>
> *Kim will drive to the P.O. and immediately pick up her duck!*
>
> *Do <u>NOT</u> put her duck on a delivery truck!*

Always pick up your duck at the post office as soon as they arrive. Some post offices will call you before or after they're open to the public to help you get your duck in record time. Never allow your local post office to put your duck on one of their local delivery trucks, or your duck may have to wait through a long delivery route in order to get to you.

These notification guidelines for you and your post office should be followed if ducklings are being shipped to you as well.

Consideration #8
Expense

If you're new to having ducks, there is considerable start-up cost involved in preparing for their arrival:

1. Brooder (heat lamp, shavings, water fount, feeder, thermometer, feather duster)
2. Duck pen construction
3. Duck house, shed or barn construction
4. General supplies: feed dishes, water buckets, heated water buckets, hoses, kiddy pools/ponds, etc.

Once you have your pens established, the cost of having a couple of ducks is pretty minimal:

5. Bedding (hay, straw)
6. Feed, calcium, grit and healthy treats
7. Sand (wintertime pen care)

The exception is when something goes wrong and your duck needs vet care.

8. Vet costs

While vet care is expensive, denying your duck medical treatment when they're ill or injured, or forcing them to succumb to home remedies is flat-out inhumane. If you broke your leg you wouldn't want your neighbor to come over and splint it for you. You'd want to get to the emergency room as fast as you could for some professional care and pain management. Your duck feels pain the same as you do and they deserve the same level of quality care that you do too. If you can't afford vet care for your ducks, then the responsible thing to do is to wait until you can before you add them to your family.

Consideration #9
Seasonal Timing

Keep the season in mind before you bring home ducklings. You'll need to keep them warm. Ducklings brought home in the early spring will need to be protected from the wind and cold until they've lost their fluff and grown their first feathers. Likewise, ducklings brought home in summer, will need to be protected from the heat. Extremes in either direction can be fatal.

Fighting between drakes wanes off in the Fall

If you're bringing home adult ducks seasonal consideration is particularly important. If additional drakes are involved, introductions are best done in the fall—when male hormonal levels have dropped and leveled out. This will help keep chasing and overexcitement to a minimum.

Many drakes get along very well from September – January, especially in colder regions, but be careful not to be fooled into believing that things will always be this harmonious. Many new Momma Ducks have been fooled by how well their drakes get along during their first year, only to discover that things aren't nearly so peaceful the following spring.

Consideration #10
Weather

Your local weather conditions will dictate some of your most difficult challenges. If you're living in the south, summer heat can be overwhelming for your ducks. If you're up north, the chill of winter can be more than you and your ducks can bear. The choice you're about to make is for the long-term, so make sure you're up for all of Mother Nature's challenges before accepting the role of Momma Duck.

Summertime Care

Keeping ducks cool is not always as easy as providing them with shade. While duck feathers help to insulate against the heat, they can only do so much, especially in extreme situations. If you're seeing excessive open-bill panting or the slight lifting and dropping of their wings as they air out their armpits and cool their blood flow, you may want to step into action.

- **Keeping cool**

Kiddy pools can heat up and become unbearable, especially if they're in direct sunlight (if so, you may want to reconsider their placement). You'll need to change the water out frequently to keep them cool and refreshing. While ice can sometimes help, its effects usually aren't very long-lasting beneath the sun. If you're going to utilize this tactic, avoid using large blocks of that can easily pinch webbed feet or toes.

Drinking water buckets should be placed in the shade. Larger buckets stay cooler longer than smaller buckets. Large chunks of ice can be safe and effective in this type of application.

Air conditioners, dehumidifiers and overhead fans can be installed in barns, but be sure to keep them clean. Filters, screens and parts should be checked routinely and maintained according to their instruction booklets to prevent the risk of fire and growth of dangerous molds.

Wintertime Care

Winter can be the hardest time to care for ducks unless you live in a climate where this cold season is obsolete. Consider wintertime care very carefully before you welcome ducks into your family.

- **Keep an open water source**

Your ducks won't care whether or not they have warm or cold drinking water available to them in the colder months, as long as it isn't frozen. I always do a quick temperature check to be sure that their heated water buckets are functioning well, so that I won't come back to find any icy mishaps.

- **Bathing and preening**

Ducks need to bathe and preen in order to fluff, seal and otherwise waterproof their feathers. Nice, tight feathers can retain a decent layer of air, which is then heated by their body. On the other hand, inadequate feather quality leads to poor insulation and poor insulation leads to shivering.

Healthy ducks can usually attend to all of their tidying needs by splash-preening from their bucket of clean drinking water; even so, occasionally, it isn't enough. If your duck is beginning to present untidy feathers or a dirty underside, it's time for them to take a real bath. A fifteen minute swim in a kiddy pool, tub or an open pond once or twice a week will usually remedy any feather problems.

Ducks shouldn't have unsupervised access to a kiddy pool that could freeze over while you're away. Ducks shouldn't be allowed to sit in small bodies of water either (which tend to be much colder than larger ponds or lakes) when there's a risk that they could ice over.

- **Warm feet in cold water**

As long as their swimming water won't freeze over, you don't need to worry about your ducks being cold while swimming. As long as they have good feather quality and we're not talking about temperature or weather extremes, ducks *love* to swim—and that doesn't change much in winter. Ducks have come up with an impressive adaptation to cold water swimming.

The arteries in their legs (which carry warm, oxygenated blood to their webbed feet) intertwine with their veins (which carry cooler blood back from their feet up to their heart again). Think of this circulation system in their legs as being *webbed* (easy to remember, right!). This webbing of intertwining arteries and veins allows the warm re-circulating blood to heat-up the colder returning blood, which helps keep their legs warm by rapidly replacing lost heat.

This heat exchange does result in the cooling of arterial blood, but since ducks don't have much soft tissue in their legs or feet, they don't have the same rich requirements as the rest of their body. The cooled blood going all the way down to their webbed feet manages to be just warm enough to keep their muscles safely oxygenated. This frugality prevents excess heat from being lost inefficiently to the surrounding cold water.

- **Snow on your aviary net**

Many people will forget to even think about their aviary net or top wire's vulnerability to snow. A wet and heavy snow can wreak havoc on your duck's overhead protection. Even the best aviary net and support structure can succumb to extreme damage if left unattended. Even a couple of inches of snow can damage or stretch top netting or wire, and it can also pull down and even break support beams and poles. If this happens, your entire duck pen can cave in on itself. Special attention will have to be placed on your duck's pen during snowstorms. You may need to leave work early or actively monitor it during your normal sleeping hours.

Snow piled on aviary nets can pull them down quickly

Weather changes tend to happen quickly, so I like to monitor my local radar images closely rather than relying on the outdated forecast of a six-o'clock weatherperson. When snowstorms are expected during the night, I set my alarm to go off every 1-2 hours depending on severity. I get out of bed every time it goes off and I check to make sure snow isn't piling up my aviary netting. If it is, I get dressed and go outside to take care of it.

It's easiest to remove snow if it's done frequently. Once the inches begin to pile up, it can take substantially longer to clear away. Snow can usually be removed by walking under your netting (or wiring) and whacking it with a broom handle, just enough to make the snow will fall down through it (keep your hood on!). Depending on the size of your pen and the intensity of the storm, this task can take minutes or even hours.

- **Snow on your electric fence**

Don't forget the weather's effect on your pen's other safety features such as electric fence lines. Snow and ice can quickly disable their effectiveness.

Shut off your electric fence charger and then circle around your pen, checking that all of the lines are clear of wintery debris. Don't forget to turn your charger back on again when you're done.

- **Sanding icy pens**

Icy pens are dangerous for your feathered friends and for you. Remember ducks' legs and feet are very delicate and easily susceptible to injury. Spread sand over any slick areas to help prevent sprained muscles and broken bones *before* you let them out into their pen. This can take some time depending on the size and slope of your pen.

Don't use any snow or ice melting salts or chemicals in or around your duck enclosure. Keep in mind, when the snow eventually melts all of these chemicals will be traveling around your yard in streams and puddles. A duck mucking around in a chemically treated puddle can quickly meet their demise.

- **Unsafe, ice-covered ponds**

During freezing temperatures many duck ponds can be partially to fully frozen. It's important to know when an icy pond is safe and when it's dangerous. Ducks get excited at the prospect of water in any season and love to dive underwater and swim and splash around. If your pond has too much ice coverage, they can get lost under the ice, become trapped and drown. This is especially true of vision-impaired ducks who can have an even more difficult time finding their way back up again.

This pond doesn't have enough exposed surface water
This pond is NOT safe for ducks.

This pond does have enough exposed surface water.
Ripples and surface movement help ducks see the open water.
This pond IS safe for ducks.

Consideration #11
Family Planning

Your female duck will lay eggs whether they're fertilized or not. If she's sharing her pen with a drake, always assume her eggs are viable. Don't take for granted that because you're not witnessing your ducks mate that it isn't happening. In some cases you just might not be seeing it (sneaky ducks!), while in others, and especially in the case of new Momma Ducks, you simply might not be recognizing it. While more experienced Momma Ducks may think I'm kidding, I can assure you I've been contacted *many times* by new Momma Ducks who mistook the mating act entirely and thought their male duck was suddenly attempting to kill their female duck.

The Birds and The Bees

The first time I witnessed a mating ritual between Young Matthew and his new girlfriend I nearly had a heart attack. While I knew exactly what they were doing, I wasn't so sure that it was safe. Even so, I soon realized that there was no reason for me to panic.

Ducks prefer to mate on water—and it's safer and not so crushing for them to do it there than on land. A drake will use his bill to grab onto the feathers on the back of your female's neck. Then he'll pull himself up onto her back. Although your female's head may sink under water temporarily; her nares will soon rise back up again and she'll catch plenty of air before dipping back under again. Experienced drakes will often extend their wings and cup and hold their girlfriend in place. On the other hand, less experienced drakes will do more "surfing" than actual mating.

This mating display ends with males circling and "tooting" in celebration while the females get straight to bathing. If they happen to mate on land, males will run around in a circle and make the same noise while females either take an "air bath" or make a beeline to their water bucket for a good splash-preen.

Deirdre "Dear Heart" courts Young Matthew

Young Matthew accepts her invitation

As long as your females are equal in size to your drakes (or not much smaller), and you don't have more than one drake piling up at one time, they'll be just fine during the act. In fact; I've noticed that it's often the girls who initiate their courtship.

Ask the Stork

A few of the most common questions I've been asked over the years are those regarding waterfowl sexuality. I remember back when I wrote the first edition of this book and an acquaintance of mine gawked embarrassingly when she hit this section. She tried to talk me out of including all these birds and bees and stork essentials, but there was no way I'd even consider it. As long as there are Momma Ducks out there asking me these questions, I'm going to continue to answer them. When she responded that no *other* duck book authors felt the urge to cover this material, I nodded and smiled knowing that this was exactly why mine needed to.

- **What's that spiral thing hanging out of my drake?**

Don't be frightened! The cork-screw looking thing dangling out of the cloaca of your drake is *not* his entrails falling out, but just his penis. Drakes normally keep their goods inside of their body until they're ready to use them and then—*tada!* It looks unusual because it's designed differently with a grooved path that his semen spiral down to get where they're going—kind of like a water park ride. Rest assured, he'll reel it back inside again in a few minutes.

- **Why are my same-gendered ducks mounting each other?**

You may see some of what appears to be mating behavior between same-sexed ducks for a couple of different reasons:

1. What you're witnessing may be a simple pecking order display. Ducks will often mount another duck to secure their own position within the pecking order hierarchy. Both males and females will exhibit this behavior with their same-gendered flock mates throughout the year.

2. On the other hand, you may very well be witnessing a same-sex encounter. Hormonal drakes will sometimes displace their over-excitement and go after another male instead of a female—especially in the spring. On occasion, you may need to protect your drakes from one another if they get a little bit crazy. Separations may be in order until hormone levels decline.

    This behavior isn't limited to drakes. If you have a healthy male-to-female ratio to prevent in-flock fighting, some of your females may get skipped over for mating. In this case don't be surprised when you walk out into your pen and find one of your females "surfing" around on the back of her girlfriend. If you see this behavior on land, you can try to encourage them out onto their pond to prevent any skeletal injuries, but as long as you're your flock members are equally sized, there shouldn't be an issue.

- **Why does my drake keep biting at my hands and wrists?**

A self-defending, frightened or angry duck will often strike at your hands or ankles because that's what's right in front of them. Injured or lame ducks are more vulnerable than other ducks and will often grab-and-pinch more frequently (and sometimes with a good twist) as an act of self-preservation. However, this is not the case when it comes to a duck who knows and trusts you. In this case, your drake is not angry at you or being mean at all, but in fact, he's probably in love with you. You're simply misreading what he's saying.

To a drake (especially a human-imprinted one) a human forearm and hand looks sort of like a female duck's neck and head. You now know that when a male initiates courtship with a female duck he uses his bill to grip onto the feathers behind her neck. If your drake is attempting to nip at your hands, he's just a little confused and doing just that. He's biting at the spot where he thinks you should have your neck feathers and trying to figure out how to hold onto you. Muscovy males can be especially diligent when it comes to this type of behavior, especially in the height of spring fever.

Be careful not to mistake this action for aggression. What you have on your hands is not an angry drake, but a bit of a passionate one. He's telling you that he loves you in one of the only ways he knows how. This is just one of those habits that you're going to have to get used to as part of your Momma Duck experience. Protective clothing like long sleeves and fingerless gloves can help ease the sting of their affections. If it gets too out of hand, try holding back a bit on some of the petting, which can sometimes stimulate hormonal behaviors. You can also try some distraction techniques like taking him on a chaperoned walk or better yet, a swim with his feathery girlfriend, so he can redirect his feelings appropriately.

Your hand and wrist are a bit duck-like in nature

- **Why are my ducks jiggling their heads at me?**

Most ducks prefer to be petted underneath the front of their bellies and then upwards towards the sides of their necks, and you'll often get a jiggle of happiness from them in response. Human-imprinted males and females ducks will both do this and it's often a precursor to a nice ducky hug. They'll jiggle, race towards you and then hop up and thrust their head over your arm or shoulder.

This is just another one of those times when your feathered friend is suddenly finding you quite attractive and is attempting to court you. If you want to tell your duck that you love them back utilizing their own language, shape your hand and wrist, so that it looks like a duck and then flash them some of that same jiggling action. They'll understand just what you're saying and will often start jiggling right back at you in response.

- **Do ducks mate for life?**

In my experience ducks, on the whole, ducks don't mate for life. In fact, they can be quite fickle. Females and males alike will often flirt and have affairs with multiple flock members. They may pick a favorite, but the second a new love interest comes along, they'll often succumb to temptation. Males are especially quick to engage with new female partners.

Miss Swan & Captain Jack on the day of their rescue

This is not to say that they don't form extremely close bonds with one another because they absolutely do. If you want your ducks to be happy, you don't want to remove their loved ones from them. While you may need to put a safety fence between two friends, you don't want to deprive them of each other's company.

In my rescue work I've often removed ducks from ponds in stages and then reunited them with their friends again later. In each instance they *immediately* recognized one another and picked up right where their friendship left off (on one occasion, three years later!). After witnessing so many happy ducky reunions I'm convinced that friends should stay together.

Planned Parenthood

When it comes to family planning, it doesn't really matter that you're ducks are mating. Unlike many other animals, pregnancy is simply not a concern with waterfowl. Although your ducks may have a daily plan when it comes to procreation, you can easily intercept their attempts with your own countermeasures; simply put, just pick up their eggs every day.

Hatching out ducklings should be taken just as seriously as when you brought home your original ducks (more so if you had no idea what you were in for at the time). You have no control over who comes out of those eggs and can easily end up with too many drakes and personality conflicts. Separations may be inevitable and this can be extremely stressful if you don't have the space for it. If you're not fully prepared for new additions, don't let your ducks hatch out ducklings—no matter how tempting it may seem.

- **Collect all eggs daily**

Make it a point to collect all of your duck eggs every day. Some ducks can be a little tricky and find amazing little hiding places for their eggs, so it's good to know the laying patterns of your females. If you're coming up short, time after time, you may want to take a better look around.

I can't tell you how many times I've been told that a duck hid her eggs and "accidentally" hatched out a dozen ducklings. First of all, this was no accident—she absolutely meant to do it. Second of all, there's no way an even halfway decent Momma Duck could be fooled this way. Most domestic ducks have to sit on their nests for 28 days straight in order to incubate them properly. You're kidding yourself if you think anyone who knows a thing about ducks is going to believe you when you say you didn't notice yours sitting on her nest day-in and day-out for four weeks. More often, people think it'll be "fun" and then realize the seismic mistake they've just made as twelve ducklings waddle by.

Unless you want this to be you, no matter how your duck protests, move her aside and take her egg away every single day. Most ducks learn pretty quickly not to get attached to their eggs; once this happens they begin leaving them behind as they move onto more interesting activities. If you have a duck who likes to bite, don't let her talk you out of it; instead, put on a pair of gloves and take them away.

Occasionally a broody duck will stay in her nest even after you remove her daily egg. If this happens, remove her from the nest and close the area off so she can't get at it. Once she's out of sight, go ahead and dismantle her nest, spreading the hay around evenly on the floor. She may be agitated at first, but she'll eventually eat and drink and move on to other healthy behaviors. Muscovy females are usually the most relentless when it comes to this kind of behavior, so be prepared to be firm.

- **Egg addling**

If you have a duck with a reproductive disorder, your vet may suggest that you don't pick up her eggs. Many ducks will stop their egg-laying after their nest is filled with 8-14 eggs; therefore, allowing them to fill their nest is nature's way of flipping off the switch.

In this case you can remove her daily egg, addle it (shake it vigorously) and write the date on the egg with a permanent marker. Do the same each additional day, addling both old and new eggs one-by-one as part of your routine. As an added security measure, candle your eggs by holding them up to a strong flashlight in a dark room. If you see veins creeping over the inside of the shell, you may want to put it in the freezer overnight before tossing it.

The idea here is that sooner or later your duck will stop her egg-laying and start nesting instead—disrupting her laying cycle. Then, once she realizes her eggs aren't viable she'll eventually abandon her nest. That's the hope anyway, but be prepared, because some ducks won't leave their nests until their rotten eggs start popping. To beat this, you can try swapping out her daily eggs for wooden ones instead. You can locate wooden eggs of similar size and weight to your own duck's eggs in craft stores. The nice thing is they tend to retain heat just like a real egg, further adding to the deception. This is enough to fool some ducks into sitting on a Pinocchio clutch.

While this strategy may prove effective, it only offers a temporary solution. Sooner or later your duck will begin her egg-laying again and the entire sequence will need to be repeated. Even worse, this strategy tends to initiate a depressing cycle of events for your duck who will grow attached to her eggs only to have her heart broken.

Hatching

If you've considered everything carefully and have the means to accommodate new additions, allowing your duck to brood a nest of eggs might be right for your family.

Be wary of giving (or selling) any of your ducklings to people who have no idea what they're in for and might toss their adult duck on a local pond when they become bored with it. If you're not careful, you can easily become the root cause of animal neglect in your own area.

- **Avoid incubating eggs**

For those who insist on hatching out ducklings, avoid incubators and let your ducks do the work. Incubation requires careful attention to temperature and humidity as well as timed knowledge on egg turning. Requirements change in stages throughout the entire duration and even the smallest of mistakes can lead to disaster.

I've been contacted by *too many* people who've hatched out ducklings as a "fun" project only to end up with seriously disabled ducklings. In every case these mishaps were caused by improper incubation techniques brought on by their own inexperience.

Human conducted incubation should only be done by experienced individuals or under their *direct* guidance. Be careful, because many people will claim to know exactly what they're doing when they actually know little more than you do. The key to detecting these imposters is they're most likely to tell you how "simple" hatching is and will usually fail to offer any detailed information. A proficient person will know that this is precision work and will be able to answer questions regarding week to week temperature, humidity and turning rates right off the cuff. Avoid assistance from people who need to look up procedures and appear to be learning from books or the internet as they go.

Be proactive and ask your mentor how many times they've hatched out an abnormal duckling and what became of their unwanted mistakes. If you ask it in a matter-of-fact tone, some amateurs will actually admit to their faults. More often, however, these so-called *experts* won't tell you about the imperfect hatchings or the number of ducklings that they have culled. Remember: The duckling you hatch out is left with a lifetime of enduring the consequences of your mistakes.

- **Let your duck do the work**

Ducks are innately designed for hatching out ducklings and this labor of love and should be entirely entrusted to them. They instinctively know what to do, how to ensure the perfect temperature and humidity and just when to roll their eggs. Of course, as with any animal, some ducks are better at this task than others and will hatch out larger broods.

If you're going to allow your duck to hatch out ducklings, consider how many ducklings you should let her hatch. Assume that every egg she sits on is viable. Do *not* account for duds. Ducks often won't start seriously incubating until their nest is full, so don't remove extra eggs. As they lay them, you can remove, addle and mark them and then put them back into the nest, or better yet swap them out with wooden eggs. In this manner, you can easily keep a lid on the maximum number of hatchlings she'll have.

Once your duck starts setting on her eggs, remember to candle (set them on an upturned flashlight in a dark room) any addled eggs for their first 5-7 days to ensure no red veins appear on the inner-shell surface. Many ducks will eventually push non-viable eggs out of the nest, but… not always.

Consideration #12
Time Investment

The next thing you need to consider is whether or not you have *time* for ducks in your life. I've seen more than my share of waterfowl care resources that boast that ducks are practically "maintenance free," but this is simply not the case, and this myth thrives at the core of the abandonment issue. It seems like a nice idea at first, but once reality kicks in many owners will dump off their pet to free up their schedules.

Personal schedule

Make sure your personal (and often changing) schedule can handle the start-up task of building a ducky safe-haven as well as daily, weekly, monthly and seasonal responsibilities. On any given day Momma Ducks should not only be prepared to spend the time accomplishing care-related tasks, but also interacting with their pets.

Healthy adult ducks need a quick attending to in the morning and a lengthier visit in the evening. Most Momma Ducks I know spend *at least* two hours a day with their feathered friends and even more on weekends.

- **Morning routines for ducks**

Morning routines begin before you go to work and usually entail fifteen to thirty minutes of time, depending upon the season and how many ducks you have. Doors are unlocked and ducks are allowed out of their evening accommodations and into their daytime enclosure. Fresh hay, food and water are provided and a little time is spent saying good-bye for the day. Be wary, ducks can be very adept at talking you into playing hooky for the day!

- **Evening routines for ducks**

When you come home, your ducks will require a follow-up routine as well. After replenishing food, providing fresh water and touching up hay again, it's time to enjoy your flock. Even shy ducks look forward to seeing you (especially if you come with treats!), so don't deprive them of your attention. Remember, this pleasant time of ducky interaction is the whole point of having feathered friends in the first place. Ducks are great stress-relievers and provide wonderful end-of-day therapy. If you give love to them, they'll send even greater love back to you too.

Young Matthew wants my time more than anything

- **Weekend routines for ducks**

Weekends will require more of your time and involvement. Keeping pens properly cleaned and maintained is best done regularly to keep tasks manageable. The longer you wait to clean out a barn, the longer it's going to take you. Depending on your water system (ponds, kiddy pools, etc), you may need to set aside extra time for its maintenance as well. None of these tasks are so overwhelming as to be unmanageable, but you need to be prepared for what you're getting into before you bring your new ducks home.

Fun weekend waddles while foraging for goodies, pleasant quacky chats by the waterside and hugs in the barn are just a few of the great things Momma Ducks don't want to miss out on. Ducks are welcome members of the family when you see all of your responsibilities as part of the joy rather than as an added burden.

- **Vet trips**

Trips to the vet aren't often needed when you have younger ducks on good diets and in safe pens, but as they get older they're more likely to need some professional help here and there, or even routinely. If your schedule doesn't allow for much leeway in this regard, this consideration can suddenly gain some extra weight.

- **Continual care for ducklings**

Unlike taking care of adult ducks in the morning and evening, ducklings should ideally be checked on frequently throughout the day, especially if you want them to imprint on you. Missing out on this valuable time with your ducklings is missing out on one of life's greater pleasures. And remember the more you bond with them now, the stronger your shared bond will be when they mature.

Consideration #13
Finding a Duck Sitter

Plans for the evening? If you're about to head out of the house and won't be back before nightfall, you'll need to consider your ducks. You may need to lock them up a little early in order to make it to the event on time, or you may need to arrive to the function a little late, after ducky bedtime. I can't tell you how many times I've had to leave a social gathering early to get home on time for ducky night-night. Sometimes I'll leave temporarily and then return again once the ducks are set for the night.

Young Matthew and Young Jeffrey don't like it when I'm late. As I've mentioned before, I have an extremely predator-proof pen; even so, the boys don't like to be outside after the sun goes down. If I'm even five minutes late, they're standing at the gate, quacking to go up into the barn.

One time I had to leave for a few days and needed my father to duck-sit while I was away. Not only did I give him a personal walk-through to show him morning and evening routines, but I also made an instructional video that demonstrated their daily routine. These days, with the waterfowl sanctuary in place, daily routines are much more complex, so we take our family vacations separately. If my daughter and I are heading out for a few days, my husband stays home with the flock, and vice versa.

Ducks are very habitual creatures, and they want to do things the way they always do things—without any improvisation. If your sitter tries to stray from the path, they can cause confusion and stress. The closer your duck sitter adheres to your ducks' normal routine, the easier it'll be for everyone involved.

Pet sitters must be trustworthy and punctual. If they don't show up before sundown to load up your ducks, your ducks could be left outside in a precarious situation. I can't tell you how many times I've been contacted by someone who lost their duck to an irresponsible duck sitter who either didn't show up on time to lock up their flock for the night, or who did an improper head count and left one poor little duck outside. Predators take full advantage of these types of mistakes. Be very wary of who you choose to help you out when you're away.

It's always a great idea to leave a checklist for your pet sitter to help ensure everything gets done correctly.

Duck Sitter's Checklist:
✓ 1. Load up all of the ducks before sundown @ 6:30 p.m.
✓ 2. Do a head count and make sure all 8 ducks are safely inside
✓ 3. Watch each duck as they load up and make sure everyone looks healthy (no boo-boos!)
✓ 4. Make sure all food dishes are full
✓ 5. Change out all water buckets and refill them with fresh water
✓ 6. Refresh any messy spots in the barn with fresh hay
✓ 7. Double check that each duck is in their proper place and with their correct friend for the night
✓ 8. Close barn window
✓ 9. Close and latch all interior gates and close and lock the main door on your way out
✓ 10. Call me as soon as you're finished locking up (cell: 888-555-3434)
*Your duck sitting list may vary depending on your own personal situation!

If you're going to be away for a few days make sure your pet sitter knows exactly how to reach you at any given time and that they're willing to bring your ducks to the vet if an emergency arises. Post the business cards of your vet and your emergency vet in your barn where they can be quickly accessed.

When I duck-sit for families who've adopted ducks from the sanctuary, I have them sign a contract that authorizes my vet to charge their credit card for an emergency care. It also stipulates the maximum amount that can be charged in the event of an emergency: *"Sky's the limit!"* While there's never been a case of an actual emergency, it's good to have a plan in place.

Consideration #14
Letting Go

Letting go is the most difficult thing a Momma Ducks will ever have to do. These feathery darlings just can't stay with us as long as we'd like them to.

Euthanasia

Although no one likes to think about it, families sometimes need to make a choice when it comes to the care of their fading duck, especially if pain or suffering that has no hope of relief is involved. I take my husband and my vet's opinions into serious consideration as well when deciding whether or not to euthanize one of my ducks. I only proceed if the decision is clear and all three of us are in absolute agreement.

- **Timing**

I can usually see it in the eyes of my duck when they've had enough of this world and are ready to move on. There's just something that changes from one day to the next that's so apparent to me. Even so, there have been occasions where I was on the wire. At these times where a borderline decision needs to be made, my husband will ask me:

1. Is there a reasonable chance your duck's health might suddenly and severely decline, leading to suffering?
2. Is there a reasonable chance your duck's health might severely decline while you're away or sleeping?
3. Is there a reasonable chance your duck might decline during odd hours when an ER vet is harder to get to?
4. Is there a reasonable chance your duck could decline suddenly and you might not make it to a vet on time?
5. Can you live with yourself if one of the above scenarios happens because you didn't euthanize your duck?

Your answers to these questions can often help you to make the right decision at the right time.

- **Together or alone?**

When the time comes to let go of one member of a mated pair or close friendship it will be time to face the decision of whether or not the healthy duck should be present during the procedure.

1. Will my surviving duck be alarmed by the sudden disappearance of their partner?

While all ducks mourn the loss of friends, it tends to be much more pronounced in small, two-duck flocks. If you have a sole survivor of a pair you'll surely be witnessing grief and loneliness in your surviving duck.

It's not uncommon for a surviving duck to mistakenly believe that the duck who has passed away is missing or lost. A duck who pines for a missing flock member can roam their enclosure searching and calling for their lost partner for weeks or even months. This is especially true when there are no other friends to help distract them from this behavior. On the other hand, if their friend has been sick for a while, they probably know it. Ducks whose friends are outwardly symptomatic will still mourn, but are less likely to react as if their partner has suddenly vanished.

If you only have two ducks and you suspect your surviving duck will exhibit a "missing friend" reaction, the option of taking them along for that final vet visit can be examined more closely.

2. Will my surviving duck be more stressed by the vet visit than by the loss?

Before bringing a surviving duck along on a final vet visit, you should consider *their* stress levels. Remember, ducks thrive on routine. If they haven't traveled much, or don't travel well and get carsick, this may not be a good idea; in fact, it may only add to their distress.

While you may be tempted to bring a surviving duck along solely for the sake of comforting a sick duck during their final moments, this usually isn't a good idea in and of itself. Ducks are often too stressed to offer much comfort during vet visits.

Together or alone is a difficult decision and there often is no right answer; there are often pros and cons for each side. Making it even more difficult to decide is the weight of your own worry and anxiety. Trust your instincts and choose the option that you believe will be least stressful for your duck.

3. Can I prepare my surviving duck for an upcoming loss?

When I have a duck who's terminally ill at the sanctuary, I'll often prepare their partner for the loss by introducing a new duck to their pen. Months later, when the inevitable comes to pass, their partner already has a new friend to help them through their mourning. This prearranged friendship averts the need for your surviving duck to vet accompaniment during that final vet visit.

4. What can I expect if I do bring my other duck along for that final vet visit?

As painful as it will be for your pet, witnessing the death of their flock mate allows them to mourn properly while preventing them any undue stress that a sudden or unexplained disappearance might cause.

Once the injections are administered and your sick duck has left this world and crossed over, your surviving duck will likely understand pretty quickly—usually within thirty seconds. Lamentation is sometimes witnessed in an open bill that trembles slightly. More often than not, a survivor will grow suddenly quiet. There's no need to stretch this event out, so once they've been given a chance to understand, it's time to get them back home to more familiar things.

5. How can I help my duck through their period of mourning?

Ducks in mourning will sometimes refuse to load up into their barn at night, believing that their friend is being accidentally left outside. Once you get them indoors, they may quack in distress or agitation while looking to you for help.

While it can be devastating to witness, remember that you're their Momma Duck and it's up to you to try to hold it together and provide some much-needed reassurances. If you have only one remaining duck, spend as much time with them as possible and encourage lots of enrichment activities—including plenty of treats, which are also effective if you're seeing any loss of appetite. The sooner you get them back into their regular routine, the less stress they'll experience.

A mirror is an excellent source of companionship for a solitary duck until a new friend can be brought home for them. This is not to be seen as "replacing" your lost duck, but rather, meeting the immediate needs of their left-behind friend. While you may not be ready, your duck most assuredly is.

- **Medical procedure**

When final moments arrive, few of us are in the proper state of mind to begin asking our vet questions about how they'll be easing our sick duck quietly over to the other side. While it may be uncomfortable to read this now, it may help make things a little less stressful for you down the road.

Most vets will use a two injection procedure when putting a duck to sleep. Some vets will give both injections in front of you while others will administer the first in a back room and then bring you your duck before giving them the second injection. For the emotional sake of my ducks, I prefer to be present for both injections, so that they're always with someone familiar. I just can't have any of my once-abandoned ducks feeling that kind of despair again at the end of their lives.

When you and your duck are ready, your vet will administer the first injection, which is an intramuscular sedative that induces euphoria, commonly Telazol. This is a mixture of Tiletamine (dissociative anesthetic) and Zolazepam (sedative). Together these two drugs induce an extremely effective sedation that approximates complete anesthesia where pain is not felt by your duck. Some ducks will flap their wings during this state and try to fly. They aren't in pain or uncomfortable, they're just in a euphoric state. I sometimes wonder where they're trying to fly to…

The second injection is administered intravenously. This one will be a type of Euthanisol and it will cause rapid cardiac arrest.

- **Cremation**

I have all of my ducks cremated and then returned to our sanctuary's cemetery where they're each properly memorialized. If you want, you can purchase a little duck-shaped urn pendant (supplier: Whisper In The Heart www.whisperintheheart.com) to hold a tiny amount of ashes, small feathers, or any other dainty item that helps you feel closer to your lost pet.

One Without The Other

Each duck will leave this world according to their own clock and while you may need time to recuperate from this loss, you may be left with a very lonely duck who simply can't wait.

- **Duck mourning**

I've personally witnessed flock depression when a member of the group passes away. Sometimes all flock members are affected, while other times just one or two ducks demonstrate concern. It depends on the personalities of your individual ducks, their particular group dynamic and the role the departed duck had within their family.

You may notice a change in diet, or witness an unwillingness to partake in usual routines or even fatigue. Some ducks will refuse to swim or frequent places where they used to go with their beloved companion while others will stick closest to those special places.

It can take some time for your flock to re-settle after the departure of one of their friends—anywhere from a few days to a few months. As powerful as your own personal grieving may be, there's nothing tougher than seeing one of your ducks suffering as well, but you have to keep yourself from tumbling into a downward spiral. Your duck is counting on you to remedy everything and they're there to help you through the loss as well.

- **Human mourning**

Bringing home a new duck can be an extremely difficult step if you're one of those Momma Duck's who worries they may be "replacing" someone. But let me assure you, this is not what's happening here. You're simply setting your own personal needs aside and attending to the emotional needs of your surviving duck.

Here are two types of emails I commonly receive through the sanctuary:

1. My duck was killed by a fox and I want another duck to replace my duck. Can I buy one of yours?

2. My eleven year-old duck just passed away and my other duck is very lonely. I'd like to find her a new friend. Can you help?

The first family isn't showing any signs of remorse at all, and they literally appear be looking to replace one duck with another duck as if they're all one and the same. The second family is clearly concerned for the welfare of their remaining duck who they've had for a long time and care for. Now let me ask you this: When you read the email from the second family, did the thought that they were trying to replace their duck even enter your mind? It didn't cross mine at all.

Don't judge yourself so harshly when bringing home a new companion. Whether it's for the sake of helping your remaining duck through their recovery, or to help in you in your own healing, your lost feathered friend won't look back at you and think you're doing some thoughtless swapping. They know you and they love you for meeting the emotional needs of their left-behind friend.

- **A Momma Duck's grief**

Grief counseling is a huge part of running my sanctuary. Momma Ducks often turn to me during these raw and hollowing moments of loss because they know that I've been there and completely understand the turmoil they're going through.

1. *Don't blame yourself:* Momma Ducks often blame themselves for the loss of their ducks, telling me what they would do differently if they had it all over again. I always ask them, *"Did you do the best you knew how to do at the time?"* This is not to be confused with what you may know now. If the answer is, *"Yes"* then it's time to forgive yourself. Take what you've learned from this experience and use it to improve the lives of your other ducks; let the loss teach you, but don't let it defeat you. That's not what your lost pet wants for you.

2. *Ducks hide things:* If you didn't notice your duck acting a little differently, or didn't put enough emphasis on any minor behavioral changes until it was too late, don't beat yourself up over it. Even the best Momma Ducks will occasionally miss a few mild symptoms. It takes an experienced eye and years of practice to outwit your tricky little feathered darlings. They like to hide things and they're very good at it. If you were deceived by their "all-is-well" act, you're not alone. Learn from it and move on, but don't blame yourself.

3. *They have no regrets:* I'm a person who believes that when we leave this world, we don't take our pain, anger or regrets with us to that heavenly place that awaits us. This being said, *even if* there was an accident or you did make a mistake, do you honestly think your duck is looking back and begrudging you for it? Or do you think they're remembering their Momma Duck and all those wonderful swims in the pool, waddles through the garden and hugs in the barn with a tremendous amount of love. Trust that they've given you the gift of forgiveness and graciously accept it from them.

4. *Remember the good times:* Getting those last few days or hours out of your mind can seem hopeless, but you have to take that step. Would you want to be remembered for your final moment on this earth, or would you prefer to be remembered for all those great moments that happened along the way? *Exactly.* Each time one of those memories of their final moments comes to mind I want you to actively think of a really great or touching memory instead. The point of this task is to allow yourself to grieve, but to do it in a positive way that honors the memory of the one you've lost.

Enrichment

Enrichment

Once you've decided to add ducks to your family you'll most likely want to engage in some fun activities together. Good Momma Ducks want their ducks to live happy and enriched lives as opposed to sitting in a pen, devoid of activities. Here are some of the fun things that Young Matthew and Young Jeffrey and all of their sanctuary friends like to do to pass the time.

Enrichment #1
My Ducky Diary

After publishing the first edition of this pet duck guidebook, I became inspired by the large number of requests I received for *more* ducky enrichment ideas. In response, I put together a fun, pocket-sized duck journal entitled: *"My Ducky Diary."*

Momma Ducks are given an entertaining and thought-provoking question about their duck for every day of the year and space to record their answers.

And, as if that isn't enough, it also gives Momma Ducks a weekly photo and description of an amusing ducky activity.

If the enrichment ideas in the following pages aren't enough for you and your ducks, this companion book is a great way to go! And... as with this book, a portion of the proceeds directly benefit the rescued ducks at Majestic Waterfowl Sanctuary.

Enrichment #2
Water

Without a doubt, water is the greatest source of pleasure for a duck, and they don't really care what form it comes in: a bucket, a pool, a hose or a pond.

Kiddy Pools

Some ducks will sit in their kiddy pool all day long, while others will only take quick, refreshing dips. One of their favorite activities is pulling dirt and mud into the water with them, so don't be disheartened when their newly cleaned, blue pool turns brown within minutes—*that's all part of the fun!* Although the water is muddy, it's still fresh and safe for your ducks to swim in and drink. It isn't until it's contaminated with duck poop that you'll need to clean it again. Kiddy pools need to be emptied and refilled with fresh water at least 1-2 times daily, depending on how many ducks you have and how much time they're spending in it. If two cleanings a day isn't enough to keep up with your flock, then consider adding an additional pool to their pen.

- **Kiddy pool safety tips:**

1. Kiddy pools should be sunk into the ground to avoid potentially serious leg and foot injuries.

2. Water sources are exciting places; avoid slippery surfaces around your pool to prevent accidents from taking place.

Ducks love it when you show up to change out their water and will soon recognize and appreciate the wonder of your garden hose. Emptying and filling pools is an enrichment activity in and of itself. Ducks are quickly drawn to any spilled water and love to play around in puddles. They pitter-patter their webbed feet up and down, splashing the water and then they wriggle their bills into the mud, looking for treats. It simply doesn't get much better than this when you're a duck. But wait... there's more! When you lift their kiddy pool out of the ground to clean it, your ducks will be thrilled to discover a goldmine of delicious snacks underneath. More on this later!

Garden Hose

The garden hose is not only an essential tool for refilling kiddy pools, but also a wonderful way to bring good cheer to your ducks.

- **Garden hose safety tips:**

1. Excitement levels can escalate quickly when a hose is unraveled in a duck pen. Be careful to avoid tripping hazards. Remember, your little friends can be quite clumsy.

2. Avoid spraying your ducks with a hose that has been lying out in the sun, or you could scorch your feathered friends. Test the temperature of the water first.

Hot days are great days to string out the hose and stir up some excitement. Set it to a light spray and aim the cold water a foot or two up into the air. Some ducks will run around and dart through the shower while others will get right to foraging in the puddles of mud that are forming beneath it. If your water source isn't arched high enough, your ducks will most likely turn their bellies into the spray of water and enjoy a cooling tummy rub as it courses down and over their webbed feet.

Adjust the spray to a lighter mist and aim the water high over their heads and watch a different, more soothing reaction. You can even add a sprinkler attachment and leave it on for a few minutes of fun.

Ponds

Walks to small ponds or streams can be similar fun-filled adventures. These happy places tend to have lots of tasty goodies for ducks to eat. They'll quickly scarf down tadpoles, crawfish, frogs and small fish along with a host of other creepy-crawly critters you probably don't want to know about.

- **Pond safety tips:**

1. Don't let your ducks into water if there's a chance that a snapping turtle could be hiding in wait. They can quickly and easily amputate your duck's foot or leg.

2. Make sure ponds are small enough that you can get your ducks back off the water again when it's time to go back to their pen.

Tip #2 is especially vital if you've brought home adult ducks who are less likely to follow your lead when you tell them it's time to go. These kind of pond adventures aren't safe for new ducks until they're *completely* settled into their new home with you.

Tours to ponds need to be done in small stages and swims are strictly off-limits until newcomers have been with you long enough to know to stick close and move along when told. You'll know when your ducks are ready for longer walks and pond excursions. If you're nervous at all about how well they'll behave (or more aptly, misbehave), then they're probably not at that point yet.

Even the best ducks sometimes refuse to come off of a pond now and then. When my boys act up, I use a long, extendable pole (swimming pool vacuum poles work great in this capacity) to coax them off of their large fenced-in pond. I slowly sweep the pole across the water, a few inches over the surface and encourage them off. After doing this once or twice, they learn to come off the water as soon as the pole makes its appearance. For larger bodies of water, you may need a kayak or inflatable boat to round up your stubborn flock.

Whatever you do, have your back-up plan ready, so you don't have to leave your ducks alone and vulnerable to predators while you go for your duck removal supplies. In addition, never let your ducks get away with their stubborn refusal to come off the water. I know they're cute, but it's vital that they learn to listen to you.

Your Swimming Pool

I'm always happily impressed with the number of Momma Ducks who allow their ducks to swim in their pools with them. If you're not offended by a little duck poop in your pool, this option just might be for you—provided you don't drink the water. No kidding, ducks in pools is simply not a safe option for families with small children who might swallow water.

- **Swimming pool safety tips:**

1. Filter intake and outtake points can be extremely dangerous. To avoid risks of drowning, never leave your duck unattended in your swimming pool.

2. Give your duck a safe way to enter and exit your pool. If they don't have one, then *stay in the water with your duck* at all times.

If you want your duck to swim in your pool with you then you'll need to make it safe for them. High levels or continued exposure to chlorine (and other pool chemicals) can cause feather damage, dry skin, peeling bills, eye irritation and when ingested... *well...* do you drink your pool water? It's just not good for them and it can interfere with healthy levels of intestinal flora.

This is why informed Momma Ducks who share their pools with their flock opt for a salt water pool system in lieu of a chlorine mechanism. Salt water systems use low amounts of salt that aren't dangerous and won't harm your beloved duck. There are a variety of salt water pool systems available on the market today and they all use the same process. Ask your local swimming pool dealer for more information.

Your bathtub

Don't laugh! Plenty of Momma Ducks bring their ducks inside for spa nights and a walk around the house.

- **Bathtub safety tips:**

1. Never leave a duck alone in a tub. They can get into all kinds of trouble and even fly out while you're in another room. Make sure all soaps and ingestible items are out of reach and stay close to the action.

2. Make sure the tub is clean of chemicals or soap, which can ruin your duck's feather quality by stripping them of their oil. Water temperature can be anywhere between cool and lukewarm.

3. Invest in a rubber faucet/spout cover to prevent accidents. You can find one of these in the baby aisle of your local store (and they do have ducky ones)!

Ducks love colorful tub toys, especially those that involve waterworks, just be sure they're safe and have no small parts that can be swallowed.

Enrichment #3
Walks & Foraging

Taking your ducks on little journeys to safe parts of your yard can be a lot of fun. If you have a garden, they'll love foraging for all kinds of bugs in it, just keep them away from your lettuce patch or you won't have any left!

Keep Your Eyes Open to Danger

Ducks are quick to see dangers before you do, so pay close attention to their body language and take an interest in what they're looking at. When you see them tip their heads up to the sky, be sure to do so yourself. If they sound an alarm quack, you need to take a good look around and figure out what's startling them and then react appropriately.

Whenever my ducks stretch their necks to look at anything, I've learned to look too. Whatever you do, stay close to your ducks and don't leave them alone for a second. If an emergency arises and you need to break away from your flock, lead them back to the safety of their enclosure before parting ways. Predators are often closer than you think and they're patient and opportunistic. They don't have a problem watching and waiting for long periods of time until the right moment presents itself; and when it does, they're much faster than your ducks—or you. Watching your ducks from across the yard or worse yet, from the window won't help them one bit when a predator drops down from the sky.

Taking New Ducks on Walks

Taking human-imprinted ducks on walks can be pretty simple business because they know you, but taking adult newcomers on walks can be quite different.

- **Feeling entirely at home**

I usually advise Momma Ducks to keep their new ducks in their pen for *at least* two solid weeks after their arrival (longer if you have a particularly shy or nervous duck) before taking them on outside excursions. Ducks who are given time to embrace their pen will often return quite eagerly to it (especially if there's fun stuff inside!).
New ducks can panic easily and take off in unexpected directions when they see or hear something out of the ordinary (and just about everything is out of the ordinary to a newcomer). Give them time to get used to the sights and sounds surrounding their duck pen before taking them for walks outside.

If your new duck is still acting nervously when you visit their pen, it's not time to take them out yet. On the other hand, if your new duck runs over to greet you or follows your other ducks over to say hello, then it's probably safe to start taking them on outside adventures. You're waiting for your duck to feel comfortable and entirely at home in their new space. Once they do, they're far less likely to panic and race off in an unforeseen direction. In fact, a scared duck will often head back to the known safety of their pen. This is *exactly* what you want. If you think your anxious duck might scatter somewhere other than towards their enclosure, you're probably asking too much of them yet.

- **Flock cohesiveness**

If you've added new ducks to your existing flock, don't let your newcomers out of their pen until you're absolutely certain they've all bonded and become a single, cohesive flock. You want to be sure there's no doubt that they'll all stick close to you and your original ducks while waddling around. The last thing you want is to be chasing multiple groups of ducks around your yard in an emergency.

- **Friends & small steps**

If you have ducks that already know the routine, your new ducks will most likely follow them while they learn the ropes. You'll be amazed how quickly newcomers figure out the way to go, especially if you have a consistent routine in place for them.

Keep their first trip outside of their pen close in proximity and brief in time. Do this multiple times to slowly build their confidence. Each time let them forage a little further away and for a little longer until you reach those areas of your yard that you would like them to frequent and enjoy.

- **Portable playpens & a helper**

If your newcomer is proving a bit timid you may want to utilize portable playpen fencing as an added measure of protection while they learn to go for walks. You can connect multiple fences together to make clear paths and play areas for your newcomers to follow. It normally only takes a matter of days for them to learn the routine, provided it's done at least once a day and occurs around the same time.

You can usually tell when it's safe to discontinue using these portable pens by your duck's behavior. I also highly recommend having an extra person standing by when dealing with ducks who are a little anxious about leaving their pen.

- **Waddle wands & hand signals**

I simply wouldn't know what to do without my waddle wand. What's a waddle wand? It can be a broom handle, a ski pole or even a long branch. Whenever I walk Young Jeffrey and Young Matthew out of their pen and up the hill to the little pond in my yard, I follow them with my waddle wand in hand. If they start to veer off course I simply use my waddle wand to gently steer them back in the appropriate direction again. The waddle wand is merely an extension of your own arm and you don't have to move it much, or even get close to them with it in order to get a good reaction.

I was surprised to discover that ducks are pretty good at understanding directional hand signals. I can point to most individuals in my flock and direct them to step forward through a gate while holding a palm up to those members who should remain where they are. Ducks can definitely learn to associate your hand signals with expected movements as long as you're clear and consistent and you use them frequently as part of their routine.

Enrichment #4
Healthy Treats

Giving your duck delicious treats is a fun and hands-on way for you to interact with each other, but remember to keep these snacks healthy.

Earthworms

No doubt about it, my ducks go absolutely crazy when they see me coming with worms. Whenever they see me trekking off into the forest with my bucket in hand, they stretch their necks up and quack with excitement. They learned early on that whenever I go down that wooded path I come back with more night crawlers than they can eat. If you have a shy duck you want to befriend, worms work every time. They just can't resist those squirming yum-yums.

When my boys were younger I'd take them on foraging walks around our small pond. I don't have an aversion to picking up worms, but after a while my hands would get pretty gross and messy, so I started using a pair of chopsticks to pick them up off the ground. It was hilarious to watch Young Jeffrey and Young Matthew eating worms off these human utensils. I used them to poke around in the grass and leaves while my boys pay super close attention and then when I stumbled upon a worm, I'd point to it with one of the chopsticks and yelp, *"A worm, a worm! I found a worm!"* They just couldn't get to their bills in there quick enough. They'd even open their wings and use them to try to push each other out of the way, racing to be the one to nab the treat first. It really was a project trying to get them to take turns.

Another fun thing to do is to dump a dozen night crawlers into an empty bucket. Then go find a non-toxic weed to pull up, leaving as much dirt in the roots as possible. Next, wet the root clump with a hose and set the plant into the bucket gently down on top of the worms. Place the bucket and its contents into a cool shady spot for about an hour. When you come back all of the worms should've disappeared into the root ball. Now it's time to play. Bring the plant into your duck pen and lay it flat on the ground. Your ducks will immediately come over to investigate the goodness and the minute they begin poking around in those roots they'll begin unburying the hidden treasures inside.

Cricket Box

Female ducks tend to be better hunters than their counterparts and often enjoy the challenge of catching fast-moving crickets more so than boys. I like making cricket boxes for my ducks because the fun can last for hours. For this activity, you can either go into the woods and turn over some stones to catch your own crickets, or you can go to a pet store and purchase a container of crickets. If you're catching your own crickets, find a small box to fill, one that's about four inches in size. Once you've finished cricket hunting, go into your duck pen.

A box full of crickets makes for tasty treats, just ask Lil Ms. Bee!

Carefully cut four small holes along the bottom edge of your cricket box, one on each of its four sides. When finished, set the container down, so that the holes are resting near the ground and acting as little cricket doors. The more crickets you have in your box, the faster they'll begin emerging and the quicker your ducks will begin having fun.

Watermelon

While it can take some ducks a little time to learn to appreciate a good watermelon, I've never known one who didn't take to it given the chance. There are few things better than a chilled watermelon on a hot, summer day. Most ducks will eat their melon right out of the rind.

Most ducks love watermelon!

Leaf Lettuce

During the winter, when grass is unavailable, ducks should have greens in their diet—they love greens. Even so, lettuce can be fun year round. If you're not good with a knife, use a pair of scissors to cut up larger leaves into smaller, safer bits. You don't want your ducks eating big leafy pieces or long, uncut stems because they can ball up in their crops or gizzards and cause digestive issues.

In warmer weather I like to float lettuce treats in water bowls and kiddy pools because when you have ducks, a quick way to make just about any treat better is to put it in water. Avoid putting food in unfiltered ponds or it can sink and decay, leading to bacterial issues.

Another fun activity is to hide lettuce treats in your duck pen before letting them outside for the day. It won't take them long to notice the goodies and to go searching for more.

Toes!

Young Jeffrey has a real taste for a very special snack—*toes!* I've learned the hard way that it's best not to wear flip-flops out to the duck pen, or it's at my own risk. I'm not the only Momma Duck to come across this either. Some ducks honestly believe that because toes lay close to the ground and wiggle a little they must be some kind of tasty treat.

Enrichment #5
Transplanting Foliage

Transplanting can be a fun spring adventure for your ducks. It's not just the new plants that are fun, but also the holes you dig to prepare for their arrival, the myriad of insects and worms that are overturned during the process and the mud puddle you make with the garden hose when preparing the cavity for its incoming plant.

Hay compost piles can seed some hearty tall grass come spring. I love pulling out large clusters of grass and then planting them into the ground inside my duck pen. My boys huddle all around me during these springtime events; they just can't get enough of it.

I wouldn't suggest planting anything you really care about in their pens because unless you put up protective fencing, they'll make quick work of it. Also be careful that you don't transplant toxic plants into their enclosures. I highly recommend that you buy a book of your local flora to help guide you in this regard as well as consulting online sources such as the ASPCA (www.aspca.org) for lists of plants that are toxic to birds.

Safety First! Ducks should never be allowed to venture anywhere near your shovel while you're actually digging. Ducks can dart in very quickly when they see a goody being unearthed and they can easily get caught between your shovel and the ground. Serious and even fatal injuries can result.

Enrichment #6
The Language of Ducks

Ducks communicate using both vocalizations and body language. If you watch and listen closely, you'll soon have a better understanding of what's going on out in their duck pen.

Vocalizations

Actually learning to speak duck is pretty fun because once you pick up on their basic lingo you'll be able to do some of your own communicating—and they'll understand just what you saying!

- **Happy quack**

The happy quack is the greatest sound you'll ever hear from your ducks. It's an open bill quacking that most often happens when you come in sight and even more so when you have a goody in your hands.

Rescued ducks Jake the Drake & Elijah laugh it up!

- **Content muttering**

Content female ducks will make vocalizations that sound like a mixture of happy muttering combined with squeaks of pleasure. Truly, it'll sound like they're having their own private conversation with themselves. They tend to do this mumbling most often while moseying around and foraging for goodies.

- **Warning quacks**

Ducks will raise the alarm when they hear or see anything out of the ordinary. Warning quacks are loud and rhythmic, as if they're counting off the seconds, one at a time. If you have more than one duck, they'll all do this together and in sync with each other. When you hear this type of quacking you should always investigate immediately and see what the trouble is.

- **Competitive boasts**

Competitive quacking tends to occur when a female duck comes within visual range of a couple of drakes. One drake will quack and then the other, each escalating their heads higher and quacking a little louder until the competition ends. My boys are human-imprinted, so they sometimes do this when I make an appearance. It's almost as if Young Jeffrey is saying, *"She likes me more!"* And then Young Matthew counters, *"No me!"* And then it goes back and forth a few times before ending.

- **Trumpet displays**

Trumpeting displays usually take place on water, but not always. Drakes will paddle their feet and lift their bodies slightly up and out of the water. Then, they stretch their necks upward and make a muffled sound in their throats before flexing their necks into a swan-like pose.

These fun trumpets are part of your drake's breeding ritual. Males will often sound one off in display to attract the attention of females and then they'll sound one off again immediately after mating.

- **Hissing**

An angry or frightened duck will sometimes charge and hiss at you. I've had a few spitfire rescues who've done this to me (usually after giving them medicine). I like to boost their confidence by immediately leaving their pen, so that they believe they've effectively chased me off.

Body Language

While you may not be able to mimic all of their non-verbal messages, being able to understand them will help you build a trusting relationship with them.

- **Tail wagging & catching rain**

Happy ducks wag their tails—it's true! Muscovy ducks exhibit this happy behavior more than any other breed, especially when vying for the attention of females (or their Momma Ducks!). Female displays also increase markedly when they're feeling particularly broody.

Muscovy ducks are often seen aiming their open bills up to the sky. Males and females do this during courtship and competing males also do this in display.

- **Splayed tail**

A duck who splays their tail feathers at you, spreading them open like a fan is saying, *"Don't touch me!"* Ducks will often do this while also opening their bills.

- **Head bobbing**

Submissive ducks bob their heads low and to the ground in the direction of dominant ducks in order to gain their acceptance. Females often bob their heads in the direction of higher ranking females and towards males as a means of establishing and reaffirming bonds, or even to flirt. Higher ranking females will often meet this bobbing with similar low-to-the-ground head bobbing, while males will usually bob their heads up and down in response.

Ducks will often respond to head bobbing even when it's you initiating the action. Whether you nod your head or use your hand as a puppet to act out the bobbing, you can often coax a loving head bob right back in your direction.

- **Head vibration**

When a boy duck gets really excited by a girl duck, he'll vibrate his head and neck in anticipation just before climbing on board. If your drake shimmies his head and neck at you, it means he loves you, perhaps a little too much, but he loves you just the same.

If you squat down in front of him and puppet your hand into the shape of a duck, he'll likely hop towards you and throw his head over your shoulder. He's really trying to mate, but can't quite figure it out, so he'll settle for a hug instead. Human-imprinted females will also express their love for you in this way.

You can initiate your own dialogue with your ducks by stretching your hand out towards your duck and then shimmying it rapidly. These subtle vibrations will often coax a hug out of your human-imprinted duck.

Fun Sounds

You can take the mimicking of your ducks to an entire new level by utilizing a few tools. When introducing new ducky sounds to your flock it's important to avoid those noises that seem to be causing distress and stick to those calls that promote curiosity.

- **Duck callers**

I thought I could improve my interspecies communication by getting myself one of those plastic duck callers. I figured it was worth a try anyway. Unfortunately, I blew in the thing and nothing happened. When I finally stopped and read the directions I learned that in order to make the caller quack, I had to sort of quack through it. That made absolutely no sense to me whatsoever. I might as well have used an empty paper towel tube and quacked through that because it would've afforded me the exact same result. It was good for a laugh anyway. Perhaps you need to spend more than two dollars to get yourself a good one, but I wasn't up to spending a few hundred bucks just to acquire a ducky voice, especially when my own is absolutely free.

- **Cell phone apps**

There are ninety-nine cent *Duck Call* apps that you can purchase for your cell phone, some of which breakdown the actual types of wild duck calls for you (i.e. feeding, greeting, chatter, welcome, come back, etc.). My boys love this little game, and they seem to like the colored screen of my cell phone too—that, or they're trying to tap the "play" buttons themselves!

- **Recorded bird-song books**

You can purchase books with sound bites of hundreds of birds and waterfowl that can be fun to explore with your ducks. Try to stay away from predatory bird sounds when playing with this kind of toy, or you can distress your ducks. It's fun to learn which species of birds intrigue them and which they completely disregard.

Enrichment #7
Welcoming New Flock Members

Introducing a new duck to your existing flock can be pretty exciting. Your ducks may react differently to one newcomer than they do to another. Always chaperone introductions, even if things appear peaceful at first. If your ducks instantly bond with the new duck you can leave them alone after a while, but continue to check back on them frequently to ensure nothing's changed in your absence.

Always keep a close eye on pecking order disputes that may rise between any of your flock members during this adjustment period. It's completely normal to see temporary squabbling—even among original flock members as pecking orders are reaffirmed. These interactions should be considered excessive if the squabbles appear to be getting too rough, too frequent, or they simply don't subside. When these conditions exist, separations are definitely in order.

More often than not, ducks need to get used to each other and there's an adjustment period involved. If so, you'll need to put a safe dividing fence between them that allows them some time to get to know each other. As long as your male-to-female ratio is correct and you have plenty of pen space for everyone, ducks tend to bond with each other within the first two weeks.

Tag

Many ducks will see a new duck and immediately run away. Your new duck will be so excited to meet their new friends and your little champions will run the other way in what almost looks like a game of tag. Sometimes it's the other way around and your duck wants to be near the newcomer, but they run away. When one duck is eager to be near the other, but the other is a little nervous, you'll see this behavior. It's relatively harmless provided you have no tripping obstacles in your pen.

You'll want to chaperone them whenever they're together and put a safe dividing fence between them when you're not there to watch. This will prevent any mishaps in the event that someone's attitude suddenly changes about their boundaries. More often than not, they just start tiring out and begin to spend their days closer and closer together.

Love at First Sight

Some ducks will instantly bond with a newcomer and want to remain together from the moment they first meet. These split second attractions may be dotted with a few pecking order pokes here and there, but are otherwise relatively painless. This is often the case when you have a solo duck who's lost a friend and you're introducing a new companion for them.

If you have multiple ducks and one duck immediately takes to the newcomer, it doesn't mean the others will. Keep a close eye on things and consider putting up a safe dividing fence when you're away. You can always put the two ducks who are getting along on one side of the fence and the remaining flock members on the other.

Aggression

It's not uncommon for pecking order rituals to arise before members become friends. This tends to occur when you welcome home a dominant duck who's not quickly put in their place. Your alpha duck may not appreciate a strong-minded newcomer, and a willful newcomer is not likely to give in easily to an existing pecking order. The more evenly matched two dominant ducks are (no matter what their gender), the longer it'll take them to resolve their issues.

Hans Solo in a brief and chaperoned confrontation with Crocodile Stanley

If things get out of hand put a safe divider fence between them. Keep them adjacent to each other, but protected from one another for a few days, giving them ample opportunity to work out their differences from opposite sides of a shared fence. Spats are normal, but if they can't work out their differences within the first minute of reintroducing them, or if it appears to be getting too rough and tumble (beware of eye injuries), separate them again and continue to try again every few days. This type of behavior is most common among males, and if they just can't work it out, permanent separations will be required—each drake in their own pen. Boys who don't get along in the same pen will often enjoy one another's company when they're kept side-by-side in neighboring pens. Friendships can eventually be forged this way, it just takes time.

Occasionally you'll get an ornery new girl whose bossiness irritates your female duck to no end and the two will squabble day-in and day-out. Put up your safe divider fence and try not to worry. Given a little time, females always seem to manage to work things out.

Introducing Ducklings to Adult Ducks

It's vital to err on the side of caution when introducing young ducklings to full-grown adult ducks unless those adults have hatched them out directly on their own. Pecking order disputes can quickly turn fatal for a small duckling. Getting new ducklings acclimated to adult ducks (and vice versa) should be done in careful stages:

1. All introductions must be chaperoned closely.

Ducklings can be introduced to their older counterparts pretty soon after their arrival *provided* you're always there to monitor everyone extremely closely. Remember, just because everything is going smoothly in front of you, doesn't mean trouble won't happen the moment you leave the room. Ducks behave differently in your presence than when you're not around (just like children); if you need to step away for a minute, take your duckling with you.

Remember: If you're going to add ducklings to your flock be sure you know their genders first, or you'll likely need to separate the boys into separate pens as they mature and begin to fight amongst themselves.

2. Increase the length and frequency of their visits.

These introductive sessions should be brief at first and then grow in length and frequency as your duckling matures. You want to be ever present during each of these sittings. Ducks can accidentally injure or drown a duckling if you're not there to intervene and protect them.

3. Ducklings should be fully feathered before joining the flock.

Provided you've been diligent about bringing your duckling out to meet your ducks on a regular basis, everyone should be prepared to become permanent pen mates by the time your duckling is fully feathered; that is, when not a single fuzzy strand of duckling fluff remains.

Ducklings can usually be fully acclimated around eight weeks of age, but it can be sooner or later depending on personalities and male-to-female flock ratios.

Remember: While it's easiest to find ducklings in the spring, introducing them to adult males during the mating season can be risky. Premature mating can seriously injure or even kill a young duckling. Keep adult male ducks away from your duckling until they're full grown and mature.

Enrichment #8
Naming Your Ducks

Naming your ducks can be a lot of fun provided you avoid commonalities like: Donald, Daisy and Aflac. If you're unsure about their gender you might want to choose a name that can be changed slightly in the case you get it wrong. It may surprise you to know that your duck will learn to know their name, so choose it wisely!

Young Jeffrey and Young Matthew were named after two close friends of mine. I used to tease both men, saying they were both secretly in love with me, each one wishing they could follow me around everywhere I went just like two little lovestruck ducks.

When I founded our sanctuary and rescues started coming in some really fun names began to take shape. One of my all-time personal favorites was our one-eyed boy: Crocodile Stanley. Both Piper and Gulliver were abandoned as ducklings before coming to my door. Piper was rescued from a drain pipe and Gulliver barely survived a seagull attack. And of course there was Ah-hamed Ibn Fahalan Ibn Alabas Ibn Rasheed Ibn Hamed (or "Eeben" for short) whose name was inspired by the movie *"The 13th Warrior"* (a Michael Crichton adaption of Beowulf) and encompasses a magnificent lineage, which every abandoned duck so richly deserves in their new life.

After meeting plenty of other Momma Ducks I've found that I'm not the only one having some real fun with names. Think it through carefully because it'll need to last them a lifetime.

Enrichment #9
Dressing Up Your Duck

There's a club of Momma Ducks out there who are having quite a bit of fun jazzing up their indoor duck diaper harnesses with all kinds of frilly accessories (see: *"Indoor Ducks"* for supplier information).

Puff in her frilly best, Photos Courtesy of Jennifer Sunshine

Costumes

Dressing up your duck in costumes can make for adorable photos while also delighting visitors; even so, remember to keep your duck's safety in mind when using them.

- **Play it safe**

1. Diaper harnesses and accessories need to fit correctly in order to avoid feather breakage and skin irritation.

2. Don't leave dressed-up ducks unattended.

3. Be careful that your accessories won't contribute to stumbling or tripping accidents.

Enrichment #10
Spring Fever

Spring is an eventful season for ducks. It marks the beginning of the season of ducky love (which then continues throughout most of the summer).

It's pretty fun to watch all that flirting going on. Girls bobbing their heads at boys like little, love-struck teenagers while the boys act like celebrities and throw themselves whole-heartedly into their love trumpets. *Good stuff!*

The real quack up (ha!) is right afterwards, the girls get right to splashing and cleaning themselves up while the boys do a bit of celebrating. They give a good love trumpet and then stretch their heads out directly in front of them, parallel to the water's surface, while zooming around in triumphant circles. Funnier yet is when they occasionally mate off-water and do this little performance on land.

Mr. Pearl takes a celebratory zoom!

Enrichment #11
Eggs

Female ducks will lay eggs whether or not you have a drake around (eggs will only hatch if they've been successfully fertilized). Be sure to collect eggs every day before cleaning and refrigerating them.

Remember: Don't dispose of unwanted eggs anywhere near your duck pen. You don't want hungry animals learning that this is a great place to find free snacks.

Enrichment for Ducks

Some enrichment activities are more fun for ducks than their human counterparts.

- **Egg counting**

Young Jeffrey is so funny when it comes to eggs. He's my little egg counter. Every day I collect the eggs and set them down in the hay near the barn door, so I can carry them up to the house when I'm ready to go. Each time he sees me do this, without fail, he comes over to the pile and pushes them all around counting each one with his bill. *How many are there, Young Jeffrey? 1-2-3?* Okay, so he's not *really* counting them, but that's what it looks like!

I've had some rescued ducks lay their first eggs while in my care, only to become brilliantly intrigued by them. *Did that come out of me?* I like to pick their egg up and move it around in the barn from place to place and watch as they come quacking over to examine it again and again with continued keen interest.

- **Egg rolling**

A few girls have surprised me by rolling their eggs back into their nests again. One of my enclosures has three pen sections, each with its own duck house. I'll often collect the three eggs from the houses and set them near the door, so I'll remember to carry them out with me when I finish my pen duties. More than once, I've forgotten the eggs there in the grass only to come back later and find all three have been carefully rolled and tucked into a nest of hay, safe inside a duck house again.

Enrichment for People

Other enrichment activities are more fun for humans than for ducks.

- **Cooking eggs**

Duck eggs have orangey yolks and are more viscous in consistency than smaller chicken eggs. Their potency is often unappreciated directly in a frying pan, but their rich flavor makes them an excellent additive to your favorite recipes. I once gathered eggs from different kinds of ducks and whipped up a half dozen small batches of scrambled eggs for a blind taste test with my family. Much to our surprise, there was a clearly noticeable difference in both the taste and consistency that hinged upon breed. If you don't believe me, try it for yourself!

- **Egg hunts & coloring**

Egg hunting can be a daily adventure if you have children, but remember to have them wash their hands right afterwards. Duck eggs come in a variety of colors ranging from white to green, but all of them take to egg dye. I like to buy dozens of egg-coloring kits and stencils when they go on sale after Easter, so that my daughter can color eggs all year round.

- **Egg art**

Some of the craftier people out there have taken egg decorating to a whole new level, making an entire hobby around the hollowing and painting of eggs. There are plenty of books on the subject and lots of fun ideas online as well.

Enrichment #12
Arts & Crafts

Ducks and art just seem to go together. Sometimes they're at the center of the action, other times they're the muse.

Bring a sketch pad and pencil with you when you visit their pen and have a little fun. Don't worry if you don't get it right at first; ducks aren't very judgmental and practice makes perfect!

Footprint Art

Human-imprinted and friendlier ducks tend to enjoy this painting activity more than their shyer counterparts. I picked up a few bottles of non-toxic, water based paint in the kids' section of my local craft store along with a couple of art canvases. I spread a thick layer of yellow paint in the center of a paper plate and then picked up Young Matthew and set his webbed feet down in it. Then I lifted him up again and set him down directly on the canvas and let him walk around a bit (with a little enticement). I did the same with red paint the following day and green the day after that. Just be careful that they've already pooped before setting them down on your canvas or you may end up with a few added colors.

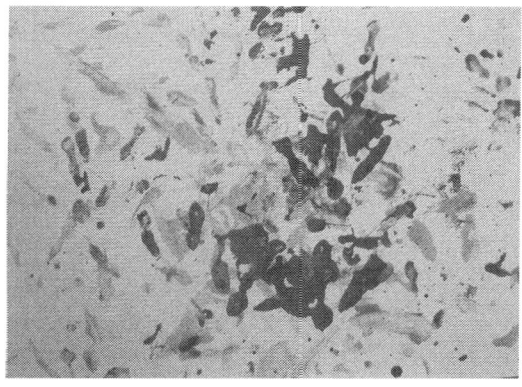 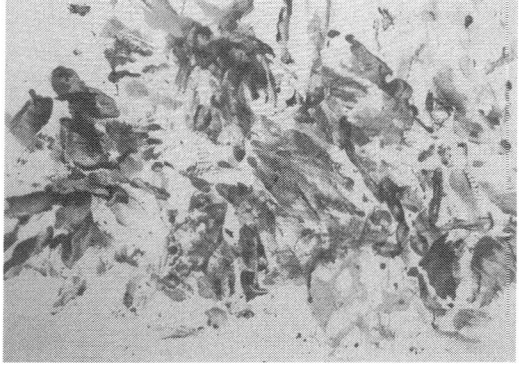

Young Matthew's painting *Young Jeffrey's painting*

Sculpture

While painting duck sculptures may seem like an activity solely for human enjoyment, once placed in duck pens, they make lovely places for worms to hide. My ducks have learned to gather around these lawn ornaments, begging me to flip them over as I walk by.

Can you tell which one is the real Jezebel?

Feather Art

Feathers that drop on the ground can be cleaned by dipping them in boiling water and then laid out to dry. You can cut them, glue them, paint them, dye them, make jewelry out of them—whatever! They make a fun project for kids. You can even paint with them, using them as your brush for interesting lines.

Photography

My ducks tend to behave more naturally when I take photos from a distance. I learned early-on that a good zoom lens is a great tool for capturing the ducky personalities.

Some of the best photo opportunities take place when your ducks are amidst their bathing routine. Water splashing takes on a whole new appearance during different hours of the day and in different seasons. Ducks often open their wings like angels during their preening and this can make for some beautiful photos. Focus in on webbed feet, bills, wings and feathers. Switching photos to black and white can add extra drama. Action sequences can make wonderful greeting cards or framed gifts.

Photographs of Lil-Bo-Peep

It's amazing what a good caption can lend to a favorite photo:

"I once caught a fish THIS big!"

"I surrender"

<u>Scrap Booking</u>

Ducky scrapbooking can be tons of fun! These artsy books are a great way to protect and share precious mementos including your favorite sketches, fun footprint art, fluffy feathers and fabulous photos. Remember to take lots of photos of your ducklings when they're little because they grow fast. Someday you'll look back at how tiny they were and you'll barely believe it.

Get as elaborate as you like with this. It's a great project for children as well. I'm sure when my daughter gets a little older, she'll take over the role of duck Record Keeper and duck Craft Project Manager.

<u>Enrichment #13</u>
<u>Sleeping</u>

Ducks love to sleep, and the longer the days are, the more naps they seem to take. It's like clockwork. Mine will even give me accusatory glances if my working in their pens accidentally wakes them up—*the little stinkers!*

Naps

On warm days, I love setting up my cot or unfurling an old blanket on the ground in my duck pen. My boys love to come over and poke around while I feign a good nap. They really are quite good at tickling.

- **1st Nap**

That point in the morning when sleeping all night really catches up to them.

- **2nd Nap**

That point in the early afternoon when their resting has really worn them out.

- **3rd Nap**

That point after lunch when a good digestive slumber seems in order.

- **4th Nap**

That point just before dinner when a healthy snooze overcomes them.

- **Bedtime**

That point when they're drowsy from all that napping.

Second nap at the sanctuary

An interesting tidbit about ducks is that they can let half of their brain sleep at a time. You can often witness this when they're tucked under their wing for a nap. As you move around their pen you may see them opening one eye to look at you. As with humans, each of their hemispheres is responsible for the functioning of the opposite side of their body; therefore, if you see their left eye peeking at you, their right hemisphere is likely awake while their left hemisphere is asleep.

When large flocks of ducks sleep, those at the center of the group will fall into a deeper slumber than those on the outskirts—who tend to let half of their brain sleep while the other half remains awake and watchful. These ducks will keep the eye controlled by their waking hemisphere faced outwards. This amazing adaptation helps protect them from predators.

Enrichment #14
Voices & Singing

The sound of ducks quacking in my backyard has truly added something wonderful to my life. I love a good ducky greeting and look forward to it every morning as I stroll down the hill to their pens.

Songs & Rhymes

Have I mentioned how much joy ducks get from the sound of their Momma Duck's voice? My boys go absolutely crazy when they hear my good morning song echoing out to them each day.

"Good morning, little duckies, I love you too!
Let's go outside today,
Let's go outside and play,
Good morning, little duckies, I love you too!"

When I open the barn door, Young Matthew and Young Jeffrey scamper around my feet while their girlfriends line up quacking at the backdoor, eager to go play outside. It sure is wonderful to be greeted with such enthusiasm every single morning.

Over the years nearly every one of my ducks has earned their own song. This is an especially good way to teach a duck their name—and it works extremely well if you've brought home an adult duck and are likely changing their name from whatever it was before.

I love to choose a song and then change out the words to suit one or more of my ducks. Some of my ducks have a half-dozen songs in their honor while others have little rhymes and ditties that I sing for them.

Enrichment #15
Becoming a Duck Whisperer

Within my first year of rescuing ducks, I learned something very interesting about them. A duck's behavior can truly tell you *a lot* about their past experiences. If you have acquired an adult duck and don't know the details of their background you can often learn more than you might expect through simple observation.

While you may not initially think of ducks being abused; sadly, it most definitely takes place. These animals have deep psychological motivations and display obvious emotions when triggered. Ducks who have experienced far less tragedy in their lives will also tell you about their histories; they'll just do so a little more subtly.

Response to Touch

The first thing to look for when observing your new duck for insights to their past, is their behavior towards people in general and their reaction to being handled.

- **Positives**

Quacky greetings, waddles of excitement and hugs and the like are all signs of a much-loved duck who likely outgrew their home before any abuses or neglect began.

Ducks who like being held, picked up and petted were quite obviously handled and doted over, while ducks who avoid this sort of contact are often simply not accustomed to it.

- **Negatives**

While ducks will usually run fearfully away from any source of stress, a duck who feels trapped will often hiss, pinch, or bite & twist in a heated tantrum. These aren't qualities of a mean duck so much as they are of a defensive duck who fears being hurt again and is attempting to protect against it. If you see this pointed behavior, you probably have a duck who had to shield themselves against some kind of abuse in the past.

Keep in mind, I'm not talking about seasonal mating behavior that can become passionately aggressive at times, but at behavior rooted in fear and anger. The difference is usually pretty unmistakable.

Response to children

Many ducks are given to children as gifts and then removed and brought to shelters (or discarded on ponds) when they became a parental burden. If your duck is fond of children, this could be why. You can often tell whether a boy or girl raised your duck just by arranging visits with family members and watching their interactions.

On the other hand, a child that wasn't monitored appropriately with a duckling may have created a "child phobia" in your duck. If your duck hisses or frights away from children in particular, this is likely the case.

Trust is earned slowly through routine and special treats. In the meantime, have someone your duck responds favorably to tend to most of the care-giving.

Response to Gender

New ducks will often respond more favorably to a man or woman depending on what they're accustomed to. If their previous caretaker was a woman, they may prefer the women of your family over the men—or vice versa if it's the other way around.

If your duck was treated poorly by a member of one gender in their prior home, they may react fearfully towards that same gender in your home. If you're noticing this behavior in your duck try to have a family member of the opposite gender initiate a bond.

In the beginning it's best to do what your duck's comfortable with whenever possible. Then, slowly, introduce other caretakers who bring special ducky treats with them. Ducks are slow to demonstrate trust. Be patient and embrace small steps in lieu of drastic measures, or you'll risk heightening reactions of fear or anger.

Enrichment #16
Visitors

You're probably thinking that by visitors I mean all the people who will flock (ha!) to your house to see your amazing ducks, but visitors can sometimes take other nice forms.

Frogs

I've discovered all kinds of interesting surprises in my duck ponds. Some days I find little drowned mice (ducks will try to eat them, by the way—blah!); other times, I find crawfish or frogs. Few things thrill my ducks more than me pulling a live critter out of one of the little ponds. My boys will quack, *"Momma, Momma, give it to me!"* while they stumble over each other and shove each other aside with their wings. Honestly, it can be a real feat getting a lost frog to safety.

I love watching ducklings interact with harmless wildlife for the first time. A frog can be a pretty amazing thing to new eyes. Get your camera ready; this could be one of those one-of-a-kind photo opportunities.

"Maybe if I give it a little poke..."

Wild Mallards

On more than one occasion our sanctuary has been visited by wild Mallards who've spiraled down for a chat. They blend in so well I probably wouldn't notice them except that female Mallards can get pretty loud. More than one visiting girl has been known to stand outside my enclosures and engage my ladies in a loud debate, explaining in no uncertain terms that her boyfriend is completely off-limits to them. And then my girls respond with an, *"Oh, yeah, well our fenced-in pond is off-limits to you!"* and it goes back-and-forth for a while until the Mallards eventually waddle up the hill to the open pond instead.

While wild Mallards can be an interesting source of discussion around the duck pond, it's best if they remain outside your duck pen. As little as they are, they can be pretty feisty (especially in springtime) and have been known to instigate fights with ducks much larger than themselves. Because they can fly, they can put your duck at a disadvantage relatively quickly.

Enrichment #17
Toys!

I know, I know. This is the moment you've been waiting for, but I wanted to save one of the really, really good ones for the end. Providing toys for your ducks to play with can be a great way to enrich their lives as well as providing you with a fun new level of interaction.

Fun Can Sometimes Be A Little Scary

Most ducks are wary by nature and often need time to adjust to new items brought into their pens. Some of the following activities may require patience or more than one attempt. Proceed slowly and try not to get discouraged if they need more time to adjust. You may find that your duck has strong feelings against one or more of these activities. If you find this is the case with your duck, use your discretion and discontinue immediately. The idea here is to introduce some fun games, not to cause them stress, alarm or discomfort.

- **Safety first**

The following enrichment activities should only be performed while you're present and directly chaperoning your ducks. Objects should be carefully inspected for quality and safety before bringing them into your duck pen. Avoid toys with sharp edges or breakable pieces.

Mirrors

Mirrors (or mirrored acrylic plexiglass sheets for added non-breaking security) are a fun source of entertainment for ducks. Although they may be wary of their own image at first, most will eventually come in for the approach.

Admiring ducky reflections can be fun!

As mentioned previously, mirrors can also be introduced to cheer up a single duck who's feeling a little lonely. Your duck will be so convinced that they have a new companion that they'll often settle down right in front of the mirror, gazing into their own eyes for hours.

Males will sometimes treat their reflection as a rival. Muscovy drakes in particular tend to put on displays in front of the mirror while doing some pacing, tail wagging, rain catching and huffing. While all this boasting can make your boy feel pretty good about himself in the short term, you don't want it to continue for too long, or he might become stressed that he can't successfully chase the other guy away. Be sure to take the mirror away after a few minutes to grant him that feeling of exhilaration. I try to avoid showing males their own reflections during the mating season to prevent them from getting overwrought with emotion that they might displace on someone else in the flock.

Cups

"Cups" is one of my favorite sanctuary games and I think my ducks would agree. This kind of fun just never seems to get dull and even the shiest of ducks can't seem to resist its allure. Just fill a row of cups with water and watch what happens. Ducks see in color, so use different colored cups to really attract their attention. I like to use transparent tinted cups, so I can see more of the snorkeling action. If you want to up the ante a little, go ahead and drop a night crawler into one of the cups. Your duck will go crazy!

Young Matthew plays a game of "Cups"

Parrot and Baby Toys

Some ducks are entertained with toys, especially if they have pieces they can safely nibble or tug on. Pet stores and baby stores can be good sources of fun gifts for your duck. Unbreakable mirrors and musical buttons can incite an even greater response from your playful duck.

Omalie plays with his toys, Photo courtesy of Chantal & Brian

Lettuce Maze

Insert leaf lettuce into a toy with holes in it, so the ducks have to work to get their healthy snacks. Be careful not to make holes too small, so bills and heads don't get stuck.

My ducks love finding green treasure in their pirate ships (ferret boats)

Plush Animals

Single ducklings are especially fond of plush animals. These wonderful and cuddly friends can provide a great deal of comfort and security to a little friend in need. Be sure there are no small parts that can be plucked off and ingested.

Lil Bo Peep snuggles up with her little plush friend

Remote Controlled Toys.

I just love sending my slow-moving radio-controlled duck out onto the pond with my ducks. The boys tend to veer away from the little bugger while the girls tend to go over to give the little guy a curious eye or an occasional good poke.

Who's your new friend?

Enrichment #18
Happy Ducks = A Happier You!

It's commonly accepted that having happy pets around can significantly reduce your own stress levels. Take time out of your day to sit and relax with your ducks. If you aim to keep your ducks happy and healthy, your ducks will do the same for you in return. The more time you spend with them, the better you'll feel—I guarantee it! I've never had pets that were so silly and so much fun. It's simply hard to have a bad day when they're around. It helps that they always look like they're smiling.

Medical Care

Medical Care

I learned very early on that the quantity and quality of medical information available to Momma Ducks is scarce and incomplete. I'm not even going to repeat what most sources will tell you to do if your duck becomes sick or injured because you and your feathered friend deserve so much better than this.

I've also found that although my vet is very well versed in duck health, many avian vets are not. Most veterinary colleges offer courses on ornithology and poultry, but not more than brief seminars on waterfowl care (if anything at all). This prepares students for a career in the poultry industry or as an avian (parrot) vet, but doesn't really prepare them for handling your duck. In addition, not all vets have a lot of duck patients, which leads to less hands-on experience with their ailments and subsequently, less experience with available treatment options.

For these reasons, I've dedicated the majority of my attention to the *Medical Care* section of this book in the hopes that it'll benefit you and your duck. Please don't make the mistake of thinking that because your duck is currently healthy you shouldn't read this portion of the book. Responsible Momma Ducks should educate themselves about the types of injuries and illnesses ducks can experience in order to better prevent them as well as learning to recognize their early warning signs. This chapter will cover medical issues that I've personally encountered as well as those I've learned about through contact with ducky friends of mine. I know it's relatively thick, but don't panic; most Momma Ducks only experience a few of these problems in the entire lifetimes of their ducks. Since you have no way of knowing which one or two these might be though, I'm going to include them all for you. Remember, no book (not even mine!) can ever replace quality vet care.

Knowledge is Power

Since many vets aren't very experienced with waterfowl, it's *your* responsibility as a Momma Duck to learn all that you can about your duck's health. Your duck may fare better if you call up your vet's office and say, *"I think my duck may have gape worm; these are his symptoms... and I've read..."* than if you say, *"Something's wrong with my duck."* Your information may give your vet a chance to do some detailed research before you and your duck come in for your appointment. It's in your duck's best interests to have an idea ahead of time of what might be going on along with possible treatment options. If your vet prescribes a different treatment regime than you expected, you'll know just the right questions to ask in response.

Signs That Vet Care is Needed

Some obvious signs that vet consultation is needed are: vomiting (yes, ducks do throw up), any kind of discharge or bleeding, the build-up of feces or fluids around the cloaca, a disinterest in their food or water, deteriorating feather quality, limping, tiredness, keeping their feathers fluffed-up or diarrhea. By diarrhea, I'm not referring to the urine mixture that passes out of your duck—and could commonly be misconstrued as diarrhea by owners of other types of pets. This is how they pass urine and is completely normal. When dealing with ducks, diarrhea is not judging how waste actually comes out of your duck's body, but rather, what it looks like once it's on the ground. Feces without shape or structure to it should be considered diarrhea.

Another clear indicator that your duck isn't feeling well is respiratory distress. If you can hear a raspy sound when your duck is breathing, if they're panting with an open bill, if you see their body heaving, or if their tail is pumping up-and-down for long periods of time, you could be witnessing signs of respiratory distress. Keep in mind, it's normal for females to pump their tails while laying their eggs, some even pant. Labored breathing is only normal during the short period when she's actually laying her egg (which is usually in the early morning), but it's abnormal in any other circumstance.

There are other less obvious signs that vet consultation is needed, such as your duck behaving unusually. Perhaps they're not interested in things that customarily appease them. Maybe they're not actively foraging, running up to greet you, or just don't seem as curious as normal and getting into their typical amount of trouble. You know your duck better than anyone else. Remember that and don't let anyone talk you out of it. Trust your instincts and seek vet assistance early on.

Keep in mind, the above list of symptoms is *not* all–inclusive, but it will give you a good starting place. Always remember to consult with your vet should any of these issues come up. Non-prescribed medicines or home remedies should never be administered unless you've consulted with your vet first.

Medication Safety

Some medications are dosed in ranges according to severity of presentation and individual tolerance. Inexperienced vets will often dose at the high end of this range rather than starting at the low or moderate end, which can put your duck's vital organs at risk (especially their liver and kidneys). Take care of your duck's long-term health by asking questions about drug safety and possible side effects.

- **NSAID medication**

NSAID (non-steroidal anti-inflammatory drugs) medications have their own inherent risks and should never be given to ducks with liver or kidney issues, or it can have fatal results. If you have an older duck, you would be wise to have their blood work checked first to make sure these organs are functioning properly before administering. Many vets will encourage a 3-4 day dosing period followed by a 1-2 day rest period to reduce any threat to your duck's kidneys or liver. If your duck is on NSAIDs for an extended period of time, periodic blood tests to monitor kidney and liver function is advisable.

- **Aspiration & injection**

Whenever your vet needs to aspirate body fluids (including drawing blood) from your duck, it's a good idea to keep them out of the water for the next 6-12 hours to help prevent the risk of harmful bacterial infections. If you need to give your duck injections, be sure to do it in the evening, before their bedtime, so they'll be ready to go out on the water again in the morning.

- **Medicating egg-laying ducks**

Whenever you medicate a female duck, discard all of her eggs for at least *eight weeks* following her last dosage (this is true of *any* medication you give her including wormers, topical ointments as well as supplements of any kind). Medications can contaminate the purity, safety and viability of eggs. Never eat them and don't allow her to hatch them out either.

- **Safe antibiotics**

Whenever your duck is feeling out-of-sorts and perhaps behaving a bit abnormally, many vets will prescribe them a 7-14 day precautionary round of Baytril® (enrofloxacin) as a preferred antibiotic regime. Over the years I've seen this particular antibiotic safely address most of my rescued flock's needs and I highly recommend it.

Dosage Verification Table

Dosages are prescribed in accordance with your duck's weight. For example, if your duck needs medication in the dose of 25-35 mgs/kg, this means they need between 25-35 mgs of medication for every 1 kg that they weigh (1 kg = 2.2 lbs.), depending on the severity of their condition and their individual tolerances. So, if your duck weighs 6.7 pounds (3 kilograms), in this scenario, they would require a dosage of 75-105 mgs of medication per dose.

Years worth of sanctuary note-taking has gone into the following table; even so, don't make the mistake of utilizing it as a home-treatment guide because that's not at all what it's intended for. There are a variety of factors and circumstances in which the doses I've provided could do more harm than good. I've *only* included it as a verification tool. In my experience there are far too many vets out there who claim they know what they're doing when it comes to ducks, but who are actually *Quacks* (I'll bet you didn't see that one coming!). If your vet prescribes something in an unusual dose, you'll have the information you need to recognize it, which will then enable you to ask questions on behalf of your duck and that's precisely what this reference table is intended for—to open a dialogue between you and your vet.

Type	Antibiotics/Antimicrobials	Dosage	Form	Frequency
	Amoxy Drop® [amoxicillin]	100-175 mg/kg	50 mg/ml	1-2x daily
	Amoxicillin	100-175 mg/kg	50, 100, 150, 200 mg	1-2x daily
	Baytril® [enrofloxacin]	5-15 mg/kg	22.7, 68, 136 mg	1-2x daily
	Baytril®	5-15 mg/kg IM	22.7 mg/ml	1-2x daily
	Clavamox®[amox. clavulanate]	50-125 mg/kg	62.5, 125, 250, 375 mg	2x daily
	Clavamox®	50-125 mg kg	62.5 mg/ml	2x daily
	Clindamycin [hydrochloride]	50-100 mg/kg	75, 150, 300 mg	1-2x daily
	Clindamycin	50-100 mg/kg	25 mg/5 ml	1-2x daily
	Silver Sulfadiazene	Small amount	1% /50, 85, 400 g	1-2x daily
	SMZ/TMP	100 mg/kg	200 mg, 40 mg/5 ml	2x daily
	Today® Cephapirin Sodium	1-2 ml	200 mg/10 ml	1x weekly
	Vetericyn® VF [hypochlorous acid]	Spritz 2-3x	.011% /4, 8, 16 oz	2x daily
	Doxycycline	10-50 mg/kg	200 mg/g	1-2x d/6-8 wks
	Doxycycline	10-50 mg/kg	50, 75, 100, 150 mg	1-2x d/6-8 wks
	Doxycycline	75 mg/kg IM	100 mg/vial	1x wk/6-8 wks
	Oxytetracycline	200 mg/kg IM (or) 2500 mg/l of H_2O (or) 2500 mg/kg of food	50, 100, 200 mg/ml	1x daily 6-8 weeks
Type	Eye Care	Dosage	Form	Frequency
	Terramycin® [oxytetracycline/poly b]	Small amount	5mg/10,000 units	2x daily
	Puralube® [mineral oil, wh. petroleum]	Small amount	150 mg, 850 mg/3.5 g	2-4x daily
	Remend® [hyasent-s]	1 drop per eye	.75% /3ml	2-3x daily
	Falcon® [tobramycin]	1-2 drops per eye	.03% /5 ml	2x daily
	Vetropolycin® [bacitray/neomy/polyc.]	Small amount	400u;3.5 mg;10,000u/3.5 g	2-4x daily
	Vetropolycin® HC [b/n/p/hc]	Small amount	1% /3.5 g	2-3x daily
Type	Wormer	Dosage	Form	Frequency
	Albon® [sulfadimethoxine]	20 ml/kg	50 mg/ml	2x daily/5 days
	Albon®	500 ml/l of H_2O	50 mg/ml	6 days
	Albon®	20 ml/kg	125, 250, 500 mg	2x daily/5 days
	Corid® [amprolium]	50-100 mg/l	96 mg/ml	5-7 days
	Corid®	50-100 mg/l	20 mg/g	5-7 days
	Cydectin® [moxidectin]	.2 ml/kg SC	5 mg/ml	1x
	Drontal®Plus [praziquantal]	5-20 mg/kg	22.7 mg/tablet	day1 & day14
	Flagyl® [metronidazole]	25-50 mg/kg	250, 375, 500 mg	1x d, 5-7 days
	Ivermectin	1-2 drops per eye	.0005-.05 mg	1x d,10-14days
	Ivomec® [Ivermectin]	.2 ml/kg SC	2.7 mg/ml	day 1 & day 14
	Levasole® [levamisole]	20-50 mg/kg	25, 50, 250, 300, 500 mg	1x
	Nemex-2® [pyrantel pamoate]	7 ml/kg	4.54 mg/ml	day1 & day 14
	Panacur® [fenbendazole]	125 mg/l of H_2O (or) 50 mg/kg of food	222 mg/g	5 days, repeat 1x on day14
	Panacur®	20 mg/kg	100 mg/ml	day 1 & day 14
	Strongid-T® [pyrantel pamoate]	7 ml/kg	50mg/ml	day1 & day14

Type	Chelating Agent	Dosage	Form	Frequency
	Calcium EDTA	30-35 mg/kg IM	200 mg/ml	2x d, 3-5 days, 4 days off, rpt.
	Cuprimine® [d-penicillamine]	30-55 mg/kg	125, 250 mg	2x d, 5 days, 4 days off, rpt.
	DMSA	25-35 mgs/kg	25, 50, 75, 100mg	3-4x d, 5 days, 11 days off, rpt
Type	**Anti-inflammatory/Pain**	**Dosage**	**Form**	**Frequency**
	Diclofenac Sodium	1-2 drops per eye	.1% / 2.5 ml	1-4x daily
	Flurbiprofen	1-2 drops per eye	.03% / 2.5 ml	2x daily
	Metacam® [meloxicam]	2-4 mg/kg	1.5 mg / ml	1-2x daily
	Pred-G® [gentamicin, prednisolone]	1-2 drops per eye	.3%, 1% /3.5, 5 ml	1-4x daily
	Rimadyl® [carprofen]	1-2 mg/kg	25, 75,100 mg	1-2x daily
Type	**Hormone Therapy**	**Dosage**	**Form**	**Frequency**
	HCG	500-1000 units/kg IM	10,000 units/10 ml	1x every 2 d, for 6 days
	Lupron® [leuprolide acetate]	200-800ug/kg IM	1 mg/.2 ml	Every 3 weeks
	Suprelorin® [deslorelin acetate]	1 implant	4.7 mg	1x, 1-3 months
Type	**Joint Care**	**Dosage**	**Form**	**Frequency**
	Adequan® [poly. glycosaminoglycan]	5-10 mg/kg IM	100 mg/ml	1x weekly
	CosaminDS®	10mg/kg	500mg / 400mg	1x daily
	Fatty Acids (omega 3)	.1 ml/kg (1:5 ratio with omega 6)	Various formulas/sizes	1x daily
	Fatty Acids (omega 6)	.5 ml/kg (5:1 ratio with omega 3)	Various formulas/sizes	1x daily
Type	**Supplements**	**Dosage**	**Form**	**Frequency**
	Ca Gluconate (dilute1:1 saline)	50-100 mg/kg IM	100 mg/ml	1x monthly
	Ca Gluconate	3300 mg/l of H_2O	Various formulas/sizes	1x daily
	Ca Gluconate	1-5 ml/30 ml of H_2O	Various formulas/sizes	1x daily
	Manganese	30-40 mg/kg food	5, 8, 10, 15, 25, 50 mg	With meals
	Tums®	125-250 mg	500, 750, 1000 mg	1x daily
Type	**Skin Care**	**Dosage**	**Form**	**Frequency**
	Granulex® V [tryps, balsam, castor]	1-2 drops	12 mg, 87 mg, 788 mg/gm	2x daily
	Benadryl® [diphenhydramine hcl]	Tiny amount	1% /28.3 g	1x
	Benadryl®	2.2 ml/kg	12.5 mg/5 ml = 2.5 mg/ml	1x
	Betadine Solution	3 ml/354 ml of sterile saline	12, 16, 32, 128 fluid oz	1x
Type	**Anti-diuretic**	**Dosage**	**Form**	**Frequency**
	Apple Pectin	100 mg	300, 500, 750 mg	1-2x daily
	Apple Cider Vinegar	15 ml/3.75 l of H_2O	Standard	2-4x daily
	Kaolin Pectin	2 ml/kg	90g/2g fl oz	2-4x daily
Type	**Anti-nausea**	**Dosage**	**Form**	**Frequency**
	Reglan® [metoclopramide]	.3 mg/kg	5, 10 mg	Every 8-12 hrs
	Reglan®	.3 mg/kg IM	5mg/ml, 10mg/2ml	Every 8-12 hrs
Type	**Anticonvulsant/Sedative**	**Dosage**	**Form**	**Frequency**
	Diazepam	.5-1 mg/kg	2, 5, 10 mg	2-3x daily
	Diazepam	.5-1 mg/kg IM	5 mg/ml	2-3x daily

Type	Nebulizing Antifungal Agent	Dosage	Form	Frequency
	F10 SC [QAC, biguanide]	4 ml/liter sterile H$_2$O	5.8% /100ml, 200ml, 1l, 5l	2-3x daily: 30 min, 2-4 wks
	Imaverol® [enilconazole]	10 mg/ml sterile H$_2$O	100 mg/ml (dilute 1:10 H$_2$O)	2x daily: 30 min, 3 wks
	Oxine® AH [chlorine dioxide]	51 ml/liter sterile H$_2$O	2% / gallon (inactivated)	2-3x daily: 30 min, 2-4 wks
Type	**Diuretic (Heart Fluid)**	**Dosage**	**Form**	**Frequency**
	Lasix® [furosemide]	.15-2 mg/kg	12.5, 50 mg	2x daily
	Lasix®	.15-2 mg/kg IM	50 mg/ml	2x daily
	Lasix®	.15-2 mg/kg	10 mg/ml	2x daily
Type	**Sedative/Pain**	**Dosage**	**Form**	**Frequency**
	Torbutrol® [butorphanol tartrate]	1-4 mg/kg	1, 5, 10 mg	4x daily
Type	**Increased Heart Contractions**	**Dosage**	**Form**	**Frequency**
	Enalapril	.2-.5 mg/kg	2.5, 5, 10, 20 mg	1-2x daily
Type	**Heart Health & Function**	**Dosage**	**Form**	**Frequency**
	L-Carnitine [levocarnitine]	1000 mg/kg of food	100, 500, 1000 mg	With meals
	L-Carnitine	1000 mg/kg of food	85, 100, 250, 454 g	With meals
	Taurine	100-250 mg/kg	500, 1000 mg	2x daily
	Taurine	100-250 mg/kg	100, 227, 500 g	2x daily
Type	**Blood Thinner**	**Dosage**	**Form**	**Frequency**
	Aspirin	5-25 mg/kg	75, 81, 100, 325 mg	3-4x daily
Type	**Blood Sugar**	**Dosage**	**Form**	**Frequency**
	Karo® Syrup (high fructose corn syrp.)	.5 ml/kg	standard	As needed
	Molasses	.5-.75 ml/kg	standard	As needed
	Gatorade® [electrolyte water]	Up to 50 ml/kg daily	standard	As needed
	NPH Insulin	.5-3 u/kg IM	U40	Every 12-48 hrs
Type	**Absorption Agent**	**Dosage**	**Form**	**Frequency**
	Activated Charcoal	2000-8000 mg/kg	standard	1x daily or as needed
	Activated Charcoal	2000-8000 mg/kg	250, 260, 280 mg	1x daily or as needed
Type	**Liver Function**	**Dosage**	**Form**	**Frequency**
	Lactulose	.2 - 1 ml/kg	3.3 g/5ml	Every 8-12 hrs
Type	**Pancreas Function**	**Dosage**	**Form**	**Frequency**
	Viokase-V® Pancrezyme [lipase, protease, amuylase]	2-5 g/kg or 1/8 tsp/kg food	71.4K, 388K, 460K usp / 113.5 g, 227 g, 340.5 g	Before meals
Type	**Oviduct Contractions**	**Dosage**	**Form**	**Frequency**
	Oxytocin	.25 ml/kg IM	10 usp/ml, 20 usp/ml	1x
Type	**Carrying Agent/Pain**	**Dosage**	**Form**	**Frequency**
	DMSO [dimethylsulfoxide]	Small amount (gel)	90% / 4 oz, 16 oz	1-2x daily
Type	**Chemotherapy**	**Dosage**	**Form**	**Frequency**
	Leukeran® [Chlorambucil]	1 mg/duck	2 mg	2x weekly
	Vincristine sulfate	.5 mg/body surface area IV .75 mg/bsa IV	1mg/ml	1x wkly, 1 wk 1x wkly, 3 wks

Type	Antifungal	Dosage	Form	Frequency
	Nystatin	300,000 iu/kg	100,000 iu/ml	2x d, 7-14 days
	Nystatin	300,000 iu/kg	500,000 units	2x d, 7-14 days
	Sporonox® [itraconazole]	5-10 mg/kg	100 mg	1-2x daily
	Sporonox®	5-10 mg/kg	10 mg/ml	1-2x daily
Type	**Antiviral**	**Dosage**	**Form**	**Frequency**
	Famvir® [Famciclover]	25 mg/kg	125, 250, 500 mg	2x day / 7 days
Type	**Reduces Blood Pressure**	**Dosage**	**Form**	**Frequency**
	Lanoxin® [digoxin]	.01-.02 mg/kg	.25, .125 mg	1-2x daily
	Vetmedin® [pimobendan]	.25 mg/kg	1.25, 2.5, 5, 10 mg	1-2x daily
Type	**Antihistamine**	**Dosage**	**Form**	**Frequency**
	Chlorpheniramine	Dilute 4 mg tablet in 237 ml (8 oz) H_2O	4 mg	1x daily

Gelatin Capsules

Some pills are *very* tiny (especially when divided into proper dosages) and difficult to get down your duck's throat. A good way to remedy this is by purchasing empty gelatin capsules. A nice, smooth, properly sized capsule can really make giving pills easy. Just insert small or partial pills inside the gel cap and fill any remaining gaps with a probiotic powder for added benefit. Now you'll be sure that any tiny pills have reached their destination.

Gel caps can also be used to administer multiple small pills at the same time (you may need to cut them to fit them inside the gel cap). This can help reduce stress levels for you and your duck during pill time.

Gel caps come in a large variety of sizes. Before ordering, it's important to figure out exactly what size you'll need without going overboard (to prevent risk of choking).

Gel Cap Size	Diameter (mm)	Length (mm)	Volume (ml)
0	7.62	21.7	.68
1	6.91	19.4	.50
2	6.35	18.0	.37
3	5.82	15.9	.30

How to Give Your Duck a Pill

It may sometimes be necessary for you to give your duck oral medication in the form of tablets or pills. Don't worry; it's a lot easier than it sounds and you don't have to fret about getting pierced by teeth the way you do with many other pets.

I've written this section as descriptively as possible to help ease new Momma Ducks through the motions, but the movements your hands are about to embark upon are actually pretty instinctive—they'll just feel right once you're underway.

If you want to practice this procedure on someone other than your duck, have a friend put a sock puppet over their hand and try it out on them.

1. **Lay out a blanket:** While learning to master this technique it's very easy to drop tablets and pills. To help keep you from having to dig through layers of hay or pine shavings for lost medication, lay an expendable blanket or towel on the ground for you and your duck to sit on before you begin.

2. **Catch your duck:** Next, you'll need to catch your duck and set them down on the blanket you've laid out (see: *"Safe Catching and Handling"*).

3. **Get your duck into position:** Kneel down over your duck, so that they're tucked safely between your knees. While getting into position it can help to place your hands on each side of their body, circling your fingers around their chest while keeping your thumbs over their wings to help keep them from flapping. Now ease yourself forward and over them until their wings are safely held in place by your legs, so they can no longer flap. Keep your feet together behind you, so they can't back out and escape.

Young Matthew is held gently between my knees

4. **Ready the pill:** Once you have your duck securely in place, position your *non-dominant* hand in front of their chest to prevent them from darting forward and escaping. Now, let go with your *dominant* hand and use it to lay your duck's pill(s) out by your side and within easy reach.

5. **Open their bill:** Now that your pill is prepped, cup the palm of your *dominant* hand beneath your duck's bill—curling your thumb up on one side and your forefinger up on the other. Gently bring both fingertips together at the same time, sliding them into the crook between your duck's upper and lower bill—at the base of their bill (as opposed to the tip). Most ducks will instantly react by opening their bill for you, but if not, use the very tips of your fingers, or a tiny edge of your fingernail to *gently* pry their bill open and apart.

   Once your duck's bill is open, they're no longer going to dart forward and escape, so take your *non-dominant* hand out from in front of them and grip onto the tip of their open upper bill, holding it gently, but firmly between your fingers—one thumb on top and two fingers side-by-side inside. These fingers will act as a wedge in between your duck's upper and lower bills, keeping them from clenching it closed again. Don't worry; they're not strong enough to hurt you if they close their bill while your fingers are inside.

6. **Tilt their head backward:** Release your *dominant* hand from the crook of your duck's bill (still holding the tip of their upper bill between the fingers of your *non-dominant* hand) and reach over for the pill, squeezing it tightly between your thumb and forefinger.

   Use your hands to gently tilt your duck's head backwards, so that the back of their head comes closer to your chest and their throat is aligned at a 45 degree angle.

   TIP: When dealing with a particularly skittish duck, I like to flip the bottom of my shirt down over their eyes to cover them. Most ducks will calm significantly when this is done.

7. **Push the pill down:** Continue gripping the tip of your duck's upper bill with the thumb and first two fingers of your *non-dominant*. If your duck is clenching, gently push your middle finger away from your duck's upper bill and towards their lower bill—wedging it a little bit open. Be careful not to force their bill open too far; you shouldn't need any more than an inch of room.

   Take the pill that's pinched between the two fingers of your *dominant* hand and slide it down inside your duck's mouth and just over the back of their tongue. Let go with your thumb and then quickly use your remaining forefinger to gently push the pill a little bit further—*barely* into the hole at the top of your duck's throat.

Gently let go of your duck's bill and let their head come back down into position. I always like to stroke their throat to help ease the pill downward. Watch for a couple seconds to make sure the pill doesn't come back up and then offer them a drink of water and perhaps a healthy treat.

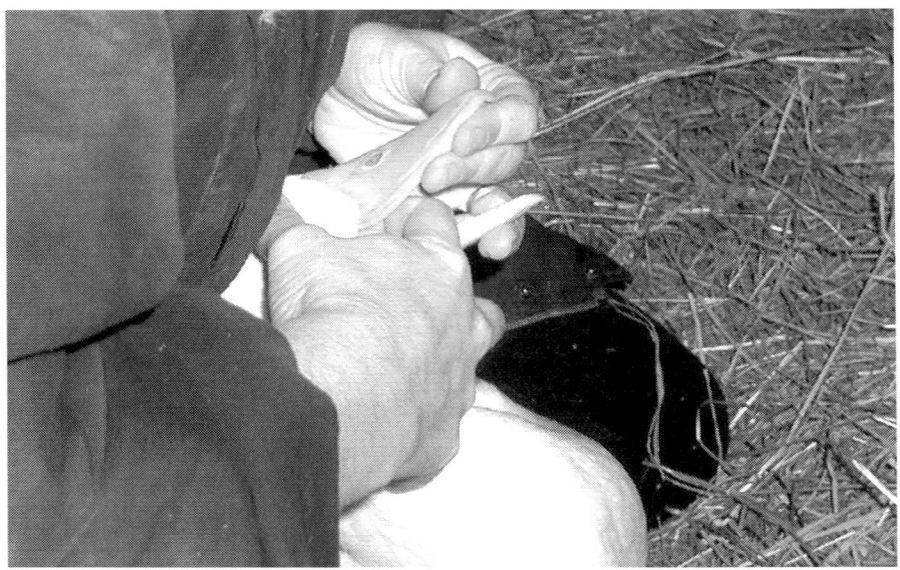

My left thumb is on the top of his upper bill with two fingers side-by-side in between.
If he was clenching, I could flex my middle finger downward to push open his lower bill a little bit.
Meanwhile, I'm pushing a pill over his tongue with my right forefinger.

Ducks as Pilling Patients

Giving a duck a pill may sound tricky at first, but once you master the maneuver, it's pretty simple and done-and-over before you can say, *"Quack!"*

In my experience there are three types of ducky reactions to taking pills:

1. *Cooperative ducks:* You may have to pry their bill gently apart, but on the whole, they take their pill without much difficulty. They're pretty self-explanatory.

2. *Biting ducks:* Some ducks will bite and pinch you as often as they possibly can until you get them steady and under control. Although *Biters* can be a nuisance, they're not the most difficult ducks to give pills to. Just be sure to wear protective clothing over your arms and you'll be fine. On the bright side, an open bill doesn't have to be pried apart. Just catch their bill in your fingers while it's open and pop the pill down. They've just opened the hatch for a nice and easy pilling session.

3. *Clenching ducks:* These ducks are the trickiest, especially for Momma Ducks new to the art of giving pills. They'll clench their bills tightly and stubbornly refuse to open them up. Ducks who've taken pills before often learn this tactic.

    There are a few tricks to get your duck to open their bill for you, and the second they do you'll need to get any finger in there as quickly as possible, before they clench it closed again. Some ducks are fast, so it may take a few tries. Whatever you do, don't lose your cool. If you get frustrated, take a break. Remain calm and don't take your impatience or aggravation out on your duck. Remember, they're afraid and just trying to protect themselves; they don't realize this is all for their own good.

a. Tickle your duck's belly feathers!

b. Dribble a little water over your duck's bill.

c. Present your duck with a bowl of water.

d. Dangle an earthworm or favorite treat in front of your duck

e. Wait patiently… eventually, you're duck will have to open up for *something*.

"No way is she getting that pill in me!"

Vet Visits & Rechecks

It's important for Momma Ducks to understand that most trips to the vet also entail follow-up visits. Because ducks are so adept at hiding their ailments, you'll need a professional eye to distinguish a recovering duck from one who's simply faking it.

Depending on your duck's particular situation weekly, bi-weekly or even monthly check-ups and tests may be in order. Of course, if your duck's situation should suddenly worsen before then, you won't want to wait that long. Call and schedule an immediate appointment to address any unexpected changes.

Surgery

Ducks have a diving instinct and will *frequently* try to hold their breath while under anesthesia. Only experienced waterfowl vets should attempt any surgery on your duck to avoid devastating losses.

- **Blood work**

A comprehensive avian blood panel should be performed and analyzed to ensure your duck is a healthy candidate for surgery and anesthesia.

- **Intubation**

Your vet should always have intubation equipment *immediately* handy during surgical procedures in case of a life-threatening emergency—*insist* upon this. Not all practices carry the small-sized tubing necessary and may not be properly prepared for a breathing crisis, so make sure they have everything they need in stock before your duck's appointment. I've had ducks stop breathing for nearly 30 minutes, multiple times during a single operation. If your vet team isn't prepared to do your duck's breathing for them, they aren't likely to survive.

- **Withhold food & water**

Vets will often recommend you withhold food from your duck 12 hours prior to surgery and water for 6-8 hours, depending on weather conditions. If you're experiencing hot weather you'll need to move your duck into a cool place before pulling their water in order to prevent the risk of dehydration or heat stroke.

Vets advise you to withhold food and water to reduce the risk of your duck vomiting and aspirating fluid during surgery. If you haven't been able to pull water for long because of the heat or if your duck is having emergency surgery, your vet can inject your duck with Reglan fifteen minutes prior to surgery. Reglan is an anti-nausea medication, which stimulates the gastrointestinal tract and encourages food to move downward, helping to prevent regurgitation.

- **Anesthesia**

Young ducks: Your vet will most likely mask down your duck with inhaled Isoflurane gas, which is often used in conjunction with injectable Dexdomitor® and Ketamine. Varying levels of injectable Torbitrol® may also be utilized to maintain the desired effect.

Endotracheal intubation prepares your duck for the use of a non-rebreathing system, which your vet team will utilize to keep them breathing via manual ventilation.

Injectable Antisedan® is used to reverse the effects of anesthesia when your duck's surgery is complete.

Older ducks, ducks of unknown age, or compromised/at risk ducks: Your vet will most likely utilize injectable Torbitrol®, Ketamine and Midazolam. As with younger ducks, they are then intubated and manually ventilated.

Your duck will wake up as these medications wear off.

- **Proper hygiene**

Whenever caring for an injured and recovering duck, it's vital that you keep their area clean and dry. Duck diapers, harnesses, cradles, wheelchairs, pine shavings, towels—all if it must be kept sanitary, especially when your duck is recovering from surgical incisions that can easily become infected, but also afterwards. Failure to keep things sanitary can result in the onset of additional medical problems that can seriously impede your duck's recovery.

- **Friendship therapy**

I just can't say it enough: *Ducks are flock animals*. It really is imperative to their recovery that they get plenty of companionship and motivation from other ducks, whether they've had surgery or not. Lonely ducks don't recover nearly as quickly as those who have daily visitors, and some forlorn ducks will even give up. A pair of ducks who have to spend their time divided from one another while one of them recuperates can both face some sad and emotional times. The more often you can get them together for visits, the better off they'll both be.

This being said, you need to protect your recovering duck from any friendly pokes, prods or mating attempts. This is *especially* true following any type of reproductive surgery. Following this type of operation your duck will need to be kept separate from other ducks for a minimum of 2-6 weeks and then possibly from members of the opposite gender for an *additional* 2-6 weeks, depending on severity.

To accomplish this, set up a playpen fence or other safe divider between the two friends to keep them together but apart during their visits. This will help prevent the surmounting of injuries. When it's time for them to part ways for a little while, remember to give any solitary flock members unbreakable, duck-sized mirrors to keep them company.

- **Post-surgical swims**

No swimming allowed! That is, not until your vet clears your duck for this activity during their post-operative check-up. When asking your vet whether or not your duck is allowed to swim, be sure to clarify whether they'll be swimming in a kiddy pool filled with tap water or a pond. Ducks are often released to swim in clean kiddy pools much sooner than in ponds.

Stress

Ducks who live their lives in duress are far more likely to become ill than ducks who live more peaceful lives. Stress widens the gateway for a number of medical issues to settle in and take hold.

- **Symptoms**

Some symptoms of mild stress may include: reduced egg production and slight behavioral changes. Some ducks will suddenly collapse into a "sit down" position, remaining seated for a few minutes. Provided they stand up again once the stressor is removed, they should be fine.

Some symptoms of acute stress may include: panting, fatigue, sudden lameness (rare), loss of appetite, weight loss, nausea, vomiting, diarrhea, listlessness, depression, disinterest in normal routines, ruffled feathers and splayed tail feathers.

- **Treatment**

Symptoms of stress often mimic those of other conditions, so eliminating anxiety as a possible cause is often a good place to begin when it comes to any treatment regime.

Environmental adjustments: Ducks can be easily stressed by even the most insignificant environmental changes. For this reason, it's best to avoid making any grand, overnight changes when it comes to their living situation; instead, changes should be made gradually. Something as simple as a different-colored food dish can seriously stress out your duck. You may have to set old and new bowls side-by-side for a few days until they realize that the new object won't hurt them.

When welcoming adult ducks into your home (especially shy ones), it's often best to avoid the temptation to hold and pet them. Give them a few days to adapt to their new environment before you begin working on your friendship. When I get new rescues, I only go into their pens to perform the most basic of tasks and then I leave again as discretely as possible. Ducks usually settle into their routine around their third day and once they do, you can begin slow and gradual interactions. The trick is to engage them without stressing them; never pushing them to do things they're not ready for, but waiting patiently for them to take a chance.

Temperature changes: Ducks can experience a great deal of stress when temperatures flux suddenly, or reach extremes. During these taxing times try to avoid piling any additional stressors onto the heap; for example, a mid-summer heat spike may not be the best time to load your duck up into the car for a ride (unless they need to go to the vet, of course).

Medical conditions: Sometimes increased stress leads to illness; other times, existing medical conditions can lead to stress. If your duck isn't behaving normally and you can't locate the source, a vet visit is definitely in order.

Medical #1
Integumentary System (Bills)

Your duck's integumentary system includes their skin, bill and feathers. In this section I'm going to cover your duck's bill.

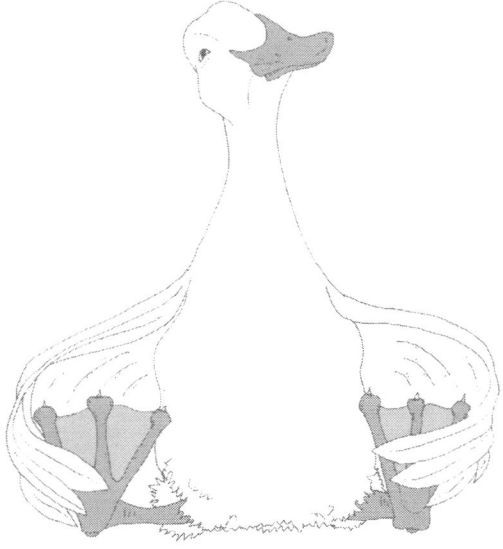

A diagram of your duck's integumentary system

While you may not think that you'll one day have a question about something as simple as your duck's bill, you may be surprised. Bills are fabulous tools for ducks, used to help them forage around in the mud and grass. Their touch receptors (found in the tip of the upper bill) are sensitive enough to easily distinguish tiny, tasty morsels from delicate grains of sand. They even have small built-in combs (called lamellae) inside that help them accomplish this sorting task. When something goes awry with a duck's bill it can range from mere aesthetics to instantly affecting their ability to eat and preen, which is why bills are such an important topic of review.

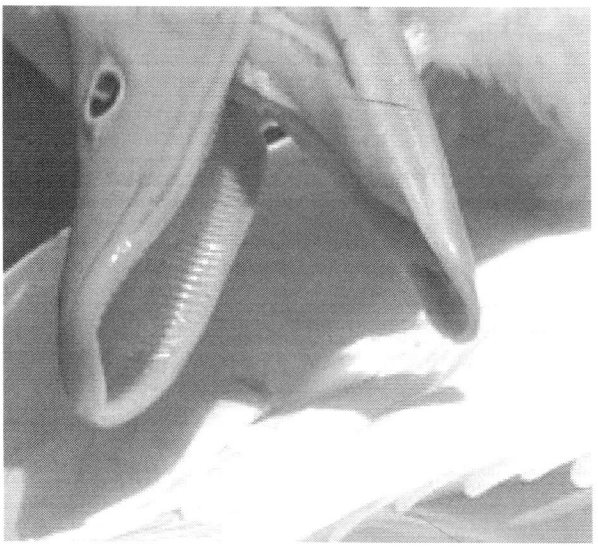

Close-up of Gulliver's bill combs

Freckled Bill

It's extremely common for little spots to appear on your female duck's bill after she matures and begins laying her eggs. These freckles are caused by hormonal changes and are completely normal and harmless. Freckles can range in color from reddish-brown to black. They can be sparse or they can cover your duck's entire bill. The old wives' tale is that the more freckles your duck has, the better layer she'll be, but there really isn't any truth in it.

The funny thing about these freckles is, for whatever reason, Momma Ducks tend to have an overnight reaction to their appearance—suddenly noticing them where they hadn't before even though they took some time to develop.

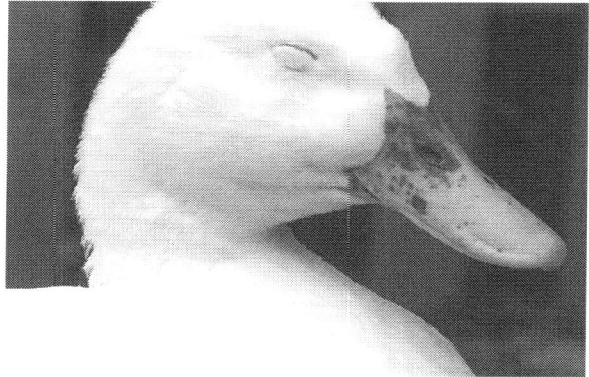
Jazzy's black freckles

Alice's freckles cover most of her bill

Jezebel's brown freckles

Peeling Bill & Rubber Bill

While many ducks will occasionally experience temporary bill peeling as a part of normal molting and shedding of old skin cells, or in dryer weather, Young Jeffrey's bill used to peel all the time.

In some cases, and in Young Jeffrey's, the constant peeling can leave portions of your duck's bill actually feeling kind of soft and rubbery, which is why it's commonly referred to as *"rubber beak"* in the parrot world, but since I'm in the waterfowl world, I prefer to call it *"rubber bill."*

Young Jeffrey's peeling bill

- **Symptoms**

Some symptoms of rubber bill may include: continual bill peeling often leaving rubbery areas of the bill exposed.

- **Treatment**

Never peel your duck's bill. While a humidifier can help a peeling bill in dry weather, bill creams aren't recommended since they can easily get on your duck's feathers during preening routines and remove their waterproof effectiveness.

1. *Diet:* The first thing you want to examine is your duck's diet. If a few of your ducks have this issue they're most likely experiencing a dietary problem (especially if your ducks aren't genetically related). If you're seeing this condition in more than one of your ducks, your choice of feed probably isn't meeting their nutritional needs. Try upgrading to a higher quality feed brand.

2. *Genetic Disposition:* If only one of your ducks is exhibiting a peeling bill and they're already on a top-notch diet, it could be that they're not foraging the same as everyone else *or* that they're simply more sensitive to vitamin or mineral deficiency. Young Jeffrey has a tendency to react to slight changes in calcium levels.

3. *Calcium Deficiency:* A shortage of calcium is often the cause of rubber bill. In this case, treatment is pretty simple. In Young Jeffrey's case, I just swapped out his regular Mazuri® Waterfowl Maintenance feed and replaced it with 100% Mazuri® Waterfowl Breeder (which has more calcium in it than the regular formula). After a few weeks I reduced his Breeder ration down to a 50/50 Maintenance-to-Breeder mix and he's still on that blend today (and 12 years old at the time of me writing this book!).

   Remember, every duck is different. Yours may require more or less laying formula to maintain a healthy bill. If your duck's bill doesn't improve and you're concerned about their calcium levels, your vet can do an ionized blood calcium level test to confirm whether or not this is the true issue or whether it might be something else.

4. *Vitamin Deficiency:* Rubber bill can also be caused by vitamin deficiencies—commonly those related to grass consumption. The reason ducks get rubber bill while geese usually don't is because geese tend to do a lot more grazing.

   Vitamin D precursors are found in the sun-dried portions of grass. Your duck converts these into Vitamin D and then into calcium. Grass also contains beta-carotene, which your duck then converts into vitamin A. When ingested at appropriate levels, Vitamin A helps your duck maintain a healthy bill. Be careful, excessive levels of Vitamin A can actually promote peeling. Consult with your vet before administering a vitamin regime that might do more harm than good for your duck.

Scratched Bill

Accidents can happen and you may discover a scratch on your duck's bill. Scratches can bleed if they're deep enough.

- **Symptoms**

Some symptoms of a scratched bill may include: a cut or scratch (minor or severe) that may result in bleeding.

- **Treatment**

Minor scratches: Clean the area with a non-stinging, wound wash a couple of times a day for the first one or two days to prevent it from getting infected. It will eventually heal and fade away.

Severe scratches: If your duck has a deep, bleeding laceration, as opposed to a slightly bleeding scratch, you'll want to seek immediate vet assistance. Wounds around the bill and mouth can become easily infected, so if the cut crosses over the edge of your duck's bill and severs into the neighboring skin, you'll also want to take them to the vet for an examination and antibiotics.

Broken Bill

A few ducks have come into our sanctuary with broken or damaged bills. If your duck breaks a piece of their bill off, pack it in ice and seek veterinarian assistance *immediately*. Bills bleed when broken, so you may need to use blood coagulant (cornstarch can be substituted if you don't have any on hand) to help control the flow until you arrive at your vet's office. Broken bills that are treated properly will eventually heal, but they won't grow back.

If the break won't seriously affect your duck's ability to eat or preen, vets will usually opt to cauterize their bill to seal the wound and prescribe an antibiotic to promote healing. Depending on the location and severity of the break they may also recommend anti-inflammatory medication, which will also provide some pain relief. Additional pain medication may also be required since bill pain can last for up to a year following the incident (often judged by their willingness to utilize it to actively forage and preen).

If the break is likely to interfere with your duck's ability to eat and preen and there's still blood supply to the area, your vet may want to try resetting their bill and wiring it back together. Dental acrylic is often applied to further protect the bill and hold things together. If your vet employs this tactic, you'll most likely be learning how to tube feed your duck to get them through the recovery period. An anti-inflammatory medication is not going to be enough to help them manage their pain in this case, so insist upon some *real* pain medication for your duck (Torbutrol® works extremely well in waterfowl).

There are two basic types of bill injuries, those that leave the tongue exposed and those that don't.

- **Non-exposed tongue**

Minor chips, cuts or breaks occurring around the edges of a duck's bill should be examined by your vet. They'll trim any "hang nail" remnants to avoid any risk of future catching or tearing. Then they'll cauterize the area with a chemical agent to stop any bleeding before prescribing appropriate medication.

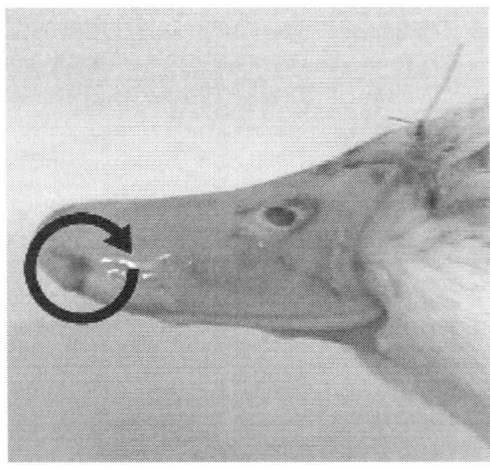
Elijah's broken bill prior to vet repairs

Elijah's bill a few months later

- **Exposed tongue**

More serious breaks may leave a portion of your duck's tongue exposed. Once fully healed, their condition may or may not interfere with their ability to eat. Most ducks will adapt and find new ways to use their remaining bill to scoop up food while others may grow weary of the effort and give up until their hunger provides more inspiration. In any case, until they master the technique, it's best to set aside timed feedings and institute a bottomless 24/7 feed dish instead. This will enable them to eat a number of small meals throughout the day as opposed to a few larger ones.

If your duck's bill injury is more serious than this and is interfering with their ability to eat, you'll need to find a new way to serve up their meals. If you have a buoyant feed (like the Mazuri® brand) you can simply pour their kibble in a bowl of water. Floating feed is a simple and effective way to promote eating. If this doesn't work, you may need to grind their feed in a food processor, which can then be served as a dry powder beside a bowl of water, or you can add water to the mix, turning it into a thick and hearty soup.

Fresh water should be made available to all ducks, at all times and this doesn't change one bit when you have a duck with an exposed tongue. It's extremely important that they can keep their tongue moist and comfortable to prevent further complications. Be especially attentive to this in hotter and drier climates/seasons. If water alone isn't providing enough moisture for your duck's delicate tongue, you can coat it with a protective layer of Chapstick® lip balm, or you can ask your vet for a tube of Optixcare Eye Lube, which can be used in the same manner.

Use extreme caution in colder weather. An exposed tongue can easily become frostbitten if not properly protected. Don't leave ducks with exposed tongues open to the elements when temperatures approach freezing (remember to consider wind chill variables). They must be locked up in a barn or shed to prevent exposure to the cold and wind and in extreme conditions they may even need to come into your house for the night.

- **Muscovy ducks with trimmed bills**

It's not uncommon to see Muscovy ducks with the tips of their upper bills cut off. Production facilities often cut and cauterize the bills of all of their ducklings to prevent males from fighting and injuring each other when they mature. Sadly, this is often done recklessly (and indiscriminately to females as well) and many ducks end up with bills that are cut back too far.

Muscovy ducks with trimmed bills (even those done improperly) usually manage to get their food down, although they're not nearly as efficient at it as their whole-billed counterparts.

Billy-cha's upper bill was trimmed back too far

He can't always pick up his treats on his own and looks forward to my help

- **Garden tools and bill injuries**

Ducks are smart, and it doesn't take them long to make the connection between your shovel and freshly turned over worms. Excited ducks have been known to *quickly* shove their bills beneath the blade of a slicing shovel or hoe—risking serious bill injuries or even amputation. They can also be remarkably sneaky, coming up behind or underneath you when you least expect it. For this reason ducks should *never* be allowed to play in the work zone.

When doing yard work keep your ducks in their enclosure or utilize portable pet playpens to ensure safety. You can move their playpen from place-to-place, giving your ducks the opportunity to explore and forage the areas you've already worked while you begin toiling neighboring grounds. In this way you can work and play side-by-side with each other without concern.

Remember, pet playpens are *not* predator proof. Dogs, coyotes and fox have been known to bolt through yards and jump into or knock over these play areas when their Momma Ducks were within twenty feet of them. Eagles and owls have also been known to swoop down out of the blue for corralled prey. *Never* leave your ducks unattended and stay within ten feet of their playpen at all times to prevent any risk of attack. Some Momma ducks build small covers for their duck playpens utilizing a lumber frame with some PVC coated welded wire mesh nailed on top. If you opt to go this route, be sure your cover can't be knocked off and fall in on top of your ducks and keep in mind… this still doesn't make your playpen predator proof; it just offers your ducks a bit of added security.

Punctured Bill

Predator attacks can result in punctures where teeth and claws pierce through a duck's bill.

- **Symptoms**

Some symptoms of a punctured bill may include: a circular hole pierced through the upper, lower or both bills, bleeding and appetite loss.

- **Treatment**

This type of wound can be treated and repaired by an experienced vet. First they'll thoroughly clean and flush out any perforations in your duck's bill and then they'll fill them utilizing dental acrylics. As with breaks, antibiotics, anti-inflammatory and pain medication may need to be prescribed.

Swollen Bill

Sudden swelling of a duck's bill is rare and requires urgent veterinary care. Your vet will take a look at the outside of the bill for any obvious cuts or punctures and then they'll look inside your duck's mouth as well.

Common causes:

1. A cut that results in a hematoma (pocket of blood).
2. A cut that results in an infection and then a subsequent abscess.
3. A damaged or infected salivary gland that results in a sailocoele (a leaking saliva gland that forms a pocket). Rarely, ducklings will hatch out of their egg with a malfunctioning salivary gland.

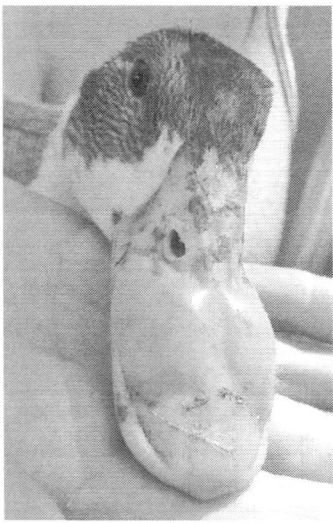

Quackers has a swollen bill, Photo Courtesy of Mandy Thrasher

- **Symptoms**

Some symptoms of a swollen bill may include: bill swelling (often "pocketed"), appetite loss and fatigue.

- **Treatment**

No matter what the cause, any delays can result in permanent damage to their bill and salivary gland. In the case of an abscess, a rupture can also result in the spreading of the infection.

Bill hematomas and abscesses are addressed similarly. If treated early, surgery is often not required; your vet will likely drain fluid out with a syringe and prescribe antibiotics and anti-inflammatory/pain medication. In the case of an abscess, they'll likely recommend culturing the fluid, so they can more accurately target any bacteria. Your vet may want you to use cold compresses in the case of a hematoma; just make sure you're clear on how long you should keep the compress in place to avoid damaging your duck's bill any further.

The tissue lining the inside of your duck's upper bill is comprised of merging groupings of salivary glands. An infected salivary gland is treated with antibiotics and anti-inflammatory/pain medication. Vets will normally start your duck on a general antibiotic, culturing for bacteria whenever possible. A damaged or malfunctioning salivary gland (or glands) may require the partial or complete surgical removal of afflicted tissue.

<u>Prosthetic Bills</u>

Snapping turtles are notorious for clamping down on a foraging duck's bill. Many ducks have survived these attacks, but the damage to their bills can be extreme. If your duck's bill is broken and damaged to the point of seriously interfering with their ability to eat, you can look into getting them fitted for a prosthetic bill.

If your vet is unable to assist you, avian vets who specialize in parrots often know how to create prosthetic bills. Another good option is to call wild raptor rescuers. They often know where to turn for quality prosthetic bills. Just keep calling and asking for referrals until you find the help your duck needs.

Prosthetic bills tend to be most successful if the line of breakage has a jagged edge as opposed to a smooth, clean one. In any case, prosthetic bills won't last forever and will need to be replaced as they wear out.

<u>Genetic Deformities</u>

Some ducklings hatch out with a twisted, curled or misaligned bill that can range from a mere aesthetic difference to actually inhibiting with their eating and preening. As with broken billed ducks, food may need to be floated on water or ground up and served to them. If the deformity actually inhibits food ingestion, vet assistance will be immediately required. As with other ducks with broken bills and exposed tongues, remember to keep your duck properly protected during cold weather.

Surprisingly, many ducks who hatch out with this kind of bill deformity live very healthy and productive lives and have no difficulty eating their meals. They often have enough of their bill to effectively preen and remain waterproof.

Sammy, Photo courtesy of Sarah McDougall

Medical #2
Integumentary System (Skin)

Most Momma Ducks don't even think about their duck's skin—so easily distracted by all those feathers! But if you want to keep your duck happy, safe and healthy, you have to pay attention to everything.

Bee Sting

Since most of your duck's body is protected by a nice layer of feathers, bee stings are pretty rare. When they do happen they tend to occur on your duck's feet, or if you have a Muscovy duck, on their face (*ouch!*).

- **Symptoms**

Some symptoms of a bee sting may include: localized swelling, discomfort (limping if stung on the feet, or blinking if stung around the face or eye).

- **Treatment**

If your duck gets stung by a bee, inspect the area carefully to make sure the stinger isn't still lodged in their skin. If so, take your duck to a well-lit area and remove it with a pair of tweezers. Next, dab the area with a *small amount* of hydrogen peroxide solution on a cotton ball and take your duck to the vet.

If the area begins to swell and your vet office is closed, you can put a *tiny* dot of Benadryl® Original Strength ointment over the sting site (keeping *very* clear of their eye if they've been stung on the face). Ideally, you want to use this cream *very* sparingly.

If swelling continues over the course of the next 1-2 hours and you still have no access to a vet, you can administer one dose of Children's Benadryl® Allergy oral suspension in the dose of 2.2 ml per kg (or 1 ml per lb). Again, this should *only* be used in an *emergency situation* when your vet isn't readily available and only in the case of healthy, adult ducks. Keep in mind that what you're doing this at your duck's own risk and it isn't guaranteed to be effective (or necessarily safe since you're using it off-label). As soon as your vet office opens, bring your duck in for an immediate exam and proper medical treatment—and be sure to tell them about any medications you've administered before consulting with them.

Frostbite

Frostbite is a real hazard for domestic ducks during freezing temperatures. Feet and bills are more vulnerable to the cold than you might think and real damage can be done if they're not properly protected from the elements.

Although their unique blood circulation helps prevent the loss of too much heat through their legs and feet, there's only so much your duck's body can handle when the weather starts getting harsh.

Prevention is the key when it comes to your ducks and the cold outdoors. Trust your instincts—if you think it might be too cold outside for them then use your good judgment and have them stay in their barn or shed for the day. Signs that it might be too cold outside include:

1. Ice forming on your duck's feathers.
2. Shivering.
3. Your duck is spending long periods of time sitting in the same place with their feet tucked underneath them and their bill buried under their wing feathers.

For their protection, it's best to keep your feathered friends *inside* during freezing rain, ice storms or high wind chills. While they can venture outdoors for brief periods, ducks shouldn't be allowed to stay there for long when temperatures drop beneath 15F degrees (20F for smaller Bantam breeds).

Muscovy ducks in particular are vulnerable to frostbite—especially on their red faces. They should only be allowed outside for brief excursions when temperatures drop beneath 40F degrees.

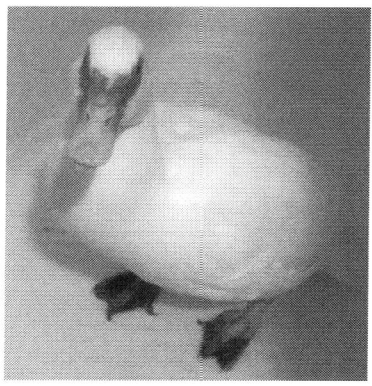 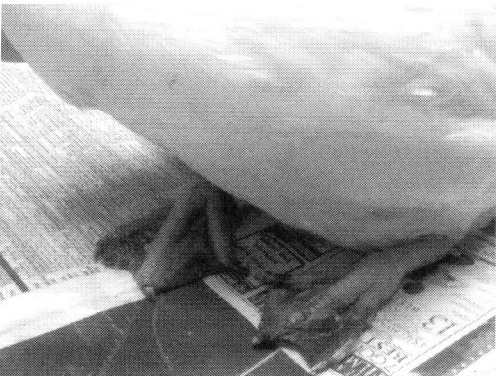

Viola's frostbitten feet / Photo Courtesy of Maggie Ciarcia-Belloni

- **Symptoms**

Some symptoms of frostbite may include: the sudden appearance of black areas on your duck's skin; this includes, but is not limited to their bill, legs and webbed feet.

- **Treatment**

Ducks suffering from frostbite need to be brought to a veterinarian for treatment as soon as possible. Mild cases are usually remedied with Granulex® drops, which have a consistency similar to molasses. It's applied twice daily to the affected areas and rapid (sometimes even overnight) improvement is often seen as it facilitates the removal of necrotic tissue. Treatment usually continues for seven days or until their skin is fully remedied and appears normal again (although there may be some scarring as well as permanent loss of toenails). Treatment in more severe cases often involves the surgical cutting away of damaged tissue and sometimes even partial foot or limb amputation. In any case, pain medication is often called for, so remember to be your duck's voice and ask for it.

Skin Coloration Changes

You may notice that your Muscovy duck's red face changes color from time to time. It may be bright red one day and then dabbled with yellow highlights the next. There's no need to worry; this is completely normal.

Muscovy ducks have beautiful red masks around their eyes and edges of their bills. These areas are far more prevalent in males than females and they become increasingly more profound with age, often extending downward over a portion of their necks.

Red caruncles often appear their brightest during the throes of passion that accompany the spring mating season. Muscovy ducks literally *brighten up* at the sight of a potential mate, or when they encounter competition for said love interest. Human imprinted Muscovies will often perk up similarly when their caretaker appears on the scene. This subtle flash of red is often overlooked in light of the myriad of vocalizations that tend to distract even the most astute Momma Duck.

During periods of calmness their otherwise ruby facial caruncles can fade in color. This is especially witnessed around the eyes and at the peaks of their bumps—most notably on the tip of the bulbous and distinguishing "bean" protuberance that lies directly over a male's bill. Color changes can be as subtle as a mild wash-out (from red to a reddish-pink), or as obvious as a color change (from red to peach, or from peach to slightly yellow). And then, as soon as they're excited again, they'll flush red with color once more.

Broody females can appear much brighter than non-laying or older girls, but then when they actually start nesting on their eggs, their blood will gradually divert from their faces down to their bellies to incubate their eggs. When this happens, their faces pale in comparison.

Provided these skin color changes are relatively symmetrical and aren't caused by weather extremes, it's all perfectly normal. Even leg and bill colors can change in accordance with these adjustments in blood flow.

Bella & Billy admire their eggs

Things to keep in mind:

1. Facial colors can change from yellow, to peach, to pink, to red as Muscovy ducks mature.
2. Color changes tend to be subtle and should be *underwhelming* as opposed to overwhelming.
3. Color changes often occur seasonally, coinciding with the mating season.
4. Color changes should be symmetrical (this is true of their bill and legs as well).
5. Sudden color changes that coincide with extreme temperatures or exposure to sun should be taken seriously.

Lacerations

There are few things more frightening than finding blood on your duck's feathers or somewhere on the ground, but accidents can happen. The best way to prevent them is to provide your duck with a safe, predator-proof pen and to keep their grounds free of foreign or sharp objects.

If your duck succumbs to a laceration, you'll need to go back to their pen and isolate the cause of the injury in order to prevent future occurrences.

- **Symptoms**

Some symptoms of lacerations may include: bleeding (minor or severe) and localized swelling around the wound.

- **Treatment**

You'll need to quickly catch and restrain your duck in order to search for the source of the bleeding. A small cut can be cleaned with wound wash while more severe lacerations need to be examined by a qualified vet. Apply direct pressure to stop any bleeding and seek out immediate treatment.

Your vet will flush out the wound, cleaning away any debris and clearing the site for careful inspection. Depending on the severity of the laceration, your duck may require stitches, which may or may not need to be done under anesthesia. While all lacerations can be serious, smooth-edged cuts caused by sharp objects can take particularly longer to heal because they're more prone to reopening. Failure to stitch them closed can prevent proper healing and drastically increase the risk of infection.

An antibiotic will most likely be prescribed for 7-14 days along with an anti-inflammatory to help control pain and swelling. Depending on location and severity, your vet may also instruct you to wash the area with a non-stinging wound wash a couple of times a day and bandage changes may also be required.

Lacerations occurring underneath your duck's webbed feet can be far more serious than other cuts and will require extra special attention to ensure they don't become infected. Ducks with foot wounds of this nature need to be set up in hygienic quarters until the laceration has fully healed. I find that private quarters (in view of other ducks whenever possible) bedded with clean pine shavings can keep things nicely sanitary during their healing phase.

Puncture Wounds

Puncture wounds tend to occur when your duck steps on something sharp while waddling along. Thorns and sharp stalks of broken plants are two common causes. Puncture wounds can also be caused by an animal bite.

- **Symptoms**

Some symptoms of a puncture wound may include: circular hole pierced into the skin, bleeding (minor or severe) and localized swelling around the wound(s). Multiple punctures (especially two found side-by-side) often indicate a predator bite.

- **Treatment**

The treatment and prevention of puncture wounds is the same as treatment for lacerations (see: *"Lacerations"*). Because puncture wounds can be deep and are far more likely to contain foreign debris (or dangerous bacteria in the case of animal bites), they should always be vet checked to prevent the formation of an abscess. Wound flushing, antibiotics and anti-inflammatory pain medications are all a vital part of your duck's treatment plan.

Abscesses

An abscess is formed when your duck's immune system reacts defensively to foreign material in their body. Some examples include: a thorn, splinter, or bacteria stemming from an animal bite (most commonly Staph). The tissue around the infectious matter becomes inflamed, swelling to encapsulate and prevent it from spreading further throughout their body. This tissue then becomes filled with pus.

Sometimes an abscess will form where you can actually see it, occasionally growing as large as an egg and stretching your duck's skin until the sudden appearance of pink flesh between their feathers catches your attention. Other times you'll have no idea something's wrong because it'll be camouflaged beneath a thick layer of fluffy feathers, or on the underside of your duck where you don't often look. This is why it's vital to always pay attention to changes in your duck's behavior. It will often be your first indicator that something is amiss.

- **Symptoms**

Some symptoms of an abscess may include: fatigue, appetite loss, weight loss and disinterest in normal activities. These changes can be very mild—almost unnoticeable. If you see your duck lazing around a bit more than usual it's a good idea to sit down with them and give them precursory medical exam. Feel around gently, searching for any swollen or painful areas on their body.

- **Treatment**

If you find any lumps or swollen areas on your duck you need to bring them to the vet for immediate treatment. Vets will often use a syringe to draw the fluid out of a minor and superficial abscess, giving your duck some instant relief. If the abscess is deeper within your duck's body cavity or is on the larger side, they'll likely suggest surgery, so they can carefully go inside to drain the fluid and clean it out properly. Depending on the location of the abscess this surgery can be relatively straightforward, or quite complicated if they need to avoid any neighboring internal organs. In any case they'll prescribe antibiotics for a minimum of 14 days to prevent infection and instruct you to keep them in very clean quarters (usually asking you to keep them out of the water) and out of reach of your other ducks.

Your duck should be rechecked in a week to confirm that the abscess in not refilling with pus. If it has, your vet will draw more of the fluid out at that time and have you schedule another follow-up appointment, so that they can continue to monitor your duck's progress.

The liquid drawn from the abscess should be clear to slightly yellow. If pus is yellow, thick or creamy in consistency the infection has advanced and may require immediate surgery. A drain may need to be inserted, but this is normally reserved as a last resort (or in the case of serious infection) since ducks are meticulous when it comes to preening and often pluck out the drain tube.

Failure to get your duck to the vet right away can result in the rupturing of the abscess. If your duck hid their abscess from you, this might be when you notice it. It's vital to get your duck to the vet for emergency care right away to avoid the further spreading of the infection and to close the open wound. Your vet will flush, drain and stitch the area before prescribing a strong dose of antibiotics and anti-inflammatory/pain medication.

Cysts

If you feel a small bump or mass beneath your duck's skin, you should have it examined by your vet.

- **Symptoms**

Some symptoms of a cyst may include: slow-growing, free-floating, bump under the skin (not attached to muscle or bone) that's smooth to the touch when rolled under the skin. Small, harmless cysts have no associated redness, irritation, or weeping while an infected or larger cyst may result in pain, inflammation, discharge and irritation.

- **Treatment**

Your vet will likely advise you to watch for any changes and schedule a follow-up visit to have them rechecked if any are seen.

If the cyst is irritated, infected, unusually large or causing your duck discomfort due to its location, your vet may recommend removal. Post-operative care requires keeping the surgical site clean to prevent infection as well as antibiotic and anti-inflammatory/pain medication for 7-14 days. In some cases, (especially with large cyst removals) additional pain medication may also be required.

Follicular Cysts

Follicular cysts tend to appear on the wings of birds, but they can occasionally turn up in more vulnerable areas. A follicular cyst occurs when a feather follicle is facing in the wrong direction. The feather that subsequently grows from this follicle is aimed incorrectly and grows inside of your duck's body instead of outside. These tiny feathers grow, break off and then form into a knot around the follicle. New feathers will continue to grow and break off, and become embedded in a fatty mass.

Although a singular follicular cyst is quite treatable, ducks with multiple, reoccurring or masses of follicular cysts may be suffering from a high level of estrogen, which may be indicative of some form of lymphoma of the reproductive system.

Follicular cysts (particularly those on the wings) can be caused by petting your duck while they're molting. This action can lead to ingrown feathers. To help remedy this, avoid petting your duck during periods of feather growth.

- **Symptoms**

Some symptoms of a follicular cyst may include: a small, pink skin lump (usually discovered on the wing), that can remain the same size or grow over time (often mistaken for an abscess).

- **Treatment**

On the wings: If your duck has a small follicular cyst on their wing your vet will likely recommend a simple surgical procedure where they remove the misdirected feather follicle and the mass surrounding it. Your duck will be prescribed an antibiotic for 7-14 days. If the cyst was on the larger side they may also need an anti-inflammatory. In either case, recovery tends to be quick and easy.

On the body: A follicular cyst that develops on your duck's body is removed similarly to those that form on their wings, although depending upon the cyst's location it can potentially be more serious. The real trouble with the locale of this kind of cyst is they can be really difficult to spot, being easily camouflaged by your duck's own body and feathers as they form and grow inside. In fact, it often isn't until they've grown quite large (sometimes as big as an egg) that you'll even discover them.

Large follicular body cysts like these can become infected, resulting in additional swelling and the accumulation of pus. This is why follicular body cysts are frequently and easily misdiagnosed as abscesses—even by good vets. Your vet will follow the protocol for treating an abscess, draining it via syringe (if they can) and prescribing antibiotics and anti-inflammatory/pain medication.

The pus should appear clear or mildly yellow in color. If your vet draws a thick, yellowy liquid with a creamy or pasty consistency from the site (indicating infection), if the mass never completely diminishes over the next two weeks, or if your duck is experiencing changes in behavior, appetite, activity level and/or temperament anywhere along the way, your vet will most likely recommend immediate surgery to get a better look at what's going on inside.

During this comprehensive surgery to clean out the abscess site, your vet will soon discover that the root cause of the issue is a reversed feather follicle. At this point they'll remove the follicular cyst and flush out the area. After closing with a few stitches they'll prescribe your duck antibiotics and anti-inflammatory/pain medication for 14 days, during which your duck will need to go back for one or two more rechecks.

As with any surgery, you'll want to keep your duck in very clean quarters and protected from other ducks who might accidentally harm them. To avoid infection they shouldn't be allowed to swim until your vet clears them during their post-operative visit.

Bruises

Not all body lumps are the result of growths or infection, some are caused by the more obvious bumps and bruises.

Young Jeffrey loves to give me hugs whenever I visit him in his pen, so I quickly noticed the lump that had suddenly appeared on the side of his neck. Since the lump hadn't been there that morning and had abruptly appeared in the afternoon, I could rule out it being a cyst or abscess. Upon closer inspection, I could see that it wasn't cut or bleeding and that the swelling was superficial—not the result of a globular mass beneath the skin. I could tell that the lump was the clear result of a good nip from his best friend and brother Young Matthew.

- **Symptoms**

Some symptoms of bruising may include: The sudden appearance of a swollen area or lump on your duck's skin and skin discoloration. Swelling decreases with healing.

- **Treatment**

It's important to keep a close eye on an injury like this, being aware of any increases in swelling—especially on the throat, where it could interfere with breathing or eating. Provided the bruise ceases to swell and doesn't interfere with normal behavior, you can simply monitor it over the next few days to make sure it gradually diminishes and disappears. If, however, there's any bleeding, if swelling continues, or if it fails to resolve itself and clear up, a vet visit is definitely in order.

Melanoma

Skin cancer is extremely rare in ducks, but when it does occur it tends to be in particular locations of the body where the skin is routinely disturbed. This can either be on their bills, which they use to forage, or around their oil glands, which get worked and prodded frequently throughout their lives.

I've often wondered about sun exposure as it relates to duck bills and Muscovy faces. I assume since melanomas can occur on human fingernails that they can also occur on a duck's bill. While I've yet to hear of a reported case of sunburn or skin cancer that was caused by the sun, I have to guess that it can happen even if people aren't emailing me about it. So, to err on the side of caution, make sure that all of your ducks always have ample amounts of thick shade in multiple locations in their pen, so that every flock member has a safe retreat from the sun's damaging rays.

- **Symptoms**

Some symptoms of melanoma may include: discolored area of the bill (not to be confused with freckles) or a mass on the bill.

- **Treatment**

Vets may be able to excise the tissue, depending on its location, but whether they can remove all of the cancer will likely be guess work. Pain medications may need to be employed and in severe or prolonged cases, euthanasia may need to be explored.

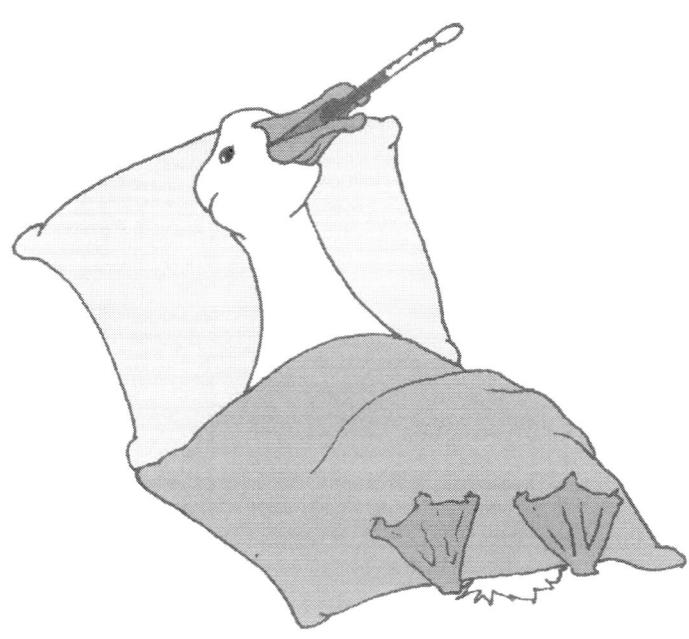

Medical #3
Integumentary System (Feathers)

Your duck's feathers are one their greatest assets, providing insulation and protection from the environment. When preened and oiled properly, they maintain waterproof effectiveness and help afford your duck their buoyancy. When they're not working properly, your duck can become chilled, overheated or may not be able to float properly. Ducks with poor feather quality who become trapped on water have even been known to drown.

Generally speaking, your duck has soft body feathers as well as rigid tail and "flight" feathers, which for the sake of clarity I prefer to call "wing" feathers since most domestic ducks can't fly. When you glance at any one of these feathers, what you're actually seeing is a divine system of interlocking hooks and barbs. On their own these bits and pieces would just fray apart, but through the use of that wonderful little comb equipped in every duck's bill, they zip back together to form a perfect seal.

Molting

The first time you see your duck molting it can be a little bit alarming. Rest assured, your duck isn't harboring a horrible parasite, nor have they contracted some rare skin disease; they're just shedding their old feathers and growing some nice new ones in their place. You'll see fresh pin feathers pushing through in no time, and their plumage should be fully restored in 2-3 weeks.

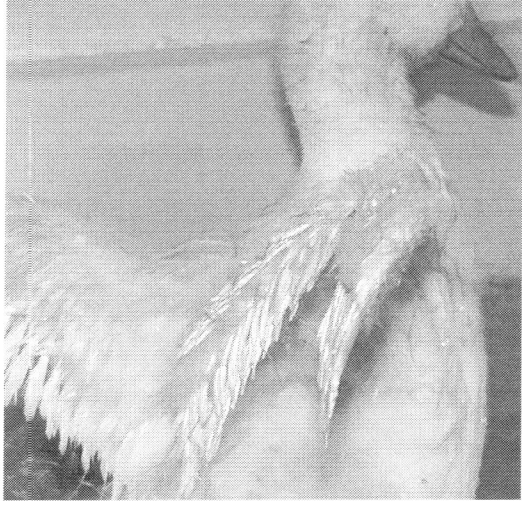

Lil Bo Peep sprouts her first wing feathers

- **Why do ducks molt?**

Feathers simply don't last forever. They become damaged and wear out. It's vital that your duck grows new replacement feathers to keep them insulated and protected from the environment—as well as waterproof.

- **When do ducks molt?**

This is always a difficult question because not only is every duck different, but males and females are different too. I've noticed that for the most part, ducks live by their own schedules. Some ducks molt "on time," while others molt early and still others molt late. Feathers dropping out of some ducks are extremely noticeable, while others seem to experience an almost transparent transformation. When and how your ducks molt often depends upon their breed, gender, genetics, climate, weather, lighting and diet.

- **Molting of sexually monomorphic ducks**

In my experience, and in our Connecticut climate, most monomorphic ducks go through two molts a year. By monomorphic I mean those breeds whose males and females have like-colored plumage. Examples include: Pekin, Cayuga, Aylesbury, Magpie, Ancona, Blue Swede, East Indie as well as some varieties of Call and Runner ducks.

1. They experience one very fluffy molt where they replace only their body feathers anytime between spring and summer. This truly varies from duck-to-duck, weighing heavily upon climate and weather.

2. Drakes go through a complete molt (body, wing and tail feathers) sometime between August and September, while females usually follow suit sometime between September and early October.

- **Molting of sexually dimorphic ducks**

In my experience, most dimorphic ducks also go through two molts a year. By dimorphic I mean those breeds whose males and females have different colored plumage (at least for part of the year). Examples include: Mallard, Khaki Campbell, Buff Orpington, Silver & Mini Appleyard, Welsh Harlequin, Saxony, Rouen as well as some varieties of Call and Runner ducks.

Males:

1. Drakes usually go through a complete molt (body, wing and tail feathers) sometime between June and July. During this time they shed their colorful feathers in exchange for more subdued and blended tones, which provide better camouflage. This is known as the *eclipse* molt and it's a quality belonging to their wild mallard predecessors who needed to be able to hide while growing their new flight feathers. Males and females often appear similar during this time.

2. Drakes go through a second molt, shedding only their body feathers in the late fall, usually around October. During this molt, they shed their earthy plumage and re-grow new and radiant-colored feathers in their place. This will prepare them for the upcoming spring mating season.

Females:

1. Females usually molt their body feathers in the spring.
2. Females go through a second and complete molt in the late summer.

- **Molting of Muscovy ducks**

Muscovy ducks only go through one molt late in the year. My drakes often molt sometime between September and October, while my females usually molt sometime between October and November (and sometimes as late as early December).

Muscovy females in particular can often get very bare (and sometimes even bald) necks for a short period during their molt. Neck feathers tend to grow back rather quickly, so if they don't begin to reappear within a week of dropping out, something else may be going on (over-mated by males, parasites, etc.).

- **Molting tidbits**

Here are a few tid-bits that can help give you some insight as to whether or not things are as they should be in regards to your duck's molting:

1. Ducks rarely molt in winter.
2. A sudden improvement in overall health or diet can spark an untimely molt.
3. Females usually stop laying eggs while they're molting.
4. Ducks usually molt rather evenly. While you may see thin areas, bald spots caused by molting are rare.
5. Molting is symmetrical. Feathers tend to drop out equally on the left and right sides of their wings and body.

- **A duck who hasn't molted**

If your duck has healthy, waterproof feathers don't worry about the timing of their molt. Just relax and let nature take its course. On the other hand, if your duck is overdue for a molt and you can tell by looking at their feathers, the problem requires further examination.

The number one cause of molting delays is malnutrition. If you're not feeding your duck quality name-brand waterfowl food, it's time to upgrade. Additional healthy veggie snacks can be served on the side, but the bulk of your duck's nutrients should come from their regular feed.

When newly rescued ducks come to our sanctuary, they commonly molt within a couple weeks of their arrival. This is especially true of malnourished or starving ducks. As soon as I place them on a nutritious diet of Mazuri® waterfowl feed, their bodies quickly react to the sudden influx of vitamins and minerals by dropping their old feathers and growing new ones while they have the chance.

Forced molt directions share striking similarities to conditions of severe deprivation. If your duck hasn't molted and someone advises you to put them through a forced molt, immediately turn and walk the other way. Directions for a forced molt often encourage putting birds through a phase of food and nutrient deprivation, followed by the sudden influx of quality meals. Many advocate a dangerous 1-2 week period of fasting followed by 4-6 weeks of small portions of crimped oats. At the end of this period, they suddenly feed large meals of grower ration. While the end result is fresh feather growth, the cost of their new plumage is malnutrition and starvation, both of which can be dangerous and even fatal. Forced molt strategies are unhealthy and should never be implemented.

- **Things to consider during the molt**

It's important to keep a few things in mind while your duck is shedding their old feathers and growing new ones.

1. Your duck's skin can become very prickly and sensitive when they're molting. Ducks who normally enjoy a good stroke over their feathers, might not want to endure a painful petting when they're feeling so tender. Most ducks will temporarily shy away and avoid unnecessary contact for a few weeks; some even become lethargic and lose a bit of their appetite. Keep an eye out to make sure they're still eating something and check for fever by occasionally feeling their bill to see if it's hot.

2. The petting and handling of a molting duck can result in the formation of follicular cysts (inward growing feather follicles) and should be avoided whenever possible—wings are especially prone (see: *"Follicular Cysts"*).

3. Non-flying ducks often flap their wings to help give them that added *umph* they need to get out of their pools and ponds. Without their primary wing feathers they often can't catch enough air to get up over the edge. Always make sure you have a stepping stone in place inside your duck's pool or pond to help them get out of the water when they're molting.

Feathers and Sunshine

Waterfowl breeders and exhibition showers are often advocates of keeping ducks out of the sun to avoid changing or fading out the colors of their feathers. East Indie, Cayuga, black Runner and black Call ducks in particular have a prism-like sheen to their ebony feathers. Breeders strive to keep this sheen as green as possible by shielding them from the sun's rays. I honestly don't understand this rational because when exposed to the sun their feathers gain an iridescent shimmer of green, blue, maroon and violet and it's absolutely gorgeous. When they flap their wings in the sunlight, you can see a virtual rainbow trapped in their feathers.

Don't deny your ducks access to the sunlight for the sake of their plumage. Your ducks are better off happy and healthy and that includes a good dose of sunshine.

Young Jeffrey has a myriad of prism colors in his feathers

Random Feathers

Some people (again… breeders & showers) will advise you to pluck out any random "unsightly" feathers—*heaven forbid!* Young Jeffrey was only a year old when he sprouted his first white feather—his first gray hair (you'd think his life was stressful or something). I wouldn't dare discomfort him with a pluck for the sake of someone else's esthetic taste. Personally, I think it gives him a very distinguished look. Let your duck keep any random mismatched feathers; they're not hurting anything.

Jeffrey sporting his distinguished white feather

Yellow Feathers

White Call, white Indian Runner and Pekin ducks (who don't have Aylesbury or Muscovy genes in the mix) don't actually have white feathers. When these ducks are healthy and well nourished they actually have a light-yellow hue to their feathers. Momma Ducks who serve ample healthy greens and veggies to their ducks will often notice that their ducks have a deeper yellow tint to their feathers than other ducks whose diets aren't supplemented with wholesome snacks. This color really stands out in the winter when your ducks can be seen against a backdrop of snow.

Impacted Oil Gland

Your duck's oil gland (or uropygial gland) is located near the root of their tail feathers. When preening you'll see them tuck their bill and roll their head in this area to gather the oil which they'll then spread all over their feathers. The feathers growing around the oil gland of a white duck often range from off-white to deep-yellow. White Muscovy drakes in particular have very yellow feathers around their oil glands. When it comes to oil glands, you should recognize what's normal for your duck and then keep an eye out for any deviances from this healthy baseline.

Although relatively uncommon, your duck's oil gland can become partially or completely clogged. If you notice a decline in the appearance of your duck's feathers, and have ruled out molting and parasites, you'll want to verify that their oil gland is functioning properly. To do this, part the feathers over their oil gland and check for any redness or swelling as well as any abnormal crusting or accumulation of oil. Again, it really helps if you know what your duck's oil gland looks like on a normal day and have a basis of comparison.

- **Symptoms**

Some symptoms of an impacted oil gland may include: redness, inflammation, tenderness, decreased feather quality, excessive shaking of tail feathers (abnormal tail wagging), unnatural oil crusting or waxy accumulation on or around the oil gland.

- **Treatment**

The visible accumulation of caked oil can be gently cleaned away with clean, warm water. Repeat this process as needed 2-3 times daily. A hot pack (not too hot!) can be held over the impacted gland, 1-2 times daily. This moist heat therapy will often help get things moving again. After removing the pack, gently massage the area for a minute or two unless it causes discomfort, in which case, stop immediately. In some cases, your vet may need to physically "milk" their oil gland to help clear the blockage and alleviate some of the internal pressure, giving your duck a bit of instant relief. Do not attempt this on your own at home.

An oil gland can become blocked for a variety of reasons, which you'll want to explore thoroughly with your vet.

1. *Infection:* Most vets will prescribe a round of antibiotics for 7-14 days as part of their treatment strategy for an impacted oil gland. If there's any swelling they'll probably prescribe an anti-inflammatory/pain medication as well. These medications will usually do the trick, but if your duck isn't improving or if their condition worsens during this treatment period, you'll need to contact your vet again right away (see: *"Infected Oil Gland"*).

2. *Overactive Oil Gland:* This occurs when your duck produces more oil than is necessary. This excess can often lead to blockages and impaction (see: *"Overactive Oil Gland"*).

3. *Stress:* If one of your ducks is being picked on by another flock member, a quiet reprieve might do them some good. Try giving them their own separate accommodations, where they're still in sight of the others for a little bit of downtime. Other common stressors include: surgery, environmental changes, loss and changes in routine. Human-imprinted ducks in particular can become stressed when their Momma Ducks are away. Stressors can result in oil blockages, which need to be treated while also providing them with unwavering routines and gentle reassurances.

4. *Hormones:* Shifts in hormone levels can sometimes influence the functioning of your duck's oil gland. These fluxes can be the result of seasonal changes in daylight hours, the onset of mating season, old age or tumors. You may be able to counteract mother nature by walking your duck up to their barn an hour or two earlier than usual when the days get longer, by cutting down on their access to mating activities and in the case of tumors, through surgery.

5. *Tumors & Ulcers:* Lumps (benign or cancerous), growths or superficial sores on or near your duck's oil gland can interfere with its normal functioning and will need to be examined by your vet right away. Surgical removal of tumors while avoiding the oil gland (whenever possible) is often recommended while open ulcers will likely require debridement and antibiotic treatment.

6. *Diet:* An improper diet can be the cause of a malfunctioning oil gland, especially one short of vitamin A. When malnutrition is a factor, stepping up your duck's feed to a higher quality brand and serving up healthy snacks can often make the difference. Consult with your vet before adding any vitamin supplements to their diet because a vitamin A overdose can result in permanent liver damage. Some vets will advise you to temporarily implement wheat into your duck's diet because it can help jumpstart their oil gland again, getting it to produce more oil. Additionally, some vets may advise you to add a little bit of fish oil to your duck's food. If you go this route, be careful not to add too much oil or it can quickly end up on their feathers—worsening an already bad situation. A better option can be to supplement their feed with a small, round cat kibble that has fish oil right in the mix.

If your duck doesn't respond to any available treatment options, the surgical removal of their oil gland is an absolute *final resort* usually reserved for serious injury to the oil gland (see: *"Ruptured Oil Gland"*). If you follow through with this operation, your duck will no longer be able to waterproof their own feathers. This means, they'll need *you* to take on the responsibility of keeping them clean and dry and they'll also need extra special protection from the heat and cold. This is a big commitment, so make sure you weigh it out carefully when discussing it with your vet. Whenever possible, it's highly advisable to seek out a second opinion.

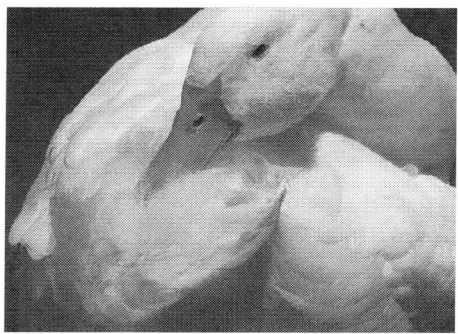

Gulliver utilizes his oil gland to preen

Overactive Oil Gland

An overactive oil gland produces more oil than your duck requires for their daily preening. The leftover oil tends to linger around the oil gland, staining light-colored feathers yellow. Provided this overabundance is normal for your duck, the only risk of having an overactive oil gland is the increased chance that it might become clogged at some point.

Ducks with misshapen or damaged bills often have a particularly difficult time preening. In their case, what appears to be an overactive oil gland may in-fact just be an underactive bill; that is, a duck who simply can't keep up with the oil their body is producing. Acknowledge this as their baseline and simply watch for any changes. Overweight ducks and ducks with leg problems or balance issues can also have a difficult time connecting with their oil glands and preening properly, in which case weight loss and stretch therapy can sometimes lead to improvements (see: *"Stretch Therapy"*). Giving your duck opportunities to bathe and preen in shallow water can give them the added support they need to balance and successfully reach their oil gland.

- **Symptoms**

Some symptoms of an overactive oil gland may include: the accumulation of excess oil around the gland and the staining of white or light-colored feathers in the immediate vicinity (often to a dark yellow).

- **Treatment**

If it's unusual for your duck to suddenly have so much extra oil lingering around their gland, you should take them to the vet for an examination. It may not be an issue with their gland at all, but rather something else entirely that's causing them to preen less frequently, causing oil build-up. Until the situation is remedied you'll likely need to help them remove some of that excess oil every day by wiping it away with a clean, disposable cloth.

Underactive Oil Gland

An underactive oil gland is one that isn't producing enough oil for your duck to waterproof their feathers properly. Limited oil flow is usually the result of a partial obstruction. As I've already mentioned, these blockages are usually attributed to environmental factors like infection, stress, hormonal fluxes, tumors, ulcers or malnutrition, but on rare occasions the unavailability of oil can also be linked to genetic factors such as an underdeveloped or small oil gland.

Inherited oil gland issues are life-long, so if your adult duck has a sudden onset of symptoms you're not looking at a genetic problem. On the other hand, if your growing duckling begins having coverage troubles as their mature feathers continue to emerge and grow they may have reached a point in their development where they've maxed out the capacity of their inherently undersized or immature oil gland.

Part the feathers over your young duck's oil gland and check for any redness, swelling, crusty or waxy build-up, or tenderness to the area. These are all signs of an impaction. If you see any of them, you're not looking at a genetic problem.

If you don't see any signs of an impaction you can take your investigation a little bit further to make sure your duck's oil gland is functioning. To do this, locate your duckling's *wick* feathers. These are the feathers that sprout right out of your duck's oil gland. Gently place your fingertips at their base. Gently slide your fingers up and along the feathers, moving in the direction of feather growth toward their tips. When you're finished take a close look at your fingers and then rub them gently together. If you see or feel a thin iridescent film on your skin, your duckling's oil gland is working. If it's difficult for you to collect a sample—if the feathers around the gland are dry, you could be looking at an underactive oil gland.

- **Symptoms**

Some symptoms of an inactive oil gland may include: decreased feather quality and the absence of oil on wick feathers.

- **Treatment**

A suddenly underactive oil gland is usually partially impacted and treated accordingly (see: *"Impacted Oil Gland"*).

On the other hand, ducks with lifelong issues that began at a certain point in their development are likely experiencing a genetic condition for which there isn't a cure. In this case, keeping their pen, house and swimming water as clean as possible will help them maintain quality feathers with minimal oil.

In either case, and whenever your duck has an issue with their feathers or oil gland, vet care should be actively sought out.

Infected Oil Gland

Older or immune compromised ducks are more prone to bacterial infections than younger and healthier ducks. Ducks swimming in unsanitary water are also at higher risk.

- **Symptoms**

Symptoms of an infected oil gland may include: redness, inflammation, tenderness, decreased feather quality, excessive shaking of tail feathers (abnormal tail wagging), unnatural oil crusting and waxy accumulation on or around the oil gland.

- **Treatment**

While less experienced vets may suggest lancing and draining the gland as a treatment option, these measures rarely prove effective and can actually lead to further infection. Instead, a qualified vet will take an oil sample from your duck's gland and send it off to a lab for culturing. While waiting for results they'll likely start your duck on a general antibiotic as well as anti-inflammatory/pain medication.

If the infection is minor (mildly visible symptoms) your vet may suggest antibiotic treatment without lab culturing for 7-14 days. Providing the situation doesn't worsen and you see quick and permanent improvement, you may not need to go any further than this. However, if the infection is more advanced (redness, swelling, tenderness etc.), don't waste time on an antibiotic that may not target the culprit bacteria.

Staph and e. coli are common culprits when it comes to oil gland infections. If either are the case with your duck, your vet may employ multiple strategies to help combat it.

1. Specific oral antibiotics are prescribed in accordance with bacterial susceptibility.

2. Vetericyn® VF spray can be used topically twice a day to disinfect the skin on and around your duck's oil gland.

3. A topical antibiotic ointment like Oxytetracycline/Polymyxin B can be applied directly to their oil gland twice a day.

4. If the bacteria is susceptible, Today® Cephapirin Sodium antimicrobial medication can be injected directly into your duck's oil gland.

To administer Today® Cephapirin Sodium, your vet will place the tip of the dosing syringe at the large pore of your duck's oil gland opening and then painlessly inject some of its salve directly into their gland. This is commonly repeated once a week for 3-4 weeks.

This down side of this type of medication is that it has an unappealing flavor, which will make the oil in your duck's gland taste less appealing for a while. It's vital that you monitor your duck's feather quality closely during this time. If their feather quality diminishes (which is pretty likely), they'll need extra protection from hot, wet or cold conditions until the treatment period ends and the medication has time to work its way back out of their oil gland.

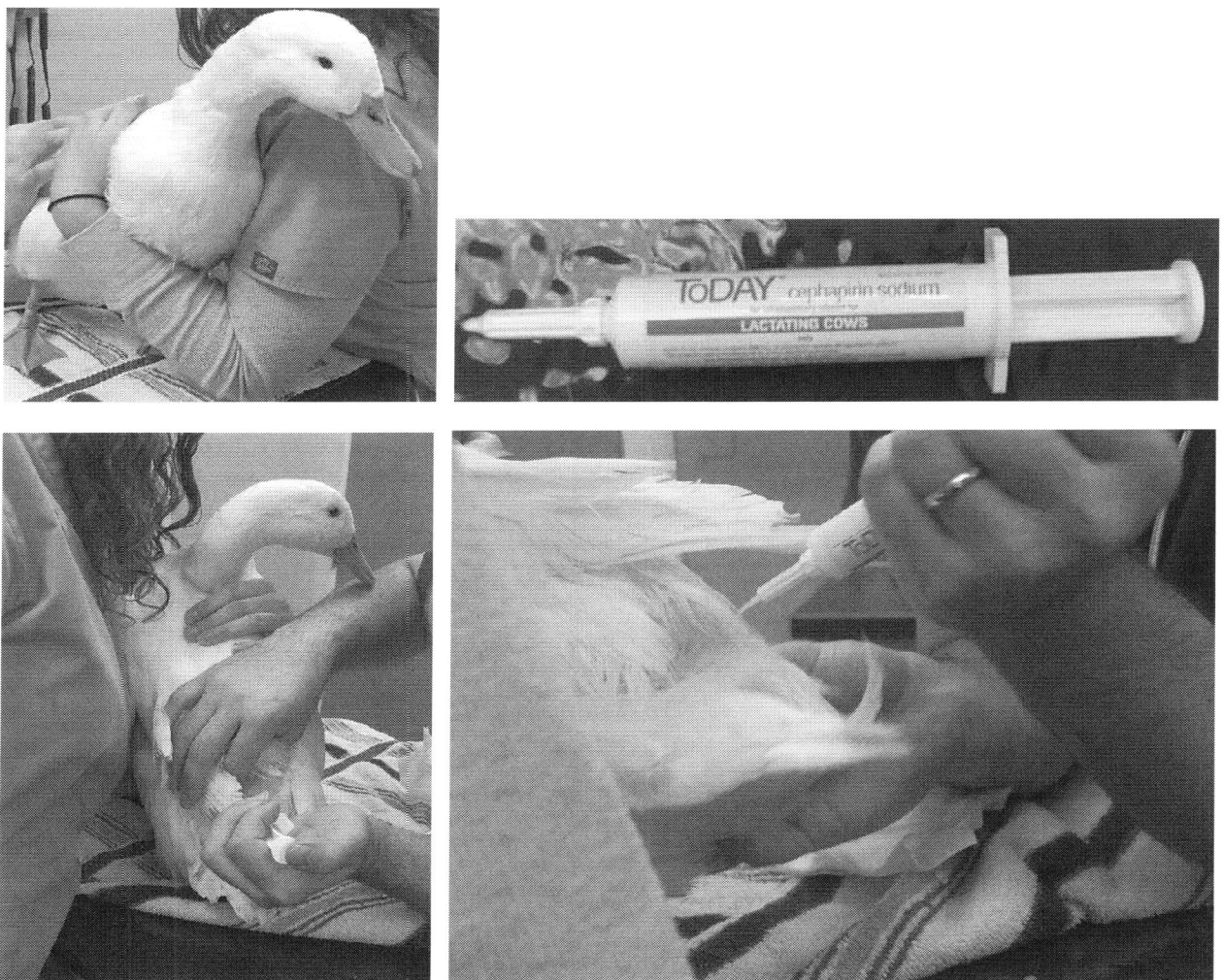

Twelve year-old Demi gets a Today® treatment to remedy a staph infection in her oil gland

Ruptured Oil Gland

A direct injury to the oil gland can be permanent and devastating. They're often caused by predator attack and can impact your duck's ability to waterproof their feathers for the rest of their life.

- **Symptoms**

Some symptoms of a ruptured oil gland may include: bleeding, tearing or visible damage of the oil gland or surrounding tissue.

- **Treatment**

Ruptured glands must be surgically repaired or removed immediately following injury; afterwards, your duck will require antibiotics, anti-inflammatory/pain medication and additional pain medication. A drain may need to be inserted for a few days. In severe cases, your duck may no longer repel water the way they did prior to the operation. This means, you'll need to take on the responsibility of keeping them clean and dry and they'll also need extra special protection from the heat, rain and cold.

Wet Feather

When a duck's feather quality declines to the point that they can no longer properly repel water, their condition is referred to as *wet feather*. Sometimes wet feather can be fully remedied; other times, it's chronic and only a full molt with new feather growth will restore your duck back to normal.

If your duck's feathers appear tattered and aren't properly "zip-locked" together, they're not going to be as effective as they should be at repelling water and keeping your duck insulated. If the root cause is addressed early enough and remedied properly, damage can be minimal; otherwise, it can seriously impact feather function. The first step to treating wet feather is to determine its cause.

Parasites: If you notice that your duck's wing or tail feathers are beginning to fray apart, you may be witnessing the first sign of lice or mites. These feather-eating parasites can cause serious damage if their numbers are left unchecked. Treatment is often as simple as a quick application of delousing powder (see: *"Lice"*) repeated again in eight days.

Over-mating: Female ducks who receive too much attention from drakes often display signs of feather damage on their wings and backs. You can improve their situation by immediately addressing your hen-to-drake ratio (adding more females) or by initiating separations to safely reduce their exposure to overzealous males.

Malnutrition: An unhealthy diet can be a major factor when it comes to feather malfunction. Ducks kept on substandard diets (consisting mostly of table scraps, generic brand/cheap feed, cracked corn and bread) are far more likely to have growth, maintenance and breakage issues than ducks who are served quality waterfowl feed. They simply can't get enough of the vitamins and minerals they need to grow and maintain vigorous feathers when they're fed junk food. While healthy veggie snacks are always a welcome addition to a wholesome diet, it's vital that their main staple be nutritionally designed for health and longevity.

Unsanitary grounds: Ducks kept in unsanitary pens are going to end up with dirty feathers. No matter how hard they work to preen and keep tidy, the continual exposure to filth (mud and poop) makes it impossible for them to keep up. You can remedy this situation by routinely cleaning their pen, house and barn. You may also need to address drainage issues in your pen, making necessary landscaping changes and utilizing sand to cover any occasional unruly spots.

Polluted swimming water: Ducks who swim and bathe in stagnant or filthy water are at risk of feather complications. As with filthy pens, dirty water can be impossible for them to keep up with. Clean all pools and ponds thoroughly (scrubbing them down) and initiate more frequent water changes.

Illness: A sick duck can suffer energy loss and nausea that prevent them from preening their feathers properly. They simply fall behind on their tidying and oiling and their feather quality goes downhill from there. During bouts of illness, you can often help your duck keep clean by placing them in the bathtub for a brief float every 1-2 days. Afterwards, set them down on a soft bed of towels and safely blow dry them. As soon as they're feeling better, they'll take over the responsibility again and your efforts will have saved them any permanent feather damage.

Oil gland issues: Trouble with your duck's oil gland can quickly lead to poor feather quality. There are a variety of causes which you and your vet will need to examine in order to ensure quick and proper treatment.

Physical challenges: Ducks with limb injuries, misshapen bills or balance issues often have greater difficulty reaching their oil glands and then stretching to other hard-to-reach places than other ducks. Sometimes you can help a friendly duck (who's used to being handled) keep clean by comfortably supporting their body weight with your hands while they preen. Another trick is to give them access to shallow water, which supports the bulk of their body weight while also allowing them to set their feet down on the ground while they preen. Some bathtub/blow drying time may also be in order.

Unnatural oil: If your duck's feathers become coated with any kind of unnatural oil or substance that they can't remove on their own (or that's unsafe for them to remove on their own and subsequently ingest), their feathers will rapidly decline. I once heard from someone who heard ducks cleaned themselves with oil and subsequently washed their duck in olive oil in an attempt to help tidy them up. Big mistake. Never use any kind of products on your duck's feathers without consulting with a vet first. If your duck's feathers become laden with any kind of foreign substance consult with a vet. They'll probably have you wash their feathers (see: *"Wet Feather Corrective Procedure"*), which may or may not need to be repeated multiple times.

Joseph came to our sanctuary with problems with his dream coat

Minor Wet Feather Resolution

When wet feather is caused by structural damage to your duck's feathers (as with parasites, over-mating and malnutrition), there's often not much you can do after-the-fact to improve their plumage situation aside from waiting for their next molt.

On the other hand, if their feathers are laden with dirt or grime, you can often resolve minor issues (and even improve a chronic situation) by giving your duck a clean space to recover. Before beginning, make sure you address the source of your duck's feather problem, or their issues will simply reoccur again.

1. Move your duck to a safe and sanitary location bedded with clean pine shavings.
2. Provide them with full access to a clean bucket of water (changed frequently) to allow for splash-preening.
3. Give your duck access to fresh and clean swimming water at least once a day (blow dry after, if necessary).
4. Protect your duck from rain, heat and cold.
5. Continue for 1-2 weeks until maximum benefits are witnessed.

Severe Wet Feather Corrective Procedure

If you're not seeing any progress in your duck's feathers within the first 5-7 days, it may be time to step things up. The following wet feather corrective procedure should *not* be attempted until you first give your duck ample opportunity to remedy their situation on their own *and* consult with a vet—*unless* their feathers are coated in some kind of substance unnatural to them, in which case this can be done immediately under vet guidance.

1. *Wash:* Place your duck into a lukewarm bath and then place a pea-sized amount of Dawn® dishwashing liquid onto the palm of your hand. I prefer Dawn® Ultra Pure Essentials (which is clear and dye-free as well as hypoallergenic) over the fancier fragranced and colored versions (even the one with the duckling on the label!).

   Rub your hands together adding a small amount of water until you have a rich lather. Gently work the lather through their feathers, always working in the direction of feather growth, from base to tip, and *never* against. Avoid the areas around their eyes and bill. If needed you can touch-up these regions later with a facecloth soaked in warm, clean water (no soap).

Foster Joseph bathing in the tub

2. *Rinse:* After bathing, drain the tub and commence with a thorough rinsing. Ideally you'll need a flexible shower head that you can bring down to your duck's level and adjust to a gentle setting in order to accomplish this. If your bathtub isn't equipped with one of these, then a plastic cup will have to do (just be sure to use clean water from the tap to rinse your duck rather than scooping up dirty/soapy tub water). Continue rinsing your duck with lukewarm water until you remove *all* of the soap from their feathers.

3. *Dry:* Lay down a couple fluffy towels and set your duck down on top of them. If your duck is standing, use another towel to gently pat their underside and soak up some of the excess, dripping water. If they're sitting, the towel beneath them will do the work for you. As the towels get wet, stack more dry towels on top or replace them entirely. Once the bulk of the water has been absorbed, it's time to take out your hair dryer for the somewhat tedious step of blow drying your duck. Keep in mind this is going to take some time, so make sure you and your duck are set up comfortably for the next hour of feather fluffing (which is a vital portion of the procedure). The good news is once your duck gets used to this pampering, they'll most likely actively help you out with some preening.

   Duck blow drying safety tips:

   a. Never use your blow dryer in or around a bathtub of water.
   b. Plug your blow dryer into a GFCI outlet for added safety.

c. Pay attention to your blow dryer's setting. *Medium* or *Low* heat settings are much safer than *High* heat settings, which can burn your duck's skin (including their bill and feet).
d. Keep your blow dryer far enough away from your duck's skin to prevent any burning.
e. Don't hover over one feathery spot for too long to prevent any burning (keep your dryer moving).
f. If your duck begins to pant, lower the heat setting and/or open a window or door to allow better airflow into the room.

You've now effectively removed all of the dirt and oil from your duck's feathers and successfully restored some of their fluff. Keep in mind, while your duck is now spotless, they can no longer successfully repel water. In essence, what you've done is given them a nice, clean palette to start with. They no longer need to struggle to get on top of filth removal; you've just done this for them. Instead, they can focus all of their energy on re-oiling their feathers, which is a slow but steady process.

4. *Wait:* Keep your duck in a very clean and dry place (preferably bedded with clean pine shavings) for a total of three days. Give them a *small* bucket of water—just large enough for splash-preening, but not so large that they can swim or immerse themselves in it.

5. *Swim:* On the fourth day place your duck back into a lukewarm tub of water (no soap) and let them splash and play and swim as much as they want to for about 10-15 minutes and then take them out and set them on towels to dry. If their feathers aren't fully repelling water yet (which they probably won't be), you'll need to blow dry them again.

Continue bathing and blow drying your duck in this manner every 1-3 days until you see maximum improvement in the waterproof effectiveness of their feathers (usually 1-2 weeks). If full waterproofing hasn't been restored by this time, you've likely improved their condition as much as you possibly can; in which case, you'll need to wait for them to go through a complete feather molt before their situation will be remedied entirely.

Close up of Cayuga Bonnie Bonster's sprouting feathers

6. *Patience:* It's important to remember that you're not likely to see an immediate improvement in your duck's ability to repel water. It can take a week or two before their re-oiling efforts add up enough to become significant. Progress may only be very slight at first, if noticeable at all, but it'll usually improve slowly over the course of the next week or so.

Do *not* repeat this procedure (except under vet advisement, when something foreign is on your duck's feathers). If their wet feather is going to improve, it'll work the first time. This procedure requires time, cleanliness, patience and attention to detail in order to have any chance of effectiveness. Repeating the procedure only sets your duck back to square one again in their re-oiling efforts.

Remember, this procedure doesn't actually restore structural damage to your duck's feathers; it merely helps remove dirt and oil, affording them a clean start. Additionally, it doesn't work in every case. If your duck's feathers are messed-up beyond repair, no amount of re-oiling will help make them waterproof or insulate them properly again. Only a complete molt can accomplish this.

Plucking a Broken Blood Feather

The bare base of a feather is called the *quill*. When a feather is alive and growing the quill has a vein in it that carries nutrients to the growing plume. At this stage of growth it's called a *pin feather* or *blood feather*. Once the feather is fully developed the vein dries up and the quill becomes hollow.

Ducks will occasionally break one of these blood feathers and since there's a vein inside it can get a little messy—especially if you have a white duck. Blood coagulants really don't work well in this situation because they don't tend to hold up for long, but they're a good temporary fix. While bleeding may slow down on its own as clotting begins, the wound is likely to re-open and bleed again during your duck's next preening session. Having a blood feather that bleeds on-and-off for days is an invitation to some potentially serious risks. In some cases, blood loss can be extreme and even fatal. In others, the malady creates a gateway for harmful bacteria to enter your duck's body right through their veins.

The most efficient way of handling a broken blood feather is to find it and pluck it out. The *entire* feather shaft must be pulled out from the skin in order for the bleeding to stop. Most Momma Ducks will agree that this task is far more of a psychological challenge than a physical one and also one that your duck isn't likely to appreciate.

1. **Get your emergency medical kit and find a helper:** Find your duck's medical kit and if possible, try to find an assistant to help hold your duck steady while you work. Ready everything you might need, so you won't have to go digging for supplies during the procedure. Lay out a pair of needle-nose pliers to do the plucking and a small towel to cover your duck's head to keep them calm. Although you probably won't need them, you should also lay out a blood coagulant (and application cotton swab) and gauze pads.

2. **Cover your duck's head with the towel:** Bring your duck to a well-lit room and place the small towel over their head to cover their eyes and help keep them calm. Talk to them gently and give them a moment to settle down.

3. **Mental preparation:** *Relax.* Read through these instructions a couple of times. This is a mental task, not a physical one. I know you don't want to cause your duck any discomfort, but if you do this right they'll be fine and so will you. This procedure is quick and the results are instantaneous.

   While most Momma Ducks can do this, if you sincerely have any doubts about committing 100% to giving your duck's feather a swift and thorough yank, put some blood coagulant right on the feather break to temporarily control the bleeding and then take your duck to the vet to have *them* pull it out for you.

4. **Locate the broken feather:**

   Body feathers are smaller and much easier to pluck than wing or tail feathers. In the case of a broken body feather, just put the fingers of your non-dominant hand (the one *not* holding the pliers) on either side of the broken feather and press slightly down against the skin and then skip forward to STEP 5.

   Wing feathers are the usual culprits when it comes to broken blood feathers. If you have a helper, have them extend your duck's wing for you. Carefully examine their wing and locate the broken feather, finding the exact spot where it comes out of their skin. This is the place where you'll want to grip the feather with your needle nose pliers—at the base of the feather, and as close to the skin as possible—*but not yet*. Just find it first.

   Estimate where the hidden root of the feather is located under the skin—it's a bump in the skin, usually about ½ inch to 1 inch back from the plucking point. Gently but firmly grip your duck's wing just *behind* this root area with your non-dominant hand (the one *not* holding the pliers). You're doing this to anchor their wing, so when you pluck out their broken feather, you won't yank their entire wing, which could dislocate a joint. In other words, hold your duck's wing in place with one hand while preparing to pluck their feather out with your other.

Tail feathers rarely break, but when they do, they're plucked similarly to wing feathers. The only difference is you'll need to gently but firmly grip the little, fleshy portion of their tail hiding underneath all those feathers in one hand while preparing to pluck out their broken feather with your other.

5. **Pull & guide the feather out:** Tighten your needle-nose pliers around the base of the broken feather as close to the skin as possible. Keep calm, take a deep breath and give the feather one firm, smooth yank, being sure to pull the feather *straight* out of its skin follicle, in the direction of feather growth. Don't hesitate or stop partway through or you'll only hurt your duck. Make a decisive pull. Pull with your dominant hand and brace their body, wing or tail with your non-dominant hand. It's only a feather, so a strong, swift pull will take it out without a fuss. Your duck may protest with a brief quack, but then it'll all be over.

If for some reason you can't get the feather completely out, if the break is too close to the skin for you to safely remove on your own, or if you just don't have the wherewithal to do this on your own, you'll need to bring your duck to the vet for immediate assistance.

6. **Apply blood coagulant with a cotton swab:** Once the feather's plucked out, the bleeding will normally come to an immediate stop. If not, you can use a small amount of blood coagulant applied with a cotton swab to stop the bleeding. Kutkit® Styps make a sanitary styptic swab that work extremely well in this capacity (supplier: AmazonSmile www.smile.amazon.com). Apply a sterile gauze pad over the wound and apply mild pressure for one minute. If the bleeding still doesn't stop, add another layer of gauze *over* the first and continue to apply pressure, then head for your vet's office right away.

Most ducks will never run into this problem, but it's a good idea to familiarize yourself with this procedure should it happen. Next time your duck is at the vet, ask them for a quick demonstration, so you'll be properly prepared in case of an emergency.

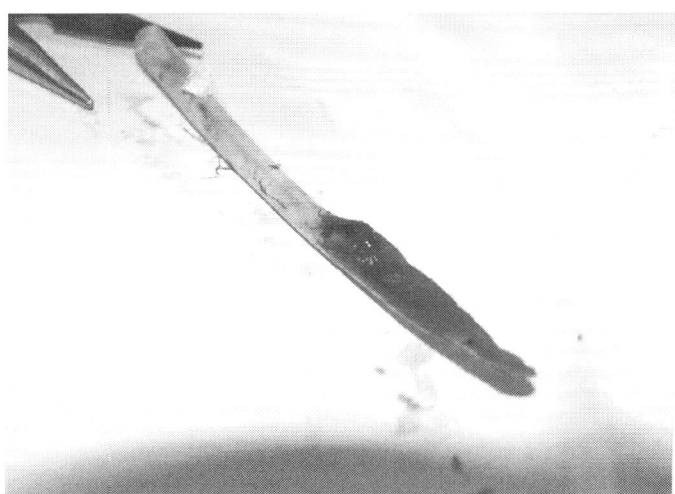

Miri's broken blood feather seconds after pulling it out

External Parasites

There are often visual signs when external parasites are thriving on your duck in large numbers. Many of them do damage to feathers, but some do damage to your duck's skin. The trouble with this second type is, if you're not parting feathers and looking around for them you may not notice their growing populations. This is why it's a good idea to do a precursory medical exam once a week while you're cuddling your duck.

Lice

Lice infestations shouldn't be an issue if you're keeping your ducks in a clean environment with plenty of access to fresh water. While bird lice are a common part of the great outdoors (carried in by wild birds) and likely to appear on even the cleanest ducks, their numbers should be low, easily kept in check by your tidy duck. Lice population explosions, on the other hand, should be taken more seriously. Ducks who are crawling with lice need a lot more access to clean bathing water and an immediate improvement to their pen and barn conditions (including changing their bedding more frequently).

Ducks with neurological issues, leg injuries or arthritis tend to have more difficulties preening their undersides than healthier ducks, which can make them more vulnerable to these pests, so be sure to do routine examinations and treatments as needed.

To aid in prevention, whenever possible, dissuade wild birds from nesting near or inside your duck pen, barn or shed. Wild birds are carriers and nests often can lead to lice population explosions.

While a few varieties of waterfowl lice suck blood, most don't and even those who do, don't do so exclusively. It's their movements over your duck's skin more than anything that causes irritation and discomfort. Rest assured, feather lice can't spread to humans or other featherless pets. They die within a week of falling off of their feathery hosts.

- **Common types of waterfowl lice**

1. *Cuclotogaster heterographa* or "head lice" are found close to the skin, near the base of head and neck feathers. While you may think it's more difficult searching for the presence of lice on a duck who isn't used to being handled, you may be surprised. When a duck gets a little stressed, their body temperature rises. A variation of only a few degrees can encourage lice to migrate away from the skin and outward along feathers to get away. Because the feathers covering your duck's head and neck are so tiny, lice often move into plain sight. They're especially easy to spot on a white or light-colored duck. If you have a duck who isn't used to being held, just pick them up and hold them for a few minutes while gently tracing a fingertip through their head and neck feathers. This simple action will usually flush head lice into view. Head lice feed on dead skin cells and feathers.

2. *Goniocotes gallinae* or "fluff lice" tend to gather in more concentrated numbers over your duck's main body, as opposed to their wings, neck or head. As their name implies, these lice gather on the fluffy base of your duck's feathers. Fluff lice feed mainly on feathers, but they do consume dead skin cells as well.

3. *Lipeurus caponis* or "wing lice" tend to hang out on your duck's wing and tail feathers, although they'll migrate further if their numbers are left unchecked. Ducks with wing lice infestations commonly have extremely deteriorated wing feathers and/or tail feathers due to the voracious appetite of these pests. Wing lice only feed on feathers.

4. *Menacanthus stramineus* (a.k.a. *Eomenacanthus stramineus*) or "body lice" are usually found on your duck's skin, especially in areas that contain sparse or no feathers—commonly preferring the vent, although they'll migrate elsewhere if their populations go unmonitored. You can sometimes see these offenders running for cover when you part your duck's feathers. Body lice feed mainly on feathers, but they do also suck blood.

5. *Menopon gallinae* or "shaft lice" are small body lice that tend to hang out on the chest, shoulder and back feathers of your duck. When you part your duck's feathers you can sometimes see them running inwards toward your duck's skin. Shaft lice feed mainly on dead skin cells and feathers, although they'll also suck blood.

- **Symptoms**

Some symptoms of lice may include: excessive scratching, damaged feathers, loss of feathers, listlessness and tireless preening. In large populations of body lice or shaft lice you may also see tiny red dots or sores where the lice have been biting and sucking blood.

- **Treatment**

You can usually find *poultry powder* at your local grain store. Read the label of whatever brand you select and make sure it specifically indicates that it's intended for lice removal on ducks. Ducks' feathers need to be treated very carefully to prevent them from losing their waterproof effectiveness, so be very careful in administering these powders and use them sparingly. This will also help ensure that your duck isn't ingesting massive amounts of pesticide while preening.

Delousing powder labels often have instructions on how to apply them to your duck's bedding, but I don't recommend doing so. Powdering your duck directly is the fastest and most effective way of remedying the issue. Any surviving lice won't be crawling back onto your treated duck and will soon die anyway. If you're worried about an infestation in your bedding, you'd be wiser to do a complete bedding change rather than attempting to remedy the problem with chemicals.

When it comes time for treatment, I like to kneel down over my ducks, with one knee on either side of them and one arm circled around in front of them to hold them in place. I then sprinkle a bit of the delousing powder into my free hand (don't forget to wear gloves) and gently work it through their feathers.

The process of treating your duck with delousing powder is actually pretty fast; the dust spreads easily through their feathers provided they're *completely* dry (never apply powder to a wet duck). Once complete, the lice will drop off quickly—many within minutes. Even so, it's best to keep your duck out of water for at least thirty minutes, allowing plenty of time for the powder to do its work before getting washed away.

For greatest success,

1. Treat all of your flock members at the same time (this includes geese and chickens too).
2. Provide plenty of access to clean bathing water (after their 30 minute waiting period).
3. Make sure their bedding and pens are clean.
4. Wait 8 days and then treat all flock members one last time to eradicate any newly hatched lice and ending the cycle.

In cases of extreme infestation Ivermectin® may also be utilized (see "Mite Treatment" for details).

Mites

Mite populations should be taken very seriously and remedied fast to prevent serious symptoms as well as the introduction of disease. Unlike lice, blood-sucking mites can migrate from your duck to you (although most can't complete their life cycle and can't reproduce).

As with lice, whenever possible, dissuade wild birds from nesting near or inside your duck pen, barn or shed. Wild birds are carriers and nests often can lead to mite population explosions. In addition, don't allow guests who have their own flocks (of any kind) to enter your duck pen directly after leaving their own pens. They need to re-dress in a fresh set of clothes and a clean pair of shoes first.

1. *Dermanyssus gallinae* or "red poultry mites" are blood-sucking in nature and are contagious to humans, able to complete their life cycle and reproduce. They're commonly introduced by wild birds and tend to live in bedding, cracks and crevices; then at night, they climb onto your duck to do their feeding (turning red with blood). Although it rarely affects ducks, these mites can carry diseases like *Salmonella gallinarum* or fowl typhoid.

2. *Ornithonyssus sylviarum* or "northern poultry mites" are blood-sucking in nature and they can be spread to humans. They're commonly introduced by wild birds, but also by rodents. These mites spend most of their time on the skin around the base of your duck's feathers especially around the vent. These mites can carry bacteria like *Pasteurella multocida*, a known cause of avian cholera, which can be fatal to ducks.

3. *Cnemidocoptes spp* (a.k.a. *Knemidocoptes spp, or Neocnemidocoptes spp*) include two varieties of mites often referred to as: "depluming mites" and "scaly-leg mites." Neither of these mites suck blood.

   a. Depluming mites burrow into the skin at the base of your duck's feathers, often leading to breakage.
   b. Scaly-leg mites burrow into skin beneath your duck's leg scales.

4. *Epidermoptes spp.* or "scaly skin mites" don't suck blood, but live on your duck's skin where they can cause skin inflammation and scabies, which can then become infected.

- **Symptoms**

1. Some symptoms of red poultry mites may include: skin inflammation, scabies (red dots, sores, scabbing and/or scaling), paleness (blood loss/anemia), listlessness, tireless preening, excessive scratching, self-mutilation, damaged feathers, feather loss, loss of feathers around the eyes or crook of the bill (where they frequent to drink body fluids), decreased egg production and increasing stress as mite populations increase.

2. Some symptoms of northern poultry mites may include any of the symptoms of red poultry mites in addition to: dark soiling around the vent feathers.

3. a. Some symptoms of depluming mites may include any of the symptoms of red poultry mites in addition to: extreme feather breakage.

   b. Some symptoms of scaly-leg mites may include: inflammation, skin crusting, deformation or discharge of the legs.

4. Some symptoms for scaly-skin mites may include: scabies (red dots, sores, scabbing and or scaling on your duck's breast, neck or head—often eventually developing into a yellowish-brown scab-crust), self-mutilation.

- **Treatment**

Injectable Ivermectin® is commonly vet-prescribed to eradicate the presence of some non-resistant mite varieties. Anywhere from 1-6 bi-weekly injections may be required, depending on the level of mite infestation.

Topical drops of Ivermectin® are often considered much safer for lightweight and bantam breed ducks as well as for younger ducks who have yet to achieve their full weight. These drops may be diluted for exceptionally small ducks.

Remember, even if you're applying topical medication to a female duck, don't eat any of her eggs for at least eight weeks following her last dosage.

Topical or injectable Moxidectin is a second alternative sometimes used to treat some varieties of non-resistant mites.

- **Building treatment**

Unlike lice who can't survive more than a week off of their hosts, mites can live up to 8 weeks between feedings. Depending on the size of your problem, your may need to set up a safe new space for your duck to remain in for the next two months while the mites naturally die off. If this isn't feasible, you can research various silicon-based chemical sprays to be used in barns, sheds and houses as well as different types of sticky traps. Remember to do some extremely careful research and consult with your vet before proceeding with any chemical alternatives to prevent the accidental poisoning (or secondary poisoning) of your duck.

Maggots

Finding maggots anywhere on your precious duck can mean any of these things:

1. There's too much decaying matter and moisture on the ground, luring in excess flies.
2. Your duck isn't cleaning themselves properly (especially around their vent).
3. Your duck has a hidden wound somewhere that needs attending.

No matter what the cause, if you find maggots on your duck, you need to get them to the vet immediately for an examination. While maggots are sometimes associated with the debridement of necrotic tissue, they can begin feeding on healthy tissue when the supply runs out.

- **Symptoms**

Some symptoms of maggots may include: visually identifiable maggots on your duck, especially around wounds or their vent.

- **Treatment**

If you find maggots on your duck, your vet will likely advise three courses of action:

1. *Bath:* Place your duck into a fresh, clean water source (kiddy pool or tub) and encourage them to clean frequently and with repeated water changes. You can use a very, very diluted Betadine® antiseptic solution (diluted to the color of weak tea) in a syringe to flush out any affected areas. Continue to draw clean solution into the syringe for flushing and re-flushing.
2. *Tweezers:* All maggots must be removed from your duck, so any that aren't flushed away have to be removed using tweezers. If any maggots are inside the vent further vet care will be required. Don't remove them on your own.
3. *Medication:* Your vet will likely administer an injection of Ivermectin® to help eradicate any missed or internal maggots and eggs. This can be repeated in 10-14 days.

Houseflies

Houseflies commonly deposit their eggs in your duck's messy hay and poop (and even on their dirty bottom) where they then hatch 1-2 days later. Additionally, they're notorious carriers of parasites and disease.

The best way to keep fly (and subsequent maggot) populations in check is not just done by keeping your duck pen clean, but also by keeping your *entire* property clean. Flies breed in all kinds of decaying organic matter—not just in duck poop. Remember to be mindful of where you place your decaying compost (which may include your duck's old hay or bedding). Additionally, it's important to keep things *dry*. Circulating barn fans can help you keep your duck's barn bedding clear of these troublesome insects.

Fly predators are a great way to safely reducing the number of houseflies on your property. These tiny wasps predate on maggots and dramatically reduce fly populations. I have them sent to me every month from April through September. I simply sprinkle the pack of 5000 around our sanctuary pens each month and houseflies are no longer an issue. (supplier: Spalding labs www.spalding-labs.com).

Flesh Flies

Flesh flies deposit larvae (not eggs) into decaying organic matter. They're also infamous for placing them into open wounds, leaving them to feast on the living flesh of mammals. Despite this fact, I've never heard of any accounts of them targeting waterfowl. If you do run into a problem be sure to take your duck to the vet for immediate treatment.

Medical #4
Musculoskeletal System (Hips, Legs, Feet & Toes)

Now it's time to go a little deeper into your duck's anatomy, down to their muscles and bones. While you may want to dismiss this section as more information than you care to know, it's actually pretty important.

Basic Leg Anatomy

It's very easy to look at a duck's legs and assume that what looks like a knee is a knee (even if the joint is backwards), or what looks like a hip is a hip. The truth is, their hip joint is tucked inside their body cavity and what you may assume is their hip is actually their knee. Meanwhile, that backwards joint you may assume is their knee is actually your duck's ankle. If you want to be able to communicate clearly with your vet, you can see where this information could be important.

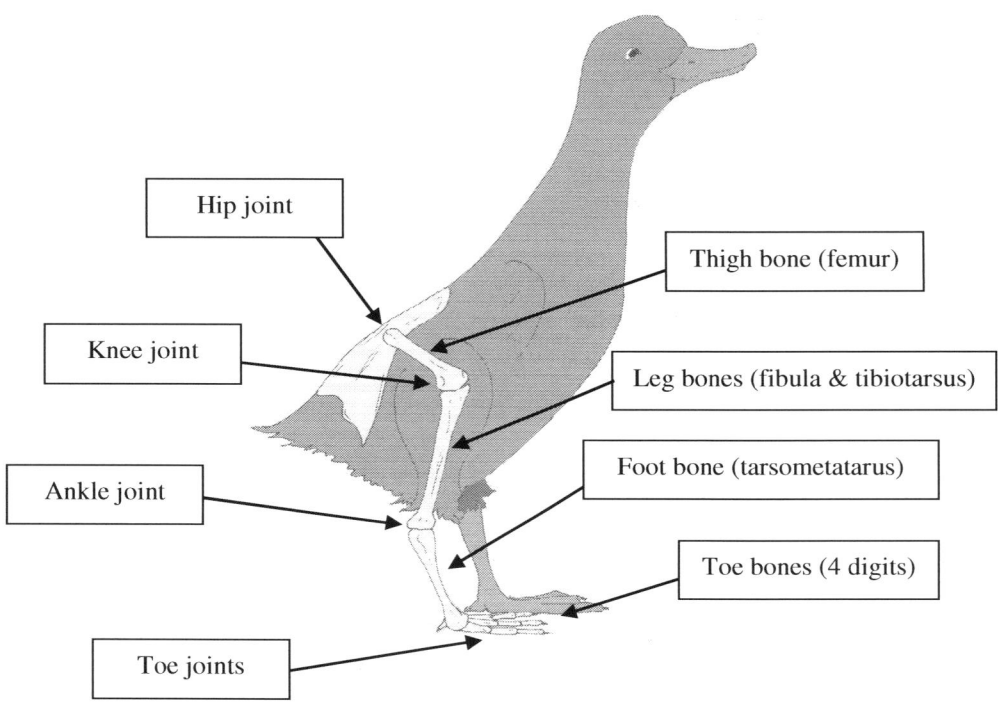

A diagram of the bones of your duck's hip, leg & foot

Therapy for Hips, Legs, Feet & Toes

Before I delve into the various types of limb conditions and injuries, I want to first review some good recovery strategies. Not every therapy is ideal in every situation, or for every duck, so remember to use your best judgment, and of course, always consult with your vet.

- **Hydrotherapy**

Hydrotherapy can play an important role in helping your duck get back on their feet again. Not only does it tend to instantly improve their mood and promote preening behavior, but it also helps take the weight of their body off of their recovering limbs.

This kind of weightless therapy is ideal for promoting the healthy healing of sprains as well as the re-strengthening of leg muscles following the mending of fractures. It can also be a part of your duck's post-surgical plan once they're incisions have fully healed and your vet has released them for this activity.

Always talk to your vet before initiating hydrotherapy as a treatment option. You'll need to address your duck's particular situation and health concerns before you can determine their readiness. If you push them to do too much too soon, you could be adversely affecting their healing rather than promoting it.

1. Keep your duck's energy levels in mind. Remember they'll need to preen after each trip to the tub. Limit the number of swims they take each day to what they can safely handle.

2. It's important to build their strength up slowly. Avoid long swim sessions in the beginning; instead, gradually increase the duration of their exercise sessions as they continue to progress.

3. The amount of swimming and moving around done during these sessions should be closely monitored. In the beginning your duck may just want to rest and float. As they continue to heal, you may need to encourage slight movements or back-and-forth tub laps.

4. Adjust the depth of the water as needed. In the beginning stages of therapy, deep water (where webbed toes can't touch the bottom) can be ideal. Water levels can be reduced as your duck progresses and grows stronger. You can steadily increase the amount of weight they're able to place on their legs, while the water still supports the bulk of their weight.

5. If your duck is going outside to their barn or shed after their swim, you want to be sure they have ample time to dry off first—especially in cold weather. I prefer to drain the tub and then set down a nice layer of towels for them to lie down on, so their bellies will dry. If you go this route, remember to swap out the wet towels with dry ones every 5-10 minutes until they no longer become wet. Ideally, you want the room to be warm enough to promote drying, without being so warm as to make them uncomfortable. If they start panting, they're too hot. Crack a window for a few minutes and give them a bowl of cold drinking water.

- **Duck cradles & wheelchairs**

Duck cradles work extremely well during recuperative periods and by simply adding wheels you can quickly turn it into a first-rate therapeutic device. In addition, wheelchairs serve as excellent solutions for ducks with permanent conditions that limit their mobility. If you have one of these simple contraptions at your disposal (or are willing to assemble one) be sure to tell your vet about it because they can guide you through how much time your duck should spend in it as well as how best to utilize it during periods of recovery.

Cradle therapy often begins with your duck being placed inside for part of their day. Your vet may want you to raise them up, so that they're feet aren't touching the floor (or so that only their tiptoes are touching) during part of that time. Your vet will also advise you when it's okay to add (or unlock) the wheels, so that your duck can begin scooting around and re-strengthening their muscles. Remember, your duck is only allowed in their cart on flat surfaces and when you're around to supervise directly.

If you want a duck cradle you're probably going to have to construct it yourself. You can get most of the materials you'll need by purchasing a *triple mesh laundry sorter with wheels* constructed of plastic piping (not metal). The only additional parts you're going to need are the six buckles with straps, which you can also find at your local department store, over in the camping section.

You'll need to do a little planning and measuring before you begin. Then, cut the plastic pipes to the appropriate size for your duck and assemble your cart (remember to account for the height of the wheels). You'll also need to do some measuring, cutting and sewing to make your duck's buckled sling out of the mesh that came with the laundry sorter. You can either make leg holes in the sling or you can pattern the mesh so that it goes between their legs. In either case, they're going to need to wear a diaper harness to prevent them from pooping on their sling.

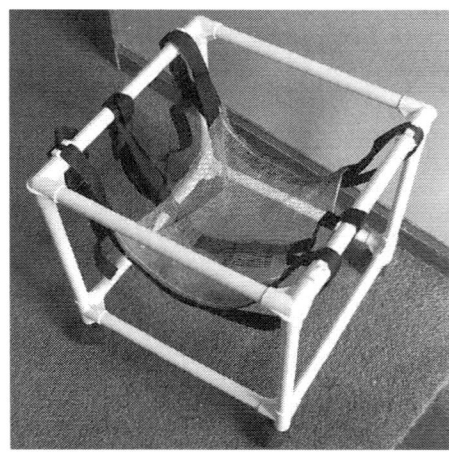 

Lemon the Duck in her wheelchair, Photo courtesy of Laura Backman

- **Recovery items**

A good diaper harness and quality duck shoes (with gripping soles) can help your duck through a variety of leg and foot issues, including post-surgical and in-home care (supplier: Nettie Kossart www.etsy.com/shop/partyfowl/).

Vinny, Victor, Ollie & Ming Mei in their duck diaper harnesses & shoes, Photos courtesy of Nettie Kossart

- **Stretch therapy**

If your duck has a long road of recovery ahead of them, you'll want to keep their muscles nice and flexible, so that they can continue to reach their oil gland, properly preen and preserve their feather quality. Stretch therapy is a great way to keep your duck nimble enough to accomplish these feats.

Coaxing your duck to reach and stretch is easily accomplished with favorite treats—worms are usually a big winner in this regard. This activity is also ideal for ducks with leg injuries who tend to be sedentary.

Dangle a worm near the left side of your duck's oil gland, encouraging them to turn their head to the left and stretch their neck back in its direction in order to eat it. Depending on the health and flexibility of your duck, you may need to gradually work your way back to this position if they can't quite reach it at first. Next, dangle another worm on the right side of your duck's oil gland, enticing them to stretch their head and neck in the opposite direction in order to get the snack.

You can make this fun and productive game a part of your duck's daily routine throughout their recovery. Ducks with permanent leg issues, who can't balance or preen easily continually benefit from this kind of stretch therapy.

- **Physical therapy, acupuncture & massage**

We live in a pet-friendly era where all kinds of holistic options are available for our feathered friends. Always talk to your vet before initiating any of these treatment protocols. They can often refer you to quality practices and individuals to help ensure the best results.

- **Weight management**

Ducks in recovery can easily gain unnecessary, added weight simply from the loss of daily exercise. While a little extra tummy growth is usually not an issue (up to ¼ lb. for smaller breeds or ½ lb. for medium-to-heavyweight breeds), anything more than this can become a problem that impedes upon their recovery because their legs need to support this additional weight. If weight gain starts becoming a noticeable issue, ration their feed (rather than it being a free-for-all 24/7 buffet), introduce healthy veggie snacks to help satiate their appetite and boredom, and if possible, safely increase their swim times to keep them as fit as you can. Most ducks will lose the excess weight they've gained once they've fully recovered and have returned back to their duck pen, resuming their normal routine again.

Cold Feet

You may notice your duck hobbling along with a limp on freezing cold days. When you pick them up to take a look, you won't see any swelling at all. While holding them in your arms you may gently flex their legs and see that all of their joints are working perfectly—no pain, no flinching, but then the moment you set them down again, there's that limp again.

On wintery days like this it's not uncommon for your duck to get cold feet and when this happens you may see them limping or repeatedly shaking their webbed feet in an attempt to get their circulation going.

- **Symptoms**

Some symptoms of cold feet may include: the sudden appearance of a limp and foot-shaking in freezing weather.

- **Treatment**

A good Momma Duck snuggle can often remedy cold feet. Bringing them inside their barn or shed is a great follow-up idea since their obviously uncomfortably cold. Once inside I like to dip their feet into their heated water bucket and then dry them off with my gloves.

If you want to bring your duck inside your house to warm them up, you can place them into a nice lukewarm bath that runs around 75 to 85 degrees Fahrenheit. If your duck starts panting, the water's too hot (remember, they have those nice feathers to help them keep warm).

Sprains

Unexpected lameness can come on quite suddenly and it can be quite alarming for Momma Ducks to witness.

- **Symptoms**

While small simple sprains may result in only mild limps, more serious sprains can be de-habilitating. I've seen ducks with sprains so severe that they were dragging their leg behind them on the ground, which is one of the symptoms for a broken leg.

If you see your duck doing this, carefully pick them up (taking their weight off of the injury) and bring them to a location with good lighting. *Without* bending any of their joints, examine their leg closely, checking from hip-to-toe for any swollen or misshapen areas. If you don't see any, you're probably looking at a sprain, but just to be sure, gently flex each one of their joints beginning at the toes and working your way up to their ankle and knee joints (never manipulate hip joints; leave this to your vet). While flexing these joints, pay special attention to their skin temperature (especially in comparison with their other leg). If you come across any hot spots, you're not likely looking at a sprain. As you continue to flex the joints keep in mind that ducks usually don't flinch from a sprain, provided you're supporting their full weight. If they do flinch, stop your precursory exam and immediately get them to the vet for further examination.

- **Treatment**

1. *Mild sprains:* If your duck is putting some weight on the leg and limping, then the best thing to do is keep them in confined quarters, safely limiting their mobility until the sprain is fully healed. To help speed-up their recovery time, you can place them in the bathtub or kiddy pool (filled deep enough for them to float in if they want to) once or twice a day. Vets often avoid prescribing anti-inflammatory/pain medication in the case of mild sprains because the slight pain is enough to signal your duck to take it easy. If you remove this minor pain pharmaceutically, they're more likely to play when they should be resting, furthering their injury. Most ducks recover from mild sprains within 5-7 days. If they're not fully functioning by then, or if their condition worsens, it's time to see a vet.

2. *Moderate sprains:* If your duck has a very pronounced limp and prefers to remain still rather than getting up to move about, you need to take them to the vet. Your vet will confirm the sprain (usually without an x-ray) and then prescribe an anti-inflammatory/pain medication. As with mild sprains, limiting their mobility and allowing them time to swim will assist in their recovery. Most ducks recover from moderate sprains in about two weeks; if they haven't fully recovered by then, you should still be seeing a remarked improvement in their limp.

3. *Severe sprains:* If your duck is remaining sedentary in lieu of walking or if their leg drags behind them when they walk because they're not able to put any weight on it, you'll want to take them to the vet for immediate care. Your vet will confirm the sprain (usually with an x-ray) and then prescribe anti-inflammatory/pain medication. As with any sprain, limiting their mobility and allowing them time to swim will assist in their recovery. If you have a cradle/wheelchair ask your vet if and when it can be utilized in aiding the healing process. The recovery time for a severe sprain can be anywhere from a couple of weeks to a few months, depending on severity and the age and general health of your duck. Although recovery can sometimes be slow, you'll often see some an improvement in their limp as they work their way through the recovery process.

Limb Amputation & Prosthetics

Many ducks with missing feet or partially amputated limbs will attempt to get up and walk, putting what they have left to good use. While it can be extremely refreshing to see them overcoming their disability, you need to prevent them from hurting themselves. The bit of tissue remaining beneath their amputated leg bone isn't designed to withstand the pressure of their body weight and left unprotected, serious injury and infection can result. To prevent this, fold a ball of cotton over the end of their amputated limb and then utilize non-adhesive, flexible *vet wrap* bandaging to secure it in place. This cushioning will help spare them painful injury, which could easily surmount their problems.

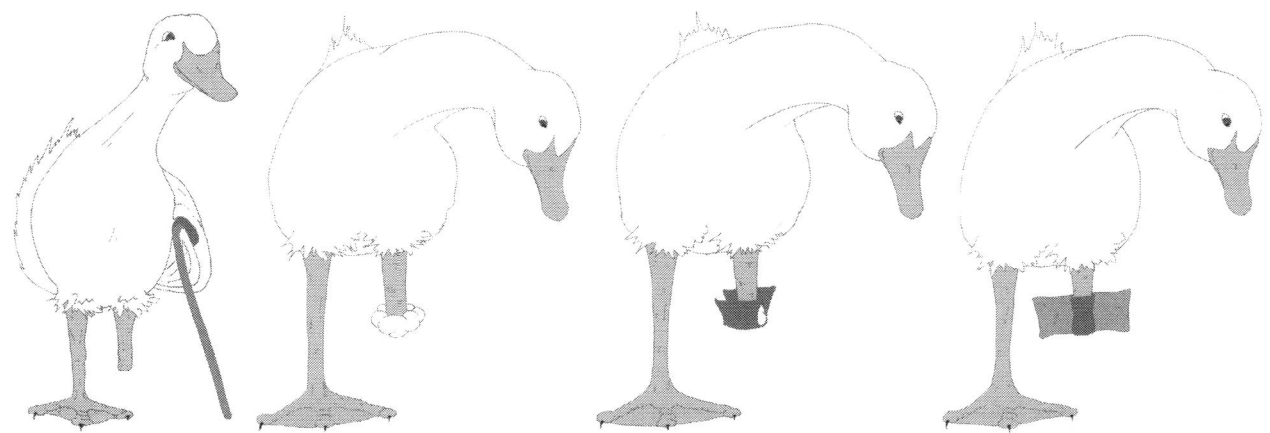

Amputated limbs must be properly wrapped to protect pressure points

Limb amputation and prosthetic webbed feet are slowly changing the lives of ducks who formerly had zero options available to get up on their feet again. Through the use of 3D scanners, amputees are being fitted for prosthetic legs created through the of 3D printers. This is an amazing medical breakthrough for pet ducks who've hatched out with misshapen limbs, who've suffered severe frostbite or who've experienced other types of irreparable damage.

Being fit for a prosthetic isn't quick and simple business. Precise measurements need to be taken in order to ensure that your duck's new leg is the same length as their existing leg. The person creating your duck's prosthetic will need to work with you and your vet to ensure they get everything right.

Prosthetics aren't currently available to everyone and they can be expensive, making prevention the key when it comes to your duck's care. Additionally, not all ducks are good candidates for a prosthetic limb. Some favorable qualities include:

1. Ducks who are human-imprinted and extremely comfortable being handled without becoming overly stressed make far better candidates for amputation surgery and prosthetics than shy and easily-stressed ducks. This is important because there's a lot of hands-on work to be done by you, your vet and the person creating their prosthesis.

2. Ducks with an energetic *"I can do it!"* attitude are more likely to recover from amputation surgery and later to accept their newly designed prosthetic, utilizing it to their advantage.

3. Ducks who are missing a foot or limb *below* the ankle joint are far better candidates for a prosthetic limb than those who've been amputated higher up their leg.

4. Young ducks often adapt to amputation and prosthetics far more readily than older ducks.

5. Ducks with other health issues often struggle with amputation surgery and prosthetics. Think carefully before proceeding.

Glory's Staph Infection...

Glory came to us along with her sister Miri. Both girls were left behind when their original family moved away without them. Neighbors took in the two girls and built them a pen to stay in, but never named them and never brought the girls to a vet, not even when Glory's ankles began to swell with brewing bacteria.

Without vet intervention, Glory's legs slowly bent outward at both ankles, seriously impacting her ability to get around easily. That's when the family relinquished the girls to our sanctuary—when they were nearly ten years old.

We immediately brought Glory to the vet and confirmed that she had suffered an unattended staph infection in both of her legs. The pus hardened and froze up her joints. Had she been treated when symptoms first appeared, she wouldn't have lost so much mobility in her legs.

Glory could walk, and was very determined to do so without any assistance from me; it just took her a little bit longer to get where she was going. I gave her plenty of access to our slope-banked pond (for easy entry & exit). It's hard to spot a physically challenged duck when they're on water and temporarily unhindered by their affliction.

So much time spent on a pond allowed Glory to keep herself clean and it kept her legs strong enough to continue using them for years to come. She did have trouble tidying up the tiny feathers around her eyes, since she couldn't use her feet and toenails to preen them the way other ducks do. About once a week I gently washed around her eyes with a facecloth soaked with clean, warm water.

Glory sure was a happy little duck who lived out the rest of her life at our sanctuary.

Glory's Vet appt.
Jan. 30th
10:30 am

x-ray & exam

Case # 92 Staph Infection

Buttercup became world famous when he took his first steps in his prosthetic leg
Photo courtesy of Feathered Angels Waterfowl Sanctuary

Dislocated Limb Joints

The dislocation of hip, knee and ankle joints is common in ducks who've fallen asleep while floating on icy waters. When they wake up they realize they're trapped in the ice and in their panic, they start struggling frantically to get themselves out. Those few ducks who do manage to free themselves, often dislocate a joint or two along the way.

Dislocations can occur in other ways including predatory attack, stumbling over potholes, tripping over obstacles, or getting their legs snagged. One of the most common causes of limb dislocations occurs when improper catching and handling techniques are employed. *Never ever* catch or hold a duck by their legs. This mistake is usually made by unsupervised children who don't know how to properly handle a duckling. While some people may shirk at this, I can tell you that I've met a number of individuals who accidentally maimed or killed ducklings when they were handling them as children and they still live with this guilt all these years later as adults. So if you or someone you know thinks it's no big deal, I assure you it *absolutely is*—both for the duckling and for the child.

- **Symptoms**

1. Your duck is suddenly unable to walk and may only barely be able to stand.
2. Your duck is using their wings to scoot along the ground, dragging one or both limbs behind them.
3. If you gently attempt to flex the joint, it doesn't feel right. (STOP immediately).
4. If you gently attempt to flex the joint, your duck flinches from pain (STOP immediately).

- **Treatment**

Take your duck to the vet immediately if you suspect joint dislocation. A serious sprain can often mimic the symptoms of dislocation to the untrained eye, so don't give up hope yet. Your vet will need to do an x-ray to confirm the diagnosis.

Sadly, vets can rarely help in this type of situation, unless it's caught and treated immediately and only if it occurs in their ankle or toe joints. If the dislocated joint can't be reset, some vets will opt to surgically fuse the joint bones together, locking the joint to prevent any further damage. This works best in ducks who have only dislocated a joint in *one* of their legs—leaving the other leg in perfect shape to take on the extra work.

Aside from exploring the option of limb amputation at the point of the dislocation, there currently isn't much more that can be done as far as treatment options. Euthanizing is a common vet recommendation, especially if your duck is experiencing pain. When pain isn't a factor, some Momma Ducks have turned their world (and home) upside down to accommodate their duck's new life. Outside ducks instantly become indoor ducks and they get carried everywhere they need to go—including the bathtub (because ducks who can't walk still *love* to swim!). Ducks who can no longer get around on their own require continual care, an abundance of love and attention, and tons of enrichment. There is no halfway about it. If you're not prepared to commit 100% to this loving relationship, for the sake of your duck, find them someone who is, or consider euthanization.

Foot & Leg Deformities

Ducklings who hatch out of their egg with foot or leg deformities can often thank humans for the mistake. While these sort of accidents can occur when a mother duck is brooding eggs, it's far more common when people attempt to incubate duck eggs (which is why I highly recommend avoiding these harmful experiments). Failure to continually monitor and manage temperature and humidity while also adhering to proper rolling techniques can lead to mild deformities that don't interfere with a duck's mobility or more serious and lifelong conditions that do.

- **Symptoms**

Hatching deformities of the limbs often present themselves as unnatural twists, bends or folds of tissue and/or bone that aren't accompanied by any signs of former injury, such as: knots (indicative of former broken bones), scar tissue, etc.

Dilly's deformed foot never got in his way. He's one of the lucky ones.

- **Treatment**

As ducks age these misshapen areas may or may not be precursors to other medical issues, often depending on their location and severity. Deformities of the joints often lead to arthritis as ducks mature, so preventative measures should be taken early on (including routine vet-monitoring and prescription treatments) to keep them on their feet for as long as possible. Other unnatural bends or twists may change the location of pressure points as your duck walks. These callous points should also be monitored closely by you and your vet to help prevent other medical issues from rising, including infection.

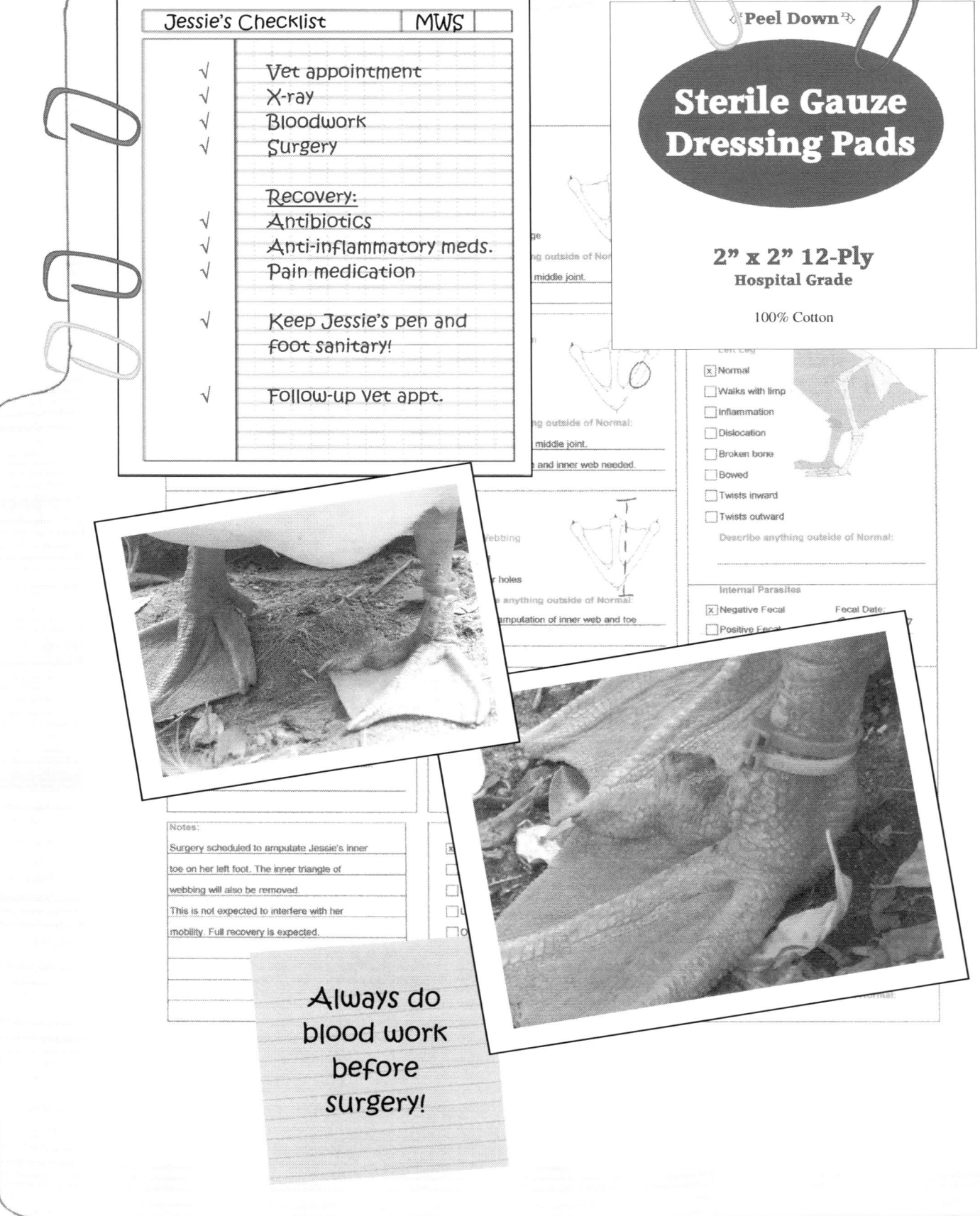

Jessie's Broken Toe...

Case # 16: Broken Toe

I went out into Jessie's pen one morning to find she had a serious toe injury, which she somehow managed to stub in her nice flat pen. The appearance of her toe alone was enough to convince me that it was broken. The open flesh around the break was swollen and warm to the touch as it began to brew with bacteria.

I rushed Jessie to the vet for immediate treatment, which included an x-ray followed by a potent round of antibiotics, anti-inflammatory medication and an additional prescription for pain management. Broken toes will sometimes fuse together without splinting, provided appropriate medications are administered and your duck is kept quiet in a small pen (to reduce their urge to go exploring). If they're not wearing a splint and there's no open wound, some swim time in the bathtub can get them off of their feet and floating, which is good for their healing toe.

In Jessie's case, the break was so severe that splinting wasn't an option because her bone would've taken at least 8 weeks to heal. Long recovery periods involving the legs or feet can be hard to pull off when you have a duck like Jessie who wants to waddle around everywhere.

Because Jessie broke her inner toe (as opposed to her middle toe), amputation of the toe and its attached webbing was the best option, promising her a speedy and uncomplicated recovery. Two-toed Jessie was back on her feet again after a brief three-week stay in our infirmary, which was bedded with clean pine shavings to prevent infection.

Jessie makes a full recovery!

Niacin Deficiency in Ducklings

Niacin (vitamin B3) deficiency along with other malnourishment issues can interfere with your duckling's rapidly developing body. Your duckling's legs, both muscles and bones, need to keep up with the ever-growing mass their increasingly supporting. Nutritional imbalances are the most common cause of their limbs no longer having the strength or ability to support their weight.

Your best defense against nutritional issues is to purchase quality brand-name duckling feed (as opposed to farm store brands). *Niacin deficiency* in particular is often the culprit in these problems.

- **Symptoms**

This type of malnourishment tends to cause issues in young ducks and ducklings. They lose the ability to support their own weight or to walk. They can literally go from walking to not-walking within hours. In early stages, legs appear normal in every regard (in later stages, legs may bow or splay outwards. When placed in water, affected ducks can swim perfectly fine with full mobility. If not treated quickly it can result in splayed legs and permanent lameness.

- **Treatment**

Protect the injured duckling by separating them from other ducks, trying to keep them in view of the others if possible and *immediately* upgrade their diet to a high-quality, brand-name feed formula. Until you can get to the vet, lightly spray some water on your duckling's new food and shake it up in a container. Then, add a teaspoon of powdered brewer's yeast (which you can find at your local health food store) to the container and shake it again. This process coats their duckling crumbles with a layer of brewer's yeast, which is very high in niacin. Prepare this mixture three times a day, in the morning, afternoon and evening. Don't allow moist feed to spoil. Throw away any uneaten portions after thirty minutes and swap in untreated crumbles in their place. This treatment plan should hold you over until you can get your duckling to the vet at which point they will commonly administer an injection of B vitamins that include niacin. They may recommend an additional multivitamin supplement; if so, they'll review proper dosages with you. Don't mess around with home remedies or concocting your own dosages. Vitamin overdoses can be fatal if you miscalculate.

If caught early enough and remedied immediately, you should see results within the first 24-48 hours and your duckling will often make a full recovery. If you don't see any improvement or if your duckling's condition worsens at any point during treatment, rush them back to the vet for re-evaluation.

Splay Leg

Splay leg (or spraddle leg) in ducklings is often the result of a slipping injury. Ducklings maintained on slick surfaces or who have insufficient bedding can lose their footing, slip and fall, twisting the position of their thigh bones in their hip sockets. It can be the immediate result of a single incident, or it can progress over multiple slips and falls. Less often, splay leg is caused by malnutrition (niacin deficiency), trampling incidents in overcrowded brooders or pens, or improper hatching techniques. While it tends to be more prevalent in ducklings, adult ducks are also susceptible (especially older ducks who are more likely to have pre-existing joint troubles like arthritis).

- **Symptoms**

Incubation error: Your duckling hatches out with this condition.

Bad fall or trampling: Your duckling suddenly can't stand and their legs are splayed out to their sides or behind them.

Minor falls or being stepped on: Your duckling's legs begin bowing outwards or twisting abnormally, but they still manage to get around. Their worsening condition often results in strength and balance issues, which can cause further slips and falls. You may start to notice your duckling resting more. This is usually the result of multiple minor slips or where a duckling is repeatedly being stepped on by other more active ducklings. These minor injuries worsen with repetition.

Malnutrition: Your duckling will spend a lot of time resting and refusing to get up. Legs worsen and may become misshapen as they continue to deteriorate.

- **Treatment**

For Malnutrition: Immediately upgrade their diet to a brand-name feed formula. Vets will commonly recommend a multivitamin and review dosages with you. Gimborn Vionate® Vitamin Mineral Powder for Pets (supplier: AmazonSmile www.smile.amazon.com) is a very good alternative if used according to the label. You can add it directly to your duck's food, but only under a vet's direct guidance. They'll need to review the Vionate® label as well as the nutritional label from your duck's waterfowl feed before determining a proper regime, so be sure to bring them both along with you. Again, (and I'll keep repeating this because it's *so* important) don't mess around with home remedies. Certain vitamin overdoses in particular can have permanent and even life-threatening results, so adhering to proper vitamin dosages is absolutely vital.

For Injury: Address any overcrowding issues in your brooder or pen to prevent further trampling incidents. Protect the injured duckling by separating them from other ducks, trying to keep them in view of the others if possible. Make sure they can reach their food and water (be extra sure there's no risk of them drowning in any water sources).

Bring your duckling to the vet for immediate treatment. Any delays can worsen the chance of a positive outcome. Your vet will safely bring your duckling's legs back into position and then brace them together using a thin strip of non-stick, flexible, self-adhesive vet wrap, which will help ensure their hip stability as they recover.

Splayed legs must be stabilized to promote healing of the hips

In more severe cases or if there is a delay in treatment, your vet may need to teach you how to slowly bring your duckling's legs a little further into midline position each day. They'll show you how to re-wrap your duckling's legs, increasing the inward tension to help promote the strengthening of their hip muscles.

During this process remember:

1. Don't limit the normal motion of the legs, or you can risk permanently freezing their hip joint.
2. Don't cut off circulation. Pay close attention to skin color and temperature.

Physical therapy is an important part of this healing and strengthening process:

1. Gently massage and flex your duckling's ankles (see: *"Basic Leg Anatomy"*) and toes regularly to prevent muscle atrophy. Do this for one minute, 3-4 times a day.

2. Cup your duckling in your hands and set them on a surface with some grip (preferably on the floor to prevent any risk of falling). If they want to sit, let them. Support them between your hands, so they don't roll to the side and then encourage them to stand. If they need help pushing up, go ahead and help them using your finger tips. This simple exercise of having them stand up will help them to safely build up their strength. These sessions should last for about a minute and should be done every two hours throughout the day, at least 6 times a day (if you can't be home to do this, you'll need to find someone who's available to step in and help). You can increase the duration of these sessions up to 2-3 minutes after the first week, just be sure not to push too hard. Take it easy and build up gradually.

3. If your duckling wants to walk, let them, but keep your hands poised and ready to prevent them from falling over. Try to promote correct walking posture, so they learn to do it right. If they can't walk normally, it's best to just have them rest, so they don't learn to do it wrong (which can be difficult for them to unlearn later).

This entire process can take as little as a week (with improvements sometimes seen on the first day) or as long as a month. Your attentiveness to detail will often determine whether your duck will walk for the rest of their lives.

Slipped Tendon

A slipped tendon (also referred to as perosis) occurs when the tendon (connecting muscle to bone) in your duck's ankle slips out of the joint. This can cause either of the long bones, above or below the ankle, to twist laterally at the joint. Subsequent shortening and thickening of these long bones may result in time.

A slipped tendon can be caused by a slipping or tripping accident, or as a result of a duck being mated too frequently by an overzealous male. Although it can happen to any duck at any age, ducks with arthritis or other joint conditions are more prone than others.

Malnutrition (niacin, manganese deficiency) is also a potential cause, but it's more likely in ducklings than adult ducks.

Symptoms

Symptoms of a slipped tendon may include: ankle inflammation, a pronounced limp that doesn't improve and often worsens with time, the effected leg may rotate inward below the ankle causing one foot to land on top of the other, further impeding their ability to walk.

Treatment

For ducklings: Immediately upgrade their diet to a brand-name feed formula. Vets will commonly recommend a multivitamin and review dosages with you. Don't mess around with home remedies or concocting your own dosages. Vitamin overdoses can be fatal if you miscalculate (see also: *Niacin Deficiency*). Protect the injured duckling by separating them from other ducks, trying to keep them in view of the others if possible.

For ducks: Slipped tendons are commonly misdiagnosed as sprains in early stages. When the sprain doesn't improve, vets will normally x-ray and pinpoint the diagnosis. Wrapping the ankle daily using waterproof adhesive bandage tape and/or vet wrap can give it good added support and improve the life of the joint, which can keep your duck waddling along for many years to come. Diligence is the key when it comes to this strategy.

Your vet may also prescribe anti-inflammatory/pain medication if the ankle joint is swollen as well as a treatment plan to prevent arthritis (see: *"Arthritis"*).

Broken Bones

If you suspect that your duck may have broken any bone in their limb (thigh, leg, foot, toe), the first thing you want to do is bring them to the vet for an immediate x-ray. Don't attempt to manipulate their bones or joints yourself; instead, try to keep them as still as possible.

- **Symptoms of a healed broken bone**

I've occasionally taken in rescues who've had hard knots on their legs, feet or toes that upon vet investigation turned out to be formerly broken bones, which had subsequently calcified and fused back together.

Qualities of a healed limb fracture:

1. Swollen areas can occur anywhere along the limb (not just in the joints).
2. There's no increased skin temperature surrounding a healed fracture.
3. The swollen area is hard and firm because it's comprised of fused bone.
4. There often isn't any pain associated with the healed area (no flinching when it's touched).
5. There are never any changes in the actual size of the knot.

- **Symptoms of a newly broken bone requiring attention**

It's usually pretty easy spotting a newly broken leg or toe bone. The outward appearance of the affliction tends to make things relatively evident. Depending on the severity of the fracture, the flesh around the break may actually be pierced by the bone and swelling is nearly always fast, progressing quickly. This is not something that slowly takes place over days, weeks or even months, but rather occurs in minutes and hours.

A broken leg bone isn't likely to be supporting any weight, which means your duck will likely refuse to stand, or they'll resort to dragging it along behind them as they use their other leg and their flapping wings to scoot along. On the other hand, a duck with a broken toe bone may not let on that they're in any pain at all and will often waddle around as if nothing's happened. Just remember, hiding their afflictions is what they do best. Just because they act like they're comfortable doesn't mean they're not in any pain.

Broken bones often result in infection—especially when left untreated. This can lead to swelling and an increase in skin temperature.

Qualities of a fresh limb fracture:

1. The outside surface area often reflects an interior fracture.
2. The skin is sometimes pierced by bone.
3. They're unable to support their weight.
4. Inflammation is fast and progresses quickly.
5. There will be an increase in skin temperature if an infection sets in.

- **Treatment**

After taking an x-ray your vet will determine the best course of action, depending on the location of the break. Hairline fractures may only require splinting, but your duck will also require a course of antibiotics, anti-inflammatory medication and a prescription for pain. *Never* splint your duck's leg on your own at home. Always seek out vet care to ensure ideal end results. Remember, any mistakes you make now can result in future lameness.

More serious fractures may require surgical realignment of the bones; in which case, surgical pins or wires may be needed to hold the bone fragments in place while they grow back together. The ends of these wires will remain outside of your duck's leg, so that your vet can easily remove them (without surgery) when the healing process is complete. In the meantime, it's vital that you keep them wrapped to prevent any accidental pokes and to keep them from pulling the wires out. You heard me right; ducks are meticulous preeners and they'll pull out even the most cleverly-bent surgical pins if given the opportunity.

In some cases bones (especially those in toes) can be reset by a vet using an acrylic splint that consists of a precise mixture of super glue and baking soda. This should never be tried at home and should *only* be performed by an experienced and qualified veterinarian who knows *exactly* what they're doing.

In any case, your duck will need to be kept still for 6-8 weeks while their bone heals. Sometimes a small and cozy pen that restricts their movement is all that's needed. In more serious cases, your duck may need to spend some of that healing time relaxing in a cradle that takes the weight off of their legs.

- **Calcium supplementation**

Vets will often recommend temporary dietary changes during the healing process to help your duck get the nutrition they need to re-grow healthy bone.

1. If they're not on it already, switch them over to 100% breeder/layer formula duck feed.
2. Make food grade calcium chips (oyster shells) available 24/7.

If your vet is concerned that low calcium levels may have caused the break, they'll recommend doing blood work to test their calcium and ionized calcium levels.

- **Egg-laying ducks**

Female ducks will often stop laying eggs (or lay irregularly) while they're mending bones, but not always. If they do lay any eggs, you'll need to examine them closely for a window into their calcium resources. Let your vet know if their eggshells are soft, bumpy or oddly-shaped, in which case an injection of diluted Calcium Gluconate may be required (see: *"Preventative Egg Binding Treatment Options: Calcium Gluconate"*).

Osteosarcoma

Osteosarcoma is a type of bone cancer that tends to occur at the end of long bones, usually around the ankle or knee joints in ducks, but occasionally in the hips.

- **Symptoms**

Some symptoms of osteosarcoma may include swelling (especially near the joint of the affected bone), limping, pain, (which may result in panting and frequent resting) and lameness.

- **Treatment**

Since the treatment of osteosarcoma involves limb amputation and chemotherapy (which is unavailable to waterfowl), there is no suggested course of action for ducks. Although pain medications can be utilized in the short-term, in the long-term euthanasia is the common veterinary recommendation.

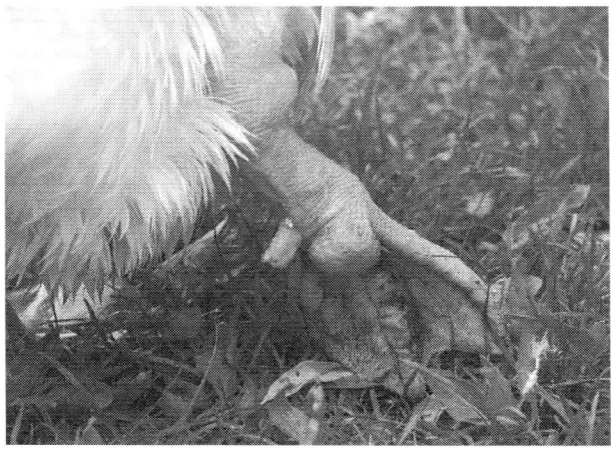

Roberta's bone cancer

Arthritis

Arthritis doesn't just afflict older ducks, it's also a notorious invader of joint injuries and infections of all kinds, which can affect ducks through all stages of their life. While there are treatments for arthritis, there are plenty of efficient preventative measures you can administer to your duck as well.

- **Symptoms**

Some symptoms of arthritis may include: joint swelling, stiffness of legs, pain, limping and lameness.

- **Treatment**

Your vet will diagnose arthritis with an x-ray. From there they may suggest a few different treatment strategies.

1. CosaminDS®: When administered daily, joint supplements can offer improvements, but it can take up to 30 days before you begin to see any results. Your vet will review dosage information with you; then, you simply break open a capsule once a day and sprinkle the appropriate amount over your duck's food.

   Some vets will also recommend giving adult arthritic ducks Omega 3 fatty acids every day. These supplements are administered daily for the duration of your duck's life to help foster healthy joints.

2. *Anti-inflammatory/pain medication:* NSAID medication can also be given on particularly bad days to help reduce any joint pain and swelling.

3. *Adequan®:* If caught in early stages, injectable Adequan® can help prevent further damage to the affected joint and prolong your duck's happy days of waddling. Adequan® is very safe for ducks and can also be administered routinely as a preventative measure for joints at risk of becoming arthritic. A small bottle of Adequan® goes a long way and to accompany it, your vet will give you a prescription for a box of 1 ml volume, super thin, 29 gauge, insulin needles (with a ½" needle). These are less expensive if purchased by the case (100 per case) and are available at your local pharmacy.

   Injections are administered intramuscularly into their chest muscle (your vet will teach you how), alternating from the left to the right sides to avoid bruising in one spot. Your vet will usually have you start by giving one injection a week for the first 6-8 weeks. After this, it can be injected weekly, bi-weekly or monthly as needed. Adequan® can also be used to help prevent arthritis in ducks who have joint afflictions and infections that are known to be precursors to arthritis. This drug truly is a miracle worker and I've seen results in as little as 2 weeks, with maximum benefits achieved within 6-8 weeks.

4. *Legend®:* Your vet may also suggest injecting Legend® into your duck's joint while they're under general anesthesia. It's a form of hyaluronate, which is normally found in high concentrations in joint fluid. It promotes healing of the joint's lining and increases the thickness of joint fluid, which then lubricates and cushions their joint. It reduces pain and inflammation in joints that are devoid of any infection.

- **Prevention**

Joint afflictions create future doorways for arthritis. Keep your duck pens safe and clear of tripping obstacles, prevent the over-mating of female ducks, separate fighting ducks, serve a nutritious diet with plenty of healthy snacks and avoid letting them get overweight. Swimming is an excellent activity to promote mobility while also relieving the strains of having to carry around their own body weight around. Ducks are much better swimmers than waddlers!

Toe & Footpad Injuries

If your pet duck tears, cuts or punctures the bottom of their foot or toes, it's absolutely vital that they get to the vet for medical treatment right away. Bacteria can quickly and easily invade your duck's body through their feet and any resulting infection can have debilitating consequences, resulting in partial or complete loss of mobility.

- **Symptoms**

Some symptoms of toe or footpad injuries may include: swelling of the foot or toe, limping or bleeding. Sometimes blood is noticed on the ground or on feathers (transferred during preening).

More often than not symptoms go unnoticed, which is why it's a good idea to routinely inspect the bottoms of your duck's feet.

- **Treatment**

Treatment for footpad injuries must be rapid and aggressive. Vets will commonly have you keep your duck in a sterile environment where they're not allowed to swim for 5-14 days, depending on severity.

For the first 3-5 days, when risk of infection is highest, your vet will likely advise you to dip and clean your duck's injured foot in an antiseptic solution 2-3 times daily. A common choice is: 3 cc. Betadine / 12 fl. oz. sterile saline (or sterile water, boiled for at least 1 minute and then cooled to room temperature), but there are other options as well including spray antiseptics.

Additionally, your vet may prescribe a salve like Silver Sulfadiazine 1% topical cream (applied topically 1-2 times daily for 10-14 days). This cream helps stop the growth of bacteria, keeping it out of surrounding skin and from entering their bloodstream. Antibiotics and anti-inflammatory/pain medication are also prescribed for 7-14 days.

Torn or Punctured Webbing

Small puncture holes through a duck's webbing are usually caused by stepping on a thorn, sharp stick or wire. If the obstacle is large enough these punctures can easily rip as your duck goes stumbling forward. The level of bleeding depends on the location and severity of the damage. Torn webbing doesn't mend or grow back, so afflictions are permanent, which is why vets don't bother stitching it. Attempt to locate and remove the cause of the incident from your duck's pen, so it won't happen again.

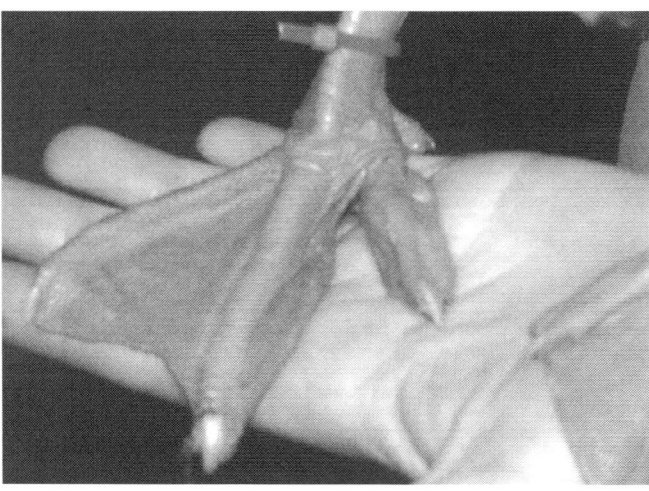

Friday was rescued with torn webbing that had already healed

- **Symptoms**

Some symptoms if torn or punctured webbing may include: bleeding (often noticed on grounds or transferred to feathers), visible holes or tears in webbing or limping (rarely and only in extreme cases where the damage also affects the tissue of the connecting toe).

- **Treatment**

Minor tears or punctures (less than a ⅛ inch in length or diameter): Minor tears or punctures in webbing normally don't require vet intervention *unless* they include damage to connecting toe tissue, which can lead to serious infections (see: *Toe & Footpad Injures*). Minor webbing tears usually don't get infected the way foot and toe pads do provided your duck pen is clean. Even so, some precautionary treatment is always a good idea.

Place your duck in freshly drawn, clean water (either in a kiddy pool or bathtub) and allow them to swim for a few minutes to cleanse the wound. Remove your duck and spray the injury using a non-stinging, antiseptic wound wash. Treat the area 2-3 times daily for 3-7 days while inspecting the injury to make sure there aren't any changes in swelling, skin temperature or color. If so, it's time to see a vet.

Clean your duck's pen and house and put down fresh bedding. Keep quarters as clean as possible to prevent infection while healing.

Medium tears or punctures (greater than ⅛ inch in length or diameter, but less than ¼ inch): Whether or not you have a vet take a look at medium-sized tears or punctures often depends on location and bleeding. If there's a lot of bleeding or if the damage affects neighboring toe tissue, it's best to see a vet who will properly clean and inspect the area as well as prescribing antibiotics. If you opt against vet care, follow the wound-cleansing instructions for minor tears then give them a clean and quiet place to recover for 1-3 days to help prevent infection, using clean pine shavings in lieu of hay or straw as bedding. Remember, smaller recovery areas encourage less walking and promote more relaxation.

Major tears or punctures (greater than a ¼ inch in length or diameter): Serious tears can bleed quite a bit. You'll need to wrap their flattened foot in a thick towel and apply direct pressure to control the bleeding while you get your duck to the vet. In these situations your vet will often clean and tidy up their webbing, removing any frayed edges that might catch and tear later, or they may even opt to surgically remove the entire triangle of webbing if the damage is severe. They'll prescribe antibiotics and possibly anti-inflammatory/pain medication if the toe is also involved in addition to laying out a wound-cleansing regimen. As with medium-sized tears, give your duck a clean and quiet place to recover, bedded with clean pine shavings.

Curled Toes

Duckling toes and webbing can become curled as a result of: broken toe bones, or malnutrition, but more commonly it's a hatching deformity caused by improper incubation technique.

- **Symptoms**

Some symptoms of curled toes can be as mild as a single toe twisting to the side, or as serious as a clenched and balled up foot. This condition can severely encumber a duckling's ability to walk, or in mild cases it may have no affect on them at all.

- **Treatment**

Take your duckling to the vet for immediate treatment. If your duckling just hatched, they need to be treated within 24 hours for best results. Fast action now can save your duck from a lifetime of immobility.

Your vet will trace the general shape of your duckling's healthy foot on a piece of cardboard (or similar material) and then cut it out. Then they'll carefully unfurl your duckling's foot. They'll flatten their foot over the cardboard cut-out and then secure it into place using a thin strip of non-stick, flexible, self-adhesive bandage (vet wrap).

Some vets will use adhesive bandaging as a splint instead. They'll unfurl the foot and gently press it flat down onto the adhesive side of a bandage that's a little bigger than their foot. Next, they'll lay a second bandage (adhesive side down) over the top of the foot. They'll press these two bandages lightly together, sandwiching your duckling's foot in-between. Lastly, they'll trim away any sticky edges. Your duckling may stumble at first, but they'll soon get used to it. Be careful to remove any water sources that could result in drowning if your duckling losses their balance and separate them from other ducklings for their own protection if necessary (preferably keeping them in view of their friends).

In either case, your vet will normally schedule a follow-up appointment the next day, where they'll remove the bandaging and check the toes to see if they've permanently unfurled. If not, they'll put on a new splint and have you re-check them again in 24 hours (continuing in this manner until the problem is remedied). Results can be seen in as little as one day, or it can sometimes take up to a few days.

If you duckling's toes curled *after* they hatched, address any dietary issues that may be causing the malnutrition, or incubator or brooder hazards that led to any broken toe bones.

Broken Toenails

If your duck breaks the tip of their toenail it'll only bleed minimally, if at all, but if they break it mid-way or even closer to the nail bed, the bleeding can more difficult to control.

Toenail breaks can sometimes be prevented by routinely examining your ducks feet. Longer toenails can be clipped or filed down, just be careful to avoid the pink quick inside. If your duck has dark toenails as opposed to light-colored, more transparent ones, and you *can't* see the quick inside, you'd be wiser to have your vet do the clipping for you.

Some ducks have fast-growing toenails that never seem to wear down, while others never have an issue with their short, stubby nails. Ducks with leg injuries that don't walk evenly with both webbed feet flat on the ground may have a couple of toenails that don't wear down naturally.

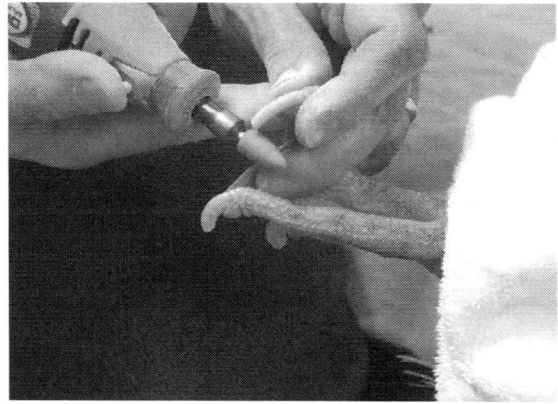

Our vet files down Dutch's long toenails

Muscovy ducks have especially fast growing toenails that are more like talons. If left unmonitored, they can really do a number on your hands and arms while handling as well as growing to the point that they curl and interfere with walking. I prefer to have out vet handle all Muscovy nail-trimmings. Some vets will use a dremel file for best results—especially when the quick is large and needs to be carefully avoided. Dremels are ideal because they prevent any splitting of the nail. Do *not* try this yourself at home!

- **Symptoms**

Some symptoms of a broken toenail may include: severed toenail, bleeding (often noticed on grounds or transferred to feathers) or limping (rarely and only in extreme cases when the nail bed is affected).

- **Treatment**

Minor toenail breaks: Bleeding is usually controlled simply by waiting for the blood to clot or by applying direct pressure. Occasionally you may need to use a blood coagulant, which you hopefully have in your duck's medicine cabinet. If not, cornstarch is a handy substitute.

Once the bleeding is controlled, you'll need to address any damage. If the toenail wasn't completely severed, cut the remaining portion off with clippers—unless you'll hit the quick and cause additional bleeding. If this is the case, bring your duck to the vet for further care because they'll be able to cauterize it if they need to.

Toenail breaks are notorious entryways for bacterial infection. Cleanse the injury using a non-stinging, antiseptic wound wash (I prefer sprays because they're easier to apply). This can sometimes loosen the clotting and result in a bit of bleeding again. If so, wait for the bleeding to stop and then put your duck in a small space bedded with clean pine shavings for 24 hours. Continue to treat the area 2-3 times daily for the next 3-7 days while inspecting the injury to make sure there aren't any changes in surrounding skin (swelling, temperature or color). If so, it's time to see a vet.

Major toenail breaks: Utilize a blood coagulant and/or direct pressure to help control the bleeding until you can get to your vet's office to have the wound cauterized. Even if you can get the bleeding to stop, major toenail breaks often continue to reopen and bleed again when your duck resumes walking around. Your vet will clean and tidy up the area, removing any pieces of nail that might get snagged and cause more damage later.

To prevent infection, your vet will likely prescribe an antibiotic. If the nail bed has been damaged, they'll also prescribe anti-inflammatory/pain medication in addition to laying out a wound-cleansing regimen for your duck. Prepare a sanitary place for your duck to recover, bedding it with clean pine shavings.

<u>Infection</u>

If you notice a knot or swollen area somewhere on your duck's legs or feet, the ability to distinguish a broken bone from an infection can really come in handy.

- **Symptoms of an infection**

If you notice any swelling on your duck's leg, foot or toe you should always bring them to the vet for an immediate examination. More often than not, swelling is caused by infection. Because of the proportion of their feet, ducks are prone to getting little cuts and scratches on their foot pads and webbing as they waddle around. These tiny abrasions can create a pathway for bacteria, which usually enters their body and then settles in around their toe or ankle joints.

You can normally feel the heat of this kind of infection by coiling your fingers around your duck's healthy leg and then doing so again around their swollen leg. The skin temperature variance between the normal joint and the infected joint is usually pretty noticeable. Inflammation caused by infection is usually relatively tender in nature—as opposed to a rock-hard, boney knot. When you gently press the skin with your fingers you should feel some give. Sometimes your duck will let you know when this area is particularly sensitive.

Ducks brewing infections of this nature will usually continue to walk until the swelling inflames to the point of locking (and possibly damaging) their joint. Until that time, although they may have a pronounced limp, they should still be able to support their own weight, bending and flexing the affected joint.

In this type of scenario, swelling tends to have a slow onset. You'll barely notice it at first, but as the days and weeks pass it'll become increasingly worse. Don't let this fool you into thinking you can take your time getting your duck to the vet. While things may appear to be moving slowly on the outside, on the inside the foundation for future lameness is quickly progressing. The questions to ask yourself are:

1. *Location:* Is the inflammation centered around a joint?
2. *Temperature:* Compare the swollen area of the afflicted leg with the corresponding area of your duck's other leg. Is there a variance in skin temperature?
3. *Tenderness:* Is the inflamed area relatively fleshy or pus filled?
4. *Sensitivity:* Is the inflammation causing your duck any discomfort or pain?
5. *Lameness:* Is your duck limping, unable to walk, or having trouble bending their leg at the affected joint?
6. *Progression:* Has the swelling been progressing slowly?

If you answered "yes" to any of these questions, you could be looking at some kind of infection.

Staph Infection

Limb infections are most often caused by staph bacteria (*Staphylococcus aureus*) and if not treated quickly they can lead to permanent joint damage, lameness and even death. Your duck's skin and mucus normally harbor staph bacteria, but it isn't until it gains access into their bloodstream through a cut or wound that it begins to cause them trouble.

In some cases, a strong and otherwise healthy duck may be able to fight off the infection, but not without dire consequences. While the infection is running rampant, the joint fills with pus and after healing, this pus hardens to a fingernail-like consistency. This hardened material locks up their joint and prevents a normal range of motion. There's no medical procedure for a duck who's struggling with this sort of lameness—it'll inhibit their mobility for the rest of their life.

Strong and healthy ducks are less likely to suffer infections than ducklings, older ducks or immune compromised ducks. Since the bacteria enters the body through a wound, ducks who are kept on soft grounds that are free of obstacles are less likely to become infected than those who traverse over rocks and sticks. Clean ducks maintained in sanitary environments are also less likely to suffer from bacterial infections.

Advanced staph infections can result in systemic infections that affect multiple organs, or the body as a whole. Examples of these include: arthritis, osteomyelitis (bone infection), synovitis (joint infection), endocarditis (infection of the interior lining of the heart) and septicemia (blood infection).

- **Symptoms**

Some symptoms of a staph infection may include: inflammation of any of the leg or toe joints.

- **Treatment**

Your vet will aspirate a sample of pus from the swollen joint and send it to a lab for susceptibility testing. If they can't get a sample of pus from the area, they can run a blood culture instead to search for any dangerous bacteria in your duck's bloodstream, which could be causing these symptoms and can eventually result in sepsis (see: *"Sepsis"*).

While waiting for lab results, your vet will probably start your duck on some form of penicillin. In a few days the lab will provide your vet with a list of effective antibiotics against the infection, and a qualified waterfowl vet will know exactly which of these are safe for your duck. Always ask your vet for copies of any tests performed on your duck and keep your own medical file at home; this way, if you ever have an after-hours emergency, you and your duck will be prepared.

Once-weekly injections of Adequan® can prevent permanent joint damage during your duck's recovery, making it a very good option.

In severe cases, surgical intervention may be required to flush out the infection and insert a drain into the swollen area. Unless your duck's situation is declining rapidly, surgery usually isn't performed until they've been on antibiotics for a few weeks without the anticipated results. Tricide® (used when an operation is being done near nerves) and Tricide-Neo® (used when an operation is *not* being done near nerves) are recommended flushing agents for staph infections. Your vet can obtain Tricide or request further information by emailing tricideinfo@yahoo.com. It comes in a small, instructional packet that includes preparation details. Tricide® can be mixed with a variety of antibiotics making it ideal for flushing out staph infections.

Your vet will likely have you flush out the post-surgical site by pushing Tricide® (or Tricide-Neo®) through the inserted surgical port. This is usually done for 3-5 days before brining your duck back to the vet to have the port removed.

Staph infections can be difficult and slow to treat, often taking 2-3 months.

- **Reading lab results**

When you get your copy of your duck's lab results, take a close look at them.

1. "S" means the bacteria they found in your duck's sample are *Susceptible* to the antibiotic listed.
2. "R" means the bacteria is *Resistant* to the antibiotic listed.

When examining the entire list, if you notice that the isolated bacteria are "S" Susceptible to *all* types of antibiotics, you could be witnessing a warning sign that the sample drawn from your duck was contaminated. It's *rare* for bacteria to be susceptible to *all* types of antibiotics. If you see this type of lab result and your vet doesn't catch it, be sure to ask them for a retest to confirm the results. Prescribing the wrong antibiotic can seriously delay treatment, which can result in the progression of infection and the worsening of your duck's condition.

Below is an example of a contaminated sample since the infection shows susceptibility to every type of antibiotic on the list. If it sounds too good to be true, it probably is.

Test Results:

AMPICILLIN	S
AUGMENTIN	S
CETIOFUR	S
CEPHALOTHIN	S
CLINDAMYCIN	S
ERYTHROMYCIN	S
GENTAMICIN	S
ENROFLOXAC	S
OXACILLIN	S
PENICILLIN	S
TRIBRISSEN	S
VANCOMYCIN	S

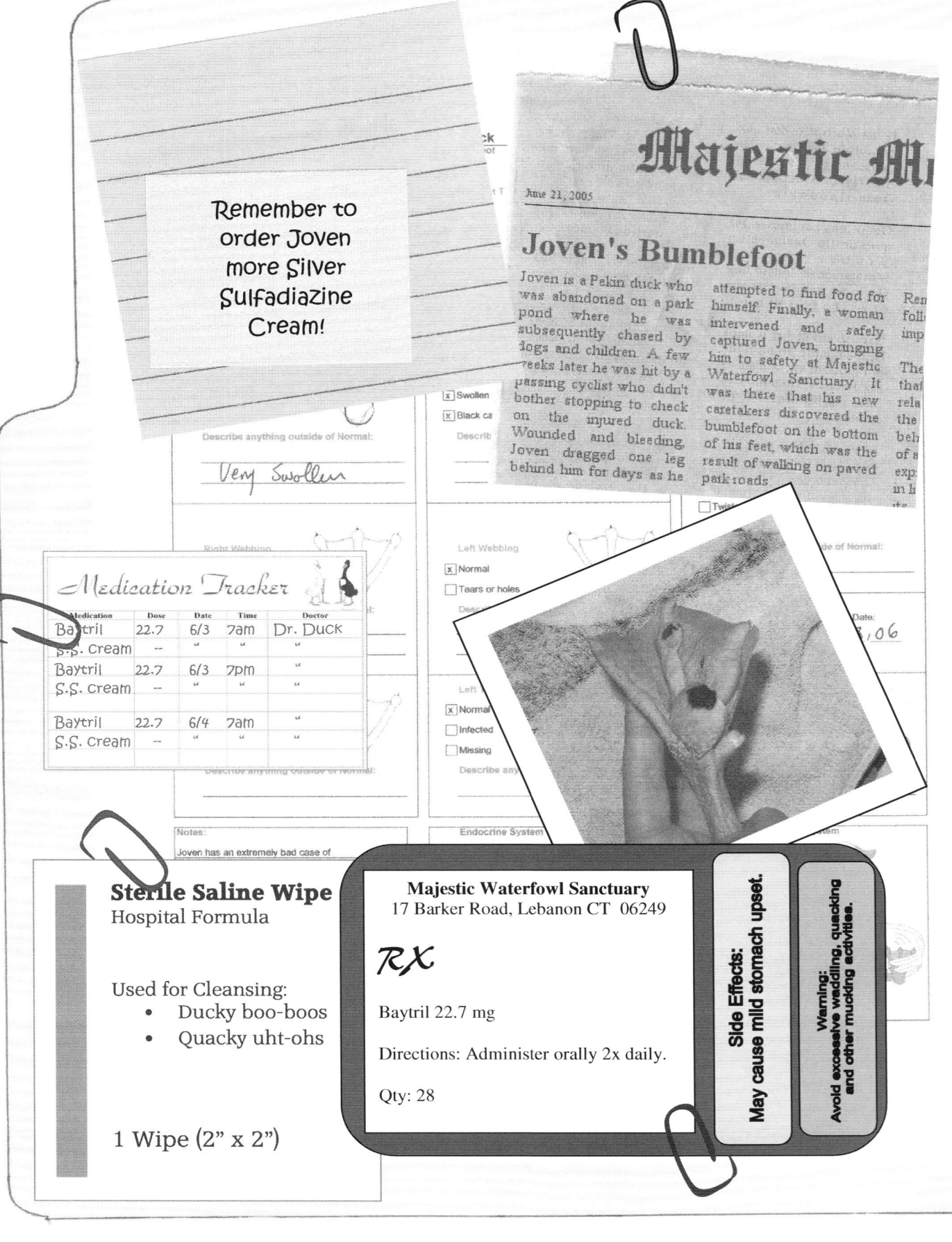

Joven's Callused Feet...

The most severe case of bumblefoot I've ever seen belonged to a rescued duck named Joven.

The bottoms of both of Joven's feet were dotted with the telltale black calluses that signify bumblefoot infections. The sores on both of his footpads were so inflammed, they had swollen to the size of quarters.

Joven's vet prescribed a twice daily regime of Baytril® (22.7 mg) along with the twice-daily application of silver sulfadiazine cream.

Joven's feet were so inflamed that his vet incorporated a one-time callous peeling into his treatment plan—once he'd been on antibiotics for a minimum of 30 days.

I encouraged Joven to soak his feet on the pond for twenty minutes and then gently peeled back any easy-to-remove black scabs, making sure to stop as soon as we felt any resistance at all (to prevent any reopening of the wound or bleeding that might lead to the introduction of new bacteria).

I continued with Joven's treatment regime of oral antibiotics and foot cream for another 90 days before his condition was fully remedied.

Bumblefoot

When a foot infection is left unattended, it commonly progresses into bumblefoot. While bumblefoot can develop anywhere along the underside of the foot or toes (except on their webbing), more often than not, it occurs at the pressure-points of the foot pads and toe joints.

Left untreated, bumblefoot can cause the restriction of motion in your duck's joints (sometimes completely locking them up) and it can further progress into osteomyelitis (infection of the bone), becoming fatal. Immediate vet intervention is definitely required.

The three most common causes of foot infections, which lead to bumblefoot are:

1. Ducks who walk on rough or rocky grounds are more likely to get the kind of cuts and abrasions on the bottom of their feet that are a gateway to infection.

2. Ducks kept on hard-packed, solid ground, cages without bedding, wire or concrete flooring are more likely to develop pressure-point calluses that eventually crack open and become infected.

3. Ducks confined to dirty or muddy pens (teaming with bacteria) and whose feet are commonly planted in excrement and sludge are more likely to end up with foot infections.

While it tends to be ducks who live in these conditions who succumb to bumblefoot, even the cleanest and best-cared for ducks can have an occasional run-in with a foot infection.

Bumblefoot can develop very quickly and ducks are extremely prone to this kind of infection. Catching and treating it before any lingering affects take hold often depends upon early detection. Make a quick inspection of the bottom of your duck's feet every week to look for signs.

The best way to prevent bumblefoot is to maintain a clean, soft and well-drained duck pen.

1. *Clean:* In warmer months, and in spacious pens, fecal matter tends to naturally work its way into the soil and decompose. Smaller pens, or favorite spots in pens, may require more of your attention in order to stay tidy. In cold weather it can be impossible to remove frozen and mounting duck poop piles, making it necessary to use plenty of sand to bury it every day—especially around water buckets where it really tends to build up. On those days when you're blessed with a temporary thaw, take advantage and shovel out whatever you can and then bury any remainder under sand. Clean up thoroughly in the spring.

2. *Soft:* Grounds should be bedded with grass or a thick layer of farmer's sand. In winter you can utilize farmer's sand and straw to help soften-up favorite pen areas. Clean up thoroughly in the spring.

3. *Dry:* Unless it's raining out, grounds should be relatively dry most of the time. Avoid keep your ducks on surfaces that are continually wet or muddy (which can be bacterial hotbeds).

4. *Give your ducks their own space:* While ducks and chickens can be penned together, there are added risks. *Staphylococcus aureus* bacteria tends to be more prevalent among chickens than ducks, which means ducks who are penned with chickens are more likely to succumb to staph infections than other ducks. This is especially true if you have a lot of birds sharing a relatively small area. In addition, chickens are less resistant to parasites and disease and can subsequently spread these to your otherwise healthy duck.

If you do want your ducks and chickens to comingle you can reduce risks of cross-contamination by building spacious pens for everyone and keeping them clean and dry.

- **Symptoms**

Some symptoms of bumblefoot may include: swollen calluses beneath your duck's feet (which often turn black), limping, pain (which may result in panting and frequent resting) and lameness.

- **Treatment**

Upon inspecting your duck's feet and confirming the diagnosis, most vets will prescribe a general antibiotic like Baytril® (enrofloxacin) for at least 14 days to address the infection and reduce swelling. Whether you'll be administering their medication once or twice a day often depends on the severity of your duck's condition.

Some vets will also recommend antiseptic foot washes, but I've found giving your duck full access to *clean* swimming water is often just as good. The more time they spend floating, the quicker their feet heal. Of course, you also need to address what caused the infection in the first place. If the grounds of your duck pen are less than ideal, they'll need to be remedied or else your duck will have a hard time healing and their bumblefoot will likely reoccur. It's vital that grounds remain soft, dry and clean. You can do this by turning over grounds and seeding grass, improving the drainage in their pen or spreading some cushy farmer's sand over the grounds (which will have to be raked routinely to remain soft).

The usage of ointments that stay on the skin, like over-the-counter QuickDerm®, or prescription Thermazene Silver Sulfadiazine cream 1%, can be applied directly to the afflicted area of the feet 1-2 times daily. Some vets will prescribe DMSO (dimethyl sulfoxide) salve, which is a carrying agent for whatever it's combined with (penicillin, enrofloxacin, meloxicam, etc.).

I prefer silver sulfadiazine cream in these situations myself because the results are often rapid, safe and thorough. Remember to always wear gloves when applying ointments to you duck's feet to prevent the unnecessary absorption of medications into your skin.

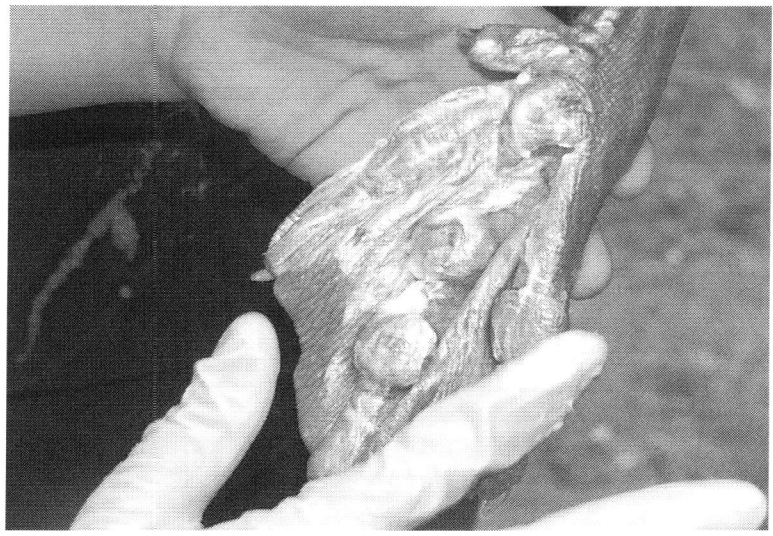

The application of Thermazene Silver Sulfadiazine Cream to infected foot pads

Most vets will have your duck come back every two weeks for follow-up visits, so they can monitor their progress until there's no more infection and your duck is as good as new again. If healing isn't progressing as it should at any point in their recovery, they may substitute or prescribe additional antibiotics to their treatment regime. In severe cases of bumblefoot, your vet may even suggest weekly injections of Adequan® to help protect your duck from joint damage.

Be wary of vets who want to immediately peel away black calluses to promote healing. This is often a strategy with parrots and other perching, caged birds, but not with waterfowl. Experienced waterfowl vets will understand that bumblefoot scabs will gently come off on their own if your duck is treated with foot cream and given ample time to soak in water. A good duck vet will see peeling or any other kind of foot surgery as last resort efforts because they'll recognize that opening a wound on the bottom of your duck's foot can quickly create a pathway for even more harmful bacteria to enter into your duck's body.

It can take anywhere from a few weeks to a few months to successfully treat bumblefoot depending on the severity of your duck's condition, the thoroughness of their treatment regime and how diligently you address any environmental causes (failure to remedy environmental factors will impede healing).

Synovitis

Synovitis is an infection of the joint (usually the knee) commonly associated with staph bacteria. As the infection worsens, the membrane around the ends of the long bones become inflamed and excess joint fluid gathers in pockets, often becoming septic. Your vet will aspirate some of the fluid and send it off to a lab to confirm the diagnosis. If left untreated it can seriously interfere with your duck's mobility, potentially destroying the affected joint.

- **Symptoms**

Some symptoms of synovitis may include: swollen and stiff joints followed by limping and the inability to walk.

- **Treatment**

Injectable or intravenous antibiotics are most effective against synovitis. This treatment is followed by a long-term regime of oral antibiotics.

Osteomyelitis

Osteomyelitis is a bone infection that is commonly caused by staph bacteria. The bacteria gain entrance through a wound that reaches the bone, or it can be carried through the bloodstream and into the bone. Once the bone becomes infected, an abscess forms in the joint, depriving the bone of its normal blood supply. In severe cases, a pus filled cavity may actually develop *inside* the bone with new bone forming around it.

The easiest way to prevent osteomyelitis is to maintain good flock hygiene, which includes keeping a nice, tidy duck pen. If your duck receives a cut or wound at any time, make sure it's treated promptly and efficiently (see: *"Lacerations"*).

- **Symptoms**

Some symptoms of osteomyelitis may include: lameness, swelling, abscess, fever, fatigue, nausea, appetite loss, behavioral changes and depression. While a mild limp is sometimes visible, more often than not, your duck will prefer resting over waddling about. When they do get up to move around, they usually won't go far before settling down again.

- **Treatment**

Treatment of osteomyelitis depends on the severity of the infection and how quickly it's discovered. It's vital that vet treatment be sought out immediately because this condition can worsen very quickly. Prognosis is highly dependent upon the timeliness of medical intervention.

Vets will often recommend an x-ray as a first step towards a diagnosis; however, the infection may not appear on the x-ray if it's still in its early stages, which is why precautionary antibiotics are an excellent strategy during the analysis process (many vets will prescribe a regime of both Baytril® and clindamycin every 12 hours).

Once osteomyelitis is successfully diagnosed, your vet will aspirate a sample of the pus from the site of infection in order to choose the correct antibiotic treatment. If the infection is in an advanced stage, injectable antibiotics are often utilized until the condition improves; then, oral antibiotics are substituted.

In mild cases, where the infection is caught early-on and treated properly, your duck can walk away without any long-term adverse affects.

A quality treatment plan includes:

1. Oral antibiotics for a minimum of 6-8 weeks to fight the bacteria.
2. Anti-inflammatory/pain medication to address any swelling.
3. Additional pain medication to reduce stress and help speed recovery.
4. Weekly Adequan® injections to protect the joint (continued 4 weeks beyond all other treatment).

In severe cases your vet may advise surgery to help drain the pus out, so that the bone can heal properly. If so, they'll also likely want to surgically remove any damaged or infected tissue. In extreme cases, amputation may be required, but this should only be performed when the infection has reached life-threatening stages.

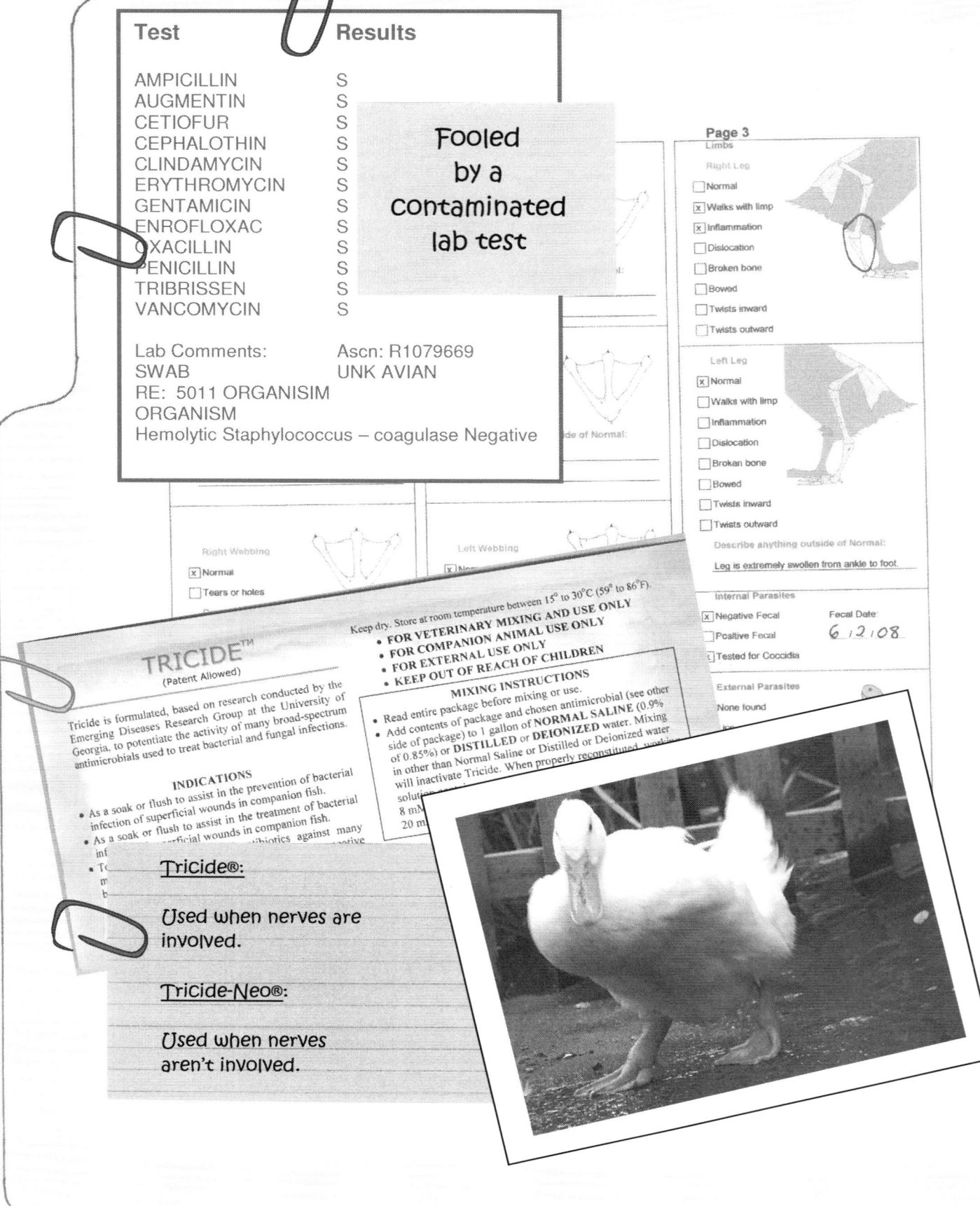

 # Roberta's Bone Cancer...

Roberta was rescued with an extremely swollen left leg, and I'm sure that was why somebody abandoned her, so that they wouldn't have to watch her suffering anymore. I fell in love with her the moment I met her, such a funny and interactive little girl.

Initial testing at the vet's indicated that it was infected with staph bacteria and desperately in need of surgical intervention. Following a preparatory round of antibiotics, she was scheduled to go in for an operation in which her affected joints would be flushed with Tricide®. The plan was to insert a port into her leg for 7 days, during which time I would continue to flush with the Tricide® twice daily before having the port removed.

Sadly, during Berty's surgery we discovered that her lab test was incorrect and what she actually had was osteosarcoma. There was a large cancerous mass encompassing her entire leg bone.

Because her condition was so far progressed, I had to make the difficult decision to euthanize Berty while she was still under anesthesia. There was no doubt her leg was causing her pain and increasing the dosage of her pain medication (Torbutrol®, which is a sedative) would have only resulted in her sleeping her days away.

Case # 66 Osteosarcoma

Medical #5
Musculoskeletal System (Wings & Tails)

Witnessing the happy flapping of wings and the pleasant shaking of tails is one of the many joys of being a Momma Duck. Occasionally, questions come up regarding these lovely little ducky parts.

Basic Wing Anatomy

And now it's time for your second anatomy lesson! This time I'm going to walk you through the basic skeletal structure of wings.

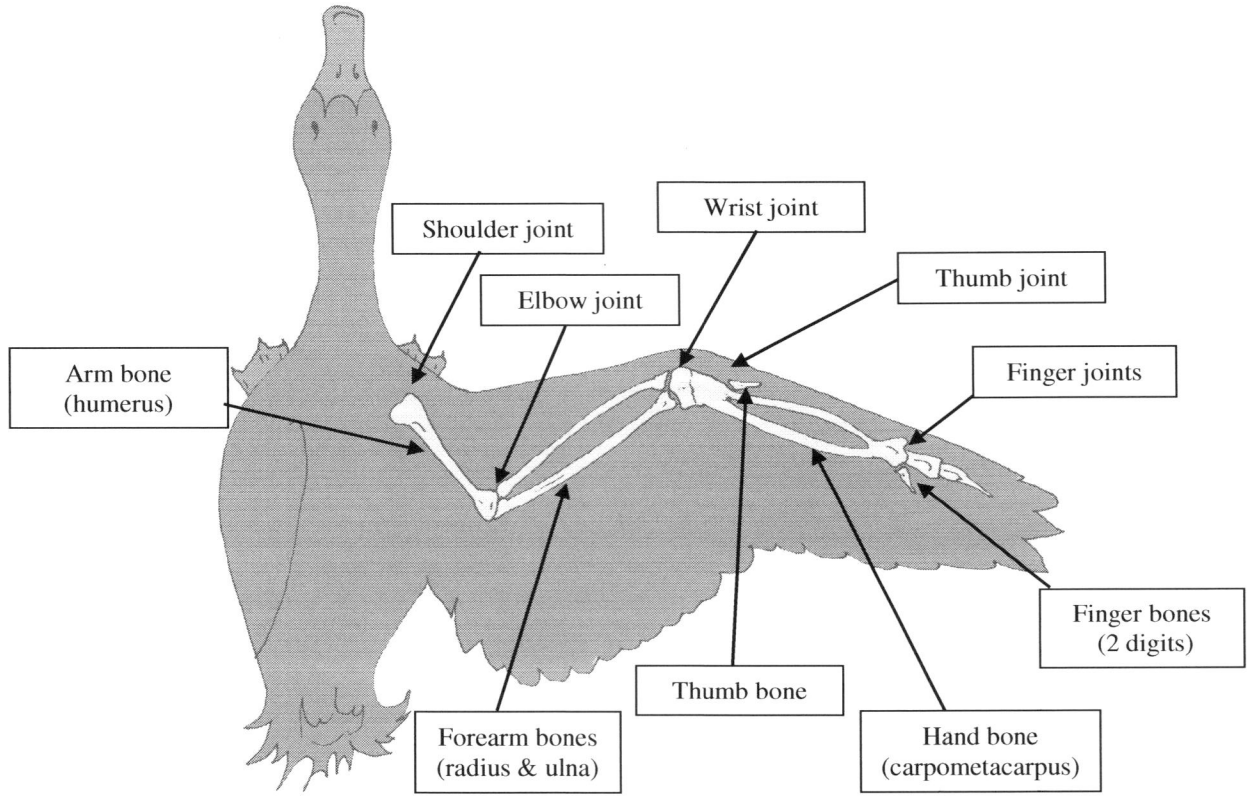

A diagram of the bones of your duck's wing

Wing Clipping

Most domestic ducks can't fly. The only exceptions are Muscovy ducks and Bantam breeds. If you don't have a full aviary to keep them contained and protected, their wings will need to be clipped every year after they molt their primary wing feathers.

Growing feathers still have blood vessels inside, so they can't be clipped until they've fully emerged and dried up, or heavy bleeding will result. If this is your first time, I highly suggest you have your vet teach you when it's safe to clip and precisely how to proceed.

Wing clipping is a lot easier if you have a helper. One person gently stretches out your duck's wing while the other uses blunt-tipped scissors (bandage cutting scissors) to safely do the pruning.

1. Extend your duck's right wing.

2. Skip over and leave 2-3 of their primary *"flight"* feathers intact at the tip of their wing—don't cut these (well... you can cut them, but their wing will look prettier when folded back up if you don't).

3. Work your way inward, towards your duck's body, cutting off the next 6-8 primary feathers an inch or so away from the skin. Do this so that the stubs are hidden and blanketed by the primary coverts, so they look pretty when you're done.

4. Repeat on your duck's left wing.

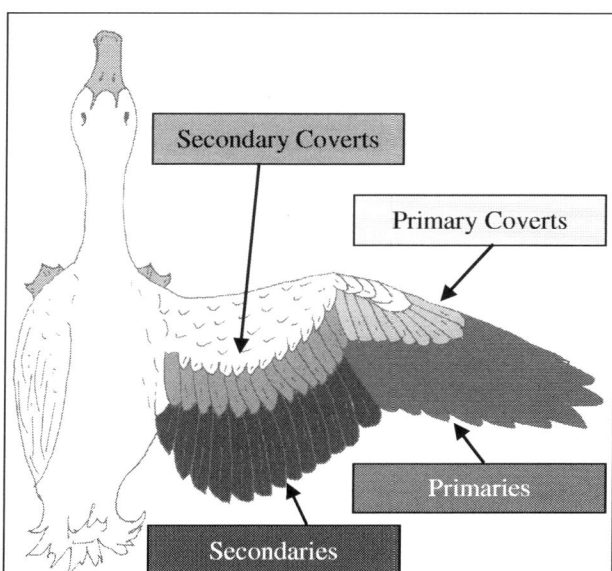 

Wing clipping: Before & after (The wrist joint is the dividing line between primary and secondary wing feathers)

Sprains

Sprained wings are relatively rare, but when they do occur it's usually the result of competitive drake fighting or females trying to escape and flap away from overzealous males.

- **Symptoms**

Some symptoms of a sprained wing may include: wing drooping.

- **Treatment**

The first thing you want to do when you see a drooping wing is bring your duck to the vet to rule out any possible fractures or dislocations. Once this has been successfully done your vet will likely prescribe anti-inflammatory/pain medication.

More severe sprains (where the wing is dangling down to the ground) may require some additional support during the recuperative period. This is done using a figure-eight wing wrap, which your vet will teach you how to do using a 2" x 2.2 yd. roll of vet wrap flexible cohesive bandage. This type of bandage doesn't have any adhesive backing, because its mesh-like fabric sticks to itself.

To apply the bandage, you'll be following a figure-eight pattern. You want to be sure to avoid twisting the bandage at any point—always keeping one side of the bandage facing inward, and the other side of the bandage facing outward. Also, you'll want to keep the flexible bandage taut (but not tight) as you work your way around.

1. Unrolling the bandage as you go, begin at the underside of your duck's wing. Then bring the bandage up and over their wing, keeping one edge of the bandage nicely tucked into the crook of the top of their wing—right near where it emerges from their body (their shoulder).

2. Then, bring the bandage diagonally down and in front, over their wing, before sending it back behind their wing and out of sight again.

3. Then, the bandage comes up and over, back into sight again, near the base of their wing, where it meets their body (their armpit). Remember to keep one edge of the bandage nicely tucked into the crook of their wing where it meets their body--*without* crumpling any wing feathers. Be careful not to pinch feathers here, or it can cause discomfort.

4. Then, the bandage comes back in front of their wing again, heading diagonally downward and toward the bend or "wrist" of their wing.

5. Roll the bandage over their wrist and then send it back behind their wing and quickly over their wing and into sight again. You have now completed the *first* figure-eight journey around their wing.

6. Repeat the above steps until you have completed 4-5 figure-eight patterns around your duck's wing. Then, finish behind their wing and cut the bandage.

7. Gently press your hands and fingers over the bandaging to lock the woven mesh together. You want to do this all over, molding the fabric securely in place.

Diagram of figure-eight wing wrap using vet wrap

To secure this bandaging in place, use a roll of elastic adhesive bandage (2" width). The application of this adhesive-backed bandage will make it more difficult for your duck to unravel their vet wrap bandaging.

Adhesive bandage and red vet wrap

1. Cut a six inch piece of elastic adhesive bandage (this length may vary depending on the size of your duck; male Muscovy ducks may require a significantly longer strip).

2. Tuck the center of the adhesive bandage strip behind the wrist of your duck's wing, sticky side facing towards the vet wrap bandage that's already in place. Avoid any direct contact with feathers as you then bring each end of the strip forward and over their wing. Rub gently all over to secure it in place.

Diagram of adhesive bandage strip overlaying figure-eight vet wrap

Wait 3 days and then remove both bandages using safe bandage-cutting scissors. *Be careful not to cut any feathers!* Allow your duck 20-30 minutes to move around freely and exercise their muscles without any bandaging. This will give you ample opportunity to see if they can hold up their wing, or if it should be rewrapped and supported for another 2-3 days.

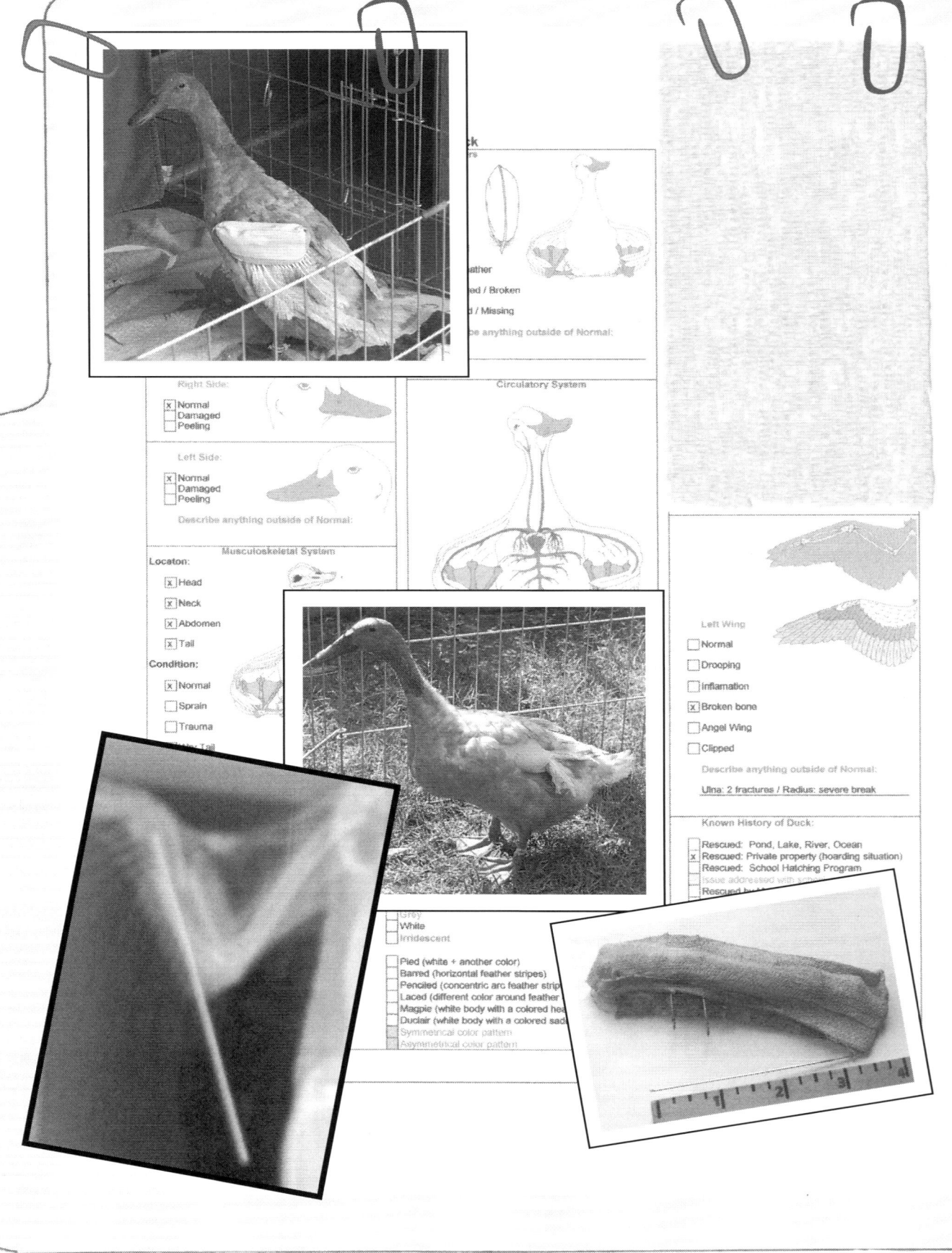

Bee's Broken Wing...

I walked out to my pens one morning and saw Lil Ms. Bee's wing drooping down to the ground. When I gently attempted to flex her wing back up into place I could feel a lack of cohesiveness and knew it was broken. An immediate trip to the vet for an x-ray confirmed that her boyfriend Marvin had accidentally injured her during an overzealous mating ritual. Her ulna was broken in two places while her narrow radius bone had sustained a serious fracture that resulted in a misalignment of the bone.

Surgery was required to brace her bones into place utilizing external pins. During the initial stages of healing I had to prevent Bee from immersing her external hardware in water, which meant absolutely no swimming allowed. I kept her water bowl shallowly filled (refreshing it frequently to keep it clean) and utilized a spray bottle to mist her feathers and promote preening activities a few times a day. During her final weeks of healing, I painted liquid bandage around the base of her pin where it came out of the skin and allowed her to bathe in clean water. This sealant helped prevent water from getting into her body and causing infection. Under vet advisement I put a thin layer of non-medicated ChapStick® around the base of her pin 2-3 times a day to create an additional moisture barrier.

Follow-up x-rays revealed that the breaks in Bee's ulna had fully healed over the course of 8 weeks while her radius had completely failed to mend. This meant that a second surgery was needed. In this operation a long pin was placed down the center of her radius, realigning the two broken sections.

I learned the hard way that ducks can (and will) do the unthinkable and actually pull out their bone pins if any part of the wire tip is left exposed. Lil Ms. Bee yanked out her six inch bone pin, botching the entire operation. During a third and more advanced surgical procedure, our vet connected her fractured radius together using a strategically bent pin and some bone cement.

Unfortunately, Lil Ms. Houdini found a way to remove this bone pin as well, leaving me with no alternative, but to permanently retire her to the sanctuary. While she has a fully-functioning wing and has returned to her normal routine, there is a chance it might give her trouble one day, in which case, a partial wing amputation may need to be explored.

Case # 112: Broken Wing

Angel Wing

Angel wing occurs when the muscles of your growing duckling's wrist can't support the weight of their newly sprouting pin feathers. As a result, their wing tips flip outward and their condition becomes noticeable. It can be linked to genetics or nutritional issues. While angel wing hinders flight in wild ducks, it's merely a harmless aesthetic condition in non-flying domestic ducks.

- **Symptoms**

Some symptoms of angel wing may include:

Ducklings: the tips of one or both wings flip outward as pin feathers sprout.
Ducks: a few wing tip feathers don't fold-up or tuck-in normally, often sticking out perpendicular from your duck's body.

- **Treatment**

If the cause is nutritional, your ducklings diet should be immediately examined, ensuring that they're on a high-quality and properly-balanced brand-name feed. Excess protein is often a contributor to this disorder (although insufficient manganese levels can also be a cause), so make sure you're serving your duckling the appropriate feed blend for their age and needs. Ask your vet or a professional at your local grain store if you need further advice. While changes in their diet will help prevent other mishaps, angel wing is irreversible by diet.

Angel wing can sometimes be corrected in ducklings when you first begin to notice symptoms. Your vet can teach you how to bandage and splint their wing(s) correctly in place using a lightweight, but sturdy slice of cardboard, which is cut to the size and shape of your duck's wing. This is held in place using vet wrap applied in a figure-eight pattern (see: *"Sprains"*).

Unless wing tips are poking your duck's eyes or causing other health problems, they should be left alone. There's no need to cut feathers in this situation (and you especially don't want to do so while they're growing and there's a vein inside).

Diagram of a wing splint held in place using vet wrap in a figure-eight pattern

Drooped Wing

Like angel wing, drooped wing occurs in ducklings. As their pin feathers sprout, their wings can't support the added weight. Drooping wing is usually the result of malnutrition, although it can be genetic.

- **Symptoms**

Some symptoms of a drooped wing may include: the drooping of a duckling's wing at the time pin feathers are sprouting.

- **Treatment**

Immediately examine your ducklings diet, ensuring that they're on a high-quality and properly-balanced brand-name feed. Make sure you're serving your duckling the appropriate feed blend for their age and needs. Ask your vet or a professional at your local grain store if you need further advice.

Drooped wing can sometimes be corrected in ducklings when you first begin to notice symptoms, treating it the same way as angel wing (see: *"Angel Wing"*).

Dislocated Wing

Ducks can be a little clumsy, often flapping their wings around before taking a good look at their surroundings. Rarely, this can result in a break or dislocation. Dislocations in the wings of females can also be a sign of overzealous mating. Examine your drake-to-hen ratio or the size of her mate in comparison to make sure she can handle her boyfriend(s). Protective separations are likely in order.

- **Symptoms**

Some symptoms of a dislocated wing may include: wing drooping, inability to tuck and fold it into place.

- **Treatment**

Immediately bring your duck to the vet for an x-ray. Once the dislocation is confirmed, your vet will need to reset the wing. Anti-inflammatory/pain medication (and possibly additional pain medication) will be in order. Your vet may also want you to wrap the wing in a figure-eight pattern for additional support (see: *"Sprains"*).

Broken Wing

Although rare, broken wings are often the result of overzealous mating. Female ducks are especially prone when males are significantly larger than them or when they're outnumbered—although this isn't always the case. Drakes penned with geese during the mating season may also be prone to this type of injury when protective ganders attack and cause damage. Ganders will often do this when they see drakes mating ducks (whether they're actually protecting females or simply getting jealous is open to interpretation).

- **Symptoms**

Some symptoms of a broken wing may include: a loose and dangling wing, a wing that can't be properly tucked and folded neatly into place.

- **Treatment**

Minor fractures: If you suspect your duck has a broken wing, a vet visit and x-ray is immediately in order. If bones are neatly aligned and the fracture is minor, something as simple as vet wrap bandaging may do the trick along with a round of antibiotics and anti-inflammatory/pain medication (see: *"Sprains"*).

Bandages can be cut away once-a-week using safe bandage-cutting scissors. Allow your duck 20-30 minutes to move around freely without their bandaging to exercise their muscles a little (this will prevent excess muscle atrophy) and then reapply new bandaging.

You should *never* wrap your pet duck's broken wing without qualified vet supervision. Their wing must be x-rayed and then bones need to be properly aligned *prior* to bandaging to avoid harmful, painful and potentially permanent medical issues.

Severe fractures: If bones are misaligned surgery may be needed to pin them into place to promote proper healing and continued use of their wing. In this case, antibiotics, anti-inflammatory/pain medication and additional pain medication is often needed to prevent infection and keep your duck comfortable.

Additional x-rays will be needed to monitor bone alignment at multiple stages of healing and your vet will also inspect the surgical site for any signs of infection. If your duck has any external hardware (bone pins coming out of their wings), they won't be allowed to immerse themselves into water, which means absolutely no swimming. To prevent any feather deterioration during this time, they can splash preen using a shallow bowl of tap water, or you can use a spray bottle to mist them a few times a day to promote preening. Pins are usually removed around week eight.

Pinioned Wing

To pinion is to amputate a duckling's wing tip (where a number of their flight feathers originate) on one side to impede their flight. This is not done on non-flying domestic ducks, which is a good thing since it's a painful and inhumane procedure, done without any anesthetic or pain medication. Basically, it would be like cutting off one of our fingers, which is in fact what they're doing.

Before coming to our sanctuary, someone mistook Marvin (a non-flying domestic Khaki Campbell drake) for a Mallard and pinioned his right wing tip. The kicker is, after putting him through this trauma as a duckling, they turned around and abandoned him as an adult, fully understanding that he could never fly or migrate away.

Wing Amputation

Wing amputation is sometimes required when a serious injury takes place. Ducks who are abandoned in public places often succumb to fishing line injuries. This unforgiving, stretch-resistant filament winds around their wings and limbs and cuts off circulation, often resulting in a slow and agonizing death unless humans step-in and intervene. Ducks who suffer severe fractures or unrelenting infections may also face wing amputation.

Wing amputation surgery can be very traumatic. Be sure to discuss whether or not your duck is a good candidate and likely to survive both surgery and post-operative care and medications before going this route.

Things to consider:

1. Ducks who are human-imprinted and extremely comfortable being handled without becoming overly stressed often handle amputation surgery better than shy and easily-stressed ducks.

2. Ducks with an energetic *"I can do it!"* attitude are more likely to recover from amputation surgery.

3. Ducks who require only partial or wing-tip amputation tend to fare better than ducks who require full wing amputation. The larger the amputation, the more difficult the recovery.

4. Younger ducks often adapt to amputation more readily than geriatric ducks.

5. Ducks with other health issues often struggle with amputation surgery.

Wry Tail

Wry tail can be mild or pronounced and is often the result of incubation errors, malnutrition or genetics (caused by two inherited recessive genes). It isn't always easy to spot in young ducklings and often becomes more noticeable as they mature. Wry tail is usually a harmless aesthetic condition, only rarely severe enough to interfere with their mobility.

Eeben has wry tail and angel wing due to nutritional issues when he was a duckling

- **Symptoms**

Some symptoms of wry tail may include: your duck's tail is off-center from the rest of their body (aiming to the left or right).

- **Treatment**

Wry tail occurring in ducklings or adult ducks can often be attributed to malnutrition. In ducklings it sometimes accompanies angel wing (see: *"Angel Wing"*) in which case, their diet should be immediately examined, ensuring that they're on a high-quality and appropriate brand-name feed. In severe cases vets may also advise a safe multi-vitamin regime.

Medical #6
Musculoskeletal System (Head, Neck & Abdomen)

Skeletal and muscular injuries are far more common in the legs and wings than in other parts of your duck's body, like their head, neck and abdomen. Even so, accidents can occur elsewhere.

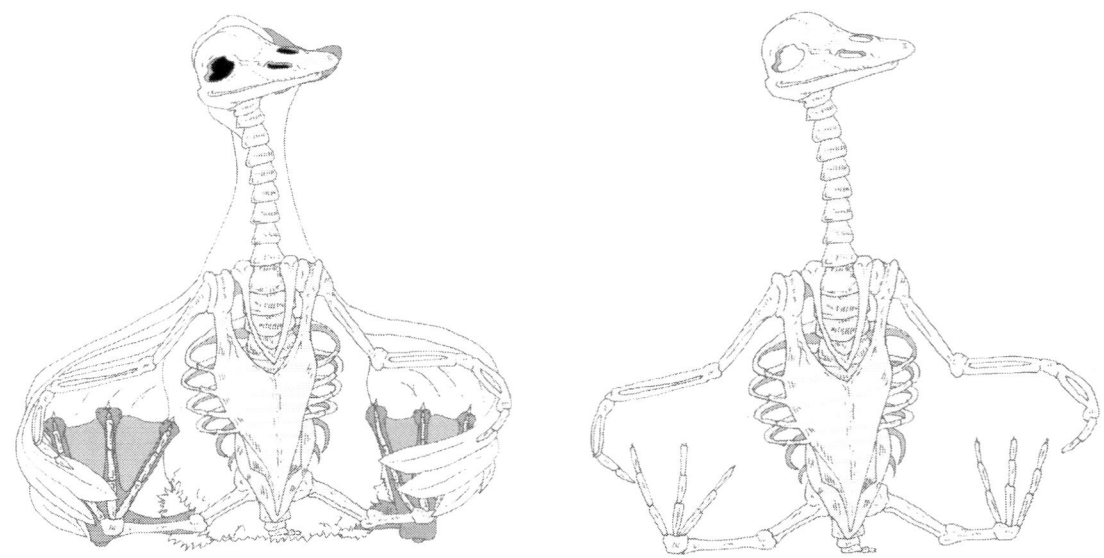

A rudimentary diagram of your duck's skeletal system

Keel split

A duck who falls from a height and then lands on their keel (or breastbone) can end up with a nasty incision when that protrusion presses and cuts into superficial tissues of muscle and skin.

- **Symptoms**

Some symptoms of a keel split may include: a straight and deep incision that runs down the center of your duck's belly as a result of an elevated fall.

- **Treatment**

Apply direct pressure using a thick stack of gauze pads or clean towel and get your duck to the vet for immediate treatment. Because the slit is so clean-cut, it'll need to be stitched up to promote proper healing. Failure to have it sutured can result in it reopening multiple times throughout the healing phase, increasing the risk of infection.

Since ducks sit on their bellies, the risk of infection is great. Your vet will put your duck on potent antibiotics, anti-inflammatory/pain medication and additional pain medication—a topical antibiotic may also be prescribed. Your duck won't be allowed to swim for 4-6 weeks until the wound is fully healed. In the meantime you can give them a bowl of clean tap water for splash-preening or you can mist them with a spray bottle a few times a day to help them preen and keep their feathers tidy.

Broken Bones

Broken spine, skull or body cavity bones can be extremely debilitating and are often fatal. They're usually the result of an extremely traumatic injury where something has fallen on them, they've experienced a major fall or they've managed to survive a predator attack.

- **Symptoms**

Some symptoms of a fractured skull includes: swelling or bleeding of the head, panting (indicative of pain), seizures, paralysis and inability to move.

Some symptoms of broken bones of the spine may include: protrusions in the neck, often marked with localized swelling, panting, paralysis and inability to move.

Some symptoms of broken bones of the main cavity: distended abdomen, swelling, panting, abdominal heaving, difficulty breathing, inability or refusal to move and loss of appetite.

- **Treatment**

Broken bones occurring within your duck's main cavity can sometimes be surgically manipulated and pinned when fractures are more complex. In any case, ducks who survive these mishaps will need to be spend a lot of time under direct supervision and in recovery cradle for 6-8 weeks (see: *"Therapy for Hips, Legs, Feet & Toes/Duck Cradles & Wheelchairs"*). Vets will usually want them suspended, so their feet aren't touching the ground during some periods of their recovery while their feet *do* touch the floor during others.

Fractured neck or skull bones are often fatal injuries; if not, humane euthanasia is often required to spare your duck any additional pain.

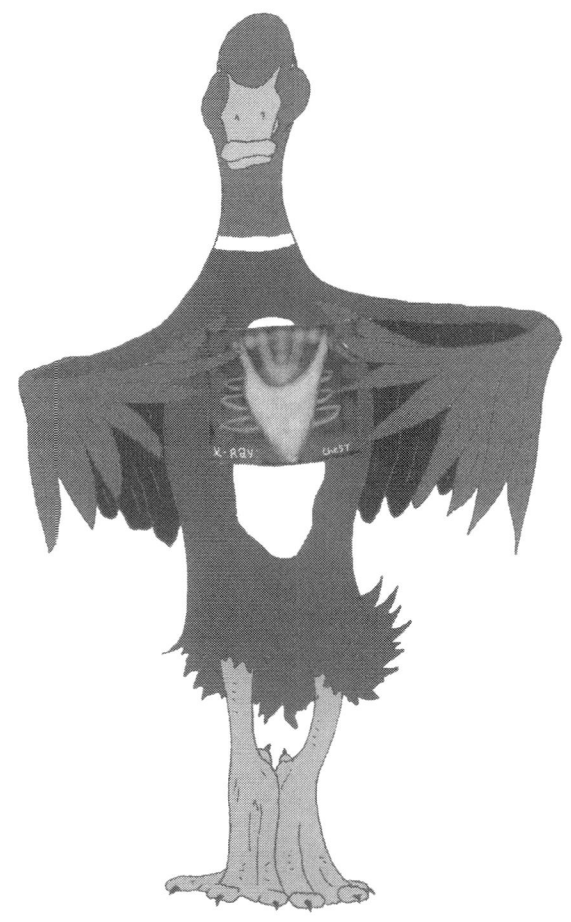

Medical #7
Reproductive System (Female)

Reproductive questions and issues aren't uncommon to Momma Ducks. While females tend to experience more complications than males, there are times when your drake may need your help as well. Even so, let's begin with the ladies.

Female Reproductive System

Your female duck's reproductive system includes their ovary, infundibulum, oviduct and vagina. Except in extremely rare instances, ducks only have one fully-developed ovary and one corresponding oviduct on their left side. Their right oviduct is nonfunctional. Your duck's eggs originate in her ovary and then take form while passing through her oviduct (her internal egg-laying tube), which look something like this:

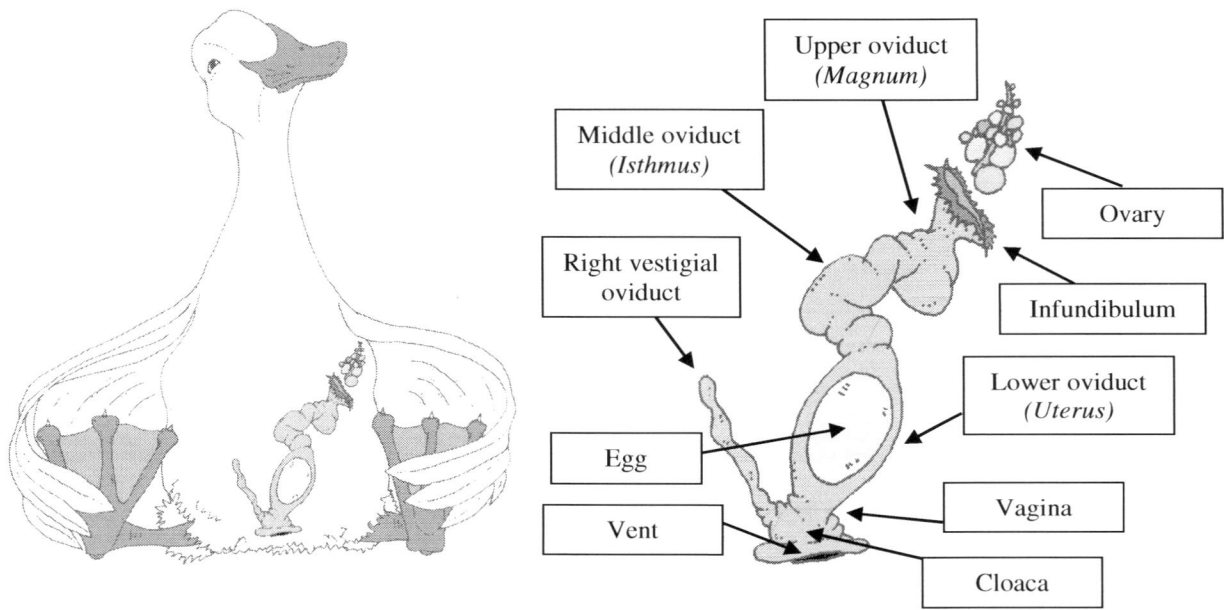

A diagram of a your female duck's reproductive system

Treatment of Reproductive Disorders in Female Ducks

Unfortunately, reproductive issues among egg-laying ducks are among the most common medical issues they face, and they can often be life-threatening. Since most reproductive disorders involve similar treatment alternatives, I'll begin by reviewing those options first.

Three common therapies implemented to temporary halt a duck's egg production are:

1. Human Chorionic Gonadotropin (HCG)
2. Leuprolide
3. Deslorelin

- **HCG injections**

HCG causes the deterioration of ovarian follicles, which inhibits ovulation. The benefit of this drug is that it *works quickly* and has few side effects if used for short periods of time. This drug is a good option for first time/one-off reproductive incidents. Three treatments are often administered in 48 hour intervals. Long term side effects may include ovarian tumors, so it's only recommended for intermittent use.

- **Leuprolide injections**

Leuprolide acetate (Lupron®) suppresses the release of gonadotropin (a hormone that regulates reproductive activity) into the body, which brings egg production to a stop. Injections are repeated about every three weeks or so. Side effects, if any, are minimal, so vets consider it very safe. One problem with Leuprolide is it may take up to several weeks to begin taking effect. This time delay can be a real issue if your duck needs an *immediate* break from her daily egg-laying routine. In addition, some ducks become immune to the treatment within a short period of time, making it only a temporary solution. It seems to have the greatest effect on young ducks who haven't been laying for long.

- **Utilizing both injections**

Many vets will administer HCG to immediately stop egg production along with a Leuprolide injection for a longer lasting effect. Combined, these two drug therapies are an excellent way of halting your duck's egg production

- **Deslorelin implants**

Deslorelin acetate (Suprelorin®) is a slow-release hormone that can either be implanted in the pectoral muscle or under the skin. It suppresses the release of gonadotropin, working similarly to Leuprolide injections and comes in various strengths (typically 4.7 mg). The effectiveness of the implant usually last between 1-3 months in waterfowl, depending on your duck's individual biology, diet and environment.

- **Expense**

The trouble with each of these therapies is they can be quite expensive. To address this issue, you can get a prescription from your vet and have it filled at a compounding pharmacy. There may be differences in shelf-lives or half-lives of these products, so be sure to ask questions and then consult again with your vet before placing your order. It's usually just a matter of using supplies a little faster and decreasing the time between your duck's injections. (supplier: Diamond Back Pharmacy, 7901 East McDowell Road, Scottsdale AZ 85257-3747, PH: 866-646-2223).

- **Salpingohysterectomy**

In severe cases, when an oviduct is ruptured or permanently damaged, when infection is too widespread to treat, or when egg binding is frequent and severe (greatly increasing the risk of other more serious medical issues like peritonitis), surgery may be your duck's only hope of survival. The procedure in which the left oviduct (the functioning oviduct) is removed is known as a salpingohysterectomy.

An abdominal incision is made and the left oviduct is removed. Your vet will need to inspect the vestigial right oviduct to verify it's truly non-functioning. There have been rare instances of the right oviduct being operative as well; in which case, it'll need to be removed also. The ovary is not normally removed because it can be difficult to reach and can bleed heavily, posing added risk.

When the oviduct is removed egg production normally shuts down due to the decline in reproductive hormones, but this isn't always the case. There is still a chance that your duck's functioning ovary could continue to produce eggs, so while they're in there, your vet will need to carefully inspect her ovary. If it has a large number of tiny egg follicles, it could be an indicator that your duck might be at higher risk for future egg production (this is true of younger ducks in particular). If this is the case with your duck, a hormone implant (Suprelorin®) can be inserted at the time of surgery.

Post-operative care includes a 3-5 day hospital stay along with intravenous fluids and nutritional support, antibiotics, anti-inflammatory/pain medication and additional pain medication. Upon returning home, your duck will need to be confined to a small and sanitary place to dissuade her from moving around too much for the first two weeks of her recovery. Clean pine shavings usually work best in this type of situation and swimming is an absolute no-no. Occasionally, in extreme cases, tube feedings may also be required until your duck resumes eating on their own again. Antibiotic, anti-inflammatory and pain medications continue for 14 days and then, at the end of two weeks, a return trip to your vet's office for staple removal and a check-up will be in order. You'll need to continue to keep your duck separated from other flock members for an additional 4-6 weeks or until they've fully recovered.

A salpingohysterectomy is often reserved as a last resort because of its complexity, extreme risk and cost, but it's sometimes necessary to prevent reoccurring and potentially life-threatening medical issues (see: *"Metritis," "Peritonitis,"* and *"Salpingitis"*). It can be particularly risky if your duck is still recovering from prior surgery. Be sure to research this option *thoroughly* before making a decision.

Very few board certified vets are experienced and successful with this operation. Confirm your vet of choice has performed this surgery successfully before on ducks—not just on birds (parrots, etc.). Be sure to ask how many of their patients actually made *complete* recoveries afterwards as well as finding out how many didn't. Your vet should be able to give you quantifiable details (as opposed to saying "a lot") while possibly even providing references.

Questions to ask your vet:

1. Surgical and post-operative risks (including any questions regarding anesthesia and intubation).
2. Post surgical hospital stay (feeding, intravenous medication, etc.).
3. Post-surgical prescription plan (antibiotics, anti-inflammatory and pain medication).
4. Post-surgical care requirements once they're back home with you again.
5. Full procedural cost (including any blood work, x-rays, post-surgical exams, etc.).
6. After-hours/weekend emergency plan (this is absolutely *vital*. Very few vets know how to perform this surgery and handle post-operative complications, so you need to know who to call no matter what the day or time).

Egg Binding

Egg binding (or egg impaction) occurs when a female duck can't pass her egg normally through her oviduct. This is often the result of an egg that can't be easily passed due to its size, shape, consistency or texture. Eggs with soft shells are often the most difficult for your duck to pass.

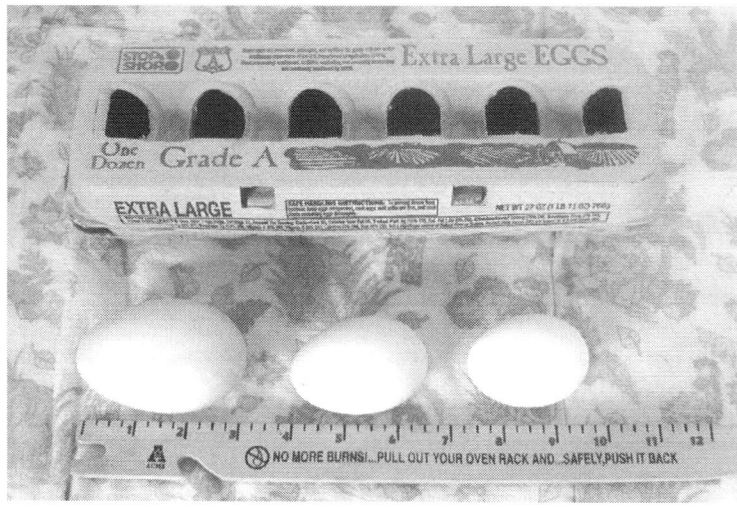

(L-R) double-yoke duck egg, normal duck egg & a store-bought chicken egg

As with other reproductive issues, egg binding can be the result of a nutritional deficiency, disease, cancer or genetic predisposition. Other ducks at greater risk include:

1. *New layers* who often lay over-sized, double-yolk eggs.

2. *Seasonal layers* who sometimes have difficulty passing their first eggs at the start of their cycle.

3. *Overweight ducks* can have more difficulty passing their eggs.

4. *Pekin ducks* have been bred to lay an unnatural amount of eggs, which can lead to additional problems. Most of my Pekins lay an egg almost every day for 4-5 years before slowing down. Their cycle only rarely stops when they molt and occasionally again for a couple months in winter.

5. *Problematic layers* have a history of laying soft-shelled eggs.

- **Symptoms**

Some symptoms of egg binding may include: resisting the urge to walk, stiff waddling, swollen vent, open-bill panting and tail pumping (tail feathers bob up and down) for extended periods of time.

Keep in mind, most of these symptoms are indicative of normal egg-laying; what you're watching out for is the prolonged continuation of these indicators. Most ducks lay their eggs within an hour, so if you see their laying behavior continuing for more than two hours, it's time to intervene (especially if this is out of character for your duck).

- **Treatment**

As soon as you notice your duck having trouble passing her egg, call your vet immediately (especially if your duck is predisposed to issues because they're a new layer, seasonal layer just starting up again, overweight, a Pekin or a problematic layer). Vets who are unfamiliar with the severity of the problem will often suggest you give your duck a little more time, placing her in a warm bath, but I've never known this to work. Worse yet, if your vet will be closed in an hour, you could end up in a really bad predicament because egg binding can be fatal if left untreated.

Vets will normally have you bring your duck in for an immediate appointment whereupon they'll give her an x-ray to make sure she's not backed up with multiple eggs (in which case they may need to put her under anesthesia to help get them out). On the other hand, if she only has one egg inside, your vet will painlessly lubricate your duck's oviduct and then give her an injection of Oxytocin to help intensify her contractions (which will result in heavier panting and increased tail-bobbing). Both of these tactics combined should help her pass her egg. Your vet will then have you take your duck home for some quiet, alone time in her favorite nesting place. Peek in on her every 15 minutes or so to make sure she's okay, but try not to disturb her.

Before leaving your vet's office, be sure to discuss an after-hours plan for your duck. The process of passing her egg can still take hours and your duck could easily run into trouble after your vet closes for the night. Now is the time to find out if anyone will be on call to help should her situation worsen. If your vet won't be available, but they give you the name of another vet who will be, *call that vet*—while you're right there in your vet's office. Explain your situation and make sure that they'll be able to help in an after-hours emergency if your duck's health deteriorates. This way, if the situation doesn't improve, everyone will be prepared. Just be sure you have copies of your duck's medical records, including the results of any recent tests.

Occasionally, you may find that the referred vet can't help out in your particular situation; even so, this is a good thing to discover while you're still there in your own vet's office. Armed with this information you can further brainstorm with your vet and devise a new plan.

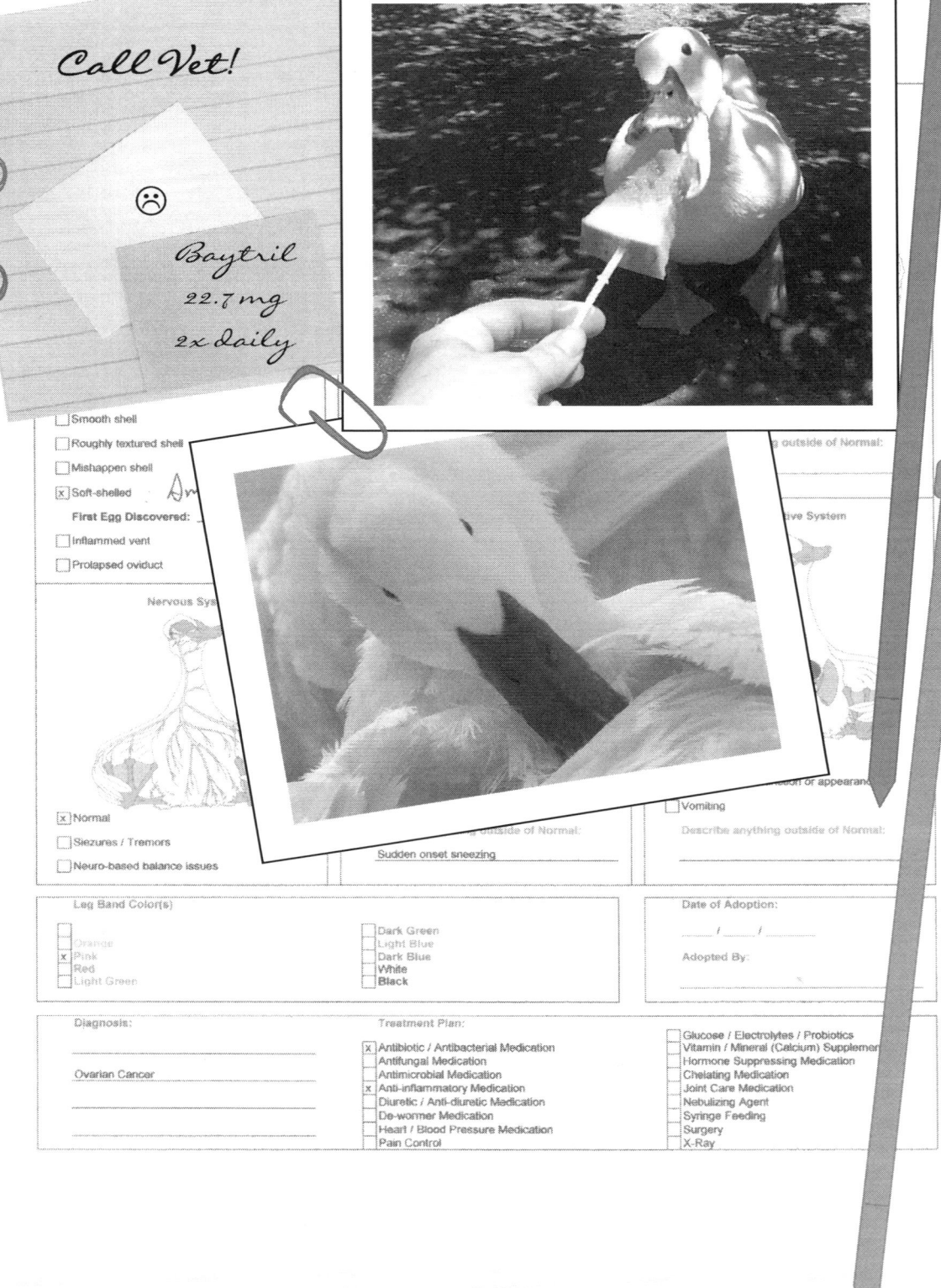

Call Vet!

☹

Baytril
22.7 mg
2x daily

- [ ] Smooth shell
- [ ] Roughly textured shell
- [ ] Mishappen shell
- [x] Soft-shelled

First Egg Discovered: _____

- [ ] Inflammed vent
- [ ] Prolapsed oviduct

Nervous System

- [x] Normal
- [ ] Siezures / Tremors
- [ ] Neuro-based balance issues

_____ outside of Normal:
Sudden onset sneezing

- [ ] Vomiting

Describe anything outside of Normal: _____

Leg Band Color(s)
- [ ] Orange
- [x] Pink
- [ ] Red
- [ ] Light Green
- [ ] Dark Green
- [ ] Light Blue
- [ ] Dark Blue
- [ ] White
- [ ] Black

Date of Adoption: ___ / ___ / ___

Adopted By: _____

Diagnosis:
Ovarian Cancer

Treatment Plan:
- [x] Antibiotic / Antibacterial Medication
- [ ] Antifungal Medication
- [ ] Antimicrobial Medication
- [x] Anti-inflammatory Medication
- [ ] Diuretic / Anti-diuretic Medication
- [ ] De-wormer Medication
- [ ] Heart / Blood Pressure Medication
- [ ] Pain Control
- [ ] Glucose / Electrolytes / Probiotics
- [ ] Vitamin / Mineral (Calcium) Supplement
- [ ] Hormone Suppressing Medication
- [ ] Chelating Medication
- [ ] Joint Care Medication
- [ ] Nebulizing Agent
- [ ] Syringe Feeding
- [ ] Surgery
- [ ] X-Ray

Alice's Ovarian Cancer ...

As Alice entered her sixth year of life she randomly began laying small, soft-shelled eggs. Prior to this time she had always been a healthy layer, so I immediately brought her to the vet to make sure she wasn't harboring any kind of hidden infection. All of her tests and cultures came back normal, but a few months later her behavior changed suddenly. While she used to lead all the other ducks from the barn to the pond every morning, she was suddenly trailing at the back of the line—and that's exactly what I told our vet. A vet who understands ducks knows that even the slightest behavioral shifts can be indicative of a concealed ailment.

Unable to find anything wrong with her, Alice began a precautionary regime of antibiotics and anti-inflammatory/pain medication for 14 days, by the end of which she was acting like her normal self again.

The following spring Alice began walking at the back of the ducky line again and we put her back on Baytril® and Rimadyl® for another 14 days. Once again her behavior returned to normal and she went about her happy business.

A few weeks later I heard some repetitive sneezing while I was out in the duck pens one morning. When it failed to stop, I followed the sound over to where Alice was swimming on the pond. Recognizing it was abnormal, I rushed her to the vet for an x-ray where she was immediately put on oxygen. Minutes later she passed away. I was in shock...

An examination of Alice's x-ray revealed that her ovary was slightly enlarged with cancer and that it had spread to her lungs. Ovarian cancer explained the change in her egg quality a year prior. It also explained her two behavioral episodes—suddenly walking at the back of the line. While we thought that the medications I had given her had aided in her recovery, she actually had gone into remission entirely on her own—*twice!*

Looking back, I realized that Alice had lived quite happily for a year following the appearance of her first symptoms, demonstrating that just because your duck has cancer doesn't mean they'll be leaving you right away or that they'll be unhealthy during that time.

Case # 182: Ovarian Cancer

Preventative Egg Binding Treatment Options

There are a few ways you can try to help prevent your duck from becoming egg bound.

- **Dietary adjustments**

Dietary adjustments can help improve a problematic layers situation. Examine your duck's diet to ensure they're on the best possible brand-name formula and that they have 24/7 access to an added calcium source. If you're serving them a mixture of regular feed and layer formula, you may need to increase the ratio of laying formula (see: *"Feeding Egg-Laying Ducks"*).

- **Lighting adjustments**

Adjustments in light can help slow down the frequency of egg production. The increase of light in spring and summer is one of the triggers that sparks your duck's reproductive cycle. Letting your duck out of their barn a little later in the morning and bringing them up again a little earlier in the evening can sometimes impede their egg-laying. If you're a fan of nightlights in your barn, you may want to turn them off for a while. Windows may also need to be shaded.

- **Environmental adjustments**

Some Momma Ducks have had short-lived success in stopping egg production by suddenly (and sometimes drastically) changing their duck's routine or environment. This is done by placing your duck in a different day pen, a new area of their barn at night (away from her usual spot), by having her spend her days or nights with different ducky companions, or even by introducing a new duck to the flock. Sudden changes like these will often pause your duck's egg-laying cycle for a couple days, but because it's *stress* that's causing this temporary cessation (and because long-term results are unlikely) I don't suggest using these tactics *unless* you have an urgent and life-threatening matter at hand.

- **Hands-off approach**

Human-imprinted females will sometimes lay more eggs when they're handled or petted by their Momma Ducks. For this reason, you may want to temporarily limit your hands-on time with your duck to help decrease her egg production. Equally, removing female ducks from the immediate presence of males can have similar effects.

- **Calcium gluconate to remedy soft-shelled eggs**

If your ducks is predisposed to laying soft-shelled eggs, you can bring her to the vet to have her calcium and ionized calcium levels analyzed. It's vital to have this blood work done before treating your duck for a calcium deficiency because low calcium levels may not be the issue at all. Genetic disposition, diet or other reproductive issues may be at hand (see: *"Metritis"* and *"Salpingitis"*). Guessing and giving your duck too much calcium can lead to organ damage and result in renal or heart disease—compounding your duck's medical issues.

If test results confirm that your duck's calcium levels are low (or on the low end of normal) your vet will likely prescribe either an oral or injectable calcium supplement. I prefer the injectable because some oral supplements can irritate your duck's throat. Injections of *diluted* Calcium gluconate are administered once-a-month by your vet. Follow-up blood work may be required to monitor calcium levels, but an improvement in egg quality is a good sign that it's working.

If Calcium gluconate injections don't improve the production of soft-shelled eggs within three months, you should discontinue use.

- **Calcium carbonate to remedy soft-shelled eggs**

You can divide a Tums® tablet appropriately and give it to your duck once daily to help remedy soft-shelled egg issues. This calcium additive should only be administered under vet guidance to ensure proper dosing. If it's going to work you should see partial to full improvement within 2-4 weeks.

- **Manganese to remedy soft-shelled eggs**

Manganese deficiency can cause your duck to lay soft-shelled eggs. Examine your feed's spec sheet (usually available on their website; if not, you can contact their customer service team and ask). Your duck should be getting 30-40 mg of manganese for every kg of duck food they consume. If the spec sheet indicates: *40 ppm* (parts per million) this translates to 40 mg per kg (many companies have more than this to account for deterioration as the feed ages). If their feed is not meeting this requirement, you can either upgrade to a new brand with higher levels, or you can make up for the shortage by purchasing chelated manganese tablets. These can be crushed and sprinkled over their food (you can lightly mist the food with water first to help it stick). Manganese *must* be dispersed evenly over their food and consumed in this manner, never by direct pilling, or you can risk a potentially dangerous overdose.

Provided you pay attention to the total manganese levels per kg, you can still serve breeder/layer formula feed to your duck, just be sure to withhold any *additional* calcium sources during treatment. This includes: calcium chips, oyster shells, multivitamins, calcium gluconate, etc. Treatment often needs to continue for the lifetime of your duck.

Manganese deficiency in growing ducklings can result in developmental issues in adults, which can result in the habitual laying of soft-shelled eggs. Unfortunately, this condition is nonreversible.

- **Hormone injections**

If your duck has recurring egg binding issues your vet will likely recommend some kind of hormonal therapy (HCG/leuprolide injections or deslorelin implants) to halt their egg production.

<u>Obturator Paralysis</u>

Obturator paralysis occurs when an egg passing through your duck's oviduct applies pressure on the obturator nerve, which runs just inside her pelvic canal. This usually occurs when the egg is soft, larger than usual or misshapen, which results in it rotating at a slower-than-normal rate down through her oviduct. This dawdling egg remains pressed against her obturator nerve for longer than it otherwise should, compressing the nerve and causing your duck's legs to splay out behind her. This leaves your duck temporarily paralyzed for a few hours until the egg moves further down and along her oviduct.

- **Symptoms**

Some symptoms of obturator paralysis may include: duck lies still with legs temporarily paralyzed and stretched out behind her for a few hours while passing her egg—usually affecting both legs simultaneously (although occasionally only affecting her left leg due to the location of her oviduct).

- **Treatment**

Provided the egg is moving along the oviduct (and not stuck), allow your duck some private time where she can remain undisturbed by other flock members and be as comfortable as possible. Keep a watchful eye, checking on her every twenty minutes or so without agitating her. Paralysis usually lasts 2-3 hours and ends with your duck slowly regaining control of her legs again. Her egg will usually make an appearance a few hours later, although it may not arrive until the following morning—during her normal egg-laying time.

If your duck isn't on her feet again by the end of three hours, and showing no improvement, it's time to take her to the vet to make sure she isn't egg bound (see: *"Egg Binding"*).

Obturator paralysis is more common in ducks who've just started laying for the first time, or in ducks who have difficulty laying. Veteran layers will occasionally experience this at the start of their annual egg-laying season. More often than not, a particular duck will be prone to this and experience it on a re-occurring basis from time to time.

Oviduct Prolapse

Occasionally while a duck is straining to expel her egg, she'll push too hard and her oviduct will come outside of her body. This can happen in varying degrees, ranging from a minor protrusion of the oviduct to major mishaps (where 4-6 inches pop outside). Ducks who are over-mated, who have a genetic tendency or who have difficulty laying (often producing soft-shelled eggs, misshapen eggs, large eggs or oddly textured eggs) tend to be more prone than other ducks—although it can happen anytime your duck becomes egg bound.

- **Symptoms**

Some symptoms of a prolapsed oviduct may include: swollen vent tissue, blood around the vent and protruding oviduct tissue (minor or severe).

- **Treatment**

Immediately bring your duck to a sanitary location, separate from any other flock members. I like to set my ducks into a clean and empty bathtub, frequently changing out their underlying bed of towels to keep the environment as hygienic as possible. Once you have her settled, call your vet for immediate assistance.

Never attempt to push the oviduct back into your duck's body yourself or you could cause permanent and irreparable damage to her oviduct. If you can't get to the vet right away, or if you have a long trip ahead of you, you need to prep her oviduct.

1. Gently mist her exposed oviduct with warm water to remove any fecal matter and debris.

2. Wait a few minutes for the area to dry naturally.

3. Place a small amount of K-Y® Jelly lubricant over any protruding tissue to keep it moist. Be certain to use a regular, non-irritating, non-heating formula and always use gloves to help prevent infection.

4. Gently mist the area again.

5. Sprinkle a small amount of granular sugar over the exposed oviduct to help reduce swelling.

6. *Never* administer anti-inflammatory medication, which can promote bleeding (pain medications like Torbutrol that don't have anti-inflammatory effects can be given as often as every 6 hours).

Once at your vet office, your duck will need to undergo anesthesia to help tuck and stitch her oviduct back in place. Sutures need to be tight enough to hold the oviduct in place, but loose enough to allow for normal egg production—never restricting this process. For this reason, purse string sutures (which won't restrict the expansion of the oviduct and cloaca) are placed around the circumference of the oviduct, allowing eggs to fit through properly.

Medications for platelet replenishment (blood loss) may or may not be necessary depending on severity, especially if there's any torn tissue. Once bleeding is controlled, anti-inflammatory/pain medication is usually prescribed along with antibiotics, topical ointment and additional pain medication for 7-14 days with one or two vet rechecks during that time.

To halt egg production during the healing phase, a fast-acting HCG injection is often given in combination with an injection of Lupron® for more long-lasting results (a Suprelorin® implant can be implemented in exchange for the Lupron®). Until these take effect, you'll want to diligently check on your duck immediately following her morning egg-laying routine to ensure her sutures are still in place. In some cases, the stress of the prolapse itself will halt egg production until hormonal therapies kick in.

The oviduct is a fast-healing portion of your duck's body and internal mending can occur as soon as 5-7 days; even so, your duck should still be kept separate from any drakes for at least 4-6 weeks (see: *"Surgery/Friendship Therapy"*). Ducks who've experienced an oviduct prolapse are at higher risk for repeat incidents, especially if their first incident was severe. Long-term hormone therapy to stop egg production may be required. If your duck doesn't respond to treatment and problems continue to arise, a salpingohysterectomy may need to be explored.

Salpingitis

Salpingitis refers to the inflammation of the upper oviduct *(magnum)* and/or the middle oviduct *(isthmus)*, which become lined with pus-filled cysts. It's often the result of a bacterial infection (commonly *E. coli*, *Salmonella* or *Mycoplasma*), or subsequent disease (see: *"Avian Cholera"*), but it can also be the secondary result of a systemic infection.

- **Symptoms**

Some symptoms of salpingitis may include: excessive open-bill panting (even when not laying eggs), difficulty passing eggs, fatigue, vent discharge (often heavy) or bleeding, frequent appearance of soft-shelled eggs, abdomen distention and occasionally, loss of appetite resulting in weight loss.

- **Treatment**

Take your duck to the vet right away. X-rays, blood work and swab culturing are often part of the diagnostic process; during which time, antibiotics and pain medications are often prescribed (vets will avoid anti-inflammatory medication if localized bleeding is suspected). Surgical debridement of the oviduct's lining is often required to remove any cysts (which, in extreme cases, can grow to fill your duck's abdominal region and wrap around their internal organs) followed by a regime of antibiotics, anti-inflammatory/pain medication as well as additional pain medication. Remember to keep your duck separate from any drakes for *at least* 4-6 weeks.

Hormonal therapies to stop egg production are highly recommended and in advanced cases, a salpingohysterectomy to remove the infected oviduct may be required.

Metritis

Metritis refers to the inflammation of the lower oviduct *(uterus)*. It's often the result of a bacterial infection (commonly *Staph*, *E. Coli*, *Streptococci*), but it can also be the secondary result of a systemic infection. Ducks who frequently lay soft-shelled, large or misshapen eggs are more prone to egg binding and therefore more likely to sustain irritation and injuries to this part of the oviduct, which then become a gateway for bacterial infections.

Not only can metritis be inflicted by the entrapment of malformed eggs, but since eggshells are formed in this area of the oviduct, any consequent damage can elicit a higher incidence of future egg deformities. This means that flawed eggs can be both a cause of metritis as well as an end result—making them a possible symptom.

- **Symptoms**

Some symptoms of metritis may include: excessive open-bill panting (even when not laying eggs), difficulty passing eggs, egg binding, fatigue, redness and/or swelling around the vent, bleeding from the vent, frequent appearance of misshapen or soft-shelled eggs, abdomen distention and occasionally, loss of appetite resulting in weight loss. Most noticeably, a duck with metritis will often expel globs of off-white gelatinous matter from her vent. Your vet will usually find much more of this substance inside her oviduct during examination.

- **Treatment**

Take your duck to the vet right away. X-rays, blood work and swab culturing are often part of the diagnostic process; during which time, antibiotics and pain medications are often prescribed (vets will avoid anti-inflammatory medication if localized bleeding is suspected).

Surgical debridement of the oviduct's lining is often required to remove any lesions followed by a regime of antibiotics, anti-inflammatory/pain medication as well as additional pain medication. Remember to keep your duck separate from any drakes for *at least* 4-6 weeks.

Hormonal therapies to stop egg production are usually enlisted, or in advanced cases, a salpingohysterectomy to remove the infected oviduct may be required.

Peritonitis

Occasionally, when a duck becomes egg bound (especially when multiple eggs are delayed in her oviduct, causing a traffic jam) some of her egg components can move incorrectly through her oviduct and end up deposited in her abdominal cavity. This condition is known as peritonitis or egg-yolk peritonitis.

Peritonitis is more common among overweight ducks, those with a genetic predisposition, those who have difficulties laying and those who tend to lay misshapen or soft-shelled eggs on a regular basis.

- **Symptoms**

Some symptoms of peritonitis may include: yolk-colored droppings, excessive open-bill panting (both when laying eggs and otherwise), fatigue, increasing abdominal distention and subsequent weight gain and loss of appetite. If your duck is eating the same amount of food as usual and gaining more and more weight, peritonitis should be considered, especially if her egg production appears erratic.

- **Treatment**

Take your duck to the vet right away for an x-ray to confirm the diagnosis. By the time symptoms appear, the condition is usually quite advanced with multiple (and even large masses) of eggs compiled in their abdomen. A comprehensive avian blood profile will determine whether your duck has a septic (yolks can easily become infected with *E. coli* bacteria) or non-septic form of peritonitis. If your duck's body successfully absorbs or encapsulates the abdominal egg mass, infection can often be avoided. Surprisingly, this is actually quite common in non-chronic situations, where eggs are only rarely deposited and don't have time to accumulate. Although infection tends to become inevitable as eggs continually mount, any single egg incorrectly deposited in the abdomen can become septic, proving fatal for your duck if left untreated.

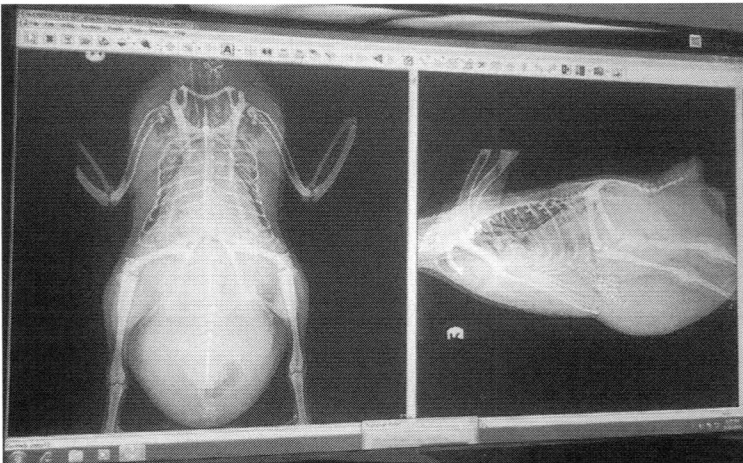

Crackers before her salpingohysterectomy, where over 20 eggs were successfully removed from her abdominal cavity
Photos courtesy of Heather Grandstaff

A potent dose of antibiotics and immediate surgery will be required to remove any eggs and clean out the abdominal cavity. Remember to keep your duck separate from any drakes for *at least* 4-6 weeks. Most vets will recommend a salpingohysterectomy be performed at the same time to prevent future instances of peritonitis. If this isn't an option, hormonal therapies to stop egg production are highly recommended.

Post-operative care for peritonitis is the same as that for a salpingohysterectomy (see: *"Salpingohysterectomy"*).

Cysts (Ovarian, Oviduct & Ovotestis)

A cyst is basically a membrane that fills with fluid somewhere in your duck's body. In relation to the reproductive tract, they can develop in the lining of your duck's oviduct or form in her ovary.

Ovarian cysts: Although often a sign of cancer when four or more cysts form in your duck's ovaries, the development of a couple of small ovarian cysts is not at all uncommon and usually harmless.

Oviduct cysts: Depending on their size and placement, oviduct cysts can have little to no impact on your duck, or they can cause major issues, actually impeding egg movement through the oviduct or negatively influencing shell formation (when occurring in the uterus region).

Ovotestis cysts: In the case where a female duck's right ovotestis becomes suddenly active, there's a slight chance it could become cystic as could her vestigial oviduct.

- **Symptoms**

Ovarian cysts are usually non-impeding, but when they're large or numerous they can cause issues. Some symptoms of problematic ovarian cysts may include: reduced egg production, abnormally small or large eggs, distended abdomen (temporary or permanent), rapid weight gain (fluid retention), abdominal heaving, excessive open-bill panting, loss of appetite and weight loss (which can be masked by fluid retention).

Oviduct cysts have symptoms similar to ovarian cysts; however, they may also include: egg binding. When occurring in the uterus section of the oviduct (where shell formation takes place) symptoms may also include: unusually thick-shelled eggs, soft-shelled eggs or misshapen eggs. In severe cases, they can even rupture the oviduct and lead to internal bleeding and peritonitis.

- **Treatment**

Ovarian cysts: Due to the high risk of hemorrhaging, surgery involving the ovary is often avoided. The presence of large or numerous ovarian cysts are also a symptom of ovarian cancer. Medicinal therapy is enlisted, which often includes: anti-inflammatory/pain medication, additional pain medication and sometimes diuretics (to reduce fluid retention in the abdomen).

Oviduct cysts and *ovotestis cysts:* In the case where cysts are interfering with normal egg production or general health, cysts can be surgically drained and/or removed. A regime of antibiotics, anti-inflammatory/pain medication and additional pain medication is administered for 14 days. Remember to keep your duck separate from any drakes for *at least* 4-6 weeks. Hormonal therapies to temporarily or permanently stop egg production are often enlisted.

In extreme cases where the left and functioning oviduct is excessively damaged by cysts, a salpingohysterectomy may need to be explored.

Benign Reproductive Tumors

Non-cancerous tumors of the reproductive system can be as minor as small nodules or as major large tissue invasions into the abdominal cavity, sometimes rupturing the oviduct.

- **Symptoms**

When large or numerous, some symptoms of reproductive tumors may include: reduced egg production, abnormally small or large eggs, distended abdomen (temporary or permanent), rapid weight gain (fluid retention), abdominal heaving, excessive open-bill panting, loss of appetite and weight loss (which can be masked by fluid retention).

When involving the ovary, some additional symptoms may include: the change of plumage, vocalizations and/or behavior from female to male.

When involving the uterus section of the oviduct, symptoms may also include: unusually thick-shelled eggs, soft-shelled eggs, misshapen eggs or unusually small or large eggs. Depending upon the permeation of the tumor(s) into your duck's abdominal cavity, other internal organs may be impacted, which can add to the range and severity of symptoms.

- **Treatment**

Surgical removal of tumors will need to be explored in a case-by-case scenario. When larger and involving the ovary or when wrapped extensively around other body organs, surgery may not be possible. On the other hand, smaller, non-invasive tumors can often be safely removed.

As with other surgeries, your duck will require a minimum 14 day cycle of antibiotics, anti-inflammatory/pain medication and additional pain medication. Hormonal therapies to temporarily or permanently stop egg production are often enlisted. Remember to keep your duck separate from any drakes for *at least* 4-6 weeks.

In extreme cases where the left and functioning oviduct is excessively damaged by a tumor, a salpingohysterectomy may need to be explored.

Ovarian Cancer

Although female ducks have only one functioning ovary, it does a lot of work, especially those belonging to Pekin ducks who have been bred to lay more eggs a year than any other breed. Cancer is a common end result to all this excessive egg-laying.

- **Symptoms**

Some symptoms of ovarian cancer may include: distended abdomen (temporary or permanent), rapid weight gain (fluid retention), soft-shelled eggs, abnormally small or large eggs, reduced egg production, the change of plumage, vocalizations and/or behavior from female to male, fatigue, abdominal heaving, excessive open-bill panting, loss of appetite and weight loss (which can be masked by fluid retention).

Ovarian cancer can eventually spread to other parts of the body (intestines, liver, spleen and lungs), which can result in seemingly unrelated symptoms.

- **Treatment**

Many types of cancer can result in large pockets of fluid around the internal organs, which are often mistaken as excess fat from the outside. Whenever your duck experiences unusual and rapid weight gain (or weight loss), it's imperative that you take them to the vet.

Ovarian cancer can be very difficult to diagnose. In most cases your vet will suspect some form of cancer, but won't be able to properly pinpoint the exact type without an ultrasound. Since there are no treatment options available for waterfowl, vets will often dissuade any unnecessary testing and simply recommend pain management instead. This regime often includes: anti-inflammatory/pain medication, additional pain medication and sometimes diuretics (to reduce fluid retention).

Oviduct Cancer

Excessive egg-laying results in higher-than-normal instances of oviduct wear and tear (including swelling, injury and subsequent repairs). These factors can contribute to the occurrence of reproductive cancers, which means heavy egg-layers (such as Pekin ducks) are often more prone than other breeds.

- **Symptoms**

Some symptoms of oviduct cancer may include: distended abdomen (temporary or permanent), rapid weight gain (fluid retention), soft-shelled eggs, abnormally small eggs, reduced egg production, fatigue, abdominal heaving, excessive open-bill panting, loss of appetite and weight loss (which can be masked by fluid retention).

- **Treatment**

Like ovarian cancer (see: *"Ovarian Cancer"*), oviduct cancer can be very difficult to diagnose without an ultrasound. Vets often recommend a pain management treatment regime that includes: anti-inflammatory/pain medication, additional pain medication and sometimes diuretics (to reduce fluid retention). Remember to keep your duck separate from any drakes to prevent potentially painful mating incidents.

Irritated Vent

If your duck has an irritated vent it could be the mark of a hard-day's work laying a difficult egg, or symptomatic of a mild and localized infection.

- **Symptoms**

Some symptoms of an irritated vent may include: external swelling, redness, bleeding or discharge.

- **Treatment**

In the case of mild irritation your vet will probably prescribe Animax® cream (Nystatin-Neomycin Sulfate-Thiostrepton-Triamcinolone Acetonide). This is an anti-inflammatory, antifungal, antibacterial and antipruritic (anti-itch) salve that you'll apply directly to the outer vent every 12 hours for 7-14 days, or until your duck has fully recovered. It will help prevent the area from becoming infected as well as helping to alleviate any discomfort. In the case of an infection, your vet will also prescribe antibiotics for 7-10 days. Depending on severity, you may need to restrict your duck's access to swimming water or ensure that they're swimming in clean tap water as opposed to pond water.

An irritated vent that's difficult to remedy, is long-lasting or re-occurring, should be examined more closely by a vet to ensure your duck's oviduct isn't injured or infected. Remember to keep your duck separate from any drakes for *at least* 2-4 weeks while she recovers completely.

Gender Change

While you may hear an occasional story about a female duck transforming into a drake, or a drake unexpectedly laying an egg, in reality, it just doesn't happen. All of these gender-bending stories can be traced back to a simple case of mistaken identity—usually where someone thought they had a boy, but then an egg suddenly appeared.

On the other hand, in instances where female ducks have been reported to turn into drakes, it usually comes down to the sudden appearance of a simple, little curly tail feather. While commonly associated with drakes, females can occasionally sprout one of these precious jewels, inspiring their Momma Ducks to believe their girl duck has suddenly transformed into a boy duck. Adding to all the confusion, she'll often take on mock-drake behavior, courting and attempting to mate other females and starting arguments with any nearby males.

- **Biological changes**

In most cases, these superficial female-to-male "transformations" are a biological response sparked by nature when there's a shortage of males around. In order to fully appreciate what's really going on, you first need to understand a little bit more about a female duck's anatomy.

Back when your female duck was still growing inside of her egg, two sex organs (one male and one female) began forming inside her. When her gender-assigning, female genes kicked in, one of these emerged into a fully-functioning ovary (usually the left one), while the other (usually the right) halted in its development. This second one is referred to as an ovotestis or a vestigial, non-functioning ovary. Only rarely does a female duck actually develop two functioning ovaries.

If you have a flock of all female ducks (or a flock with older or injured males who can no longer mate or properly protect their females), it's not unheard of for nature to step in and jumpstart the benign ovotestis in one (or more) of them. This switch from utilizing her dominant ovary to using her awakening ovotestis, leads to a drop in estrogen production.

Interestingly, many male characteristics aren't determined by male hormones at all, but by the absence of female hormones. Once a female duck no longer produces estrogen, her body naturally reverts to a default setting of male plumage. In addition, the no-longer dormant ovotestis begins producing steroids. The sudden presence of these male hormones is responsible for the drake-like traits and behaviors you're now witnessing in your female.

If a drake is later added to the flock, this female will *sometimes* revert back to utilizing her dominant ovary and eventually molt her curly tail feather, falling back into her natural place within the flock again. This reaction to a lack of males is not limited to ducks. Many species of birds experience similar transformations in nature. Female chickens have actually been known to go through vocal changes and begin crowing when there are no roosters around. Rarely, some birds will even change color in addition to behavior to match those of the opposite gender.

- **Henopause**

Having no males around isn't the only time females will sprout a curly tail feather. It isn't uncommon for older females who are no longer laying eggs to sprout a curly tail feather as their functioning ovary retires. I like to refer to this as *henopause.*

Female ducks being treated with hormone injections or implants to disrupt their laying cycles often grow these curly tail feathers.

Miri sprouts a drake-like curly tail, but she's still most definitely a girl!

- **Tumors**

If you have a younger female and males are present in your flock and she's *still* sprouting a curly tail feather, a timely visit to the vet is in order to determine why her vestigial ovary has suddenly kicked into gear. It can sometimes be a sign of some kind of tumor or growth interfering or damaging her main ovary.

- **Male role reversal**

It's much more common for females to take on male attributes, then for males to take on female qualities. When males switch to more female characteristics, it's often caused by testicular tumors, which means a visit to the vet is definitely in immediate order.

Medical #8
Reproductive System (Male)

When it comes to male ducks, reproductive issues are far less common. Producing eggs is hard work and drakes are spared from this laborious task and all of its associated physical tolls. When less things can go wrong, there's far less to worry about; even so, some attention to detail is required.

Male Reproductive System

The basic reproductive anatomy of a drake includes their testicles, deferent ducts (vas deferens), seminal vesicles and penis and it all looks something like this:

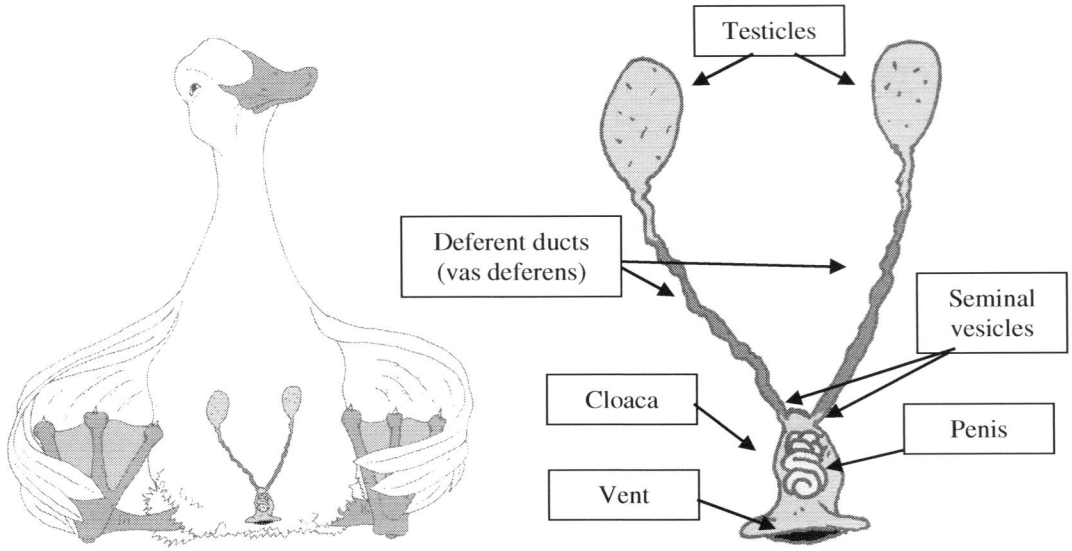

A diagram of your male duck's reproductive system

Prolapsed Penis/Phallus

While many novice Momma Ducks often mistake the corkscrew-shaped organ precariously dangling from their drake's vent as his entrails, it's actually his penis. It's perfectly normal to see your drake's boy parts tumble out onto the ground and drag behind him (especially after mating). Provided he pulls it back inside his body again soon afterwards, you have nothing to worry about.

The top three causes of a prolapsed phallus (phallus/penis paralysis) are:

1. Bacterial infection.
2. A lack of swimming water, or unsanitary swimming water (resulting in infection).
3. Over-stimulation/exertion (often occurring in the spring or when new females are introduced).

However, other factors may include: genetic tendency, obesity, testicular tumors, lower gastrointestinal issues (diarrhea, ventricular blockage, straining), illness and old age.

*Photo of a Pekin duck's penis
(for the sake of privacy, I won't say whose!)*

- **Symptoms**

Some symptoms of a prolapsed phallus may include: inability to quickly retract the phallus, continual phallus protrusion (just the tip or a few inches), vent redness, swelling, bleeding, dark or discolored necrotic tissue—any of which may affect energy levels, appetite and weight.

- **Treatment**

A prolapsed penis is very rarely fatal provided it's properly attended to. Bacterial infections are the usual culprits and a round of antibiotics and anti-inflammatory/pain medication for 7-14 days will often do the trick provided your drake has ample access to swimming water (especially clean tap water) and is given a break from mating by separating him from any females.

A topical antibiotic ointment like Bacitraycin Plus® can also be applied to the protruding penis and external vent 1-2 times daily to keep the area moist and help stave off infection. If an additional antibiotic is *not* needed, Vaseline® petroleum jelly can be substituted to aid in moisture retention.

The more time your boy spends floating in clean tap water, the more likely he is to recover quickly, so keep his kiddy pool as fresh as you can and encourage him to swim as often as possible. To help prevent infection you'll also want to keep his pen and house as tidy as possible during his recovery, so remember to actively remove any piling fecal matter and lay down fresh bedding frequently (which you should be doing anyway)—especially in his favorite resting spots, where he'll be spending a lot of time.

Lots of time on clean water is just what the doctor ordered

If attended to immediately, a prolapsed penis will usually retreat back into your drake's body without a few days and without any further hang-ups, but there are instances when it won't. The longer your drake's penis remains outside of his body, the less likely it is to make a permanent retreat and the more prone it is to infection. If your drake's penis doesn't respond to continued medication or worsens (especially in hotter months where flies and infection pose a greater threat), or if tissue begins to swell, bleed or become necrotic, you need to get him back to the vet for an immediate partial penectomy.

- **Penectomy**

During a penectomy, your vet will surgically remove the exposed tip of the penis. In older drakes, or in cases where the prolapse is likely to re-occur again (exposing the next section of penis to the great outdoors), vets will often shorten the phallus enough to prevent it from ever falling outside of their cloaca in the future—leaving them with about an inch of tissue. Only experienced waterfowl vets who know exactly how to perform this delicate operation properly (and have done so successfully before) should be allowed surgical access to your drake's private parts.

Inexperienced vets often don't know to gently pull out and expose the entire length of penis all the way down to its base before beginning. This is necessary because a drake's penis fills with lymph fluid in order to enlarge before mating (which in a prolapsed situation doesn't retract again properly). If your vet simply cuts off the exposed tip, following surgery, the lymph fluid will withdraw and your drake can be left with excess loose skin dangling from the end of his penis, which results in necrotic tissue and infectious complications.

Post-surgical medications include antibiotics, anti-inflammatory/pain medication and additional pain medication. Recovery takes 7-14 days, but drakes should be kept separate from females for at least 4 weeks to prevent any mating activity.

If surgery is done correctly, post-surgical complications are drastically reduced, but they still may include:

1. Appetite loss.
2. Internal irritation and swelling.
3. Inability to urinate or pass fecal matter.

If your duck isn't passing waste, excess inflammation could lead to intestinal blockage. In this case, topical Flurbiprofen or corticosteroids may be prescribed to further reduce inflammation and pain. Follow-up barium x-rays may also be required to monitor intestinal function. Retained feces may need to be evacuated followed by a single cloacal flush using a cortisone enema. Dietary changes may also be suggested by your vet until your drake is back on track again.

In the case of a post-operative infection, a cloacal swab culture should be performed to help identify the bacterial culprit. This will help ensure that the proper treatment regime is prescribed.

Testicular Cancer

Unlike ovarian cancer in female ducks, testicular cancer in drakes is actually pretty rare. When it does occur, there's usually a genetic tendency for it.

- **Symptoms**

Some symptoms of testicular cancer may include: inability to quickly retract the phallus, phallus prolapse (varying degrees), distended abdomen (temporary or permanent), rapid weight gain (fluid retention), fatigue, abdominal heaving, excessive open-bill panting, weight loss (which can be masked by fluid retention) and the change of plumage, vocalizations or behavior from male to female.

As the tumor continues to grow it can press on other organs and invade other areas resulting in seemingly unrelated symptoms (often pressing on the kidney and causing increased frequency in urination).

- **Treatment**

There is no treatment for testicular cancer in ducks. Leuprolide injections are sometimes used as a means to decrease tumor size and prolong life, but it's not a cure. Anti-inflammatory/pain medication and additional pain medication should be enlisted to ensure comfort, so your drake can enjoy the last chapter of his life with you.

Testicular Cysts & Benign Tumors

Drakes usually don't have issues with tumors or cysts unless they're genetically inclined. Rarely do cysts or tumors become symptomatic or require surgery.

- **Symptoms**

Some symptoms of cloacal cysts or tumors may include: inability to quickly retract the phallus, phallus prolapse (varying degrees), vent redness, swelling, bleeding, any of which may affect energy levels, appetite and weight.

Some symptoms of testicular cysts or tumors may include: distended abdomen (temporary or permanent), rapid weight gain (fluid retention), fatigue, abdominal heaving, excessive open-bill panting, loss of appetite, weight loss (which can be masked by fluid retention) and the change of plumage, vocalizations or behavior from male to female.

- **Treatment**

Cysts can be surgically drained and/or removed and tumors excised. Depending on the level of invasiveness, cyst/tumor removal may or may not involve the affected testicle. In an attempt to avoid major surgery in older drakes, your vet may suggest leuprolide injections as a means to decrease tumor size.

A regime of antibiotics, anti-inflammatory/pain medication and additional pain medication is administered for 14 days. Recovery tends to be fast; occurring in as little as 5-7 days; even so, your drake should be kept separate from any females for at least 4 weeks.

Y. Jeffrey's Privates...

When Young Jeffrey was eleven years old he began to have chronic trouble reeling in his "fishing line." Under vet guidance, I started him on a round of antibiotics (Baytril®) along with anti-inflammatory/pain medication (Rimadyl®) while using Vaseline® to prevent any drying or chaffing. In addition to this medical regime, our vet sent a fecal sample off to the lab for culturing.

Under anesthesia our vet carefully tucked Young Jeffrey's penis back inside his body and placed a few stitches outside his vent to help keep everything inside. Torbutrol was added to his list of medications to manage any pain or discomfort he might be feeling. Unfortunately, Young Jeffrey managed to pull out his stitches by the following afternoon, demonstrating that this "stitch-in-place" tactic simply doesn't work well with ducks.

A few days later Young Jeffrey's fecal culture came back negative for bacteria, but it did indicate elevated yeast levels. Vinegar is a natural way to help reduce your duck's yeast count, so under vet advice, I added regular white vinegar to his drinking water (16 ml Vinegar/1 liter water).

Young Jeffrey's situation tended to flux back and forth--even after his health issues had been addressed and normalized. Some days his phallus would be safely tucked inside, other days it wasn't. Proximity to females didn't seem to influence his condition either way, so there was no point in separating him from them.

As summer approached I knew the risk of a serious infection would only increase, so after discussing his situation thoroughly with our vet, I decided a penectomy would be in Young Jeffrey's best interests.

The surgical procedure was a complete success, removing all but a short bit of his penis to prevent it from tumbling outside anymore. He was pretty quiet for the first three days of his recovery, his pain managed with Torbutrol® and Rimadyl®, but then by day four, he was more like himself again. Two weeks after that, he left my sunroom and went back outside to his own enclosure again where he immediately swam out on his pond and began mating all of his ladies. Honestly, you'd never know he had this surgery judging by his behavior!

Testosterone Overload

While high levels of testosterone in drakes is a normal part of spring fever, an overload of this hormone can lead to some serious health issues.

- **Symptoms**

Some symptoms of testosterone overload may include: over-aggressive mating activity, increased urination, loss of appetite and excessive thirst.

Too much testosterone can also bring about the enlargement of your drake's internal testicles, resulting in phallus prolapse, which can then lead to a counter-intuitive *disinterest* in normal mating behaviors.

- **Treatment**

Separate: To reduce your drake's testosterone levels, the first thing you'll want to do is separate him from the company of other ducks. This means giving your boy a nice, quiet retreat where he can't see or hear any of his feathered friends. This time away from competing males and alluring females will often help control and reduce his hormone levels. If you only have two ducks, you can certainly give your healthy and well-behaved duck a mirror to keep them company, but avoid giving your testosterone-loaded drake a mirror, or it'll just get him worked up again.

Limit handling: As heartbreaking as this may be, you'll need to avoid handling and petting your duck as much as possible during this special time out, especially if he's human-imprinted; if you don't, you'll risk another hormonal influx. You can of course still talk to him and enlist low-energy level enrichment activities to prevent boredom and loneliness.

Restrict daylight: Since increased daylight hours are nature's way of influencing your drake's testosterone levels in the first place, you may want to bring your boy into a barn or house where you can control the lighting. Simply shave 2-3 hours off of his daily exposure to sunlight utilizing light switches and window shades. Keep the blinds closed for an extra hour in the morning and then shut off the lights 1-2 hours before sundown at the end of the day. Continue this way for 3-7 days, or until his symptoms wane off and he becomes more recognizable to you again. *Never* seclude your drake in complete darkness in an attempt to speed up the process. Not only is this inhumane, but you'll also risk his testosterone surging out of control again once you move him back outside—the variance being entirely too great.

Once your boy is symptom-free you can go ahead and bring him back out to his pen again, keeping him separate, but in view of other ducks. After an additional 7-14 days you can attempt to reintroduce him to his flock mates once more. While he may be overzealous at first, he should simmer down and level out. If not, you may need to separate him again, keeping him in sight of others until his hormones subside.

Medical tests: In stubborn or extreme cases, x-rays and/or ultrasounds may need to be performed to rule out testicular tumors and cysts as the pressing source of his problem.

Hormonal treatment: Leuprolide injections can be explored to reduce testosterone production, but this is normally reserved for drakes who have lingering physical symptoms (such as phallus prolapse).

Medical #9
Nervous System (Eyes & Ears)
===

Your duck's nervous system includes their brain, spinal cord and nerves. These components help them to see, hear, feel, taste and smell their world—although it's not fully understood how well they can actually smell. I once heard they can smell about half as well as a turkey vulture. Can they pick up the scent of earthworms hidden under leaves? *Who knows!*

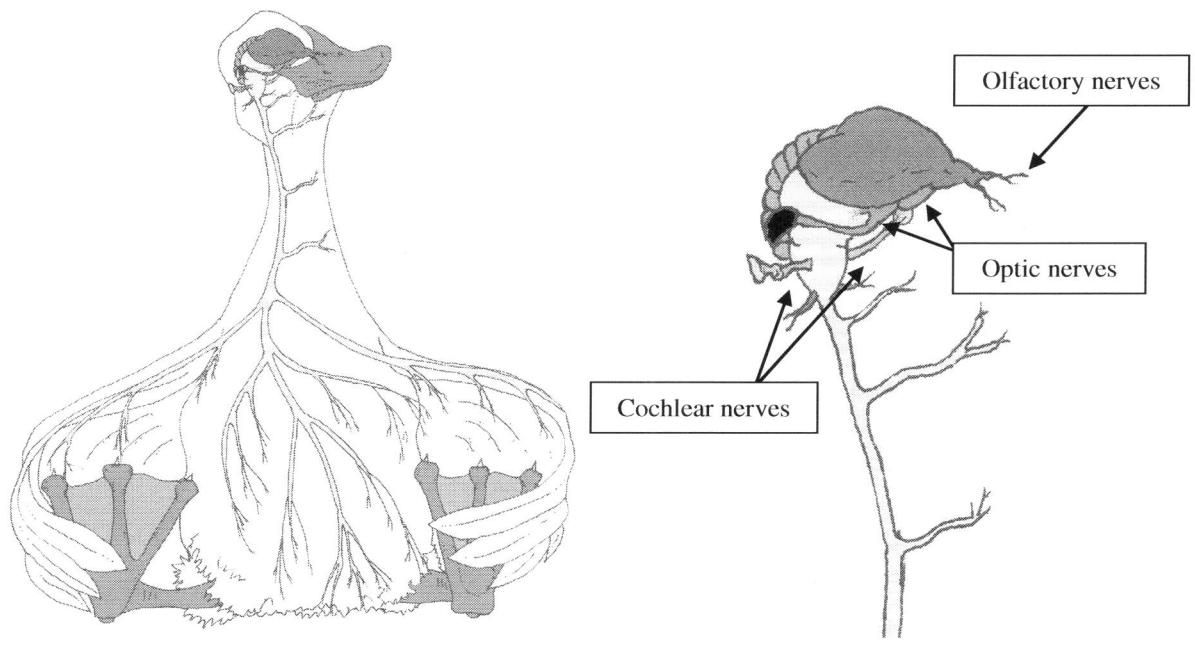

A rudimentary diagram of your duck's nervous system

Ears

Your duck may not have fancy external ears the way we do, but they can hear just as well as you can—maybe even better. I know my gang can hear a crinkly bag of lettuce in my hands the moment I step outside the house.

Hearing Impairment

Most birds have a reflex whereupon a flap of skin obstructs their external ears the second they open their bills until a few seconds after they close it again. This helps protect their inner ears from their own booming voices (which those of you with female ducks will quickly appreciate). Some species of birds can go completely deaf during this time. It's unknown how much hearing ducks lose while quacking and if males and females experience this differently. While reflexive hearing loss in response to quacking may be normal, hearing impairment resulting from trauma, disease or genetics is not. Fortunately, it's also pretty uncommon in waterfowl.

- **Symptoms**

Some symptoms of hearing loss may include: a duck who fails to notice you until they actually see you—often startling suddenly when they make visual contact.

- **Treatment**

While there are no ducky hearing aids, birds have the uncanny ability to replace hair cells on the cochleas of their inner ears, which means hearing damage may not always be permanent. Until then, let your duck see you before approaching.

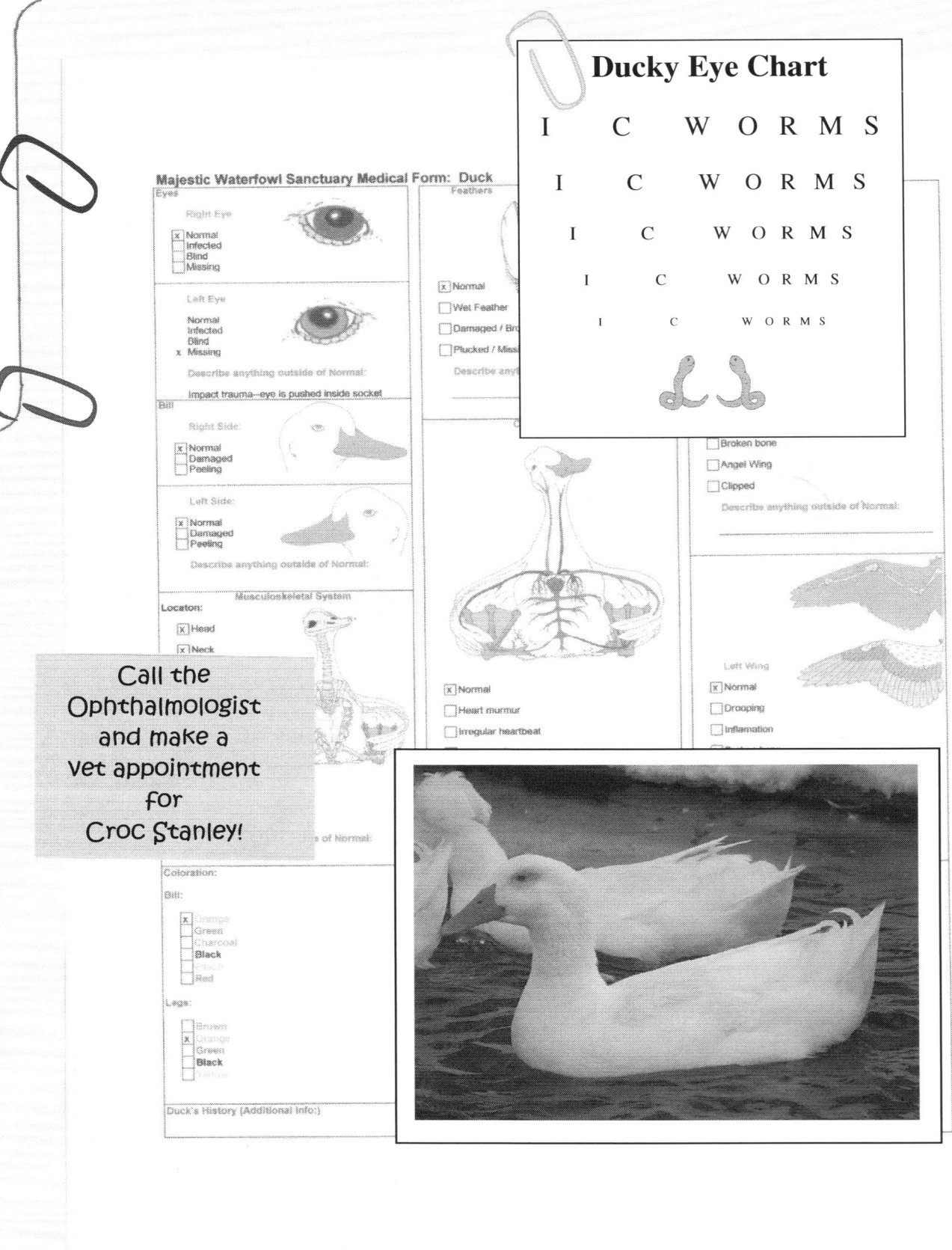

Croc's Missing Eye...

Crocodile Stanley came to our sanctuary with what appeared to be a missing eye. A trip to the vet confirmed that his eye was there, just poked inside the socket. Impact trauma is not uncommon when male ducks are allowed to battle it out or when males get too rough with females.

In Croc's case, surgery wasn't required because he didn't exhibit any pain reflexes during his vet examination, but some years later we had a female duck named Murdoch who flinched whenever the vet touched the feathery area around her effected eye. Like Croc's eye, hers was also poked inside the cavity. In her case, however, surgery to remove eye remnants, seal off exposed nerve endings and stitch the eyelid closed was required to alleviate her discomfort.

Although Crocodile Stanley's afflicted eye never gave him any trouble, it was important to watch for any signs of infection, especially in the hotter months of summer.

The only consideration I really had to keep in mind when caring for Croc on a daily basis was to stay within his field of vision. He wasn't a fan of surprises, so it was important to make some noise whenever his good eye wasn't on me; that way, he would know I was approaching.

Case # 82: Missing Eye

The eyes of birds may be among the most highly developed and efficient of all animals during daylight hours. Indeed, your duck's eyes are pretty amazing for a number of reasons:

1. *Size:* Birds have large eyes in relation to their body size. Not only do bigger eyes contain more light receptors, but they're also able to support a larger retinal image.

2. *Form:* Ducks can contract *two* muscles in their eyes that control lens *and* corneal curvature. This function allows them to see clearly while submerged underwater.

3. *Color perception:* While you have red, blue and green photoreceptors (cones) in your eyes that enable you to see in color, your duck has more of them than you do. This allows them to see colors more richly and fully, which in turn makes it possible for them to better discriminate between colors. Where you may see a visiting robin as having only one solid shade of orange on his belly, your duck can differentiate a variety of orange hues making each bird unique and distinguishable. As if this wasn't awesome enough, your duck also has a fourth type of cone, which enables them to see ultraviolet light! Now you see why you should include colored objects in and around their pen to stimulate visual interest. Enrichment activities in particular become much more interesting when you pay attention to a vast array of color options.

4. *Panoramic view:* While most ducks can barely see the tip of their own bill, their panoramic vision does allow them to see to the sides, above and behind them—possibly as two separate images *(imagine that!)*.

5. *Function:* Your duck uses their left and right eyes differently. Their left eye is normally used for distant activities like watching for predators (and keeping an eye on their Momma Duck!) while their right eyes is usually reserved for close-up pursuits like foraging. This differentiation occurs while they're still in their egg and is a result of their body position in relation to lighting. Because of the way they're curled up inside, their right eye is normally exposed to more light than their left.

Eyelids

Your duck has three eyelids, the upper and lowers as well as a third nictitating inner membrane that originates in the front corners of both eyes. This transparent film acts like protective goggles, safeguarding their corneas while they're swimming or poking their heads underwater. If you take a close look at your duck while they're napping you'll see that their lower eye lid does most of the work, coming up to cover the bulk of their eye's surface area (as opposed to your own where the upper lid covers down to protect your eye).

Eye Crust

Ducks with certain types of disabilities (including those with neurological problems, balance issues and limb disabilities) often can't coordinate their movements well enough to groom properly. While healthy ducks can easily manipulate their webbed feet and use their toenails to assist in delicately preening the tiny feathers around their eyes, ducks with mental and physical challenges may not be so adept. As a result one or both of their eyes can get a little messy.

- **Symptoms**

Some symptoms of eye crust may include: mild caking of normal discharge and dirt around the eye(s).

- **Treatment**

Actively keeping an impaired duck's eyes nice and clean can really help prevent unwanted infections. Some ducks may need one or both of their eyes cleaned daily, others weekly and still others only randomly here and there—often depending on the season and availability of clean swimming water.

To tidy-up the feathers around your duck's eyes dip a clean washcloth into a bowl of lukewarm water until it's soaking wet. Gently hold your duck in place (or kneel down over them to keep them still) and then use a small portion of the towel to gently wipe the feathers around their eyes, being careful not to actually touch their eyeballs or any connective tissue. Your strokes should be slow and tender. Never scrub their feathers and always move the washcloth in the same direction as their feather growth.

If your duck's feathers are caked down or hard, hold the water-soaked washcloth gently in place over their eye and allow the warm water to permeate through and soften the crusty build-up. As their feathers begin to feel pliable, slowly begin wiping their feathers clean of debris. Manipulate the washcloth frequently, so that you're always holding a clean section of fabric against your duck's feathers and re-dip it into the warm water often to keep it laden with water.

In more acute cases, you may not be able to get their eye completely clean in one sitting and may have to come back to it later in the day or over the course of a few days. Some ducks just need a head start before being able to complete the task on their own. If you're having trouble getting or keeping their eyes clean, if build-up is quickly returning, this may be an indication of an infection; in which case, you should take them to the vet for an examination.

Eye Infection

Eye infections aren't all that uncommon among ducks and they can occur in one or both eyes. To keep the infection from spreading any further and to prevent the possibility of permanent damage or visual impairment, it's a really good idea to get them to a vet right away.

- **Symptoms**

Some symptoms of an eye infection may include: keeping their eyelid(s) closed, loss of feathers around the eye(s), inflammation, irritation, discoloration, discharge and caking in or around the eye.

- **Treatment**

For superficial cases, vets will commonly prescribe Vetropolycin® (Neomycin Polymyxin B Sulfates Bacitracin Zinc) antibiotic eye ointment to be applied directly onto the infected eye or eyes 2-3 times a day for 7-14 days, or until their eyes have completely cleared. In acute or chronic cases, Vetropolycin HC® (with hydrocortisone 1%) may be substituted.

When there's a lot of caking involved, many vets will recommend flushing your duck's eye clear of debris with sterile saline solution before applying the eye ointment. Sterile saline ampoules (also referred to as sterile saline *pods* or *vials*) are a good item to have in your duck's emergency medical kit for these kind of situations. You simply break one open, treat one or both eyes and then discard. I prefer these tiny disposable vials over bottles of saline because you eliminate the risk of contaminating bacteria gaining entrance into the container.

In more extreme cases of infection, swab culturing (bacterial & fungal), antibiotics and/or anti-inflammatory/pain medication may also be required.

To help reduce the recovery period for eye infections, provide your duck with plenty of access to freshly drawn, clean tap water.

Eye Trauma

Mild eye trauma is not all that uncommon among ducks. While actively foraging a stalk of straw, blade of grass, bit of dirt, or other random object can unexpectedly impact your duck's eye.

More often, eyes get poked by other ducks. Mild trauma is usually the result of an occasional, misdirected and accidental jab of a bill. On the other hand, severe trauma (which is far more prevalent during the mating season) often occurs when drakes are left to fight amongst themselves, or when females are being over-mated by males.

- **Symptoms**

Some symptoms of eye *mild* eye trauma may include: tiny bubbles or foam forming in the corner of your duck's eye, partially/fully closed eyelid, mild swelling, slight damage to the tissue surrounding the eye. Mild eye trauma usually only occurs in *one* eye.

Some symptoms of *severe* eye trauma may include: eye foam, partially/fully closed eyelid, swelling, tissue damage, bleeding and the actual loss of an eye (poked into its socket). Severe eye trauma usually only occurs in one eye, but it can occur in both eyes—especially when overzealous drakes are left uninterrupted. When both eyes are damaged the injuries sustained are usually *not* symmetrical.

- **Treatment**

The first step of treatment is to determine the cause of your duck's affliction. Look around their barn and pen and make sure there's nothing dangerous sticking out at your duck's eye level. If fighting or over-mating is the culprit, separations are definitely in immediate order.

Your vet will want to do a close-up exam of your duck's eye to make sure there aren't any corneal scratches that might impact their vision or become infected. They'll do this by placing fluorescein (orange dye) into their eye, then turning out the lights and taking a closer look with a blue light; any damage will appear green.

Vets commonly treat any lens damage with a prescription of Remend® corneal repair gel. These thick eye drops are administered directly onto your duck's afflicted eye or eyes 2-3 times a day for 7-14 days, or until they've completely healed. In some instances your vet may recommend flushing your duck's eye clear of debris with sterile saline solution prior to application. Your vet will likely want to see them again for a follow-up visit in a week to check their progress and to make sure infection doesn't set in, in which case antibiotics will be required.

As with any injuries, keep your duck in a clean environment during their recovery period, being especially diligent about keeping any water sources they're immersing their eyes and face into as clean as possible to help prevent the risk of infection.

In more severe cases anti-inflammatory/pain medication may also be required. Rather than treating any pain and swelling orally with a pill, most vets will have you administer this medication directly to your duck's eye for maximum effect. A prescription of Flurbiprofen .03% Ophthalmic Solution (NSAID) can be picked up at your local human pharmacy, commonly packaged in a 2.5 ml bottle. Your duck is given one drop per eye, twice daily for 7 days. While rare, if your duck exhibits a pain reaction to these drops (shaking their head or excessive blinking for more than a few seconds or any other unusual rubbing behavior) discontinue use immediately and flush their eyes with sterile saline (pain should subside within 1-2 minutes). Ideally Flurbiprofen should only be used for short periods of time and then discontinued to minimize the risk of negative side effects (which may include impaired vision).

Irritated Tear Duct

Eyelids that no longer line up properly together or that fail to fully cover your duck's cornea (commonly caused by a poking injury) can lead to dryness of the eye or the overstimulation of tear production, either of which can result in tear duct irritation or infection.

- **Symptoms**

Some symptoms of an irritated tear duct may include: "pocketed" swelling of the tear duct, eye dryness, watery eyes and discharge (when infected).

- **Treatment**

If you see a swollen pockets beneath your duck's eye bring them to the vet for an immediate exam to avoid the risk of infection and permanent visual impairment. They'll flip down their lower eyelid and locate the swollen tear gland.

Irritated tear ducts are often treated with irrigating eye drops or sterile saline administered 2-3 times daily. Keeping their swimming and drinking water clean will help prevent the risk of infection. Your vet may also prescribe a non-antibiotic eye lubricant like Puralube® Vet Ointment twice daily for 7-14 days.

Infected tear ducts are treated the same as eye infections (see: *"Eye Infection"*).

Sinusitis

Bubbles that appear in the corners of your duck's eyes on a regular basis that are *not* caused by an impact injury can be an indication of a sinus infection.

- **Symptoms**

Some symptoms of sinusitis may include: swollen cheeks, partially closed eyes, white nare discharge, imbalance, disorientation, appetite loss, weakness, and tiny, long-lasting bubbles originating in the corners of your ducks eyes (usually both) that do *not* respond to eye trauma treatment (see: *"Eye Trauma"*). These bubbles are *not* accompanied by any signs of physical trauma. In other words, their eyes look open and healthy in all other regard.

- **Treatment**

Your vet will likely prescribe Falcon® Tobramycin Ophthalmic Solution 0.3% (which usually comes in a 5 ml bottle). Most vets will advise you to administer two drops per eye every twelve hours for 7-14 days. Baytril is often commonly prescribed along with an antihistamine like Chlorpheniramine (dissolve a 4mg tablet in 8 oz. of drinking water changed daily).

Eye Dryness

Eye dryness often occurs in both eyes simultaneously unless there is an affliction directly affecting one eye (blocked tear duct, cyst, etc.).

- **Symptoms**

Some symptoms of dry eyes may include: feather loss around the eyes, excessive scratching/rubbing around the eyes, abnormal blinking, discharge and a partially or fully closed eyelid.

- **Treatment**

Most vets will begin the exam by checking your duck's eyes for any signs of infection or injury. Once both have both been successfully ruled out they'll likely proceed with a tear production test (or Schirmer's test). To do this, they tuck the end of a tiny strip of filter paper painlessly into your duck's eyelid (I say painless, but your duck still won't appreciate it). If your duck is particularly squiggly, they may give them a topical anesthetic first. The paper is then removed and the level of tear absorption is measured.

If your duck's tear production is low, your vet will prescribe a non-antibiotic eye lubricant like Puralube® twice daily for 14 days to see if the feathers around your duck's eyes begin to re-grow. Eye lubricant may need to be continued seasonally or indefinitely, depending on whether the cause is environmental or biological.

Giving your duck plenty of access to fresh, clean tap water can also help improve their dry eyes. A good way to do this is by adding a few water buckets to their pen—after all, what's more fun for a duck than sticking their face into a bucket of water! Like their kiddy pool, these additional water sources should be changed 2-3 times daily for cleanliness and ideal affect.

Cataracts

Even the most attentive Momma Ducks may not notice the slow onset of cataracts for quite a while. Since they tend to develop in one eye 6-8 months before appearing in the other, there often aren't any noticeable behavioral changes for some time. To avoid this oversight (no pun intended), it's important to take a once-a-month look into your duck's eyes.

- **Symptoms**

Some symptoms of cataracts may include: cloudy, grayish-white opaque discoloration in the pupil (that begin small and expand to cover the entire pupil over time), blurry vision, poor night vision and eventual blindness.

There are four basic types of cataracts:

1. Age-related cataracts (which occur in older ducks)
2. Traumatic cataracts (which are caused by impact or injury)
3. Secondary cataracts (which are caused by infection, diabetes, glaucoma, malnutrition, or exposure to toxins)
4. Congenital cataracts (which are inherited)

Beyond this, cataracts are classified by the location of lens affliction:

1. Anterior cataracts (front of the lens)
2. Nuclear cataracts (center of the lens)
3. Posterior cataracts (back of the lens)

There are various levels of each of these three classifications and operability depends on your duck's particular diagnosis. Some types progress rapidly and require timely diagnosis and fast treatment to avoid blindness while others progress more gradually. No matter what the case, when you notice cataracts in your duck's eyes, a trip to an ophthalmologist vet is definitely in order.

Dierdre Dear Heart's cataract eye

- **Treatment**

Age-related cataracts: If your older duck is developing cataracts they're most likely age-related; in which case, surgery is the only means of correcting their vision.

Traumatic cataracts: If you have a young duck who's sustained an eye injury, this could be the cause of their cataracts. This is why it's so important to bring your duck to the vet for an exam whenever they've received an accidental poke. Taking care of your duck's cornea right away can help prevent visual impairment down the road.

Secondary cataracts: If you have a young duck who hasn't suffered any eye trauma your vet will need to perform some tests and ask you a few questions in order to determine their cause, so they can treat them accordingly.

1. **Infection:** Swab culturing of the eye to rule out fungal and bacterial infection.

2. **Diabetes:** Comprehensive avian blood panel to rule out diabetes (and further rule out infection).

3. **Glaucoma:** Tonometer (puff of air) to rule out glaucoma (hardening/thickening of the cornea).

4. **Malnutrition:** Provided your feathered friend is on a healthy, duck-designed, brand-name menu, your vet will be able to rule out malnutrition as a source of the problem. If this is not the case, bring the ingredient label from your duck's feed bag along with you for your appointment. If malnutrition is the issue, your duck's feed will need to be immediately upgraded to a quality name brand and a multi-vitamin supplement may also be in order.

5. **Toxins:** Your vet may ask you questions about any chemicals you may be using around your yard. You'll need to rule these out as a source or your duck's cataracts will continue to worsen and other flock members may run into similar problems.

Congenital cataracts: If you have a young duck who has not suffered any eye trauma and who's clear of infection, diabetes, glaucoma, malnutrition or toxins then you could be looking at an inherited condition.

Unless you're dealing with age-related or congenital cataracts, you can often halt their progression by pinpointing and treating their root cause. Keep in mind this won't reverse any cataracts that have already developed, but it can keep things from getting any worse for your duck.

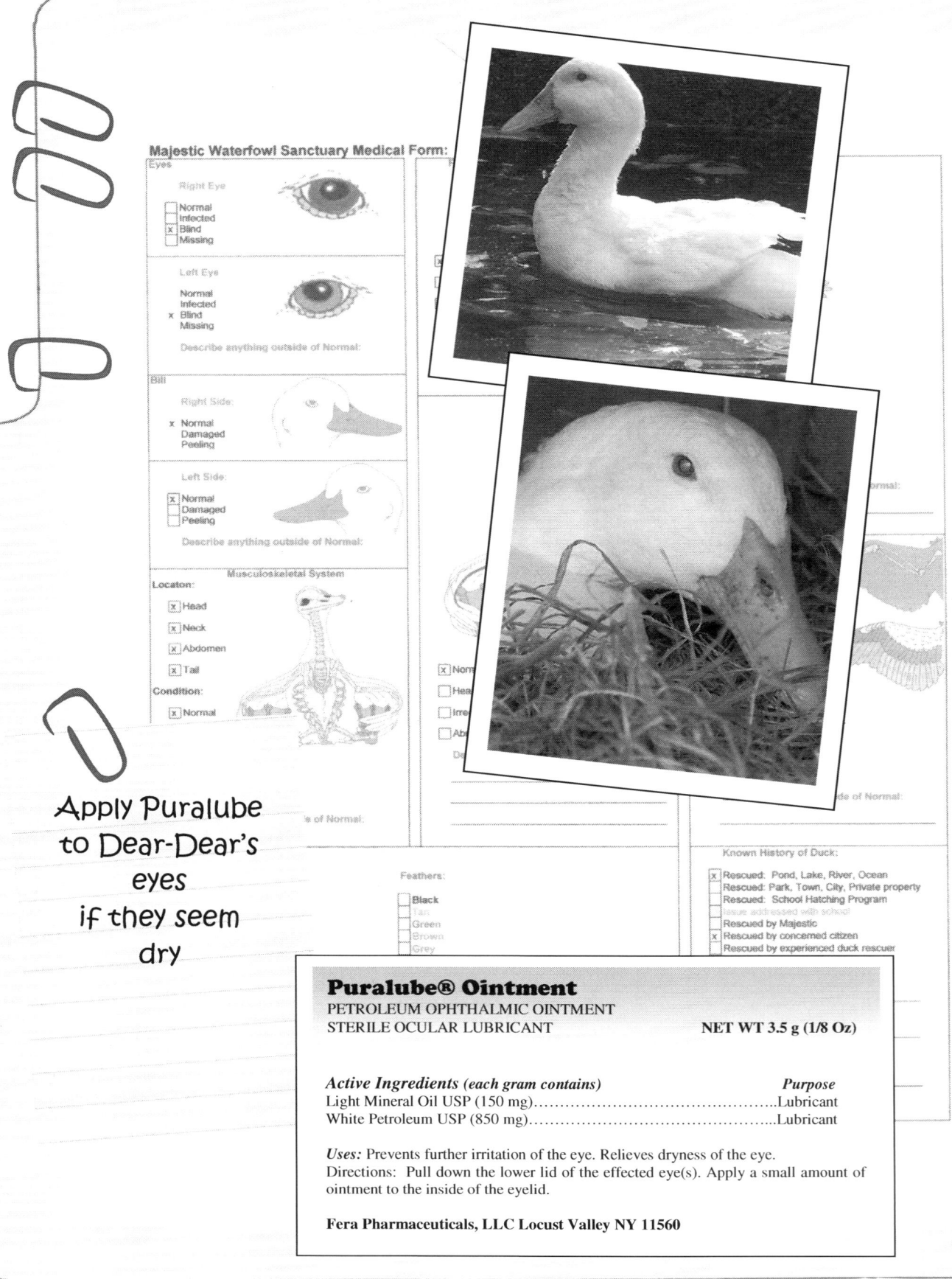

Dierdre's Cataracts...

Case # 133 Cataracts

In her later years Deirdre "Dear Heart" lost her vision to cataracts in both eyes. While I wished we could've surgically restored vision in at least one of her eyes, she had other medical issues that made it extremely difficult, including having a bad reaction to anesthesia. The risk was simply too high.

While I couldn't give Dear-Dear back her eyesight, I aimed to make the end of her days with us as enriching as possible and this included bringing her as many special treats as I could sneak by the other ducks.

While she was extremely proficient at finding her food and water bowls and her way to and from the barn and pond everyday, the one thing she couldn't do well was tell when I was attempting to sneak her a little goody. Inevitably, the other ducks would catch on to what I was up to and come running over to get in on the action. Their excited vocalizations motivated Deirdre to jump into action, suddenly foraging for the treats she couldn't see.

This was how I learned that the flock's quacks provided Deirdre with the vocal cues she needed to understand it was snack time. Not only did the other ducks tell her when goodies were being handed out, but the intensity of their racket let her know exactly what kind of treats were being served. She could easily distinguish between vocalizations for lettuce and those for freshly-gathered nightcrawlers.

Deirdre's flock ended up keeping her belly warm and happy, proving that blind ducks benefit greatly from having good friends around.

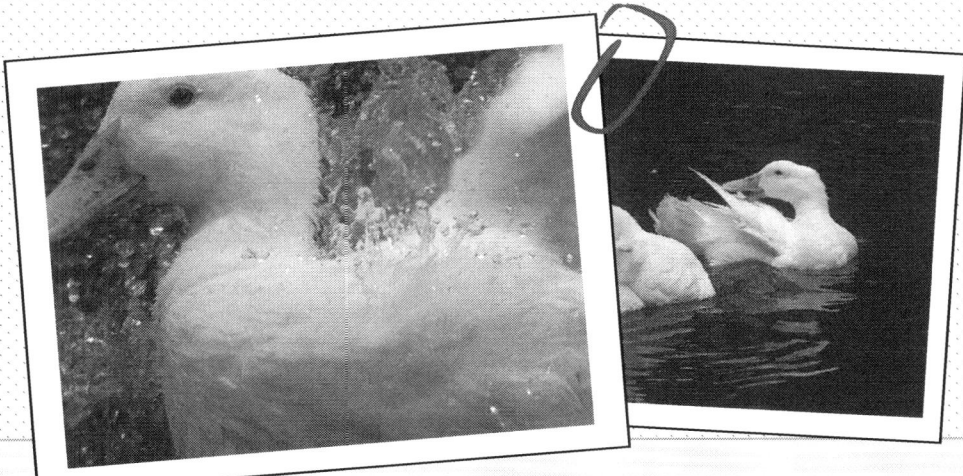

Depending on the type and location of your duck's cataracts, they may or may not be operable. Cataract surgery is tricky business to begin with because duck eyes are so small. Your duck's eye surgeon will need to keep their pupil dilated throughout the surgery in order to operate successfully. This is easier said than done. If your duck has any *optic atrophy* (reversible damage) or *optic neuropathy* (irreversible damage) preventing their pupils from dilating properly, this could actually work to their advantage, making them an even better candidate.

When cataract surgery *is* possible, it should only be performed by an a qualified avian veterinary ophthalmologist who's also experienced with the ins-and-outs of waterfowl anesthesia. More so, it should only be done if it's expected to restore your duck's vision to an effective degree. Because ducks do best when their time under anesthesia is limited, many vets will recommend limiting cataract surgery to just one eye, repairing the worst of the two.

To prepare your duck for surgery, your vet will most likely prescribe eye drops to reduce any inflammation and help prevent the risk of post-surgical infection. Pred-G® is a common choice. A week before surgery you'll begin administering one drop a day into the eye (or eyes) that will be operated on. Side effects may include stinging for 1-2 minutes after application. Depending on your duck's particular situation you may be able to avoid steroid eye drops and use a non-steroidal drop like Diclofenac Sodium Ophthalmic Solution instead. Ask your vet which type of drops are more appropriate for your duck.

The operation itself normally only lasts an hour or two and your duck can usually return home that same day. Surgery in waterfowl doesn't include the implantation of an artificial lens, so ducks tend to have slightly blurry or far-sighted vision in their post-operative eye. Objects within 3-4 feet are often hazy, while objects farther away are much clearer.

Post-surgically, your vet will increase the frequency of the Pred-G® dosage to 3-4 times per day for 6-8weeks. In addition, they'll prescribe pain medication for the first 2-3 days as well as anti-inflammatory/pain medication for the first 7-14 days.

While your duck is recovering you'll need to keep them in sanitary quarters for 6-8 weeks (clean pine shavings are ideal). To further prevent the risk of infection, you'll need to keep your duck from submersing their eyes completely under water, so swimming is not allowed. Your duck should only have a shallow water bowl of water for drinking and splash-preening. The bowl should be cleaned (preferably by dishwasher) at least once a day and their water should be refreshed every 2-3 hours.

Provided nothing goes wrong during this initial grace period, your vet will usually clear your duck for swimming activities upon their one-week checkup. Swimming is only allowed in freshly drawn tap water—*never* in a pond. You can either give them some swim time in a clean kiddy pool, or you can let them play in your bathtub as long as you change it out as often as needed in order to keep it as sanitary as possible.

Blindness

Blindness can be the result of age, injury (commonly inflicted by other ducks), genetics, cataracts or disease. After an initial vet examination to properly assess the situation, you should continue to visually inspect afflicted eyes on a regular basis to watch for any signs of decline that might require further vet attention.

Blind ducks can live very enriched and productive lives; you just need to help them do it.

- **Transitioning**

Ducks can demonstrate signs of fear, aggression or depression during the onset of blindness—or if blindness is sudden, during the period immediately following their loss of vision. As with people, this can be a very difficult time for them, but there are things you can do to help ease their transition.

- **Pen safety**

Implement any necessary pen changes to ensure the safety of your visually-impaired duck. Take a close look around and try to pinpoint any areas that might be dangerous for them. Pens should always be clear of any rocks, sticks, ramps or tripping obstacles that could lead to limb and toe injuries, even more so when you have a duck who's losing their sight. You may need to modify or enlarge entryways into their duck house or lay a mat down over their doorjamb for the day to keep them from stumbling while waddling in and out. In addition, remove anything your duck might fall off of or bump their head into. Make sure all plants, bushes and trees are well-pruned. You don't want your duck accidentally running into branches or foliage, which could lead to serious injuries. Inspect their pen daily, keeping ground surfaces smooth and free of debris.

- **Simplicity**

Make sure the position of houses, pools, water buckets and food bowls are in the most efficient places and easily accessible to your duck.

- **Routine & consistency**

While ducks with normal vision thrive on routine, blind waterfowl absolutely rely on it. Always keep food and water bowls in the same location in your duck's pen. For that matter, strive to keep *everything* consistent in their pen. Don't move things around or you'll cause disorientation and a possible accident. Environmental consistency provides them with the most security. If you do need to make any changes, do so gradually.

If you're accustomed to serving your duck's meals at certain times of the day, you'd be better off initiating a change and making it available 24/7, so they always know where to find it. If you do insist on a feeding schedule, keep to a strict schedule. If they eat all of their food, leave their empty food dish in their pen rather than removing it.

When it comes to pen visits, try to keep a relatively regular schedule, so your duck will know when to expect you and what you'll be doing during these visits (topping off food bowls, changing out pools, or coming for hugs). While enrichment activities can be fun, avoid hastily introducing strange new things that could be frightening.

- **Rubber mats**

Blind ducks use the feeling of the ground under their feet to help them recognize where they are in their pen. Be creative and help them utilize their sense of touch. Having distinguishable grassy zones and sandy areas can help them get their bearings.

Placing rubber mats in certain locations of your duck's pen is one way of providing your duck with some good tactile signals that tell them where they are. Utilize different mat textures to define different things. Mats with raised lines might indicate food and water bowls, those with raised dot patterns might surround their pool and mats that are smooth may circle a tree or post you don't want them to accidentally bump into. Mats can also be successfully utilized to create paths from one place to the next. Just remember to keep them in the same place to avoid any confusion.

- **Water safety**

Practicing water safety is a smart way to help prevent an accidental drowning. Remember, ducks who can't get themselves out of water can become hypothermic (even in warmer seasons) and even drown (see: *"Drowning"*). Blind ducks are even more prone to this type of accident because they can't visually formulate other ways of getting out.

Female ducks who can't see are more likely to become overwhelmed during mating rituals as are subservient drakes who are forced to compete with heartier males (especially in deeper water). Blind ducks are also more apt to stumble into a freezing pool in winter and become trapped in ice. Remember to drain and fill unused swimming holes with hay or safely cover them over when they're not in use.

There are three good strategies to help keep blind ducks safe when you're not around to supervise swim times:

1. *Shallow pool:* Replacing deep pools with shallow pools is often a good idea. A smaller kiddy pool is easier to get out of then a bigger one. If you have a few ducks, replace one large kiddy pool with a couple of smaller and shallow ones.

2. *Gated pool:* In extreme cases (especially where overzealous drakes or particularly panicky ducks are concerned) you can place their pool in a gated-off section of their pen. During the spring and summer when males can get a bit unruly, you can either keep them all off the pond entirely when you're not around to directly chaperone, or you can use the gate to separate males from females.

3. *Sloped-bank pond:* If you're able to do it, building a special pond with a gradient embankment to meet your duck's new health needs is a great way to go. Ducks can safely walk into their new pond and easily get back out again. Close monitoring is in order until they master their new pond's location and can enter and exit easily.

How to Build a Slope-Banked Pond

Dig a small cavity into the ground with a slightly inclined ramp at one end (no more than 30 degrees).

Set a PVC pipe into the wall of the deep end of the pond, just beneath the lip and at the point where the water will naturally want to overflow once the pond is full. Set the pipe so that it carries excess water to the perimeter fencing of your pen, so that it'll drain right through the wire, exiting your pen and pouring outside (rather than flooding your pen or making a swamp). You can bury the pipe if you want to; just make sure it's set right for the water to drain properly before you do.

Next, hand-apply a thick mix of concrete (so it holds its shape and sticks to the sides) to form a 2-3 inch-thick lining all around (sides and bottom). At the same time, I highly recommend making a one-foot concrete lip all the way around your pond to keep your duck from playfully excavating all of the surrounding soil and pulling it into the water while they're swimming. This lip will also will give them a reliable signal when they're getting close to the water's edge.

The great thing about this type of pond is you can clean it simply by running a hose down into the deep end. Just turn the faucet on and allow the fresh water to flush out and replace the old water. You'll still need to bail it out with a bucket and shovel out any debris that has collected, but for the most part, it's a pretty low maintenance system.

In colder regions, you may run into some cracking over the course of the winter, but the cracks can be quickly re-faced every spring with minimal effort.

Homemade slope-banked pond

- **Companionship**

If you have two ducks, your sighted duck will guide your visually-impaired duck anywhere and everywhere they need to go. This type of relationship is ideal for Momma Ducks who can't be around all the time as well as being great for ducky morale.

If you only have one duck and they're beginning to lose their vision, adding a companion while they still have their ability to see can really help them through the transition. If you already have a male duck you should add a female to prevent any unnecessary fighting. If you already have a female duck, it's still a good idea to add another female to keep a vigorous boy from overwhelming her.

If your duck is unexpectedly blinded you may not want to add a new flock member until they've settled down and adapted to their new situation to prevent any excess change and stress.

- **Exercise and stimulation**

Blind ducks still need their exercise to stay fit and healthy. It's vital that they keep moving and remain actively entertained as opposed to becoming under-stimulated, lethargic and depressed.

If your duck has a partner, their friend will usually keep them happily on the move, but if you have a solitary duck, you may find their emotional state quickly waning as they shun otherwise normal activities (this is especially true in the case of sudden, unexpected blindness). If you begin to notice this decline, you'll need to spend a lot more time with them, coaxing them into safe activities and chaperoning closely until they build-up their confidence. You can encourage foraging by routinely placing healthy treats on the ground around them, setting them further away as they become more active.

- **Harness and leash**

As with any other duck, blind ducks should never be let out of their pen without direct, adult supervision. Walks out of the safety of their pen can be especially stressful for visually-impaired ducks. They can react in unforeseeable ways to unusual sounds and situations and place themselves in danger if you don't have complete control. Use your best judgment and if you insist on taking them on excursions out into your yard, invest in a quality and well-fitted duck harness and leash first (see: *"Indoor Ducks"* and *"Therapy for Hips, Legs, Feet & Toes/Recovery Items"*).

Once you've fully harness-trained your special-needs duck and have had plenty of practice inside their pen, you can begin taking them outside. Start out small at first. Don't go far and don't stay out too long. Design a regular routine, so your duck will know exactly what to expect and when to expect it. Take them along the same path each time to build familiarity, and then slowly add to their journey as they become more and more comfortable with it. Failure to keep things consistent will only stress out your duck, impeding their progress and shattering their confidence. They'd be better off remaining in their pen where they feel nice and safe, than forced outside for irregular, anxiety-ridden walkabouts.

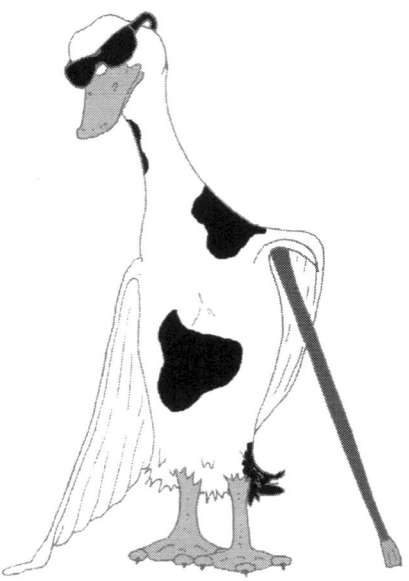

- **Signal sounds**

When approaching your blind duck's pen it's a good idea to use familiar sounds to let them know you're coming. Personally, I like to belt out a good song as I head out to my pens (whether I have blind ducks or not!), but you can make just about any kind of noise you want as long as it's unobtrusive and doesn't stress anyone out.

It's easy to inadvertently startle a blind duck, even when they know you're somewhere nearby. To help keep your duck advised of your position you can either talk, hum or whistle while you work, or you can come up with other ways to let them know where you're. Wearing jewelry that jingles (and can't fall off in your duck pen) or weaving your shoelace through a little bell are both creative ways that continually give away your location.

Be creative with sound-making. You can create specific signals for meal times, treats or enrichments. You can even devise special auditory cues to let them know when they're about to be petted or picked up; this way, they expect the physical contact before it actually happens and aren't alarmed.

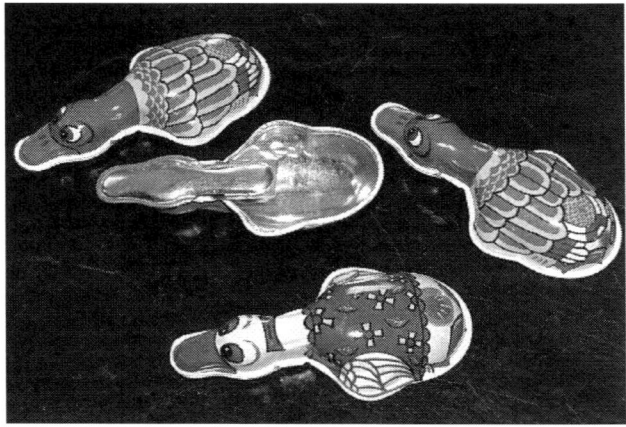

Duck clickers can provide auditory cues for blind ducks

Medical #10
Nervous System (Brain & Spinal Cord)

Neurological conditions can be congenital (inherited) or environmental in nature, and while they tend to have a variety of symptoms, seizures are among the most common.

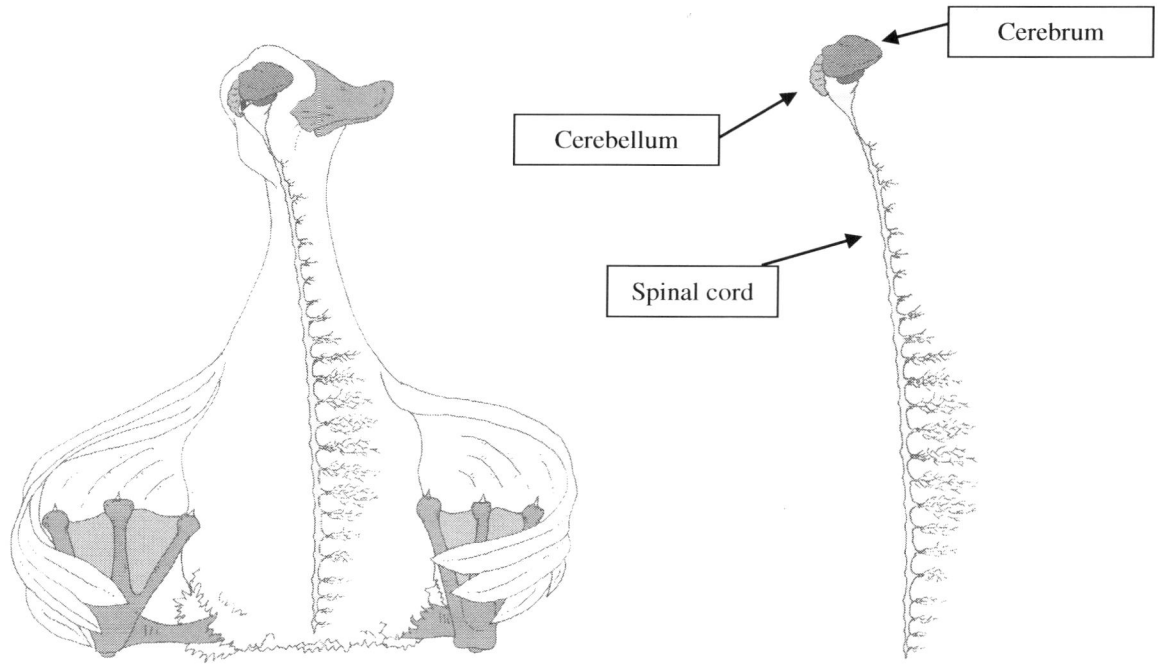

A rudimentary diagram of your duck's brain and spinal cord

Seizures

Partial seizures involve only one hemisphere of the brain. *Simple partial seizures* usually result in localized tremors often seen in a wing or leg, while *complex partial seizures,* grip more of the brain's hemisphere and can result in a loss of consciousness. *Generalized seizures* engage both hemispheres of the brain and impair consciousness.

Seizures can be caused by: rapidly increasing fever, low blood sugar (diabetes), malnutrition, infection and parasites that cause deprivation (tapeworm), temperature extremes (heat stroke and hyperthermia), severe trauma, organ failure and neurologically-based conditions. Ducks who pass away from a wide array of illness and diseases will often end their lives in the final convulsions of a seizure, losing consciousness as they go.

- **Symptoms**

Some symptoms of seizures may include: convulsing, twitching, lying on their back while paddling their feet in the air, the stretching and stiffening of the neck (straight forward or curling behind them over their back), loss of motor control, evacuation, odd vocalizations and loss of consciousness. These events can range from mild to severe, presenting frequently or rarely depending on their underlying cause.

- **Treatment**

If your duck or duckling is experiencing seizures you need to bring them to a vet right away. To keep up their strength until you get there, you can give them a dose of Karo® syrup (high fructose corn syrup) immediately following each seizure, or in the case of poison ingestion, you can give them warmed molasses instead. These are administered via oral syringe.

Vets will often treat your seizing duck with fluids and glucose, an anticonvulsant/sedative (Diazepam) and nutritional support while also running a comprehensive avian blood panel to check body function (especially liver and kidneys).

Ducks can often survive environmentally caused seizures with little or no permanent damage if the source of the problem can be effectively eliminated and provided they receive immediate vet treatment.

Congenital Neurological Disorders

Ducklings can hatch out of their eggs with inherent brain or spinal cord disorders, which often result in neurological complications.

- **Symptoms**

Some symptoms of neurological disorders may include: balance issues, impaired motor control, circling and seizures. These symptoms can be mild or acute, having minor or major implications.

- **Treatment**

Individual cases should be carefully examined and reviewed with a qualified vet to determine if your duck's special needs can be met through supportive care and medications, or if they have a real quality-of-life issue, in which case euthanasia may need to be explored.

Brain & Spinal Cord Tumors

Brain and spinal cord tumors are both pretty rare in waterfowl. When they do occur, results can be mild or severe depending on their location and speed of growth.

- **Symptoms**

Some symptoms of brain tumors may include: seizures, excessive open-bill panting (indicating a painful headache or dizzying nausea), appetite loss, difficulty remembering their way or finding normal things (like their food dish), trouble balancing and impaired motor control.

Some symptoms of spinal cord tumors may include: impaired motor control, balance issues, excessive open-bill panting (indicative of pain) and a visible deformity of the spine.

- **Treatment**

There is no treatment for brain or spinal cord tumors. Surgery is often considered too invasive. If your duck is managing well and still has their mobility and appetite, pain medication can be given as supportive care until it comes time to humanely euthanize.

Environmental Neurological Disorders

Most neurological disorders are environmentally based. Common causes include: disease, malnutrition, incubation errors, severe trauma and ingestion of toxins.

Neurological Disease

Duck Viral Enteritis, Duck Viral Hepatitis and Avian Encephalomyelitis can all have neurological implications, which may or may not be reversible depending on the promptness and effectiveness of treatment (see: *"Lymphatic-Immune System"*).

Metabolic Bone Disease (Vitamin Deficiency)

While metabolic bone disease (MBD) is more often seen in the limbs, it can also result in abnormal bone degeneration of the spine, resulting in nerve compression. MBD is usually caused by malnutrition and is rarely inherited.

- **Symptoms**

Symptoms of MBD of the spine may include: weakness, tremors, seizures, swollen joints, paralysis and pain (which may manifest in a refusal to participate in normal activities). These symptoms tend to intensify with disease progression.

- **Treatment**

Immediately examine your duck's diet, ensuring that they're on a high-quality and properly-balanced brand-name feed. Make sure you're serving your duck the appropriate feed blend for their age and needs. Ask your vet or a professional at your local grain store if you need further advice. In severe cases, ask your vet about vitamin supplementation, being mindful of safe dosages. MBD is often reversible if caught and treated in a timely manner.

Incubation Errors

Sadly, many neurological issues actually begin while ducklings are still tucked inside their little eggs. Improper incubation techniques are the number one cause of neurological issues among ducklings and most of these blunders are inflicted upon them by inexperienced and unqualified humans.

- **Symptoms**

Some symptoms of incubation errors resulting in neurological issues may include: newly hatched ducklings who demonstrate seizures, paralysis, spinning in circles, balance issues and muscle coordination deficits.

- **Treatment**

Sadly, most vets won't even touch ducklings in this predicament other than to offer euthanasia. If your duckling is a real fighter with mild symptoms, you may be able to find a vet willing to provide some supportive care including fluids, glucose, an anticonvulsant/sedative and nutritional support.

Brain & Spinal Cord Trauma

Most injuries involving the head and spine can commonly be attributed to human error. Ducklings dropped through human mishandling can result in skull and spine fractures, spinal compression, brain swelling and hemorrhaging that can lead to a lifetime of disability. Young children who squeeze ducklings too tightly in their hands can also cause these types of injuries.

- **Symptoms**

Some symptoms of brain and spinal cord trauma following an accident may include: bleeding, swelling, seizures, dizziness, spinning in circles, impaired motor control, balance issues, sudden onset paralysis, excessive open-bill panting (indicative of pain), unwillingness to move or engage in normal activities.

- **Treatment**

Depending on the age of the duckling and the severity of the accident your vet may be able to treat trauma with anti-inflammatory/pain medication as well as providing supportive care including fluids, glucose and nutritional support. Depending on the situation, recovery may be partial or complete.

Tricia's Toxins ...

One morning I went outside and noticed that Tricia wasn't her normal perky and bossy self. Usually she's an instigator who likes to stir up all kinds of trouble. It wasn't like her to be so still and quiet, never mind to ignore her food dish. I immediately brought her to the vet who quickly determined that she was either harboring a hidden infection, or more likely, had ingested dangerous hepatoxins from a spring algae bloom.

While our sanctuary's duck pond is clear of this kind of trouble, the stream that feeds it travels through multiple properties and forested areas before arriving at our pens. It was important to explore what might have drifted downstream when determining her diagnosis.

After drawing blood for a comprehensive avian blood panel, our vet had me start Tricia on a precautionary round of antibiotics, which consisted of 250 mgs of Clavamox® twice daily for 14 days.

I also began treating Tricia with activated charcoal to help absorb any toxins. To accomplish this I mixed 1 teaspoon of the powdered charcoal with a few cc's of a strawberry flavored Ensure® Plus Nutritional Shake once a daily for three days (via syringe). It was vital that I wait at least 2 hours after giving her antibiotics before giving her the charcoal.

Because she wasn't eating, Tricia required timed syringe-fed meals, which consisting of: Ensure® Plus, Oxbow Critical Care™, Avi-Culture® probiotics and Iams® Maximum-Calories canned cat food.

The final bit of therapy was to give Tricia 2.5 mgs of Torbitrol® every night at bedtime to help make sure she could rest comfortably and get a good night's sleep. This is vital to a duck's recovery.

Our vet strategy included a recheck in 7 days with a plan to x-ray and perform a fecal culture if adequate improvement wasn't seen. Fortunately, by the time she went back to the vet, she was showing nice signs of improvement. She didn't exhibit any signs of discomfort when the vet palpitated her pelvis or abdomen this time around.

Tricia's appetite returned the following week and she made a complete recovery!

Case # 164: Poisoning

Ingestion of Toxins

Over the years, I've responded to dozens of emails regarding rapid onset seizures in pet ducks. In every single case I was able to successfully trace the source of the problem back to accidental poisoning simply by asking for photos or descriptions of their yards.

Ducks who come out of their pens to play in your lawn aren't the only ones at risk. If you have potentially hazardous materials in your yard, they often have a way of being tracked into your duck pen. This is why it's so important for you to know which items in and around your home and yard might be toxic to your feathered friends.

Putting aside the chemicals you commonly understand to be dangerous if consumed by your duck (household chemicals, paints, solvents, gasoline, oil, pesticides, herbicides, rodent poisons, snail/slug bait, etc.), there are a few other items that you might not be considering.

1. *Pressure treated lumber:* This lumber is treated with chromium, copper, and arsenic (CCA). Over time they can leach into the surrounding soil or water (if immersed). Although people tend to focus on the arsenic, all three of these components are toxic. While there are disputes over how large doses have to be and how long they need to be consumed in order to cause disease, I advise to err on the side of caution. Avoid sinking beams into ponds or soil. Instead, mount them on top of concrete footings to prevent any leaching. Always sweep up any sawdust after cutting boards to prevent accidental ingestion of toxins.

2. *Fertilizer (lawn & garden products):* Lawn, flower, plant and tree fertilizers contain a myriad of unsafe chemicals for your duck including zinc and iron. Avoid treating any areas in or anywhere around your pens. Rain wash and foot traffic can easily carry these unsafe chemicals into your duck's pen.

3. *Ice/snow melt & salt:* Avoid treating your driveway with chemicals or salt. When the spring thaw comes, these substances can easily be carried into puddles in your duck's pen—and no duck can resist a good puddle, no matter what poisons linger inside. Ingestion of these chemicals can be fatal. A puddle of water contaminated with salt from your driveway can result in toxic effects known as sodium ion poisoning. Even if these puddles dry up before your duck has access to them, they can seep into the soil and resurface following the next rainstorm. Try to avoid applying poisons anywhere in your yard because they have a nasty way of spreading around. They can be washed through rainfall, snow melt, made airborne by wind, or treaded by foot into other areas of your property, seriously threatening the lives of your ducks.

4. *Fireworks:* It's not uncommon for people to light off fireworks in their yards in summer (just make sure your ducks are safely locked up for the night, so you won't spook them). If you're one of these people remember to carefully clean up any remainders *immediately* thereafter. Fireworks can contain a variety of heavy metals and chemicals, which can leach into puddles or soil.

5. *Blue-green algae (cynobacteria):* Blooms of blue-green algae can contain hepatoxins and/or neurotoxins that can be fast-acting and fatal. Pay attention to the condition of any natural ponds that your ducks have direct or indirect access to, considering the course of any overflow or traveling streams.

6. *Compost piles:* Your compost heap should always be fenced off with a generous barrier between it and your duck's foraging space. These piles of decomposing and decaying organic matter can potentially harbor fatal mycotoxins.

7. *Mulch:* While a nice decorative touch to your lawn, pine and cedar mulch (among other varieties) can be very dangerous for your duck. While it may look pretty on the surface, there are often dangerous molds brewing underneath. Ingestion of these molds can lead to rapid renal failure. In addition, some mulch products are treated with chemicals and colorants that may be dangerous for your duck.

8. *Mushrooms (fungus):* Many species of mushrooms are poisonous if ingested. Watch for them growing *anywhere* in your yard and pull them completely out of the ground when you find them. Dispose of them

properly (in a trash barrel) to restrict their spread. Mushrooms can grow very fast and appear practically overnight. By removing them quickly, you can prevent their spores from traveling into your pen areas.

9. *Plants, flowers & berries:* Ducks are infamous plant and berry eaters. Keep a close eye on what's growing in and around your pens and yard. A guide to poisonous plants in your area is an invaluable tool. Before buying or transplanting any foliage into your enclosures, be sure to read up to make sure that it's non-toxic and safe for your ducks. *When in doubt, pull it out!* Removing toxic plants before they can seed and reproduce can help stop invasive problems down the road.

10. *Cigarettes (chewing tobacco, nicotine patches/gum):* I once had a visitor sit down in one of my pens during a sanctuary tour and light-up a cigarette. I couldn't get that thing extinguished and her escorted off the premises quickly enough. While it's completely unacceptable to smoke in the middle of an animal sanctuary, it's acceptable in your own backyard. If you or any of your visitors are smokers, tobacco chewers, or using nicotine gum or patches, be sure that these products aren't dropped, discarded or spit into the ground where your ducks might possibly ingest them (remembering that these things can travel through your yard when it rains). Cigarettes contain approximately 3.5 mg of nicotine, while nicotine gum has 2-4 mgs, and an ingested nicotine patch can release 5-15 mgs of nicotine over the course of 16 hours. A five pound duck can be poisoned by as little as 2.5 mgs of nicotine with a fatal dose being around 20 mg.

11. *Matches:* The tips of unlit matches contain potassium chloride, which can cause terrible stomach pain if ingested by your duck. If you're a smoker, lighting off fireworks or starting campfires, be sure that matches aren't dropped or left on the ground where your ducks can find them.

12. *Human food:* Many of the food items you're eating are not ideal and potentially harmful for ducks. Check out the label before you decide. Chemicals like artificial preservatives, colors, flavorings are only a few of the items on the list that may be an issue for your duck. High sugar and fat contents can also result in immediate problems. Keep processed food, chocolate, grapes, dairy products and other food items out of reach of your ducks—especially if you have an indoor duck that tends to get into things when you're not looking.

13. *Poisoning:* While I wish I didn't have to include this one, I've heard of a few instances where someone's neighbors poisoned their ducks. In some cases they knew they had angry neighbors while in others, they simply had no idea. The best way to prevent this is to keep your ducks from roaming around on other people's property. Whenever you let your ducks out of their pen they need to be directly chaperoned, being careful to keep them well away from anyone harboring any ill-intentions.

14. *Balloons, ribbons & wrapping paper:* Parties are fun, but remember to pick up any leftover remnants in the yard before letting your ducks out to forage. While most party items don't contain toxic dyes, pieces of popped balloons are colorful and attract immediate attention. If ingested they can cause suffocation or intestinal blockage. The same is true of curly ribbons and wrapping paper.

Not everything bad for your duck is found in your lawn; sometimes a toxin turns out to be an ingredient in your duck's prescribed medication. If your duck has a bad reaction to any of their medication, stop administering and immediately consult with your vet.

- **Symptoms**

Some symptoms of poisoning may include: rapid onset seizures, vomiting, diarrhea, disorientation, balance issues, paralysis and loss of motor control.

- **Treatment**

If you suspect your duck has ingested a toxic substance, seek out immediate vet assistance—especially if they're symptomatic. Seizures and vomiting are commonly the first symptoms you'll see. You can help give supportive care for the seizures on the way to your vet (see: *"Seizures"*).

Vets will often treat poisoned waterfowl with activated charcoal, fluids & glucose, an anticonvulsant/sedative (Diazepam) and nutritional support while also running a comprehensive avian blood panel to check body function (especially liver and kidneys). Ducks can often survive a poisoning with little or no permanent damage *if* they're treated immediately and the source of the poisoning is located and removed to prevent re-exposure. Once home again, you may need to administer further treatments of activated charcoal (capsules) and warm molasses (via oral syringe) to your duck to help absorb and remove any lingering toxins.

Hardware Disease

The ingestion of metal (or metal-plated) objects is known as *Hardware Disease*. Ducks are hopelessly attracted to the beautiful and shiny objects that fall into the grass and glitter in the sunshine. This can include: screws, nuts, bolts, nails, staples, bits of wire, coins, aluminum foil (gum wrappers), jewelry, pins, pen parts—you name it, they'll eat it. Once ingested, these metal tidbits remain inside your duck's body, sometimes causing internal damage while their metal-plating erodes away and is absorbed into their bloodstream.

Although hardware disease can be difficult to treat, it's entirely preventable. Avoid wearing jewelry in your duck pen and make weekly inspections of their enclosure, barn, houses and pools. Ducks are nibblers, so pay close attention to any small metal objects (staples, etc.) that can be pulled out and ingested. As an added measure, you can periodically sweep in and around their pen with a metal detector and/or a rolling magnetic broom, which you can purchase from your local hardware or home supply store.

Avoid running lawn mowers, weed-wackers, chainsaws, etc. in the vicinity of your ducks. I'm continually baffled by people who dress-up in all kinds of protective eye goggles and gear and then proceed to work right next to (or inside) their duck pen—while their ducks are in it! Feathers aren't effective safety gear and won't protect them from any shrapnel launched in their direction. In addition to putting your duck in immediate danger, it's also an effective way to shoot unsafe objects directly into their pen. Always lock ducks up safely in their house or barn whenever you're cutting grass and weeds around their pen and be sure to aim your lawnmower's blower out and away whenever doing a pass, so that any hidden objects won't get thrown inside.

- **Symptoms**

Some symptoms of hardware disease may include: difficulty standing or walking, fatigue, decreased appetite, seizures or watery green (almost fluorescent) droppings.

If you see your duck swallow a metal object, take them to the vet right away. Proactive treatment can significantly increase the likelihood of successful treatment. Once they become symptomatic, hardware disease can be increasingly more difficult to treat.

- **Treatment**

If your duck exhibits symptoms of hardware disease take them to the vet for an immediate x-ray. If it doesn't show any sign of metal objects, your duck may have successfully passed the item, but may still be suffering from metal poisoning. In this case, blood is drawn to test for lead and zinc toxicity. Results can take up to a week, and if your duck is highly symptomatic they may not make it that long. In this type of scenario vets will commonly recommend you begin chelation therapy until results are confirmed or clearly ruled out.

On the other hand, if the x-ray *does* show a metal object lodged inside your duck's digestive tract, your vet will want to run blood work to check any effects before proceeding with chelation therapy.

Some objects are considered less harmful due to their shape or consistency. In this case, your vet may recommend giving the item a chance to pass on its own. To monitor the progression they'll have you come back for follow-up x-rays on a weekly or bi-weekly basis for the next 2-4 weeks. If the object doesn't pass, it may move to a more ideal location for surgery or your duck's body might naturally encapsulate it—surrounding it in tissue and sealing it off. In this case, it may never harm your duck at all. Follow-up blood work should be enlisted to ensure your duck's organs are unaffected and functioning properly.

On the other hand, some objects are like ticking time-bombs and may require immediate removal whenever possible. This includes objects that are: sharp, made of lead (or lead-plated), or which are causing (or could quickly cause) severe health issues.

Ideally, endoscopic surgery (going down through the throat or up through the cloaca) is the safest way to go, but depending on the location of the object, it isn't always possible. Sometimes more invasive surgery needs to be weighed against waiting to see if the object will move through their digestive tract to a more ideal location. The hope is that this new position does allow for an endoscopic procedure.

Laparoscopic alternatives are currently being explored by some vets to remove objects from the gizzard through small incisions in the body cavity. This is much less invasive and can be successful especially if the object is removed soon after ingestion.

Lead Poisoning

Lead paint chips and lead shot from guns aren't the only sources of lead poisoning. Because so many domestic ducks are abandoned on public ponds, many of them risk ingesting fishing tackle (lead sinkers and old lures).

When lead is ingested, it gets into the gizzard and begins to erode. As it does, it enters the bloodstream and stores in your duck's body, often with fatal results.

Prevention is the best course of action when it comes to lead poisoning. Over the years I've heard from quite a few people who realized after-the-fact that they build their duck pen over lead-contaminated soil or who discovered too late that their pond or the well supplying their duck's with water held a dark secret.

1. *Test your water:* If there's a risk of contamination, or if your duck is exhibiting symptoms, have your natural pond and water sources tested for lead toxicity. If lead levels are high, you can often consult with the testing company or a local university about safely and effectively remedying the problem. If you want to run a simple test yourself you can purchase your own testing kids pretty inexpensively just be sure to read and follow the instructions carefully (supplier: Gempler's www.gemplers.com).

2. *Test Your Soil:* You can also have the soil of your pen site tested. If lead levels are high you can consult with professionals who will often advise topsoil excavation and safe refill. Be sure to dispose of any contaminated topsoil safely and legally to prevent issues elsewhere.

- **Symptoms**

Some symptoms of lead poisoning may include: seizures, anemia, vomiting, general weakness, rubber legs (instability), appetite and weight loss, drooping wings, marked immune deficiency, difficulty breathing, open-bill panting, excessive drinking, dehydration, pale-colored bill and bright green diarrhea.

- **Treatment**

Bring your duck to the vet for immediate treatment, which includes an x-ray (to see if a lead object is inside them), a comprehensive avian blood panel and lead testing (which involves additional blood work). If not discovered in its early stages, lead poisoning can result in permanent damage and successful treatment may not be possible. Your vet will likely recommend euthanasia to prevent any further suffering in this situation.

When discovered in time, lead needs to be removed from your duck's system as quickly as possible through forced vomiting (emesis) utilizing injections (emetics) and/or by increasing digestive function using laxatives. Surgery will be immediately required if the lead object is still inside your duck (see: *"Hardware Disease"*).

Calcium EDTA solution is a heavy metal chelating agent. It's given to your duck as an injection or as an IV treatment. So as not to encumber you with complex chemistry, suffice it to say that it'll go into your duck's body and bind with heavy metals. The agent then leaves their body through the urinary tract, taking some of the heavy metals along with it.

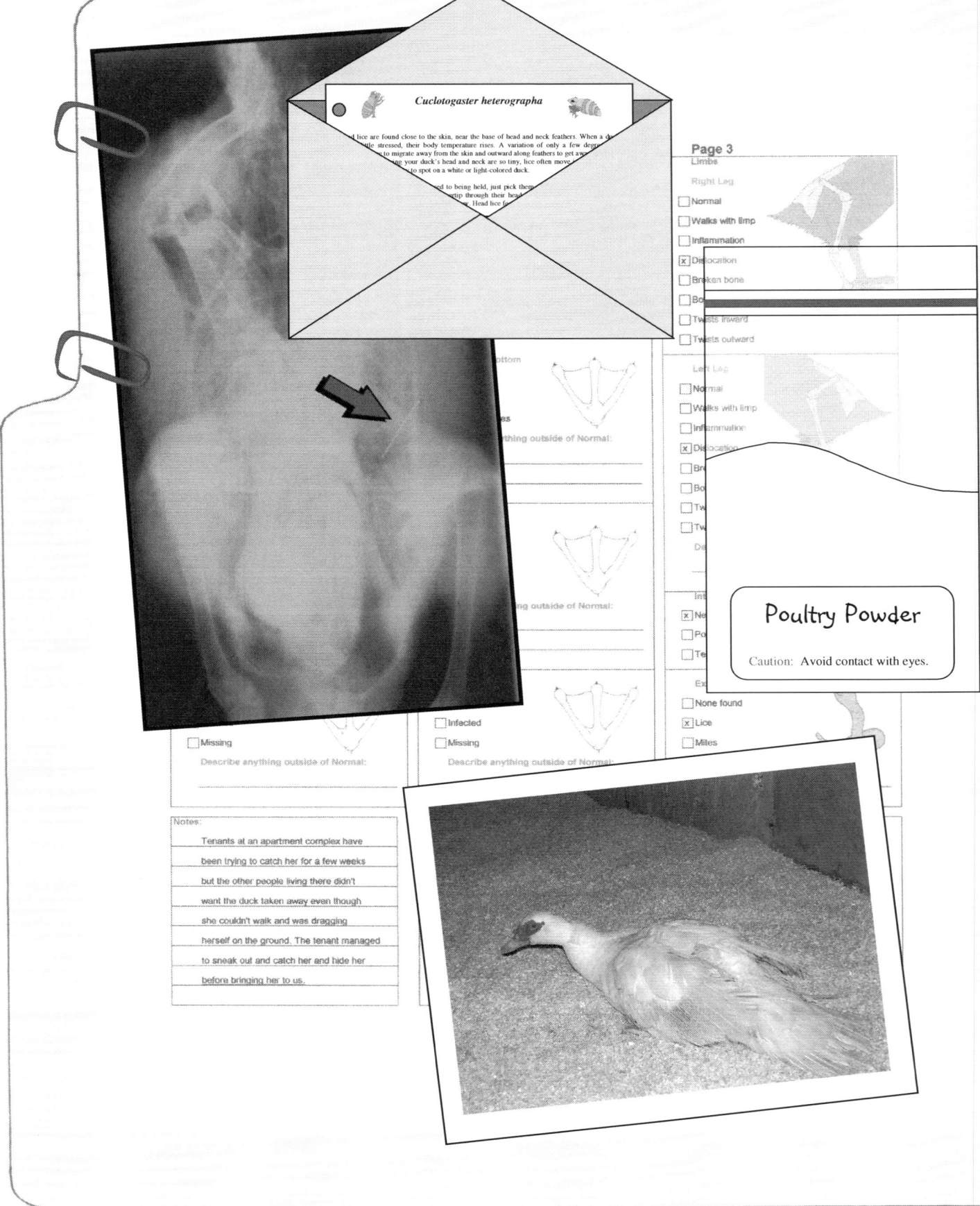

Daphnee's Needle ...

Daphnee was a Muscovy duck who was dropped off and attempting to survive on a small pond at the center of an apartment complex. She was brought to us one October when some residents there noticed she couldn't walk.

An x-ray confirmed that both of her ankles and knees were dislocated. This kind of injury occurs when ducks stay out on water in cold water in an attempt to avoid predators. Eventually they succumb to sleep and the ice encroaches around them. When Daphnee woke up and found herself in this snare, she panicked and struggled to get herself free, dislocating her own joints to do so.

The sad thing is, no one took notice of her tragic predicament—that she was dragging herself around on the ground, until the following October. In the meantime, she faced starvation and a feather lice infestation because she couldn't stand up to preen her underside properly. By the time she came to our sanctuary she was in pretty sad shape, but I rolled out the red carpet by getting rid of her lice, filling her belly with good food, taking her swimming and letting her visit with our other ducks.

Because Daphnee was a Muscovy, I knew she would grow new flight feathers that would enable her to fly around her pen, getting her to and from our barn and slope-banked pond. Wings and water remedy the need for all that walking. Sadly, the x-ray also revealed that Daphnee had swallowed a sewing needle. She must've discovered it on the shores of that pond, saw it glimmering there in the sunlight and found it too alluring to resist.

Ducks are prone to swallowing metal objects. While hardware disease can sometimes be treated, this wasn't the case with Daphnee. The needle in her intestine was like a ticking time bomb, threatening a painful demise the moment it pierced through her intestinal wall. Unfortunately there was no safe way to remove it, so in light of all of her injuries, I decided to euthanize her to spare her any more pain. This kind of decision are among the most difficult for Momma Ducks to make, but at times, there are just no alternatives.

Case # 66: Hardware Disease

The trouble with Calcium EDTA is it can be very difficult to get your hands on in short notice. You'll often have to call local human hospitals or a compounding pharmacy to track it down.

Your vet can teach you how to administer these injections yourself.

1. Inject intramuscularly twice-daily for a total of five days.
2. Treatment stops for four days.
3. Then, treatment picks up again: twice-daily for another five days.
4. Retest your duck's blood for lead levels and proceed forward under direct vet advisement.

Side effects of Calcium EDTA include diarrhea and vomiting. Since it also removes other minerals from the body, excess loss of calcium (hypocalcemia) can result. Calcium levels should be closely monitored by your vet, especially in egg-laying ducks. Calcium sources (oyster shells, calcium chips, supplements, etc.) should be withheld during treatment and for a couple hours afterwards (to control their intake levels) before being reintroduced again.

Zinc Poisoning

Zinc poisoning is different from lead poisoning in that zinc is able to work its way out of your duck's system, provided the source of contamination is successfully removed. Zinc poisoning is entirely preventable if you understand its causes. In addition to keeping foreign objects out of your pens (zinc plated nuts, bolts, etc.) there are other things to consider.

1. *Galvanized wire:* Zinc is used in the process of making galvanized wire fencing. You can use non-coated galvanized wire for applications entirely above ground, but for underground applications (digging predator barriers) or those in or near water you'll want to go with a protected PVC coated wire.

2. *Plating:* Zinc can be found in the coating of many metal pet dishes. Avoid metal food containers at all costs. Always use plastic or rubber buckets and bowls in your duck pens.

3. *Water:* As with lead, you can proactively test your water sources for zinc toxicity if there's a risk of contamination, or if your duck becomes symptomatic. You may need to go through a testing company for this because zinc naturally exists in water (it's the *level* of zinc that's important); also, home testing kits can be expensive. When having your water tested remember to specifically request zinc level testing since it's not normally included in most company-offered packages. If they discover high amounts of zinc in your water, the testing company should be able to provide you with resources for solutions.

4. *Soil:* Before building your duck pen consider the site carefully. Remnants of paint or chemicals poured into the soil can cause zinc toxicity (among other problems) making former workshop areas poor locations. Fertilizers are also high in zinc. Prior garden sites or orchards can harbor high levels of zinc that can quickly make your duck ill. Remember to consider that prior property owners may have treated the grounds differently before you. If you're concerned, or if your duck is symptomatic, test their soil for zinc. When positive for zinc, topsoil may need to be excavated and replaced.

5. *Feed recalls:* A bag of feed coming from an improperly formulated batch can lead to all kinds of problems. If your duck has zinc poisoning and you've successfully ruled everything out, it's time to inspect their dinner—especially if multiple ducks are symptomatic.

    Feed manufacturing companies do make mistakes. If you suspect your duck's feed could be the source of the problem, stop serving from your current bag and buy a new one. If you're sticking with the same brand, make sure to compare the lot numbers on both bags and purchase from a different batch. Contact the manufacturer if you need help finding or understanding this information on their packaging.

    You can have a sample of feed tested at a local university or by an independent lab for confirmation (feed companies often won't test until they receive multiple complains, but you can try). If results are conclusively positive for excessive zinc levels you'll need to immediately follow-up with the manufacturer.

- **Symptoms**

Some symptoms of zinc poisoning may include: seizures, anemia, vomiting, general weakness, rubber legs (instability), appetite and weight loss, drooping wings, marked immune deficiency, difficulty breathing, excessive drinking, dehydration, pale-colored bill and bright green diarrhea.

Because symptoms for lead and zinc poisoning are the same, vets will commonly recommend testing the blood for both—unless you're certain you can rule either of them out (it's often easier to rule out lead).

- **Treatment**

In addition to isolating and eliminating the cause of the zinc poisoning, you'll need to bring your duck to the vet for immediate treatment. Your vet will x-ray (to see if an object is inside them), draw blood for a comprehensive avian panel along with taking additional blood for the zinc test. Zinc poisoning is usually easier to treat than lead poisoning provided it's caught in time. Medication and follow-up blood tests will be needed once the process begins to verify that your duck's zinc levels are being effectively reduced.

In cases where zinc toxicity is relatively low and the source has been successfully removed, vets may attempt to increase your duck's urine flow with a crystalloid solution that will help flush the excess zinc out. If your duck's zinc levels are high enough to warrant further intervention, a chelating agent is commonly prescribed to bring their levels back under control. Injections of Calcium EDTA solution (see: *"Lead Poisoning"*) are the most common and effective treatment.

A less effective treatment is D-Penicillamine (or Cuprimine). It's dosed orally and also helps draw zinc out of the body. The trouble with this drug is it can be near impossible to get your hands on. Most human pharmacies don't stock it and won't special order it due to the low demand and high cost, so you may have to try hospital or compounding pharmacies.

If neither of these treatments are readily available where you are, your vet may instruct you to purchase over-the-counter DMSA (dimercaptosuccinic acid). Vets will commonly prescribe a dose of 25-35 mgs/kg daily. This means a 5 pound duck with high zinc levels would do best on a dose of 75 mgs daily, while a duck with lower zinc levels might do better on a dose of 50 mgs daily (remember: 1 kg = 2.2 lbs). DMSA is also a good option to get your duck started while you wait for a special order of Calcium EDTA solution to arrive.

DMSA is often given to your duck on an empty stomach for maximum absorption. Side effects may include nausea, so it's advisable to divide pills and space them out over the course of the day. Many vets will advise you to split the dosage into two, three or four doses (with three or four being most preferable). You can either dose morning, noon and night OR you can dose every eight hours over a twenty-four hour period. If nausea and loss of appetite become an issue you may need to reduce the overall dosage a bit. Discuss this possible outcome with your vet before beginning a treatment regimen, so you're prepared for any scenario.

DMSA is often administered with rest periods in mind. Ducks are often dosed for 3-5 days depending on their zinc levels, their recommended dosage and their individual tolerance. Most vets will go with a three-day dosage period; however, if your duck is having exceptional difficulty tolerating DMSA (which is rare), they can be dosed every other day for five days. While you may be tempted to pull gel capsules apart and sprinkle the DMSA over your duck's food, it actually has a very bad taste (and odor), which will discourage your duck from eating it. This is one pill you'll just have to pop down their throat.

Following this 3-5 day treatment period comes a 3-11 day rest period (with 11 days being ideal). Not only will this give your duck time to recover from any nausea experienced, but it'll allow their body time to recover from the loss of glutathione (which is their body's own natural chelator responsible for pushing heavy metals outside of their cells). Once glutathione is naturally restored in their body, the next dosing period of DMSA can begin.

Basically, you want to ensure your duck's dosing cycle provides them with enough medicine to counteract their elevated zinc levels without risking their overall health. This in mind, an experienced vet will advise a special mix of vitamins for your duck during the rest periods between DMSA dosing. These supplements will restore those healthy minerals that are incidentally bound and removed from their body along with the zinc. They include iron, calcium and magnesium.

All of these treatment options draw calcium from the body, so again, calcium levels in egg-laying ducks should be monitored closely. Calcium sources should be removed at dosing times and then re-introduced a couple of hours afterward or in the case of DMSA treatment, their calcium should be removed during their 3-5 day dosing cycle and then reintroduced during their 3-11 day rest period.

While DMSA is an over-the-counter drug, *never* attempt to treat your duck at home without direct vet supervision. Dosages of DMSA and intermittent multivitamins need to be carefully measured, catering to your duck's particular needs in order to ensure success and help prevent fatality.

Medical #11
Respiratory System

Your duck's trachea, lungs and multiple sets of air sacs make up their respiratory system.

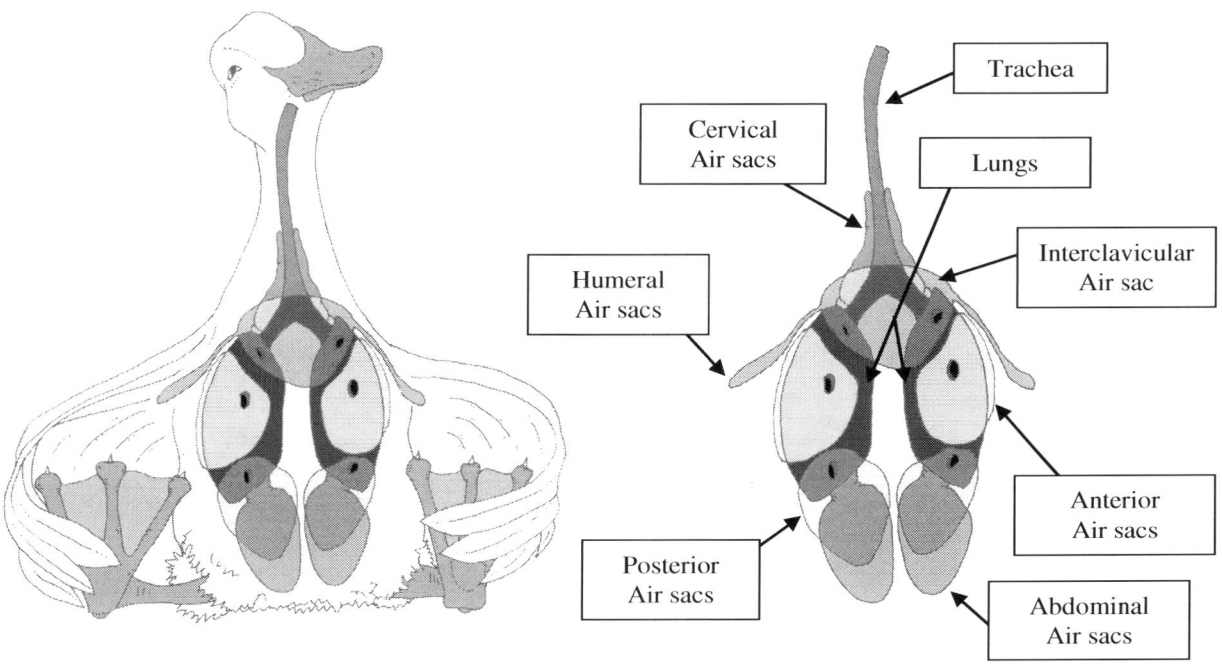

A diagram of your duck's respiratory system

Chronic Respiratory Disease

Mycoplasma gallisepticum is the bacteria responsible for Chronic Respiratory Disease (CRD). Infected egg-laying ducks pass the bacteria onto their ducklings by course of their eggs. Ducks harboring the bacteria are often latent carriers, not becoming symptomatic or contagious until they become stressed—then it begins to spread to other flock members through the air and by direct mucus contact.

- **Symptoms**

Some symptoms of CRD may include: difficulty breathing, coughing, sneezing, gurgling, fatigue, nasal discharge, eye bubbles, head shaking, appetite loss, weight loss and decreased immune deficiency.

- **Treatment**

Bring your duck to the vet for antibiotic medication. Treatment normally continues for 14 days or until your duck is no longer showing symptoms. While this will improve their situation, it's not a cure and future flare-ups (although milder in comparison) may occur—especially during stressful times.

Aspergillus

Aspergillus flavus is a pathogenic mold (from the same genus as *Aspergillus parasiticus*) that often grows on decaying hay, vegetation, corn, wheat, grains and wood chips. Once inhaled, aspergillosis can develop in the lungs and air sacs of your duck (or you). Ducklings, older ducks and immune compromised ducks are most susceptible.

Unclean feed and water areas often spark growth of these two molds. Ducks are messy eaters and often spill pellets, which can quickly become covered with this greenish-blue mold. Splash-preening around water buckets and into surrounding hay can also incite development. Cleaning up messy spots on a daily basis can help prevent dangerous disease outbreaks in both you and your ducks.

Aspergillus molds are far more prevalent during hot and humid weather, so it's important to be extremely diligent during these times of the year.

If you notice aspergillus mold growing anywhere in your barn or pens:

1. Move your ducks to another area of their pen to prevent inhalation of disturbed particles.
2. Ensure proper ventilation—especially if you're indoors.
3. Remove all contaminated material.
4. Thoroughly clean and sanitize the location.
5. Disinfect any involved food bowls or water buckets (be sure to let food bowls dry thoroughly before refilling).

Disposable face masks (painter's masks) are commonly seen as ineffective against the tiny mold spores, but they certainly can't hurt if you'd like to wear one as a precaution.

- **Symptoms**

Some symptoms of aspergillosis may include: difficulty breathing, excessive open-bill panting, fatigue and fever.

- **Treatment**

Take your duck to the vet for an x-ray and swab culture to confirm the diagnosis. It used to be that ducks with aspergillus didn't stand much of a chance. Those who did survive often had to endure long and grueling drug therapies that put their vital organs at risk. Today there are multiple treatment options for you and your vet to explore.

Drug Therapy: A prescription of antifungal medication will be in order. Vets will usually prescribe itraconazole because it has the fewest side effects and doesn't interfere with feather growth the way some other antifungal medications do.

Antifungal medications are very potent and can make your duck very ill; they can even cause death if the doses are too high. Frequent vet visits and follow up x-rays will be needed to closely monitor the healing of your duck's lungs and air sacs. Close attention to their blood chemistry is also necessary to prevent liver damage. Blood is commonly drawn every two weeks to monitor levels and make comparisons—adjusting dosages whenever necessary.

Nebulizer Therapy: The great thing about nebulizer treatment is its safety. Set a special place aside in your barn or shed and drape plastic to create a tent (a 6' x 6' x 6' area is ideal). Select a disinfectant solution that can be used as a nebulizing agent and pour it into a vaporizer for your duck to inhale. Always follow product directions and safety instructions. Before beginning any treatment regimes for your duck, it's absolutely vital that you take them to a qualified vet first.

If used properly and under direct vet guidance, nebulizing agents can be both safe and effective against a number of types of bacteria, viruses and molds.

1. F10® SC Veterinary Disinfectant can be purchased in smaller, more economical sizes and also works as an effective nebulizing agent (supplier: Berry Zoo Direct www.bigreptileworld.com).

    F10® SC Treatment:

    a. Fill a vaporizer with a diluted mixture of F10® SC and sterile water.
    b. Place your afflicted duck into their tent and run the vaporizer for 30 minutes.
    c. Your duck can return to their normal routine in between treatments; they don't need to stay in the tent.
    d. Repeat this treatment 3 times a day, every 8 hours.

e. Only treat afflicted ducks. Remove healthy ducks from the treatment area during administration.
   f. Continue treatment for 2-4 weeks under vet supervision.
   g. Your vet will probably want to see your duck every other week for x-rays to monitor their progress (unless conditions worsen, in which case more frequent check-ups will be required).

2. Oxine AH® is purchased by the gallon; it's a cleaning agent as well as safe in nebulizing applications (supplier: AmazonSmile www.smile.amazon.com).

   Oxine® AH Treatment:

   a. Fill vaporizer with a diluted mixture of *inactivated* Oxine® AH and sterile water.
   b. Place your afflicted duck into their tent and run the vaporizer for 30 minutes.
   c. Your duck can return to their normal routine in between treatments; they don't need to stay in the tent.
   d. Repeat this treatment 3 times a day, every 8 hours.
   e. Only treat afflicted ducks. Remove healthy ducks from the treatment area during administration.
   f. Continue treatment for 2-4 weeks under vet supervision.
   g. Your vet will probably want to see your duck every other week for x-rays to monitor their progress (unless conditions worsen, in which case more frequent check-ups will be required).

3. Imaverol® is purchased in 100 ml bottles with each ml containing 100 mgs of Enilconazole.

   Enilconazole Treatment:

   a. Fill vaporizer with a diluted mixture of Imaverol® and sterile water.
   b. Place your afflicted duck into their tent and run the vaporizer for 30 minutes.
   c. Your duck can return to their normal routine in between treatments; they don't need to stay in the tent.
   d. Repeat this treatment 2 times a day, every 12 hours.
   e. Only treat afflicted ducks. Remove healthy ducks from the treatment area during administration.
   f. Continue treatment for 3 weeks under vet supervision.
   g. Your vet will probably want to see your duck every other week for x-rays to monitor their progress (unless conditions worsen, in which case more frequent check-ups will be required).

Pneumonia

Pneumonia is the result of a bacterial, fungal, parasite or viral infection, which attacks your duck's respiratory system and causes fluid to accumulate in their lungs.

- **Symptoms**

Some symptoms of pneumonia may include: difficulty breathing, wheezing or gurgling, coughing, sneezing, nasal discharge, excessive open-bill panting, abdominal heaving, fever, fatigue and loss of appetite.

- **Treatment**

Breathing difficulties should always be taken very seriously. Bring your duck to the vet immediately. They'll confirm the diagnosis by listening to your ducks lungs (and air sacs), taking their temperature and possibly performing an x-ray.

Upper respiratory infections like pneumonia require immediate antibiotic intervention. Vets will commonly jump-start their treatment by administering an injectable dose (commonly Baytril®) right away, while sending you home with a prescription of oral antibiotics to be given over the course of the next 10-14 days. During this time, try to keep your duck out of extreme temperatures to reduce their stress levels and minimize their recovery time.

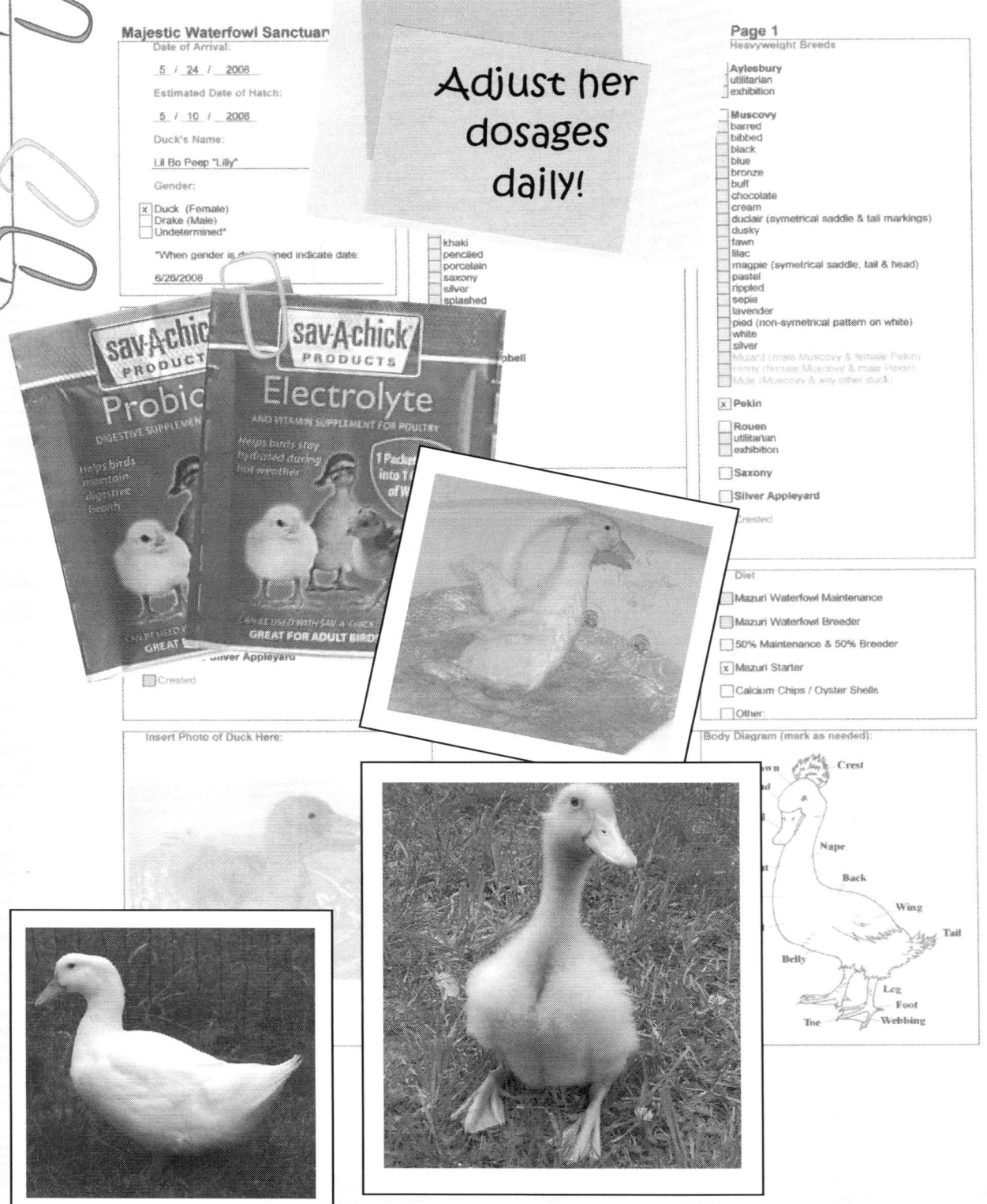

 # Lilly's Pneumonia...

I knew there was a problem when Lil Bo Peep arrived at the sanctuary. It's always a bad sign when a duckling is continually panting with an open bill, even worse when their legs, feet and bill are all hot with fever as hers were.

I arranged for an immediate vet visit where she was diagnosed with pneumonia and given a prescription of Amoxi Drops®, which is a safe alternative for developing ducklings who weigh less than 4 pounds. The tricky thing about medicating a duckling is their rapid growth rate. You'll need to weigh your duckling every day and your vet will need to give you a dosing chart that tells you how much medicine to administer as your hatchling grows. Once ducklings cross the 4 lb. marker, you can switch them over to Baytril® (discuss the risks involving younger ducks with your vet first).

Fever is the body's means of fighting infection. Cool baths should be used with discretion and discussed with your vet to determine appropriate temperature, frequency and duration.

During recovery it's vital to keep your duckling eating and drinking. Sometimes sprinkling a bit of food in their bowl of water is enough to inspire them to eat and drink; other times, you may need to set them into a shallowly-filled tub. Just fill your tub with an inch of water (or 2 inches for larger ducklings) and then sprinkle a bit of food around. This will usually get them going; if not, you'll need to contact your vet about tube feeding.

Like every other duckling, Lil Bo Peep grew extremely fast, and she simply wasn't well enough to consume enough food to keep up with her body's continual demands (not to mention she was already suffering from malnutrition when she arrived). As a result, she had a difficult time supporting her own weight and would often rest on her ankles. It was vital to keep her swimming as much as I could during this time, so that her leg muscles would develop properly. Being in the water also enabled her to stand and walk around correctly; I adjusted the water level to encourage this as she continually grew.

Eventually, Lil Bo Peep overcame her pneumonia and malnutrition and grew strong enough to waddle around like every other duck at the sanctuary. She blossomed into a healthy and happy Lilly.

Aspiration Pneumonia

Aspiration pneumonia occurs when your duck accidentally inhales liquid, food, blood or vomit down into their trachea and lungs.

- **Symptoms**

Some symptoms of aspiration pneumonia may include: gurgling when breathing, coughing, trouble swallowing, hoarseness, shortness of breath, panting and fever (if an infection sets in).

- **Treatment**

The aspiration of a small amount of water will usually work itself out. If your duck exhibits symptoms for more than two hours, or if their condition worsens (even mildly), it's time to call your vet for help. In extreme cases where food, blood or vomit is aspirated, a favorable outcome is far more unlikely and vet assistance should be sought out immediately.

Your vet will confirm the diagnosis by listening to your ducks lungs and possibly performing an x-ray. Antibiotics (commonly Baytril®) may be required to prevent infection, hinder the formation of lung abscesses and avert the risk of related tissue necrosis. In severe cases, your duck may need to be put on oxygen to help them breathe.

Air Sac Injury & Infection

In addition to a set of lungs, your duck also has a complex system of air sacs throughout their body. Complete air movement in and out of their body takes place over the course of two of their breaths. An injured or ruptured air sac will often change the buoyancy of your duck.

- **Symptoms**

Some symptoms of an infected air sac may include: difficulty breathing, wheezing, coughing, excessive open-bill panting and abdominal heaving.

Symptoms of a ruptured air sac may also include: a duck who floats incorrectly in water (unbalanced).

- **Treatment**

Vets will confirm the diagnosis by listening to your duck's lungs and air sacs and by performing an x-ray. If they discover a punctured air sac there's not much they can do other than prescribe antibiotics to help prevent the risk of infection during healing.

90% of all air sac injuries in adult ducks tend to remedy themselves on their own (provided antibiotics are prescribed). While they usually return back to normal they occasionally remain collapsed. As long as your duck isn't having any difficulty breathing there's often no need to intervene any further.

About 10% of all air sac punctures require more invasive intervention. Younger ducks seem to have more trouble recovering from ruptures than mature ducks. In these more difficult cases, an open catheter is often inserted and sutured into place to assist in your duck's recovery.

Air Sac Mites

Cytodites nudus are small mites that can appear in the trachea, bronchi, lungs and air sacs of ducks. Air sac mites are spread to other ducks through coughing and subsequent inhalation.

- **Symptoms**

Some symptoms of the presence of air sac mites may include: coughing, sneezing, wheezing, loss of voice, excessive open-bill panting, head shaking, clicking sounds in air passages, abdominal heaving, weakness, weight loss and pneumonia.

- **Treatment**

Air sac mites can colonize your duck's air passages and cause life-threatening blockages, so immediate treatment is vital. Your vet will confirm the diagnosis by looking down your duck's throat, by tracheal swab and by fecal testing.

Injectable Ivermectin® is commonly prescribed to eradicate air sac mites. Anywhere from 1-6 injections administered every 14 days may be required for up to 6 weeks depending on the level of infestation. Be sure to sanitize all water buckets and food bowls daily during the treatment period.

Avian Chlamydia

Avian Chlamydia *(Chlamydophila psittaci)* is extremely rare in small, closed flocks—especially when ducks are content and kept in nice clean pens. It's far more likely in larger flocks, where ducks are overcrowded in pens, or in circumstances where ducks are highly stressed—often striking immune compromised and older ducks first. The bacterium that causes Chlamydia is commonly spread through the direct ingestion of fecal matter of infected birds although it can come through direct inhalation. Once inside the body, they usually settle in the mucus membranes where they instigate numerous and often seemingly irrelevant respiratory or digestive infections that are actually systemic in nature.

- **Symptoms**

Some symptoms of avian Chlamydia may include: eye discharge, bubbles or caking, nasal discharge, sneezing, fatigue, fever, ruffled feathers, diarrhea, loss of appetite and weight loss.

- **Treatment**

Chlamydia can be difficult to diagnose, especially in mild cases. Your vet will often need to run comprehensive blood work, x-rays (looking for lung lesions, air sac thickening or the enlargement of organs) as well as performing a fecal and/or cloacal swab culture. Once successfully diagnosed, all flock members must be treated and quarantine measures should be set in place to avoid spreading the disease any further.

Your duck will be placed on a vet-monitored medicated diet containing 1% Chlortetracycline (CTC) for 45 days. You can switch them over by mixing medicated pellets with their regular food for a few days, but you can't actually begin counting treatment days until they're fully converted over and consuming a 100% medicated diet. If your duck is laying eggs, ask your vet about achieving appropriate dietary calcium percentages.

In addition to a change in diet, your vet will prescribe one of these antimicrobial treatment options:

1. *Oral doxycycline:* 10-25 mg/kg can be given orally as a test to see if your duck can handle the dosage without throwing-up. If they *can't* tolerate this dosage, injectable options may need to be explored. If they *can* stomach it, treatment can continue in the proper increased dosage, 1-2 times daily for 6-8 weeks.

2. *Injectible doxycycline:* This can be administered intramuscularly once-a-week for 6-8 weeks although it may cause some irritation at the injection site.

3. *Oral oxytetracycline:* This can be added to their drinking water *or* to their duck food for 6-8 weeks.

4. *Injectible oxytetracycline:* This can be administered intramuscularly every 24 hours for 6-8 weeks.

5. *New alternatives:* Ask your vet about any new and breaking treatment regimes. Doxycycline medicated feed or other injectable formulas may be available through compounding pharmacies.

While treatment can save your duck's life, it won't fully cure them. They'll still remain a latent carrier, with possible random flair-ups and the potential to shed bacteria and spread disease to other hosts—*including humans (psittacosis).*

Following the 45 day treatment period, repeat a fecal culture to confirm the bacteria is no longer present. Quarterly tests can be performed to continually monitor any bacterial shedding.

<u>Whistling</u>

My Young Matthew is a whistler. Whenever he inhales through his tiny nares I can hear a lingering whistle clinging to his every breath. This endearing little trait has been ever-present since his duckling days and has never been accompanied by any other symptoms. While regular and life-long whistling is harmless in a duck of good health, the sudden onset of whistling can be an early indicator of a respiratory issue, so pay close attention.

Remember, it's always advisable to seek out vet assistance at the onset of any unusual symptoms because ducks are masters when it comes to disguising their illnesses. By the time symptoms appear, ailments tend to already be well underway.

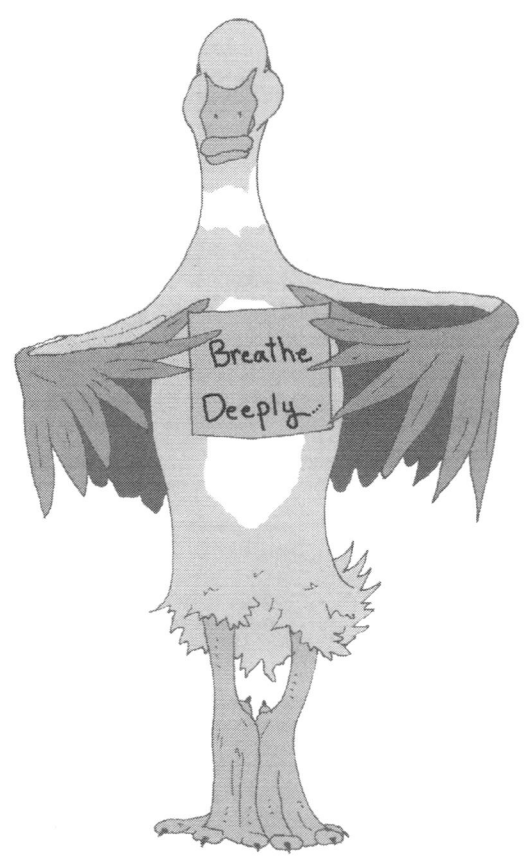

Medical #12
Digestive System

Your duck's esophagus, crop, proventriculus, gizzard, spleen, liver, intestines, pancreas, ceca (or caeca) and vent are all components of their digestive system.

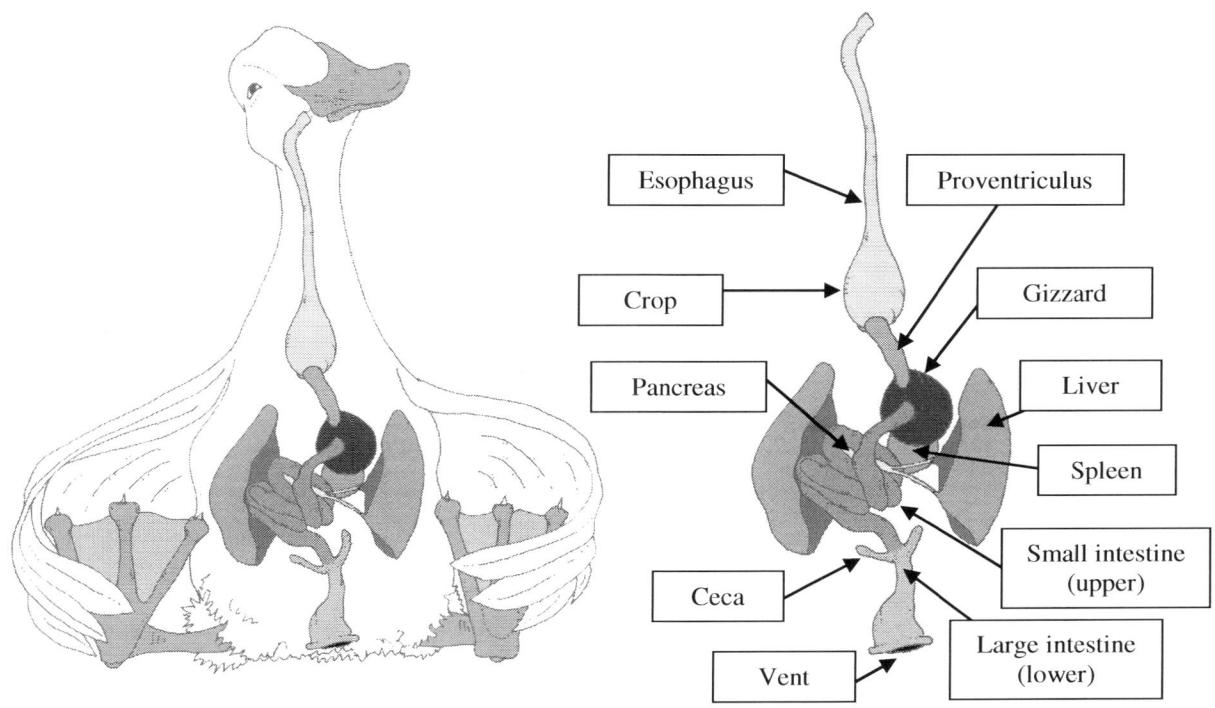

A diagram of your duck's digestive system

Malnutrition

Malnutrition doesn't simply mean your duck isn't getting enough food; it can also mean that the *quality* of the feed your serving doesn't contain the right amounts of vitamins and minerals they need to stay healthy.

- **Symptoms**

Some symptoms of malnutrition may include: excessive weight gain (although it may seem counterintuitive, ducks who are malnourished often try to eat *more* food in order to compensate for nutritional deficiency), weight loss, fatigue, poor immunity to disease or parasites, routine healthy complications, seizures (often seen first in leg tremors), angel wing and wry tail.

- **Treatment**

Immediately examine your duck's diet, ensuring that they're on a high-quality and properly-balanced brand-name feed. Make sure you're serving your duck the appropriate feed blend for their age and needs. Ask your vet or a professional at your local grain store if you need further advice. In severe cases, your vet may recommend a temporary regime of vitamin supplementation, being mindful of safe dosages.

Internal Parasites

Most Momma Ducks dread the thought of their little feathered friends carrying visitors along with them. These unwanted guests can include a wide variety of worms, protozoa, lice and mites. The good news is proper hygiene and maintenance goes a long way when it comes to protecting your ducks. This means keeping any questionable visitors out of their duck pen, which includes any human guests who may have just trekked through their poultry pen and picked up some freeloaders in the treads of their sneakers. This is when a sanitizing footbath outside your barn door is in good order.

Some symptoms that may be indicative of the presence of internal parasites include:

1. Your duck is eating normally, but unable to maintain a healthy body weight.
2. Your duck has a body so small that it's ill-proportionate to the size of their neck and head.
3. Your duck has chronic diarrhea.
4. Your duck is behaving unusually, often with a little lackluster towards normal activities.

If you're seeing any of the above symptoms you should bring a fecal sample to your vet to test for the presence of parasites. If it comes back positive you'll want to act quickly to control any further spread to other flock members and to their grounds.

- **Avoid home treatment plans**

When it comes to parasites and your duck, avoid guessing. Administering routine or precautionary worming doses is a bad idea because you can mess with their immune system. Don't assume your duck has parasites, or treat them for it if you haven't had them tested first, and *never* give your duck worming medication without vet guidance.

I've personally seen and heard a lot of conflicting information about worming ducks using over-the-counter products and most of it's absolutely *wrong*. I don't care if you're reading it in a book, exploring the topic on the internet or hearing it from an employee at your local grain store—no matter what the source, if they don't have a vet degree, assume they're off the mark and bring your beloved duck to the vet instead. *Why?*

1. Your vet will prescribe safe worming medication that addresses the particular type of parasite present in your duck.

2. Your vet will determine your duck's precise weight to ensure safe and correct dosages are administered.

3. Your vet will determine the level of infestation. This knowledge regarding your duck's parasite count will assist you in devising counter measures in regards to their pen (larger numbers require more drastic action, including multiple cleanings).

4. Water additive, over-the-counter general wormers aren't as effective as prescription wormers.

5. Many over-the-counter wormers are intended for large animals making dangerous overdoses a real risk. (There's a vast difference between the dosages for the 300 pound horse listed on the package label and your little 6 pound duck).

- **Treating the entire flock**

If any member of your flock tests positive for parasites, you'll want to treat everyone in order to fully eradicate the issue—especially those sharing the same pen. Ducks in different pens should be tested to make sure you haven't tracked any guests in on the bottom of your boots. If you have a larger flock, random testing will often give you a good picture. Try to obtain fecal samples from some of the older and more immune compromised ducks for accurate insight.

Your vet will need to know the weights of all of the ducks who'll require parasite treatment. You can usually bring them into your vet for a free weighing on their front office scale.

- **Follow-up testing**

The final step to eradicating parasites is to confirm they're really gone. When your vet is prescribing wormer medication remember to ask when you should submit another fecal sample to make sure the problem has been fully addressed. Low parasite counts are often easy to eliminate if you've cleaned up properly, but larger counts may take a few tries. In any case, if you haven't fully wiped them out, you should at least see a reduction in their numbers and this is a good step in the right direction. Keep working at it and you'll surely get there.

- **Preventing invasion**

The presence of parasites can *sometimes* be a sign that you're not keeping your duck pen as clean as you should be. If it's difficult to keep their pen clear of fecal matter you probably have too many ducks in too small of a space. Either increase their pen size or clean their enclosure, houses and barn more frequently.

A muddy, wet environment is also conducive to worms that thrive in moist habitats. For this reason you want your duck's outside pen area to drain properly after rainstorms. Clean, dry and sunny pens all help prevent the outbreak and spreading of parasites. Routinely moving water buckets and kiddy pools to new areas of the pen can also help prevent problems.

- **Earthworms acting as hosts**

Even when precautionary measures to keep pens clean and dry are taken, natural exposure is entirely possible. While earthworms sometimes carry eggs of parasitic worms, these pests are far less likely to establish themselves in a clean and dry environment. The risk of infection isn't so threatening that your ducks shouldn't be allowed to enjoy them (good luck stopping them anyway!).

If you're purchasing your night crawlers in lieu of gathering them yourself (ensuring clean collections sites), be careful to consider the source before carrying them up to the register.

Removing Parasites from Barns and Pens

While your ducks are on worming medication and shedding their parasites:

1. Remove and replace their bedding every day throughout the entire treatment period and shovel up any piles of poop you see in their pen—especially in favorite resting spots. Discard it a safe distance from their enclosure.

Once your ducks complete their treatment:

1. Immediately clean and sanitize their barn, shed and any duck houses (discarding any bedding) using a freshly mixed bleach solution comprised of 1 part bleach and 9 parts water. This should be allowed to sit for at least 10 minutes. Rinse and let the area dry thoroughly before letting your ducks back inside.

2. Drain and similarly sanitize any artificial ponds, kiddy pools, food dishes and water buckets.

3. Food grade diatomaceous earth (or "dearth") can be fed daily under vet advisement as 5% of your duck's total diet (this means *everything* they eat, not just what's in their feed dish) for 7-60 days to help eliminate the re-ingesting of hookworms, roundworms, pinworms, tapeworms and whipworms.

4. Remove any lingering parasites from the grounds of your duck enclosure. *How?*

There are three common ways to remove worms that might be lingering in the grounds of your duck pen.

1. *Dearth:* Food grade dearth can be effective at decreasing parasite populations in your duck pen. It's safe for your ducks as long you use actual *food grade* dearth. Do *not* use any other quality of dearth around your ducks, or it could be extremely harmful—even fatal.

Use a single-mesh strainer to sprinkle it over the grounds of your duck pen. Do *not* do this while your ducks are in the pen to avoid accidental inhalation. When parasites try to cross the dearth it causes them serious injury and often kills them. This method is most effective in small count parasite populations.

2. *Topsoil removal:* Once your ducks are free of worms, remove all of the infected soil to a depth of 8-12 inches. Replace this topsoil with new, uninfected soil, seeding new grass if desired. As soon as you're finished you can return your ducks back to their pen.

3. *Controlled burning:* Parasites can't withstand the intense heat of a burning fire, but you obviously have to be *extremely* careful with this one. Remove your ducks far away from their pen along with any duck houses, pools, buckets, etc. Use a hose to thoroughly soak down any areas you want to keep safe including all fencing, wooden posts, flammable fixtures, etc. Afterwards, keep this hose within easy reach and readily available at all times while you're working.

Using a propane weed burner (which provide a very controlled burn if used according to instructions) you can safely and methodically cover the grounds of your duck pen.

- **Additional cleaning tips**

1. Worms are vulnerable to sunlight and drying; use this knowledge to your advantage when fighting infestations.

2. Worms can be extremely transmittable, so be sure to clean and sanitize all tools, gear and equipment thoroughly and adhere to a strict quarantine routine (especially regarding the bottom of your boots) until the problem is thoroughly resolved. Utilizing disposable polyethylene boots with elastic cuffs that quickly pull-over the tops of your shoes or boots can be helpful in controlling their spread (supplier: FarmTek www.farmtek.com).

3. Worming medications can effectively remove parasites from your duck's body, but they don't necessarily kill them in all of their life stages. They basically enable your duck to expel them, which means there could be living parasites or eggs in your duck's fecal matter. Practice caution to avoid the re-infection of your duck or the spreading these worms to other pens or any other species of birds in or around your home.

Capillary Worms (Roundworm/Nematode)

Capillary worms are a type of hairworm (or threadworm). Eggs of capillary worms are transmitted from bird-to-bird through direct fecal ingestion or indirectly via the consumption of earthworms. Their presence in your duck is determined by a fecal exam. Humans can't become infected with these parasites.

1. *Capillaria anatis (a.k.a. C. brevicollis, C. colaris, C. anseris, C. mergi):* This species of capillary worms thrive in the ceca of your duck. The ceca are two dead-end intestinal avenues (known individually as the cecum or caecum) that extend outward from the junction between the small and large intestines.

2. *Capillaria caudinflata* and *Capillaria obsignata*: These two species of capillary worms thrive in the small intestine (and sometimes in the ceca) of your duck.

3. *Capillaria annulata* and *Capillaria contorta*: These two species of capillary worms thrive in the crop and esophagus of your duck.

- **Symptoms**

Symptoms of capillary worms are often unapparent until they've reached a level of infestation. They tend to be more noticeable in ducklings and immune compromised ducks.

Some symptoms of *C. Anatis, C. caudinflata* and *C. obsignata* may include: diarrhea, weight loss, fatigue and reduced egg production.

Some symptoms of *C. Annulata* and *C. contorta* may include: weight loss, fatigue, chronic coughing and in severe cases, pneumonia.

- **Treatment**

Your vet will most likely prescribe Panacur® *(fenbendazole)* to treat your duck for capillary worms (although some may prescribe Levasole® *levamisole*).

Common Panacur® treatment regime:

1. A single dose of Panacur® is administered orally.

2. This is followed by a 2 week waiting period during which time no treatment is administered.

3. Following the 2 week waiting period, another single and final dose of Panacur® is administered.

4. Thirty days after this second treatment, a follow-up fecal test should be done to ensure the parasites have been successfully eradicated.

5. If follow-up fecal testing reveals that parasites are still present, your vet may opt to administer a single dose of injectable Ivermectin. This should resolve the issue for good.

Liquid Panacur® is ideal for measuring out such small, duck-sized dosages, but if your vet doesn't have access to it, or if you're uncomfortable giving medicine via oral syringe, you can also get Panacur® granules. If your duck is a good eater at meal times, you can simply dampen their duck feed a little bit and then sprinkle the medicine over the top. If you have a fussier eater, you can sprinkle it over the top of a few pieces of watermelon in a bowl (or whatever other snack your duck will consume in its entirety).

Cecal Worms (Roundworm/Nematode)

Heterakis spp are intestinal or cecal worms. Cecal worms thrive inside the ceca of your duck and their eggs are transmitted from bird-to-bird through direct fecal ingestion or indirectly via the consumption of earthworms. Their presence in your duck is determined by a fecal exam. Humans can't become infected with these parasites.

- **Symptoms**

Some symptoms of cecal worms may include fatigue and reduced egg production. Although usually harmless, large numbers of these worms can cause the thickening of the cecal walls, which can eventually lead to hemorrhaging and death.

Rarely, a duck can become infected by a protozoan carried by cecal worms, which can cause serious damage to their liver and ceca. This is called Blackhead Disease or *Histomoniasis*. Symptoms include: decreased appetite, fatigue, yellow droppings as well as avoidance of other ducks and normal routines. This condition is very uncommon in ducks (who tend to be immune to it), but it's deadly without treatment.

- **Treatment**

While some vets will utilize Panacur® to treat cecal worms, many will opt to prescribe Strongid-T® *(pyrantel pamoate)* instead.

Common Strongid-T® treatment regime:

1. Administer a single dose of Strongid-T®.

2. This is followed by a 2 week waiting period during which time no treatment is administered.

3. Following the 2 week waiting period, one single and final dose of Strongid-T® is administered.

4. Thirty days after this second treatment, a follow-up fecal test should be done to ensure the parasites have been successfully eradicated.

Strongyloides (Roundworm/Nematode)

Oesophagostomum avium are a type of threadworm that thrive in your duck's ceca. Their eggs are transmitted from bird-to-bird through direct fecal ingestion. Their presence in your duck is determined by a fecal exam. Humans can't become infected with these parasites.

- **Symptoms**

Some symptoms of strongyloides may include: weight loss, fatigue and diarrhea.

- **Treatment**

Either Panacur® or Strongid-T® may be prescribed to treat strongyloides. A second fecal sample should be submitted 3-4 weeks after treatment to ensure they've been thoroughly eradicated.

Ascaris (Roundworm/Nematode)

Ascaridia spp are a type of roundworm that thrive inside your duck's small intestine. Eggs of these intestinal worms are transmitted from bird-to-bird through direct fecal ingestion or indirectly via the consumption of earthworms. Their presence in your duck is determined by a fecal exam. Humans can't become infected with these parasites.

- **Symptoms**

Some symptoms of ascaris may include: fatigue, diarrhea and emaciation.

- **Treatment**

Panacur® is often prescribed as treatment. A second fecal sample should be submitted ten weeks after treatment to ensure they've been thoroughly eradicated.

Subulura (Roundworm/Nematode)

Subulura spp are a type of roundworm. Some species thrive inside your duck's small intestine while others flourish in their ceca. Eggs of these intestinal worms are transmitted from bird-to-bird through direct fecal ingestion or indirectly via the consumption of beetles and cockroaches. Their presence in your duck is determined by a fecal exam. Humans can't become infected with these parasites.

- **Symptoms**

Some symptoms of Subulura may include: decreased egg production.

- **Treatment**

Panacur® is often prescribed as treatment. A second fecal sample should be submitted ten weeks after treatment to ensure they've been thoroughly eradicated.

Tetrameres (Roundworm/Nematode)

Terameres spp are a type of roundworm that thrive inside your duck's esophagus. Eggs of these intestinal worms are transmitted from bird-to-bird through direct fecal ingestion or indirectly via the consumption of beetles and cockroaches. Their presence in your duck is determined by a fecal exam. Humans can't become infected with these parasites.

- **Symptoms**

Some symptoms of tetrameres may include: vomiting, green-colored feces and weight loss.

- **Treatment**

Panacur® is often prescribed as treatment. A second fecal sample should be submitted eight weeks after treatment to ensure they've been thoroughly eradicated.

Gizzard Worms (Roundworm/Nematode)

Amidostomum anseris and *Acuaria spp* are gizzard worms and as their name implies, they thrive inside the gizzard of your duck. They're more common in geese than in ducks, so if you have a mixed flock, your ducks may be more prone to this parasite. They're also more common in malnourished flocks confined to unclean pens. The presence of this parasite can lead to decreased immunity in your ducks as well as death depending on the level of infestation. Eggs of gizzard worms are transmitted from bird-to-bird through direct fecal ingestion or indirectly via the consumption of earthworms. Their presence in your duck is determined by a fecal exam. Humans can't become infected with these parasites.

- **Symptoms**

Some symptoms of gizzard worms may include: fatigue, loss of appetite and emaciation.

- **Treatment**

Panacur® is often prescribed as treatment. A second fecal sample should be submitted thirty days after treatment to ensure they've been thoroughly eradicated.

Gape Worms (Roundworm/Nematode)

Syngamus trachea) is a type of roundworm known as gape worm and they thrive inside your duck's trachea. Eggs of gape worms are transmitted from bird-to-bird through direct fecal ingestion or indirectly via the consumption of earthworms, snails, slugs and insects. Your vet will often confirm their presence by looking down your duck's throat, where they can usually be seen. They can also verify their presence by fecal exam. Humans can't become infected with these parasites.

- **Symptoms**

Some symptoms of gape worms may include: gasping, choking, shaking of the head like they're trying to get something out of their throat, appetite loss and emaciation. Left untreated they can result in suffocation.

- **Treatment**

While some vets will utilize Pancur® to treat gape worms, many will opt to prescribe Ivermectin instead.

Common Ivermectin treatment regime:

1. Administer a single dose of Ivermectin.
2. This is followed by a 2 week waiting period during which time no treatment is administered.
3. Following the 2 week waiting period, one single and final dose of Ivermectin is administered.
4. Thirty days after this second treatment, a follow-up fecal test should be done to ensure the parasites have been successfully eradicated.

Eyeworms (Roundworm/Nematode)

Oxyspirura spp are a type of roundworm known as eyeworms. They're very rare, but when present they thrive in the membranes, ducts and sacs that surround your duck's eyes. Eggs of eyeworms are transmitted from bird-to-bird through direct fecal ingestion or indirectly via the consumption of cockroaches. Your vet will often confirm their presence by performing an eye exam. They can also confirm their presence by fecal exam. Humans can't become infected with these parasites.

- **Symptoms**

Some symptoms of eyeworms may include: swollen, itchy, sticky or watery eyes, feather loss around the eyes (from continual scratching), restlessness, conjunctivitis and even blindness.

- **Treatment**

Vets commonly prescribe a one-time treatment of Ivermectin® eye-drop solution, which they'll prepare and administer for you. In addition to a follow-up eye exam, a second fecal sample should be submitted five weeks after treatment to ensure they've been thoroughly eradicated.

Fluke Worms (Flatworm/Trematode)

Cyathocotyle bushiensis, *Sphaeridiotrema globulus* and *Sphaeridiotrema pseudoglobulus* are all types of intestinal fluke worms that thrive inside your duck's lower intestine and ceca. Even mild Fluke infestations can lead to cecal ulcers, hemorrhaging and death. They're usually found in wild waterfowl (including Muscovy ducks) or in domestic ducks who have access to natural lakes or ponds. Ducks become infected with these flatworms after consuming infected freshwater snails or dragonflies. The presence of these fluke worms can be confirmed by fecal exam.

Prosthogonimus spp are fluke worms that thrive in your duck's oviduct. The presence of these fluke worms can be confirmed by fecal exam or by a cloacal swab and culture. Humans can't become infected with any of these species of parasites.

- **Symptoms**

Some symptoms of all of these fluke worms may include: loss of appetite, weight loss, fatigue, fever, diarrhea and dehydration.

Some symptoms of oviduct fluke worms may also include: green discharge that stains the vent feathers, a decrease in egg production, soft-shelled eggs, peritonitis, abdominal tension and the appearance of worms in an infected duck's eggs.

- **Treatment**

Fluke tend to die off in 2-4 months, but you should still treat your duck because they can do plenty of damage in the meantime. Drontal Plus® *(praziquantel)* is commonly prescribed.

Common Drontal Plus® treatment regime:

1. Administer a single dose of Drontal Plus®.

2. This is followed by a 2 week waiting period during which time no treatment is administered.

3. Following the 2 week waiting period, one single and final dose of Drontal Plus® is administered.

4. Thirty days after this second treatment, a follow-up fecal test should be done to ensure the parasites have been successfully eradicated. In the meantime, prevent your duck from accessing infected ponds or lakes.

Tapeworms (Flatworm/Cestodes)

Amoebotaenia cuneata (a.k.a. A. sphenoides), Choanotaenia infundibulum, Davainea proglottina, Raillietina spp are all very uncommon in ducks, but when they do occur they thrive inside your duck's small intestine. Eggs of these flat tapeworms are transmitted from bird-to-bird through direct fecal ingestion or indirectly via the consumption of earthworms, bugs, flies, slugs, ants or beetles. The presence of tapeworms can be confirmed by fecal exam. Humans can't become infected with these species of parasites.

- **Symptoms**

Some symptoms of tapeworms may include: loss of appetite, weight loss, fatigue, seizures, decreased egg production and diarrhea.

- **Treatment**

Drontal Plus® is commonly prescribed as treatment. A second fecal sample should be submitted four weeks after treatment to ensure they have been thoroughly eradicated.

Trichomonas

Trichomonas gallinae are one-celled protozoa that can infect the back of the throat and crop of your duck. Ducks become infected after drinking water that's contaminated with saliva or droppings from an infected host bird (especially pigeons or raptors who consume pigeons) or via direct transmission from bird-to-bird through fecal ingestion. They usually infect younger or immune compromised ducks, causing inflammation and ulceration of the esophagus. The presence of trichomonas protozoa can be confirmed by fecal exam or by swabbing the mouth or crop for culturing. Humans can't become infected with this species of protozoa.

- **Symptoms**

Some symptoms of trichomonas, if noticeable at all, may include: diarrhea, fatigue, loss of balance and excessive gulping or swallowing motions, especially while eating. It can also cause inflammation and distension of the crop as well as rotten breath. If left untreated they can spread and result in liver abscesses.

- **Treatment**

Flagyl® *(metronidazole)* is commonly prescribed to treat trichomonas.

Common Flagyl® treatment regime:

1. Administer Flagyl® every day for 5-7 days.

2. Thirty days after this second treatment, a follow-up fecal test should be done to ensure the parasites have been successfully eradicated.

Coccidia

Eimeria spp. is a one-celled protozoa referred to as coccidia. They infect the cells that line your duck's intestines. They're found in ponds, streams, lakes and other natural bodies of water all over the world. They're deposited in the feces of wild ducks and geese and since waterfowl love to dabble in water, they can easily ingest these parasites. The smaller the water source and the more wild waterfowl visiting it (and pooping in it), the higher the risk of a coccidia infection. Once your flock is infected, they can continue to spread it through direct fecal ingestion. The presence of coccidia protozoan can be confirmed by fecal exam, but you have to specifically request it (because it's not always tested as part of the normal testing package). Humans can't become infected with this species of protozoa.

Vets who are inexperienced with waterfowl will sometimes falsely assume that fowl coccidia is similar to canine coccidia and a product of filthy living conditions (that result in unavoidable fecal ingestion). If your vet jumps to the conclusion that your perfectly tended, clean and tidy duck is being kept in similar adverse living conditions you'll now understand upfront where they're coming from.

It's part of a duck's natural tendency to dabble in puddles. All it takes is a little rain to fall upon grounds frequented by wild waterfowl and you quickly have puddles that embody infected fecal matter. Even the cleanest of ducks can't resist a good puddle and may become incidentally infected, which is why it's a good idea to do periodic fecal exams if your ducks are at risk of exposure.

- **Symptoms**

Some symptoms of coccidian may include: diarrhea (sometimes with blood), loss of appetite, weight loss and fatigue.

- **Treatment**

    Albon® *(sulfadimethoxine)* is commonly prescribed for individual cases while Amprolium soluble powder is mixed into drinking water when multiple ducks need to be treated.

Common Albon® treatment regime:

1. Administer Albon® twice daily for 5 days. If you need to treat a large flock it can be added to their only source of drinking water for 6 days (this works best if you keep them away from all other water sources until the treatment period has ended).

2. Thirty days after this second treatment, a follow-up fecal test should be done to ensure the parasites have been successfully eradicated.

Oversized Pebble Consumption

Your duck's digestive system doesn't work the same way ours does because ducks don't have teeth (an evolutionary development to reduce excess weight, which is necessary for flight). Instead, they swallow small pebbles, which temporarily lodge in their gizzard (stomach muscle) and do their grinding for them as food passes through. These tiny stones normally measure less than a ¼ inch, but occasionally ducks will pick up larger pebbles and attempt to swallow them—sometimes successfully. If your duck is exhibiting this behavior, it can be indicative of digestive issues, which they're attempting to self-correct.

- **Symptoms**

Some symptoms of oversized pebble consumption include: Ducks who pick up pebbles with diameters of over ½ inch or more with the intention of eating them. They'll often roll them around inside their bills, trying to set them up to go down their throat.

- **Treatment**

Give your duck a bowl of grit, which you can purchase from your local grain store. Given access to a healthy alternative, many ducks will pass on the larger pebbles. If they do continue to hunt down oversized stones, however, bring them to the vet for an immediate check-up.

Lost Voice

Your duck's trachea branches apart into two bronchi just above their lungs. Immediately over this fork is their syrinx, which enables them to make their celebrated vocalizations.

A lost voice can be caused by:

1. *Ingestion:* Ducks will sometimes swallow a nut or pebble that's a little too big for their own good, or a scratchy bit of stick, which can cause a throat injury. The ingestion of these or other objects can sometimes result in temporary, or even permanent vocal impairment (especially if it's still lodged there).

2. *Infection:* Respiratory illnesses or infections can sometimes result in a lost voice, which is usually temporary.

3. *Intubation:* Surgical intubation can lead to throat irritation. It's not unheard of for a duck to come out of anesthesia without a voice, which is nearly always temporary.

4. *Injury:* A duck who catches their neck in the weave of fencing wire or survives a predatory attack focused on their throat will sometimes sustain vocal damage, which can be temporary or permanent depending on severity.

Can you hear me now?!

Mercy's Hunger Pains...

Case # 122: Refusal to Eat

Most newcomers are starving when they arrive at our sanctuary and will gorge down food the second they see it. Mercy was different. Whoever abandoned her obviously fed her table scraps because she turned her bill up at everything else. Stubborn newcomers often give up to their hunger and delve into their healthy waterfowl food by their second day, but not Mercy. She wouldn't have it.

Most ducks mimic the behavior of other flock members, so our first strategy was to put her where she could see other ducks eating their food. No luck. But... I did notice that she was a very active forager, hunting for goodies around her pen, which is surely what kept her alive during her period of abandonment. With this in mind, I began offering her some wild berries, grass, insects and worms—things she recognized as food, to keep her going until she took to her new food. The trick was to offer her enough natural goodies to sustain her, but not so much as to remedy her appetite and dissuade her from tasting her bagged feed. When this strategy proved ineffective against her willpower, I came up with a new plan.

I ground up her Mazuri® feed in a food processor and then poured it into her bowl. When teaching your duck to eat it's important to train them using their regular food bowl, so that as you change out their diet, the bowl will still remain familiar to them. I added enough water to the ground feed to turn it into a thick soup and then gently stirred in a handful of nightcrawlers while Mercy watched—YUM! She could barely contain herself and quickly delved into the fabulous soup, unintentionally eating the ground feed along with the worms. This accustomed her to the flavor of her new food. Over the next two days I repeated the same procedure only I didn't grind the Mazuri® quite as finely and I reduced the amount of water I put into the mix, making it a little thicker. I also stirred in more worms to really encourage her to go at it, indiscriminately gulping down worms and food alike. By the 4th day, I was able to present her with a regular bowl of feed mixed with just enough water to make it a soup, without any worms in it. She searched frantically for a moment and even gobbled down a few incidental pellets before realizing it wasn't so bad after all. Moments later she dug into her new food with a passion and the rest was history.

- **Symptoms**

Some symptoms of a lost voice may include: your duck opens their bill to quack, but no sound comes out, unusual vocalizations (squeaks) and hoarseness.

- **Treatment**

Bring your duck to the vet for antibiotic medication to address any current infection or risk of infection resulting from tracheal injury. Anti-inflammatory/pain medication is also prescribed to reduce and swelling and help provide comfort. If your duck just had surgery, they're likely already on both of these medications, in which case, just be sure to let your vet know what's going on, so they can follow-up properly at future check-ups.

In most cases of a lost voice, your duck's quack will begin to return within 2 weeks, provided they're promptly seen and treated by a vet.

Remember: You know your duck's environment better than anyone. Take a moment and consider if there's any chance they may have swallowed an unsafe object (screw, coin, nail, paperclip, etc.). If so, they should have an immediate x-ray done to make sure it isn't lodged anywhere inside of them, which might lead to further and more serious issues (see: *"Hardware disease"* and *"Zinc Poisoning"*).

If your duck's not attempting to quack at all (and this is unusual for them), take them to the vet right away. The absence of a quack can be very severe. Their silence could be a sign that their health is deteriorating rapidly; in which case, x-rays, blood work, antibiotics and/or other tests and treatments may be required.

Eggshell Craving

Whenever your duck is craving anything unusual it should be examined more closely because dietary deficiencies are often at the heart of the matter. Female ducks who lay eggs are usually the ones who'll crave eggshells because they're a good source of calcium. Once your duck learns to eat eggshells, it can be a difficult (and messy) habit to break.

- **Symptoms**

Some symptoms of eggshell-craving may include: eating their own or other duck's eggs, especially soft or thin-shelled eggs (which are easier for them to break).

- **Treatment**

1. Immediately examine your duck's diet, ensuring that they're on a high-quality and properly-balanced brand-name feed formula that's an appropriate blend for their age and needs.

2. If they're not already on a 100% ration of layer/breeder formula, you may want to do so right away.

3. Be sure female ducks have an added source of calcium (oyster shells or calcium chips) available in its own separate bowl 24/7.

If you've already done each of these things, you may want to visit your vet and have your duck's blood calcium level checked, especially if she's laying soft-shelled eggs. If it's low, a calcium additive may be in order (see: *"Preventative Egg Binding Treatment Options/Calcium Gluconate"*).

Feather Craving

Feather craving is another symptom of nutritional deficiency; it can be a sign that something important is missing from your duck's diet.

- **Symptoms**

Some symptoms of feather craving may include: the frequent consumption of shed feathers.

- **Treatment**

Immediately examine your duck's diet, ensuring that they're on a high-quality and properly-balanced brand-name feed formula that's an appropriate blend for their age and needs. Mixing crimped oats in with their regular feed can also help. If the behavior continues take your duck to the vet for a check-up and review multivitamin additive options.

Feather Biting

Sometimes ducks will obsessively nibble and bite at feathers in a particular area of their body. They don't actually ingest any of these feathers, but they do tend to damage and even break them. This behavior has nothing to do with malnutrition and everything to do with localized pain or discomfort.

- **Symptoms**

Some symptoms of feather biting may include: patches of pin-feathered skin on your duck's body, localized areas of broken feathers and preening efforts that focus too intensely on specific body parts.

- **Treatment**

In order to effectively treat your duck you'll need to find out what's causing their discomfort. Your duck is already pointing the way and showing your vet exactly where it hurts. Some possibilities may include: parasites, arthritis, muscle sprain, broken bone, localized infection or irritation. A comprehensive avian blood panel, x-ray or swab culturing (when applicable) can usually offer further insight. When the source remains undetermined, your vet will likely prescribe antibiotics and anti-inflammatory/pain medication for 7-14 days to see if your duck's situation improves any.

Appetite Changes

Appetite changes can be indicative of a wide variety of ailments and should be monitored closely. While drastic differences are more readily apparent (and are often a late-stage symptom), gradual differences are just as important—even more so, because early detection can equate to a rapid response time and proactive treatment.

There are times when appetite fluxes are completely typical. The best way to recognize these is to pay attention to your duck and learn their own personal habits. Once you know their regular patterns, you'll be able to discern normal behavior from abnormal behavior.

Common times when appetites tend to flux include:

1. When ducks are molting, their appetites often decrease as their pinfeathers evolve (which can be uncomfortable and often negatively impacts their appetite). This is usually followed by a period of appetite increase as their feathers emerge. When all is said and done and their molt is complete, their appetite should return back to normal again.

2. Ducks often eat substantially less in the heat of summer.

3. Ducks tend to eat more near the end of fall as they prepare themselves for winter, putting on a nice layer of fat. They often continue to consume large amounts of food through winter in order to maintain this insulating weight.

4. In the spring ducks tend to eat less as their appetites wane off; this helps them shed their unneeded winter weight in preparation for warmer weather.

5. Ducks may experience appetite increases when they're laying eggs and require a higher intake of calories.

- **Symptoms**

Some symptoms of appetite changes may include: mild or sharp increases or decreases in food consumption.

- **Treatment**

If your duck is exhibiting an unseasonable or unusual interest or disinterest in their food, it definitely merits you taking a closer look. In these situations it's best to feed your ducks separately, so you can measure exactly how much food you put in their dish and how much they're actually consuming. This can give you more quantifiable information for your vet.

Vets commonly begin with a general exam, looking into their throat and taking their temperature. This is usually followed by sending a fecal sample off to a lab to rule out parasites, which can affect your duck's appetite either way. Just to be careful, most vets will also start your duck on a round of antibiotics for 7-14 days to address any infectious sources (which you can stop 24 hours later if your duck ends up testing positive for parasites, substituting the required treatment instead).

Blood work, x-rays and swab or fecal culturing can be enlisted if you still don't have answers and your duck continues to behave abnormally or decline.

Medication & Appetite Loss

Some medications can result in a loss of appetite. If you notice that your duck's eating habits have changed since taking their medication, be sure to alert your vet and then try a few counter measures.

- **Make food available 24/7**

If your duck is experiencing a loss of appetite, make sure they have food available to them 24/7, so they can eat at any point during the day that they're feeling up to it.

- **Adjusting the dosage**

While your vet may tell you to give your duck medication twice a day, some medications remain effective in higher doses given once a day (rather than 12 mg twice a day, they can get 24 mg once a day). Whether or not this can be done depends on the half-life of the particular medication in question and the likelihood of increased risks or side effects associated with a higher dose. Your vet will know whether it's safe to proceed or not. Once you have their approval you can give your duck their medication once a day instead of twice, which gives them a longer recovery time in between administration, which can really help their appetite.

If your duck still isn't thriving, your vet may want to reduce the dosage or switch medications entirely, so be sure to keep them in the loop.

- **Dosing at bedtime**

It can be advantageous to give your duck their medicine at night, right before they go to sleep, so that they have their full appetite back by morning and continue to eat and graze normally throughout the entire day.

- **Measuring food consumption**

If your duck is losing weight in response to medication, try to measure how much they're actually eating. Institute meal times and afford them separate quarters while they're eating, so you can accurately measure their food consumption.

Post-Surgical Appetite Loss (Intubation Irritation)

Sometimes an intubation tube can cost post-surgical swelling, irritation and localized pain in your duck's throat, which may prevent them from wanting to eat. This appetite loss can last up to two weeks.

- **Symptoms**

Some symptoms of intubation irritation may include: loss of appetite following surgery (often complete) and hoarseness.

- **Treatment**

Be sure to let your vet know that your duck isn't eating right away. Their post surgical care probably already includes antibiotics and anti-inflammatory/pain medication, but your vet may want to prescribe additional pain medication as well.

Bacterial Infection & Appetite Loss

Unexplained appetite loss and stomach pain can be indicative of a bacterial infection of the digestive system, especially in older or immune compromised ducks who can succumb more easily.

- **Symptoms**

Some symptoms of bacterial infection of the digestive system may include: disinterest in normal activities, seclusion from flock mates, remaining in the same place for long periods of time, fatigue, nausea, vomiting, loss of appetite (often complete, including resisting favorite treats), weight loss, diarrhea, stomach pain (often preferring to stand up rather than lay down on their belly) and sometimes even phallus prolapse in males.

Bacteria are sometimes large enough to be seen in your duck's fecal matter, especially in severe cases. It often resembles tiny, spiraling noodles (which can look like some kind of parasitic worm to the untrained eye). If you see this, collect a sample and bring it to your vet.

- **Treatment**

If symptoms are relatively mild, vets will normally prescribe a general antibiotic for the first 7-14 days. If you don't see any improvement with in the first 7 days, or if your duck's condition worsens, you could be looking at a resistant strain of bacteria.

If symptoms are more severe, if you find evidence of bacterial growth in your duck's fecal matter, or if your duck isn't responding to antibiotic treatment within 7 days, bring a fecal sample to your vet right away and ask them to do a culture (or your vet can do a cloacal swab if you prefer). It's important to do this early-on because it can take 7-10 days for the culture to grow and reveal the culprit; in the meantime your vet will probably try switching your duck to a different antibiotic. Many vets will begin with **SMZ/TMP** (sulfamethoxazole trimethoprim) oral suspension while also recommending a comprehensive avian blood panel as well, which can reveal further insight.

Any time your duck is on medication or experiencing unusual symptoms it's a good idea to include probiotics as part of their treatment plan; this is especially true of digestive issues involving harmful bacteria. Increasing the number of supportive bacteria in your duck's intestines can really help them in the battle (see: *"Probiotics"*).

Once the culture results are in, your vet will prescribe the appropriate medication to address the sensitivity of the specific bacterial strain found present.

Remember to be careful not to spread harmful bacteria to other flock members. Wash your hands thoroughly and avoid tracking it from pen to pen on the bottom of your shoes.

Syringe Feeding

Ducks sometimes need long-term assistance with feedings, while other times they just need someone to jumpstart their digestive system, coaxing them to eat again.

Until you can get to your vet for quality nutritional supplies, you can grind your duck's food into a powder using a small food processor. Just before you're ready to begin feeding your duck, add enough water to draw the food up into an oral syringe. The trouble with this procedure is that ground feed tends to thicken quickly as it soaks up water, clogging your syringe and making things difficult (which is why this is only a temporarily solution, holding you over just until you can get more syringe-compatible ingredients). Be sure to have extra water handy, so you can keep loosening the consistency of the mix.

- **Recipe**

The following ingredients maximize your duck's calorie and nutritional intake:

1. ½ can of Iams® Maximum-Calorie canned cat/dog food (purchased at your vet office).

2. 3 tablespoons of Oxbow Critical Care™ Herbivore Recovery Food (purchased at your vet office).

3. 1 teaspoon Avi-Culture® probiotic powder (rotate with Rezealiant Living Feast powder).

4. Slowly stir in a few tablespoons of Ensure® Plus (strawberry or vanilla, *not* chocolate) until proper consistency is achieved for syringe feeding.

5. In the case of diarrhea, you can also add 1-2 tablespoons of organic applesauce baby food.

- **Amounts**

Most ducks need to consume between 10-12% of their body weight every day (on the higher side for egg-laying ducks). The average duck (weighing approximately 5-7 lbs) needs between 60-90 ml of the above food recipe a day. *Never* go over 90 ml in 24 hours. You can administer up to 30 ml per feeding, 3 times a day, or if your duck is uncomfortable with this amount (they'll tell you when they've had enough) you can offer them smaller meals more frequently throughout the day. Most ducks will accept between 10-25 ml per feeding (based on their size) before putting up a *real* fuss about it, which is when you should stop to prevent regurgitation.

I find that most of my medium-to-large-sized ducks will tolerate about 21-24 ml per feeding before insisting that I give them a break. Listen to your duck. There's a recognizable difference between normal fussing and increased struggling, which suggests that they're full. Always err on the side of caution until you better understand your duck's digestive limitations.

As an example, I use a 3 ml oral syringe, and refill it 7 times (for a total of 21 ml) every four hours (6:00 a.m., 10:00 a.m., 2:00 p.m., 6:00 p.m.) to help keep a medium-to-large duck's energy level up. Then I give them a break and let them rest undisturbed overnight before beginning again the following morning. I always have a bowl of food and water available to them 24/7, so they can begin eating on their own whenever they want to.

- **Instructions**

In some ways, syringe feeding is very similar to giving your duck a pill (see: *"How to Give Your Duck a Pill"*).

1. Open your duck's bill.
2. Place the tip of the oral syringe just over and past their tongue—*never* down into their throat.
3. Push the food out of the syringe.
4. Wipe any excess food away from your duck's bill and off the outside of the syringe using a small facecloth.
5. Refill the syringe and repeat, giving your duck breaks in between as needed.

Once you get the hang of it, syringe feeding is pretty quick and only mildly invasive, which means even a squeamish Momma Duck can pull it off. While aspiration of food is uncommon (and often indicative of a mix that's a little too watery), it can occur and should be attentively treated (see: *"Aspiration Pneumonia"*).

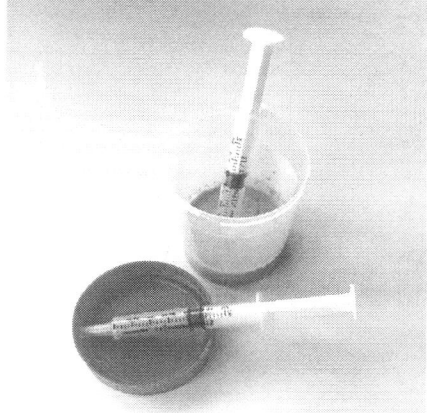

Prepared mixture

This feed blend can be stored in your refrigerator in a sealed container for up to 24 hours before discarding. To protect the integrity of the vitamins & supplements in the mixture, do *not* use your microwave to reheat it; instead, warm the food before each feeding by setting the covered container into a bowl of hot water for a few minutes. Stir the mixture to help ensure it has an even temperature throughout and then test it to make sure it's not too hot.

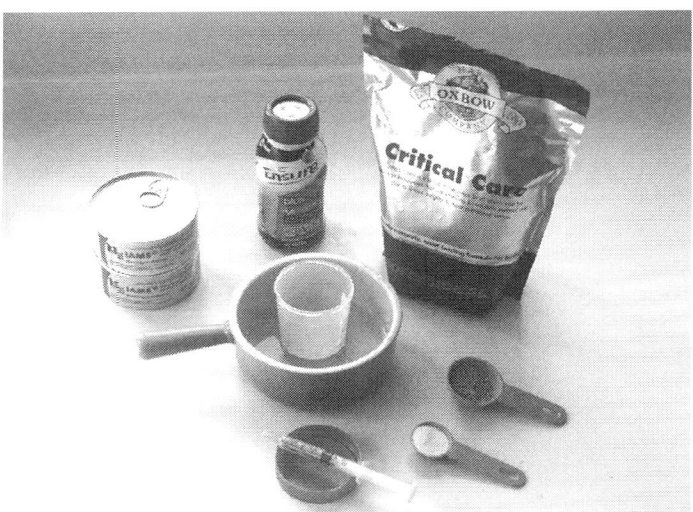

Warm the refrigerated mixture in a bowl of heated water prior to feeding

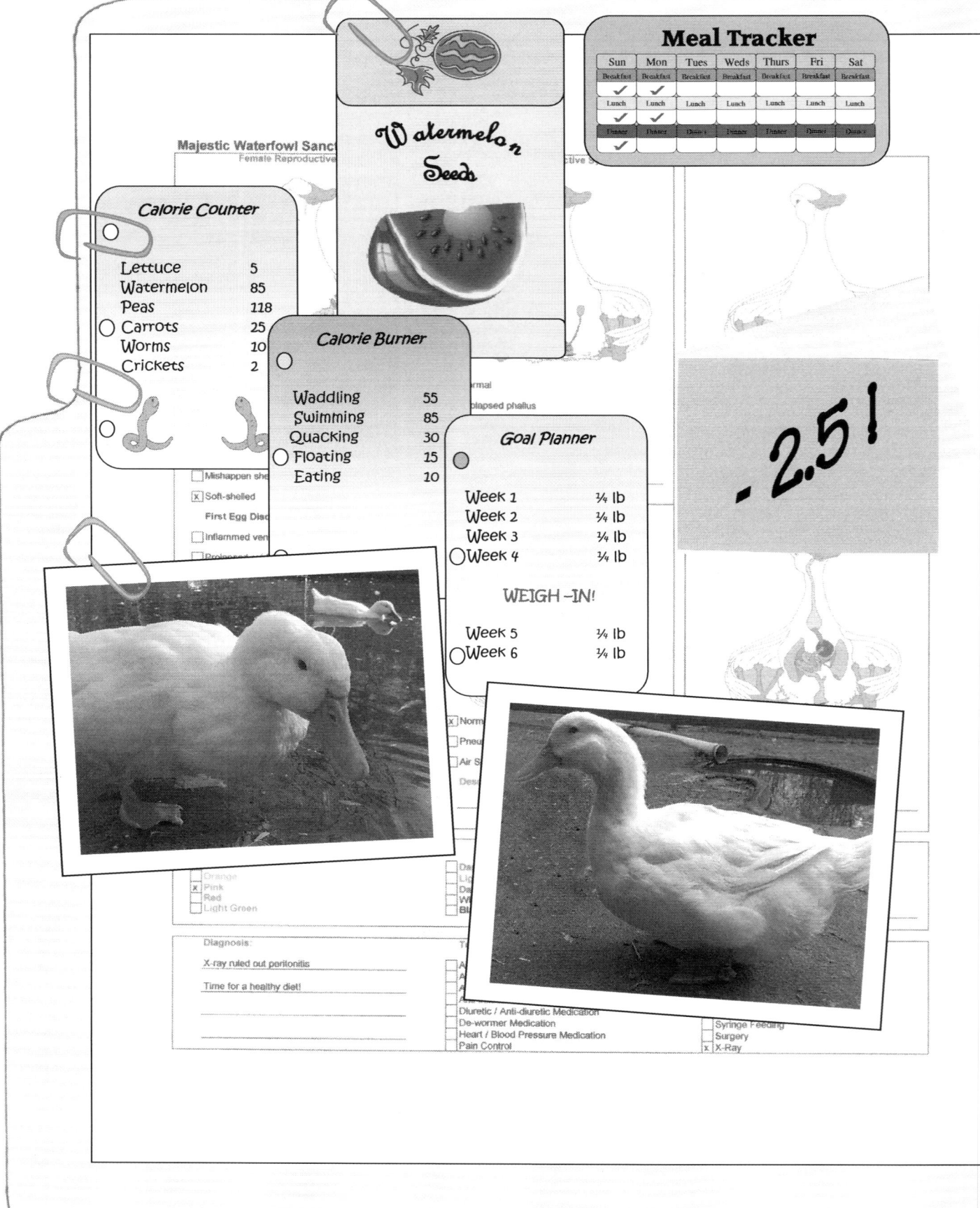

Have Mercy...

When Mercy first arrived at our sanctuary she refused to eat anything, but a year later you'd never know she was once starving! She had clearly been abusing the free-choice meal system.

Some ducks will gain weight due to hidden tumors, fluid retention or other health problems. Being a notorious soft egg-layer, I wanted to make sure Mercy wasn't suffering from any internal egg-laying issues (peritonitis) before we began. Once given the all-clear, it was time for my 9.9 pound Mercy-Lulu to lose a vet-advised 2.5 pounds. This would help prevent future health complications, which might include: joint issues, diabetes or renal disease.

When fed exclusively, Mazuri® recommends feeding 25-30 grams of their feed for each kilogram your duck weighs. Mercy's starting weight was approximately 4.5 kg, which amounts to a daily recommended intake of 112.5 grams of feed (approximately 1/2 cup). While 1/2 cup of feed may be enough to meet Mercy's nutritional needs, I didn't want to shock her system too drastically, or have her feel completely miserable, so I opted to offer her 1/2 cup of feed three times a day instead, working well above recommended minimums. If she hit a plateau I could always reduce her servings to 1/3 cup of food three times a day until she lost her ideal, vet-recommended weight.

Although her main meals were served on a timed basis, I also introduced a bottomless bowl of freshly chopped and shredded vegetables that included goodies like leaf lettuce, carrots, peas and tomatoes. This dish was monitored carefully and kept full and fresh through all hours of the day, so she wouldn't feel the need to gorge at mealtimes.

As an additional tactic, I moved Mercy and her boyfriend Piper to a different pen that promoted further activity due to its proximity with interesting neighbors and the opportunity to exercise on a larger pond.

Mercy lost her first pound after one month of dieting at which point she could once again greet me with little hops of excitement!

Case # 123: Overweight

Tube feeding

While the same feed mixture and dosages are often utilized, tube feeding is a little more invasive than syringe feeding, which is why most Momma Ducks prefer not to do it if they don't have to (including me!). Still it has its benefits:
1. Most medium-to-large ducks will get three 30 ml meals 2-3 times a day, making it more convenient.
2. Tube feeding isn't as messy because you're pushing all the food down into the tube at once using one large syringe, rather than stopping to repeatedly refill a small syringe.
3. If done *correctly,* the risk of aspirating food is completely eliminated.

The downside of tube feeding is it can result in throat irritation if it's done incorrectly. If you decide to go this route, your vet will need to give you the proper supplies and then teach you how to slide the tube properly down your duck's esophagus.

Dietary Aids

There are additional ways you can help support a sick duck during their recovery; just be sure to check with your vet *first* because not all therapies are ideal in every situation.

- **Energy water**

Substituting electrolyte water (Sav-A-Chick® Electrolyte packets) with your duck's regular drinking water can give them a little extra boost. If your duck *is* eating well and in good health, avoid using these types of products, which can cause nutritional imbalances.

- **Healx® Booster**

Some vets will advise you to give Healx® Booster to your duck when they're sick, weak or immune compromised. Healx® is a liquid suspension comprised mainly of organic red palm fruit, which can be administered via oral syringe and has active antimicrobial properties. You prepare it similarly to baby food, warming it in water before giving it to your duck. Be sure to get proper dosages from your vet.

- **Vibrant Health® Rainbow Vibrance**

Vibrant Health ® Rainbow Vibrance is a nutritional powdered supplement intended for humans that can be added to your duck's special diet during periods of syringe or tube feeding. Have your vet inspect the label, so they can determine proper dosages for your duck.

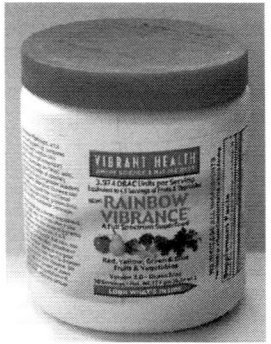

Probiotics

Probiotics contain helpful digestive bacteria, which you can give to your duck whenever they need a little digestive support. Probiotics are an excellent way to boost and protect intestinal flora when:

1. Your duck is on medication.
2. Your duck is experiencing appetite loss or other unusual symptoms.
3. Your duck is sick or fighting an infection.
4. Your duck is recovering from surgery.
5. Your duck's immunity to disease has temporarily or permanently dropped.
6. Your duck is showing signs of their age.
7. Your duck is stressed.
8. Your duck is molting.
9. Your duck has been exposed to parasites or disease.

My favorite brands are:

1. **Avi-Culture:** (supplier: National Bird Designs www.nationalbirddesigns.com/shop.html). Probiotics store indefinitely in your freezer, so it's best to purchase them *before* you actually need them; this way, you'll always have them on hand.

2. **Rezealiant Living Feast:** (supplier: MannaLife International www.mymannalife.com). This is a powerful, nutrient-dense nutritional product. Each serving contains naturally occurring vitamins, minerals, antioxidant compounds, amino acids, enzymes, essential fatty acids, fiber, probiotics and phytonnutrients. It's actually a human probiotic and nutritional supplement, but I've seen it do wonders for ducks fighting bacterial infections.

3. **Vibrant Health ® Green Vibrance:** (supplier: AmazonSmile www.smile.amazon.com). This is another nutritional supplement intended for humans that also contains probiotics.

Under vet guidance, you can either sprinkle these powders over your duck's food, add them to a syringe feeding recipe or fill empty gel caps.

Sav-A-Chick® probiotic packets (which are added to drinking water) are another handy option, but are often only available in grain stores in spring and summer.

If you don't have any of these on hand and are in a pinch, you can syringe-feed your duck some yogurt containing *L. acidophilus*.

Excess or Rapid Weight Gain

Some ducks will have the opposite problem when it comes to appetite and will overeat and gain too much weight. Remember, weight gain is common and acceptable when occurring just before winter, provided that your duck takes that excess weight off again in the spring (which most do).

- **Symptoms**

Some symptoms of excess weight gain may include: rapid or slow weight gain (ducks often hide this under fluffy feathers, so watch for any increased difficulty getting around).

- **Treatment**

Because excessive weight gain (especially rapid) can be indicative of conditions and diseases like peritonitis, organ failure or cancer, it's best to take your duck to the vet for an immediate x-ray and blood work to ensure you're just dealing with chubbiness.

Copy down any meal instructions from your duck's feed bag and then bring it and the ingredient label to your vet appointment. Once you confirm there are no other health issues involved, this information will help your vet formulate a weight loss plan designed specifically for your duck.

Dehydration

Excessive drinking (especially in conjunction with diarrhea) is often a sign of dehydration. You can check to see if your duck is dehydrated by lifting one of their wings. In the crook of their "armpit" you'll find a flap of skin. If you press this skin between your fingers and it doesn't spring back into place, your duck may be dehydrated (you can also do this test on the back of their leg shank).

- **Symptoms**

Some symptoms of dehydration may include: excessive thirst, excessive panting, airing out the armpits, pale bill and eventual seizures.

- **Treatment**

Take your duck to the vet right away for subcutaneous fluids and possible IV rehydration. Vets will often have you keep your duck in a cool place during recovery, out of direct sunlight. Electrolyte water is often temporarily substituted with regular drinking water and made available to them at *all times*.

If your duck still isn't drinking normally, you can administer up to 50 ml/kg of water via oral syringe per day under vet guidance. Keep in mind you need to subtract out any water they *are* drinking from this total amount in order to keep from going overboard. Also consider that this amount is based on ideal conditions regarding temperature and exertion. As with syringe feeding, you can spread these fluid dosing sessions out based upon your duck's particular needs and preferences. Most ducks will tolerate between 10-25 ml of water every 2-3 hours without putting up too much of a fuss. Be careful not to squirt too much down their throat too rapidly, or they can aspirate the fluid. I find it best to use a 3 ml oral syringe when administering water in this fashion, allowing them to take a few breaths in between each filling. If they do aspirate fluid you'll hear gurgling sounds when they breathe. If this occurs, stop immediately and give their body time to absorb the liquid. If it doesn't work itself out within the next 2 hours, you'll want call your vet. They may need to go in for subcutaneous or IV fluids to give them a break from syringe dosing (see: *"Aspiration Pneumonia"*).

Diarrhea

Diarrhea can be indicative of a wide array of illnesses and infection, ranging from mild to severe. Diarrhea is often the body's way of removing toxins from the system, so depending on its severity, your vet may or may not want to interfere with this function—especially in the short term. They may want to lessen the symptom more than alleviate it, depending on the cause.

Female ducks in particular will often come off their nests following their normal egg-laying routine and pass a rather poignant bout of diarrhea. Unless you're seeing other accompanying symptoms, this is usually normal.

- **Symptoms**

Some symptoms of diarrhea may include: consistent and abnormal loose bowel movements.

- **Treatment**

A look at your duck's overall health and symptoms will be necessary in order for your vet to determine the most appropriate course of action. They'll often want to run a comprehensive avian blood panel and begin with a round of antibiotics in addition to other supportive care.

Adding pectin to your pet's diet is a safe and often effective way to help tighten up your duck's poop, and there are a few alternatives to accomplishing this.

1. Syringe feed a couple of tablespoons of organic apple baby food to your duck each day until symptoms improve.

2. Adding appropriate amounts of organic apple cider vinegar to you duck's drinking water can improve your duck's condition. This product ferments, so remember to change their water frequently. As an extra bonus, it may also soothe irritated intestinal lining.

3. Kaolin Pectin oral suspension (found at farm supply stores) can be administered 2-4 times daily.

4. Apple Pectin tablets can be given to your duck once daily, or twice daily (every 12 hours) in more serious cases.

Side effects for each of these products include constipation, so only use them under the direct guidance of your veterinarian. Kaolin Pectin Suspension may cause stomach cramping. If you see a decline in your duck's appetite, discontinue immediately and consult your vet.

Remember, diarrhea can lead to dehydration. Monitor your duck's drinking habits carefully to ensure normal behavior. If your duck is spending too much time (or all of their time) at the water bucket, bring them back to your vet immediately.

Crop

When your duck eats, their food travels down their esophagus and into their crop. From this sac, the food then moves downward into their gizzard. Crop issues are rare among ducks who are cared for properly and who are maintained on a healthy diet; they're more common among abandoned ducks, older ducks, immune deficient ducks and ducks with neurological issues.

A *slow crop* is one that functions at a decelerated rate, which is usually caused by infection, impaction or injury, although there are a few other factors that can negatively influence muscle control.

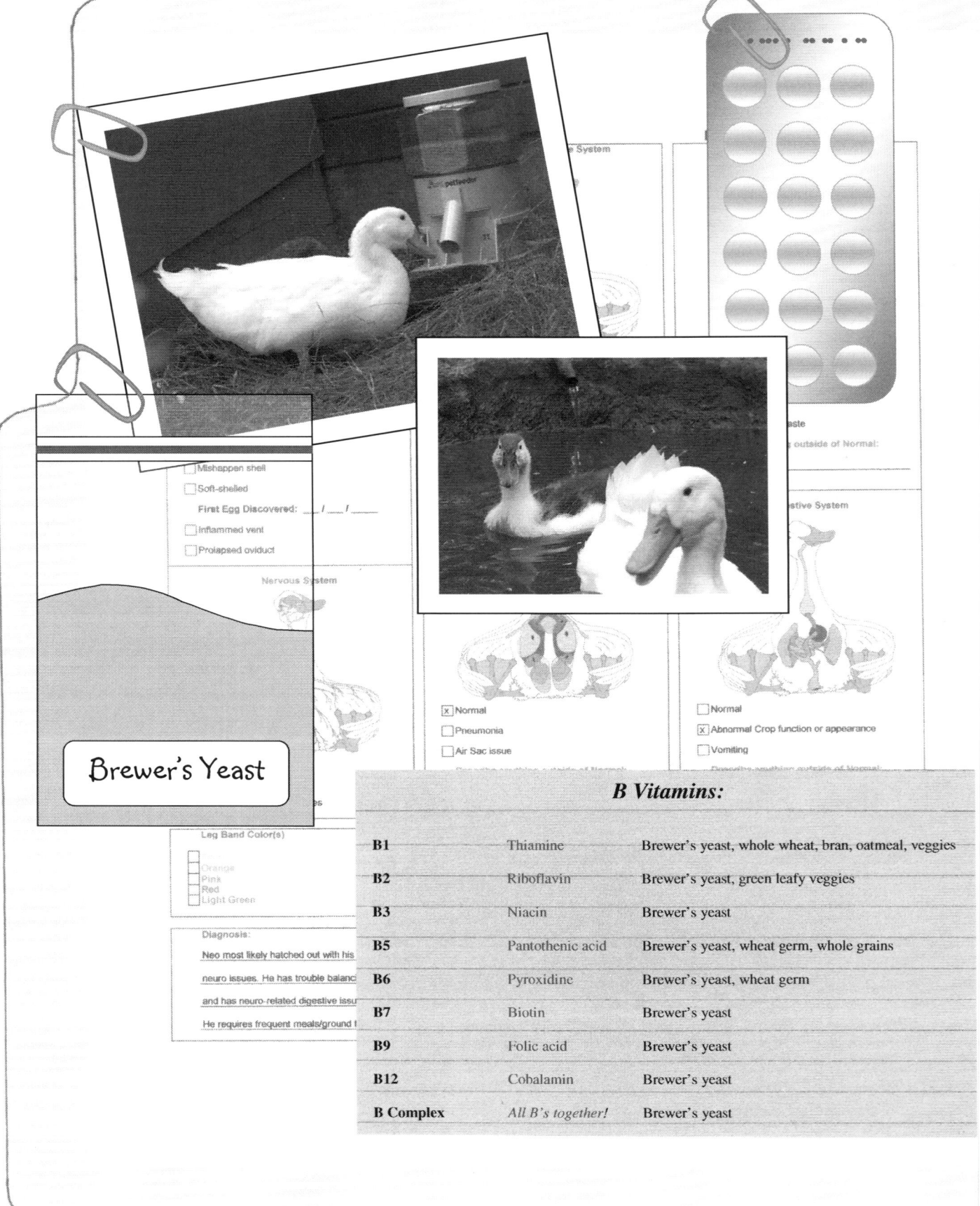

Neo's Crop...

Neo arrived at our sanctuary with a distended and pendulous crop; in fact, it was so engorged he had difficulty balancing his body as he walked and often fell down.

A vet visit confirmed that Neo's crop issues could be attributed to his congenital neurological issue, which impeded proper muscle function. Even so, the fact that he was abandoned to fend for himself certainly didn't help his situation any. Poor Neo would starve for days and then gorge when park visitors came to feed him, further taxing his digestive system.

To help in his digestive function, I immediately placed Neo on a diet of ground Mazuri® Waterfowl Maintenance food, but the trouble with this was he was also suffering from starvation anxiety. Whenever I put food in his pen, he would immediately gorge, refusing to stop until all the food was gone. To address this issue, I placed an automated feeder in his pen, which spurt out a half cup of ground feed every hour for 16 hours. Neo quickly learned that food was reliably forthcoming and that he no longer needed to stress over its availability. From that point on I could simply put out a bowl of ground food into his pen, enough to last him the whole day.

The ground food moved easily from his crop to his gizzard, remedying his pendulous crop. After three months on this diet, we slowly increased the coarseness of his food, grinding it less and less until he could safely eat regular-sized pellets.

Because Neo's crop issues were ultimately neurologically based, his digestive tract never quite functioned as smoothly as other ducks. For this reason, Brewer's yeast was supplemented as a part of his dietary plan to help improve nerve function and offer him a little more assistance.

Neo also had a bit of a learning disability, so to aid him further I introduced a duckling named Switch to his enclosure. An instant friendship was forged between them and little Switch often aided Neo in finding happy things to do in his pen. The buddy system tends to work very well with ducks.

Specialized Crop Diet

The best way to assist your duck when they're experiencing any kind of crop issue is by grinding their feed into more easily digested crumbles. To accomplish this you can pour their feed into a food processor and let it run until it's pulverized. I like to do large batches, which I store in sealed containers, so I don't have to keep coming back to it again and again.

The second dietary strategy is to feed your duck small amounts at frequent intervals throughout the day. This limits the amount of the food in the crop at any one time, allowing it to move more freely into the gizzard.

Combined together, these two approaches are the best therapy for aiding proper crop function. Depending on whether your duck's condition is temporary or chronic, this diet may need to be maintained for the short term, or for the rest of their lives (as with neurological issues).

If your duck has just recovered from a temporary crop condition and their healing phase is complete, gradually increase the size of their feed crumbles by running it for less time through the food processor. Offer slightly larger portions at each mealtime (so they learn to leave some of their food untouched, discouraging gorging behavior). Continue in this manner until you have them back on their regular routine and eating normal-sized feed pellets again. If at any time their crop doesn't empty out properly, reduce the size of their crumbles again as well as the amount of food you're offering at each interval feeding. Give your duck some more time to recover and then proceed forward again; this time, a little more slowly.

- **Additional Tips**

1. Make sure clean water is available 24/7.

2. Be sure your duck has ample access to grit to aid in their digestion.

3. Foster digestive enzymes by adding probiotics to your duck's diet.

4. Help control and prevent bacterial, fungal and yeast growth by adding apple cider to your duck's water *(15 ml per gallon under vet guidance)*.

- **Automated feeders**

Interval feeding can be very difficult for the working family. Fortunately, you can purchase automated feeders for your duck that will dispense specific amounts of food at pre-programmed times. Some are battery operated, while others are electrical and need to be plugged in. I haven't found a model yet that can endure direct exposure to weather, so pay attention to size and how well it'll fit into your duck's house or barn.

Crop Stasis (Sour Crop)

Food normally leaves the crop and moves towards the gizzard soon after being eaten. When the crop stops emptying and becomes distended with fermenting food and fluids it's referred to as *crop stasis* (*sour crop* or *crop infection*). In most cases, crop stasis is caused by contagions directly associated with the crop, including bacterial infection, fungal infection, viral infection and most commonly, yeast infection. Less frequently, other factors can contribute to crop malfunction and subsequent secondary infection. These can include: stress, sudden dietary changes, kidney disease, diabetes, parasites, dehydration, poisoning (especially heavy metals), genetic predisposition and neurological disorders.

- **Symptoms**

Some symptoms of crop stasis may include: distended crop, sour breath, drooling, dehydration, increased or decreased appetite, fatigue and weight loss (which can eventually result in malnutrition, emaciation and seizures).

When palpitating the crop, gurgling sounds can often be heard and even felt.

- **Treatment**

A vet examination is urgently needed when your duck has a crop issue, during which time a number of tests may be performed to isolate the cause:

1. *X-ray:* to ensure there's no blockage (see: *"Crop Impaction"*).

2. *Crop culture:* to isolate the source of infection (your vet will slide a very narrow and flexible device painlessly down your duck's throat to get the sample).

3. *Fecal exam:* to rule out parasites.

4. *Blood work:* to look for signs of infection (also to test for zinc or lead poisoning, which can result in crop distention).

5. *Crop flushing:* Warm saline is often utilized as a flushing agent to remove lingering, undigested matter and help normalize crop PH.

6. *Subcutaneous fluids:* to rehydrate (only if your duck is dehydrated).

Until lab results come back confirming the culprit, your vet will likely advise a few strategies to keep your duck digestively comfortable:

1. *Crop massage:* There is an actual method to massaging the crop—never pushing the crop itself upward. Failure to massage the crop correctly can result in immediate choking or aspiration pneumonia. Your vet will need to teach you how to do this properly, ensuring the safety of your duck.

2. *Probiotics:* Adding helpful bacteria to your duck's diet can help boost digestive enzymes.

3. *Apple cider:* Adding proper amounts of apple cider vinegar to your duck's water helps inhibit bacterial, fungal and yeast growth.

4. *Antifungal/Antibiotic:* An antifungal oral suspension like Nystatin and/or antibiotic medications may be prescribed twice daily to jumpstart treatment until lab results arrive. If results are confirmed, treatment can continue for 7-14 days.

5. *Crop flushing:* Follow-up vet appointments may be required to re-flush the crop with warm saline.

6. *Crop Care:* Reglan® oral solution is commonly prescribed to help restore normal crop function while also relieving nausea.

7. *Rehydration:* Electrolyte water may need to be swapped for regular drinking water if your duck is dehydrated. Repeat vet appointments for subcutaneous fluids may be required during the recovery phase.

8. *Specialized Diet:* Some helpful adjustments will need to be made to their diet, which will help immensely with digestion.

Crop Impaction

A crop can become obstructed when a foreign object (hardware disease), clump of food (often caused by starvation and subsequent overeating), parasites, growths or tumors block the passage leading out of the crop (the top of the proventriculus). This blockage prevents food from properly "draining" out of the crop and moving down towards the gizzard.

Ducks who are allowed to graze on the cut grass of freshly mown lawns have a higher likelihood of encountering this kind of impaction as wads of grass form a ball in their crop (which is even more likely if the grass is wet).

- **Symptoms**

Some symptoms of a crop impaction may include: distended crop, drooling, dehydration and increased or decreased appetite.

- **Treatment**

Under vet guidance, sometimes a pea-sized amount of cat hairball remedy will help lubricate any grass or food that's blocking your duck's crop, enabling it to pass. This should only be given when you're absolutely sure that a food item is at the core of the problem. The last thing you want to do is lubricate a foreign object, encouraging its movement further into the body, which can inhibit endoscopic removal later.

Bring your duck to the vet for an x-ray, which will help determine the nature of the blockage. Your vet will then have a better understanding as to whether the object needs to actually be removed (via flushing or surgery) or encouraged to pass and digest.

Most vets will recommend a specialized crop diet for 1-2 weeks following removal of the impaction.

Pendulous Crop

A pendulous crop is a chronic condition whereby the crop muscles have become permanently weakened, losing their ability to effectively contract and push food downward towards their gizzard. This leads to a life-long condition in which every time your duck eats, their crop functions at a decelerated rate and distends abnormally in response.

Cases of pendulous crop can range from mild to severe. The most common cause of this malady is the lack of medical response to incidents of crop stasis or impaction. When left untreated these conditions continue to worsen, stretching crop muscles until they lose their ability to properly contract again.

Occasionally, the root cause of a pendulous crop is less obvious. Genetic predisposition to crop ailments or neurological disorders that affect associated muscle control and contractions can lead to long-term disabilities. Repetitive starving and gorging behaviors can also result in a pendulous crop. This is commonly observed in abandoned waterfowl who never know when their next meal is coming.

Neo was rescued with a pendulous crop

- **Symptoms**

Some symptoms of a pendulous crop may include: a clearly visible and permanently distended crop, which appears even worse after eating.

- **Treatment**

There is no treatment for a pendulous crop, but you can modify your duck's diet to help improve their condition and aid in their digestion. Some improvement in crop size is often witnessed, but it's usually a direct result of smaller, more easily-digestible meals. If your duck suddenly gorges on whole-sized food again, their condition is likely to re-appear full-force.

Crop Injury

The wall of your duck's crop is very thin and can be prone to injury if you're not careful; this includes punctures and tearing (and even burning, so never allow your duck to consume any hot food or liquids).

- **Symptoms**

Some symptoms of a crop injury may include: partially digested food or fluids oozing out of a wound in your duck's chest as well as associated bleeding.

- **Treatment**

Rush your duck to the vet for immediate surgery. Antibiotics, anti-inflammatory/pain medication along with additional pain medication is often required. Syringe or tube feeding may be required for 2-4 weeks, followed by a specialized diet where your duck's regular food is ground up for them and served in small, but frequent intervals. This can continue for another 2-4 weeks or until healing is complete and your duck's eating habits and crop function return to normal.

Fatty Liver Hemorrhagic Disease (Hepatic Disease)

Fatty Liver Hemorrhagic Disease (FLHD) or *Hepatic Disease* is a slow-progressing condition where liver tissue is gradually replaced with fat, which results in organ enlargement and eventual hemorrhaging.

Liver disease can be caused by: vitamin deficiency (calcium), malnutrition (low-grade or inappropriate feed formulas), ducks who are pushed to unnaturally grow or lay eggs, high estrogen levels, medications (like Metacam® and Rimadyl®), metal toxicity and poisoning. It can also be the result of genetic predisposition and old age.

- **Symptoms**

Some symptoms of liver disease may include: abdominal distention, diarrhea, loss of appetite, fatigue, consistently discolored droppings (often bile green), pale bill, disorientation, balance issues, tremors and seizures. Enlarged liver can press on other internal organs resulting in other seemingly unrelated symptoms.

- **Treatment**

Liver disease is confirmed by blood work and x-rays. While there's no cure, if discovered in early stages, your vet will examine the particulars of your duck's diet and likely advise a few changes to help keep them going for as long as possible. This dietary strategy may include: increased carbohydrates, fiber, vitamins and minerals (especially B-complex) and decreased fat and protein levels.

If your duck happens to be overweight, a plan to help them take off some of that excess burden will also be incorporated into their health plan. In addition, your vet's plan may include Lactulose supplementation to reduce blood ammonia levels and Lipotropic nutrients to help promote the breakdown and export of fat from the liver.

Avoid any home remedies and vitamin concoctions that aren't vet approved at all costs. Unsafe strategies (milk thistle, red clover and burdock—among others) or improper dosages can easily prove toxic and result in rapid decline and fatality.

Aspergillus Parasiticus (Aflatoxicosis)

Aspergillus parasiticus is a carcinogenic mold (from the same genus as *Aspergillus flavus*) that grows on feed, hay and vegetation and produces extremely dangerous aflatoxins (chemicals), which can result in liver cancer.

- **Symptoms**

Some symptoms of aflatoxicosis may include: liver damage, liver cancer, nausea, vomiting, decreased immunity, hemorrhaging and seizures.

- **Treatment**

There is no effective treatment for aflatoxicosis caused by *Aspergillus parasiticus*. Supportive care often includes antibiotic and antifungal medications, plasma transfusion as well as nutrition and hydration therapies. These strategies can be enlisted to preserve quality of life until humane euthanasia is required.

Botulism

Botulism is caused by bacterial outbreaks (*Clostridium botulinum*), which tend to occur in decaying organic matter and stagnant water. When either of these are ingested, the bacteria can quickly make your duck fatally ill. Ducks are extremely susceptible to this disease, and it only takes a small amount to be life-threatening.

Wound Botulism refers to the same bacteria entering your duck's body via their bloodstream rather than through their digestive system.

Preventative measures include keeping your duck's water clean by changing their water every day (or keeping it filtered and circulated) and by keeping their grounds clear of rotting organisms (both plants and animals). It's not that uncommon to find a dead frog, fish or mouse floating in your duck pond or kiddy pool. If you see this, remove and dispose of the carcass and then immediately perform a complete water change after cleaning their pool (or keep your ducks off of the water for a day or two, allowing streams to naturally circulate the water, making it safe again). Likewise, if you find a small animal on the ground in your duck pen, shovel it up along with any maggots, insects and associated soil, which can also harbor fatal bacteria.

- **Symptoms**

Some symptoms of botulism may include: weakness, paralysis of the neck (a.k.a. *limberneck*), wings and/or legs and excessive panting. Death often occurs quickly, usually within a day or two.

To test for the presence of botulism, *gently* push down on your duck's head. If they provide any resistance, their neck muscles aren't paralyzed. Of course, this test needs to be repeated at regular intervals in order to be reliable.

- **Treatment**

If symptoms appear, vet treatment must be sought out immediately in order to save your duck's life. There often isn't time for confirmation testing, so precautionary treatment must begin immediately. Supportive care including nutritional and IV support along with antitoxin medication and antibiotics is required. If you can help your duck through the first 48 hours, they'll most likely survive; however, they won't become resistant, which means future incidents can still occur.

Medical #13
Urinary System (Renal System)

Your duck's kidneys and ureters make up their urinary (or renal) system.

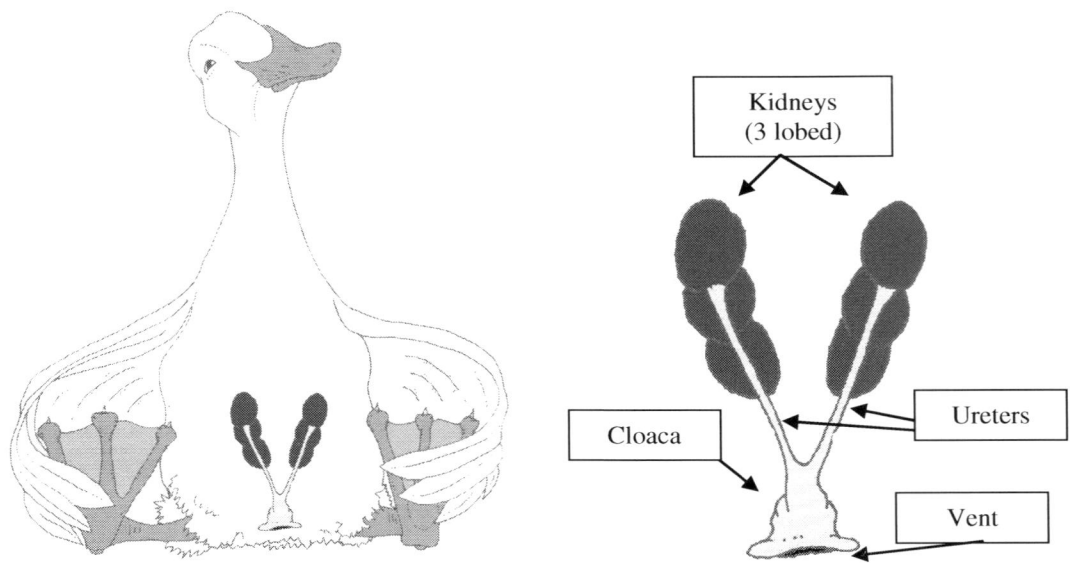

A diagram of your duck's urinary system

Renal (Kidney) Disease

Symptoms of renal disease often appear quite suddenly because it's difficult to notice the early warning signs. One day you can have a happily waddling duck and the next they just don't want to leave their nest. Their health can decline to the point of no return by the end of the day or with 1-2 weeks.

Renal disease can be brought on by: bacterial, viral or fungal infections, toxins, medications, heavy metals, vitamin D poisoning, vitamin A deficiency, urinary infections/obstructions, trauma, cysts and tumors.

- **Symptoms**

Some early symptoms of renal disease, which may be difficult to detect may include: decrease in appetite, slight weight loss, fatigue, diarrhea and increased thirst.

Some late-stage symptoms of renal disease (which are often precursors of renal failure) may include: anemia, complete loss of appetite, extreme weight loss, seizures, refusal to participate in normal activities, diarrhea, excessive drinking, severe dehydration, instability (wobbly legs), muscle weakness, pale bill & legs (often fading to an unnatural pale yellow), fluffed up feathers (especially around the neck and face), drooping wings (some days worse than others) and depression.

- **Treatment**

In the case of severe symptoms, euthanasia should be sought out, but if symptoms are mild, you may have time to determine the cause and find out if your duck's condition is reversible. Your vet will likely suggest the following courses of action if your duck's condition merits investigation:

1. *Dietary examination:* Every aspect of your duck's diet needs to be immediately scrutinized including feed bag labels (for ingredients and vitamin/mineral content) and for quality (making sure it's free of any mold). Any multivitamins, supplements or medications your duck is taking also need to be considered.

2. *Trauma:* X-ray to look for urinary obstructions, tumors, cysts or signs of injury.

3. *Infection:* Comprehensive avian blood panel and fecal/cloacal culturing will help pinpoint any infections. Your vet will likely prescribe potent antibiotics to try to combat possible infection while you wait for results.

4. *Metal poisoning:* X-ray (to look for swallowed objects) and additional blood work to test for zinc and/or lead poisoning. Depending on the severity of your duck's symptoms, your vet may or may not want to start your duck on chelation therapy while you wait for results.

While waiting on test results, supportive fluids for dehydration will likely be required. Subcutaneous injections are commonly done every 2-3 days in your vet's office while you wait. In more severe cases, you may need to drop your duck off for IV catheterization and then come back and pick them up later (or stay and sit with them if your vet allows it). A plentiful tube feeding can also be a great bonus for your duck while they're there.

If you're uncomfortable doing tube feedings on your own, you'll need to syringe-feed your duck in between vet tube feeding appointments to keep them as strong as possible while you're waiting for a diagnosis (see: *"Syringe Feeding"*).

In addition to the normal syringe diet, your vet may have you include other ingredients:

1. *Anemia:* Liquid Vitamin B supplementation (your vet will give you this in an oral syringe).
2. *Anemia:* Iron (crushed over-the-counter pill).
3. *Diarrhea:* Organic apple baby food.

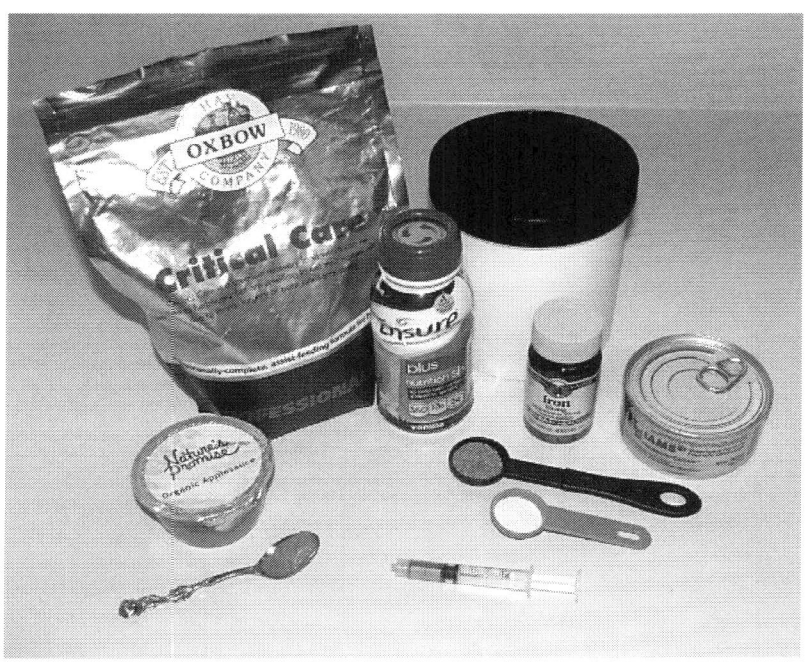

A syringe diet for ducks with renal issues can be specifically tailored to their needs

Medical #14
Circulatory System (Cardiovascular System)

Your duck's heart, veins, arteries and blood make up their circulatory system.

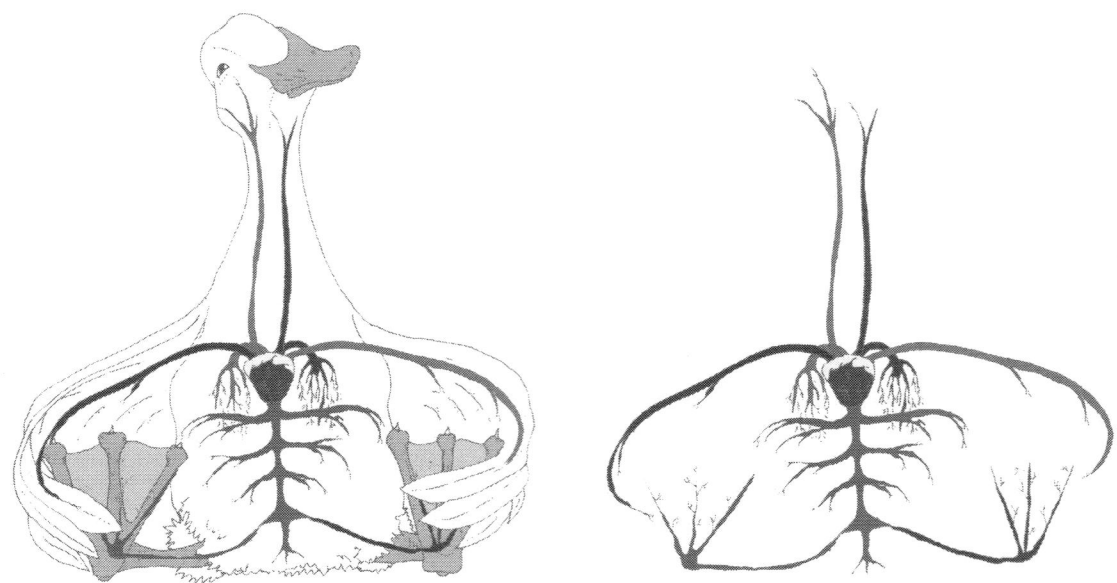

A rudimentary diagram of your duck's circulatory system

Heat Stroke (Hyperthermia)

It's a good thing ducks love water because they don't perspire and a nice, cool pond can really help keep their body temperature in check. The same way feathers are designed to help insulate your duck against the cold in winter, they work to protect them from the heat in summer, but sometimes the sun is simply more than they can handle.

While many ducks have to contend with hot weather, heavyweight ducks seem to have the most difficulty dealing with it. Ducks cope with the heat by rapidly increasing the flow of blood to their legs and feet where it's able to escape their bodies. Gentle wing fluttering (or what I like to refer to as: *airing out their armpits*) is a way to manipulate their feathers to expose areas of skin, which also helps to release excess heat. To further combat high temperatures, ducks will begin open-bill panting to promote the cooling evaporation of moisture in their mouths while also effectively reducing their core temperature by pushing refreshing air throughout their complicated system of lungs and air sacs, which are embedded among their muscles, organs and bones.

I can't tell you how many times I've gone out in my pens and seen my ducks panting in the hot sun instead of moving underneath one of their thick shade trees or taking a swim out on the cold pond. I have to assume that they look a lot hotter than they really are (that or they're just too lazy to get up and move). Even so, I usually take pity on them and mist them with the hose or coax them out onto the water.

Heat stroke occurs when your duck can no longer regulate their own body temperature and it rises out of control. Kiddy pools and small ponds can quickly get hot in summer and may need cold water added to them (or complete water changes), so they can continue to provide relief. Make sure all of your ducks have access to swimming and drinking water along with plenty of access to shade.

Ice is a great way to cool down your kiddy pools and water buckets in the heat of summer. You can use all kinds of containers to make blocks of ice in your freezer. For extra fun, freeze bite-size pieces of watermelon or lettuce inside. Just be careful the ice cubes aren't so big as to risk any pinching injuries. You don't want your duck's legs getting caught between a huge block of ice and the edge of their pool. Ice chips served in a bowl of cold water is another great way to beat the heat. Just be sure to give the ice a few minutes to melt down in size to reduce any risks of choking.

Jocamo & Yolanda keeping cool in summer

- **Symptoms**

Some symptoms of heat stroke may include: excessive panting, wing fluttering (airing out their armpits), excessive thirst, hot bill and feet, vomiting, loss of consciousness and seizures.

- **Treatment**

Heat stroke can quickly become fatal. If your duck is showing any signs of trouble, immediately remove them from the sun and bring them into a cool location. Apply towel-wrapped ice packs beneath both of their wings for 60 seconds and then remove them again. Continue to place them on-and-off again as needed every few minutes without leaving them in place for too long. Place a bowl of cool water in front of them to help them rehydrate and maybe even take them for a cooling bath in your tub.

Keep them out of the sun for the rest of the day, encouraging plenty of fluid intake. Call your vet immediately if symptoms don't improve or if their situation worsens.

Hypothermia

Hypothermia is the opposite of hyperthermia and it occurs when your duck can no longer regulate their core body temperature and it begins to drop out of control. Ducks with feather quality issues or who have difficulty staying dry, underweight ducks, lightweight ducks and ducks who aren't properly protected from the cold are at higher risk than others.

- **Symptoms**

Some symptoms of hypothermia may include: shivering, shallow breathing, fatigue and loss of consciousness.

- **Treatment**

Immediately bring your duck to a nice, heated location and offer them lukewarm water to drink. The best way to heat up a cold duck is with a blow dryer. Remember to keep the setting on *"low"* and avoid focusing the airflow on any one spot while also keeping far enough away to prevent any burning. If your duck is wet, continue until they're completely dry.

Keep them out of the cold for the rest of the day, encouraging plenty of warm fluid intake. Call your vet immediately if symptoms don't improve or if their situation worsens.

Heart Attack (Myocardial Infarction)

Ducks have relatively large hearts in comparison with their body size and they beat a lot faster than yours or mine (anywhere between 200-400 beats per minute!). Heart attacks usually take place when a coronary artery is blocked by a blood clot, and they tend to occur in older duck and ducks with existing heart disease (overweight or stressed ducks are at an even higher risk). They're usually fatal, but occasionally a duck can survive one without you even knowing that it happened. If any heart damage was sustained, you may begin to notice symptoms.

- **Symptoms**

Some symptoms of a heart attack may include: difficulty breathing, drooling, loss of balance, weakness, pale bill and/or leg coloration and seizures.

- **Treatment**

Take your duck to the vet for immediate treatment. They'll likely need to be put on oxygen and other supportive care including pain medication. Depending on the cause and any damage done, heart medications will be required including Enalapril, which lowers blood pressure and aspirin, which is a blood thinner. Heart attacks are normally confirmed by blood work, x-ray and sometimes by ultrasound.

Cardiomyopathy (Heart Muscle Disease)

Cardiomyopathy is the deterioration of the heart muscle, which makes it difficult for your duck's heart to pump their blood and usually results in eventual heart failure.

Cardiomyopathy can be caused by: malnutrition, viral infection, genetic predisposition, heart valve disorders, diabetes, excessive weight gain, hyperthyroidism, or tissue damage from a prior heart attack.

There are three forms of cardiomyopathy:

1. *Dilated:* The main chamber of your duck's heart becomes enlarged and less effective at pumping (this is the most common form).

2. *Hypertrophic:* The main chamber of your duck's heart begins to abnormally thicken and stiffen.

3. *Restrictive:* Your duck's heart muscle loses its suppleness, inhibiting expansion.

- **Symptoms**

Some symptoms of cardiomyopathy may include: loss of appetite, fatigue, shortness of breath, raspy breath sounds, drooling, panting, distended abdomen, coughing, leg paralysis, pale leg color, abdominal heaving, loss of balance, sudden collapse.

- **Treatment**

Although cardiomyopathy is not common to ducks, the diagnosis of a deteriorating heart muscle does occasionally come up. Unless your duck is symptomatic, it's usually discovered by accident during routine exams when your vet listens to your duck's heartbeat. Cardiomyopathy is confirmed by further testing, which may include: blood work, x-rays, electrocardiogram (ECG), atropine response test and/or an ultrasound.

Commonly prescribed medications include:

1. *Lasix:* This is a diuretic. It helps reduce fluid around the heart (Lasix has a short half-life and must be administered every 12 hours to be effective).

2. *Digoxin:* This slows the heart's beating and helps increase the force of heart contractions.

3. *Enalapril:* This is an Angiotensin-Converting Enzyme (ACE) inhibitor, which lowers blood pressure.

4. *Pimobendan:* This is sometimes prescribed instead of Enalapril in the case of dilated cardiomyopathy. It often provides rapid and significant improvement in your duck's level of activity.

5. *Taurine and L-Carnitine:* These supplements can sometimes improve life expectancy. They normally have the greatest effect when your duck is nutritionally deficient in this area. Be careful to examine their entire diet before supplementing and always consult with your vet before initiating treatment.

Heart Murmur

Most heart murmurs are insignificant, occurring in completely healthy hearts, with completely normal blood flow. Only occasionally are they indicative of blood flowing through damaged heart valves.

Different types of valve diseases can result in varying types of complications, which may include: valve prolapse, degeneration or thickening. These issues can in turn lead to blood regurgitation or backflow, which (in some cases) can lead to eventual heart failure.

Heart murmurs can be caused by: congenital deformity, old age, or damage from a prior heart attack.

Marvin has a heart murmur, which has proven harmless to date

- **Symptoms**

Some symptoms of a heart murmur may include: fatigue, difficulty breathing, sudden weakness—dropping suddenly to the ground (especially when stressed) and not being able to get back up right away.

- **Treatment**

If your vet detects a heart murmur that isn't affecting your duck's overall well-being, they'll advise you to keep your eye on their situation and immediately inform them of any changes in breathing or decreased energy levels. If you want to know more than this, you can schedule an ultrasound.

When a heart murmur is affecting behavior, your vet will prescribe the same medications used to treat cardiomyopathy (see: *"Cardiomyopathy"*). Treatment also includes keeping your duck as tranquil and stress-free as possible, while still allowing them to live an enriched and social life.

Congestive Heart Failure

A duck with congestive heart failure has a heart that simply doesn't pump blood as well as a duck who has a normal heart. When the kidneys receive less blood, they can't function properly and filter out excess fluid like they usually do. This causes an abundance of fluid build-up in the body, especially in the lungs and liver.

- **Symptoms**

Some symptoms of congestive heart failure may include: difficulty breathing, excessive panting, abdominal heaving, fatigue, irregular or rapid heartbeat, coughing, leg swelling, nausea, distended abdomen, lack of appetite and weight gain (fluid retention).

- **Treatment**

Congestive heart failure is commonly confirmed by blood work, x-ray and ultrasound. Prescribed medications are the same as those used to treat cardiomyopathy (see: *"Cardiomyopathy"*).

Ducks who are diagnosed with *end stage* heart failure usually have less than six months to live. Even so, heart medications can keep them pretty happy and comfortable right up until the end. Whenever I have a rescued duck who's diagnosed with end stage heart failure, my vet gives me a needle syringe that's preloaded with the correct dose of injectable Lasix. If at any point they go into respiratory distress, I can simply inject it into their pectoral (chest) muscle to alleviate their symptoms within a minute or two. This medication then affords me time to get in touch with my vet regarding increased oral Lasix dosages, or if we're already past this point, to their office where we can attend to humane euthanasia, preventing any further pain or discomfort.

Endocarditis

Endocarditis occurs when bacteria (usually staph) from your duck's body gains access into their bloodstream through a wound and then travels to previously damaged portions of their heart (the interior lining or valves). Ducks with heart murmurs, congenital deformities, or who have experienced a heart attack are far more likely to experience this than healthy ducks.

- **Symptoms**

Some symptoms of endocarditis may include: fever, fatigue, heart murmur, panting, shortness of breath, coughing, weight loss, pale bill or legs, abdominal swelling, leg swelling and blood in the urine.

- **Treatment**

Left untreated, endocarditis can have life-threatening results (further spread of infection, organ damage and heart failure), so it's vital to get your duck to a vet right away if you're seeing symptoms. Your vet will diagnose the condition with x-rays, blood work (including culturing), ECG and/or an ultrasound.

Potent intravenous antibiotics will be required for 3-5 days to target the particular bacteria involved in the infection. Your duck's vitals will need to be continually monitored during their hospital stay. Oral antibiotics will be needed for an additional 2-6 weeks depending on severity.

Anemia

Anemia is a condition where you duck's blood doesn't contain enough healthy red blood cells, which are responsible for binding and carrying oxygen through the body. Anemia can be inherited, or it can be the result of iron deficiency, malnutrition (vitamin C or B_{12}), metal toxicity, kidney disease or blood loss (internal or external).

- **Symptoms**

Some symptoms of anemia may include: fatigue, rapid heartbeat, difficulty balancing, pale bill or legs, decreased immunity, seizures, discolored urine, and restlessness.

- **Treatment**

Your vet will diagnose anemia by running a comprehensive avian blood panel. If the cause is nutritional or genetic, dietary adjustments will need to be made, ensuring your duck is on a high-quality, brand-name waterfowl feed that's appropriate for their age and gender needs. Vitamin and iron supplements may also be required and will need to be administered under vet supervision to prevent dangerous overdoses.

In the case of metal toxicity, chelation therapy will be required (see: *"Lead Poisoning"*). If their anemia is the result of internal bleeding, the source will need to be located and remedied before your duck's condition will improve.

Sepsis (Septic Shock)

Sepsis (or septic shock) is a condition caused by a blood infection (or septicemia), which is often the result of a staph infection that enters your duck's body through an inflicted wound or cut—or by way of osteomyelitis (bone infection) or pneumonia (although other bacteria or fungi can be responsible). Ducklings, older and immune compromised ducks are more likely to succumb to sepsis than other ducks.

- **Symptoms**

Some symptoms of sepsis may include: fever, chills, excessive panting, loss of appetite, vomiting and diarrhea.

- **Treatment**

Left untreated, sepsis can have life-threatening results (organ damage), so it's vital to get your duck to a vet right away if you're seeing symptoms. Your vet will diagnose the condition by doing a blood culture where they check for the presence of bacteria.

Potent intravenous antibiotics will be required for 3-5 days to target the particular bacteria involved in the infection. Your duck's vitals will need to be continually monitored during their hospital stay. Oral antibiotics will be needed for an additional 2-6 weeks depending on severity.

Thymic Lymphoma

Thymic lymphoma is cancer of the white blood cells or lymphocytes, which originate in the interior of the thymus glands (see: *"Lymphatic-Immune System"*). It's extremely rare in waterfowl.

- **Symptoms**

Some symptoms of thymic lymphoma may include: swollen neck, fever, fatigue, weight loss, excessive panting, coughing and difficulty breathing.

- **Treatment**

If your duck suddenly losses weight without any changes in their diet, you should always take them to the vet (the same is true if they suddenly gain weight). Thymic lymphoma is diagnosed through a combination of tests including: blood work, x-ray, ultrasound and a physical exam.

New treatments for lymphomas may include Leukeran® tablets (chlorambucil) given orally twice a week as well as vincristine sulfate administered by IV on a weekly basis. The bad news is long-term success hasn't been reported with either of these... *yet*. Even so, a positive result for lymphoma doesn't always require immediate euthanasia when the diagnosis is made. Some ducks thrive happily for a year or more provided that pain management and other supportive care is actively taken into consideration.

Lymphocytic Leukemia

Lymphocytic leukemia is a cancer of the white blood cells or lymphocytes, which originate in the bone marrow. It can occur acutely or chronically, but both are pretty rare in waterfowl.

- **Symptoms**

Some symptoms of *acute* lymphocytic leukemia may include: loss of appetite, weight loss, fever, fatigue, abdominal swelling, swollen neck (enlarged lymph nodes), excessive panting, and immune deficiency.

Some symptoms of *chronic* lymphocytic leukemia may also include: anemia.

- **Treatment**

Lymphocytic leukemia is diagnosed through a combination of tests including: blood work, x-ray, ultrasound and physical exam. It's treated similarly to thymic lymphoma (see: *"Thymic Lymphoma"*).

Medical #15
Endrocrine System

Your duck's thyroid gland, pineal gland, pituitary gland, pancreas, ultimobranchial gland, ovary/testes, adrenal glands and parathyroid glands are all components of their endocrine system. These glands release hormones into their bloodstream.

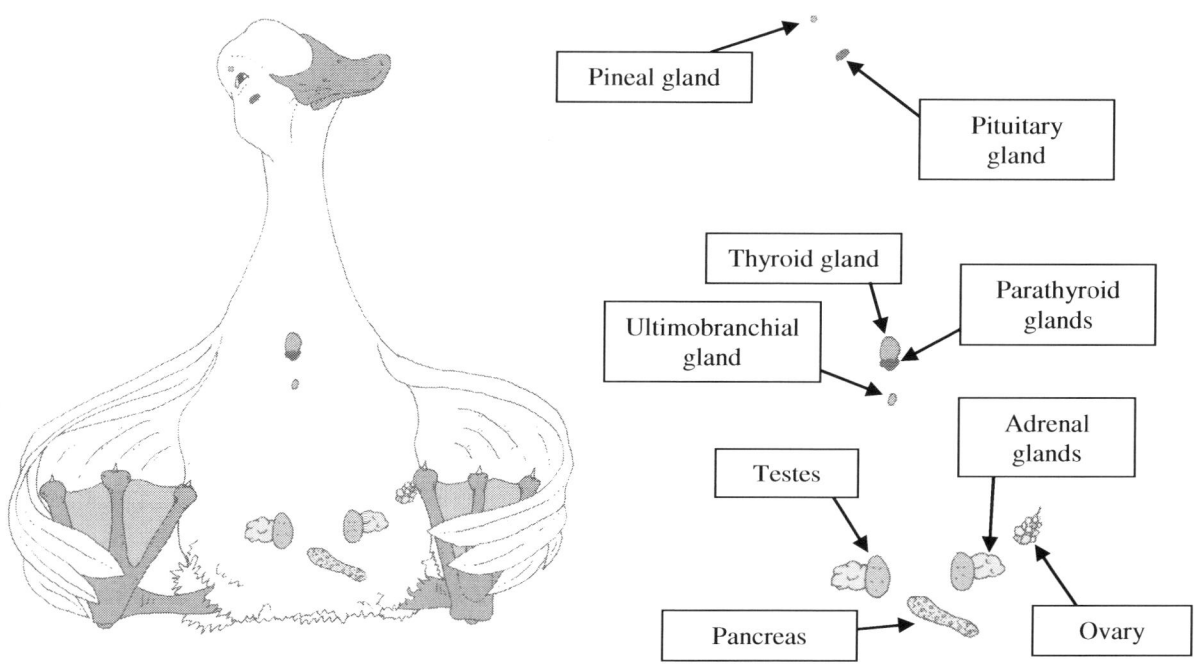

Diagram of your duck's endocrine system

Endocrine Disorders

Aside from occasional gender-benders when a female duck's ovary stops functioning, the endocrine glands usually don't give ducks any problems.

- **Symptoms**

Some symptoms of endocrine disorders may include: metabolic issues (abnormal body temperature, energy levels, growth rates and appetite).

- **Treatment**

Sudden or drastic changes should be closely examined by a vet. A comprehensive avian blood panel is highly recommended in these instances. Endocrine disorders are often untreatable in waterfowl, aside from examining and improving their overall diet and nutrition as well as their living conditions (reducing stress) whenever possible.

Hypothyroidism (Underactive Thyroid)

Hypothyroidism occurs when the thyroid gland doesn't release enough hormones.

- **Symptoms**

Some symptoms of hyperthyroidism may include: slow metabolism, weight gain, fatigue, depression and constipation.

- **Treatment**

Sudden or drastic changes should be closely examined by a vet. A comprehensive avian blood panel is highly recommended in these instances. Endocrine disorders are often untreatable in waterfowl, aside from examining and improving their overall diet and nutrition as well as their living conditions (reducing stress) whenever possible.

Hyperthyroidism (Overactive Thyroid)

Hyperthyroidism occurs when the thyroid gland releases more hormones than are necessary.

- **Symptoms**

Some symptoms of hyperthyroidism may include: fast metabolism, increased appetite, weight loss, nervousness and diarrhea.

- **Treatment**

Sudden or drastic changes should be closely examined by a vet. A comprehensive avian blood panel is highly recommended in these instances. Endocrine disorders are often untreatable in waterfowl, aside from examining and improving their overall diet and nutrition as well as their living conditions (reducing stress) whenever possible.

Endocrine Cancers

Different endocrine glands exhibit different symptoms when invaded by cancer and most of these symptoms go unnoticed until the cancer has progressed into advanced stages, often spreading to other body organs, or growing large enough to press on and interfere with other organs. At this point tumors can probably be seen on an x-ray and definitely by ultrasound. The good news is that most of these cancers (with the exception of ovarian cancer) are extremely rare in ducks; although this could be because they go undiagnosed and are therefore unreported.

- **Symptoms**

1. *Thyroid cancer:* Swollen throat, lump on the throat, difficulty swallowing, hoarseness, wheezing, coughing, difficulty breathing and excessive open-bill panting.

2. *Parathyroid cancer:* Excessive open-bill panting (indicative of abdominal pain), nausea, vomiting, fatigue, bone fractures, loss of appetite, refusal to engage in normal activities. Most of these symptoms are caused by elevated calcium levels in the blood (hypercalcemia).

3. *Ultimobranchial cancer:* Unknown, but symptoms may appear similar to those of Thyroid or Parathyroid cancers.

4. *Adrenal cancer:* Excessive open-bill panting, abdominal heaving, distended abdomen, rapid weight gain (fluid retention), refusal to engage in normal activities, loss of appetite, weight loss (which can be masked by fluid retention) and in some cases, high blood pressure and high blood sugar.

5. *Pituitary cancer:* Fatigue, high blood pressure, irregular heartbeat, blindness, refusal to engage in normal activities and open-bill panting (indicative of headache pain).

6. *Pineal gland cancer:* Your duck's pineal gland is located in the middle of their brain. Cancerous tumors can be slow-growing (pineocytoma) or fast-growing (pineoblastoma). Some symptoms may include nausea, vomiting, open-bill panting (indicative of headache pain), refusal to engage in normal activities, visual problems, increased fluid in the brain, memory loss (having trouble remembering normal routines) and seizures.

7. *Pancreatic cancer:* Abdominal distention, rapid weight gain (fluid retention), nausea, vomiting, excessive open-bill panting, diarrhea, pale-colored poop, high blood sugar, loss of appetite, weight loss (often masked by fluid retention) and refusal to engage in normal activities.

8. *Ovarian cancer:* (see *"Ovarian Cancer"*).

9. *Testicular cancer:* (see *"Testicular Cancer"*).

- **Treatment**

There are no treatment options for endocrine cancers in waterfowl. Pain management should be explored until the time for humane euthanasia has arrived.

Diabetes

The pancreas produces insulin and glucagon, which together regulate and balance blood glucose levels.

Type 1 Diabetes: When your duck's immune system attacks the pancreas until it can no longer supply enough insulin to keep blood sugar levels down. This type of diabetes often has a quick onset, with the sudden appearance of symptoms.

Type 2 Diabetes: When your duck's body builds an unnatural resistance to insulin and the pancreas can no longer produce enough to keep blood sugar levels in check. This type of diabetes often has a slow onset, with the gradual appearance of symptoms.

- **Symptoms**

Some symptoms of diabetes may include: increased appetite, excessive thirst, weight loss, fatigue and when progressed, seizures.

- **Treatment**

Until you can get your duck to the vet, low blood sugar issues can be addressed by syringe feeding Gatorade® every 4 hours. If you can get them to drink it on their own, you can serve it up right in your duck's water bowl.

While untested in ducks as far as I know, I have discussed the option of insulin with vets and have been advised that they would likely begin with NPH (Neutral Protamine Hagedorn) insulin, which is often used on diabetic parrots.

Pancreatitis

Inflammation of the pancreas is referred to as pancreatitis. Acute pancreatitis occurs when the digestive enzymes it produces become active while still inside the pancreas—irritating and potentially damaging itself. In acute cases, symptoms appear suddenly and often last for days. Chronic cases are usually the result of abdominal injury, with symptoms developing gradually. Other causes of pancreatitis may include: high calcium levels, genetic predisposition, infection and pancreatic cancer.

- **Symptoms**

Some symptoms of pancreatitis may include: excessive panting (indicative of abdominal pain), nausea, vomiting, diarrhea, weight loss and seizures.

- **Treatment**

If left untreated pancreatitis can result in malnutrition, infection, diabetes, kidney failure, respiratory issues, pancreatic cysts and cancer. Take your duck to the vet right away for a comprehensive avian blood panel, x-rays and possibly an ultrasound.

Pancreatitis can be agonizing, which means some good pain medication will definitely be in order. Pancreatic enzymes (pancrezyme) can be prescribed by your vet and added to your duck's food to help them pre-digest their meals.

Some serving adjustments will need to be instituted in order for this therapy to be effective:

1. Your duck will need to be served their meals individually rather than relying on a 24/7 feeding system.

2. Add a small amount of water to your duck's food and then stir in the appropriate, vet-prescribed amount of pancrezyme powder.

3. Allow the mixture to sit for 15-20 minutes and then serve.

If your duck disproves of the flavor and refuses to eat, ask your vet about utilizing tablets before meals instead.

Some additional dietary changes may also be in order. Ducks with pancreatitis shouldn't be fed layer or breeder formula feed or be given calcium additives, which can all induce seizures. High fat feed formulas (growing formulas) are also not ideal for ducks with pancreatitis.

If your duck suffers from pancreatic seizures, your vet may advise giving them Gatorade® or electrolyte water every 4 hours for 2-3 days or until they fully subside.

Medical #16
Lymphatic-Immune System

Your duck's lymphatic system consists of their thymus and bursa of Fabricus (which atrophies with age and no longer exists in adult ducks). The immune system is *part* of the lymphatic system and has no related organs.

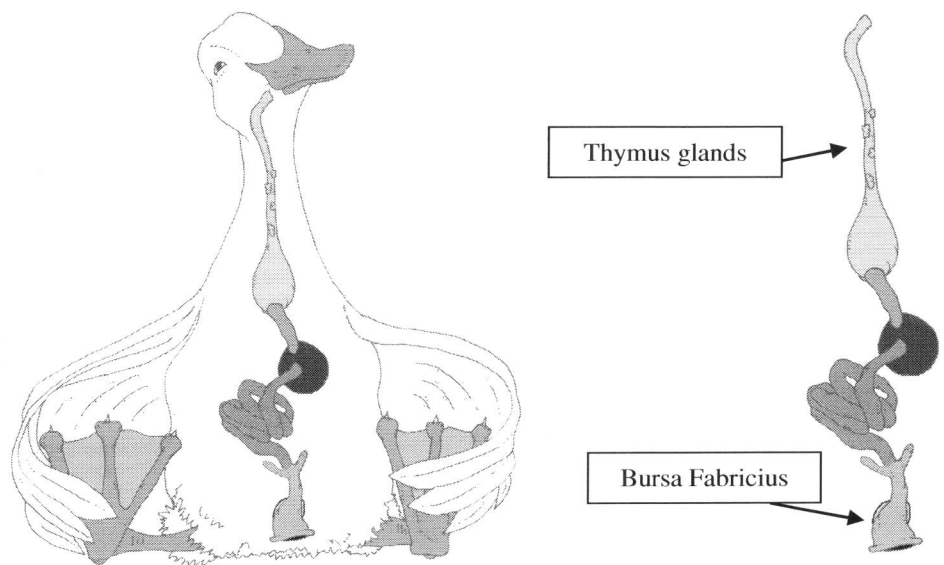

A diagram of your duck's lymphatic system

Fever

Your duck's normal body temperature runs around 105-106F (vet visits can cause stress, which may elevate their temperature slightly).

An elevated temperature is a clear indicator that something's wrong with your duck. Some causes of fever may include: infection (viral, bacterial, fungal), conditions that cause inflammation (often relating to reproductive organs in female ducks), cancerous tumors, abscesses, parasite infestations, heat exhaustion and medication (side effects).

- **Symptoms**

Some symptoms of a fever may include: your duck's bill feels noticeably hot and sometimes their feet as well (especially in ducklings), open-bill panting, loss of appetite, weight loss, fatigue and dehydration.

- **Treatment**

Whenever your duck is exhibiting a fever, they should be brought to your vet for an immediate examination. Failure to seek out treatment can allow the underlying issue to continue unchecked, which can be fatal. During the exam, your vet will ask you questions to help pinpoint the source of your duck's increased body temperature. Be sure to mention any recent behavioral changes, including those relating to egg-laying and appetite. If any other flock members are exhibiting similar traits, be sure to mention them as well.

A general oral antibiotic (like Baytril®) is often prescribed for 7-14 days to address any hidden infection. In the case of a high fever your vet may jumpstart your duck with a potent dose of injectable Baytril® while they have them in their office.

Ask your vet if your duck should be quarantined from other flock members and if so, for how long. If your duck could be contagious and you're approaching an off-hours or holiday weekend, ask them for a few extra pills in case one or two of your other ducks become suddenly ill (just enough to hold you over until their office is open again). Remember to have your emergency vet plan ready, in case your duck's condition declines after normal business hours.

If your duck doesn't respond to the antibiotics, vets will often run a comprehensive avian blood profile to help see what's going on as far as your duck's white blood cell count as well as ensuring their organs are still functioning properly (and if not, what countermeasures need to be taken). X-rays (and sometimes ultrasounds) can also be enlisted to give your vet further insight into the source of the problem. If your vet suspects that the fever is an inflammatory response they may prescribe anti-inflammatory/pain medication.

Fever is a natural reaction to help your duck's body counteract infectious disease. For this reason, feverish ducks shouldn't be placed into cold baths as a home remedy. Forcibly cooling your duck can interfere with their regulatory mechanisms and should be avoided *unless* you're so advised by your vet. You can, however, provide your duck free access to cool, clean swimming water, giving them the option to self-cool if they want to.

Immune Deficiency

As your duck enters their geriatric years you may notice a decrease in their immune system. Bacterial infections are far more common in elderly ducks than they are in their younger counterparts. Stressed ducks, including those who've lost their mates, can also experience dips in their immune systems, especially if they have no other ducks around to keep them company. Remember ducks are flock animals who thrive in each other's presence and often become depressed in solitary situations.

- **Symptoms**

Some symptoms of immune deficiency may include: more frequent trips to the vet for a variety of issues ranging from bacterial infections, fever, pneumonia, general illness—all the way over to parasite infestations (just to name a few).

- **Treatment**

If your duck is nervous or stressed, attempt to alleviate those stressors that are affecting them, bringing serenity back to their pen as well as to their immune system. If your duck is lonely, giving them a new ducky companion can often lift their spirits, which in turn can positively influence their immunity. In addition, examine their diet and make sure they're on a brand name feed formula best suited for their age and needs. Probiotics can be added to an elderly or immune compromised duck's diet to help boost their capabilities. You may even wish to discuss vitamin and mineral supplement options with your vet.

Thymic Carcinoma (Lymphosarcoma)

Thymic Carcinoma is cancer that occurs on the outer epithelial cells of the thymus glands and it's *extremely* rare in waterfowl. Older or immune compromised ducks are more susceptible as well as those with a genetic predisposition.

The Bursa of Fabricius is the primary site for B-cell production in ducks while their thymus glands are the primary site of T-Cell production. B-cell and T-cells are types of white blood cells that fight off infection. While cancer of the Bursa of Fabricius is seemingly unreported in ducks, there have been isolated cases of thymus gland cancers.

- **Symptoms**

Some symptoms of thymic carcinoma may include: swollen throat, lump on the throat, chronic coughing, difficulty breathing, difficulty swallowing, wheezing, hoarseness and excessive open-bill panting.

- **Treatment**

Thymic carcinoma is diagnosed by blood work, x-ray, ultrasound and physical exam, although it can only be truly diagnosed through biopsy.

Treatment for lymphosarcoma may include Leukeran® tablets (chlorambucil) given orally twice a week. The bad news is long-term success hasn't yet been reported. Even so, a positive result for lymphoma doesn't always require immediate euthanasia when the diagnosis is made. Some ducks thrive happily for a year or more provided that pain management and other supportive care is actively taken into consideration.

Viral Disease

Now I'm going to cover some of the big-time viral diseases out there. You'll most likely *never* see any of these, but you may hear about them and want to know more. If so, you can read about them here. For the most part, these viruses tend to occur in large populations including hatcheries, private collections and zoos, especially in regions prone to outbreaks. If you keep your duck pen nice and tidy and avoid overcrowding or bringing in newcomers without quarantining them first, you should never experience any of these issues.

Duck Viral Enteritis (DVE) / (Duck Plague)

Duck Viral Enteritis is a highly contagious disease among waterfowl. It's instigated by a herpes virus that causes vascular damage and results in hemorrhaging and rapid death. The virus spreads from duck-to-duck through direct contact or by way of the environment, commonly through water (especially in slow-moving or stagnant ponds).

DVE usually only surfaces among wild populations (often non-migratory), large flock situations (zoos or private collections) and in localized geographical areas—with outbreaks tending to occur in the spring. DVE is *rarely* heard of among a couple of backyard pet ducks.

The best preventative measures include:

1. Muscovy and Mallard ducks in particular appear to be more susceptible to DVE than standard domestic ducks. The sudden death of Muscovy or Mallards while other breeds remain unaffected can be an indicator of DVE. Even so, proper quarantine measures should be taken before adding *any* new waterfowl to your flock. The incubation period of DVE is 7 days or less, so keep newcomers separate from your own flock for 2-4 weeks before introducing them to your own ducks.

2. Whenever possible, prevent your ducks from intermingling with wild waterfowl (especially large flocks or if you live in an area where DVE is prevalent).

3. A live and weakened virus vaccine can be administered to ducks at risk, but it appears to be less effective on Muscovy and Mallard ducks.

- **Symptoms**

Symptoms of DVE may include: overall weakness, disinterest in normal routines, appetite loss, extreme thirst, diarrhea (sometimes bloody and staining their vent) and sudden death. More often than not, symptoms go unnoticed and ducks are suddenly found deceased.

- **Treatment**

If caught in very early stages, hospitalization including IV fluids, nutritional support and potent pain medication can sometimes be effective, although most vets will recommend humane euthanasia instead. Ducks who do recover from DVE are immune to re-infection, but are still carriers and can spread the disease to other waterfowl.

Duck Viral Hepatitis (DVH)

Duck Viral Hepatitis tends to occur in ducklings under a month old and is transmitted from duck-to-duck via fecal ingestion. DVH is fatal and highly contagious with ducklings becoming symptomatic within 1-2 days of transmission. Hatcheries and serious breeders often immunize their ducks against DVH to prevent upsetting losses.

The best preventative measures include:

1. Continued injections of inactivated vaccine into breeding adults can prevent outbreaks. Ducklings at risk can receive injections into their webbing on their first day of life with immunity coming 3-4 days later.

2. Avoid the comingling of ducklings with adult ducks for 4-6 weeks to prevent transmission.

- **Symptoms**

Some symptoms of DVH may include: fatigue, loss of appetite (which is highly unusual in ducklings), balance issues, lack of motor coordination, arching of back, seizures (often while lying on their back, with feet paddling in the air), followed by rapid fatality.

- **Treatment**

There is no treatment for DVH, although some ducklings can live through outbreaks (especially with supportive care). Ducklings who do survive, continue to carry the virus and can spread it to others for another two months. For the safety of other ducklings, Famciclovir (Famir®) is often prescribed as an antiviral agent to help prevent future breakouts and spreading.

Avian Diphtheria (Fowl Pox)

Avian Diptheria is a virus spread by mosquitoes, which occurs very rarely in ducks. The disease is usually slow-developing with outbreaks that range from mild to severe. Once infected, ducks can often infect each other through direct contact, whereby the virus gains entry into another duck's body and bloodstream.

- **Symptoms**

Some symptoms of avian diphtheria may include: missing feathers with skin warts, foot or leg warts, dark bill lesions (near the base of the bill) and respiratory difficulty (if bill lesions block the upper throat).

- **Treatment**

There is no treatment available. Mild cases will sometimes run their course and then fade away while more severe cases can be more problematic. Supportive care including pain medication will need to be sought out. There are vaccinations to help prevent outbreaks, but they're often only used in large commercial applications.

Avian Encephalomyelitis

Avian Encephalomyelitis is a virus that's spread through the ingestion of fecal matter. It's extremely rare among waterfowl because they harbor natural antibodies.

- **Symptoms**

Some symptoms may include: head, neck and wing tremors, loss of balance, lack of muscle coordination, disinterest in normal activities and paralysis.

- **Treatment**

There is no treatment available, but some ducks will survive with supportive care. Preventative vaccinations are available, but since ducks tend to be naturally immune it's *never* recommended.

Avian Proventricular Dilatation Disease (PDD)

Avian Proventricular Dilation Disease is believed to be caused by more than one virus including *Avian bornavirus* (ABV), which attacks the nervous system. This eventually leads to secondary symptoms, including damage to the proventriculus (the passageway connecting your duck's crop to their gizzard).

PDD is usually spread through direct fecal ingestion, or potentially from mother ducks to their ducklings via their eggs. I say this very loosely because in actuality, random PDD testing on wild ducks, geese and swans has *yet* to show instances of infection in Mallard ducks, which means you really don't have anything to worry about. If you have a mixed flock including geese or swans and one of them becomes infected with PDD (which is extremely unlikely), the odds that they could infect your ducks is practically zero. So why do I mention this disease at all? Because people ask me this question all the time, and if you're one of them, you too can rest easy now.

- **Symptoms**

Some symptoms may include: vomiting, severe weight loss, delayed crop movement, the passing of undigested food in the feces, diarrhea, seizures, blindness, muscle weakness and lack of interest in normal activities.

- **Treatment**

PDD is normally confirmed by your vet through crop biopsy, blood testing, and endoscopic exam. The presence of AVB can be tested by a cloacal swab culture. There isn't much in the way of treatment aside from administering non-steroidal, anti-inflammatory/pain medication, an anticonvulsant/sedative and nutritional and fluid support.

West Nile Virus (WNV)

West Nile Virus is spread by mosquitoes and is very rare in waterfowl. It's more prevalent in particular regions and during certain times of the year (July to September in the U.S.).

- **Symptoms**

Some symptoms of WNV may include: fever, excessive panting, fatigue, vomiting, appetite loss, sudden muscle weakness, partial paralysis, muscle tremors and seizures.

- **Treatment**

WNV is confirmed by blood test. Treatment includes supportive care, which includes IV fluids, pain medication, anticonvulsant/sedative, antibiotics to prevent secondary infection and possible tube or syringe feedings.

Newcastle Disease Virus (NDV)

Newcastle Disease is a highly contagious virus (*paramyxovirus*), which is passed from bird-to-bird through ingestion of feces or bodily discharge or through inhalation; even so, it's pretty rare among waterfowl, especially in closed flocks.

The best way to prevent the introduction of NDV into your flock is by quarantining any new birds (any species) for a minimum of 2 weeks (4-6 weeks if there's a high risk of exposure) to ensure they don't become symptomatic before allowing them to intermingle with your ducks.

- **Symptoms**

Symptoms of Newcastle Disease may include: excessive panting, difficulty breathing, coughing, sneezing, diarrhea (often discolored), loss of appetite, weight loss, nasal and eye discharge, fatigue, muscle tremors, paralysis, shaking/twisting of the head and neck, drooped wings and circling behavior.

- **Treatment**

Newcastle Disease is confirmed by blood test. Once your duck becomes symptomatic there is no treatment, only supportive care, which includes: IV fluids, pain medication, anticonvulsant/sedative, antibiotics to prevent secondary infection and possible tube or syringe feedings. Oxine AH in a nebulizer is sometimes enlisted, although it's uncertain if it actually provides any assistance. There are vaccines available to help prevent some strains of NDV, but since ducks aren't usually at risk, they aren't always readily available or recommended.

Avian Influenza (Bird Flu)

Avian influenza is a naturally occurring viral infection among birds. Most strains aren't harmful at all; in fact, it's currently only the H5 and H7 strains that are of concern. Many wild birds are carriers although they may never exhibit symptoms. The virus can be passed onto ducks via the ingestion of fecal matter or bodily discharge.

The only way to prevent an infection among your flock is to keep your ducks in a fully closed environment, where no wild birds have any access into their pen or barn. Since most ducks aren't kept in a *completely* closed environment, you can achieve peace of mind by understanding that outbreaks are extremely rare among healthy pet ducks kept in sanitary conditions, especially in the U.S.

- **Symptoms**

Some symptoms of avian influenza may include: unusual and involuntary movements, circling behavior, deformation of the neck, lack of interest in food or water, blindness, diarrhea and nasal or eye discharge. Death usually occurs soon after the onset of symptoms.

- **Treatment**

Your vet can perform a cloacal swab, virus isolation test for the H5 and H7 strains of avian influenza. They'll need to send the sample to a state approved, regulatory lab. It usually takes about five days to receive test results.

There's no treatment for avian influenza, only supportive care, which includes IV fluids, pain medication, anticonvulsant/sedative, antibiotics to prevent secondary infection and possible tube or syringe feedings. Oxine AH in a nebulizer is sometimes enlisted, although it's uncertain if it actually assists.

Bacterial Disease

Now it's time to move onto some of the major bacterial diseases out there. You'll most likely *never* see any of these among your small flock of ducks because, as with the previous section of viral diseases, they tend to only occur in large populations including hatcheries, private collections and zoos, especially in regions prone to outbreaks. If you keep your duck pen nice and tidy and avoid overcrowding or bringing in newcomers without quarantining them first, you should never experience any of these issues.

New Duck Syndrome/Disease (Infectious Serositis)

Riemerella Anatipestifer infection (a.k.a. *Pasteurella Anatipestifer*) is a bacterial disease that tends to affect younger ducks under eight weeks old. Transmission from duck-to-duck can occur by inhalation, or by entryway into the bloodstream via cuts in the bottoms of their webbed feet. If left untreated the infection can become systemic, involving multiple organs, which is why the disease is sometimes referred to as *Duck Septicemia*.

The best way to keep bacteria out of your duck pen is to prevent it from being introduced. This is done by keeping things tidy and making sure anyone entering your duck pen has clean shoes and clothing. If they have flocks of their own (waterfowl, chickens, turkeys, pheasants) be sure they don't unwittingly bring contaminants into your duck pen. Vaccines are available and can be explored if you believe your young ducks are in particular risk, but these are mostly used in breeder situations and are rarely recommended.

- **Symptoms**

Some symptoms of New Duck Syndrome may include: weakness, limp neck, head/neck tremors, spasms, refusal to participate in normal behaviors, lack of motor coordination, balance issues, nasal discharge, coughing and sneezing.

- **Treatment**

If your young duck is exhibiting symptoms take them to the vet right away. Blood culturing can confirm bacterial presence, but treatment is required immediately—often leaving no time to wait for results. Supportive care including penicillin and subcutaneous fluids (or IV fluids) and tube/syringe feedings may be in order.

Avian/ Fowl Cholera

Avian cholera (a.k.a. *Fowl cholera*) isn't very prevalent in domestic ducks the U.S. It's more common among wild waterfowl and introduced via wild birds and rodents who carry *Pasteurella multocida* bacteria. Ducks become infected through direct contact, fecal ingestion or by drinking contaminated water. Blood-sucking northern poultry mites *(Ornithonyssus sylviarum)* can also be responsible for bacterial introduction and spread.

Preventative measures include:

1. Inoculation may be available. Ask your vet if you believe your duck may be at risk of exposure.
2. Avoid allowing your ducks to comingle with wild waterfowl, especially if you're in a region where avian cholera is prevalent.
3. Keep wildlife out of your pens; this includes rodents and birds.
4. Keep pens and barns clean and water sources fresh and sanitary to prevent parasite and bacterial invasion.

- **Symptoms**

Some symptoms of avian cholera may include: loss of appetite, diarrhea (sometimes bloody), trouble breathing, nasal and eye discharge, seizures and circling behavior.

- **Treatment**

Avian cholera is confirmed by blood test, but since most infected ducks don't survive their first twelve hours, supportive treatment must be immediately sought out as soon as symptoms appear. It's often treated with SMZ/TMP oral suspension antibiotics, but when bacteria prove resistant, injectable penicillin, streptomycin and/or dihydrostreptomycin may do the trick. Any other flock members will need to be treated proactively.

Salmonellosis (Food Poisoning)

Salmonellosis is a type of food poisoning that occurs when ducks are infected with Salmonella bacteria (and there are many strains of it). Infection can crop up when ducks ingest food, water or feces (commonly from wild birds or rodents) contaminated with the bacteria. Older ducks and immune compromised ducks are more likely to succumb.

Some strains of salmonella are also harmful to humans, especially those found in the feces of ducklings, so be sure to wash your hands carefully after handling any new arrivals.

Keep wild birds and rodents out of your pens whenever possible and keep food and water sources clean and fresh to help prevent bacterial contaminants.

- **Symptoms**

Some symptoms of salmonella may include: diarrhea, fever, nausea, refusal to participate in normal activities, open-bill panting.

- **Treatment**

Your vet will confirm salmonellosis by fecal exam. Ducks usually require supportive care that includes subcutaneous fluids (and in severe cases, IV fluids). In the case of secondary infection, they may also need antibiotics. Treatment often continues for 3-4 weeks, depending on severity.

Reticuloendotheliosis

Reticuloendotheliosis is caused by a virus of the same name, which is transmitted by mosquito (although it isn't very contagious). This virus was once limited to mammals until research scientists stuck their fingers in the mix and bridged the gap. It targets the reticuloendotheial system (or mononuclear phagocyte system), which is mainly located in your duck's spleen and is responsible for destroying harmful bacteria that enters their body.

- **Symptoms**

Some symptoms of reticuloendotheliosis may include: weight loss, pale bill and legs, immune deficiency, abnormal feather growth, partial paralysis (sometimes sporadic) and benign and malignant tumor growth involving the thymus glands.

- **Treatment**

There is no treatment available although supportive care can increase your duck's chances of survival. Long-term effects can include thymic lymphoma.

Medical #17
Surviving Predatory Attack

If you haven't predator-proofed your pen properly and your duck succumbs to an attack you'll need to stabilize them using the knowledge I've given you in prior sections. Once you've accomplished this, get them to a qualified vet as soon as you possibly can.

Ducks are very resilient and will often survive a close encounter with a predator provided you get them safely through their first few hours *and* start them on potent antibiotics to address any dangerous bacteria passed through bites and scratches.

If you have other ducks, make sure another family member ensures they're all safe and accounted for. Once a predator knows where to find a free meal, they'll be back. It's usually just a question of when.

Medical #18
My Ducky Medi-Tracker

To assist you in tracking and recording your duck's physical description, history, symptoms, vet visits, medical care and prescriptions, I've created a health journal just for them.

My Ducky Medi-Tracker utilizes a simple check-box system to record all of the vital details about your feathered friend. Whimsically illustrated and designed as a companion to this book, the Medi-Tracker makes an excellent addition to your duck's medical kit.

Waterfowl Rescue

Waterfowl Rescue

People contact me from all around the world, asking how to safely capture and assist abandoned domestic ducks in their area. Since the need for this information is so prevalent, a chapter on waterfowl rescue is definitely in order.

Domestic ducks aren't adapted to survive in the wild, and abandoning an unwanted duck (setting it "free") on a local pond is inhumane. While I'm guessing most people who do it aren't intending to be cruel, but simply have no clue what lies in store for their ducks, that's no consolation for these sad feathered friends who've been left behind.

Most domesticated ducks can't fly to avoid predators and they're certainly no good at running. They have no claws, and no teeth to defend themselves, which literally makes them *sitting ducks*. Most succumb to predation, acts of human cruelty and malnutrition (and then starvation in the leaner months). They suffer from exposure to harsh elements, becoming frostbitten, or actually freezing right into the ponds they're sitting on in winter.

And if all of this isn't enough, there's also the emotional trauma involved. Ducks depend on their human family for everything—food, water, shelter and routine. When all this is ripped out from under them, it terrifies them, especially human-imprinted ducks who are simply distraught when abandoned by the people they love.

This is when people like you and me notice the problem, roll up our sleeves and commit ourselves to lending a hand to get them out of the mess they're in and back where they belong—with a loving and devoted family.

Rescues #1
Abandoned Ducks

Unless it's an emergency and the duck's life is in immediate danger, there are a few steps you need to take before embarking on a rescue.

1. Ask around and confirm the duck is truly abandoned and doesn't belong to anyone. You don't want to get in trouble for stealing someone's pets (even if they're where they don't belong).

2. You're going to need to find a *safe* place to bring the duck after you rescue them. Whether you take them temporarily until you find that place, or permanently adopt them depends on you.

3. If the duck is injured or looks compromised in anyway, find a vet who can see them following their rescue.

4. Some ducks are easy to capture while others are elusive. The ease of rescue often depends on their personality and where they're located. If you need help, round up some reliable friends to give you a hand.

5. If the ducks are on public property, notify the police the day you're going to do the rescue to prevent any interference from "concerned" citizens (honestly, you won't believe what some people are willing to do).

6. But most of all: Get written permission from the property owner, town official or park foreman (depending where the duck is located) *before* you attempt to capture the duck (or notify the police). No one will bother you once you have this in hand, and if they do, *you* can call the police for assistance.

Sample letter:

"I noticed that there are (two) domestic ducks at (location). These ducks were most likely former pets who were dropped off and abandoned. They're non-flying and when the other ducks and geese migrate in the fall these ducks will be left behind and will most likely die over the course of the winter. Even worse, if any other irresponsible pet owners see them there, it could entice them to drop off their own pets as well. You could end up with a real problem on your hands if I don't remove them quickly. I would like your permission to come in and safely remove the ducks from this public place and deliver them to a safe and loving home, which I have lined up, ready and waiting."

This sensible line of logic usually works with reasonable people who want the best for the animals (although in some cases you may be asked to sign a liability waiver). Just remember to send a *thank you* note after the ducks have been safely rescued, letting them know that the ducks are now in a nice new home. It's a nice way to close the relationship and remain in good graces.

Rescues #2
Rescuing Ducks on Water

One universal truth about trying to rescue skittish ducks on water is they usually don't realize that they need to be rescued. You can't blame them; they're living in the moment and have no idea of the inherent dangers involved.

Large Bodies of Water

As you'll soon realize, ducks are very adept at diving under the water when they get scared and then popping up again anywhere between six and twenty feet away in any direction. Ducks will continue to dive and resurface until they get tired; at which point, they won't dive nearly as deep or swim nearly as far. The early stage of rescuing is often just a ploy where you slowly attempt to tucker them out (without overstressing them too much). Once their dives become superficial, you can easily scoop them up in a large butterfly net and bring them safely to shore.

If you have access to a kayak, canoe, rowboat or jet ski, the rescuing will go a lot faster and will be much less frustrating for you. A jet ski is preferable to a motor boat because it has incredible maneuverability and doesn't have a dangerous propeller, which means you can safely and easily capture even the fastest duck.

Jet Ski

- **Two-seat jet ski**

A two-seat jet ski enables a passenger to catch the duck with a butterfly net while someone else operates it, which is ideal in rescue situations. To prevent equipment damage in shallow or rocky water, it helps if you have someone else in a kayak near shore who can keep the duck out on deep water during the rescue.

- **Single-seat jet ski**

While a single-seat jet ski is less ideal and puts more responsibility on the operator, an experienced person can still manage to net a duck. The other option is for the operator to herd the duck to shore where rescuers are waiting. Again, this type of equipment can be used in combination with a kayak to prevent damage from rocky shorelines.

Kayaks, Canoes and Rowboats

There are instances when kayaks, canoes and row boats can effectively herd a duck onto shore and into a staged pen area. These tactics tend to work best on smaller bodies of water where you can corner the duck and force them up onto land (ducks can usually easily out-swim you on larger bodies of water).

Consider your shoreline wisely before embarking on the rescue and use the landscaping to your advantage. Some ponds have existing fencing or steep banking in some areas that you can use to your advantage to help corner the duck once they've come off the water. It's equally important to consider any dangerous obstacles or situations; you don't want a frightened duck to stumble over treacherous rocks or worse yet, to run out into a neighboring street where they might be hit by a passing car.

Luring Ducks to Shore

Not everyone has access to water equipment, but this doesn't mean you can't lure the ducks off of the water and up to you. Ducks generally thrive on routine and tend to fear anything out of the ordinary *unless* they're extremely hungry or human-imprinted and very trusting of people. If the ducks you plan to rescue are relatively skittish you'll need to do some prep work before you attempt to capture them.

1. Begin by feeding the ducks routinely at the same time every day (preferably in the early morning, when they're really hungry if you can). Lure them further and further up onto land. Try to get them at least 15-20 feet from shore if you have room.

2. Once the ducks are used to coming a good way up onto shore, have a helper slowly walk the shoreline between the ducks and the water. At first the ducks will flee back to water, but eventually they'll get used to having someone harmlessly come between them and their perceived safety. If you don't have a helper, you can work on circling around the ducks yourself while you're feeding them, getting them used to having you come between them and the water.

3. Lay bamboo stakes (or long sticks) on the ground, mapping out where you'll eventually stage your U-shaped pen area. They need to learn to ignore foreign objects, allowing their appetites to prevail. It's a good idea to get them familiar with the pet carrier you'll be using on rescue day too. Start by setting it off far and then bring it in closer every day.

4. If anyone will be helping you on rescue day, have them show up for a few feedings, so the ducks get used to other people lingering around, or have other people visiting the area participate in this exercise with you.

Once you've eased the ducks through these four steps and they'll come up for food anyway, you can begin preparing for their actual rescue.

<u>Rescue Pen Assembly</u>

Your on-shore duck pen can be made a number of ways. Here's a relatively inexpensive one that travels well and sets up easily.

Supplies needed:

1. One 80' x 6' deer fencing barrier
2. Ten 4' bamboo posts
3. Bag of fifty heavy-duty zip-ties (a.k.a. cable ties)
4. Bag of bottom fencing stakes
5. One rubber mallet

Here's what you do:

1. Weave the first 4' bamboo post through one end of the deer fencing, starting at the top of the 6' netting and working your way down. Leave 2' of netting draping down at the bottom.

2. Zip-tie the bamboo post securely into place and then snip off any excess zip-tag ending.

3. Unroll the plastic fencing 10 feet and then weave and zip-tie the next bamboo post similarly into place.

4. Continue zip-tying bamboo posts every 10 feet until 7 posts are in place.

5. Unroll the last 20 feet of netting and weave and zip-tie the 8th post into place at the end.

The finished fence should look something like this:

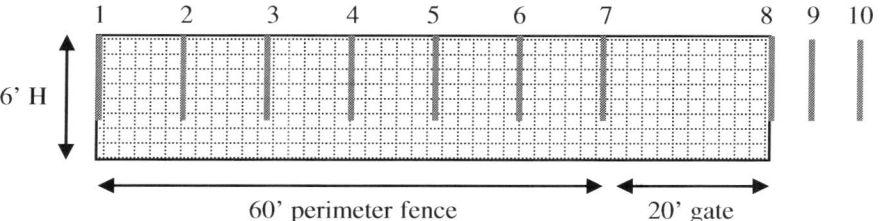

Roll the fencing carefully back up and bring the two extra bamboo posts, the fencing stakes and the rubber mallet along with you to the rescue site (along with a pet carrier for the ducks).

Once at the site:

1. Unroll and set up your portable pen on shore, making sure the 20' gate opens up towards the pond and seals the pen closed properly when shut. You can set it up in a square or in a U-shape, whatever works best in your situation.

2. Pound the first 7 bamboo posts firmly into the ground using the rubber mallet. *Don't* pound post #8 into the ground.

3. Open the gate and gently push bamboo post #8 into the ground, just enough to hold it in place while you're assembling the rest of the pen.

4. Space out the two extra bamboo posts (# 9 and #10) in the pen's gateway between post #1 and post # 7 and pound them into the ground. These will eventually help support the closed gate.

5. Lay the extra 2 feet of bottom netting onto the ground, so that it drapes *inside* of the pen and then pin it down with the fencing stakes (don't worry about the extra 2' of fencing draping from the gate).

6. Set up your pet carrier, so that it's ready in the pen.

7. Place the rubber mallet on the ground near post #1.

Rescue Time!

You now have temporary pen in place. Send one person to hold bamboo post #8, standing as far away from the pen as possible while keeping the gateway wide open. This person is the *gatekeeper* and they're going to need to remain perfectly still and wait for the ducks to come up on shore.

The person who usually feeds the ducks (this is probably *you*) is the *feeder*. When everything's in place, the feeder can begin luring the ducks up onto shore and as deep into the pen as possible. It's best to do this when they're really hungry, so you may want to skip a day of feeding and then head out early in the morning the next day before anyone else fills their tummies.

Once the ducks are deep in the pen, the gatekeeper will need to close the gate as efficiently as possible without startling the ducks back into the water. This is usually done by making a wide girth down and away from the pen's mouth as they pass by before broaching back up again to seal the gate. Sometimes the gatekeeper needs to sprint suddenly forward if they feel the ducks are about to turn and bolt back down towards the water. Once they've made it to post #1, they can grab the mallet and pound the #8 gatepost into the ground. The two free-standing bamboo posts will help brace the gate once it's closed.

If you can get anyone else to help that day, this is the perfect time to send them running in to stand on the 2 feet of draped netting that's dangling from the gate—pinning it to the ground *outside* of the pen. These are your *goaltenders*.

The feeder now becomes the *catcher* and begins cornering the ducks against the soft fencing and loading them safely into the pet carrier. The faster they can do this, the more likely they'll catch all of the ducks before they find their way out.

The gatekeeper remains on the outside center of the 20' gate, sliding back and forth as needed and guarding it to prevent any ducks from escaping and catching any who try. They can hand off any captured ducks to the catcher inside the pen, who can then load them into the pet carrier (see: *"Safe Catching and Handling"*).

While this may sound a little complicated, it's really quite easy and most people using this system eventually get their duck although it can take more than one attempt—especially if ducks aren't prepped properly before attempts are made. If you can, practice the routine a few times in your backyard.

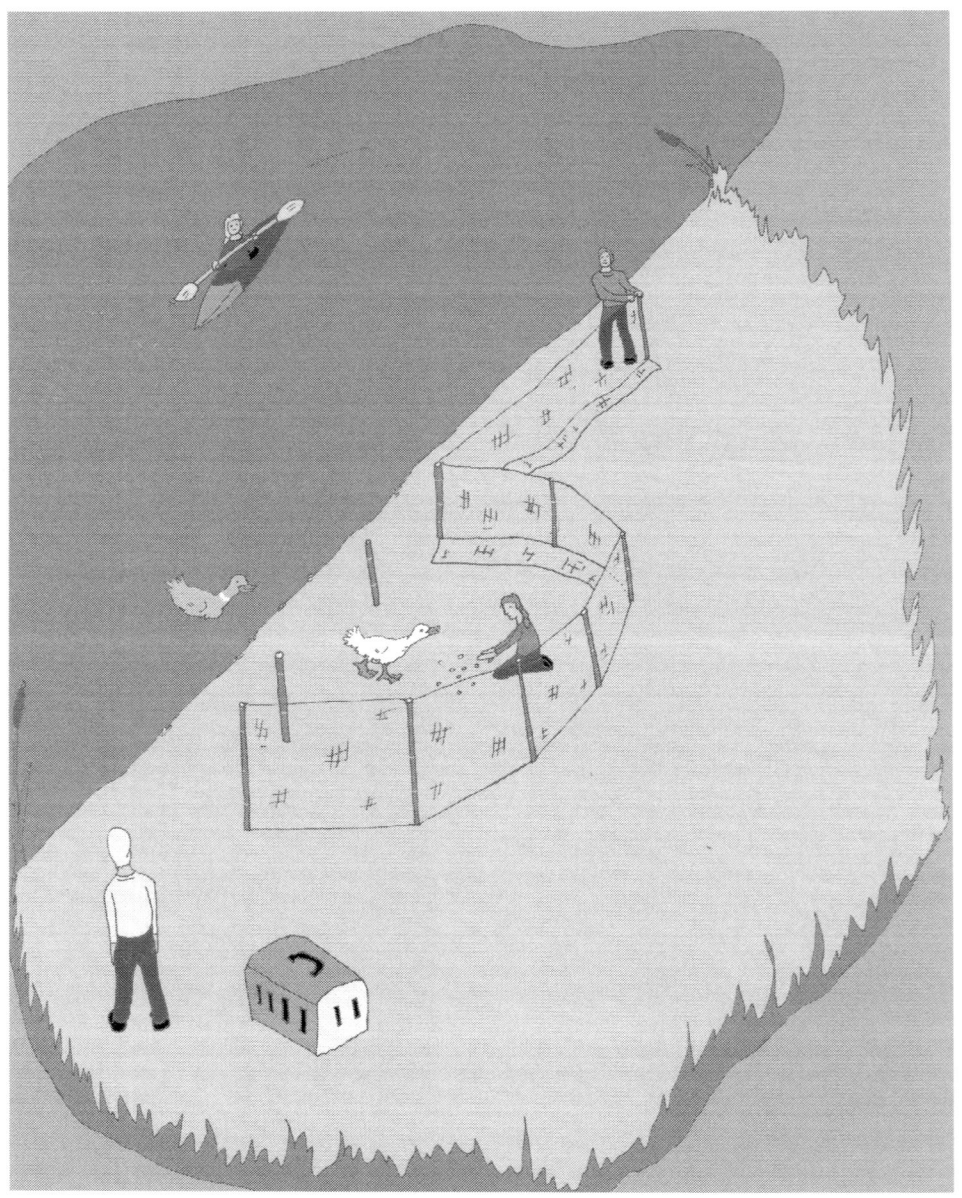

Land rescues are done by luring ducks up onto shore into staged pens

Rope Over The Water Rescue Method

When dealing with smaller bodies of water you can often catch ducks by setting up a temporary pen and using a length of rope to herd ducks up into it. Two people work together, each taking an end of the rope and working their way around the pond and towards the staged pen. Keep the rope line taut and close to the surface of the water as you go. It helps if you have one or two helpers ready to catch the ducks once they're inside.

Using rope to herd a duck into a staged pen

Rescuing Tips

Catching ducks can be a bit of a *learn-as-you-go* skill, but there are a few tricks I can tell you ahead of time to help give you a good jump on things.

- **Fake left, grab right**

A handy and universal trick to catching ducks is to *fake left and grab right*. If the duck is running along the fence line trying to escape, you can usually fake them into turning right into your arms. Use this technique more than once if you need to, or trick them into heading into a set of helping hands.

- **I thought you had him!**

Never rely on one another to catch the duck; instead, everyone needs to give it their best at all times—never giving up until the duck is actually in someone's hands. The most common duck rescuing mistake is, *"I thought you had him!"* If two of you both manage to get your arms around the duck at the same time—all the better! So don't give up too soon.

- **We've got a flier!**

Sometimes a duck will take flight when you're about 4-5 feet away and encroaching in on them for the capture. They can only lift themselves a few feet off of the ground and don't steer well, so if they take off, just get directly in front of them, open your arms and catch them kind of like you'd catch a football, only being careful of their neck and head. Then quickly get them safely to the ground and sit over them to hold them in place until someone can bring a pet carrier to you. Ducks will normally try to fly in the direction of the water when attempting this escape maneuver.

- **Never grab a duck by the legs**

Never, ever grab a duck by the legs or wings—not under any circumstances, or you could risk permanently injuring them. If necessary, you can grab a duck *gently but firmly* around the *base* of their neck while you or someone else gets control of their wings.

- **Don't flinch**

Don't be afraid; ducks can't hurt you. Honestly, the worst direct injury you might get from a duck is a pinch, poke or accidental scratch. Last minute flinching can lead to escapes. As a final defense, ducks tend to flap their wings right before being caught. The moment you close your eyes and turn your face away, they take advantage and make a break for it. It's what they do. Keep your face and eyes on the duck at all times, and show no fear because there's nothing to be afraid of.

Ideal Catching Times

The best time to rescue a duck is between 8:00-10:00 a.m. The sooner you can get there, the less likely anyone else will have already fed them breakfast.

You'll usually only get a few chances to catch a duck on any given day. If you don't get them by the second or third try, it's time to pack-up and call it a day.

Don't get discouraged if you don't get all of the ducks on your first attempt. Give them a rest and go back and feed them for a few more days to re-establish their trust and then try, try again! Catching a wary duck can sometimes be frustrating, but if you keep at it, you can usually get them. When colder weather comes and ducks get hungrier they're often easier to lure in and catch.

Rescues #3
Wild Waterfowl

I've received a lot of inquiries regarding the rescuing of wild waterfowl over the years and sadly, most of them never needed any help in the first place. Most people contact me about ducklings or eggs that they've removed from a nest and brought home with them, not understanding that they probably haven't helped at all or that what they've done is illegal. That's right, in the U.S. wild ducks and ducklings are protected by the Migratory Bird Treaty Act, which clearly states that it's *illegal* for unlicensed individuals to keep them for any length of time, and this actually goes onto include their eggs and feathers too.

If a wild duck or duckling is in urgent danger, you may carefully and humanely capture them and arrange for their *immediate* transfer to a licensed wildlife rehabber, or to a vet who's working in conjunction with a rehabber. If the duckling isn't in pressing danger, but you're concerned about them, avoid the temptation of disturbing them and contact a wildlife rehabber for advice *before* actually intervening. Don't assume that ducklings have been abandoned just because you don't see their mother around. Often times, the mother is nearby waiting for you to leave before coming back. Likewise, *never* pick up any "abandoned" eggs in the hopes of incubating them yourself. Any small mistakes you make can lead to a lifetime of disabilities. This isn't a game and again, it's *illegal*.

I know how darling little ducklings are, but it's important to keep *their* best interests in mind, setting aside your own personal desires. Wild ducklings need to be taught to forage for natural foods and they need to learn to exercise their wings so they can fly one day; they can't do either of these things in your house. It's also vital that they don't imprint on humans (this means *you!*), or they won't fair well in the wild. They may not act appropriately around other ducks and become outcasts, or they may seek out other humans once released, which could prove disastrous (not everyone has good intentions when it comes to wild ducks). On the other hand, a certified rehabber has the training and know-how to take care of a wild duckling and ensure that they can be released safely back into the environment.

I'm also occasionally asked for help regarding adult wild ducks. All I can say in this regard is, unless the duck is somehow incapacitated and unable to fly, you'll need access to some pretty fancy gear (net guns, jet ski, etc.) as well as some experienced help before proceeding. While I may know my stuff when it comes to rescuing non-flying ducks, not much of it applies to those who can simply lift-off and get away.

Wild Duck Emergency

As a preparative measure, begin to take notice of business cards of licensed wildlife rehabbers in your area. They're often available at your vet's office, humane society or pet supply stores. Take their card, or copy down their information, so that you'll have it if you ever need it. Their card will usually indicate the types of animals they're licensed to handle. Proactive internet searches can also help prepare you for a wildlife emergency. Rehabbers often operate out of their own pocket, so reach out and find people to support in your area to help keep them going; just be sure to visit them first to make sure they're running a clean and respectable service. Good rehabbers often have a wonderful network of connections and can give you the names of other nearby rehabbers that handle all kinds of wildlife.

- **Safe Place**

Place the duck in a protective pet carrier (if you don't have one you can use a closable cardboard box with plenty of penny-sized breathing holes) lined with hay or an expendable dry towel—free of any loose strings that might result in toenail tangles or accidental ingestion. Avoid using newspaper for bedding since it can remove precious oils from a duck's feathers.

You want your temporary guest to be warm and cozy, but not hot. Remember adult ducks have feathers that are excellent insulators. Ducklings should be kept warm and draft free, but still well-ventilated.

While it might be tempting, try not to disturb your visitor. Let them rest quietly in a closed-off room until you can arrange for their safe transfer to a rehabber. Be extremely cautious that neither children nor family pets have access to them in the meantime.

- **Water**

Place a small bowl of drinking water in the corner of the duck's pet carrier as soon as you have them settled in a private room. If you've rescued a duckling, you want to be careful they can't fall and drown in their water bowl, so keep it small and shallow.

Once you have the duck or duckling resting safely in a protected location with drinking water, your highest priority is to contact rehabbers and find someone who can take them as soon as possible. The quicker you get them there, the more likely they are to survive.

- **Food**

If you've just rescued a wild duck or duckling avoid feeding them until you've received advice from a certified rehabber (or if you can't find one right away, try contacting a vet who's experienced with waterfowl) because some species have specialized diets.

Wild ducks: If you can't reach a qualified person within 2-3 hours of their rescue, you can offer actual duck food to a fully feathered adult duck.

Wild ducklings: If you can't reach a qualified person within one hour of their rescue, you can offer them actual duckling crumbles, or better yet, live meal worms (which you can find in most pet stores). Offer them a few at a time and allow them to eat as much as they want. Continue offering them the meal worms every hour until you're able to find help.

- **Drive & donate**

Once you find a certified rehabber willing to take the duckling, you'll need to get them there right away. It's bad manners to ask a rehabber to drive to you and then to take care of the animal as well. You should bring the duck to them and remember to always donate!

Index

A

Abacot Ranger ducks, 140
abandoned ducks, 408
abdominal bones, 288
abdominal injury, 288
abscess, 223
ABV, 401
Acuaria, 357
acupuncture, 249
addling eggs, 167
Adequan, 263
adrenal cancer, 394
adrenal glands, 393
aflatoxicosis, 383
aggression, 186
air conditioner, 161
air conditioning, 86
air sac mites, 349
air sac, infection, 348
air sac, injury, 348
air sacs, 343
Albon, 360
algae bloom, 334
alligator, 64
alpha male, 102
Amidostomum, 357
Amoebotaenia, 359
amputation, limb, 251
amputation, wing, 286
Ancona ducks, 134
anemia, 390
anesthesia, 210
angel wing, 284
ankle, 246
appetite loss, 366, 367
appetite, changes, 365
arm, 278
arteries, 386
arthritis, 263
arts & crafts, 190
ascaridia, 356
Ascaris, 356
Aspergillus flavus, 343
Aspergillus parasiticus, 383
aspiration, 202
aspiration pneumonia, 348
Australian Spotted ducks, 129
auto feeder, 40
automated feeders, 378
avian bornavirus, 401
avian chlamydia, 349
avian cholera, 403
avian diphtheria, 400

avian influenza, 402
avian proventricular dilatation disease, 401
aviary net, snow, 162
Avi-Culture, 373
Aylesbury ducks, 141

B

baby toys, 198
balloons, 335
bantam, 120
bantam breeds, 126
barred feathers, 124
bathing, winter, 161
bathtub, 178, 179
bean, 87
bear, 63
bedding, 84
bee sting, 220
behavior, seasonal, 160
bibbed, 122
bill, 212
bill injuries, 217
bill, broken, 215
bill, deformed, 219
bill, freckles, 213
bill, hematoma, 218
bill, peeling, 213
bill, prosthetic, 219
bill, punctured, 218
bill, scratched, 215
bill, swollen, 218
bill, trimmed, 216
bio-security, 156
bird flu, 402
biting, 165
blackhead disease, 355
bleach solution, 353
blindness, 325
blood, 386
blood feather, 240
blood infection, 391
blood work, 209
blow dryer, safety, 238
Blue Seal, 26
Blue Swede mixed ducks, 136
Blue Swedish ducks, 135
bobcat, 61
body language, 184
body lice, 242
body temperature, 397
bone cancer, 262
bone disease, 331
bone infection, 274

boots, 248
botulism, 383
brain, 329
brain trauma, 331
brain tumor, 330
bread, 37
breastbone, 288
breed colors, 122
breed standards, 121
brewer's yeast, 258
broken leg, 260
brooder, 46
brooder temperature, 49
bruises, 225
Buff Orpington ducks, 137
bumblefoot, 272
burdock, 383
bursa of Fabricus, 397

C

caeca, 351
calcium chips, 34
calcium gluconate, 296
calcium, bones, 262
Call ducks, 126
canizie, 123
canoe, 409
Capillaria, 354
capillary worms, 354
cardiomyopathy, 388
cardiovascular, 386
carpometacarpus, 278
caruncles, 87
cat, 65
cataracts, 320
catching ducklings, 90
catching ducks, 90
catching rain, 184
Cayuga ducks, 138
ceca, 351
cecal worms, 355
cerebellum, 329
cerebrum, 329
cestodes, 359
chain link, 81
charge & retreat, 154
checklist, duckling, 51
checklist, duck sitter, 170
chickens, 272
children, ducklings, 254
chlamydia, avian, 349
chlamydophila psittaci, 349
chlorine, 178
chlortetracycline, 349

Choanotaenia, 359
chocolate, 38
chondroitin, 263
chronic respiratory disease, 343
cigarettes, 335
cardiovascular system & diagram, 386
checklist, before-you-go, 52
checklist, duck sitter, 170
circulatory system & diagram, 386
clean water, 99
cloaca, 384
cloaca, female, 290
cloaca, male, 306
cnemidocoptes, 244
coccidia, 360
cold feet, 249
companion animals, 154
compost pile, 334
concrete ponds, 92
cork-screw penis, 164
costumes, 188
coughing: See parasites & respiratory system
cracked corn., 30
cradle, 247
CRD, 343
cremation, 173
crested ducks, 125
crickets, 181
crop, 351, 375
crop diet, 378
crop impaction, 380
crop injury, 382
crop stasis, 379
crop, burned, 382
crop, infection, 379
crop, pendulous, 381
cuclotogaster, 242
cups, 197
curly tail feather, 117
Cyathocotyle, 358
cysts, 224
cysts, ovarian, 301
cysts, oviduct, 301
cysts, ovotestis, 301
Cytodites nudus, 349

D

Davainea, 359
dearth, 32, 353
deferent ducts, 306
dehumidifier, 161
dehydration, 374
depluming mites, 244
dermanyssus, 243
deslorelin, 291
diabetes, 395
diaper harness, 111, 248
diarrhea, 201, 375
diary, 176
dietary aids, 372
digestive system & diagram 351
dimorphic ducks, 228
disabled duckling, 167
disease, bacterial, 402
disease, resistence, 23
dislocated limb, 254
diving instinct, 209
dog, 65
dosages, 202
double-laced feathers, 124
doxycycline, 349
drake to duck ratio, 116
drakes, fighting, 101
drakes, multiple, 104
drakes, pair, 100
drakes, separating, 104
dress-up, 188
Drontal Plus, 359
drowning, 91
duck callers, 185
duck feed, 25
duck house, 77
duck identification, 106
duck plague, 399
duck septicemia, 402
duck sitter, 170
duck sizes, 120
duck virus enteritis, 399
duck virus hepatitis, 400
duck weights, 121
duck, rescue, 409
duckling diet, 26
duckling, bedding, 48
duckling, checklist, 51
duckling, drafts, 46
duckling, feeder, 39
duckling, food, 50
duckling, growth, 53
duckling, heat, 49
duckling, housing, 46
duckling, illness, 55
duckling, lameness, 258
duckling, naps, 53
duckling, pecking, 54
duckling, swimming, 52
duckling, water, 50
ducklings and ducks, 187
ducklings, acquiring, 151
ducklings, benefits, 148
ducklings, catching, 90
ducklings, holding, 90
ducklings, incubating, 167
ducklings, supervision, 51
ducklings, transitioning, 55, 56
ducklings, with ducks, 150
ducks, acquiring, 152
ducks, benefits, 150
ducks, catching, 90
ducks, expense, 159
ducks, recognition, 166
ducks, transport, 156
duclair, 122
DVE, 399
DVH, 400

E

eagle, 66
ear flaps, 313
ears, 313
earthworms, 180
East Indie ducks, 127
eclipse molt, 228
egg binding, 292
egg impaction, 292
egg, odd-shaped, 34
egg-laying issues, 292
eggs, 189
eggs, addling, 167
eggs, incubating, 167
eggs, medication, 244
eggs, soft-shelled, 296
eggshell, eating, 364
eggshell, soft, 34
eggshell, texture, 34
Eimeria, 360
elbow, 278
electric fence, snow, 162
electric fencing, 76
emergency, wild duck, 415
encephalomyelitis, 400
endocarditis, 390
endocrine system & diagram, 393
endocrine, cancer, 394
endocrine, disorders, 393
endoscopy, 337
energy water, 372
enilconazole, 345
eomenacanthus, 242
epidermoptes, 244
esophagus, 351
estrogen, 304
euthanasia, 171

Euthanisol, 173
exotic ducks, 120
eye dryness, 320
eye infection, 317
eye trauma, 318
eyelids, 317
eyes, 315
eyeworms, 358

F

F10-SC, 344
failing oil duct, 237
falcon, 66
fans, 161
feather art, 191
feather biting, 365
feather colors, 122
feather duster, 49
feather eating, 365
feather loss, eyes, 320
feather, broken, 240
feathers, 227
feathers, damaged, 236
feathers, faded, 230
feathers, sunlight, 230
feathers, yellow, 231
feed bowl, 39
feed dispenser, 39
feed expiration, 31
Feed label, 29
feed recalls., 31
feed research, 28
feed storage, 32
feed, medicated, 26
feed, milling, 29
feed, quality, 28
feed, U.S. brands, 26
feed, UK brands, 27
feeder, duckling, 39
feeding schedule, 38
feet, black, 221
feet, circulation, 161
feet, warm, 161
female reproductive system & diagram, 290
femur, 246
fenbendazole, 355
fencing, 72
fencing, inside, 81
fencing, underground, 74
fencing, unsafe, 81
Fenland/Fancy Feed, 27
ferrtilizer, 334
fever, 397
fibula, 246

fighting, 102
fighting, signs, 100
figure eight wing wrap, 280
finger, 278
fireworks, 334
fish, 64
fisher cat, 63
Flagyl, 360
flatworm, 359
flesh flies, 245
FLHD, 382
flies, 245
flock size, 112
flock, all females, 115
flock, all males, 114
flock, M/F pair, 115
flock, multiple males & multiple females, 116
flock, one male & multiple females, 116
flooring, 80
fluff lice, 242
fluke worm, 358
fly predators, 245
follicular cysts, 224
food poisoning, 403
foot circulation, 249
foot deformity, 255
foot infection, 267
foot, swelling, 267
footpad injury, 263
foraging, 179
forearm, 278
fowl pox, 400
fox, 61
freckles, 213
free-ranging, 67
frogs, 195
frostbite, 220

G

gape worms, 357
garden hose, 177
garden hose safety, 177
Garvo, 27
geese, 113
gelatin capsules, 206
gender change, 303
gender id, ducklings, 117
gender id, ducks, 117
gender id, feathers, 117
gender id, Muscovy, 119
gender id, quack, 118
gender selection, 113
gizzard, 351

gizzard worms, 357
glucosamine, 263
gonadotropin, 291
goniocotes, 242
grain, 30
Granulex, 221
grapes, 38
grass, 89
greens, unhealthy, 36
grey, 122
grieving, 174
grit, 34
group labeling, 30

H

hair dryer, safety, 238
hairworm, 354
hardware cloth, 83
hardware disease, 70, 336
hatching deformity, 255
hatching, ducklings, 167
hatching, prevention, 166
hawk, 66
hay, 84
HCG injections, 290
head bobbing, 184
head injury, 288
head jiggling, 165
head lice, 242
head vibration, 184
Healx Booster, 372
hearing, 313
hearing, impairment, 313
heart, 386
heart attack, 388
heart failure, 390
heart murmur, 389
heart valves, 389
heat lamp, 49
heat stroke, 386
heat, winter, 87
heated barns, 87
heavyweight, 120
heavyweight breeds, 141
henopause, 304
hepatic disease, 382
Heterakis, 355
hinny, 144
hip, 246
hip injury, 258
hissing, 184
histomoniasis, 355
holding ducks, 90
homosexuality, 164
Hooded Ranger ducks, 140

hormone implants, 291
housing, shade, 77
human imprinting, 148
humerus, 278
hydrotherapy, 246
hygiene, surgery, 210
hyperthermia, 386
hyperthyroidism, 394
hypothermia, 387
hypothyroidism, 394

I

ice/snow melt, 334
icy pens, 162
icy ponds, 163
Imaverol, 345
immune deficiency, 398
immune system & diagram, 397
imprinting, 148
imprinting, filial, 148
imprinting, sexual, 149
incubating eggs, 167
incubating, improper, 167
incubation errors, 331
Indian Runner ducks, 131
indoor ducks, 111
infectious serositis, 402
inflamed vent, 303
infundibulum, 290
injection, 202
insulation, 88
integumentary system & diagram 212
intestinal worms, 355
intestines, 351
intubation, 209
intubation, irritation, 367
irregular pied, 123
isthmus, 290
Ivermectin, 358

J

jet ski, 409
joint care, 263
joint supplements, 263

K

kayak, 409
keel split, 288
Khaki Campbell ducks, 132
kiddy pool safety, 176
kiddy pools, 92, 176
kidney disease, 384
kidneys, 384

knee, 246
knemidocoptes, 244

L

lab results, reading, 269
laced feathers, 124
lacerations, 222
lamellae, 212
lameness, duckling, 258
laparoscopy, 337
laying formula, 35
laying issues, 292
lead poisoning, 337
leg bands, 106
leg deformity, 255
leg infection, 267
leg paralysis, 297
leg, diagram, 246
leg, swelling, 267
Legend, 263
lettuce, 182
Leuprolide, 291
levamisole, 355
levasole, 355
lice, 242
lice, lame ducks, 242
life expectancy, 109
light, egg-laying, 296
lightweight, 120
lightweight breeds, 131
limb dislocation, 254
lipeurus, 242
litter, 85
liver, 351
liver disease, 382
loneliness, 210
lonely duck, 112
lost voice, 361
lungs, 343
Lupron, 291
lymphatic system & diagram, 397
lymphocytic leukemia, 392
lymphosarcoma, 398

M

maggots, 245
magnum, 290
magpie, 122
Magpie ducks, 133
male reproductive system & diagram, 306
Mallard ducks, 130
Mallards, wild, 196
malnutrition, 351

manganese, 297
massage, 249
matches, 335
mate for life, 166
mating ritual, 163
mating season, 188
mats, rubber, 325
mazes, 198
Mazuri, 26
Mazuri Europe, 27
MBD, 331
meal worms, 416
medicated feed, 349
medication, eggs, 244
medications, 202
medicine cabinet, 23
Medi-Tracker, 406
melanoma, 226
menacanthus, 242
menopause, 304
menopon, 242
metritis, 299
metronidazole, 359
mice, 34
middleweight, 120
middleweight breeds, 134
milk thistle, 383
Mini Appleyard ducks, 128
mirrors, 112, 197
misting systems, 86
mites, 243
molting, 227
monomorphic ducks, 228
motion sensor lights, 76
mottled feathers, 124
mourning, duck, 173
mourning, human, 173
mulards, 144
mulch, 334
mule, 144
Muscovy ducks, 143
Muscovy gender, 119
Muscovy mixed, ducks, 144
Muscovy, frostbite, 221
musculoskeletal system & diagram, legs, feet & toes, 246,
musculoskeletal system & diagram, wings & tail, 278
musculoskeletal system & diagram, head, neck & abdomen, 288
mushrooms, 334
Mycloplasma gallisepticum, 343

N

naps, 192
nares (nostrils), 41
NDV, 401
nebulizer, 344
neck injury, 288
nematode, 354
neocnemidocoptes, 244
nerves, 329
nervous system & diagram, eyes & ears, 313
nervous system & diagram, brain & spinal cord, 329
neurological disease, 330
neurological disorders, 330
new duck disease, 402
new duck syndrome, 402
newcastle disease, 401
newspaper, 415
newspaper, bedding, 156
niacin deficiency, 258
nicotine patches/gum, 335
night crawlers, 180
northern poultry mites, 243
no-spill water bowl, 157
NSAIDs, 202
Nutrena, 26
nutrient packets, 50

O

obturator paralysis, 297
Oesophagostomum, 356
oil gland, impacted, 231
oil gland, infected, 234
oil gland, overactive, 233
oil gland, ruptured, 236
oil gland, surgery, 236
oil gland, underactive, 233
olfactory nerves, 313
Omega 3, 263
opossum, 64
Organic Feed Co., 27
ornithonyssus, 243
osteomyelitis, 274
osteosarcoma, 262
ovarian cancer, 302
ovarian tumor, 301, 305
ovary, 290, 304
ovary, endocrine, 393
ovary, vestigial, 304
over-mating, signs, 100
oviduct cancer, 302
oviduct prolapse, 298
oviduct tumor, 301
oviduct worms, 358
oviduct, diagram, 290
oviduct, left, 291
oviduct, right, 291
oviduct, vestigial, 290, 291
ovotestis, 304
owl, 66
oxalic acid, 36
Oxine AH, 345
oxyspirura, 358
oxytetracycline, 350
oyster shells, 34

P

Panacur, 355
pancreas, 351, 393
pancreatic cancer, 395
pancreatitis, 395
pancrezyme, 396
paramyxovirus, 401
parasite counts, 352
parasites, burning, 354
parasites, dearth, 353
parasites, external, 241
parasites, grounds cleaning, 353
parasites, internal, 352
parasites, removal, 353
parasites, sanitizing, 353
parasites, symptoms, 352
parasites, topsoil, 354
parathyroid cancer, 394
parathyroid glands, 393
parrot toys, 198
Pasteurella anatipestifer, 402
PDD, 401
pebble eating, 34, 360
pecking order, 54, 102, 150
Pekin ducks, 142
pen location, 57
pen materials, 59
pen size, 68
pen supports, 70
pen, doors, 72
pen, fencing, 72
pen, instructions, 69
pen, rescues, 410
pen, roofing, 70
penciled feathers, 124
pendulous crop, 381
penectomy, 308
penis, 164, 306
penis prolapse, 306
people food, 335
peppered feathers, 124
peppermint oil, 32

Peritonitis, 300
perosis, 260
pet carrier, 25, 156
petting, egg-laying, 296
petting, hormones, 165
petting, sensitivity, 230
phallus prolapse, 306
pharmacy, compounding, 291
photography, 191
physical therapy, 249
physical therapy, duckling, 259
pied, 123
pill administration, 206
pin feather, 240
pine shavings, 84
pineal cancer, 395
pineal gland, 393
pineoblastoma, 395
pineocytoma, 395
pinion, 286
pituitary cancer, 394
pituitary gland, 393
plants, toxic, 335
playpens, 102
plush toys, 199
pneumonia, 345
poison ingestion, 334
poison, safeguarding, 334
poisoning, 335
poisons, 334
pond safety, 177
pond, slope-banked, 326
ponds, 95, 177
pool safety, 178
portable playpens, 82, 102, 180
poultry powder, 243
poultry wire, 82
praziquantel, 359
precautionary worming, 352
predator attack, 405
predator barrier, 75
predator deterrents, 59
predator skirt, 75
predators, hidden, 60
predators, list, 60
predators, table, 67
preening, winter, 161
preformed pond liners, 93
pressure treated lumber, 334
primary coverts, 279
primary feathers, 279
probiotics, 373
prolapsed penis, 306
prosthetic bill, 219
prosthetic, leg, 251

Prosthogonimus, 358
protozoa, 359, 360
proventriculus, 351
psittacosis, 350
pumps, 98
puncture wounds, 223
Purina, 27
puzzle mats, 80
pyrantel pamoate, 355

Q

quack, female, 118
quack, male, 118
quacking, 183
quarantine, 155
QuickDerm, 273

R

raccoon, 62
radius, 278
Raillietina, 359
raisins, 38
rat, 34, 64
red clover, 383
red face, Muscovy, 221
red poultry mites, 243
renal disease, 384
renal system & diagram, 384
reproductive system & diagram, female, 290
reproductive system & diagram, male, 306
rescue, duck, 409
respiratory system & diagram, 343
reticuloendotheliosis, 404
Riemerella anatipestifer, 402
rippled feathers, 124
rodents, 32, 34
rope, rescue, 413
Rouen, 145
roundworm, 354
rowboat, 409
rubber bill, 213

S

sailocoele, 218
salivary gland, 218
salmonella, 403
salmonellosis, 403
salpingitis, 299
salpingohysterectomy, 291
sand, 162
sanitizing, bleach, 353

Saxony ducks, 146
scaly leg mites, 244
scaly skin mites, 244
sculpture, 191
secondary coverts, 279
secondary feathers, 279
seeds, 30
seizures, 329
seminal vesicles, 306
separating ducks, 99
sepsis, 391
septic shock, 391
septicemia, 391
sequential production, 28
sexual behavior, 164
shade, 85
shade cloth, 85
shade trees, 85
shaft lice, 242
shipping ducks, 157
shoes, 248
shoulder, 278
Silver Appleyard ducks, 147
silver sulfadiazine, 273
sinusitis, 319
skeleton, diagram, 288
skin, 220
skull injury, 288
skunk, 64
sleeping, 192
slipped tendon, 260
slipping, 99
slow crop, 375
Small Holder Range, 27
smell, sense of, 313
snake, 64
snapping turtle, 63
snow-melting chemicals, 163
solar fencing, 76
sour crop, 379
spangled feathers, 124
Sphaeridiotrema, 358
spinal cord, 329
spinal injury, 288
spinal trauma, 331
spinal tumor, 330
splashed feathers, 124
splay leg, 258
splayed tail, 184
spleen, 351
splint, wing, 284
splinting, bones, 261
spraddle leg, 258
sprains, 249
spring fever, 188

staph infection, 268, 272
Staphylococcus, 268
stepping stones, 230
sticky eye, 317
straight run ducklings, 117
straw, 84
stress, 211
stress, egg laying, 296
striped feathers, 124
Strongid-T, 356
strongyloides, 356
Subulura, 356
sulfadimethoxine, 360
summertime care, 160
supplement, powder, 372
Suprelorin, 291
surgery, 209
surgery, food & water, 210
swimming, 176
swimming pool, 178
swimming water, 91
swimming, duckling, 52
Syngamus, 357
synovitis, 274
syringe feeding, 368
systemic infection, 268

T

table, gel cap sizes, 206
table, predators, 67
tail wagging, 184
tail, crooked, 287
tapeworm, 359
tarsometatarus, 246
tear duct, irritated, 319
Telazol, 173
temperature flux, 211
testes, endocrine, 393
testicles, 306
testicular cancer, 309
testicular cyst, 309
testicular tumor, 305, 309
testosterone, excessive, 312
Tetrameres, 357
threadworm, 354
thumb, 278
thymic carcinoma, 398
thymic lymphoma, 391
thymus, 397
thyroid cancer, 394
thyroid gland, 393
tibiotarsus, 246
Tiletamine, 173
tobacco, 335
toe, 246

toe biting, 182
toe injury, 263
toenail trimming, 266
toenail, broken, 266
toes, curled, 265
tongue, 216
toys, 196
trachea, 343
transporting ducks, 156
trematode, 358
Trichomonas, 359
Tricide®, 269
tripping, 99
trout, 123
trumpeting, 184
tube feeding, 372
Tums, 296

U

ulna, 278
ultimobranchial cancer, 394
ultimobranchial gland, 393
ureters, 384
urinary system & diagram, 384
uropygial gland, 231
uterus, 290

V

van deferens, 306
veins, 386
vent, 351, 384
vent, female, 290
vent, inflamed, 303
vent, male, 306
vet, 21
vet exams, follow-up, 209
vet wrap, 279
viral disease, 399
vitamin packets, 50
vitamin powder, 259
vocal damage, 361
vocalizations, 183
vocalizations, Muscovy, 119
vomit, car sick, 156

W

walks, 179
water, 40
water bucket, heated, 43
water bucket, rubber, 42
water dispenser, 42
water feature, 91
water fount, 42
water fount heater, 42
water fount, duckling, 41
waterfowl, wild, 414
watermelon, 181
weasel, 62
webbed feet, 88
webbing, puncture, 264
webbing, torn, 264
weight gain, 374
weight management, 249
weighted bowl, 41
welded wire mesh, 83
Welsh Harlequin ducks, 139

west nile virus, 401
wet feather, procedure, 238
wet feather, resolution, 237
wet feathers, 236
wheelchair, 247
whistling, respiratory, 350
wild duck emergency, 415
wild ducks, 120
wildlife rehabber, 415
windows, 81
wing clipping, 278
wing clipping, diagram, 279
wing lice, 242
wing wrap, 280
wing, broken, 285
wing, diagram, 278
wing, dislocated, 285
wing, drooped, 285
wing, flipped, 284
wing, splint, 284
wing, sprain, 279
wintertime care, 161
WNV, 401
wormers, over-the-counter, 352
worming, flock, 352
wound wash, 24
wrist, 278
wry tail, 287

Z

zinc poisoning, 340
Zolazepam, 173

Do you have a predator-proof duck pen?

Are you looking to welcome a feathered friend into your family?

Visit us at: **www.majesticwaterfowl.org**

Help provide safe and loving homes for domestic ducks & geese—

Help change a life today!

The author makes no representation, warranty, or guarantee in connection with any guidance provided anywhere within this book. The author expressly disclaims any liability or responsibility for loss or damage resulting from its use or for the violation of any federal, state or municipal law or regulation with which such guidance may conflict. Any guidance is general in nature. In addition, the assistance of a qualified professional should be enlisted to address any specific circumstances.

Printed in Great Britain
by Amazon